THE UNITE

SUPREME COURT

★ ★ ★

The United States Supreme Court

THE PURSUIT OF JUSTICE

Christopher Tomlins, Editor

★ ★ ★

Developed in cooperation between

HOUGHTON MIFFLIN COMPANY

and THE AMERICAN BAR FOUNDATION

Houghton Mifflin Company

BOSTON · NEW YORK

2005

For information about permission to reproduce selections from
this book, write to Permissions, Houghton Mifflin Company,
215 Park Avenue South, New York, New York 10003.

Visit our Web site: www.houghtonmifflinbooks.com.

Library of Congress Cataloging-in-Publication Data

The United States Supreme Court : the pursuit of justice / Christopher
Tomlins, editor ; Developed in cooperation between
Houghton Mifflin Company and the American Bar Foundation
p.   cm.
Includes bibliographical references and index.
ISBN 0-618-32969-2
1. United States. Supreme Court — History. 2. Constitutional History
— United States.   I. Tomlins, Christopher L., date.
KF8742.U55 2005
347.73'26'09v — dc22   2005040315

PRINTED IN THE UNITED STATES OF AMERICA

QUM 10 9 8 7 6 5 4 3 2 1

Contents

Contributors

PAUL FINKELMAN University of Tulsa College of Law

WILLIAM E. FORBATH University of Texas School of Law

DAVID C. FREDERICK Kellogg, Huber, Hansen, Todd & Evans,
P.L.L.C., Washington, D.C.

HOWARD GILLMAN University of Southern California

STEPHEN E. GOTTLIEB Albany Law School

CHARLES F. HOBSON The Papers of John Marshall,
College of William & Mary

WYTHE W. HOLT, JR. University of Alabama School of Law

MAEVA MARCUS Documentary History of the Supreme Court
of the United States, 1789–1800

LUCAS A. (SCOT) POWE, JR. University of Texas School of Law

LINDA PRZYBYSZEWSKI University of Cincinnati

NORMAN L. ROSENBERG Macalester College

WILLIAM G. ROSS Cumberland School of Law, Samford University

KATHERINE FISCHER TAYLOR University of Chicago

CHRISTOPHER TOMLINS The American Bar Foundation

MARK TUSHNET Georgetown University Law Center

MELVIN I. UROFSKY Virginia Commonwealth University

MICHAEL VORENBERG Brown University

KEITH E. WHITTINGTON Princeton University

WILLIAM M. WIECEK Syracuse University College of Law

Acknowledgments

This book is the outcome of a highly productive cooperative effort between the Houghton Mifflin Company and the American Bar Foundation. Houghton Mifflin provided the initial impetus by inviting me to develop a concept for the book, design and oversee the project that would bring it to fruition, recruit the contributors, and edit their work. The American Bar Foundation, a research institute dedicated to social-scientific study of law, legal institutions and legal processes, and also my home institution, ensured that I would have the time and research assistance required to complete the job. To both, and notably to Gordon Hardy, former Director of Electronic Publishing and General Reference at Houghton Mifflin, and to Bryant Garth, Director of the American Bar Foundation at the time this project came before the Foundation's governing board, I extend my warmest appreciation.

This book recounts the history of a unique institution: the Supreme Court of the United States. As such, the book is the collective product of the historians, political scientists, legal academics, and professional lawyers whose names appear on the list of contributors immediately preceding this acknowledgment. All are scholars who have devoted the better part of their careers to exploring the history of law and of courts in the United States and elsewhere, and particularly the history of the United States Supreme Court. Their wealth of expertise enables us to explore the Court and its activities over the full span of its existence and across a broad range of topics that opens the Court to a wide public audience.

Law is, of course, central to the study of legal institutions and processes, but its technicalities can be an obstacle to an appreciation of the social, political, and cultural significance of an institution like the Supreme Court. The contributors to this volume have as far as possible eschewed the technicalities of legal doctrine in order to bring the Supreme Court and the Constitution alive in the most direct and accessible way. They have chosen the broadest range of perspectives — those of history, politics, and legal practice, of course, but also of popular and material culture. Their efforts make the book as complete an account of the Court as one could wish.

To complement the history it presents, this book also provides essential supplementary information: biographies of every justice and an accounting of the Court's budget since its inception. Much of this information was gathered and compiled by a trio of dedicated American Bar Foundation research assistants — Crina Archer, Greg Prieto, and Mike Frisch. Their efficiency, enthusiasm, energy, and active interest made the project a pleasure to direct. The first and longest serving of the three, Crina Archer, deserves particular mention for her manifold organizational skills.

At Houghton Mifflin, Gordon Hardy commissioned the project, read and commented on all the chapters, and provided endless helpful advice. I could not ask for a more supportive colleague with whom to work. Wendy Holt and Brandi Archer stepped in to oversee production of the book itself. Manuscript editors Evelyn Pyle and Beth Fuller made many wise suggestions that have improved the book in its entirety.

As well as overall editing, I am responsible for illustrations research, with considerable help from Crina Archer and Greg Prieto. I am particularly grateful to Jerry Goldman, founder of Northwestern University's *Oyez* project, for making the project's illustration files available to us; to Clare Cushman of the Supreme Court Historical Society for her interest and advice; to Timothy Crowley, Esq., for the loan of a rare artifact; to Jay Stratton in the Office of the Curator of the Supreme Court of the United States; and to innumerable archivists and librarians throughout the country for their patient advice and assistance. Crina Archer wrote the biographical appendix, and Crina Archer and Mike Frisch researched the Court's budget. Errors that remain in the appendixes, or elsewhere, are fully my responsibility.

Introduction

Characterizing the Supreme Court

Morally and legally, the Supreme Court of the United States is the most authoritative branch of the federal government; institutionally, the least powerful. "John Marshall has made his decision," Andrew Jackson is reputed to have said after the Court suggested in *Worcester v. Georgia* (1832) that the federal government was obliged to ensure that the Cherokee were protected from the state of Georgia's intrusions on their quiet enjoyment of their lands. "Now let him enforce it." These particular words are apocryphal, but what Jackson actually said on the occasion conveyed the same meaning, albeit in less pithy language: "The decision of the supreme court has fell stillborn, and they find that it cannot coerce Georgia to yield to its mandate."

Jackson's dismissal of the Court's significance in this instance is reminiscent of Stalin's later description of the pope — a general without tanks. History offers us a subtler verdict. On one hand, it has indeed been the Court's fate throughout its existence to make decisions of great moment that must nevertheless depend on others' resources for meaningful effect. On the other hand, time and again, the Court — a secular papacy — has shown that its declaratory capacity can be determinative, not only of legal matters but also, quite decisively, of political and social outcomes. The outcomes have sometimes been disastrous, as in *Dred Scott*, or admirable, as in *Brown*, or deeply controversial, as in *Bush v. Gore*. That outcomes are readily observable, however, is indisputable.

Perhaps for the very reason that its authority to effect outcomes indirectly looms much larger than its actual instrumental capacities to do so directly, the Court has quite carefully guarded both itself and the processes by which it works from the unmediated gaze of outsiders. Like Oz's wizard, much of the Court's public authority lies in appearances. Appearances begin with the Court's own appearance — familiar in the modern era as the "marble, Roman palace" that opened for business in October 1935, physically reconstituting the Court *outside* the Capitol for the first time, as a clearly separate and equal third branch of the federal government. "It is a magnificent structure," noted Howard Brubaker, a *New Yorker* commentator, "with fine big windows to throw the New Deal out of." Brubaker's words underline the Court's legal authority (just as the sequel Court-packing controversy would expose its institutional vulnerability to a determined president), but the metaphor of *de*fenestration was apt: Those fine big windows were not for looking in from the outside, and they shed little light on the Court's shrouded backstage.

This most morally authoritative branch of the government is also, in its interior workings, the least transparent. Unlike the open, messy, partisan chaos of Congress and unlike the brass-band dignities and occasional peep-show notorieties of the presidency, the Supreme Court sits deliberatively apart in its palace, physically separated not only from the other institutions of government but also from the crudities of the Washington street by a mountain of steps and a phalanx of columns. The justices are presented as the nation's most elevated practitioners of law's mysterious science, not flamboyant politicians (or trial lawyers) but closeted "high priests" engaged in the interpretation of "mandarin texts." Appearing at their bench from behind curtains that bar the inner workings of authority from the public gaze, the justices appear as one, bound together in an essential uniformity of dress and deportment: austere, remote, dignified, and virtually indistinguishable in anonymous black robes. In the 1930s musical comedies *Of Thee I Sing* and *I'd Rather Be Right* (Plate B.6),* all nine justices were made to look exactly alike.

If this apparently homogenous institution has a recognizable face, it is almost invariably that of the chief justice. The nine identical justices of the 1930s stage were all made to look exactly like then Chief Justice Charles Evans Hughes. As the essays presented here indicate, every chief justice has had clear opportunities to lead the Court over which he presides. Some have proved masters of the institution; others, completely ineffectual. Nonetheless, there are clear limitations on the extent to which a chief justice may go in impressing his personality or interpretive preferences on the collectivity of the bench, particularly a bench that has included from time to time such brilliant but intemperate others as Stephen J. Field, George Sutherland, or Felix Frankfurter. The chief justice has means to influence the Court's agenda but nonetheless casts only one vote. As several authors here show, the story of successful judicial leadership on the Court is more one of astute maneuver in a collegial realm of sharp personalities than of institutionally assured ascendancy.

Nor does the chief elevate himself above his colleagues without risk. The magnificently authoritative robes worn by the first justices were abandoned by their successors in favor of homogenous black. Chief Justice

---

* Plates A.1–A.15 follow page 146; Plates B.1–B.15 follow page 370.

Rehnquist's modest attempt to mark the chief justice's distinctiveness by embroidering his robes with a commander's distinguishing stripes, which he wore to preside over the impeachment trial of President Clinton, earned him pundits' ridicule as much as respect. It did not help that the inspiration was a costume designed for the character of the British Lord Chancellor in a production of Gilbert and Sullivan's mocking *Iolanthe.*

The abiding characteristic of the Court's appearance, in short, is not individuality but an elaborate, all but impenetrable uniformity of convention, practice, and ritual. Impenetrability extends even to the conventions and practices of disagreement. Readers will discover here repeated accounts of intense debate, disagreement, and even personal clashes among justices. Yet by design and in function, the Court is the embodiment of a principle of separation of government and governance from the undue influence of human impulse. The public assurance of legitimate rule in a constitutional democracy is, after all, rule not by men, but by law. The Court's role is to ensure, and itself to stand for, the enduring appearance of that separation. That it is itself composed of men (and, lately, women) who disagree with one another requires that it make particularly athletic efforts to conceal its humanity, efforts not required of the other branches, where maximal self-exposure all too often is considered the key to career success. On the Court, the disembodiment of decision making — its appearance at most in converging or diverging "opinions" — is necessary if judicial disagreement is to be rendered allowable amid law's supposed certainties.

At work, the Court is an alchemist, self-consciously transmuting the living ideas of a panel of men and women, and their staffs of law clerks, into collective pronouncement. But the Court's public pronouncements set conditions of constitutional legality on action. They do not, at least formally, explore political possibility or seek compromise. They are, as far as possible, carefully shorn of personality. The Court's "work" transforms the ideas of men into statements of law. Hence, the Court's work must be shrouded — if not in absolute secrecy, then in enormous discretion. Exposure of the Court's labors of transformation would undo the rule-of-law principle that inhabits American constitutional democracy and shrouds the men and women whose daily activities make and continually remake it.

Good history should engage with an institution's myths and practices, not simply reproduce them. An earlier book in this series pointed out how common images of the presidency exaggerate the impact and the magnitude of the personal. "Everything a president does," Alan Brinkley wrote, "seems to much of the nation to be larger than life." Common images of Congress may similarly overemphasize its sausage-making, logrolling approach to governance. To engage properly with the history of the Supreme

Court requires close examination of its myths and images. Here, as we recount the Court's history critically, we watch its members over time continually constructing and reconstructing the law's rules and their own procedures for making them. We gauge the extent of the Court's involvement in politics; we analyze how it has been perceived over time and how it presents itself.

Throughout, we can be sure of only one thing, which is emphasized at the outset, repeated by example throughout the chronological chapters that provide an account of the cycles that characterize the Court's career across more than two centuries, and repeated again in the later chapters that probe the Court's place in American legal culture: The path the Court has followed — the way it has turned out — was not foreordained. The Court has traditions that at one and the same time wrap it in a formality that protects its capacity to be closeted and secretive and portray an institution of abiding continuity. This notwithstanding, the Court has no single incarnation, no essence. At the creation of the Republic, it was not clear what precisely the Supreme Court would look like, what its role would be, or whether it would successfully assert a place for itself among the institutions of the federal government. Ever since, the Court can and has changed dramatically — cyclically — in character and authority. The Court, in other words, is not a constitutional given, an inevitability. Its current incarnation, as at every moment during its history, is a construct of the human choices made by its members, and alternatives always exist to choices made. All the same, traditions that suggest an abiding continuity are an extremely useful resource — perhaps even the Court's most powerful weapon. They provide the cover that reassures and, in so doing, allows change to occur. From beginning to end, we may say, the history of the Supreme Court of the United States provides cogent proof that appearances matter.

—CHRISTOPHER TOMLINS
The American Bar Foundation

Part I

THE FIRST SEVENTY YEARS

★ ★ ★

Birth to Near Death

THE SUPREME COURT OF THE UNITED STATES WAS CALLED TO order for the first time in February 1790. First mooted three years earlier, at the 1787 Constitutional Convention, a design for the Court was established in the Judiciary Act of 1789 and in President Washington's first appointments. In this first part, we encounter the reasons for the creation of a federal court system with a Supreme Court at its apex, the political debates and disagreements that shaped the Supreme Court's initial jurisdiction and powers, and the personalities of the key players on and off the early Court. We see the Court struggle to assert itself during its first decade, planting seeds here and there that would come to fruition during the long career of Chief Justice John Marshall. We see the Court adapt successfully from the nationalism of the Marshall era to the very different nationalism of Chief Justice Roger Taney, only to fall into near irrelevance and impotence as a result of its own hubris. Only seventy years after the Court came into being, its disastrous decision in *Scott v. Sandford* (1857) reduced the Court to the lowest point in its history, consigning it to a position of complete impotence and irrelevance during the nation's deepest crisis — the crisis of slavery, secession, and civil war.

1

The Establishment of the Federal Court System

1787–1791

W E HAVE BECOME ACCUSTOMED to thinking that every democratic government worthy of the name must look like ours — an executive, an independent legislature, and above all a separate judiciary branch that looks and operates very much as our own federal court structure does. This notion seems so straightforward as to be an expression of first principles, universally agreed on, resisted only for malign motives. It is something of a paradox, then, to discover that the origins and establishment of the U.S. government, and particularly of the Supreme Court and the entire judiciary department, lie not in the straightforward application of transcendent first principles but squarely in the politics of the new United States in the 1780s and 1790s.

Contrary to the belief deeply embedded in American political culture that the Framers were farsighted, essentially politically disinterested patriarchs who planned for the ages and set up a fair, neutral government that had an apolitical court system as its safety valve for political excesses, the important decisions that established the new national judiciary in 1787–1791 were intensely political, hotly contested deals made to solve immediate political problems. If different political views and compromises had prevailed at the time, a different judicial structure would have resulted, one perhaps unrecognizable to us today. The judicial system that emerged from the Founding era's compromises was in important respects ungainly and awkward, contemporaneously regarded simultaneously as wise and yet temporary. That system has mostly endured, but mostly through political happenstance rather than planning.

Problems of the Confederation: Development, Debt, Dissent, and Dignity

Development

The Framers of the Constitution were essentially the globalizers of their time. Their primary concerns, both in establishing a much stronger and more centralized national government for the United States and in making a separate judiciary a third branch of that government, were developmental in nature, that is, commercially and internationally oriented.

After the long bloody years of revolutionary war, the 1783 Peace Treaty unexpectedly awarded the victorious United States all the vast British land between the Appalachian Mountains and the Mississippi River south of the Great Lakes. Great Britain hoped to saddle the new nation with all the problems inherent in a distended territory full of unconquered hostile natives and bordered by an antagonistic but feeble Spain to the west and south and by Britain itself to the north. Spain's acquisition of Louisiana in 1763 gave it the capacity to control use of the Mississippi for transportation and trade. Britain retained nine forts along the northern boundary, all within the territory supposedly ceded (the sites included Mackinac Island, near the junction of the northern three Great Lakes, and what are now the cities of Detroit, Toledo, and Oswego), guaranteeing it control of both the lucrative fur trade and any American commerce along the St. Lawrence River. Both Spain and Britain were adept at inciting the hostile Indians within the United States. They also correctly judged that the emergent nation suffered from economic exhaustion and military insufficiency.

"Localism"

The Framers understood the nation's precarious position but regarded the settlement and commercial exploitation of the new interior region, and economic development in general, as the solution to its weakness. They imagined that, by satisfying the "West's" full growth potential, along with continued growth in the states along the seaboard, they would enrich themselves while simultaneously producing the workers, the revenue, and the kinds of wealth that would make the nation strong.

Development was hindered, however, by what they called "localism"—by self-preferential treatment, anticommercial sentiment, and commercial rivalries between and among the states, which thought of themselves as nations. Indeed, under the form of government the United States had before 1789, the states were nations. The Articles of Confederation gave each a veto in Congress. At crucial moments during the 1780s, the vote of a single small state had denied Congress what it sought. Congress had neither the power to tax nor the power to raise an army. Under the Confederation, the United States had neither an executive nor a permanent judiciary.

Out-of-state landowners, merchants, and debt holders sometimes thought themselves discriminated against in "local" dealings. Take the case of Robert Morris of Pennsylvania, the nation's wealthiest merchant and greatest land speculator. As the Confederation's Superintendent of Finance, Morris had successfully maintained the nation's wartime finances and had simultaneously reaped immense personal profit from his office. In a 1783 debt suit, a North Carolina jury returned a verdict against him for more than three times the amount of the debt for which he had been sued. In a second North Carolina verdict against him four years later, Morris again thought himself cheated and discriminated against by a locally biased jury. Such "localism" obtusely hindered commercial dealings, growth, and national effectiveness, the Framers felt, and they wanted to terminate it.

International Respect

In order to attract the capital necessary for development, the Framers calculated that the interest of foreign investors — bankers and merchants in Great Britain and the Netherlands — had to be awakened and secured and that the dominant world powers in western Europe had to be convinced that the United States was a genuine, respectable nation.

There were several components to the Framers' notion of "respect." The most important was commercial. Before investment would begin to flow, the nation and thousands of U.S. citizens had to act responsibly in meeting millions of dollars in outstanding debts, even though both nation and citizens were desperately poor in cash terms.

But there were other components, too. To a European, a real government had respect for foreign dignitaries, providing them with a national court to which they could take disputes. Embarrassingly, two incidents in the 1780s, involving members of the Dutch and Spanish ambassadorial entourages, had to be dealt with by the Pennsylvania courts (Philadelphia was then the nation's capital), since the United States had none of its own. More generally, the European powers simply failed to take very seriously the democratically governed, feuding, and executive-free former British colonies. Democracy was new on the world scene. Europeans had kings, scenes of regal splendor, armies and navies. The economically depressed, armyless United States seemed ungovernable, headless, and likely to fall apart.

Debt and Democratic Dissent

In fact, many Framers were no fonder of democracy than they were of localism, particularly as democracy seemed to be breeding dissension within the United States, largely over economic issues. With the onset of the Revolution, hard money had flowed overseas. Paper money had been issued, but its value had evaporated quickly. The long struggle with the British was expensive, farms were ravaged, slaves were run off, and soldiers essentially went unpaid. By the end of the war the states had turned to heavy taxation to pay their war debts, which the people found tremendously burdensome. Britain meanwhile punished the "victor" by shutting off the lucrative American trade with the British West Indian colonies. In the South — the economic bulwark of the new nation — three poor crop years in succession, a drastic drop in tobacco prices, and the recall of paper money combined with the ravages of the war to throw the region, and hence the nation, into a deep depression, beginning in 1784 and lasting into the 1790s. The average farmer had many debts and taxes but nothing with which to pay them. State courts suddenly filled to overflowing with debt suits. Many people just left town; hordes of folks in numbers amazing to observers began to pour across the Appalachians.

Debtors plastered legislative venues with petitions for relief. Blessed with a heightened consciousness of their own power, thanks both to a revolutionary ideology of democracy that released their own desires for self-governance and to their success in fighting for and winning freedom, the debtors saw, in many cases, that heightened power explicitly recognized in new democratic state constitutions. Debtors influenced several state legislatures to issue more paper money and to relieve the tax burden. As the depression dragged on, the debtors forced legislative postponement of some debts and acceptance of relatively worthless property as a tender for other debts. In the South, it helped that powerful planters were among the largest debtors. At the height of the depression, in 1785–1787, ordinary folk exercised their recently won right of revolution by forcing the temporary closure of courts in South Carolina, Maryland, Connecticut, and Virginia (where a courthouse was razed). An upcountry South Carolina judge summed it up: "[T]he people would not suffer . . . creditors to sue debtors."

"The people" reinforced this attitude by marches and tumults in New Jersey and Pennsylvania, by holding the New Hampshire legislature captive for five hours, by causing the Rhode Island legislature to overturn a state court decision declaring that state's paper money act unconstitutional, and by rising in armed revolt in western Massachusetts. Shays's Rebellion — its goals were to close the courts and to "petition" the legislature for debt relief — created fear and havoc from late summer 1786 to early summer

1787, well after the beginning of the Constitutional Convention. The national government had no troops and no power to deal with these bitter protests or to overturn the prodebtor soft-money policies with which many states had assuaged them. Propertied commercial elites and many others were thoroughly alarmed, on both counts.

"British Debts" and International Investment

Another set of debt issues—the "British debts"—seemed to the Framers equally to call for a stronger national government. The dogged resistance that many Americans offered to British creditors, along with the many ways that state legislatures, judges, and juries backed up debtor intransigence, were highly alarming to those with developmental interests. Debtors and democracy (influencing state legislatures and courts) seemed to have run riot.

Local courts functioned as the debt-collection agency of last resort. Because of the turmoil attendant upon the collapse of British authority, courts in many of the colonies had closed before the Revolution broke out. Pursuant to international law, once hostilities started, the courts remained closed to enemy aliens. This left merchants in London, Liverpool, Glasgow, and other British trading cities holding a very large bag of unpaid and now uncollectible debts for sums that had been advanced against farms and future crops for the purchase of fine clothes and other commodities produced in the mother country. One knowledgeable estimate places the total value of the tens of thousands of debts at £5,000,000. Virginians alone owed about 45 percent of the total, with another 35 percent owed in the other Southern colonies and the remaining fifth scattered unevenly throughout the Northern ones.

During six and more years of actual hostilities, especially in Virginia, North Carolina, South Carolina, Pennsylvania, New Jersey, and New York, and along the seacoast, towns and farms were pillaged, torched, and destroyed. Savannah, Charleston, Philadelphia, and New York were occupied by the British for much or all of the war. Economic devastation was severe, and animosities ran high.

Every state—from anger as well as from dire financial need—passed laws confiscating at least some Loyalist property, and most states passed laws specifically impeding the ability of British creditors to recover their debts. Several states closed their courts to British creditors, Pennsylvania and New York suspended executions on debt judgments, Virginia and Maryland made their essentially worthless paper money a tender for British debts paid into their state treasuries, and New York denied wartime interest on them. Courts still open to British creditors allowed juries to deduct some or all of the wartime interest on the debts, or deducted it themselves. Most courts allowed the settlement of decedents' estates, discharging all creditors who did not timely file claims despite the inability of British creditors to file.

The 1783 Peace Treaty was essentially negotiated for the United States by two mercantile-oriented lawyers who saw debt issues from the standpoint of creditors: John Jay of New York and John Adams of Massachusetts. Thus it contained language that "Creditors on either Side shall meet with no lawful Impediment to the Recovery of the full value in Sterling Money of all bona fide debts heretofore contracted." If enforced, this would cancel all the wartime statutes and practices restricting the collection of British debts and prevent any new ones.

Many Americans greeted the news of this provision with disbelief and rejection. British creditors and their agents who attempted to collect debts were met with physical violence from New Hampshire to North Carolina. Spurred by strong popular sentiment and by debtor pressure during the lengthening depression, several state governments simply ignored the treaty and passed new legislation impeding the collection of British debts.

Most state courts enforced these laws. Massachusetts and Connecticut, for example, embraced the deduction of wartime interest; South Carolina continued the closure of its courts until 1785 and then postponed payments through installment laws; British creditor litigants in Pennsylvania found it almost impossible to collect; and the courts of Virginia, Maryland, North Carolina, and Georgia refused to open themselves to British creditors. New York courts refused to overturn a statute allowing owners of realty to recover rents and damages from the wartime British occupiers of New York City property. North Carolina and Pennsylvania courts in 1787 and 1788 denied Loyalist claims to confiscated land. Led by Patrick Henry and Richard Henry Lee, the Virginia legislature in 1783, 1784, and 1787 defeated bills that would have repealed all statutes and practices contrary to the treaty, although, like South Carolina's, the 1783–1784 bills would have set up installment payments. In 1785 and 1786, that legislature also defeated bills to open the courts to British creditors.

Although the British were also refusing to comply with portions of the Peace Treaty, the states' open nullification of debt repayment caused a host of bankruptcies in Great Britain and protests from the British government. A plea from Congress in 1787 for the repeal of legislation contrary to the treaty resulted in compliance from all states north of the Mason-Dixon line (except New Jersey and New York, which complied only in 1788, after the Constitution was ratified), but only from Maryland and North Carolina to the south. Even then, courts and juries in Connecticut, Pennsylvania, New Jersey, and New York continued to deduct wartime interest.

Americans who represented the creditor element were sorely beset by this state of affairs. It operated to prevent the further extension of credit from European bankers and merchants whether to the United States, to the individual states, or, more particularly, to any individual developer who desired to open up the territory beyond the Appalachians.

The Constitutional Convention, Federal Courts, and Creditors

Debtor Elements Not Represented at the Convention

A distinct polarization of viewpoint on the debt issue in the United States occurred in the late 1780s. Governor William Livingston of New Jersey, a delegate to the Constitutional Convention, put it this way: "The interest of the creditor coincides with that of the community. Not so the interest of the debtor. The former desires no more than his own. The latter wants to pocket the property of another." The popular debtor uprising caused great fear among Livingston's sort for the safety of their accumulated wealth, as well as for the entire system of commerce and credit. Merchant Charles Pettit of Pennsylvania thought that the popular element wanted "[a] total abolition of all Debts both public and Private and even a general Distribution of Property." Many decided that the answer was a much stronger national government, and a convention was called to meet in Philadelphia.

The powerful popular debtor elements were opposed to any centralization of national authority. Several elite spokesmen for them refused to accept seats at the convention, including four signers of the Declaration of Independence — Thomas Nelson and Richard Henry Lee of Virginia, Samuel Chase of Maryland, and Abraham Clark of New Jersey — as did Patrick Henry of Virginia, Erastus Wolcott of Connecticut, and Willie Jones of North Carolina. In Massachusetts, Samuel Adams, an opponent of Shays's Rebellion but no representative of creditors, also refused election, while John Hancock, prodebtor in his sympathies, was not offered a place. Some others opposed to a strong national government, such as Robert Yates and John Lansing of New York and John Francis Mercer and Luther Martin of Maryland, left the convention.

The Framers who met in Philadelphia during the broiling summer of 1787 spoke largely for the interests of creditors and commercial development, not those of debtors and democracy. "The evils we experience," said Elbridge Gerry of Massachusetts, "flow from the excess of democracy, . . . the danger of the levelling spirit." He wanted to "secure . . . the commercial and monied interest." James Madison of Virginia thought that, "more perhaps than anything else, . . . interferences . . . with the security of private rights, and [with] the steady dispensation of Justice" had "produced this convention." Governor Edmund Randolph of Virginia, in introducing Madison's Virginia Plan for a stronger national government, observed that when the Confederation was formed, "no commercial discord had arisen among any states — no rebellion had appeared as in Mass[achuset]ts — foreign debts had not become urgent — the havoc of paper money had not been foreseen — treaties had not been violated." He too located the cause of all these difficulties in "the turbulence and follies of democracy."

Alexander Hamilton of New York framed the issue succinctly: "[I]n every community where industry is encouraged, there will be a division of it into the few & the many. Hence separate interests will arise[.] There will be debtors & Creditors &c." The specific, recent experience of difficulty by the creditor interest to which Gerry, Madison, Randolph, and Hamilton all referred was brought up by other Framers again and again throughout the Convention. Democracy had to be reined in, "localism" stifled, the conditions for commercial transactions, trade, and national dignity reinforced. The delegates mostly agreed that a more centralized national government with separate executive and judiciary branches was necessary to accomplish these goals. National power to maintain an army, to tax, and to control commerce was a given.

Adoption of a Strong, Less Democratic Central Government

Disagreements among the Framers at the Convention were largely over matters *other* than national strength and economic development. They fought over which parts of the union would have power in the Congress — large states or small states — and they disagreed mightily about slavery. The Convention solved both of these issues to general satisfaction through the "Great Compromise," which gave small states equal representation with the larger ones in the powerful new national upper house, or Senate, while also allowing slaves to count (as three-fifths of a person) for purposes of determining the number of members each state would have in the new lower house, or House of Representatives. (Voters, however, were only those enfranchised by the states, which excluded slaves, women, the poor, and those with little or no property.) After this important deal, creditor-oriented representatives of small states such as William Paterson of New Jersey (a lawyer for British creditors) and Oliver Ellsworth of Connecticut shifted over to favor the strengthened national government that most members of the Convention wanted.

Democracy was restricted in the final document. The president would be selected through a complicated, remote electoral college system; senators would be chosen by the legislatures of the states. No thought was ever given to popular election of federal judges. The one-year term for members of the Continental Congress, and their eligibility for only three in any six years, were both omitted in favor of infinite reelectibility, with two-year terms for members of the new lower house, six-year terms for senators, and four-year terms for presidents. Judges were awarded life tenure. The debtor-influenced democracy of the states was also hemmed in. States were forbidden to coin money, to make anything but gold and silver a tender for debt, or to make any law impairing the obligation of contracts (that is, canceling or postponing debts). Provision for organizing, arming, and disciplining state militias — the most democratic institutions in the union, owing to the lack of property qualification on membership and election at large of lower-ranking officers — was given to Congress. Localism was also attacked by provisions requiring the states to give "full faith and credit" to the acts and adjudications of one another and homogenizing the "privileges and immunities" of state citizens. To make state subordination clear, laws made by Congress and national treaties were rendered "the supreme law of the land," and state judges were specifically required to be bound by them.

The national government was immensely strengthened. Congress was given the power to levy taxes and duties on imports, to coin money and to regulate its value, to raise and support an army and a navy, to call out the state militias, and "to regulate Commerce with foreign Nations, and among the several States." Congress was allowed to make all laws "necessary and proper" to carry out its powers. The president became commander in chief, was expected to be assisted by a cabinet of executive officers, would make regular reports and recommendations to Congress, and would see that the laws were "faithfully executed." The president and the Senate shared both the treaty-making power and the appointment of ambassadors, other executive officers, and federal judges.

The Vague but Powerful Judiciary Article

There remained the significant issue of a federal judiciary. Madison argued that neither state courts alone, nor appeals from them into a federal court, would be sufficient to handle the national judicial business: "What was to be done after improper Verdicts in State tribunals obtained under the biased directions of a dependent Judge, or the local prejudices of an undirected jury? . . . [T]he Courts of the States can not be trusted with the administration of the National laws. The objects of [national] jurisdiction are such as will often place the General & local policy at variance." Federal trial and appellate courts were, he thought, absolutely necessary, with a broad jurisdiction.

Against him were arrayed South Carolina planters John Rutledge and Pierce Butler, who were debtors themselves (Rutledge was hopelessly in debt), and debtor representative Luther Martin of Maryland. They argued that no federal trial courts were needed — perhaps precisely because of the reasons Madison gave. They persuaded the Convention to deny the establishment of any lower federal courts in the Constitution. Madison and James Wilson of Pennsylvania responded quickly with a motion leaving it to Congress to decide whether lower federal courts would be needed. In the end, the judiciary article of the new Constitution — Article III — authorized only "one" Supreme Court, giving Congress the power to set up lower courts if necessary.

What were those "objects of [national] jurisdiction" that Madison thought so necessary to give "the steady dispensation of justice" but that he anticipated would be so divisive? Unlike the detailed descriptions of the powers of the Congress and the president the Convention argued about so ceaselessly, Madison and the Convention were content with a vague, inclusive statement of the jurisdiction that the new federal court(s) would exercise. His motion "that the jurisdiction of the national Judiciary shall extend to all cases arising under the Nat[iona]l laws: And to such other questions as may involve the Nat[iona]l peace & harmony" was accepted by the Convention, the second phrase being agreed to on at least three separate occasions without debate.

In fact, little debate is recorded on any aspect of the federal judiciary, and no debate whatsoever is recorded on the extent or nature of its jurisdiction. The Convention's Committee of Detail made great efforts to specify what questions involving "the national peace and harmony" meant. Nevertheless, a studied vagueness remained. The impulse to assuage foreign lenders in the face of intense popular feeling by providing forums for debt recovery not subject to local debtor agitation probably accounted for much of the prevailing vagueness. As the Anti-Federalist commentator "Brutus" would point out, vagueness allowed for broad interpretation and thus for assertions of jurisdiction in instances not specifically anticipated but thought necessary by the federal judges considering a particular situation. Where authority was wanting "or ambiguously expressed," Brutus warned, the courts were enabled "to supply what is wanting by their own decisions." So doing, the courts "will not confine themselves to any fixed or established rules, but will determine, according to what appears to them, the reason and spirit of the constitution." The legislature would have no capacity to set aside a judgment, because the Constitution gave it to the courts to decide in the last resort. The judicial power would thus operate "to effect . . . an entire subversion of the legislative, executive and judicial powers of the individual states. Every adjudication of the supreme court, on any question that may arise upon the nature and extent of the general government, will affect the limits of state jurisdiction. In proportion as the former enlarge the exercise of their powers, will that of the latter be restricted."

The pressing necessity to assuage foreign debtors, plus the needs of development in general, were responsible for the delineation of most of the heads of federal jurisdiction. "Judicial power shall extend," Article III stated, not only to "all cases" arising under laws passed by Congress but also to "all cases" arising both under the Constitution itself (suppose, for instance, a state persisted in making something other than gold and silver a legal tender for debts) and under "Treaties made, or which shall be made," the latter phraseology expressly intended to include suits under the Peace Treaty. Federal courts were also given jurisdiction over controversies between citizens of different states (solving the local prejudice Robert Morris thought he had been subjected to in North Carolina) and between citizens of a state and foreign citizens (allowing British creditors to bypass the state courts).

More controversially, state sovereign immunity was apparently waived to allow federal courts jurisdiction not only over "controversies between two or more States" but also for controversies between a state and foreign citizens (thus, federal courts were allowed to hear challenges to laws like those of Virginia and Maryland, which permitted discharge of British debts by paper money payment into their state treasuries), and "between a State and Citizens of another State" (covering the widespread effects of emissions of paper money, or impressment of goods or livestock during the war). Everybody agreed that federal courts should have admiralty jurisdiction, not only because of the lack of wartime uniformity in state courts' handling of prize cases within that jurisdiction, but also because most important commerce involved the high seas, and admiralty courts existed worldwide to apply a relatively uniform body of international law in commercial or other disputes arising on the sea. National dignity was proclaimed by giving the Supreme Court jurisdiction over cases involving ambassadors.

The last additions made to Article III by the Convention expressly extended both federal court jurisdiction to equity cases, in which juries did not sit, and the Supreme Court's "appellate" jurisdiction to questions of both law "& fact." In the civil law system of most of Europe (as opposed to the common law, which predominated in the United States and Great Britain), "appellate" jurisdiction meant a review of a lower court decision in the reviewing court by a new trial, without a jury. James Wilson — a member (with Rutledge, Ellsworth, and Randolph) of the Convention's Committee of Detail, as well as Robert Morris's personal lawyer and, according to his biographer, an "irrepressible speculator" in land—assured a questioning Framer that such was precisely what the change was meant to achieve. In state courts and even in any lower federal courts, troublesome British-debt jury verdicts that either were for less than the amount owed or failed to include wartime interest could thus be overturned upon review by the new Supreme Court—a final method of triumphing over the angry democracy of popular dissent in British-debt cases. Trial by jury was less important than development, commercial viability, and national dignity. Wilson and Rutledge (and later Ellsworth and Paterson) would all be among the early appointees to the Supreme Court.

Disclosure of Prodebtor Strength in the Ratification Process

National Upset over the Judiciary Article

When the Convention finally finished its work and disclosed its document to public scrutiny in September 1787, opposition exploded. Most controversial was the overall nationalizing and antidemocratic spirit of an instrument whose drafters had voted overwhelmingly to impose a property qualification on the officeholders of the new government (an instruction favored by Madison but eventually disregarded by the Committee of Detail). A fair share of the opposition concentrated more precisely on the powers claimed for the national government in Article III.

In the context of depression, widespread breaches of the Peace Treaty, and continuing opposition to the satisfaction of British creditors' claims, the vagueness of Article III's jurisdictional grants, along with the power of Congress to multiply lower federal courts at will and the document's implicit lack of faith in state courts and juries, seemed to many to mean the subversion of the state courts. George Mason, a Convention delegate who had refused to sign the final document, and Patrick Henry, whose half-brother John Syme was the single largest British debtor in Virginia, summarized the arguments on the floor of the Virginia Ratification Convention. Mason warned: "The inferior courts are to be as numerous as Congress may think proper. . . . Read the 2d section [the jurisdictional provisions of Article III], and contemplate attentively the extent of the jurisdiction of these courts, and consider if there be any limits to it. I am greatly mistaken if there be any limitation whatsoever, with respect to the nature or jurisdiction of these courts." Henry declared: "[T]he trial by jury is gone: British debtors will be ruined by being dragged to the federal court, and the liberty and happiness of our citizens gone, never to be recovered." Such "dragging" could ruin a poor litigant who had won a jury verdict: Mason noted that such a person could be forced to retry the case before the Supreme Court, possibly five hundred miles distant, and "[h]e must bring his witnesses where he is not known, where a new evidence may be brought against him, of which he never heard before." Further, many thought that the references to "all" in Article III meant that federal courts would now have exclusive jurisdiction over all issues of federal law (whatever that might mean, in the absence of any national laws or regulations in 1788) and all cases brought by foreigners.

Backtracking on the Judiciary by Defenders of the Constitution

Worried now that their document might fail of acceptance, Federalist defenders of the Constitution began to backtrack on particulars, hoping to retain the very broad judicial powers contained in Article III. Promising repeatedly in print and in the state ratification conventions that Congress would set right all the difficulties, the defenders specifically said that Congress would guarantee civil juries and prohibit the Supreme Court from reviewing juries' factual determinations and that federal jurisdiction would be rendered inexpensive and nonoppressive. They stressed that national jurisdiction was concurrent, not exclusive, meaning that plaintiffs could choose either federal or state court. The defenders were silent on the contentious "citizenship" jurisdictions over foreigners and over suits between citizens of different states. "I will not say it is a matter of much importance," Madison (their first propounder) muttered in the Virginia Ratification Convention.

The Federalists did not back off, however, on their developmental designs, making it clear that the elimination of difficulties in securing credit was the principal reason for the "citizenship" jurisdictions and indeed for the whole federal judiciary. Randolph, in the Virginia Convention, noted bluntly: "[T]he [national] judiciary . . . are to inforce the performance of private contracts. The British debts, which are withheld contrary to treaty, ought to be paid. Not only the law of nations, but justice and honor require that they be punctually discharged." Framer Hugh Williamson of North Carolina said in an essay: "It is provided in this system that there shall be no fraudulent tender in the payment of debts. Foreigners with whom we have treaties will trust our citizens on the faith of this engagement, and the citizens of different states will do the same."

Hamilton, writing in *The Federalist Papers* as Publius, made the same point, and as bluntly. The federal judiciary "ought to have cognizance of all causes in which the citizens of other countries are concerned." It was "essential to the preservation of public faith." Strong independent federal courts were, he thought, "requisite to guard the constitution and the rights of individuals from the effects of those ill humours which the arts of designing men, or the influences of particular conjunctures, sometimes disseminate among the people themselves," which in turn have a tendency "to occasion . . . serious oppressions of the minor [i.e., creditor] party in the community. . . . I allude to the fraudulent laws which have been passed in too many of the states." Others even threatened force and violence on the subject. Framer and future Chief Justice Oliver Ellsworth warned: "[W]e see, how necessary for the union is a coercive principle. . . . The only question is, shall it be a coercion of law or a coercion of arms?. . . I am for coercion by law, that coercion which acts only on delinquent individuals."

Narrow Passage of the Constitution

Popular opposition was not assuaged by the coordinated and forceful arguments of the Federalist proponents of the Constitution. It is probable that a majority of U.S. citizens in 1787–1788 opposed adoption. But the Constitution was submitted by the Convention and the Continental Congress to conventions in each of the states, not to a general public vote. Instead of the unanimity required by the Articles of Confederation, the Convention set nine states as the number needed for ratification and the commencement of the new government. Three small states — Delaware, New Jersey, and Georgia — ratified quickly and unanimously, but many states, including all the large states whose concurrence with the new government was politically necessary, experienced serious difficulty over ratification.

In Pennsylvania, the last week of a session of the state legislature occurred just following the end of the Constitutional Convention. Even though another session was to begin in October, a majority hastily called for a ratification convention. To protest this undue swiftness, opposing members of the legislature refused to attend. Because their absence would prevent the vote for a ratification convention, two absentees were confronted by a mob led by the captain of one of Robert Morris's ships and physically forced to attend the assembly. Once the Pennsylvania Ratification Convention began, in December, Federalists steamrolled the Constitution through. Their opponents claimed in print that ratification had occurred only because of the Federalists' force and haste and that a majority of Pennsylvanians opposed the Constitution. The opponents proposed many amendments.

When the New Hampshire convention met in February 1788, Federalist supporters discovered that a majority of delegates were opposed. The supporters had the meeting postponed to June. By then, a few more supporters had been elected. Eight opponents were absent on the day of the final vote, being plied with alcohol; Federalists were willing to accept suggested amendments; and the Constitution passed by 10 votes out of 104 cast.

Majorities against the Constitution were elected to the conventions of each of the other key big states — Virginia, Massachusetts, and New York — but a similar pattern obtained. In Massachusetts, many of the opponents lived in the forty-six townships that could not afford to send them to Boston. The opponents who did attend were subjected to pressure by desperate Federalists who, as in every state, used "every ploy that would help achieve their goal" (to quote a historian of the Massachusetts Ratification Convention). Samuel Adams and then John Hancock were persuaded, grudgingly, to come over to the Federalist side. But none of this was enough. The Federalists had to accept the suggestion of several amendments to the Constitution in order to gain a 21-vote victory out of 355 votes cast.

Virginia and New York Federalists got their conventions scheduled for the summer of 1788, predicting, accurately, that by then decisions in other states would have provided momentum for adoption. This pressure was important, but a majority was obtained in Virginia (10 votes out of 168 cast) only after Randolph switched sides and only after the Federalists were once again willing to accept a list of suggested amendments. In New York, where Governor George Clinton was strongly opposed and a large majority against had been elected, the same thing happened. By then, nine states had ratified, so a union had been formed, and New York faced the danger of isolation. Melancton Smith, an important opponent, was won over to reluctant support, and Federalist acceptance of suggested amendments led to ratification by 3 votes out of the 57 cast. Even after Virginia and New York became the tenth and eleventh states to join the union, North Carolina (another large state) and Rhode Island rejected the Constitution by huge majorities.

John Quincy Adams remarked in 1839 that the Constitution "had been extorted from the grinding necessity of a reluctant nation." Gouverneur Morris, a Federalist Framer from Pennsylvania, described the ratification process in a speech in the Senate in 1802 in similar terms: "The passions of the people were lulled to sleep; State pride slumbered; the Constitution was promulgated; and then it awoke, and opposition was formed; but it was in vain." Dissent against the Constitution was widespread and vociferous. More than two hundred amendments were put forward by the various ratification conventions. Eighty amendments proposed important alterations to the judiciary, almost all of which arose from the controversies over debts and democracy. New York, Virginia, and the Pennsylvania

dissenters would have limited any lower federal courts to admiralty jurisdiction. New York, Virginia, North Carolina, and the Pennsylvania dissenters would have eliminated the "citizenship" jurisdictions over foreigners and citizens of differing states. Massachusetts, New Hampshire, and
Maryland would have placed minimum amount-in-controversy limits on
these two jurisdictions and a higher limit on appeals, thereby at least keeping those with small debts out of a potentially distant federal court. Maryland would have required trials by jury in all actions on debts or contracts.
Virginia would have eliminated all British-debt cases by allowing jurisdiction over "no case where the cause of action shall have originated before the
ratification of this Constitution."

Some Federalists in the First Congress, which met in the spring of 1789,
were unwilling to cater to opposition strength or sentiment. Wiser and
more clear-headed Federalists, such as Oliver Ellsworth, knew that the future of the shaky national union depended on concessions and compromises. Too many people were opposed to the Constitution to be ignored.
The dilemma was to cater to them without seriously crippling the union
and, especially, the national judiciary.

The Judiciary Act of 1789

Failed Alternative Judicial Systems

The very sparseness of language in Article III allowed for many possible
judicial systems. Three were proposed in the Senate in the spring of 1789.
Virginia had selected two Anti-Federalist senators, a result engineered by
Patrick Henry to undo, if possible, the effects of ratification and to advance
the amendments suggested by the Virginia Ratification Convention. During judiciary committee deliberations, one of these senators, Richard
Henry Lee, was converted to the scheme that would eventually pass by the
canny compromises and persistent persuasiveness of its principal drafter,
Oliver Ellsworth. But Lee felt duty-bound to join with his colleague
William Grayson to bring Virginia's desires to the Senate floor when debate
on the judiciary opened on June 22. Lee had moved for independence in
1776 and was probably the best-known person in the Senate. He and
Grayson proposed to limit the jurisdiction of the lower federal courts to admiralty cases. Thus, the state courts would be the trial courts of the federal
system and, except for admiralty, all issues would come to the Supreme
Court either on appeal from the states or as an original trial. After full debate, the Senate voted this system down on June 24, as did the House when
the scheme was proposed in August.

Then William Samuel Johnson of Connecticut and a few others introduced a second scheme, the *nisi prius* system, which would have only one federal court, a Supreme Court, composed of a large number of judges. These judges — as occurred contemporaneously in England — would ride out on circuit, singly or in small groups, into the states to sit at the trials of cases. They would return collectively to the seat of government to deliberate, consult, and ultimately decide difficult reserved questions of law. Johnson argued that such a system would be inexpensive, saving litigants and witnesses the costs of travel to the center, and would create instant uniformity of law. After a half-day's debate, the Senate on June 24 also rejected *nisi prius*. Neither rejection was inevitable, however. Had either *nisi prius* or the Virginia plan been adopted, the national judicial system would have been unrecognizable to us today.

The Ellsworth Plan: Restrictions on Federal Power Accepted

The scheme adopted was principally the work of Oliver Ellsworth, who deserves to be called the "Father of the Judiciary." Having taken to the Convention a great many ideas developed in conversation with his strong Federalist friends in Connecticut and Massachusetts, Ellsworth nevertheless understood in the wake of the ratification process the need for genuine compromise. He made drastic concessions to the opposition interests, and early in committee deliberations — by April 24 — these, plus his forceful, insistent style of argument, convinced Lee to favor his proposal. Lee's support was decisive, for he was clearly the most important opponent of strong central government on the committee.

The major points of Ellsworth's compromise were as follows. First, severe limits and restrictions would be placed on federal court jurisdiction. Cases "arising under" the Constitution, laws, or treaties would be tried in state courts, and appeal would be allowed to the Supreme Court *only* (1) from *final* decisions in the *highest* court of a state, and (2) where the state court had ruled *against* the federal law in question. These provisions conceded much to the dignity of state courts, assuring Anti-Federalists that those courts would not be superseded by the federal scheme.

Second, the "citizenship" jurisdictions, involving foreigners or out-of-state citizens, would be given to the federal courts, but cases would be subject to a $500 minimum amount-in-controversy limitation. This provision eliminated at one stroke about half the British debts from federal court, including all of the smallest ones most troubling to Anti-Federalists. Appeals in these cases to the Supreme Court were subjected to a $2,000 amount-in-controversy limitation, protecting litigants who won (up to that amount) from traveling to the seat of government.

Finally, Supreme Court appellate jurisdiction would occur *only* by "writ of error," a mode of appeal limiting the appellate court to *questions of law only,* so that no jury verdicts would be overturned.

In return, there would be many federal courts, in three layers. District courts, consisting of a single federal judge each, would sit three times a year in each state. The jurisdiction of these courts would be limited to noncontroversial cases: admiralty, petty crimes, and cases dealing with the revenue (customs and taxes). This would bring the new national government into each state. (Bending over backward to please Anti-Federalists, and despite the Constitution's seeming grant of exclusive federal jurisdiction over all admiralty cases, Ellsworth's bill allowed state courts to grant maritime remedies that the common law was competent to give.)

The United States would be divided into three circuits, and circuit courts would sit twice a year in each state. (To please Anti-Federalists, no states were divided in drawing the circuit boundaries.) The circuit courts would try all the important and controversial cases — the "citizenship" cases (above the $500 limit) and federal crimes — as well as hearing appeals from the district courts. Also listening to sharp Anti-Federalist criticism, the bill established an "assignee" limitation, prohibiting the assignment of a cause of action to a citizen of another state in order to create federal jurisdiction where none existed between the original parties. To save money and to bring important judges to these cases, the circuit courts would not be staffed with their own judges but would each consist of two of the six Supreme Court judges and the local federal district court judge. With such important judges, appeals from their decisions would likely be fewer.

Finally, a Supreme Court, consisting of a Chief Justice and five associate judges, would sit twice a year at the seat of government; its members would also ride circuit twice a year. Its jurisdiction would be mostly appellate, from both state courts and federal courts. In instances of ambassadorial litigation, suits between two or more states, and suits involving a state as defendant when sued by a citizen of a different state, it would have original jurisdiction. Knowing that these last suits would cause immense controversy, the bill's drafters lodged them in the Supreme Court.

Federal writs of habeas corpus would lie only to prisoners in federal custody, not also to prisoners in state custody. Federal writs of mandamus would lie only to federal officers.

The last element in the compromise emerged two weeks later, probably from Lee's insistence that the Federalists keep all the promises they made during the ratification contest. What if a British-debts plaintiff or, more likely, an out-of-state plaintiff wanted to sue in state court? Ellsworth's answer was to make the "citizenship" jurisdictions concurrent.

"Citizenship" jurisdiction cases would be allowed either in state court or, above the amount-in-controversy limit of $500, in federal court. Defendants in "citizenship" cases in *state* court could transfer them to federal court, but only before trial. Thereafter litigants in such cases must abide the choice. No appellate jurisdiction from state courts to the Supreme Court would be established for those in "citizenship" cases who had chosen state court. This limitation remains today.

In addition to the meliorations already mentioned, no provision was made for the transference of any "British debt" case already pending on state court dockets, meaning that there would be no "retroactive" application of federal jurisdiction to such cases. The right to trial by jury in civil cases was upheld throughout.

Although Federalists were pleased with the three tiers of courts, with the large number of federal judges, and with the placing of federal officials in every state ("you carry Law to their Homes, Courts to their doors — meet every Citizen in his own State," as Paterson's notes for his June speech defending the scheme show), they were uneasy with the whole. From their standpoint, it was a weak bill, mostly a hope for the future.

Ellsworth's choice to escalate the presence and numbers of federal officials rather than grant the courts all the power they could have been given was tactically brilliant, but nevertheless had been a choice made from weakness. The state courts would still try many important cases, including both "federal question" cases and some of those between citizens of different states. Many British-debt cases would not be tried at all. The British were furious and protested regularly (to no avail) during the 1790s.

The basic outlines of the federal judiciary had been determined. Congress nevertheless spent two more months tinkering, adjusting the details, and most of those changes moved in the same direction as had Ellsworth's compromises: restricting the power of the federal courts. Several minor changes established that the Senate, like the Anti-Federalists, was opposed to federal judges' sitting without juries and trying or reviewing factual determinations.

Not all the changes were restrictive. Probably as a stopgap measure arising from the Senate's failure to bring in a bill defining federal crimes, the federal courts were allowed to hear common-law crimes (that is, crimes defined by the courts, not by the legislature). Although, as noted, the writs of habeas corpus and mandamus were restricted to federal instances, the powers of federal courts to issue the other peremptory writs (that is, "demanding" writs, or unappealable mandatory orders) were left open-ended. Potentially, this could allow broad use of the writs of injunction, prohibition, and certiorari, the latter to withdraw a case from a lower court at the reviewing court's insistence, the others to give certain kinds of orders to lower courts. This could cause much trouble if state courts were considered "lower." Except for the open-endedness of the writs provision, however, these items were minor, and the possible use of peremptory writs to extend federal power was an unknown quantity entirely in the future.

Overall, Ellsworth's compromise strategy worked well. A judiciary act much more restrictive of federal judicial powers than Federalists had desired was passed by both houses of Congress in September and was immediately signed into law by President George Washington. Anti-Federalist strength had forced Ellsworth and a Federalist Congress to keep the backtracking promises Federalists had made about the judiciary during the ratification campaign. It had ensured preservation of much of the state courts' authority and dignity, and it had ensured that several important debt-case-related restrictions would be placed on the jurisdiction and activity of the new federal courts. The new structure was full of nationalizing potential, but the fact in 1789 was one of restriction and limitation of power.

Immediate Denial of Alteration of the Judiciary, 1789–1791

Many Federalists saw the Judiciary Act of 1789 as a puzzling and temporary measure, "an experimental law," as Congressman Fisher Ames of Massachusetts put it, passed only "in the confidence that a short experience will make manifest the proper alterations." Federalists desired a much more fully empowered judiciary, and in August 1790 the House of Representatives authorized Attorney General Edmund Randolph to study the act in operation and propose changes to it. Anti-Federalists also desired changes: Senator William Maclay of Pennsylvania wrote Patrick Henry in September 1789 that the Virginia plan, restricting the lower federal courts to admiralty, had many friends in Congress and might still pass. But events that occurred in the fall of 1790 and the winter of 1791 stopped all important changes, forcing contemporaries to appreciate the compromising wisdom of Ellsworth.

Anti-Federalist Upset at Peremptory Writs

When North Carolina finally entered the union, Robert Morris and his lawyers used two of the peremptory writs to try to transfer to federal court the 1787 verdict in which, he claimed, he had been grossly ill-used by a North Carolina jury. After that verdict had been handed down, Morris had appealed it to the Superior Court, North Carolina's highest court, but had allowed his appeal to lie on the court's docket. Then, in September 1790, his lawyer persuaded three of the newly appointed Supreme Court justices — John Rutledge and James Wilson, who had served on the Convention's Committee of Detail, and John Blair, also a Framer — to sign two writs: one of injunction, preventing the North Carolina court from acting further in the case, and one of certiorari, transferring the case to the North Carolina federal circuit court. Both writs implied that the highest court in North Carolina was inferior to a middle-level federal court; moreover, both writs were commands, not requests. Neither the North Carolina court nor the lawyer for Morris's opponent was notified, much less asked beforehand.

This high-handed procedure seemed to confirm to Anti-Federalists all the charges they had raised against the Federalists. Federal courts would make state courts useless in ordinary cases, such as this contract case; states were inferior to the federal government in ordinary matters; the federal government would exercise its power peremptorily; and no matter what restrictions might have been placed on federal court power in the Judiciary Act, broad construction of federal power rendered them worthless, as the Anti-Federalist commentator Brutus had foreseen. Morris, on the other hand, thought that the federal courts had been instituted to redress localistic state court discrimination against developers and merchants.

In November 1790, the North Carolina Superior Court refused to obey the writ and sent an angry explanation to the legislature, which approved the Court's action in an equally angry resolution. The strong words of the judges and the legislature made national news, accelerating Anti-Federalist upset at the very moment Treasury Secretary Alexander Hamilton was proposing both an excise tax on whiskey and federal assumption of the remaining state Revolutionary War debts. Anti-Federalists did not like these actions and asserted that the federal government lacked authority to undertake them. The Supreme Court justices allowed the unobeyed certiorari writ to rest. When similar requests for certiorari came in 1791 to Wilson as circuit judge in Virginia and to James Iredell as circuit judge in Georgia, both writs were denied. Iredell stated that there was no federal authority to issue the writ. Once again, vociferous Anti-Federalist resistance had turned back an attempt to garner broad powers for the federal courts.

Randolph's Report, the Benson Amendment, and Impasse

On New Year's Eve 1790, Randolph submitted his report on the judiciary. Federalists were aghast. Randolph was strongly committed to union and thought that clashes between the states and the federal government, such as that in the North Carolina instance, would be the force of dissolution. Wanting to avoid as many such clashes as possible, Randolph brilliantly and thoughtfully proposed the termination of concurrent jurisdiction between state and federal courts. He proposed that six categories of jurisdiction be made exclusively federal, including cases involving rights created by Congress. All other cases involving questions arising under the Constitution, laws, or treaties could be transferred from state courts to federal courts by request of either party before trial, but would otherwise remain forever in the state courts. Randolph thought that the nation should not be bound by state decisions on federal subjects, so that erroneous state court decisions about federal subjects could be remedied by future federal court decisions. But to preserve union, he argued, no federal interest was so strong that it should be allowed a second chance in a federal court (including appeals); the uniformity of federal law was not as important as state court dignity. Finally, with the North Carolina instance fresh, he would carefully limit the power of federal courts to issue peremptory writs. No friend of British-debt avoidance, Randolph would have allowed the Supreme Court to review issues of fact.

Federalists thought that state courts that denied creditors their due deserved no such dignity and respect. The Federalists were unwilling to allow any chance that state court decisions on federal law or federal interests — as they viewed creditors' interests — might be final and unappealable to federal courts. They countered with a short amendment to the Constitution, proposed by strong Federalist Congressman Egbert Benson of New York, on March 1, 1791. Benson's proposal would have made each state supreme court a federal court, whose judges were selected by the states but paid by the national government, and who would have tenure during good behavior.

Thus did the Federalists make their point that matters committed to the state and federal judiciaries were not separable into two distinct spheres, but rather were inescapably joined, and that federal supremacy in the resulting clashes was inevitable. To try another plan, as Randolph proposed, could result, Benson's amendment warned, in an arrangement that destroyed state courts and their independence altogether. Anti-Federalist claims that Federalists sought, one way or another, the subordination of the states to the national government were, it seemed, correct.

Neither Benson's amendment nor Randolph's plan ever surfaced again. At least for the moment, both Federalists and Anti-Federalists were content to accept Ellsworth's compromises. The next round of clashes over the power of the federal courts would commence in the spring of 1800, when it became clear that Thomas Jefferson would become the third president of the United States but with Federalists still in control of Congress. Some important changes would occur, mostly in the manner in which the Supreme Court conducted its business, but when the dust settled with the failure of Justice Samuel Chase's impeachment in 1806, the outcome of that round too was to leave the basic structure of the federal courts intact as it had been established under the Judiciary Act of 1789. So it remains.

—WYTHE W. HOLT, JR.

FOR FURTHER READING AND RESEARCH

For detailed treatment of the context and drafting of the Judiciary Act of 1789, with citations for most of the quotations used here, see Wythe Holt, " 'To Establish Justice': Politics, the Judiciary Act of 1789, and the Invention of the Federal Courts," *Duke Law Review* (1989), 1421–1531. The other quotations I have used may be found in Max Farrand, ed., *The Records of the Federal Convention of 1787*, 2v. (New Haven, 1911); and Jacob Cooke, ed., *The Federalist* (Middletown, Conn., 1961), 521–557.

For further information on political, economic, and legal issues during the period, see Gary B. Nash, *The Urban Crucible: Social Change, Political Consciousness, and the Origins of the American Revolution* (Cambridge, Mass., 1979); Joseph Ernst, *Money and Politics in America 1755–1775: A Study in the Currency Act of 1764 and the Political Economy of Revolution* (Chapel Hill, N.C., 1973); Merrill Jensen, *The New Nation: A History of the United States During the Confederation 1781–1789* (New York, 1950); Allan Nevins, *The American States During and After the Revolution* (New York, 1924); Allan Kulikoff, *The Agrarian Origins of American Capitalism* (Charlottesville, Va., 1992); Christopher L. Tomlins, *Law, Labor, and Ideology in the Early American Republic* (New York and Cambridge, 1993); Wilfred J. Ritz, *Rewriting the History of the Judiciary Act of 1789: Exposing Myths, Challenging Premises, and Using New Evidence*, Wythe Holt and L. H. LaRue, eds. (Norman, Okla., 1990); Terry Bouton, "A Road Closed: Rural Insurgence in Post-Independence Pennsylvania," *Journal of American History* 87 (2000), 855–887.

For the Robert Morris case, see Wythe Holt and James R. Perry, "Writs and Rights, 'clashings and animosities': The First Confrontation between Federal and State Jurisdictions," *Law and History Review* 7 (1989), 89–120.

For federal criminal common law, see Wythe Holt, "The First Meeting of the Federal Circuit Court in New York: A Federal Common Law of Crimes?" *Second Circuit Redbook*, 1990–1991 Supplement (1990), 19–25. For the first attempt to revise the Judiciary Act, see Wythe Holt, " 'Federal Courts as the Asylum to Federal Interests': Randolph's Report, the Benson Amendment, and the 'Original Understanding' of the Federal Judiciary," *Buffalo Law Review* 36 (1987), 341–372. For that revision of the Judiciary Act most desired by members of the first Supreme Court, see Wythe Holt, " 'The Federal Courts Have Enemies in All Who Fear Their Influence on State Objects': The Failure to Abolish Supreme Court Circuit-Riding in the Judiciary Acts of 1792 and 1793," *Buffalo Law Review* 36 (1987), 301–340.

2

The Earliest Years   1790–1801

Laying Foundations

THE SUPREME COURT OF THE UNITED STATES is the Constitution's most novel and least-defined creation. Everything the Constitution has to say on the matter appears in a single phrase of one sentence in the first clause of Article III. "The judicial Power of the United States, shall be vested in one supreme Court and in such inferior Courts as the Congress may from time to time ordain and establish." In Article III, the shortest of the articles establishing the three branches of government, delegates to the Constitutional Convention set out a few rules — federal judges would have life tenure and their salaries could not be diminished while they continued in office — and vaguely described the jurisdiction encompassed by the federal judicial power but left the most controversial question — whether courts inferior to the Supreme Court were needed — for Congress to answer. As such, no one could predict how the institution might develop, least of all those in Congress called on to put flesh on the constitutional bone.

Establishment of a National Judiciary

The first Congress, more attuned to the politics of the day than the Framers had been and very much aware of the opposition to the judiciary article during the ratification debate, kept these considerations in mind when it enacted the Judiciary Act of 1789. The act organized the national judiciary in three tiers: district courts, circuit courts, and the Supreme Court. Each tier was assigned a jurisdiction that did not exhaust the full measure of the constitutional grant. Despite Herculean efforts to design a federal judicial system without arousing the antagonism of the state judiciaries, those involved recognized the difficulty of achieving such a goal. Their scheme of organization, they realized, should therefore be characterized as experimental and perhaps temporary in nature. Appointed under the 1789 act, John Jay (Plate A.1), the first chief justice of the Supreme Court, captured the sentiment exactly: "It is pleasing to observe that the present national Government already affords advantages, which the preceding one proved too feeble and ill constructed to produce. How far it may be still distant from the Degree of Perfection to which it may possibly be carried Time only can decide. It is a Consolation to reflect that the good Sense of the People will be enabled by Experience to discover and correct its Imperfections."

When President George Washington took office in 1789, the institution of the Supreme Court was completely unformed. Washington did not know even the number of justices he would be required to appoint. Within a few months, however, the basic contours of the third branch had begun to emerge from the Senate committee charged with considering the matter. The Supreme Court would consist of a chief justice and five associate justices and would convene at the federal capital on the first Monday in February and the first Monday in August to hold two annual sessions. Below the Supreme Court would be two levels of lower courts. At the lowest level, the Judiciary Act created for each of the states a federal district court that would have its own presiding judge, who lived in the district and would exercise jurisdiction over admiralty and maritime causes and minor federal crimes. At a higher level would be circuit courts, which, unlike today's circuit courts of appeal, were to be primarily courts of original jurisdiction — trial courts — for major federal crimes and civil cases of higher monetary value. Appeals from the district courts made up a minor portion of their dockets. Each state would have one circuit court, and the states were grouped into three circuits: eastern, middle, and southern. The Judiciary Act provided that no judges would be appointed to the circuit courts. Instead, twice a year, two Supreme Court justices would attend the circuit court in each state, with the district judge from that state as the third member of the bench. The act set the number of justices at six, so that two could be assigned to each circuit in the spring and in the fall.

By failing to require a separate set of judges for the circuit courts, Congress limited the expense of the federal judiciary about which many states had complained during the ratification process. But Congress claimed to have more positive reasons for the omission: Sending Supreme Court justices to all the states would be good for the new government and good for all the citizens. As then Senator William Paterson, who would later become a justice, noted, circuit courts would benefit the populace by carrying "Law to their Homes, Courts to their Doors."

The appointments that President Washington made to the Supreme Court reflected his desire to ensure that the new judicial system succeed.

While the judiciary bill made its way through Congress, the president had several months to think about possible candidates — and to feel political pressure as well. The president himself decided on the qualities he wanted. He did not choose men solely on the basis of legal knowledge but instead looked for nominees with a wider experience of the world. Support for the Constitution was essential. He also took into account character, training, health, and public renown. Geographical diversity, according to Washington, was another necessity, not only because the justices would have to ride circuit but also because he wanted to avoid arousing jealousies among the states. Participation in the Revolution, finally, weighed heavily in Washington's calculations: The greater the sacrifice, the better the chance to obtain federal office.

The salary attached to the position of justice made nomination to the Supreme Court attractive. The drafters of the first Compensation Act had proposed salaries of $4,500 and $4,000 for the chief and associate justices, respectively — the highest salaries for new federal officials other than the president and vice president. But fearing the envy of state judges who did not get paid nearly as much and predicting that federal judges would have less work (a prediction quickly proved wrong), the House of Representatives lowered the chief's salary to $3,500 and the associates' to $3,000. In the Senate, however, the salaries again were raised to $4,000 and $3,500, where they remained until 1819. The president signed the Compensation Act on September 23, 1789, the day before the Judiciary Act became law. The salaries appeared generous, but the Compensation Act made no provision for payment of the justices' expenses while traveling to and from the Supreme Court, living in the nation's capital for the Court sessions, and riding circuit. After the first year, the justices found that they had very little money left from their annual salary. The news got out, and the job of Supreme Court justice became much less desirable.

The First Supreme Court

How did Washington choose the first six nominees to the Supreme Court? He instructed those interested in appointment to write to him but always returned noncommittal answers. He consulted with senators and congressmen about possible candidates from their states, and he talked to his closest friends and advisors about specific individuals. One question he consistently asked was whether a potential nominee would be likely to accept an appointment. In his view, if too many people turned down the federal offices tendered them, the new government would be harmed in the eyes of its citizens.

As Washington winnowed down the field, service on a state judiciary became the criterion that seemed to gain most in importance. Vice President John Adams had emphasized the desirability of such experience: "It would have an happy effect," he wrote, "if all the judges of the national supreme Court, could be taken from the chief Justices of the several states. The superiority of the national government would in this way be decidedly acknowledged. All the judges of the states would look up to the national bench as their ultimate object." Washington clearly valued Adams's advice: Five of his six nominees to the Supreme Court had held high judicial positions in their states.

The president sent his first six nominations to the Senate on the day he signed the Judiciary Act. John Jay, his choice for chief justice, headed the list. Only forty-three years old when he was appointed, Jay, a native of New York, had already had an extraordinarily full life. A successful practicing attorney, Jay got caught up in the political efforts meant to resolve the colonies' dispute with Great Britain. Immediately after independence, he became the first chief justice of New York's newly formed state Supreme Court of Judicature. But Jay soon left New York. Elected to the First and Second Continental Congresses, he was unexpectedly chosen president of Congress, then appointed minister plenipotentiary to Spain, and a few years later selected as one of the commissioners to negotiate a peace with Great Britain.

Jay had hoped to withdraw from the public arena once peace was concluded, but the Confederation Congress named him secretary of foreign affairs, and he did not refuse to serve. He remained secretary of foreign affairs until Thomas Jefferson succeeded him as secretary of state on March 22, 1790, six months after Jay had assumed the chief justiceship. Washington chose a statesman rather than a renowned legal scholar to head the Supreme Court in the expectation that Jay would play a greater role in the political development of the institution than in its jurisprudence. Indeed, during the early years of the Republic, Jay became a close and trusted advisor to the president, involved in affairs of state unconnected to the judiciary.

Washington's five nominees to be associate justices had similar qualifications, although their experience was not as extensive as Jay's, especially in the arena of diplomacy. In order to establish seniority, the president supplied different dates for each of the commissions of the justices, who were all confirmed by the Senate on the same day. The most senior associate was John Rutledge of South Carolina, a lawyer trained at the Middle Temple in London, who had risen to be governor of his state and chief justice of the South Carolina Court of Chancery. William Cushing, second in seniority, differed from the others in that he had no national experience but had achieved prominence in his home state of Massachusetts, where, after independence, he had become chief justice of the Superior Court of Judicature (later named the Supreme Judicial Court). Third in line came Robert Hanson Harrison of Maryland. Much to Washington's disappointment, Harrison never served on the Supreme Court. Becoming ill in January 1790 on his way to New York, the first capital of the United States, Harrison withdrew and returned his commission.

Next in seniority was James Wilson, the man many had thought would be chief justice. Broadly educated at the University of St. Andrews, Scotland, Wilson came to America imbued with the spirit of the Scottish and English enlightenment — perfect preparation for the patriot cause. After studying law, he developed a flourishing practice and devoted himself to opposing English rule. He signed the Declaration of Independence as a representative of Pennsylvania. During the Revolution, Wilson immersed himself in political theory, history, and philosophy, and his preeminence in these fields was recognized both by the American Philosophical Society, which elected him a member in 1786, and by the Pennsylvania legislature, which chose him as a delegate to the federal convention in 1787. Wilson's contributions to the framing of the Constitution are widely considered second only to James Madison's, but his subsequent career on the Supreme Court did not fulfill the promise of his earlier achievements. President Washington showed himself prescient when he declined to nominate Wilson as chief justice. Continually distracted by financial problems, Wilson spent time in debtors' jail even while he was associate justice. His exceptional intellectual ability made little impression on his judicial brethren, and he died in disgrace while still on the bench.

The most junior member of Washington's initial group of nominees was John Blair of Virginia. Having studied in London, Blair returned to his native state to practice law and became an active patriot. His long judicial career began immediately after Virginia's independence, and he served as a judge on various state courts, becoming chief justice of one and then chancellor of another. With Washington and Madison, Blair formed part of Virginia's delegation to the federal convention and strongly supported the Constitution. At the time of his nomination to the U.S. Supreme Court, Blair had just been appointed by the state legislature to be one of five judges of the new Virginia Supreme Court of Appeals.

Washington made one additional appointment to fill the vacancy created when Robert Harrison returned his commission. Under the circumstances, the president needed to act quickly. Fortunately, he had someone in mind. James Iredell of North Carolina had been a wartime state attorney general, superior court judge, and a leading proponent of the federal Constitution at his state's two ratifying conventions. Washington believed that it would be expedient to nominate a North Carolinian to allay that state's doubts about the Constitution, and Iredell's name had been suggested to him. Satisfied that Iredell's character and experience suited him for the job, Washington nominated Iredell to the Supreme Court on February 8, 1790. The Senate confirmed the nomination on February 10, but Iredell did not receive his commission until March 3. Although this was too late for the Court's first meeting, it meant that a full bench was available for the spring circuits.

During the remainder of his two terms in office, Washington filled a further five vacancies: Thomas Johnson replaced John Rutledge in 1791; in 1793, William Paterson took Johnson's place; when John Jay was elected governor of New York in 1795, John Rutledge received a recess appointment as chief justice and served one term but was not confirmed by the Senate; Samuel Chase became John Blair's replacement in 1796; and a few months later, the Senate confirmed Oliver Ellsworth as chief justice.

During his term, President John Adams dealt with three more vacancies. On the death of James Wilson in 1798, Adams nominated Bushrod Washington; Alfred Moore became a justice in 1799 when James Iredell died; and in January 1801—three months after the resignation of Ellsworth in October 1800 and after John Jay had first declined nomination by Adams and confirmation by the Senate to a second term—John Marshall was appointed chief justice. In all, then, twelve men sat on the Supreme Court bench in its first decade. Six had served in the Continental Congress, four in the Confederation Congress, and two in the U.S. Congress. Only five of the justices had not seen service in a national congress, but all had been delegates to their states' ratification conventions. Samuel Chase was the only justice who had not participated in either the Constitutional Convention or his state's ratifying convention. With backgrounds like these, it is not surprising that the justices felt some proprietary relationship to the new order.

As the year 1790 began, the justices embarked on their business in a spirit of discovery: Each action they took would be a test of the blueprint for governing outlined by the Constitution and the First Congress. Fully conscious of the significance of every decision they made, the justices invested much thought in even the smallest administrative detail.

At the initial February term of the Supreme Court, which took place at the New York Merchants Exchange (Plate A.2), administrative matters were the only things on the agenda. A great many city dignitaries attended the session, but what unfolded was hardly exciting. The commissions of the justices and the attorney general of the United States, Edmund Randolph, were read; a Court clerk and a crier were appointed; seals were adopted for the Supreme and circuit courts; and a rule for the admission of attorneys to the Supreme Court bar (one that remains in effect to this day) was announced. Another rule promulgated, that "all Process of this Court, shall be in the Name of the President of the United States," caused some comment because it equated the president with the English king, but Congress did not change it. In the second week of the term, the Court convened for three days, admitted attorneys on each of those days, and then adjourned until August. At some point during the session, the justices decided on their circuit assignments. Jay and Cushing took the eastern, Wilson and Blair got the middle, and Rutledge and Iredell rode the southern — by far the longest and most difficult circuit to traverse.

The Justices on Circuit

Before they set out on their circuits, Washington informed the justices that he believed that the "stability and success of the National Government" depended to a large extent on the "Interpretation and Execution of its Laws." Therefore, he thought it "important that the Judiciary System should not only be independent in its operations, but as perfect as possible in its formation." He wanted the justices to tell him about any problems they encountered, so he and the legislature could correct them. James Madison, a member of the Congress that passed the Judiciary Act, also believed that the organization of the judiciary was deficient and expressed the hope that "the system may speedily undergo a reconsideration under the auspices of the Judges who alone will be able perhaps to set it to rights." Although they did not take advantage of the president's invitation frequently, the justices can on occasion be found freely communicating their feelings about how the new system was working and what changes were needed to improve it.

Prominent among their concerns was circuit riding. The justices may have appreciated intellectually the benefits that were to accrue to the new nation from their attendance at courts in every state, but the realities of travel in the late eighteenth century made circuit duties burdensome. Already committed to attending the Supreme Court in the nation's capital during the two worst months of the year, February and August, the justices were required to spend another six months — three in the spring and three in the fall — attempting to reach the scheduled circuit courts. Rutted roads, muddy trails, and swollen or frozen rivers often made these trips a nightmare. Once arrived at their destination, the justices usually found themselves in public lodgings that were at best crowded and uncomfortable. William Cushing once slept with twelve lodgers to a room; James Iredell complained that one could meet unexpectedly "a bed fellow of the wrong sort." To add insult to injury, the justices had to pay their own expenses.

Objecting to more than the physical discomforts of their rounds on circuit, the justices questioned the propriety — maybe even the constitutional propriety — of requiring the same individuals to serve as both superior and inferior court judges in the same cases. When all six justices were in New York for the August 1790 term, they discussed their scruples about the circuit system and agreed that Chief Justice Jay would draw up a letter to the president. In that draft, Jay wrote exclusively and at length about the unconstitutionality of assigning Supreme Court justices to hear matters of original jurisdiction that had not been enumerated in the two categories of cases specified in Article III of the Constitution. When the justices made their protest public in a letter sent to the president and Congress in August 1792, however, they merely alluded to this problem, noting that their dual appointments as circuit and Supreme Court judges would impair both the impartiality of the Court and public confidence in the institution. They concentrated their fire on the burden of being required to spend so much of their time away from home and family and in such unpleasant conditions. Congress responded to the complaints in March 1793 by passing a Judiciary Act amendment that required the attendance of only one Supreme Court justice at each circuit court, thus reducing, but not eliminating, the burden of circuit riding.

Practical impediments notwithstanding, the justices took their circuit duties seriously; they were frequently the only representatives of the new national government that citizens would see and prepared carefully. At the opening of each court, the presiding justice gave a charge to the grand jury; derived from English practice, this custom remained in use during the colonial era and made its way intact into the new Republic. These often-lengthy disquisitions — part sermon, part political discourse, part jurisprudential essay — allowed the justices to explicate the laws and structure of the federal government to grand jurors. In his initial appearance at the New York circuit court, for example, Chief Justice John Jay discussed why and how the United States had been formed, the theoretical basis for its organization, the obstacles with which it had to contend, and the difficulties it would face. But he did his best to appeal to people of all persuasions, to enlist their sympathy for a great experiment: "If the most discerning and enlightened Minds may be mistaken relative to Theories unconfirmed by Practice_ if on such difficult Questions men may differ in opinion and yet be Patriots_ and if the Merits of our opinions can only be ascertained by Experience, let us patiently abide the Tryal, and unite our Endeavors to render it a fair and an impartial one." In this charge — the first ever given under the new Judiciary Act — Jay put his finger on what would become throughout the history of the Supreme Court the subject of recurrent controversy: judicial review. "A judicial Controul, general & final, was indispensable. The Manner of establishing it, with Powers neither too extensive, nor too limited; rendering it properly independent, and yet properly amenable, involved Questions of no little Intricacy." Though clearly cognizant of the difficulty of the issue, it probably did not occur to the Court's first members that the nation would still be wrestling with the problem two hundred years later.

In this same charge, Chief Justice Jay identified another issue that would plague the justices throughout the 1790s: the practical effect of the separation-of-powers doctrine as enunciated in the Constitution. When the U.S. government began operations in early 1789, separation of powers was a new and relatively untried political concept. By the end of the eighteenth century, Jay observed, there was unanimous agreement among "wise and virtuous Men" that the powers of government should be divided into "three, distinct, independent Departments_The Executive legislative and judicial." But the chief justice quickly noted that "how to constitute and ballance them in such a Manner as best to guard against Abuse and Fluctuation, & preserve the Constitution from Encroachments, are Points on which there continues to be a great Diversity of opinions, and on which we have all as yet much to learn."

Justices in Extrajudicial Roles

The Constitution having wedded a system of checks and balances to the separation-of-powers doctrine, the justices had to not only determine the impact of this combination of doctrines on the cases that came before them but also consider what it meant for their own behavior as individuals. As Congress and the president often asked the justices to act in ways not wholly in keeping with an independent judiciary engaged only in judicial work, they had to develop guidelines that would govern the activities they would undertake.

Aware that debate at the Constitutional Convention had counterposed the need for an independent judiciary to the desire to use the talents of eminent men, the justices articulated a distinction between the Court as an institution and its members as individuals. The Supreme Court as an institution would follow scrupulously the separation-of-powers doctrine to make sure that nothing would interfere with its impartial adjudication of cases and controversies properly presented. But as individuals, its members would participate in a wide variety of activities that might be looked on as compromising their independence as an institution.

From the beginning of the decade, Congress and the president freely used the justices where necessary for the good of the nation. Passed on August 12, 1790, legislation dealing with the reduction of the public debt made the chief justice a commissioner of the Sinking Fund along with other high government officials. Congress believed that the work of this commission was so important that its members had to be worthy of the public trust. No one in Congress objected to using a justice in this manner. Indeed, shortly thereafter, a different statute named the chief justice an inspector of coins for the United States Mint—another job that required the public's confidence.

The president, too, had occasion to take advantage of the wisdom of the justices. In the summer of 1793, as the war of the French Revolution raged in the Atlantic, the United States found its neutrality endangered by the conflicting demands of the belligerent powers: France and Great Britain. The Washington administration decided to seek the advice of the Supreme Court on a number of questions about the interpretation of the nation's treaties and statutes, as well as the law of nations. As Secretary of State Thomas Jefferson wrote to the justices, the president would be "much relieved" if he could refer these matters to the Supreme Court because the justices' collective knowledge, experience, and authority would "ensure the respect of all parties." But before Washington could do this, he had to know "whether the public may, with propriety, be availed of their *advice on these questions.*" In their official reply to the president, the justices emphasized the Constitution's separation-of-powers doctrine as an obstacle to their complying with his request: "The Lines of Separation drawn by the Constitution between the three Departments of Government__their being in certain Respects checks on each other__and our being Judges of a court in the last Resort__are Considerations which afford strong arguments against the Propriety of our extrajudicially deciding the questions alluded to."

History has taken the justices at their word, and the Supreme Court, as a separate and independent institution, has never given an advisory opinion. The justices, however, do appear to have given the executive advice, hinting that in this particular instance involving the foreign policy of the United States, the government would appear stronger if the executive adopted neutrality rules, to be followed later by endorsement by Congress and the Court. President Washington and his cabinet learned that cases were in the pipeline in which the judiciary might supply the answers to some of the questions that they had put to the Supreme Court. That is indeed what transpired: In a series of cases beginning with *Glass v. Sloop Betsey* (1794), the Supreme Court established that the federal courts had jurisdiction as courts of admiralty to deal with many of the issues raised by the president's questions. The justices may, however, have rued the day they announced that decision. For the next several years, the greater part of their docket would be taken up with prize cases.

Presidents Washington and Adams both used the justices in another extrajudicial capacity: as special envoys to European powers. Diplomatic relations between the United States and England had become so tense by early 1794 that Washington determined to send Chief Justice John Jay, because of his extensive experience in diplomacy, to negotiate a peaceful settlement of numerous controversies. Jay successfully concluded the Treaty of Amity, Commerce, and Navigation (popularly known as the Jay Treaty), which was signed on November 19, 1794, but he did not return to the United States until the end of May 1795. In 1799, President Adams nominated Chief Justice Oliver Ellsworth to be one of three ministers plenipotentiary to France, sent to seek an end to the quasi-war with that nation. Arriving in Paris in March 1800, Ellsworth worked out a commercial convention that was ratified by the Senate in February 1801. In each instance, however, the absence of the chief justice caused much hardship for the other justices. They had to continue presiding over the circuit courts, and the chief's absence meant one less justice to sit on the Supreme Court bench during its sessions. In Ellsworth's case, the European mission had an even more unfortunate result: Ellsworth's health was broken, and in October 1800, while still in Paris, he resigned from the Supreme Court. Adding to these very practical effects of the extrajudicial missions was the unease caused by the underlying problem of justices engaged in work that might someday come before the Court in the ordinary course of litigation.

The justices themselves did not seem excessively troubled by giving advice in their individual capacities on subjects that might later appear in cases on the Court's docket. Justice William Cushing lobbied Congress to enact the first federal crimes act because he had already presided over a prosecution for piracy with no law to guide him. Chief Justice Jay consulted with Secretary of the Treasury Alexander Hamilton and Senator Rufus King about measures the federal government might take to deal with opposition to the whiskey excise. Jay wrote to Washington, setting out his opinion on the constitutional power of Congress to punish counterfeiting and to repair post roads. The chief justice also drafted a neutrality proclamation that he sent to the president. (The text of the proclamation later issued by Washington did not, however, follow Jay's draft.) Justice Iredell conspired with his brother-in-law Senator Samuel Johnston to get Congress to change the law governing the assignment of circuits; other justices urged congressmen to end the system of circuit riding altogether. Chief Justice Oliver Ellsworth, days after joining the Supreme Court, advised his former colleague Senator Jonathan Trumbull that President Washington should resist the request of the House of Representatives for documents relating to the negotiation of the Jay Treaty, which the House wanted to examine before it would vote any funds for implementing the treaty. "The claim of the House of Representatives to participate in or control the Treaty making power is as unwarrented as it is dangerous," Ellsworth wrote. Toward the end of the 1790s, when

Congress was involved in reforming the whole judicial system, Justices William Paterson and Bushrod Washington drafted a complete judicial reform bill and presented it to a congressional committee. When it had finished its work on the bill, the committee asked Paterson for comments and suggested that he show the bill to the other justices.

The Court's Decisions

The earliest substantive opinion given by the Supreme Court, *West v. Barnes* (1791), interpreted a congressional statute in a manner that caused hardship to some litigants. The decision so upset Justice Iredell that he wrote to the president, asking that the details of the case be made known to Congress so that the law could be changed as soon as possible. *West v. Barnes* addressed a procedural question: Was a writ of error that did not come from the Supreme Court valid? Argued in August 1791, the second term of Court held in Philadelphia but the first held in the Court's quarters in the new City Hall (Plate A.4), the case appeared to be of little importance. The plaintiff-in-error had a writ signed and sealed by the clerk of the circuit court in Rhode Island, but the defendant's counsel protested its validity, maintaining that, although the Judiciary Act did not specify from what court a writ of error should issue, section 14 authorized the federal courts to issue writs "agreeable to the principles and usages of law." Past usage required that the writ issue from a higher court to a lower one. Another section of the Judiciary Act, however, suggested that Congress might have had something different in mind. Section 23 stated that a writ of error would stay the judgment of a lower court only when a copy of the writ was filed for the adverse party in the lower court clerk's office within ten days after judgment was entered. If writs of error could be obtained only from the Supreme Court sitting in Philadelphia, litigants in the remote areas of the country could never have the benefit of this section, because it was physically impossible to fulfill its requirements in ten days. Only those able to meet the ten-day deadline could obtain stays of execution of judgment. Congress surely did not intend to treat litigants in this inequitable fashion.

In deciding on the writ's validity, the Court had to choose whether to construe the statute strictly or to allow equal access to justice for citizens residing in all parts of the country. In seriatim opinions—the custom in the early 1790s—the justices unanimously ruled the writ of error invalid. If they had not, they would have been interpreting section 23 to mean that, if Congress allowed only ten days to lodge the writ, Congress must have meant to allow circuit courts to issue writs to themselves—a conclusion not consonant with past usage.

Although they were sensitive to the problems that their decision would cause for writ-seeking litigants who lived far away from the capital city, the justices believed that correction could come only from the legislature that wrote section 23; Congress, not the Court, had to provide the remedy. As Justice James Iredell observed, "It is of infinite moment that Courts of Justice should keep within their proper bounds, and *construe*, not *amend*, acts of Legislation." He fully expected Congress to change the law immediately. When it did not, Justice Iredell continued all cases in his circuit in which section 23 was implicated and sent a letter to President Washington, revealing his action and requesting the president to urge Congress to act. Eventually, Congress did make different provisions for writs of error.

In another series of cases not long thereafter, the justices again had occasion to weigh what action would be appropriate for the Court and what they might do as individuals. Fraught with even greater significance, the *Invalid Pensions Cases*, as they are collectively known, also brought the concept of judicial review into play. Congress enacted the Invalid Pensions Act ("An Act to provide for the settlement of the Claims of Widows and Orphans barred by the limitations heretofore established, and to regulate the Claims to Invalid Pensions") in March 1792, and the first opportunity the justices had to react to it was on circuit in the spring. No federal bureaucracy existed, so Congress, in this act, assigned to the circuit courts the task of hearing the claims of disabled Revolutionary War veterans and ascertaining whether a pension was deserved and in what amount. Once a decision was made, it was to be forwarded to the secretary of war, who would investigate the claim for fraud. He would then send his determination to Congress, which would review it and choose whether to include it in the final pension list.

The justices did not agree on how to respond to the act. All thought the statute unconstitutional on its face, but only the judges of the Circuit Court of Pennsylvania refused to hear any veterans' claims — the first instance of judicial review in a federal court. The judges of that circuit — Justices Wilson and Blair and U.S. District Judge Richard Peters — wrote to President Washington that they believed the act unconstitutional because examining invalids' claims was not a judicial duty. Moreover, the statute subjected the court's determinations to revision by the executive and legislative branches, an authority not contained in the Constitution. Judges on the eastern and southern circuits also addressed letters to the president with their views on the Invalid Pensions Act, although no veteran appeared in their courts to press a claim. These judges agreed with the Pennsylvania circuit court that the plain text of the statute appeared to assign unconstitutional business to the circuit courts. Nevertheless, the judges of the New York circuit court agreed to carry out the task imposed on them, because they were able to devise a way to read the act that would bring it within the bounds of the Constitution. Chief Justice Jay, Justice Cushing, and U.S. District Judge James Duane explained that the statute should be read as giving the pension duties to commissioners who had been described in their official rather than personal capacities. The judges were the commissioners identified, and they would conduct the review of pension claims in that role; court would be adjourned, and the invalid veterans could then appear. The judges noted that this reading was proper in view of the benevolence of the object of the act, because it allowed them to achieve Congress's purpose and show their respect for that branch of government.

Whether the opinion of the judges of the Pennsylvania circuit or of the New York circuit would prevail in the Supreme Court remained unknown for almost two years. The Court first looked at the issue after Attorney General Edmund Randolph moved for a mandamus to order the Pennsylvania court to hear the claim of William Hayburn, an injured veteran. The Court postponed a decision until it became moot because Congress enacted a new statute. But in this second Invalid Pensions Act, passed in February 1793, Congress directed the attorney general and the secretary of war to seek an adjudication before the Supreme Court to decide whether pensions granted under the 1792 act were valid. On February 17, 1794, in an unreported case, *United States v. Yale Todd*, the justices ruled that Todd's pension, which had been approved by judges performing their duties as commissioners, had no legal validity. With no rationale for the decision announced, no one knew whether this was the first time that the Supreme Court had declared a statute unconstitutional or whether the Court had based its ruling on statutory interpretation. From the available evidence, it seems clear that the justices did not strike down the Invalid Pensions Act. If they had, all pensions granted under the act would have been rescinded. Instead, only those veterans who had received pensions after hearings before judges sitting as commissioners had to apply again. Those invalids whose claims had been heard by the district judge of Maine, who wielded the powers of a circuit judge because no circuit court met in that state, kept their awards.

The Supreme Court had further opportunities later in the 1790s to exercise the power of judicial review, but before the Court dealt with those cases, it had to answer one of the most important and controversial constitutional questions to arise in that decade, a question that continues to haunt our constitutional jurisprudence today: Could an individual sue a state in a federal court? Article III of the Constitution provides that the judicial power of the United States "shall extend . . . to Controversies between two or more States" and "between a State and Citizens of another State." Article III also grants original jurisdiction to the Supreme Court in all cases "in which a State shall be Party." During the Constitutional Convention, the subject of state suability elicited no debate, but after the Constitution was sent to the states, that subject became a bone of contention. At their ratifying conventions, several states proposed amendments that would have removed from the Constitution what appeared to be a grant of federal jurisdiction over suits brought by individuals against states. None, however, was adopted. Instead, in section 13 of the Judiciary Act of 1789, Congress gave the Supreme Court original but not exclusive jurisdiction over controversies "between a state and citizens of other states, or aliens."

In the 1790s, eight suits against states were brought in the Supreme Court. In the most famous of these, *Chisholm v. Georgia* (1793), the Court announced its belief that the Constitution mandated federal jurisdiction over suits brought by individuals against states. The decision was not greeted favorably by many of the states, and the ruling inspired the Eleventh Amendment, which was ratified in order to overturn *Chisholm.* Yet in two cases brought to the Court before *Chisholm,* two states — Maryland and New York — entered appearances after subpoenas were issued against them. Maryland settled its case out of court, but *Oswald v. New York* eventually went to trial in 1795. The jury verdict was in favor of the plaintiff, and New York appropriated funds to satisfy the judgment against it.

Even Georgia, which demonstrated its disregard for the Court by not appearing to defend itself against Chisholm's charge that the state owed him money, changed its mind after the Court held that it had jurisdiction and ordered Georgia to show cause why a default judgment should not be issued. At the following term of court, counsel hired by Georgia asked for a postponement. At the next term, counsel argued that judgment should not be entered against the state. The justices thought otherwise and directed that, at the subsequent term, a jury be empaneled to determine how large a sum was owed to Chisholm as a result of Georgia's "breach of promise and other defaults." Before that happened, however, Georgia settled with Chisholm. Simultaneously, the state instructed its representatives in Congress to seek a constitutional amendment eliminating the grant of federal jurisdiction over individuals' suits against states. If Georgia had been as determined to defy the Court as later judges and historians have depicted, the state could have ignored the Supreme Court's judgment. Instead, Georgia chose to satisfy Chisholm's claim and to work within the new federal system to achieve its larger ends.

Congress duly sent to the states a constitutional amendment that explained that the judicial power of the United States should not be "construed to extend" to suits against states by citizens of another state or by aliens. The Eleventh Amendment was ratified by the requisite number of states in less than a year, but the sentiment that had produced it seemed by then to have eroded, for some of the states forgot to notify the federal government that ratification had occurred. Nor did the federal government show any interest in the fate of the amendment. Not until 1798 did the secretary of state receive notice of all the ratifications, leading the president to announce the amendment officially adopted. Until then, the Supreme Court had continued to hear suits against states. Only in February 1798, after the president's announcement, did the justices strike the remaining suits against states from the docket.

What goes unnoticed in the usual commentary about the negative reception of the Court's decision in *Chisholm* is the authority accorded the Court's action. States and citizens accepted the ruling and chose constitutional means to demonstrate their disagreement with it. Moreover, at the same time that Georgia denied the Court's jurisdiction in *Chisholm,* the state looked to the Supreme Court to enforce its rights in another case, *Georgia v. Brailsford* (1794). *Brailsford* is also notable for a second reason: The first, but not last, jury trial to take place in the Supreme Court resulted from adjudication of this suit.

That *Chisholm* did not deal a deathblow to the respect shown for the third branch of government can be shown by the anticipation with which the country, over the next several years, awaited two Supreme Court decisions of great constitutional import. Exercising the power of judicial review, in *Ware v. Hylton* (1796) and *Hylton v. United States* (1796), the Court resolved two issues of major importance. *Ware* concerned the right of British creditors to recover pre–Revolutionary War debts owed to them by Americans. Article 4 of the Definitive Treaty of Peace (1783), which ended the war between Great Britain and America, guaranteed that "creditors on either Side shall meet with no lawful impediments to the Recovery of the full Value in Sterling Money of all bona fide Debts heretofore contracted." British debts had existed in all the states, and many debtors in the North had repaid them. In Virginia, however, where merchants and planters owed more than £2,000,000, state courts had been hostile to British creditors since the Revolution, and debtors steadfastly refused to settle their accounts. Various statutes enacted by the Virginia General Assembly during the Revolution permitted debtors of British subjects to avoid fulfilling their obligations; these debts stood opposed to the treaty provision. The primary act at issue in *Ware v. Hylton* was a 1777 act for sequestering British property, which allowed the debtor to make his payments to the Virginia state loan office instead of his British creditor.

When the federal courts opened in 1790, British creditors were able to pursue their claims in the circuit court in Virginia. As the legal issues in every British debt case were the same, the parties agreed that whatever was decided in *Ware v. Hylton* would cover all the cases. The defendant debtors raised five pleas. A circuit court decision in Richmond in 1793, where Chief Justice Jay, Justice Iredell, and U.S. District Judge Cyrus Griffin were sitting, found for the plaintiff creditor on all counts but one. The court held that the defendant had not yet paid his debt to the plaintiff and rejected various defenses, including two state statutes put forth by Hylton to show that the debt no longer existed. The most interesting argument concerned the fourth plea, in which the defendant asserted that, because the British had violated the peace treaty by carrying off American property (slaves) and not evacuating the western posts, he did not have to fulfill his obligations under the treaty. Jay and Iredell made it very clear in their opinions that only the president and Congress, not the judiciary, had the power to declare that a treaty had been abrogated, which had not happened in this instance. If the treaty required it, Hylton had to pay his debt.

The court ruled in the defendant's favor on one issue: In his second plea, Hylton claimed that he had retired part of his debt by making a payment into the state loan office. In opposition, the plaintiff maintained that Article 4 of the peace treaty combined with the supremacy clause of the Constitution (Article VI, clause 2) voided the Virginia sequestration law and entitled him to recover the full sum owed. Justice Iredell and Judge Griffin agreed with the debtor. In order for all lawful impediments to the recovery of bona fide debts to be removed in keeping with Article 4 of the treaty of peace, they ruled, Virginia would have had to repeal its statutes dealing with British debts. But the state had not done so. They supported the plaintiff's constitutional claim, that the treaty was supreme, but not the conclusion he drew from it. Although the right of a British creditor to reclaim his debt was explicit, that was only a general conclusion. By interpreting the words of Article 4 of the treaty in conjunction with the actions of the Confederation Congress and the Virginia legislature, the court held, with regard to this specific lawsuit, that the plaintiff retained his right to recovery but not for that part of the debt that Hylton had already paid into the Virginia loan office.

Chief Justice Jay disagreed with this rationale. Having been one of the American negotiators of the peace treaty, he thought he knew what Article 4 meant. "Creditors," he wrote in his dissenting opinion, "should (as I understand the article) be restored to the free exercise of their rights as *creditors*, and . . . all impediments which hostile laws had interposed to prevent or suspend the recovery of their debts, should be done away." Thus, the treaty annihilated all actions taken during the Revolutionary War under the Virginia statute authorizing loan office payments. The defendant must be responsible for the full amount of the debt. On the basis of the circuit court's ruling on the second plea, the plaintiff sought review in the Supreme Court.

Jay's participation in consideration of *Ware v. Hylton* on the circuit court level brought negative comment from those who thought it improper that one of the authors of the treaty should sit as a judge and determine a litigant's rights under it. Later in the 1790s, similar objections would greet the nominations of Jay and Ellsworth to be envoys abroad, where they might negotiate treaties that subsequently could come before the Supreme Court. The criticism did not derail those appointments, but the various activities that the justices undertook as individuals always were open to the same objection. At the end of the decade, sentiment against extrajudicial activities culminated in several attempts to enact legislation or pass a constitutional amendment forbidding judges to accept any other federal offices while they continued on the bench. All the measures failed, but the complaints persisted.

As it happened, by the time *Ware v. Hylton* reached the Supreme Court, Chief Justice Jay already had resigned his position to become governor of New York, an office to which he had been elected while in England and while he still held the title of chief justice. At the February 1796 term, only five justices held commissions; a new chief justice had not yet been appointed. Justice Iredell, who was in attendance, did not participate, because he had sat on the case in the court below. Although there was no official prohibition keeping the justices who had decided cases as circuit judges from voting at the Supreme Court level, the justices informally had adopted a practice of recusal—not followed in every case—to mitigate their misgivings about serving as both trial judge and judge of last resort in the same suit. After an entire week of oral argument, in which John Marshall made his first and only appearance in the Supreme Court as an advocate (he represented Hylton), the remaining four justices handed down a judgment in agreement with Chief Justice Jay's circuit court opinion. They upheld the British creditor's right to recover the full amount of the debt, invoking the supremacy clause of the Constitution and declaring that Article 4 of the peace treaty superseded Virginia's sequestration act.

Having exercised judicial review to void a state statute, the Supreme Court, at the same term, passed on the constitutionality of a federal statute, the Carriage Tax Act of 1794. Before enacting the legislation, Congress had considered the constitutional validity of such a tax, questioning the extent of Congress's own taxing power in general and debating whether the specific duty imposed on carriages was a direct or an indirect tax. Opponents and proponents of the statute all sought to bring it before the Court for an authoritative decision on these questions. In order to do so, the participants had to resort to a legal fiction because no one who had refused to pay the tax owned enough carriages to fulfill the statutory amount in controversy necessary to invoke the jurisdiction of the Supreme Court. The government prevailed on Daniel Hylton — the defendant in the British debts case — to become the defendant in the tax case, and it was agreed that the government would pay all Hylton's expenses in bringing the suit. The United States then sued Hylton for the unpaid taxes on 125 carriages. Hylton's defense was the unconstitutionality of the Carriage Tax Act.

One day after its decision in the British debts case, the Supreme Court, in *Hylton v. United States,* held the Carriage Tax Act constitutional. Under the Constitution, a direct tax had to be apportioned according to a census of each state. Persuaded by the argument of Alexander Hamilton, who was recruited to present the government's case before the Court, no justice thought that the carriage tax was a direct tax. All the justices acknowledged that they were engaged in an exercise of judicial review, weighing the congressional statute against the Constitution. They knew they had the power to overturn the act, if necessary. But although there were critics of the substantive decision in *Hylton,* the Court's power of judicial review was not questioned.

The justices remained steadfast in their belief that the exercise of judicial review formed a legitimate part of their constitutional mandate, even as the exacerbation of political tensions in the final years of the decade called that power into question. After the passage of the Alien and Sedition Acts in 1798, judicial review became a focal point of partisan debate when the justices on circuit refused to permit juries to consider the constitutionality of that legislation. The Kentucky and Virginia Resolutions of 1798 and 1799 specifically questioned the constitutionality of the Alien and Sedition Acts and asserted that each state should judge for itself the constitutional validity of congressional statutes. Other states failed to support the resolutions, however, and several state legislatures repudiated their theory of state nullification, placing the power of judicial review with the federal courts where it belonged under the Constitution.

In the late 1790s, the Supreme Court did not need to wield the power of judicial review in many instances. Most of the cases on the Court's docket concerned nonconstitutional issues. Admiralty, property, commercial practices, debt: These were the kinds of suits that kept the Supreme Court busy in the second half of the decade. Although these cases did not produce many memorable decisions on major points of law, they allowed the Court to clarify crucial procedural rules and to set out guidelines for litigants and lawyers. What constituted the record that was to be sent up to the Supreme Court? How should litigants establish the diversity of citizenship necessary to invoke the jurisdiction of a federal court in common law cases? Which party would be responsible for court costs? Could attorneys legitimately claim fees as part of a damage award? All these questions were answered in the course of adjudicating otherwise minor cases. But one case decided at the August 1798 term did have great constitutional significance. In *Calder v. Bull,* in considering whether an act of the Connecticut legislature granting a new trial for the probate of a will was in conflict with the Constitution, the Supreme Court determined that prohibitions on "ex post facto" laws were confined to criminal proceedings only.

During these years, the Court varied its practice in delivering opinions. At the start of the decade, the justices had adopted the English tradition of announcing opinions seriatim, each judge speaking in turn. After Oliver Ellsworth assumed the position of chief justice, however, the Court began to issue "opinions of the Court"—that is, one opinion announced by the chief justice or by the senior associate justice if the chief were absent. Even in the first half of the decade, the Court had on occasion delivered a single, brief opinion in a case, which Supreme Court Reporter Alexander James Dallas styled an "opinion by the Court," and once the Court drew attention to its use of the single opinion to achieve a political purpose. In *Glass v. Sloop Betsey,* the case establishing that the admiralty jurisdiction of the federal courts extended to both instance and prize, the Court emphasized the unanimity of its decision by beginning each paragraph of its decree with words like "This Court being decidedly of opinion." Late in the 1790s, the Court used opinions by the Court more frequently, but the practice of delivering opinions seriatim was not entirely abandoned. In *Calder v. Bull,* for example, the justices announced their opinions seriatim. Only after the ascension of Chief Justice Marshall to the bench did the practice finally disappear.

The Judicial Path Forged

As the decade drew to a close and political opposition to the Federalists increased, ferment for judicial reform grew. It appeared possible that Vice President Thomas Jefferson would defeat President Adams in the election of 1800 and that his Republican Party would become the majority in Congress. Federalists saw expansion of the judiciary as a way to preserve both the Federalist presence and Federalist principles in government. It took little more than a year to craft and enact a new judiciary bill.

The Judiciary Act of 1801 greatly expanded the jurisdiction of the federal courts and, to the justices' immense satisfaction, eliminated the system of circuit riding. In its stead, six new circuit courts and sixteen new circuit judgeships were created, which President Adams hastily filled before leaving office. Considered as an attempt to rectify the problems brought to light by the experience of the federal courts in the 1790s, the 1801 act seems reasonable. But politics sealed its fate, and it was repealed one year later.

President Adams and the Federalists nevertheless left an enduring mark on the Supreme Court in the person of John Marshall. Committed as firmly to the principles of the new Constitution as the earliest justices had been, Marshall built on the foundation laid by the Courts of Chief Justices Jay, Rutledge, and Ellsworth and brought to the Supreme Court "the Energy weight and Dignity," in the words of Chief Justice Jay, "which are essential to its affording due support to the national Government."

The goal of strengthening the new federal government had animated the Court throughout its first decade. Although its caseload was small by modern standards (depending on the criteria used, between 100 and 120 actions reached the Court in the whole period), the Court had handled its duties with great sensitivity to the national and international repercussions of its decisions, leaving a number of precedents that have stood the test of time. The justices worked to establish the Court as an institution worthy of being at the head of the third branch, and by 1801, despite some missteps, it had become one. It remained for Marshall and those who followed him to realize the Court's full potential.

—MAEVA MARCUS

FOR FURTHER READING AND RESEARCH

A wealth of additional information, in the form of primary sources and scholarly essays, can be found in Maeva Marcus, ed., *The Documentary History of the Supreme Court of the United States, 1789-1800* (7 volumes to date) (New York, 1985–2004). A magisterial treatment of the period in which the fledgling Court developed, albeit one that largely ignores the Supreme Court, is Stanley Elkins and Eric McKitrick, *The Age of Federalism* (New York, 1993). Julius Goebel produced a thorough, scholarly history of the Court's first decade in *Antecedents and Beginnings to 1801* (New York, 1971), volume 1 of the *History of the Supreme Court of the United States* (the Oliver Wendell Holmes Devise). A shorter, more readable history is on offer in William Casto, *The Supreme Court in the Early Republic* (Columbia, S.C., 1995). Ralph Lerner's "The Supreme Court as Republican Schoolmaster," *Supreme Court Review* (1967), 127–80, is a classic statement of the Court's role in the developing political culture of the early Republic.

3

The Marshall Court 1801–1835

Law, Politics, and the Emergence
of the Federal Judiciary

W HEN CHIEF JUSTICE ELLSWORTH resigned in October
1800, President John Adams nominated former Chief Justice John Jay to fill the vacancy. Jay declined the appointment, pleading poor health and the unlikely prospect of a reform that would give the judiciary sufficient "energy, weight and dignity." Under pressure to act quickly because of the impending change of administrations, Adams then turned to Marshall, his secretary of state, and said, "I believe I must nominate you." He submitted Marshall's name to the Senate on January 20, 1801. Despite some grumbling from Federalists who thought that Justice Paterson deserved to be promoted, the Senate confirmed the appointment on January 27. The new chief justice presented his commission and took the oath of office on February 4, when a quorum of justices assembled in a "half-finished Committee room" on the first floor of the Capitol for the first Supreme Court session held in the city of Washington. Having little business to transact, the Court adjourned on February 10. For the remaining three weeks of the Adams administration, Marshall continued to serve as secretary of state and stayed on as acting secretary through March 4, Thomas Jefferson's first day in office as president.

Marshall was commissioned chief justice at the age of forty-five, having acquired broad experience as a statesman and lawyer. A veteran of the Continental Army, he established a highly successful law practice after the war, served in the Virginia legislature, and sat on the state's executive council. As a delegate to the state ratifying convention in 1788, Marshall participated in a debate on the Constitution unmatched in forensic talent arrayed on both sides of the question. During the 1790s, he publicly defended the measures of the Washington administration, most conspicuously the controversial Jay Treaty of 1794, which attracted notice beyond Virginia and earned him a reputation as a leading Federalist. Unwilling to give up his lucrative practice, Marshall turned down several appointments to federal office, including that of attorney general, before accepting Adams's nomination to be commissioner to France in 1797. That assignment launched his rapid ascent to the inner circle of the Adams administration, culminating in his judicial appointment. As a legislator and executive officer in both the state and federal governments and as a practicing lawyer in regular contact with the judiciary, Marshall came to the bench thoroughly versed in the political processes and workings of government and with a sensitive understanding of the nature and boundaries of legislative, executive, and judicial power. "Experience of men and affairs," wrote an admiring twentieth-century judge, gave Marshall "a hardheaded appreciation of the complexities of government, particularly in a federal system."

Marshall, the longest-serving chief justice, sat on the Supreme Court until his death in July 1835. Scholars consider his chief justiceship to be the pivotal epoch in the history of the federal judiciary — a moment when the institution, poised between receding into relative insignificance or developing into a truly coordinate department of government, took a decisive step in the latter direction. During his tenure, the Supreme Court successfully asserted its claim to be the guardian of the Constitution and the arbiter of conflicts arising from the clash of federal and state sovereignties. This claim embraced the "duty" to consider the Constitution as paramount law in its ordinary function of adjudicating cases and to invalidate acts held to be repugnant to that law.

The Marshall Court did not invent "judicial review" (a term coined in the twentieth century) but developed and refined the practice by using the traditional methods of statutory interpretation to expound the Constitution. The essential core of the Court's constitutional law consisted of a "nationalist" reading of the Constitution, giving effect to the enumerated and implied powers of the federal government and to the restrictions and prohibitions on the state governments.

Conflict and Accommodation, 1801–1810

Mandamus, the Repeal of the Judiciary Act, and *Marbury v. Madison*

If Marshall's appointment owed something to political expediency and to the president's tendency to act impulsively, there can be no doubt that Adams had taken the full measure of the man who was now to preside over the Supreme Court. Since joining the cabinet as secretary of state in May 1800, Marshall had become the president's most confidential advisor (next to Abigail). Earlier, on a diplomatic mission to France in 1798, the Virginian had gained national renown in defending the nation's honor and dignity against the insulting behavior of Talleyrand and his anonymous agents, "X, Y, and Z." Soon afterward, Marshall had distinguished himself in Congress as the administration's ablest advocate, notably in a speech defending the president's extradition power under the treaty with Great Britain. That speech displayed argumentative skill of the highest order and confirmed a reputation for legal and constitutional exposition that Marshall had gained (in a losing cause) as counsel in the case of *Ware v. Hylton* (1796), his only appearance as a lawyer before the Supreme Court.

Had Marshall, in turn, taken full measure of the situation confronting him? The prospects for the federal judiciary were scarcely auspicious in 1801. In the high political excitement accompanying the Republicans' transition to power following the electoral defeat of the Federalists, the judiciary became the focal point of the victorious party's resentment and mistrust. Memories were fresh of the federal courts' vigorous enforcement of the Adams administration's efforts to suppress internal dissent during the war crisis of 1798 and 1799, most conspicuously in prosecuting, fining, and jailing Republican newspaper editors on indictments brought under the notorious Sedition Act. Federal judges also rendered themselves obnoxious by delivering grand jury charges that intemperately denounced opposition to government and exhorted the citizenry to support the administration's policies.

These harangues drew forth Republicans' angry rebukes to judges who had been "converted into political partisans." Republican antagonism toward the judiciary intensified when the lame-duck Federalist Congress in February 1801 passed a judiciary act creating sixteen new circuit court judgeships. Until the last hour of his administration, Adams and the Senate were busily nominating and confirming circuit judges and, in addition, forty-two justices of the peace created by the recently enacted law establishing a government for the District of Columbia. To Republicans, this was a brazen attempt by the defeated party to perpetuate its control of government through the judiciary. As Jefferson bitterly remarked, "There the remains of federalism are to be preserved & fed from the treasury, and from that battery all the works of republicanism are to be beaten down & erased."

The "midnight" appointments set in motion a sequence of events that brought the judiciary to the brink of crisis, from which it emerged more or less intact, thanks to a prevailing spirit of moderation and accommodation. In this first test of his chief justiceship, Marshall demonstrated the attributes of leadership that would serve him well throughout his tenure.

It happened that the commissions of Adams's appointees as justices of the peace for the District of Columbia had not been sent out before the expiration of the administration. Assuming that he had discretion to revoke the appointments because the commissions had not been delivered, President Jefferson made nominations of his own on March 5, reappointing many of Adams's nominees while reducing the number of justices to thirty. Among those whom Jefferson did not reappoint was one William Marbury (Plate A.5). Marbury sought legal redress in the Supreme Court, which under the Judiciary Act of 1789 was authorized in special cases to issue writs of mandamus to government officers. (In mandamus proceedings, the plaintiff applied directly to the Supreme Court.) At the Court's December 1801 term, Marbury's lawyer moved for a rule to Secretary of State James Madison to show cause why a writ of mandamus should not issue commanding him to deliver Marbury's commission as justice of the peace. On December 18, Chief Justice Marshall announced the Court's decision to grant the rule and assigned the case to be argued at the next term. Republicans indignantly denounced the Court's action on Marbury's behalf as an unwarranted judicial intrusion into executive matters, a politically motivated attempt to embarrass the new administration. Whatever doubts the president and his political majority might have entertained about the propriety (and legality) of repealing the Judiciary Act of 1801 were now discarded. After a protracted debate, Congress by a party vote enacted the repeal in March 1802.

The repeal, and a subsequent judiciary act adopted in April, abolished the circuit courts established under the 1801 act and restored the former system by which circuit courts were composed of Supreme Court justices and judges of the U.S. district courts. This legislation also provided for an annual meeting of the Supreme Court, commencing the first Monday in February. Thus, after granting Marbury's motion for a rule to show cause in December 1801, the Supreme Court did not meet again until February 1803. Clearly, the political branches were not eager for the Supreme Court to take up the mandamus case. In the meantime, before arguments in the case could be heard, the Supreme Court justices in the spring of 1802 faced a dilemma that exposed them to the risk of a direct confrontation with the administration: whether to hold the circuit courts established by the recent legislation. By attending the circuits, the justices would signify their acquiescence in Congress's authority to reinstate circuit riding by Supreme Court justices. Chief Justice Marshall himself doubted the constitutionality of the measure, believing that Supreme Court justices could not perform circuit duty without separate and distinct commissions as circuit justices. In order to determine their course of conduct, the chief justice solicited the views of his brethren, holding himself "bound by the opinion of the majority." On learning that a majority considered this question as fully settled by the practice of riding circuit from 1789 to 1801, Marshall readily assented, remarking that "policy dictates this decision to us all." The justices averted a showdown by attending their circuits in the fall of 1802.

At the February 1803 term, the Supreme Court heard Marbury's lawyer argue the case for issuing the mandamus. No counsel appeared for Madison, the Jefferson administration from the outset having refused to recognize the proceedings. On February 24, two weeks after hearing arguments, Chief Justice Marshall delivered the Court's opinion. *Marbury v. Madison* affirmed that Marbury had a legal right to his commission. His appointment had been confirmed and his commission signed and sealed. The opinion also agreed that a mandamus was the proper remedy. But the Court ultimately denied relief on the ground that it lacked jurisdiction to issue the writ. Although the Judiciary Act of 1789 authorized the Supreme Court to issue writs of mandamus to government officers, the Court ruled this provision void as purporting to enlarge its original jurisdiction beyond that prescribed by Article III of the Constitution.

The decision in *Marbury v. Madison* was thus a victory for the administration. In the short run, however, the opinion only exacerbated opposition to what Republicans regarded as an overweening and partisan judiciary. The Court, so its critics vehemently protested, had flouted judicial propriety by giving an opinion on the merits of the case, gratuitously charging the administration with having acted unlawfully, before ultimately deciding that it had no jurisdiction to issue the mandamus. By contrast, the Court's assumption of authority to declare a law of Congress unconstitutional — for which *Marbury* subsequently achieved near mythic status as the precedent establishing "judicial review"— provoked scarcely a murmur of comment at the time.

Difficult as it was for Republicans to perceive anything but hostile intent in *Marbury,* Chief Justice Marshall had no desire to provoke a confrontation with the Jefferson administration. Instinctively cautious, Marshall was acutely aware of the judiciary's weakness and vulnerability. His overriding concern in the first years of his chief justiceship was to ensure the judiciary's survival, then to elevate its status and authority. To accomplish his goals, he directed a prudent retreat by the judiciary away from "politics" and into its proper province of "law." The Supreme Court's function, he declared in *Marbury,* was solely to decide on individual rights, not to inquire into executive conduct where the executive had proper discretion. "Questions in their nature political, or which are, by the constitution and laws, submitted to the executive, can never be made in this court," he added. The Court had already demonstrated a willingness to abide by this principle in upholding the new administration's foreign policy goals in cases arising from the quasi-war with France. By attending their circuits after the repeal of the judiciary act, the Supreme Court justices further signaled withdrawal and accommodation. On his own first circuit in 1802, the chief justice pointedly confined his grand jury charge to points of law "without the least political intermixture" and stated his fixed determination not to allow his charges to be published.

What the uproar over *Marbury* obscured was that Marshall was attempting to cleanse the judiciary's tarnished reputation. Short of dismissing Marbury's request without comment — an unacceptable alternative because it would be seen as abject capitulation — the Supreme Court could not have avoided Republican censure in deciding the mandamus case. In declaring that the secretary of state had no discretion to withhold Marbury's commission but was legally bound to deliver it, the Court was denounced for meddling with executive prerogatives — that is, for overstepping the boundary between law and politics that the opinion attempted to define. In this respect, *Marbury* was a failure in the short run. But, as became clearer in subsequent years, the Marshall Court had looked beyond the immediate case to deliver a statement that has resonated ever since about the rule of law. If, in the context of 1803, the statement appeared to be a bold challenge to executive power, the Court, in denying itself jurisdiction, conveniently avoided having to order the secretary of state to deliver the commission, an order that almost certainly would have been ignored. The mandamus case, commentators have noted, showed the chief justice to be an adroit tactician who managed to uphold the claims of judicial power without directly clashing with the administration.

Marshall's affirmation of judicial review in the second part of *Marbury* has also been seen as a brilliant tactical maneuver, another bold assertion of judicial power (this time directed at the legislative) that succeeded because the result favored the administration. In no sense, however, did the chief justice impose a controversial institution on an unwary people whose attention was diverted elsewhere. In 1803, most politically articulate Americans, Federalists and Republicans alike, accepted the notion that courts were empowered in certain instances to declare legislative acts unconstitutional. In keeping with his aim of strengthening the judiciary by shedding its image as a partisan institution, Marshall appealed to a broad consensus — to "certain principles, supposed to have been long and well established" — in making the argument for judicial review. These principles, in essence, were that a written constitution was intended to be a check on governmental power, that a constitution was supreme law, and that, in deciding cases, courts were duty-bound to enforce this supreme law whenever it conflicted with ordinary legislation. "It is emphatically the province and duty of the judicial department to say what the law is," Marshall famously declared, but these words implied no claim to judicial supremacy in expounding the Constitution, no authority to bind the other departments of government in cases that did not take the form of a legal dispute. Other than stating the minimal case, *Marbury* settled little concerning the meaning and scope of judicial review. A clearer definition of the Marshall Court's application of the doctrine would gradually unfold in subsequent cases.

In its first exercise of judicial review, the Marshall Court was able to present itself as a high-minded, impartial tribunal concerned solely with expounding law. The decision was an act of self-denial, a refusal to accept jurisdiction conferred by Congress. At the same time, in the case of *Stuart v. Laird* (1803), decided just a few days after *Marbury*, the Court underscored its determination to withdraw from the political realm, pointedly refusing to reconsider the constitutionality of circuit riding by Supreme Court justices. This was the same question the justices had confronted in the spring of 1802 and answered by attending their circuits. *Stuart v. Laird* formalized that earlier agreement and offered further assurance that the Supreme Court would not interfere with the policy goals of the administration.

Impeachment

In the wake of *Marbury*, Republican rancor toward the judiciary remained high, signified by impeachment proceedings against federal judges. The Constitution provides for the removal of judges found guilty of "treason, bribery, other high crimes and misdemeanors." In the early 1800s, there was as yet no fixed consensus on the meaning of the impeachment provision: whether it was to be narrowly restricted to criminal activity or broadly applied to embrace obnoxious or unpopular behavior. In February 1803, while *Marbury* was pending, the House impeached John Pickering, a New Hampshire Federalist district judge who was notoriously alcoholic and probably insane. Despite misgivings among Republicans about impeaching a judge who was obviously unfit but had committed no crime, the Senate convicted Pickering in March 1804. This action encouraged radical Republicans who wanted to use the impeachment process to remove judges regarded as politically hostile to the administration. On the day of Pickering's conviction, Congressman John Randolph initiated proceedings against Supreme Court Justice Samuel Chase. Irascible, overbearing, and partisan, Chase had made himself a convenient target by his intemperate conduct of sedition and treason trials during the Adams administration and more recently for a grand jury charge that denounced the Jefferson administration and expressed contempt for democracy. The House approved impeachment articles, but in March 1805, the Senate failed to convict Chase by the necessary two-thirds majority. The acquittal of Samuel Chase — the only Supreme Court justice to be impeached — owed much to his able defense but also to evident division among Republicans over the use of impeachment as a means of removing political opponents from office.

The Treason Trial of Aaron Burr

Apart from establishing a precedent restricting grounds for impeachment to criminal conduct, Chase's acquittal signified a triumph of moderation that was reinforced by the rejection of proposals to amend the Constitution so as to enable the president to remove federal judges by joint address of the House and Senate. Rapprochement between the political and judicial branches was interrupted in 1807, however, by the treason trial of Aaron Burr, which took place on Chief Justice Marshall's circuit in Richmond. In response to Burr's military expedition to the Southwest in the fall of 1806, the government vigorously prosecuted the former vice president and his followers for provoking war against Spain with the traitorous design of detaching the West from the United States. Before Burr's trial began, the Supreme Court, in *Ex parte Bollman and Swartwout* (1807), released two of his confederates from imprisonment on petition for habeas corpus, an action seen as a deliberate attempt to frustrate the executive's attempt to suppress the conspiracy.

In the ensuing circuit court proceedings against Burr, Chief Justice Marshall angered Jefferson by issuing a subpoena *duces tecum* requiring the president to produce papers Burr had requested as material to his defense. At the close of the trial, Marshall delivered an elaborate opinion narrowly defining treason and excluding most of the testimony, which in effect compelled the jury to acquit Burr. Republican papers predictably denounced the chief justice for twisting the law to allow a traitor to go free. Once again, there were calls for reform of a partisan judiciary that seemed to ignore the people's will with impunity. But the furor over the Burr trial eventually subsided, and aside from verbal assaults, the judiciary emerged relatively unscathed. Congress again failed to act on proposals to make easier the removal of judges from office and also refused to amend the law of treason.

Accommodation

The Burr trial marked the last direct confrontation between administration and judiciary before the 1830s. Although tensions persisted throughout the remainder of Jefferson's presidency, accommodation gradually replaced outright conflict. By 1807, Jefferson had three of his own appointees—William Johnson, Brockholst Livingston, and Thomas Todd—sitting on the Supreme Court. In the common cause of upholding national authority, the administration and the federal courts needed each other.

As it attempted to steer a neutral course in the midst of the Napoleonic Wars, the government depended on the courts to enforce its stringent embargo laws interdicting trade with the belligerent nations—laws that were openly resisted and repeatedly denounced as unconstitutional, particularly in New England. While interpreting these laws strictly to preserve the rights of individuals against abuse by government officers, federal judges never questioned the power of Congress to enact such legislation; indeed, a Federalist judge in New England forcefully upheld the constitutionality of the embargo. Courts, for their part, were powerless to enforce their orders without the assistance of the executive department. When the state of Pennsylvania resisted a federal court decree, Chief Justice Marshall, in *United States v. Peters* (1809), forcefully sustained the Supreme Court's ultimate right to determine the jurisdiction of the federal courts. In response to the state's continued defiance, President Madison pointedly reminded the governor that the federal executive was legally bound to carry into effect any federal court decree "where opposition may be made to it."

Fortified by this endorsement of federal judicial power against an assertion of states' rights, the Supreme Court, in *Fletcher v. Peck* (1810), for the first time nullified a state law as repugnant to the Constitution. (In *Ware v. Hylton* [1796], the Court had not, strictly speaking, declared the Virginia sequestration law unconstitutional but had held that payments into the state's treasury under that law did not constitute a lawful discharge of debts owed to British subjects.) *Fletcher v. Peck* was also the first of a line of decisions interpreting the clause of the Constitution prohibiting the states from passing laws "impairing the Obligation of Contracts."

Nationalism and the Consolidation of Judicial Power, 1811–1824

In 1811, President Madison filled two Supreme Court vacancies created by the deaths of William Cushing and Samuel Chase. Succeeding Cushing was Joseph Story of Massachusetts, who had already served a term in Congress and had argued *Fletcher v. Peck* before the Court. Only thirty-two (the youngest ever to serve on the high court), Story achieved a stature on the Marshall Court second only to the chief justice himself. Story was an indefatigable legal scholar and publicist, author of numerous treatises, who in 1829 became the first Dane Professor of Law at Harvard. Chase's seat went to Gabriel Duvall of Maryland, who had been comptroller of the treasury since 1802. Of the seven justices on the Supreme Court (a seventh seat had been added in 1807), five had been appointed by Republican presidents. Marshall and Washington were the only Federalist holdovers. Party affiliations were virtually meaningless, however, as Marshall and his brethren enjoyed an unusually harmonious relationship and were united by fundamental agreement on basic values embodied in the Constitution. With no further changes in personnel taking place until 1823, the Marshall Court during the next dozen years achieved its highest degree of internal stability and unity and made its most enduring contributions to American constitutional law.

By 1810, the Supreme Court was sitting in the basement room below the Senate chamber that was to be its home until the Civil War (Plate A.6). When the British burned the Capitol in 1814, the Court moved to temporary quarters until returning to its customary location in 1819. The annual term commenced the first Monday in February (moved to the second Monday in January, beginning in 1827) and continued to the middle of March. The Court met daily (except Sunday) from eleven to four, hearing arguments that often went on for hours and could extend over two or three days. Many cases attracted large audiences that crowded into the gallery to hear the great legal gladiators of the day: William Pinkney, Samuel Dexter, Thomas A. Emmet, Daniel Webster, and William Wirt, to name only the most prominent. Their forensic duels were a favorite entertainment for Washington society, whose season coincided with the opening of the Supreme Court. No argument excited greater public interest than *McCulloch v. Maryland* (1819), which extended over nine days and employed the talents of six distinguished counsel, the Court having suspended its customary rule restricting the number of lawyers to no more than two for each party. Story pronounced Pinkney's argument in that case the greatest speech he had ever heard: "His eloquence was overwhelming. His language, his style, his figures, his arguments, were most brilliant and sparkling."

Marshall as Leader of the Court

The best indicator of Marshall's effectiveness as a leader was the Court's remarkable internal unity. From the outset, Marshall adopted the practice, begun by Ellsworth, of a single majority opinion of the Court — most often delivered by the chief justice himself — in place of seriatim opinions from each of the justices. Marshall's particular skills were ideally suited to molding a small assemblage of individual justices into a collective entity that spoke with a single authoritative voice. Endowed with a mind of the first rank, Marshall possessed acute powers of logic, analysis, and generalization that enabled him to quickly master complex legal issues with discerning comprehension. He was not the most learned lawyer on the Court (that honor went to Story), but his mastery of the law was certainly equal to his high judicial station. The chief justiceship, as Story noted, was "the very post where weakness and ignorance and timidity must instantly betray themselves and sink to their natural level."

Along with intellect and learning, an abundance of charm and sociability also served Marshall well. He exuded warmth, geniality, kindness, and unaffected modesty in his personal and social relations. Marshall introduced another innovation: the practice of sharing the same boardinghouse during term time, which allowed for the full play of his personality in a setting that seamlessly mixed official business with the pleasures of social life. After concluding each day's session in court, the justices resumed deliberations over dinner and wine at their Capitol Hill lodgings. Sharing living quarters and meals encouraged a frank yet cordial exchange of views, fostered collegiality, and helped to advance the goal of reaching a true opinion of the Court. The justices lived "very harmoniously and familiarly," said Story, mooting "questions as they are argued, with freedom" and deriving "no inconsiderable advantage from the pleasant and animated interchange of legal acumen." The usually ascetic justices were known on occasion to stretch their rule of drinking wine only in wet weather. Marshall would sometimes ask "Brother Story" to "step to the window and see if it does not look like rain." And if Story informed him that the sun was "shining brightly," the chief might reply, "all the better; for our jurisdiction extends over so large a territory that the doctrine of chances makes it certain that it must be raining somewhere."

Marshall did not lead by imposing his will on supposedly weaker associates; his brethren, in fact, were highly capable and independent-minded jurists. The key to his leadership lay in his openness to argument and persuasion, his willingness to subordinate his own views if necessary to obtain a single opinion of the Court. An engaging intellectual humility enabled Marshall to defer, when necessary, to the superior learning of others. In both courtroom and conference chamber, Marshall was a patient and attentive listener, not merely soliciting but also demanding arguments. If the Court most often spoke through the chief justice, the opinion was the product of collaborative deliberation, carried out in a spirit of mutual concession and accommodation. To be sure, the single opinion of the Court had the effect of projecting unity when in fact the justices were divided. Unless the opinion was said to be "unanimous," the size of the majority was usually hidden from view.

The internal dynamics of this collegial institution encouraged silent acquiescence by justices who dissented from the majority. On one occasion, for example, Story suppressed a strong urge to deliver his own opinion, noting that "Judge Washington thinks (and very correctly) that the habit of delivering dissenting opinions on ordinary occasions weakens the authority of the Court, and is of no public benefit." Dissenting opinions did occur, to be sure, though usually prefaced with an apology from the justice for disagreeing with his colleagues. Of the Marshall Court justices, the most independent-minded was Justice Johnson, who has been called "the first dissenter."

Constitutional Nationalism

During the dozen years following the War of 1812, Marshall and his brethren were united in the common cause of upholding national power and enforcing the Constitution's restrictions on state sovereignty. In a series of unanimous or near-unanimous decisions, the Supreme Court affirmed the "implied" powers of Congress, broadly interpreted Congress's power to regulate commerce, struck down state laws that were repugnant to the contract clause or that conflicted with the principle of federal supremacy, asserted broad jurisdiction to decide cases arising under the Constitution and laws of the United States, and sustained its appellate power over the state judiciaries. Most of these cases originated in the state courts and came to the Supreme Court by writ of error, as provided by section 25 of the Judiciary Act of 1789. Section 25 empowered the Court to hear appeals from a state's highest court in cases that involved a "federal" question — that is, when a state court denied a party's right claimed under the federal Constitution or a federal law or treaty.

These nationalizing decisions provoked impassioned denunciations of the Marshall Court, founded on the doctrine of states' rights, a potent ideology that found expression in all sections of the young nation before hardening into a political dogma associated with the South and the defense of the peculiar institution of slavery. But although posing a continual challenge to the exercise of federal judicial power, states' rights opposition to the Court was sporadic and local, never gaining ascendancy in the country at large. As Pennsylvania had discovered in resisting *United States v. Peters* in 1809, a state or a region that felt particularly aggrieved by a Supreme Court decision would find little support elsewhere.

In its first important constitutional case after the War of 1812, the Supreme Court emphatically upheld its power to review state court decisions. *Martin v. Hunter's Lessee* (1816) arose from the Virginia Court of Appeals' refusal to obey the Supreme Court's mandate in an earlier case sustaining, on the basis of national treaties, the rights of those claiming land formerly belonging to British subjects. The state court judges contended that the Constitution did not confer federal appellate jurisdiction over the state tribunals and that section 25 was therefore unconstitutional. Justice Story for the Court established his credentials as a judicial nationalist in a masterly opinion that firmly anchored appellate jurisdiction to the nature and logic of the Constitution.

Then, in 1819, three major decisions invalidating state laws provided a stunning display of constitutional nationalism. In *Dartmouth College v. Woodward*, the Court held that the colonial charter incorporating Dartmouth College was a contract protected by the Constitution and struck down New Hampshire's laws converting the New England college into a state-controlled university. The Court also invoked the contract clause in *Sturges v. Crowninshield*, this time against a New York insolvency law that discharged debtors from future liability on assigning their property to creditors.

Marshall spoke for the Court in these two cases and again in the third of this term, *McCulloch v. Maryland*, considered by many to be the greatest of his constitutional utterances. In the course of upholding Congress's power to incorporate the Second Bank of the United States and denying the state of Maryland's right to tax the bank, Marshall embarked on an exhaustive inquiry into the extent of federal power, the limits on state sovereignty, the nature of the federal Union, and the principles of constitutional interpretation. Because of its implications for matters beyond the national bank itself — including, ominously, a proposal to prohibit the introduction of slavery into the territories — *McCulloch* unleashed a torrent of hostile criticism by states' rights adherents, nowhere with greater intensity than in Virginia. The attacks so alarmed Marshall that he undertook an anonymous extrajudicial defense of *McCulloch* in a series of newspaper essays.

Hardly had the controversy over *McCulloch* subsided when the Supreme Court in *Cohens v. Virginia* (1821) once more offended Virginia's sensibilities by assuming jurisdiction to hear an appeal brought by two brothers prosecuted in a state court for unlawfully selling tickets to a lottery drawn in the city of Washington. This case elicited from Chief Justice Marshall a comprehensive analysis of the constitutional foundations and extent of federal judicial power. In particular, he read the judiciary article of the Constitution as conferring on the Supreme Court broad jurisdiction to decide cases involving the conflicting powers of the federal and state governments — in effect, responding judicially to states' rights champions who denied the Supreme Court's adjudicatory role in maintaining the federal system.

The same 1821 term saw the Court provoke the wrath of Kentucky. *Green v. Biddle* invalidated the state's land laws allowing compensation to settlers who had been ousted by nonresident titleholders. For the Court, Story ruled that Kentucky's laws violated the 1789 compact by which Kentucky had separated from Virginia. This compact, said Story, was a contract protected against impairment by state legislation. Although it granted a motion for reargument on the ground that no counsel for the claimants had appeared, the Court reaffirmed its decision at the 1823 term, Bushrod Washington giving the opinion.

By upholding the exercise of national power, striking down state laws, and asserting a supervisory role over the state courts, the Supreme Court aroused the antagonism of localist forces in the national legislature. A number of proposals came before Congress to curb the Court's powers by repeal of section 25, by amending the Constitution to give the Senate appellate jurisdiction in cases in which a state was a party, and by enlarging the number of justices to ten and requiring the concurrence of seven to pass on the constitutionality of state and federal acts. This last measure, sponsored by a Kentucky senator angered by *Green v. Biddle,* brought forth a private communication from Marshall to the influential Speaker of the House, Kentuckian Henry Clay. The politically astute chief justice warned Clay of the danger of enacting "a general law of great and extensive influence to effect a particular object." This timely intervention no doubt had its effect. That neither this nor any other attempt to reduce the Court's powers succeeded owed much to Marshall's superb political skills and testified once more to his leadership in overseeing the Supreme Court's transformation into a tribunal of great prestige and authority.

The high tide of constitutional nationalism continued through the 1824 term. *Gibbons v. Ogden* saw the Court for the first time expound Congress's power to regulate commerce in the course of considering the validity of New York laws that restricted steam navigation on the state's waters to vessels licensed by the Livingston-Fulton monopoly. The chief justice's expansive reading to the commerce clause came close to adopting the view that Congress's power was exclusive. The Court struck down the monopoly laws, though ultimately basing its decision not on the commerce clause but on the narrower ground of collision with a federal statute. *Gibbons* had important consequences for the growth of a national economy, for it ensured that steamboat navigation on the coastal and inland waters of the United States would be opened to free competition. In *Osborn v. Bank of the United States* (1824), the Court invalidated another state attempt to tax the bank — in this instance, Ohio, which despite *McCulloch* had continued to insist on its constitutional right to lay such a tax. Once again, Marshall read the Constitution as conferring broad jurisdiction on the federal courts, this time to provide front-line judicial protection to federal instrumentalities, and restated the principle of national supremacy to uphold the bank's exemption from state taxation.

Accommodation and Retreat, 1825–1835

Until the mid-1820s, all the important cases that had required the Supreme Court to perform the delicate task of determining the limits on state powers had resulted in an abridgment of state sovereignty. Although the Court's nationalizing activism had stirred up opposition to its assumed role as arbiter of the federal system, anti-Court sentiment had never gained ascendancy in Congress, signifying an underlying agreement among the American people to preserve the integrity of the institution. But this consensus, clear enough in retrospect, was by no means evident to the chief and his brethren. Hence, whether by coincidence or for reasons of expediency, the Marshall Court in its last decade began to render opinions more favorable to state power. These years also saw cracks open in the Court's monolith, as separate and dissenting opinions appeared more frequently.

The death of Brockholst Livingston in 1823 signaled the first breach in the nationalist consensus. Smith Thompson of New York succeeded to Livingston's seat at the 1824 term. Two years later, Thomas Todd died, to be replaced by Robert Trimble of Kentucky. Trimble himself died in 1828 after serving only one term, and Bushrod Washington, then the Court's longest-serving justice, died the next year. President Andrew Jackson filled these two vacancies with John McLean of Ohio and Henry Baldwin of Pennsylvania, both of whom joined the Court at the 1830 term.

An early sign that the Court's unanimity, if not unity, could be broken appeared in *Gibbons,* when Justice Johnson announced that he would henceforth give his own opinion in major constitutional cases. Thompson and Trimble also served notice that they would follow an independent course. Johnson, Thompson, and Trimble became part of a four-vote majority that, in *Ogden v. Saunders* (1827), upheld the validity of state bankruptcy laws that operated prospectively on contracts. For the first and only time in his tenure, Chief Justice Marshall was compelled to dissent in a constitutional case.

The Court continued to issue decisions nullifying state laws, but its nationalist voice was now muted by dissents. Thompson, for example, dissented in *Brown v. Maryland* (1827), which voided a state law imposing a license fee on importers. Johnson and Thompson dissented in *Weston v. City Council of Charleston* (1829), which held that a city tax on stock of the United States unconstitutionally interfered with Congress's power to borrow money. In *Craig v. Missouri* (1830), Marshall could muster only a bare majority — Johnson, Thompson, and McLean dissenting — to rule that state loan office certificates were "bills of credit" prohibited by the Constitution.

The *Craig* dissents particularly pained Marshall, deepening his apprehension about the breakdown in the Court's internal unity and cohesiveness. Concerned as he was about threats from Congress to the Court's appellate jurisdiction, he now feared (referring to *Craig*) that the Court itself would relinquish its supervision of the state courts. Section 25, he gloomily predicted, "is to be repealed, or to use a more fashionable phrase, to be nullified by the Supreme court" — not during his tenure, he hoped, "but accomplished it will be, at no very distant period."

The "revolutionary spirit" within the Court also manifested itself in the rupture in the justices' communal living arrangements, which for so many years had served to promote harmony as well as efficiency. If the justices "scatter ad libitum," the chief worried, many cases would remain undecided, and those the Court did decide would "probably be carried off by seriatim opinions."

Ironically, whatever unity the Court now displayed occurred in cases upholding state laws. In *Willson v. Blackbird Creek Marsh Company* (1829), a commerce clause case, a unanimous Court declared that a state law authorizing construction of a dam across a navigable creek was a legitimate exercise of regulatory power that did not interfere with Congress's "dormant" power to regulate commerce. The Court also unanimously agreed, in *Providence Bank v. Billings* (1830), that a state law imposing a tax on corporations was not repugnant to the contract clause. Finally, in *Barron v. Baltimore* (1833), the Marshall Court's last constitutional case, the justices were of one mind in rejecting a Baltimore wharf owner's complaint that the paving and regrading of city streets destroyed the commercial value of his property and thus amounted to an uncompensated "taking" of private property prohibited by the Fifth Amendment. The Bill of Rights, said Marshall, was intended to restrict the federal government, not the state governments.

Chief Justice Marshall did manage to rally his brethren for an emphatically nationalist opinion in *Worcester v. Georgia* (1832), which held that Georgia laws asserting sovereignty over the Cherokee Indians were repugnant to the federal Constitution, laws, and treaties. In truth, however, this decision underscored the impotence of the Supreme Court in the face of determined political majorities. In championing the rights of the Cherokee, the federal judiciary encountered resistance not only from a single state but also from the Jackson administration, which favored a policy of removing Native American peoples inhabiting the eastern states to lands west of the Mississippi River. Once again, as in its earliest years, the Marshall Court confronted a hostile president with a large popular mandate.

Of *Worcester*, Jackson allegedly remarked, "John Marshall has made his decision, now let him enforce it." There is no proof that the president uttered this statement, but it accurately reflected the attitude of an administration that bitterly resented the Court's interference in the Cherokee business. The case was ultimately resolved by a compromise in which Georgia pardoned a missionary to the tribe prosecuted under the state's laws but did not yield its sovereign pretensions. The Cherokee in turn gave up further legal efforts to prevent their removal from ancient tribal lands. While avoiding a confrontation with the executive department, the Court preserved its authority in the immediate case, although it could do nothing for the Cherokee beyond affirming the tribe's legal and constitutional rights. At least the judicial department, said Story, could wash its "hands clean of the iniquity of oppressing the Indians, and disregarding their rights."

The chief justice's difficulty in maintaining a unified Supreme Court coincided with — and seemed symptomatic of — a larger crisis of union that overshadowed his final years on the bench. Nothing portended the mortality of the Constitution and union more ominously than "nullification," a South Carolina doctrine that asserted the right of a state to declare federal laws — in this instance, the tariff — unconstitutional and nullify their operation within the state's borders. To Marshall, this constitutional heresy was "so extravagant in itself" that he could scarcely "believe it was seriously entertained by any person." If nullification represented the new constitutional truth, what, he asked, was the point of replacing the Articles of Confederation with the Constitution? Left unspoken was a further question: Had all the labor of the Supreme Court in support of constitutional nationalism been in vain? At the height of the nullification crisis in 1832, the aging jurist confided that he was yielding "slowly and reluctantly to the conviction that our constitution cannot last." He foresaw the end of a union that had "been prolonged thus far by miracles."

Until a few months before he died in July 1835, Marshall had enjoyed remarkably good health. He had never missed a Supreme Court term, even surviving a painful operation for bladder stones at the age of seventy-six. At one point, he contemplated retirement but decided to stay on after Jackson was reelected in 1832. Although temperamentally cheerful and optimistic, Marshall in his final years experienced a profound sense of failure — a failure of his vision of the Constitution and union and of the vital role played by the Supreme Court in maintaining a strong and efficient national government. His pessimism was justified. The Civil War stands as devastating testimony to the failure of the experiment in federal union devised in 1787, which the Marshall Court had labored to preserve. Marshall could not know that the union would be reestablished and flourish stronger and more consolidated than ever before. But in a real sense, it was a new union, a new nation, a new Constitution, and a new Supreme Court that emerged after 1865.

Constitutional Law and the Marshall Court

Nationalism

The Marshall Court characteristically used judicial review to void acts enacted by state legislatures. In one class of cases, centering on the clause declaring that the Constitution and laws of the United States were the "supreme law of the land," state legislation was struck down as repugnant to the exercise of a power vested in the federal government. The leading "federalism" cases — *McCulloch v. Maryland* and *Gibbons v. Ogden* — are also notable for their liberal reading of the powers delegated to the federal government. In championing national power, however, the Marshall Court was not a precursor of modern liberal nationalism and the twentieth-century regulatory state. Although denounced by states' rights proponents as "consolidationist," seeking to destroy the state governments and concentrate all power in the general government, the Court viewed its mission as promotion of an energetic and efficient government to carry out the great national purposes outlined in the Constitution. To Marshall and his brethren, the federal government was chronically vulnerable to the aggressive encroachments of the state governments. The internal pressures that undermined the authority of the central government and loosened the bonds of union in turn exposed the United States to external threats by foreign powers. The nationalist perspective of the Marshall Court hence inclined not forward to the nation-state that emerged after the Civil War but backward to the 1787 idea of a union whose objectives were primarily conservative and defensive. The Constitution was designed to establish an equilibrium between the federal and state governments, but this equilibrium was in continual danger of breaking down in favor of state power. The Court's nationalism is best described as defensive or negative: resisting the superior force of state sovereignty rather than augmenting federal power.

McCulloch, the preeminent expression of Marshall Court nationalism, is a case in point. In the first part of the opinion, Chief Justice Marshall articulated the basic tenets of constitutional nationalism in upholding Congress's power to incorporate a national bank. He began with the premise that the Constitution was the constituent act of the people of the United States, not a compact among sovereign states. From this he derived the principle that the general government, "though limited in its powers, is supreme within its sphere of action." Such a government possessed only enumerated powers, but the Constitution did not exclude incidental or implied powers by confining the government only to "expressly" delegated powers.

Whether the government could create a corporation, which was not among the enumerated powers, depended on the construction of the Constitution. Here Marshall set forth another nationalist principle—that the Constitution marked only the "great outlines," designated only the "important objects," leaving the multiplicity of subordinate governmental powers to be deduced by a fair and reasonable construction. In determining the nature and scope of the delegated powers, said Marshall in a memorable phrase, "we must never forget, that it is *a constitution* we are expounding," by which he meant that the Constitution was not to be read as a detailed blueprint for governing. The chief justice thus prepared the ground for erecting another nationalist pillar, the doctrine of "implied powers," which held that a government of "ample powers" must be presumed to have "ample means" to execute those powers, even if the means were not spelled out in the Constitution.

It followed that Congress should have broad discretion in selecting the means for executing its designated powers, a principle of construction founded not only in reason but also in the clause of the Constitution granting Congress power to pass all laws "necessary and proper" for executing its enumerated powers. After a detailed exposition of this clause, Marshall formulated a rule for determining the constitutionality of implied powers: "Let the end be legitimate, let it be within the scope of the constitution, and all the means which are appropriate, which are plainly adapted to that end, which are not prohibited, but consist with the letter and spirit of the constitution, are constitutional."

McCulloch eloquently affirmed the doctrine of implied federal powers, but this meant only that Congress could select reasonable means for carrying into effect an enumerated power. Marshall did not mean to suggest that Congress, in addition to its delegated powers, could tap a vast reservoir of other powers that were not expressly granted but could be implied because Congress was the legislative branch of the national government. The essential defensive aspect of *McCulloch* became more evident in the second part of the opinion, when Marshall invoked the principle of national supremacy to deny Maryland's right to tax the national bank. Such a tax was a prime example of state aggression on federal authority, an illustration of the powerful centrifugal tendencies that continually threatened to dissolve the union. National supremacy, as Marshall envisioned it, was not an offensive weapon to encumber or obstruct the operations of the state governments but rather a conservative and defensive principle to enable the general government to exercise freely its limited powers and to resist state encroachment on its jurisdiction.

Marshall's adoption of so-called broad (a term he did not use) construction of the Constitution was also defensive. He did not so much affirm a broad construction of Congress's powers as reject a "strict" construction (urged by Maryland's counsel) that would confine Congress only to those means that were absolutely or indispensably necessary. Strict construction, argued Marshall, would emasculate the general government: prevent it from performing the important functions entrusted to it. A government so tightly tethered would scarcely be more effective than Congress under the former Confederation.

Defense was also a principal motif of *Gibbons,* another exemplar of Marshall Court nationalism, which was notable for its spacious reading of Congress's power to regulate interstate and foreign commerce. No part of the Constitution has proved a more fertile source of national power than the commerce clause — this was the constitutional foundation on which Congress erected the federal regulatory state that emerged in the twentieth century. Not surprisingly, therefore, *Gibbons* has been cited as the leading precedent for this development. Again, however, its main significance at the time lay in limiting the exercise of state power — the state of New York's monopoly on steamboat navigation on its waters. Indeed, the situation in regard to steamboat navigation in the 1820s was reminiscent of the retaliatory commercial restrictions enacted by the states under the Articles of Confederation. In reaction to New York's monopoly, some states passed laws forbidding steamboats licensed by New York to navigate their waters, while others began to grant their own steamboat monopoly rights.

Marshall expounded the commerce clause as conferring plenary power on Congress to regulate commerce, a power "complete in itself" that could "be exercised to its utmost extent." The chief justice stopped short of adopting the view that Congress's power was exclusive, although he acknowledged the great force of that argument. Again, in affirming an extensive scope for the commerce power, he was not being aggressively or gratuitously nationalistic but responding to counsel's reliance on strict construction to minimize the reach of the commerce clause and assert a "concurrent" power in the states to regulate commerce.

Marshall devoted a good portion of his opinion to denying the validity of the concurrent-power doctrine, concluding with another censure of strict construction and its baneful consequences:

> Powerful and ingenious minds, taking, as postulates, that the powers expressly granted to the government of the Union, are to be contracted by construction, into the narrowest possible compass, and that the original powers of the States are retained, if any possible construction will retain

them, may, by a course of well digested, but refined and metaphysical reasoning, founded on these premises, explain away the constitution of our country, and leave it, a magnificent structure, indeed, to look at, but totally unfit for use.

This passage nicely captures the tenor of Marshall Court nationalism, which was to protect and defend the general government against persistent antifederal forces that imperiled the "more perfect Union" formed by the Constitution of 1787. Defensive nationalism was pragmatic and flexible, giving broad scope to federal power while leaving ample room for the exercise of state power. *Gibbons,* for example, recognized a broad area of reserved state regulatory powers ("police" powers), which served as the basis for the Court's sustaining of the state law in *Willson v. Blackbird Creek Marsh Company.*

The Contract Clause and Property Rights

In another line of cases, the Marshall Court nullified state laws that unconstitutionally violated the private rights of individuals. Unlike the federalism cases, in which the offending state law conflicted with a federal power and therefore yielded to the principle of national supremacy, the state law in these cases came within the Constitution's prohibitions and restrictions on the states. To Marshall, the most important prohibition was that against laws impairing the obligation of contracts; under his guidance, the contract clause became the Supreme Court's chief weapon to restrain state interference with property rights. It was the constitutional expression of the doctrine of "vested rights," the belief that the rights acquired by individuals under the law — notably, the right to the security and free enjoyment of property — were to be regarded as inviolable, not to be infringed by governmental power. As the Constitution's principal guarantor of vested rights, the contract clause functioned in a way somewhat similar to the role undertaken by the Fourteenth Amendment and the "incorporated" Bill of Rights in the twentieth century. To a remarkable degree, the Marshall Court succeeded in making the original Constitution, through the contract clause, serve as a charter of rights that protected the American people from the acts of their state governments. As the chief justice remarked in *Fletcher v. Peck,* "the constitution of the United States contains what may be deemed a bill of rights for the people of each state."

As in the federalism cases, so too in the contract clause cases: The Marshall Court's purpose was not to anticipate the modern American future but to preserve the Constitution of 1787, to fulfill its intention to protect private rights. State violations of those rights during the 1780s had been an overriding concern of the Framers. Particular attention had been directed at paper money and tender laws, at laws permitting citizens to offer specific property instead of money in payment of debts, and at laws that provided for installment of debts and postponed executions for debts. The Court gave a broad scope to the contract clause, bringing laws within its purview that the Framers probably never thought of in 1787. Still, it was an essentially eighteenth-century "republican" concern about the insecurity of private rights in state legislatures ruled by arbitrary and capricious factions that lay behind the Court's contract clause decisions. The chief justice and his brethren were not conscious modernizers attempting to clear the path for the triumph of capitalism and corporations. To be sure, the core of their jurisprudence — the sanctity of property and contractual rights — could be harmonized with or adapted to the demands of an emerging capitalist economy, but this was more unintended consequence than deliberate design of their constitutional law.

The Marshall Court first interpreted the contract clause in *Fletcher*, which arose from Georgia's 1795 sale of thirty-five million acres of its Yazoo lands (most of present-day Alabama and Mississippi) to several New England land companies. These companies hastily sold the lands to third parties throughout the country. The next year, 1796, after it was revealed that all but one of the Georgia legislators had exchanged their votes for shares in the land companies, a newly elected legislature rescinded the sale. When the case came up for decision in 1810, Chief Justice Marshall for the Court disallowed the act rescinding the Yazoo sale. He ruled that the state's grant of land was a contract protected by the Constitution. The rescinding act of 1796, which deprived innocent third-party purchasers of rights acquired under the sale, impaired the obligation of that contract and was therefore void. The decision established a precedent for the principle that a state land grant was a contract and that the contract clause protected public (those in which a state was a party) as well as private contracts between individuals. The chief justice based his broad reading of the clause on its general language, which made no distinction between private and public, and on its manifest intention to shield persons and property "from the effects of those sudden and strong passions" to which state legislatures were exposed. The Court reaffirmed the principles of *Fletcher* two years later in voiding a New Jersey law repealing a tax exemption on land formerly belonging to Indians.

In *Dartmouth College v. Woodward* (1819), Marshall built on *Fletcher* to extend the reach of the contract clause to embrace corporate charters. Like a land grant, a corporate charter was a grant of property by public authority and thus constituted a contract. In this case, the Court ruled that the charter granted to Dartmouth College by the British Crown in 1769 was a contract protected by the Constitution and that New Hampshire's laws reorganizing and assuming control of the college were unconstitutional.

To reach this conclusion, the Court had to meet the objection that the charter created a public corporation for public purposes and was therefore subject to state control. Examining the charter, Marshall found that Dartmouth College originated as a private "eleemosynary" (charitable) corporation and retained that character despite the application of its funds to broad public purposes, such as education. The private rights protected by the charter were those of the corporation itself as the "assignee" of the rights of the original founders and donors. Marshall conceded that protection of corporate rights may not have been contemplated by the framers of the contract clause, but if a rare or unforeseen case had no part in establishing a constitutional rule, that circumstance in itself did not except such a case from the operation of the rule. Again, the general language of the contract clause evinced an intention that it should have a comprehensive reach. Nothing in the wording or in the nature and reason of the case itself could justify restricting the meaning to exclude rights conferred by a corporate charter. Characteristically, Marshall used a literal, or "plain meaning," construction to the Constitution's words, placing the burden of proof on those who would construe them in a narrower sense.

Dartmouth announced a principle of constitutional law that applied not only to charitable corporations, such as private colleges, but also to business corporations. By creating a wide scope for unfettered entrepreneurial activity, the principle suited the requirements of a burgeoning capitalist economy. Still, the larger purpose of Marshall and his brethren was not simply to carve out a capacious zone of legal immunity for corporations but rather to make a statement about the inviolability of private rights in the exercise of state power and the duty of judges under the Constitution to prevent these rights from being sacrificed to the fluctuating policies of legislative majorities.

This purpose was also evident in the Court's broad interpretation of the contract clause to invalidate state bankruptcy and insolvency laws that discharged debtors from liability for debts. To be sure, the enhancement of property and creditor rights resulting from this interpretation stimulated foreign investment in the American economy and promoted the growth of an internal common market. In the principal case, *Sturges v. Crowninshield* (1819), Marshall encountered the same objection put forward in *Dartmouth* that such laws were not on the Framers' minds in 1787, that the contract clause was intended to embrace only the mischiefs complained of at the time. Once again, he construed the contract clause's general language to show that it was not directed at particular laws but instead was "intended to establish a great principle that contracts should be inviolable." The intention of the Constitution, as gathered from its words, was to guard against the manifold and unforeseen ways that ingenious legislators might violate the obligation of contracts.

Marshall spoke for a purportedly unanimous Court in *Sturges*, but in fact, the justices were badly divided. Although they agreed that laws acting retrospectively on prior contracts, as in this case, were unconstitutional, the justices split on the question of prospective bankruptcy laws. This division emerged publicly in *Ogden v. Saunders* (1827), when the Court by a 4–3 majority upheld the constitutionality of such laws. Adhering to the construction he had urged in previous cases, Marshall in dissent insisted that the words and intention of the contract clause did not support a distinction between retrospective and prospective laws.

Despite his setback in *Ogden*, Marshall was largely successful in sustaining a broad reading of the contract clause to make it an effective barrier to state interferences with the vested rights of property and contract. As it happened, the Court after 1827 upheld the state legislation in cases brought under the contract clause, but this concession to state sovereignty was not inconsistent with the pragmatic jurisprudence that characterized the federalism cases.

A good example is *Providence Bank v. Billings* (1830), in which the Court held that a Rhode Island law laying a tax on a state bank was a legitimate exercise of its taxing power. Marshall rejected the argument that the bank's corporate charter, as a contract protected by the Constitution, exempted it from state taxation. Conceding that taxation could destroy the bank, the chief justice declared that the Constitution "was not intended to furnish the corrective for every abuse of power" by state governments. Although convinced that the contract clause should have extensive application, Marshall recognized the potential of pushing arguments based on that clause to such extremes that would hamper the ability of state governments to perform their ordinary functions.

In the same spirit, he rejected counsel's argument in *Barron v. Baltimore* (1833) that some of the Bill of Rights amendments should be applied to both the state and federal governments. Were the proposition sustained, the Supreme Court would have gained a vastly enlarged scope for the exercise of judicial power against state interferences with private rights. In declining the offer, Marshall employed the same principles of construction he had used to support an enlarged interpretation of the contract clause to argue for a restrictive application of the Bill of Rights to the federal government alone.

The Legacy of the Marshall Court

The Marshall Court created a body of constitutional law that endeavored to promote the energetic and efficient operation of the federal government and to enforce the Constitution's protections for private rights. Yet perhaps its most fundamental and enduring achievement was to solidify the practice of judicial review, first invoked in *Marbury v. Madison,* so that it became a regular and continuously operating principle of the American constitutional system. As a specific instance of judicial review, *Marbury* was somewhat anomalous, for it struck down a law of Congress, which did not happen again until 1857. All subsequent exercises of the power under Marshall were applied to state laws. In those cases, the Marshall Court, though not by conscious design, carried judicial review beyond its original incarnation as an extraordinary, rarely invoked defense of fundamental law toward the now familiar idea of judicial exposition of the constitutional text. Marshall and his brethren applied the principles and methods of statutory interpretation to the Constitution itself, treating it in much the same way that judges construed ordinary statutes. In this way, the Constitution became "legalized," that is, amenable to routine judicial exposition and implementation. In a subtle, almost imperceptible, way, the Constitution shed its extraordinary, "fundamental" quality as foundational political law and took on the character of an ordinary law, the kind of law that could run in the court system, one that judges could construe in the course of routine adjudication of lawsuits.

Constitutional law in the United States became simply another branch of law—like commercial law, contracts, and property—with its own set of doctrines and leading cases. Like other fields of law, constitutional law emerged and developed as a result of adjudication, the adversarial process by which parties advance and contest legal claims in courts of law. By assimilating constitutional exegesis to adjudication, the Marshall Court was able to infuse its constitutional pronouncements with the qualities of an ordinary legal judgment and thereby persuade the American people to accept such pronouncements not as politics but as so much *law.*

From the outset of his tenure, Chief Justice Marshall recognized that the effectiveness of the Supreme Court would depend on its capacity to generate acceptance as a tribunal that impartially pronounced "law" and renounced any claim to decide "political" questions. The separation of law and politics, indeed, was the key to the judiciary's rise to coordinate status with Congress and the executive as one of the three capital powers of government. Precisely because it conducted itself as a legal tribunal, the Supreme Court under Marshall acquired the prestige and authority to be entrusted with the power to decide great public questions. Crucial to this development was the Court's appropriation of the Constitution as its special preserve. Marshall and his brethren built up the institutional strength of the Court by tapping into the American people's reverence for the Constitution. As the guardian of the Constitution, the Court made itself the voice of the people's permanent will. By 1835, the mystique was essentially in place, the justices Olympian sages, jealous protectors of the Constitution, far above the turbulent waters of politics. This mystique remains the basis of the Court's extraordinary power, largely explaining why an institution composed of unelected judges with lifetime appointments can credibly claim to serve the ends of democratic government.

The emergence of judicial power in the United States during Marshall's day could not have occurred without the willing acceptance—even complicity—of the American people. In the confusion, uncertainty, and instability that characterized republican government, the people and the politicians they elected to office increasingly referred great public questions to courts for disposition in a rational, orderly, and impartial way.

As the perceptive French observer Alexis de Tocqueville noted in the 1830s, "Scarcely any political question arises in the United States that is not resolved, sooner or later, into a judicial question." Many of the great cases that came up to the Marshall Court began life as political issues in the state and federal governments. Before it took the form of *Fletcher v. Peck*, the sale of the Yazoo lands was embroiled in Georgia politics and was a hotly debated topic in the U.S. Congress. *McCulloch v. Maryland* affirmed the constitutionality of the Bank of the United States in 1819, but this matter had first attracted attention as early as 1791 in the debates of the First Congress. The controversy over the future of a small New England college, resolved in *Dartmouth College v. Woodward,* had begun mired in the political and religious factionalism of New Hampshire. The Cherokee Nation, which had accoutered itself as a well-organized and well-financed interest group with influential political and legal friends in Washington, pleaded its case in the political arena long before turning to the Supreme Court.

The Marshall era was "foundational" in making the Supreme Court an arena for the resolution of fundamental questions and an equal partner in the tripartite scheme of government; in developing the authority to expound the Constitution and apply it as law in the ordinary course of adjudication; in making enforcement of the Constitution primarily if not exclusively a judicial responsibility; and in creating the field of constitutional law and propounding enduring principles of that law. Yet the Marshall Court was a far cry from the Supreme Court familiar to Americans of the twenty-first century. Only in matters of form does the modern Court still bear any resemblance to an ordinary court of law. Having virtually complete control over its docket, the Court no longer decides routine private lawsuits, acting rather on "a roving commission seeking out important constitutional questions." By definition, it takes on only the weightiest public causes, the decision of which involves it in policymaking in ways scarcely distinguishable from legislating. In the Marshall era, by contrast, the Supreme Court remained essentially a legal institution, an appellate court for deciding ordinary cases at law. The constitutional adjudication for which it has been remembered was in fact a rare if not extraordinary exercise of judicial power. Despite periodic bursts of activity, the Marshall Court can hardly be described as "activist" in the modern sense. Most of the time, it quietly pursued its strictly legal business, far removed from the controversies that agitated the public arena. Of course, it was during these long periods of quiescence that the Court solidified its institutional identity and authority in a way that conditioned Americans to accept its role in making constitutional law as well.

In early-nineteenth-century America, the experiment of a compound federal republic had scarcely yet begun, the role of the judicial department in particular was still largely undefined, and constitutional law was mostly uncharted, virgin territory. Situated in this historical context, the Marshall Court enjoyed a unique freedom to be creative, to write on a virtually clean slate, and to make the precedents that would be the starting point for subsequent judicial inquiry.

Constitutional interpretation as practiced by the Marshall Court had a pristine quality, directly and immediately tied to the text of the Constitution itself, with no accumulated gloss of precedents to block its view. In the person of its chief justice, the Marshall Court formed a living link with the generation that wrote the Constitution and thus could reasonably claim to possess a Framer's knowledge of its meaning and intent. To paraphrase Oliver Wendell Holmes, the Marshall Court represented "a strategic point in the campaign of history," and part of its greatness consisted of its "being *there*." Without question, Chief Justice Marshall and his associates made the most of their historical moment.

—CHARLES F. HOBSON

FOR FURTHER READING AND RESEARCH

The Supreme Court under Chief Justice Marshall is covered in two massive volumes: George Lee Haskins and Herbert A. Johnson, *Foundations of Power: John Marshall, 1801–15* (New York, 1981); and G. Edward White, *The Marshall Court and Cultural Change, 1815–35* (New York, 1988). These are, respectively, volume 2 and volume 3–4 of the *History of the Supreme Court of the United States* (the Oliver Wendell Holmes Devise). The former emphasizes the Court's endeavor to separate law and politics, while the latter explores the ways in which the Court's jurisprudence was shaped by republican ideology. More recently, Johnson has published *The Chief Justiceship of John Marshall 1801–1835* (Columbia, S.C., 1997), a volume in a series, of which he is the general editor, on the chief justice-ships. R. Kent Newmyer, *The Supreme Court under Marshall and Taney* (Arlington Heights, Ill., 1968), remains the best brief survey. Newmyer's *John Marshall and the Heroic Age of the Supreme Court* (Baton Rouge, La., 2001) is at once a model ju-dicial biography and an illuminating history of the Marshall Court. Jean Edward Smith, *John Marshall: Definer of a Nation* (New York, 1996), is a lively and percep-tive biography. Charles F. Hobson, *John Marshall and the Rule of Law* (Lawrence, Kans., 1996), is an intellectual biography that emphasizes Marshall's grounding in the common law.

4

The Taney Court   1836–1864

The Jurisprudence of Slavery and the Crisis of the Union

ROGER BROOKE TANEY served as chief justice from 1836 until 1864, making him second in length of service among all chief justices, behind only John Marshall, his immediate predecessor. From the moment he took the center seat until the Civil War began, Taney dominated the Supreme Court. Until secession altered the status of the Court, and Taney's role on it, the Court reflected his views, values, and prejudices.

On the eve of Lincoln's election, Taney was an angry proslavery ideologue and aggressive Democratic partisan whose constitutional nationalism was tied to the federal government's support for slavery. In 1860, everyone on the Court, except Justice John McLean, shared Taney's views. With Lincoln's election, the formation of the Confederacy, and the subsequent war, Taney emerged as a Southern nationalist in sentiment and a fellow traveler of secession. But during the war, rapid changes on the bench, as well as Taney's extreme hostility to Lincoln and the Union cause, destroyed his ability to lead the Court. When he died in 1864, Taney still held the center seat on the bench, but he was no longer the "chief" of the Court.

Despite his dominance on the Court, Taney was never able to command the level and depth of support that Marshall had enjoyed. Political and economic change, compounded by the growing conflicts of sectionalism and slavery, simply precluded the unanimity that Marshall had often achieved. Justice Joseph Story, who served with Taney from 1836 until 1845, was far more of a nationalist than Taney, and his prestige and scholarly skills enabled him to challenge Taney's Jacksonian jurisprudence, even if he could not defeat it. On the other extreme, Justice Peter V. Daniel, although a Jacksonian Democrat, was so fanatical an advocate of states' rights that he frequently dissented even though the chief justice and a majority of the Court were themselves extremely solicitous of states' rights. Justices John McLean and Benjamin R. Curtis both rejected the relentlessly proslavery stance of the Taney Court and unsuccessfully challenged the Court majority in such cases as *Prigg v. Pennsylvania* (1842) and *Dred Scott v. Sandford* (1857).

Taney is best remembered for his stridently proslavery, racist opinion in *Dred Scott v. Sandford*, certainly the most memorable and important case during his tenure on the Court. Some have argued that *Dred Scott* was an aberration that should not mar his otherwise distinguished service on the bench. But in fact, Taney's opinion in *Dred Scott* dovetailed neatly with his long-held views on the rights of free blacks, his overwhelmingly proslavery jurisprudence before and after that case, and his subsequent opposition to Lincoln, the Union cause, and emancipation. The decision also reflected the proslavery racism of the Court as a whole: Only two justices dissented from Taney's opinion.

After Taney's death, Senator Charles Sumner of Massachusetts opposed placing his bust alongside all the other departed justices. "If a man has done evil during his life," Sumner told his Senate colleagues, "he must not be complimented in marble." Sumner noted that England had never honored the hated Chief Justice Jeffries, "famous for his talents as for his crimes." Like Jeffries, Sumner argued, Taney had been "the tool of unjust power." He had "administered his last justice wickedly, and degraded the judiciary of the country, and degraded the age." He was not to be remembered by a marble bust; rather, Taney was to be dealt with in the works of scholars, where, Sumner confidently predicted, "the name of Taney is to be hooted down the page of history."

Since Sumner gave that speech, Chief Justice Taney's reputation — and that of his Court — has fluctuated. His twenty-eight-year tenure on the Court was significant. He wrote many important opinions and endorsed others written by his brethren. Much of his jurisprudence, especially on economic issues, has been held in high regard. But in the end, his reputation, and that of the Taney Court, turns on *Dred Scott*. If no longer "hooted down the page of history," Taney and his brethren must be understood as deeply marred by their proslavery jurisprudence before the war. Similarly, Taney's reputation, although not that of a majority of the Court, is equally marred by his hostility to the Union and to freedom during the Civil War.

Taney and His Court's Personnel

Roger Brooke Taney was born in 1777, the second son of a Maryland planter. Knowing that his older brother would inherit the plantation, Taney turned to law and politics, serving in the Maryland legislature as a Federalist and then, after he left the Federalist Party during the War of

1812, as a National Republican. In the 1820s, he was the state attorney general and a supporter of Andrew Jackson's presidential bids. In 1831, Jackson appointed him U.S. attorney general.

As an adult, Taney educated and manumitted virtually all his own slaves. In 1818, he successfully defended Jacob Gruber, a Methodist minister prosecuted in Maryland for preaching sermons that had antislavery implications. Despite his personal generosity toward his slaves and his defense of Gruber, Taney was never an opponent of slavery and as a mature adult always opposed granting any rights to free blacks. Indeed, during his tenure as U.S. attorney general, Taney wrote an unpublished "Opinion of the Attorney General" in which he argued that African Americans in the United States had no political or legal rights except those they "enjoy" at the "mercy" of whites. As he would years later in *Dred Scott*, Taney ignored the fact that African Americans had voted in a number of states at the time of the ratification of the Constitution and continued to do so in the 1830s. His attorney general's opinion also concluded that the Declaration of Independence was never meant to apply to African Americans, who were not, in his mind, entitled to the natural rights of "life, liberty, and the pursuit of happiness." During his tenure as attorney general, Taney supported the constitutionality of state laws — known as black seamen's laws — which prohibited free black sailors from entering most Southern states.

Once on the Supreme Court, Taney's views on race and the rights of free blacks would become increasingly important and controversial as slavery became the central issue of American politics. At the time of his appointment, however, Taney had gained greater notoriety in an altogether different cause — Andrew Jackson's war against the Bank of the United States. As Jackson's attorney general, he had drafted the president's message vetoing the recharter of the Bank of the United States. This made him the ideological, as well as political, enemy of nationalists, former Federalists, and members of the emerging Whig Party. While serving as interim secretary of the Treasury, Taney compounded his notoriety by initiating the redistribution of government funds from the Bank of the United States to "pet banks," often owned by men who supported Jackson.

Jackson nominated Taney to replace Marshall as chief justice in December 1835, and the Senate confirmed him in the spring of 1836. Taney looked like the anti-Jacksonians' worst nightmare: a smart, articulate ideologue strategically positioned to eviscerate Chief Justice Marshall's constitutional nationalism. After Taney's confirmation to the Court, Whigs and nationalists feared that he would do just that.

Taney also had the personnel on the Court to modify or completely reverse Marshall's jurisprudence. By the time Andrew Jackson appointed Taney to the bench, the "Marshall Court" was no longer the bastion of

Federalist/Whig nationalism it once had been. Jackson had already appointed John McLean (1829), Henry Baldwin (1830), and James Wayne (1835) to what was a seven-man court. Taney became the fourth Jacksonian on the Court, thus ensuring a majority for his political and jurisprudential perspective. The nomination and confirmation of Philip P. Barbour (done on the same days as Taney in 1835 and 1836) made the Court even more Jacksonian in character.

In 1837, after Taney's first term on the bench, Congress created two more seats, which Jackson filled with John Catron and John McKinley. Thus, starting with the 1838 term, the new nine-man court contained seven Jacksonian Democrats who could easily outvote the two remaining Marshall Court justices: Smith Thompson and Joseph Story. By 1846, the entire Court was made up of Jacksonians: Samuel Nelson had succeeded Thompson in 1845, and Levi Woodbury replaced Story in 1845. Other changes — Peter V. Daniel (1841) replacing Barbour, Robert Grier (1846) replacing Baldwin, and John A. Campbell (1853) replacing McKinley — brought no ideological alteration. Indeed, with the exception of Justice Benjamin Robbins Curtis, who served from 1851 to 1857, and John McLean, who moved away from the Democrats on issues of race, slavery, and the commerce clause early in his Court career and became a Republican in the 1850s, the Court remained thoroughly Jacksonian until Lincoln began to remake it during the Civil War.

Taney's Court was not only Jacksonian but also dominated by proslavery Southerners aided by "doughfaces"—Northern men with Southern principles. From 1837 until 1861, the Court always had five Southern justices and four Northerners. Throughout this period, at least two, and sometimes three, of the Northerners were doughfaces, who voted consistently to support slavery and Southern states' rights. The most important doughfaces were Robert Grier of Pennsylvania, Samuel Nelson of New York, and Levi Woodbury of New Hampshire. Woodbury had higher political ambitions and believed that his stridently proslavery decision in *Jones v. Van Zandt* (1847) would gain him a spot on the Democratic presidential ticket. However, his early death prevented this.

Combined, the doughfaces and the Southerners created a Court that was easy for Taney to lead. His leadership was subtle: equal parts tact and willingness to involve other members of the Court in its most important decisions. As G. Edward White has noted, "Taney preferred to influence others through the power of suggestion rather than of persuasion." Unlike Marshall, Taney often assigned the task of writing important decisions to others: In more than twenty-eight years as chief justice, Taney wrote only about 270 majority opinions himself, averaging fewer than 10 a year. But he also wrote only 12 dissents — fewer than one every two years. In other words, directly or indirectly, Taney was almost always able to sway the Court to his views.

Even those who despised his political and legal views found him irresistibly charming. Justice Samuel F. Miller, a partisan Republican appointed by Lincoln, served with Taney during the chief justice's last two terms on the bench. Miller later wrote of his earliest encounter with Taney:

> I had never looked upon the face of Judge Taney, but I knew of him. I remembered that he had attempted to throttle the Bank of the United States, and I hated him for it. . . . He had been the chief Spokesman of the Court in the *Dred Scott* case, and I hated him for that. But from my first acquaintance with him, I realized that these feelings toward him were but the suggestions of the worst elements of our nature; for before the first term of my service in the Court had passed, I more than liked him; I loved him.

Economic Development

Aside from its decisions on slavery, race, and the Civil War, the Taney Court is best remembered for its economic decisions, particularly those that dramatically altered the balance of state and national powers created by the Marshall Court. The Taney Court did not completely destroy the Marshall Court's jurisprudence, as some Whigs had feared, but often severely modified it. Three 1837 cases — *Charles River Bridge v. Warren Bridge, New York v. Miln,* and *Briscoe v. Bank of Kentucky* — all decided during Taney's first term, set the stage for the jurisprudence of the newly remade Jacksonian Court.

In *Charles River Bridge,* Taney, writing for a 4–3 majority, allowed the states to promote economic and industrial development in an age of rapid technological change. The case pitted a newly chartered entity against an established, vested economic interest. The case began when the Charles River Bridge Company sued to prevent the construction of a new, competing bridge, to be built by the Warren Bridge Company.

The Charles River Bridge Company's charter had evolved out of an exclusive franchise to operate a ferryboat on the Charles River between Boston and Charlestown, Massachusetts. The company claimed that the exclusivity carried over to the bridge and hence that, in chartering a competing bridge, the state of Massachusetts was abrogating preexisting chartered rights in violation of the contracts clause of the Constitution. This was certainly a plausible theory, one that Story, Thompson, and the newly appointed Jacksonian, John McLean, accepted. In his dissent, Story asserted, "I stand upon the old law . . . in resisting any such encroachments upon the rights and liberties of the citizens, secured by public grants." But Taney and the other three Jacksonians on the seven-man court offered a more flexible approach to the contracts clause, concluding that "any ambiguity in the terms of the contract" or corporate charter "must operate against the adventurers [stockholders] and in favor of the public." The end result was to strengthen state governments by giving them more latitude in regulating their economies and to allow new technologies and industries to compete with and often supplant older ones.

In *Miln,* the Court seriously modified the Marshall Court's commerce clause jurisprudence and substantially enhanced the powers of the states to interfere with interstate or international commerce. The case involved a New York law requiring that ship captains report to state authorities all passengers brought into the state. Miln was the consignee of a ship whose master failed to make a report, and Miln was then fined $15,000. Miln argued that the New York law interfered with interstate commerce. Certainly, this would have been the outcome if the Court had followed Marshall's doctrine, as set out in *Gibbons v. Ogden* (1824). But with Barbour writing its opinion and Story alone in dissent, the Court upheld the New York law by creating an entirely new constitutional doctrine, asserting that the New York law was a "regulation . . . of police." Under this newly created "police powers" doctrine, states were allowed to regulate aspects of interstate and international commerce carried on within their own jurisdictions, as long as Congress had not regulated the activity.

Lurking in the background to this case was the issue of free black sailors. Starting in 1822, South Carolina and other Southern states had passed laws allowing for the arrest of free black sailors who entered their ports. In *Elkison v. Deliesseline* (1823), a circuit court case, Justice William Johnson had declared that such laws were unconstitutional but found that he did not have jurisdiction in the case immediately before him. While Jackson's attorney general, Taney had supported such laws in an opinion he wrote for the president. Now, in *Miln,* with Barbour as his amanuensis, Taney was able to create the doctrine necessary to allow such laws.

The police powers doctrine would remain a permanent part of American federalism and constitutional law. In *Cooley v. Board of Wardens of Port of Philadelphia* (1851), the Taney Court would reaffirm the doctrine in allowing the port of Philadelphia to require that ships involved in interstate commerce hire a local pilot to guide the ship to a dock. Ultimately, *Miln* and *Cooley* set the stage for local regulation of interstate and international commerce in the absence of federal regulation. This was one of Taney's most lasting contributions (or alterations) to constitutional law and illustrates a significant break with the Marshall Court tradition.

By the same 6–1 vote, with McLean writing the majority opinion, the Court in *Briscoe v. Commonwealth Bank of Kentucky* upheld the right of a state-chartered bank to issue bank notes. This narrowed the implications of Chief Justice John Marshall's opinion in *Craig v. Missouri* (1831), which had prohibited states from issuing paper money. Logically, if the Constitution prohibited a state from issuing currency, a state could not charter a bank to do what the state itself could not do. However, McLean distinguished between a bank issuing notes and a state issuing currency.

This decision dovetailed with Jacksonian opposition to the federally chartered Bank of the United States, which Taney had helped destroy. More important, *Briscoe* enhanced the power of the states to regulate their economies. The Constitution prohibits the states from issuing "bills of credit," and in *Craig v. Missouri* (1831), Marshall had held that Missouri could not issue "certificates" that could be used to pay state taxes and other debts. Kentucky adopted a similar program, but instead of issuing the certificates directly, it chartered a bank, which was entirely owned and operated by the state. This bank then issued notes, which it loaned to borrowers and which circulated as currency within the state.

McLean asserted that the bank notes were not "bills of credit" because they were not technically backed by the full faith and credit of the state. Disingenuously, McLean asserted that this paper money was simply currency issued by a private bank that simply happened to be owned and operated by the state.

The case was directly tied to Taney's role in the demise of the Bank of the United States. In 1832, President Jackson had vetoed the recharter of the Bank of the United States. Taney drafted that veto. One result of the bank's demise was the elimination of the only form of currency to circulate nationally, bank notes issued by the Bank of the United States. Another result was a severe shortage of specie (gold and silver) in circulation. In order to cope with these problems, in part caused by Jackson and Taney, Kentucky had developed its system of issuing currency through the state bank. By effectively reversing the Marshall Court on this issue, McLean, Taney, and the other Jacksonians on the Court were able to provide a constitutionally permissible way for the states to cope with the economic chaos the Jacksonians themselves had created. Any other result might have forced the Jacksonians to either change their position on banking and currency policy or risk losing their political majority.

In a bitter dissent, Story noted that the "Mr. Chief Justice Marshall is not here to speak for himself." Had he been, he would surely have found the statute unconstitutional. Story's dissent illustrates how quickly the Taney Court had asserted itself as a new power, ready to modify or abandon

Marshall's jurisprudence to fit the circumstances and politics of Jacksonian America.

Gradually, the Taney Court moved from rigid support for states' rights to a more flexible approach. This may have been a sign of growing sophistication on the part of the Court, perhaps reflecting a realization that doctrinaire Jacksonian economic policy might not always work, perhaps also a response to the stark reality of economic crisis in the aftermath of the Panic of 1837.

Thus, despite his general deference to state regulation, Taney encouraged interstate economic development. In *Bank of Augusta v. Earle* (1839), for example, Taney held that a bank chartered in one state might do business in another unless specifically prohibited from doing so. Here, Taney enhanced interstate business while at the same time continuing to acknowledge the authority of the states to regulate their economies. The ruling allowed states to exercise regulatory authority but required them to do so explicitly, by specifically banning out-of-state corporations from doing business within their jurisdictions. Then, in *Swift v. Tyson* (1842), Justice Story, writing for a unanimous Court, asserted that in commercial cases, the Court would develop a national common law. This meant that in commercial litigation, the federal courts could develop their own common-law rules and would not have to rely on state rules. *Swift* made sense in a vibrant, expanding economy in which few lawyers or businessmen would have any idea what the common law was in other states. It was a dramatically nationalistic decision, reminiscent of the Marshall Court at its most expansive moments.

Taney's expansion of federal jurisdiction in *Propeller Genesee Chief v. Fitzhugh* (1852) also illustrates an increasingly sophisticated, nondoctrinaire approach to economic development. Here, he reversed the Marshall Court's doctrine, enunciated by Justice Joseph Story in the *Thomas Jefferson* (1825), which had allowed the states to regulate traffic on inland waters. That decision had resulted in an impossible set of differing and sometimes contradictory rules in the nation's water commerce. Taney concluded that federal admiralty jurisdiction extended to all navigable rivers and lakes, not just to those affected by "the ebb and flow of the tide." Taney understood that the Great Lakes "are in truth inland seas. Different States border on them on one side, and a foreign nation on the other. A great and growing commerce is carried on upon them . . ." Thus, as Harold M. Hyman and William M. Wiecek noted in *Equal Justice Under Law* (1978), "Taney discarded the English tidewater rule of Admiralty jurisdiction that Story had imported into American law," replacing it with a more pragmatic test: navigability. "The *Genesee Chief*," these authors concluded, "ranks with *Charles River Bridge* as a triumphant marriage of technological development and legal advance, based on a realistic appraisal of the policy consequences of adopting one rule of law or another."

Decisions expanding national power were not the norm for the Taney Court. In the *License Cases* (1847), the Taney Court upheld the right of states to ban the importation of liquor; *Cooley v. Board of Wardens* (1851) reaffirmed the concept of state police powers first articulated in *Miln*. Both decisions reflected Taney's general deference to the states. However, in the *Passenger Cases* (1849), the Court slightly modified the police powers doctrine by striking down, on commerce clause grounds, state laws taxing immigrants. In the 5–4 vote, the justices split in odd ways. McLean, Grier, Wayne, and Catron, the most moderate Jacksonians on the bench, voted to strike down the law. They were joined by McKinley, a states' rights, proslavery ideologue from Alabama, who argued that the "migration and importation" provision of the Constitution, which had prohibited the banning of the African slave trade before 1808, also prohibited the states from taxing immigrants. This decision weakened the states by limiting their power to regulate immigration. Taney dissented, arguing that this case should follow the rule set out in *Miln*. In another dissent, Justice Daniel, the most stridently proslavery and states' rights member of the Court, complained that the decision would undermine the right of the slave states to "repulse" or "tax the nuisance" of free blacks who might try to enter them from "Jamaica, Hayti, or Africa."

Taney was also unable to carry the Court the first time it heard *Pennsylvania v. Wheeling and Belmont Bridge Company* (1852). The case involved a railroad bridge built between Virginia and Ohio across the Ohio River. The bridge was so low that steamboats were forced to lower their smokestacks to get under it. Not surprisingly, the Court voted 7–2 to support Pennsylvania's claim that the bridge was a "nuisance" that impeded interstate commerce. Taney and Daniel dissented. Before any action could be taken, Congress passed a law declaring that the railroad bridge was a "lawful structure" and a "post road," which Congress had the right to regulate. In a second suit, the Court upheld the act of Congress by a vote of 6–3. The three dissenters — McLean, Wayne, and Grier — often voted to support a nationalist view of the Constitution. Here, they argued that Congress's commerce power did not extend to building an obstruction over the water. The majority, which included four who had voted against Taney in the first case, had the better argument: Virginia could not obstruct commerce; nor could a private railroad or bridge company, but Congress could.

On economic issues, the Taney Court usually supported the states and private interests and opposed a nationalistic view of commerce and congressional power. The Court enforced a nationalist interpretation of the commerce clause and the contract clause only when a state clearly overstepped the powers of Congress or clearly interfered with commerce, as in the *Passenger Cases* and the first *Wheeling Bridge* case. In those cases, Taney dissented, refusing even there to limit the states. Thus, the Court generally allowed the states great flexibility in determining how their economies should develop.

Slavery and Race

Defenders of Taney and his reputation, such as Felix Frankfurter, stress his economic decisions. On issues of race and slavery, they portray him as a moderate, stressing his defense of Rev. Jacob Gruber in 1818 and the manumission of his own slaves. But first as attorney general and then as chief justice, Taney protected slavery and undermined the rights of free African Americans at every turn. Equally important, during the Civil War Taney hindered Lincoln's attempts to uphold the Constitution and keep the Union intact.

Dred Scott is correctly seen as the most important decision Taney wrote on race and slavery. Defenders of Taney complain that this admittedly bad and unfortunate decision has been used unfairly to destroy his whole reputation. Chief Justice Charles Evans Hughes said in 1931 that *Dred Scott* was a "well-intentioned mistake." Yale law professor Alexander Bickel called it a "ghastly error." Political scientist Henry J. Abraham still calls *Dred Scott* a "monumental aberration" and thinks it "a pity that Taney is so often remembered by that case."

Taney's defenders are, however, wrong. Well before *Dred Scott,* Taney had taken strong positions in support of slavery and against free African Americans. Far from an aberration, *Dred Scott* can be seen as the logical culmination of Taney's ideas on race and slavery. Moreover, his opinion denying any rights to free blacks — even those who voted and held office in some Northern states — was hardly "well intentioned."

Since joining the Court, Taney had dealt with slavery in a number of decisions. His first major encounter came in 1841, when the Court heard both *United States v. The Amistad* and *Groves v. Slaughter.* The *Amistad* was the first great slavery-related *cause célèbre* to reach the Supreme Court, although the case had little impact on the Court's jurisprudence over slavery. *Groves,* on the other hand, was a rather mundane case involving the interstate sale of slaves, which raised no great political issues but was fraught with important constitutional questions affecting slavery and the economy.

The *Amistad* was a Spanish schooner filled with slaves newly (and illegally) imported to Cuba from Africa. While being transported from one part of Cuba to another, the slaves revolted, killing most of the whites on board, and demanded that the two surviving whites, who had been the purchasers of the "slaves" in Cuba, transport them back to Africa. The two Cubans sailed east during the day but at night reversed course, heading north and west, in hopes of reaching a Southern state in the United States. Instead, the craft ended up in Long Island Sound, where a Coast Guard vessel interdicted it. Various suits arose over the status of the vessel and the Africans on it. In an opinion by Justice Joseph Story, the Supreme Court eventually ruled that the blacks had been illegally taken from Africa, could not be held as slaves under Spanish or American law, and should be returned to Africa. Taney silently concurred in Story's opinion. By 1841, even many proslavery advocates found the African trade to be immoral and a violation of natural law as well as bad public policy. Thus, Taney's acquiescence in freeing the *Amistad* Africans cannot be seen as antislavery.

On its face, *Groves v. Slaughter* did not raise pro- or antislavery issues either. It was essentially a commerce clause case, a suit between slave sellers and slave buyers. Mississippi's 1832 constitution prohibited the importation of slaves for sale. This was not an antislavery provision but rather an attempt to reduce the flow of capital out of the state. Slaughter, a professional slave dealer, sold slaves in Mississippi and received notes signed by Groves and others. Groves and his codefendants later defaulted on the notes, arguing that sales of slaves in Mississippi were void. Speaking for the Court, Justice Smith Thompson of New York determined that Mississippi's constitutional prohibition on the importation of slaves was not self-executing and that absent implementing legislation, the prohibition in the Mississippi constitution was inoperative. Thus, he held that the notes were not void. This was a reasonable result based on commercial rules and was consistent with the outcome in *Bank of Augusta v. Earle* (1839). In that case, Earle and other Alabamians refused to honor their own bills of exchange on the ground that they had been bought by an out-of-state bank. Taney had ruled that out-of-state banks could operate in any state, in the absence of an explicit act of the legislature to the contrary. Similarly, in *Groves*, Justice Thompson held that the Mississippi purchasers could not hide behind a clause of the state constitution and refuse to pay the notes they signed for the slaves they purchased, without an explicit statute in Mississippi banning slave sales. This result was "neutral" with regard to slavery.

Indicative of what would become his highly partisan approach to slavery throughout his career on the Court, Taney wrote a separate concurrence, insisting that the federal government had, in any case, no power over slavery. This was one of only fourteen concurring opinions that Taney wrote in his twenty-eight years on the bench. Taney's opinion dealt with an issue that was not directly before the Court. Clearly, Taney did not want to leave any implication that Congress might regulate slavery under the commerce clause. He declared that "the power of this subject [slavery] is exclusively with the several States; and each of them has a right to decide for itself, whether it will or will not allow persons of this description to be brought within its limits from another State, either for sale, or for any other purpose . . . and the action of the several States upon this subject cannot be controlled by Congress, either by virtue of its power to regulate commerce, or by virtue of any other power conferred by the Constitution of the United States."

Taney's separate opinion is consistent with his other decisions that allowed the states to regulate economic development. These are the decisions that Felix Frankfurter and other supporters of Taney admired so much. However, *Groves* at least suggests that Taney's commercial jurisprudence may have had a hidden goal: the protection of slavery and of the right of the states — especially the Southern states — to regulate this aspect of their economy. In that sense, Taney's opinion in *Groves* dovetails perfectly with his "opinion" as U.S. attorney general on the rights of free blacks. Written to advise President Jackson on the constitutionality of statutes adopted by most Southern coastal states prohibiting free blacks (from other states or the British Empire) from entering their jurisdiction, Taney in effect had argued that, because blacks had no rights and could be reduced to slavery at the whim of white society, the Southern states were free to exclude free blacks from their jurisdiction as they chose.

Some of Taney's most important decisions, giving states greater control over their economies, are sandwiched between his "opinion" as attorney general and his opinion in *Groves*. This suggests that slavery was in the background of Taney's economic decision making, that his desire to protect slavery influenced his commercial jurisprudence. He wanted to give the slave states great autonomy in regulating slavery and at the same time make sure that the federal government would not interfere with slavery.

The opinions in *Groves* also included a concurrence by Justice McLean and dissents from Story and McKinley. McLean took a position that was a mirror of Taney's. The chief justice used the case to reaffirm that the federal government could not abolish the domestic slave trade. McLean used his opinion to assert that the states emphatically had the right to ban slavery and prohibit anyone from bringing slaves into their jurisdiction. McLean noted that the states could not ban "the cotton of the south, or the manufactured articles of the north," but he asserted that "the power over slavery belongs to the states respectively. It is local in its character, and in its effects."

This position was not simply one of Jacksonian states' rights. Rather, it was the beginning of a constitutional argument against the theory that slavery was a national institution — a proposition that Taney would later support in *Dred Scott.* Justices Story and McKinley dissented from the Court's decision, believing that the notes were void. Story, who was often uncomfortable with slavery, perhaps felt that this was a chance to reject the idea of enforcing the sale of human beings. McKinley, writing from his proslavery states' rights position, believed the constitutional clause to be self-executing.

In *Prigg v. Pennsylvania* (1842), the Court heard its first case involving the fugitive slave clause of the U.S. Constitution. Edward Prigg had seized a black woman and her children in Pennsylvania and removed them to Maryland without complying with a Pennsylvania state law. At least one of the children had been born in Pennsylvania and was clearly free under that state's laws. The woman, Margaret Morgan, had been born of parents who were once slaves in Maryland, but no one had ever claimed her as a slave and she had grown up "free." Prigg was subsequently convicted of kidnapping under Pennsylvania's 1826 personal liberty law, for failing to obtain a proper writ from a state judge before removing the African Americans from the state. In a sweeping victory for slavery, which shakes to the core his antislavery reputation, Justice Story struck down the Pennsylvania law, upheld the federal Fugitive Slave Law of 1793, and further declared that slave owners had a constitutional right to seize their slaves anywhere they found them, without resort to any sort of legal process, as long as the seizure could be done without a breach of the peace.

In reaching these conclusions, Story swept aside both the free-state birth of one of the children and Morgan's prima facia claim to freedom. He also ignored the potential for kidnapping created by this decision. Story's goal in *Prigg,* as in *Swift v. Tyson,* decided earlier that term, was to create a federal common law. Here, he made slavery part of the federal common law and in essence said that slave owners could seize any black person, anywhere in the country, and claim that person as a slave, without interference from any state official or court.

Story's opinion also asserted that the federal government could not require state officials to enforce the Fugitive Slave Law of 1793, although he urged them to do so as a matter of patriotism, moral obligation, and (unenforceable) constitutional duty. Taney rejected this part of Story's opinion in another of his rare separate opinions, arguing that the states should be free to pass laws that aided in the return of fugitive slaves. He phrased this argument in terms similar to his economic arguments. He rejected the notion that the fugitive slave clause, and the 1793 federal law adopted to enforce it, prevented the states from passing parallel enforcement legislation. Instead, he argued that "by the national compact, this right of property [slavery] is recognized as an existing right in every state of the Union." Thus, the states were free to protect slavery. When it came to slavery, Taney supported state power for the Southern states, rejecting the right of the free states to protect the rights of free African Americans. But this should no longer seem surprising. Since his days as attorney general, Taney had believed that free blacks had no rights that any government had to protect.

Justice McLean dissented, arguing that the free states had the right to protect the liberty of their free black citizens. His was a lone voice in favor of liberty on a Court that was by now overwhelmingly proslavery. Justice Story, who held the "New England seat" on the Court, was allegedly opposed to slavery, but his opinion in *Prigg* was overwhelmingly supportive of bondage. After Story's death, his son argued that this decision was in effect antislavery because under it, the states were able to opt out of helping to return fugitive slaves. But Story himself understood this, and shortly after the opinion was delivered, he wrote to a Southern senator, urging that Congress create throughout the nation federal "commissioners" who could issue warrants under the Fugitive Slave Law. Congress followed this advice to the letter, passing the Fugitive Slave Law of 1850. Abolitionists were certainly not impressed by any notion that *Prigg* was secretly antislavery. In his home state of Massachusetts, abolitionists began to call Story the "Slave Catcher-in-Chief for New England." Were it not for *Dred Scott*, Story's opinion in *Prigg* would be remembered as the most important proslavery opinion in the Court's history.

Taney wrote his first majority opinion in an important slave case in *Strader v. Graham* (1850). Strader's steamboat had transported Graham's three slaves from Kentucky to Ohio, where they disappeared. Kentucky law held a steamboat operator liable for the value of any slaves who escaped by boarding the boat without written permission of the owner. Strader, however, argued that the blacks were free because Graham had previously allowed them to go to Indiana and Ohio. Speaking for a unanimous Court, Taney ruled against Strader, arguing that the status of the African Americans could be decided only by Kentucky, which had ruled they were slaves. Kentucky was free to ignore the laws of Ohio and Indiana on this question.

In *Strader*, Taney in effect asserted the right of a state to decide the status of African Americans within its jurisdiction. Presumably, had Graham's slaves asserted their liberty in Indiana or Ohio, those states would have freed them. But Taney hedged on this issue, declaring that "every State has an undoubted right to determine the *status* or domestic and social condition, of the persons domiciled within its territory" except as "restrained" by the Constitution. This wording clearly applied to fugitive slaves, which the Northern states could not declare free, but it also held open the possibility that slave owners had other federal rights to carry their slaves into the North or the federal territories. What was implicit here later became explicit in *Dred Scott*.

Dred Scott v. Sandford

Dred Scott was the slave of a military physician resident in Missouri, Dr. John Emerson. Emerson had taken Scott to Fort Snelling, in present-day Minnesota—at the time, free territory under the Missouri Compromise. Emerson had also taken Scott to the free state of Illinois. Scott later returned with Emerson to Missouri. After Emerson's death, Scott sued Emerson's widow for his freedom on the ground that he had become free through his residence in a jurisdiction where slavery was illegal and that once free, he was always free. After nearly eleven years of litigation in state and federal courts, the Supreme Court finally decided the case in 1857. Although all nine justices wrote opinions, Taney's was the "Opinion of the Court." In his sweeping, fifty-five-page opinion, Taney sought to settle the nation's divisive political questions of slavery and race in favor of the South.

Taney might have dealt with Dred Scott's claim to freedom in a very simple way. Scott had lived in free jurisdictions and might have been able to claim his freedom in those places. But he did not do so. Therefore, Taney might have relied on the precedent in *Strader v. Graham* to affirm the decision of the Missouri Supreme Court that Scott was still a slave. Taney could simply have declared that when Scott moved back to Missouri, he lost whatever claim to freedom he might have enjoyed under the Missouri Compromise. Initially, in fact, this is what the Supreme Court planned to do, with Justice Samuel Nelson of New York writing a narrow opinion denying Scott's freedom. In taking this position, the Court would have said that states were free to ignore the impact of federal law—the Missouri Compromise—or other state law on the status of slaves.

In the end, however, the Court refused to decide the case on narrow grounds. Southerners wanted the Court to resolve the festering issue of slavery in the territories in favor of their section by striking down the prohibition on slavery in the Missouri Compromise. Congressman Alexander Stephens, for example, pressured Justice James Wayne, a fellow Georgian, to take such a position. Similarly, President-elect James Buchanan pressured some justices to settle the territorial question, again in favor of the South, which would relieve Buchanan of the political difficulties presented by turmoil in the territories. In February 1857, the four Southern associate justices asked Taney to write a comprehensive opinion. Even without Taney's vote, these four easily outvoted the two concurring Northerners: Samuel Nelson, and Robert Grier of Pennsylvania. The two Northern dissenters, John McLean of Ohio and Benjamin Robbins Curtis of Massachusetts, had no impact on who wrote the majority opinion. By this time, as Don E. Fehrenbacher has shown, Taney had "become privately a bitter sectionalist, seething with anger at 'Northern insult and Northern aggression.'" Thus, the change of votes on the Court allowed him to write "the opinion that he had wanted to write all along."

Three aspects of Taney's opinion made it infamous: his denial of congressional power to regulate slavery in the territories, his application of the Fifth Amendment to protect the property claims of slave owners in their slaves, and his conclusion that free blacks had no legal rights under the Constitution. In a tortured interpretation of the Constitution's clause on territorial jurisdiction, Taney ruled that the Missouri Compromise's ban on slavery in the territories was unconstitutional. Article IV of the Constitution empowered Congress "to dispose of and make all needful rules and regulations respecting the territory or other property belonging to the United States." Despite the apparent grant of power in this clause, Taney denied that it had anything to do with the territories owned by the United States in 1857. Rather, Taney declared that the territories clause of Article IV "was a special provision for a known and particular territory, and to meet a present emergency, and nothing more." Taney's argument was strained and unconvincing: "The language used in the clause, the arrangement and combination of the powers, and the somewhat unusual phraseology . . . all indicate the design and meaning of the clause" was to be limited to the territories the government owned in 1787. He continued:

> It does not speak of *any* territory, nor of *Territories,* but uses language which, according to its legitimate meaning, points to a particular thing. The power is given in relation only to *the* territory of the United States — that is, to a territory then in existence, and then known or claimed as the territory of the United States. . . . And whatever construction may now be given to these words, every one, we think, must admit that they are not the words usually employed by statesmen in giving supreme power of legislation. They are certainly very unlike the words used in the power granted to legislate over territory which the new Government might afterwards itself obtain by cession from a State.

With these words, Taney struck down the Missouri Compromise, a major piece of congressional legislation that had been the keystone of sectional compromise for more than a generation. By implication, Taney also struck down the Kansas-Nebraska Act of 1854 and portions of the Compromise of 1850.

Second, Taney ruled that a ban on slavery in the territories violated the Fifth Amendment's due process clause. Taney asserted that "the Constitution recognizes the right of property of the master in a slave, and makes no distinction between that description of property and other property owned by a citizen" and that therefore, "no tribunal, acting under the authority of the United States, whether it be legislative, executive, or judicial, has a right to draw such a distinction, or deny to it the benefit of the provisions and guarantees which have been provided for the protection of private property against the encroachments of the Government." In essence, Taney held that slavery was a protected species of property and that, under the Constitution, the Congress could not deprive any citizen of this kind of property.

By implication, this interpretation prohibited any territorial legislature from banning slavery. This pleased Southerners but angered Northerners. It flew in the face of the Northwest Ordinance, the Missouri Compromise, and all other laws in which Congress had banned slavery from federal territories. Moreover, the use of the Fifth Amendment seemed to some people cynical and ironic. That amendment, after all, asserted that no person could be denied life, liberty, or property without due process of law. Taney stressed the "property" in slaves and protected it but ignored the obvious possibility that the amendment might ban slavery in all federal jurisdictions because it denied people liberty without due process.

Taney might have stopped here. These parts of the decision alone had given the South an enormous victory. But he did not stop. Instead, he tackled an aspect of the case that was unnecessary for the larger decision or the political victory of the South. It concerned the issue of race and the place of blacks in American culture and society.

Dred Scott had brought his case to the federal courts under diversity jurisdiction. Mrs. Emerson had sold her interest in Scott to her brother, John F. A. Sanford, who lived in New York. In 1854, Scott sued Sanford for his freedom in federal court.*

Sanford argued that Scott was "a negro of African descent; his ancestors were of pure African blood" and as such, he could not be a citizen of Missouri or of the United States and could not sue in federal court. United States District Court Judge Robert Wells rejected this plea, concluding that *if* Scott was free, he was a citizen of the state in which he lived, for purposes of federal diversity jurisdiction. When the case reached the Supreme Court, Taney reexamined this plea and the response of Judge Wells.

Again, Taney might have answered this plea with a narrow but fully sufficient analysis. He could have said that in Missouri, free blacks were not citizens. He might have noted that under Missouri law, free blacks could not vote, testify against whites, move into the state, own certain kinds of property, or enter certain professions and that they lacked a wide variety of other legal rights normally associated with citizenship. In *Strader v. Graham,*

---

* John Sanford's surname was recorded as Sandford in the Supreme Court decision as a result of a clerical error. The case has been known as *Dred Scott v. Sandford* ever since.

Taney had asserted that "every State has an undoubted right to determine the *status* or domestic and social condition, of the persons domiciled within its territory." Taney might easily have applied this logic, determining that Scott could not sue in diversity because even if free, he could never be a citizen of Missouri. This argument would have surprised no one and would have allowed Taney to dismiss the case for want of jurisdiction without ever getting to the issues of slavery in the territories. Or, Taney might have used this analysis along with his argument that the Missouri Compromise was unconstitutional.

But in *Dred Scott*, Taney was in no mood for restraint. This was his chance to settle the issues of slavery in the territories, to strike out at the North, and also to settle once and for all the place of blacks in American society. Taney, the seething sectionalist, hoped to place blacks beyond the pale of legal protection in the United States. This would head off the growing concern for black rights in the Republican Party and even in the mainstream of the North. After *Dred Scott*, Taney could be certain that blacks would not appear before his Court — or any other federal court — as plaintiffs, defendants, or attorneys. By 1857, blacks had been admitted to the bar in Maine, Massachusetts, Ohio, and New York. It seemed only a matter of time before a black lawyer from one of those states brought a case into federal court. This was something Taney could not allow.

Thus, Taney argued that free blacks — even those allowed to vote in the states where they lived — could never be citizens of the United States and have standing to sue in federal courts. Taney offered a slanted and one-sided history of the Founding period that ignored the fact that free blacks had voted in a number of states at the time of the ratification of the Constitution. Although Taney was aware of black voters in 1787, the chief justice nevertheless argued that at the adoption of the Constitution, blacks were either all slaves or, if free, were without any political or legal rights. He declared that blacks

> are not included, and were not intended to be included, under the word "citizens" in the Constitution, and can therefore claim none of the rights and privileges which that instrument provides for and secures to citizens of the United States. On the contrary, they were at that time [1787] considered as a subordinate and inferior class of beings who had been subjugated by the dominant race, and, whether emancipated or not, yet remained subject to their authority, and had no rights or privileges but such as those who held the power and the Government might choose to grant them.

Taney concluded that blacks were "so far inferior, that they had no rights which the white man was bound to respect."

In *Dred Scott,* Taney hoped to end all controversy over slavery in the territories and the place of African Americans in the United States. But he wanted to accomplish this by giving the South a sweeping victory and by thoroughly vanquishing any notion of black rights. Taney delivered his *Dred Scott* opinion only a few months after the Republican Party had nearly won the presidential election on a platform that endorsed the "self evident" principles in the Declaration of Independence that all people "are created equal, that they are endowed by their Creator with certain unalienable Rights, that among these are Life, Liberty, and the Pursuit of Happiness." But Taney asserted that the Republican platform was historically and constitutionally wrong. Taney wrote in *Dred Scott:*

> In the opinion of the Court, the legislation and histories of the times, and the language used in the Declaration of Independence, show, that neither the class of persons who had been imported as slaves, nor their descendants, whether they had become free or not, were then acknowledged as a part of the people, nor intended to be included in the general words used in that memorable instrument.

At one level, Taney may have been right. Many of the Framers — and certainly the vast majority of the Southern Framers — did not intend to provide for racial equality through the Declaration of Independence. Thus, when considering the intentions of some of the nation's founders, Taney's assessment seems correct:

> But it is too clear for dispute, that the enslaved African race were not intended to be included, and formed no part of the people who framed and adopted this declaration; for if the language, as understood in that day, would embrace them, the conduct of the distinguished men who framed the Declaration of Independence would have been utterly and flagrantly inconsistent with the principles they asserted; and instead of the sympathy of mankind, to which they so confidently appealed, they would have deserved and received universal rebuke and reprobation.

His understanding of the intentions of the Southern Framers at the Constitutional Convention seems equally correct:

> It is impossible, it would seem, to believe that the great men of the slaveholding States, who took so large a share in framing the Constitution of the United States, and exercised so much influence in procuring its adoption, could have been so forgetful or regardless of their own safety and the safety of those who trusted and confided in them.

Yet in the end, Taney sought to prove too much, especially by relying on an intentionalist argument. His historical argument was narrow, partisan, and unsophisticated. He ignored the black soldiers who fought for the patriot cause. He refused to consider that African Americans voted in a number of states in the 1780s. He was oblivious to the connections between the Revolution, the Declaration of Independence, and the ending of slavery in the North. His opinion was not designed to persuade opponents of slavery that he was right; rather, it was written to bludgeon them (Plate A.8). Ultimately, he severely miscalculated. Rather than acknowledge the complexity of slavery and race relations in a nation that was half slave and half free, Taney simply tried to sweep away opponents of slavery. He failed miserably. Northern anger over the opinion fueled the Republican Party and helped put Lincoln in the White House.

Six other justices agreed with Taney in almost all aspects of the case, and each wrote a concurring opinion. Curtis and McLean dissented. Their dissents pointed out the historical inaccuracies and logical inconsistencies of Taney's opinion.

Dred Scott undermined support for the Court and its credibility. The Republicans made the next two elections — the congressional election of 1858 and the presidential election of 1860 — a referendum on *Dred Scott*. The most articulate critic of the decision, Abraham Lincoln, became the party's nominee in 1860 and carried every free state but New Jersey, which he split with Stephen A. Douglas.

Ultimately, *Dred Scott* was an abysmal failure that undermined the prestige of the Court while accomplishing none of Taney's goals. Rather than destroy the Republican Party, Taney's opinion was a significant factor in making it the dominant political organization in the nation for two generations. Rather than guaranteeing the constitutional security of slavery, Taney's decision led to the political success of the first serious antislavery political party in the nation's history. Rather than consigning African Americans to the status of noncitizen, the decision set into motion events that led to the Fourteenth Amendment, which specifically guaranteed the citizenship of blacks.

Curtis left the Court after *Dred Scott*. His bitter dissent in that case was a devastatingly accurate critique of Taney's misrepresentation of history and constitutional law. Never before had Taney been taken to task so thoroughly by another member of the Court — but then, never before had he written such an intellectually suspect and politically divisive opinion. However, Taney could not forgive Curtis for his dissent, and relations were so poor between the two that Curtis resigned from the bench after the term ended. He was replaced in 1858 by another doughface from New England,

Nathan Clifford. McLean remained the only opponent of slavery on the bench until his death in 1861.

The Fugitive Slave Law, Secession, and Civil War

After *Dred Scott*, the Taney Court heard two more cases involving fugitive slaves: *Ableman v. Booth* (1859) and *Kentucky v. Dennison* (1861). Both cases involved issues of federal supremacy and states' rights. Taney spoke for a unanimous court in both cases, and they are both jurisprudentially sound. However, they are ideologically inconsistent. In *Ableman*, Taney disowned all notions of states' rights because the theory was being articulated by a free state in defiance of the Fugitive Slave Law of 1850. In *Dennison*, he rediscovered the viability of states' rights — even when asserted by a free state — in order to protect the slave states from federal interference on the eve of the Civil War.

In *Ableman*, Taney rejected Wisconsin's attempts to remove from federal custody the abolitionist Sherman Booth, who had helped a fugitive slave escape. Taney refused to consider the constitutionality of the new Fugitive Slave Law of 1850, even though it was substantially different from the 1793 law upheld in *Prigg*. As in *Dred Scott*, Taney made no attempt to persuade those who doubted the constitutionality of the 1850 law that his position was correct. Instead, he asserted without argument that the law was valid, even though it denied alleged slaves a jury trial or the right to testify in their own behalf. Taney also dismissed Wisconsin's states' rights arguments as though he had never heard of the idea of states' rights. Taney's *Ableman* opinion was a sweeping endorsement of federal power and the supremacy of the Constitution and the Supreme Court's interpretation of it. Chief Justice Marshall could not have written a more thorough assertion of the authority of the Supreme Court. Taney wrote this ultranationalist opinion to protect slavery from the antislavery states' rights ideas of the North.

In *Kentucky v. Dennison*, however, Taney changed his tune once again. This case was a suit by the state of Kentucky to force Governor Dennison of Ohio to extradite a free black named Willis Lago, who had helped a slave woman escape from Kentucky. The obvious proslavery result would have been to side with Kentucky. This would have also been consistent with Taney's opinions in *Prigg*, *Dred Scott*, and *Ableman*, in which he rejected states' rights in favor of federal protection of slavery. But by the spring of 1861, when the Court decided the case, seven slave states had already left the Union, and Abraham Lincoln was about to become president. Sympathetic to the Southern cause, Taney avoided writing an opinion that would have given the federal government the legal authority to force state governors to act. Thus, in an opinion reminiscent of Marshall's tactics in *Marbury v. Madison,* Taney castigated Governor Dennison but refused to order him to act.

Taken together, the line of cases from *Prigg* (or even *Groves v. Slaughter*) to *Dennison* shows that *Dred Scott* was neither uncharacteristic nor an aberration. These cases show that *Dred Scott* was part of Taney's larger jurisprudential goal of protecting slavery and the South whenever he could. By this time, Taney—and the majority he commanded—had lost all theoretical mooring. He could flit back and forth from states' rights to federal supremacy. When it benefited slavery—as it did in *Strader v. Graham*—Taney was happy to allow the states to determine the status of people within their jurisdiction. When it did not, as in *Dred Scott,* Taney denied states that capacity. To have done otherwise would have allowed free blacks in Massachusetts, Rhode Island, or New York to sue in federal court. Taney was interested not in constitutional principles but only in proslavery and pro-Southern results.

When the Civil War began, Taney applied this constitutional jurisprudence to protecting opponents of the Union. He would remain on the Court until his death in 1864. During these final few years as chief justice, Taney did everything in his power to thwart Abraham Lincoln's policies. In *Ex parte Merryman* (1861), heard in his capacity as circuit court judge, Taney denounced Lincoln for the military arrest of a Marylander who was organizing Confederate troops, destroying bridges, and in other ways making war against the United States. Lincoln ignored Taney's fulminations and kept Merryman in Fort McHenry.

Meanwhile, Taney privately compared enlistment in the Confederate army to enlistment in the patriot army during the Revolutionary War. He prepared what historian Don Fehrenbacher accurately characterized as "gratuitous opinions that were never called into use, holding several acts of the federal government unconstitutional." This included an opinion, sitting in his desk should such a case reach him, declaring conscription unconstitutional. Refusing to recognize the nature of the Civil War, Taney dissented in the *Prize Cases* (1863), which upheld the right of the U.S. government to interdict shipping in and out of Confederate ports. He also opposed the taxation of judicial salaries to help pay for the war. He was, in some ways, the Confederacy's greatest ally in Washington.

By the time he died, Taney was a minority justice, ignored by the president and Congress, held in contempt by the vast majority of his countrymen, and respected most in those places that proclaimed themselves no longer in the Union. Taney's obvious tilt toward the Confederacy showed that he had traveled far from the days when he had advised Andrew Jackson on how to suppress nullificationists. Indeed, he had become one himself.

In the Court of History

The Taney Court's reputation is directly tied to that of its chief justice. He dominated the Court like no other chief except Marshall. Taney's reputation as a justice is mixed. At his death, few had anything good to say about him, yet today it is clear that his impact on the law was great. For the first twenty years of his tenure, he guided the Court successfully, steering the development of important constitutional doctrines, especially in economic matters. Yet Taney is best remembered for *Dred Scott*, the most infamous decision in American constitutional history.

Taney's defenders, such as Felix Frankfurter and Carl B. Swisher, have insisted that *Dred Scott* did not exist in isolation but must be seen in the context of his entire career. In this they were entirely correct. They then proceeded to examine Taney's economic decisions and concluded that their greatness trumped *Dred Scott*. *Dred Scott*, they concluded, was a great man's aberration. But in fact, Taney's defenders had reached their conclusion by doing exactly what they said should not be done: They looked at *Dred Scott* in isolation — in this case, in isolation from Taney's other decisions on slavery, race, and the Civil War. When Taney's whole career is examined, *Dred Scott* emerges clearly as the apex in a series of decisions designed to strengthen slavery, protect the South, and, after 1861, undermine the cause of the Union. Taney was creative in finding legal solutions to questions about banking, commerce, and transportation, but he refused to apply these creative talents to the development of a jurisprudence that could defend fundamental liberty and human rights. That failure will always overshadow his successes.

How, then, do we evaluate the Taney Court and its chief justice? Clearly, the Court under Taney had a profound impact on the shaping of the American economy. However, it is rather less clear whether Taney himself was necessary for that result. For example, had President Jackson promoted John McLean to the chief justiceship, it is likely that many of the same kinds of economic decisions would have been written. In that regard, a McLean Court would not have looked much different from the Taney Court. However, in the area of slavery, race, and the coming of the Civil War, McLean would have been a very different chief justice.

In the end, then, it is Taney's jurisprudence on slavery, race, and secession that matters most. Here, the chief justice failed to provide meaningful leadership for the Court or the nation. In the end, Taney must always be remembered more for *Dred Scott* than for his opinions about the economy. Indeed, *Dred Scott* has come to stand for all that can go wrong in a Supreme Court decision and all that did go wrong under the proslavery Constitution. *Dred Scott* remains the most infamous decision in American constitutional history, and its author suffers accordingly, for his jurisprudence denied fundamental liberty and human rights to millions of Americans.

Taney's blunt language in *Dred Scott* made men like Senator Sumner hate him. But it was Taney's cynical proslavery, pro-Southern jurisprudence, and his aggressive attacks on freedom, even in the North, that gave Sumner reason for that hatred. However much we may admire Taney's personal grace, his clever opinions on commercial issues, and his sometimes brilliant analysis of constitutional issues, his racism, proslavery dogmatism, and secessionist sentiments will remain his legacy. Whenever the name Taney comes up, there will always be the echo of hooting.

—PAUL FINKELMAN

FOR FURTHER READING AND RESEARCH

The most comprehensive history of the Taney Court is still to be found in Carl B. Swisher's *The Taney Period, 1836–1864* (New York, 1974), volume 5 of the *History of the Supreme Court of the United States* (the Oliver Wendell Holmes Devise). The book was Swisher's last, published posthumously, and reflected scholarly ideas and concepts popular four decades earlier, when Swisher had published what remains the only serious biography of Taney, *Roger B. Taney* (New York, 1935). But though dated in many ways, particularly in its discussion of slavery and the *Dred Scott* case, *The Taney Period* offers the reader unparalleled detail.

More accessible, and much more current in its analysis, is Harold M. Hyman and William M. Wiecek, *Equal Justice Under Law: Constitutional Development, 1835–1875* (New York, 1982). Although published only eight years after the Swisher volume, this book reflects current interpretations and evaluations. A very short but excellent history of the period is R. Kent Newmyer, *The Supreme Court Under Marshall and Taney* (Arlington Heights, Ill., 1968).

Many important specialized books cover aspects of the Taney Court. Don E. Fehrenbacher's massive tome, *The Dred Scott Case: Its Significance in American Law and Politics* (New York, 1978), remains the standard work on that case. More accessible is Paul Finkelman, *Dred Scott v. Sandford: A Brief History* (Boston, 1993). The Taney Court's other major slave cases are discussed in Paul Finkelman, "Story Telling on the Supreme Court: *Prigg v. Pennsylvania* and Justice Joseph Story's Judicial Nationalism," *Supreme Court Review 1994* (1995), 247–294; and Howard Jones, *Mutiny on the Amistad* (New York, 1987). On economic development under Taney, see Stanley I. Kutler, *Privilege and Creative Destruction: The*

Charles River Bridge Case (New York, 1978). The best judicial biography for the period is R. Kent Newmyer, *Supreme Court Justice Joseph Story: Statesman of the Old Republic* (Chapel Hill, N.C., 1985).

There are competent biographies of other members of the Court, but no solid modern biography exists for Taney. For a critical appraisal of Taney, see Paul Finkelman, "'Hooted Down the Page of History': Reconsidering the Greatness of Chief Justice Taney," *Journal of Supreme Court History* vol. 1994 (1995), 83–102.

Part II

THE SECOND SEVENTY YEARS

★ ★ ★

How to Be "Supreme"?

AFTER CHIEF JUSTICE TANEY'S DEATH, THE COURT'S MOST URGENT task was, crudely, to become "supreme" again — to recover the standing that it had earned prior to the 1850s. At first under Salmon P. Chase, and then under the capable if obscure Morrison Waite and Melville Fuller, the Court slowly won back sufficient legitimacy to be recognized once more as an influential voice beyond the realm of executive and legislative government — indeed, as the appropriate arbiter of the boundaries that should pertain between government power and individual rights. Still, the Court was cautious, often confusing dogma for authority, often appearing obtuse and unimaginative in the face of the era's challenges: industrialization and class warfare, racism and segregation, and the rise of the trusts and corporate power. Unlike later successors, the Court of this period rarely offered a lead on the era's great issues, coming late to an acknowledgment of the promise of reform. Yet although hesitant, the Court under Chief Justices White and Taft did begin groping for modernity — this during an era when constitutional scholars have conventionally found little good to say about many of its decisions. The Court also demonstrated that there were other ways to live up to its name. During Taft's tenure, the Court achieved a revolution in self-management: For the first time, it established organizational control over the federal court system and, just as important, its own docket. Most important, the Court gained congressional approval for a home of its own. A life in borrowed space under the Capitol dome compromised the Court's capacity to project supremacy as the leading institution of the third branch. Gaining its own grand space was a good indicator that the Court was branching out.

5

The Chase Court   1864–1873

Cautious Reconstruction

W HATEVER TANEY'S FAILINGS might have been as chief justice, at least he died on an auspicious day: October 12, 1864, when voters in Taney's home state of Maryland adopted a new constitution abolishing slavery. As the New York socialite George Templeton Strong observed, "two ancient abuses and evils were perishing together." Taney, whose *Dred Scott* decision of 1857 had declared that Congress lacked the power to prohibit slavery in a territory, much less a state, and that African Americans remained "a subordinate and inferior class of beings" with "no rights which the white man was bound to respect," was finally gone. And President Abraham Lincoln, who since the beginning of the Civil War had been cajoling Union border states to abolish slavery, finally had a victory. The way was clear for freedom — and for a new Supreme Court.

Circumstances in Maryland suggested some of the challenges that the new Court would face. In the first year of the war, Lincoln and Taney had clashed over the case of John Merryman, a Maryland militiaman who had been imprisoned without trial for recruiting soldiers for the Confederacy in an area where Lincoln had suspended habeas corpus rights. Acting in his capacity as circuit justice, Taney had issued an ex parte decision demanding Merryman's release on the basis that only Congress could suspend habeas corpus. Lincoln had ignored the ruling, and Congress eventually passed legislation upholding such arrests. In *Ex parte Vallandigham* (1864), a majority of the Supreme Court upheld Lincoln's wartime authority to curtail civil liberties. Taney reviled what he saw as a perilous shift away from civilian and state authority and toward national, military despotism. "I have outlived the Government . . . which has conferred so many blessings upon us," he wrote just before his death. "The times are dark with evil omens and seem to grow darker every day."

On the eve of Taney's death, the fate of the Union remained uncertain. Military victory for Union forces was by no means ensured. During the summer, the near success of a Confederate raid led by General Jubal A. Early on Washington, D.C., reminded Northerners how fragile their security was. The Union army had scored major victories in the fall, especially when Union General William T. Sherman took Atlanta. But closer to Washington, Confederate General Robert E. Lee's troops still eluded those of Union General Ulysses S. Grant. Meanwhile, the Union destruction of slavery and states' rights, the twin engines of the secessionist impulse, remained incomplete. Even in the loyal states, such as Taney's Maryland, Unionists continued to struggle to maintain the upper hand. A month after the emancipation vote in that state, for example, a Union general there had been forced to prohibit the apprenticeship of African American minors to their former masters — an arrangement sustained in Maryland state courts.

Besides the implementation of emancipation, the war had provoked a host of other issues that would require the attention of the post-Taney Court. In the 1863 *Prize Cases,* for example, the Union blockade of the Confederacy had resulted in a complex set of rulings addressing the very legality of the war itself. By a bare majority, the Court ruled that the blockade was, for the most part, constitutional and embraced a duty to defer to "the political department of the government" in time of war. But it also raised, without resolving, piecemeal doubts about the extent of war powers by hinting that some of the ships stopped by the blockade did have a legitimate claim against the government.

Nor had the Court resolved the constitutionality of the wartime financial measures passed by the era's Republican-dominated congresses. Although most Northerners conceded that the new national systems of banking, taxation, and currency were necessary in order to wage the war, some Northerners were bound to challenge the measures if they were maintained in peacetime.

Finally, and most important, the new Court would have to play a crucial role in bringing secessionist states back into what Lincoln called their "proper relations" with the Union. By the time Taney died, Unionists in a number of states, including Louisiana, Arkansas, and Tennessee, had begun the process of reconstructing their state governments and state constitutions so that their states could reclaim their powers and send representatives and senators to Washington. As the president, Congress, and the states struggled for control over reconstruction, the Court would have to take sides.

Whatever position the Court took on these matters, it faced an additional uphill battle: restoring its own reputation. The high esteem and position that the Court had attained under John Marshall had slowly withered under Taney until dropping precipitously after *Dred Scott*. The limited public outcry that greeted Lincoln's dismissal of Taney's *Merryman* decision accurately reflected the diminished stature of the Court and its chief justice. During the early years of the war, Taney was the only well-known justice on the Court, and old age and infirmities kept him away from most of the proceedings. Most of the other justices were also well past their prime. A majority of the Court's members had been born before 1800. Although the Court now held sessions in more hospitable surroundings — in 1861, it had moved from a cramped room in the Capitol basement to the refurbished former chamber of the Senate (Plates A.6 and A.7) — seats in the audience were usually empty. The Court was supreme in name only. As far as most Americans were concerned, the real action of lawmaking took place only in Congress and the White House.

The New Chief Justice

The desire to restore the Court's eminence, as well as to reverse Taney's course on slavery and states' rights, guided Lincoln's choice of a new chief justice. As one of the best-known antislavery lawyers and politicians of his generation, Salmon P. Chase was an obvious contender. Born in New Hampshire but raised in Ohio by his uncle, an antislavery clergyman, Chase returned east for college at Dartmouth and legal training in Washington, D.C., under William Wirt, the U.S. attorney general. Chase then traveled back to Ohio, setting up a legal practice in Cincinnati.

Although not particularly successful or skillful at his profession, he eventually gained fame as an antislavery lawyer, defending many fugitive slaves and the abolitionists who aided them. In 1837, he argued his most famous case, in defense of James Birney, who would later run for president as a candidate of the abolitionist Liberty Party. Birney's servant, Matilda, had escaped from slavery in St. Louis, and Birney was accused of violating a state law against harboring fugitives. Chase lost the case but won national attention. He soon found that he had a stronger taste for politics than for law. After promoting the short-lived Liberty Party, Chase helped to found the Free-Soil Party, which was committed to stopping the spread of slavery. A coalition of Free-Soilers and antislavery Democrats nominated Chase for U.S. senator in 1849, and he was elected by the state legislature. His oratory was lackluster compared to that of other antislavery senators, most notably William H. Seward of New York, but he was a principled and skilled politician. Having joined the newly formed Republican party, he was elected governor of Ohio in 1855, and in 1860, he was a candidate for the presidential nomination. But that honor went to Lincoln.

After winning the election, Lincoln selected Chase to be his secretary of the Treasury. Lincoln never trusted Chase, who continued to hunger for the presidency and formed alliances with Lincoln's critics, especially the radical Republicans. But Lincoln calculated that Chase could do less damage from within the administration, so he kept him in the cabinet, despite Chase's repeated attempts to resign and his campaign to displace Lincoln in early 1864 as the presidential nominee of the "Union Party," the wartime name adopted by the Republicans. The president finally accepted Chase's resignation in the summer of 1864, after it was clear that Chase's candidacy was doomed. To smooth the departure, the president may have hinted to Chase or his allies that Chase might become chief justice when Taney died. Taney obliged Chase four months later. Justice Noah H. Swayne, who had been Lincoln's first appointee to the Court, was preferred by many, including a majority of the Court and the cabinet. Swayne was undeniably a more able, experienced jurist, and his antislavery credentials were at least as strong as Chase's. But Lincoln, who supposedly said that he "would sooner eat flat irons" than appoint Chase, recognized that giving Chase the position would placate the radicals and — at least for the moment — harness the Ohioan's presidential scheming.

Chase was the fifth justice appointed by Lincoln in a politically divided Court. Five Democrats remained from before the Civil War: James M. Wayne, John Catron, Samuel Nelson, Robert C. Grier, and Nathan Clifford. Chase and three other Lincoln appointees — Noah Swayne, Samuel F. Miller, and David Davis — were Republicans. The fifth Lincoln appointee, and tenth justice overall, was Stephen J. Field, a Democrat. (Congress had created a tenth federal circuit in California and Oregon in part to shore up the pro-Union majority on the Supreme Court.) Although the justices were expected to be nonpartisan, their political affiliations came to shape many of their decisions, especially those involving policies launched by Lincoln or the Republicans in Congress.

On taking his new position, Chase faced two daunting tasks. First, as a former member of the Lincoln administration, he naturally felt impelled to defend the government against constitutional challenges to the means by which it had prosecuted the war, even though he recognized the legitimacy of some of the opposition's arguments. Second, he knew that he must quickly establish his authority among his fellow justices in order to gain their respect and to manage the Court effectively during his term. That maneuver would also be difficult, for although his political career had made him more of a celebrity than his associates, he had little of their experience and expertise as a jurist.

The opportunity to make headway in both endeavors came early, in the case of the *Circassian* (1866). Only three weeks after Chase was sworn in, the Court heard arguments challenging the Union navy's capture of the *Circassian*, which had been sailing for New Orleans. In the *Prize Cases*, the Court had upheld the right of the Union government to seize noncombatant ships sailing to or from enemy ports. But when the *Circassian* had been captured, New Orleans was not technically hostile; it was in the process of falling into Union hands. This was the first major constitutional challenge to the Lincoln administration under Chase's watch, and the new chief justice used the occasion to assert his authority. He voted to sustain the action of the Union blockade, and he decided to author the majority opinion, even though he had little experience in international law. He worked long into the nights, studying admiralty law and drafting and redrafting his opinion. The product — a clever argument distinguishing the port of New Orleans, which was still hostile, from the city, which was not — allowed the Court to support the Union war effort without appearing to deviate from the principle of the *Prize Cases*. Chase won the support, and perhaps even some admiration, of his fellow justices. Only Nelson, the most conservative Democrat on the Court, dissented.

Among other things, the *Circassian* case revealed Chase's desire to show that he was in charge. In assigning the writing of opinions, he may at first have gone so far as to assign all decisions, regardless of whether he was in the majority. Eventually, however, he followed the procedure set by John Marshall. If Chase was in the majority, he assigned only the majority opinion, sometimes to himself. If he was in the minority, he did the same for the minority opinion, whereas the most senior justice in the majority assigned the majority opinion.

Differences in opinion among the justices could be fierce, but Chase kept the tone of conferences civil. He encouraged the justices to be sociable with one another, regardless of their politics and principles. He dutifully attended dinner parties hosted by his associates, although he never much enjoyed acting the part of a socialite. To his credit, he did not play favorites with his colleagues or hold grudges against them. He could become distracted by his presidential ambitions, but at least in his early years as chief justice, he kept his political machinations out of the Court.

If Chase had a consistent failing, it was his tendency toward defensiveness born from his lack of judicial experience. It was difficult enough for him that he did not receive the deference from his fellow justices to which he had grown accustomed from underlings when governor and Treasury secretary; he also had to suffer with the knowledge that he was not as qualified as some of those he now led. Occasionally, his defensiveness led him to be too argumentative with other justices or to scold them with unwarranted harshness if he suspected them of doubting his stature. On one occasion, for example, when he heard a rumor that Justice Miller had complained of the way that

Chase had been assigning opinions, the chief went out of his way to find and rebuke his fellow justice.

Civil Liberties

Military Arrests — Again

In the 1864 *Vallandigham* decision, the Taney Court had rejected the position its chief justice had embraced in *Ex parte Merryman* and had instead supported policies and actions of the Lincoln administration that, in peacetime, it might have regarded as unconstitutional. Nevertheless, the justices remained divided along partisan lines on the proper scope of military authority. Unsurprisingly, Republicans tended to uphold Lincoln, whereas Democrats tended to criticize him. By 1866, the Civil War was over, and both Lincoln and Taney were dead. But the question of military power, especially over civilians, remained very much alive, in part because some wartime treason cases had not yet been fully resolved and in part because the military courts in the occupied South, including those operated by the newly created Freedmen's Bureau, were continually being criticized as unconstitutional. *Ex parte Milligan* (1866) offered the Court an opportunity to draw the boundaries of military authority.

In 1864, Lambden P. Milligan had been arrested in Indiana on charges of treason (Plate A.9). Tried and convicted by an army court, Milligan was sentenced to death. Lincoln had kept Milligan in prison rather than allowing the sentence to be carried out, but Lincoln's assassination led President Andrew Johnson to jettison clemency and go forward with the death penalty.

Milligan's attorneys, who included a sitting congressman, a former U.S. attorney general, and a brother of a Supreme Court justice, argued that trials of civilians by military commissions went beyond the letter of the law of the Habeas Corpus Act of 1863 and beyond the spirit of the law of the Constitution. All the Democrats but one took the side of Milligan. All the Republicans but one took the side of the government. The Democratic exception was Wayne, who had authored the majority opinion in *Vallandigham* and now upheld that position by affirming the power of military courts. The Republican exception was David Davis, who eventually left the party and became a political independent. Davis wrote the 6–4 majority opinion, which ruled the military trial of Milligan unconstitutional. In words that would later be enshrined by champions of civil liberties, Davis opened his opinion with the declaration that "the Constitution of the United States is a law for rulers and people, equally in war and peace. . . . No doctrine, involving more pernicious consequences, was ever invented by the wit of man than that any of its provisions can be suspended during any of the great exigencies of government."

Despite Davis's high-minded opening, the *Milligan* decision had only limited impact. Davis and the majority upheld military trials for soldiers. More important, the opinion suggested that the only real problem in Milligan's case was that a civilian had been tried by a military commission in a *loyal* area where civil courts still operated. By implication, disloyal areas were fair territory for military trials of civilians. That meant that *Milligan* did not necessarily undermine the authority of military courts then operating in formerly rebellious areas of the South. Indeed, the four years after the decision saw some five hundred military trials of civilians in the occupied South, a number that did not include the hundreds of proceedings against civilians by the Freedmen's Bureau courts during the same period.

To be sure, the *Milligan* decision helped cast doubt on the idea that "military necessity" always excused the abridgment of civil liberties. But it left open the possibility that "military necessity" could be found pressing enough in certain circumstances to allow for some abridgment. The minority's dissent in *Milligan*, authored by Chase, argued that Congress could define those circumstances — that it could declare when the crisis was severe enough to expand the reach of military tribunals. Even the majority opinion suggested that a point might come when military necessity trumped personal liberties, although it was vague on how to determine when that point had been reached. It merely stated that, in loyal areas where civil courts still operated, this point had not yet been reached. Thus, the door was still open for future Courts to draw new boundaries of military jurisdiction.

Test Oaths

The matter of military commissions was not the only civil liberties issue to come before the Chase Court. The Court also had to rule on the constitutionality of test oaths, another highly partisan issue arising from the war and central to the course of Reconstruction. In December 1863, Lincoln had suggested a policy whereby all but high-ranking Confederates might obtain amnesty if they took a simple oath upholding the Constitution and the Union. The remainder would have to seek amnesty through a presidential pardon. More radically inclined Republicans, however, preferred that amnesty be given only to those who took an "iron-clad" oath, swearing that they had never aided the rebellion, and that amnesty be left in the hands of Congress. By the time the war ended, no single, sweeping piece of legislation concerning amnesty had been adopted as law. (Lincoln had pocket vetoed the only amnesty act passed by Congress, embedded in the so-called Wade-Davis bill, which specified an "iron-clad" oath.) However, Lincoln and then Andrew Johnson after him used their pardon power liberally, much to the dismay of congressional Republicans.

Although no overarching amnesty law had been created during the war, certain state and federal entities had developed their own policies, setting the stage for a judicial challenge. The federal Supreme Court, for example, required attorneys practicing before it to take the iron-clad oath. Missouri required the same of its clergymen. The first of these laws was challenged by Augustus H. Garland, a former Confederate congressman; the second was challenged by a Catholic priest named Cummings. In 1867, the Court ruled on both cases — *Ex parte Garland* and *Cummings v. Missouri* — and declared the iron-clad requirement unconstitutional.

The "Test Oath Cases," as the two cases were jointly known, revealed even more clearly than *Milligan* the partisan split on the Court. All six Democrats supported the majority opinion, authored by Field, whereas all four Republicans supported the dissenting opinion, authored by Miller. Field argued that, because they penalized people for past political actions, the test oaths were ex post facto laws and bills of attainder, both of which were prohibited by the Constitution. In his dissent, Miller pointed out that past actions could and often should be considered in determining whether someone was qualified for a certain profession or office. Field won the day; as a result, many expected that white Southerners would win Reconstruction because Republicans would no longer be able to proscribe former Confederates from political office or crucial professions. The Test Oath Cases, along with *Milligan,* would shut the door on Republican Reconstruction.

In fact, just as *Milligan* had kept cracks open for trials by military commissions, so the Test Oath Cases failed to keep out iron-clad oaths. Republicans at the state level and in federal departments chipped away at *Garland* and *Cummings* by imposing iron-clad oaths regardless of the Supreme Court decision. Then two sweeping blows were struck against the Test Oath Cases by Congress, first in the Reconstruction Act of 1867, which imposed an iron-clad oath, and next in the Fourteenth Amendment, ratified in 1868, which affirmed that oath and gave all pardoning power to Congress rather than to the president. When it came to civil liberties, congressional Republicans would not be restrained by a Court controlled by Democrats, even if the chief justice was a Republican.

The Court admitted its defeat in 1868 in *Ex parte McCardle.* William McCardle had been arrested for writing editorials in Vicksburg, Mississippi, against Reconstruction. He appealed to the Court to overturn the arrest on the basis of an 1867 Habeas Corpus Act. By the time the Court issued its decision, Congress had repealed the parts of that act that allowed appeals such as McCardle's to be made to the Supreme Court, but the Court still could have found a way to claim jurisdiction and reaffirm its commitment to civil liberties. Instead, Chase's ex parte opinion denied jurisdiction because of the changes that Republicans had made to the new Habeas Corpus Act. Lest it appear that the Court was now controlled by Congress, Chase asserted that Congress could not narrow the Court's appellate jurisdiction as defined in the 1789 Judiciary Act — although the rest of the *McCardle* opinion allowed Congress to do just that.

Chase flexed the same muscle again in *Ex parte Yerger* (1869). In that case, Edward Yerger, who had been arrested by military authorities in Mississippi for stabbing to death a Union army officer, requested a writ of habeas corpus so that he might be tried by a civilian court. Because Yerger's attorneys invoked only the 1789 Judiciary Act, not later habeas corpus acts, Chase could — and did — grant his request. U.S. military authorities might have challenged Chase's argument by keeping Yerger in a military prison and contending that Congress could indeed narrow the Court's jurisdiction. But instead, they allowed Yerger to be tried by a civilian court.

Reconstruction: A New Federalism?

Although much of the time at loggerheads, the Chase Court and Congress labored hard to avoid confrontations over the fundamental question of whether the Court's authority was absolute and immutable. Indeed, the only clear consensus between the Court and Congress during the immediate postwar period was that the process of Reconstruction should be guided by caution and flexibility and should avoid staking positions on bedrock principles that might in turn provoke fundamental conflict.

If any one principle might have been sufficiently well established to guide the course of Reconstruction regardless of the twists and turns of expediency, it was surely the idea that the power of the nation had now gained decisive ascendancy over those of the states. In fact, the experience of the Chase Court exposed not the withering of states' rights ideology but rather its tenacity — at least to the extent of sustaining belief in the necessity of limiting national power. During the Chase years, tension within federalism — between the states and the nation — was far more visible than tension within the national government — between the Court and Congress. To be sure, many Americans held that the triumph of national over state power was the most important of the "fruits of victory" earned by Union triumph in the war. But many others persisted in arguing that the war had not fundamentally changed the nature of the Republic's federalism.

The Court's approach to the thorny question of paper money revealed its own ambivalence in embracing the notion that a fundamental alteration had occurred in federalism. The Constitution granted Congress the power "to coin Money, [and] regulate the Value thereof" but said nothing about creating *paper* money, the value of which was not tied directly to precious metal. In 1862, wartime necessity had led Congress, with the approval of Chase, then the Treasury secretary, to pass an act creating a national paper currency, popularly known as "greenbacks." Seven years later, in *Veazie Bank v. Fenno* (1869), a case involving prohibitive federal taxation of state currency, Chase ruled that the federal government had the power to not only tax state currency but also outlaw it altogether.

If observers detected a new nationalism in Chase's 1869 *Veazie* opinion, however, they were mistaken. Chase sounded a very different tune in *Hepburn v. Griswold* (1870), also known as the *First Legal Tender Case.* Griswold objected to Hepburn's paying an 1860 debt in wartime paper currency, worth less than the original debt. The specific laws in question were the Legal Tender Acts of 1869, but the larger issue was Congress's power to issue paper currency. Although he had helped create such a currency as Treasury secretary, Chase now took the side of the hard-money advocate, the creditor Griswold. "Whatever benefit is possible" from national paper, Chase argued, "is far more than outweighed by the losses of property" and other "evils which flow from the use of irredeemable paper money." Chase suggested that Congress could issue only a currency that had the least-disruptive effect on personal and state property. Such a standard narrowed congressional power too much, Justices Miller, Swayne, and Davis argued in dissent.

Two years after *Hepburn v. Griswold,* the Court reversed its position on paper money and upheld Congress's power to issue currency, a move that some modern scholars have interpreted as evidence that the Court was committed to the principle of national over state power. But the overturning of *Griswold* was less about a shift in principle than an unexpected change in personnel. In 1866, radical Republicans in Congress had attempted to reduce the number of justices from ten to seven by passing legislation that would keep their enemy, President Johnson, from replacing John Catron, who had died in 1865, or replacing the next two justices who might resign.

The move was in part political, but it also stemmed from a desire, shared by Chase, to make the Court more efficient. In 1867, James Moore Wayne died, reducing the number of justices to eight. Realizing that an even number of justices could lead to deadlocked decisions, Congress in 1869 voted to increase the number of justices to nine. Robert Grier soon resigned, opening the way for the new president, Ulysses S. Grant, to appoint two justices. Critics accused Grant and the Republicans of trying to pack the Court, but the charge was unwarranted. The act was mainly an effort to avoid a deadlocked Court and to ease the burden on Supreme Court justices: In that vein, the act also called for the creation of nine new circuit court judgeships. (Supreme Court justices still served on the federal circuit courts, a duty that would burden them until the 1890s.) Grant nominated former Attorney General and Secretary of War Edwin M. Stanton, who was approved by the Senate but died only days after his confirmation. Grant also nominated the sitting attorney general, Ebenezer R. Hoar, but the Senate rejected him. Finally, Grant nominated the Republicans William Strong and Joseph P. Bradley, both of whom were quickly confirmed. But before they took their seats, Chase and the Democrats on the Court had struck down the Legal Tender Act in *Hepburn*. In 1871, the two Grant appointees joined with the other Republicans on the Court to reverse the *Hepburn* decision in *Knox v. Lee* and *Parker v. Davis*, also known as the *Second Legal Tender Cases*. The Republicans, who generally approved of paper currency, added another justice to their ranks when Grant replaced Samuel Nelson, who resigned in 1872, with Ward Hunt. The majority was now propaper, but the chief justice, once the most important Republican on the Court, was not part of it.

Nor, for that matter, could the chief justice be identified any longer as a Republican. Until 1868, Chase had clearly been in the Republican camp — at least in public. A Republican presidential contender in 1860 and 1864, Chase's firm positions on the immorality and the illegality of slavery and racial discrimination had earned him a reputation as one of the most radical of Republican leaders and certainly the most radical member of Lincoln's cabinet. In his early years as chief justice, he used his position to implement the antislavery vision he had developed before the war. On circuit in Maryland in 1867, Chase delivered the most powerful antislavery statement ever given by a chief justice. The case, *In re Turner*, involved a prejudicial labor contract between former slave Elizabeth Turner and her former master. Chase ruled that such contracts were prohibited by the Thirteenth Amendment, which abolished slavery, and by the first clause of the Civil Rights Act of 1866, which granted whites and blacks "full and equal benefit" of the law.

Initially, Chase had also led the Court into taking the radicals' position on the preeminence of national over state power. He wrote the majority opinion in *Mississippi v. Johnson* (1867) and a concurring opinion in *Georgia v. Stanton* (1868), both of which foiled efforts by Southern states to outlaw the Reconstruction Act of 1867. In the first case, Southerners asked the Court to keep the president from enforcing the act, which they claimed was unconstitutional. The Court replied that it had no authority to intervene, even if the act were unconstitutional. The Court took the same stance in *Stanton*, although in that case, the target was not the president but the secretary of war. Finally, in *Texas v. White* (1868), the Court went even further, arguing that the Reconstruction Act and all similar congressional laws were constitutional. Chase's majority opinion claimed that Texas — and, by implication, every ex-Confederate state — was not yet restored as a state and thus had no standing to sue. Texas had not left the Union, Chase argued, but "the government and the citizens of the State, refusing to recognize their constitutional obligations, assumed the character of enemies, and incurred the consequences of rebellion."

Yet despite Chase's genuine commitment to Reconstruction and to "equality before the law" — the nineteenth-century belief in the unconstitutionality of laws or actions creating a legal disability for a class of people — his loyalty to the Republicans was tenuous, even though it was they who were doing the most to enact these policies. In 1868, the chief justice began to turn his back on his radical allies and to form alliances with the Democrats.

The Presidency: Chase's Unrequited Ambition

The move was not as incongruous as it might seem. Chase had been a Democrat during his early political career in Ohio, and although he had parted company with most Democrats over slavery, he still shared their preference for hard over soft money, as he revealed in the legal tender cases. During the Civil War, Chase had privately explored creating a new party — a fusion of antislavery Democrats and Republicans — that would elevate him to the presidency. That dream had died during the first years of the presidency of Andrew Johnson, who also had attempted such a fusion but had managed to drive the two parties apart by alienating the radicals who had gained control of the Republican party.

By 1868, the lure of the White House was as strong as ever for Chase. But with fusion no longer a possibility, and with other candidates, especially Grant, in a better position to receive the Republican nomination, he had no choice but to court the Democrats. In his public comments outside of Court, he began to soften his position in favor of Reconstruction and racial equality. On the question of black suffrage, for example, he argued that voting requirements should continue to be left to the states, even if that led to some black disfranchisement. (A year later, Congress passed the resolution for the Fifteenth Amendment, which prohibited states from disfranchising on the basis of race; the amendment was ratified in 1870.) As the presiding officer in the impeachment trial of President Johnson — a position that went to the chief justice by the terms of the Constitution — he undermined the radicals' efforts to institute procedures that would have decreased his influence in the trial and increased the chances of Johnson's conviction. Chase used his power in the Johnson trial sparingly, however, and he was in no way responsible for Johnson's acquittal by a narrow margin. Nonetheless, he must have been pleased by the result. Had Johnson been convicted, he would have been replaced by the president *pro tempore* of the Senate, Benjamin Wade, Chase's longtime rival from Ohio, who would then have been a strong candidate for reelection in 1868. Johnson's survival meant that Chase's path to the presidency remained open.

Ultimately, however, Chase's campaign for the Democratic nomination, ably managed by his daughter Kate, was unsuccessful. The nomination went instead to the former governor of New York, Horatio Seymour, whose loyalty to the Democrats had been more steadfast. A Democrat had a good chance of winning the election: Seymour would eventually lose to Grant by only a narrow majority of the popular vote. So Chase's failure must have done much to drain his spirit and strength. He grew weak and in 1870 suffered the first of a number of debilitating strokes. The presidency was no longer within reach. He would have to finish his days as the chief justice of a Court composed of a majority of Republicans, whom he had spurned, and a minority of Democrats, who had spurned him.

Reconstruction Defined

Isolated and with rapidly failing health, Chase fell back on the antislavery principles that had guided him through most of his political career. Two 1871 cases involving the sale of slaves prior to the Thirteenth Amendment — *White v. Hart* and *Osborn v. Nicholson* — provided an occasion for Chase to reveal that his moral core remained intact. In both cases, all the justices but Chase joined the majority opinion, authored by Swayne, which argued that slave-sale contracts had to be honored even though slavery had been abolished. To suggest otherwise, argued Swayne, whose reputation as a justice hostile to slavery was at least as solid as Chase's, was to contravene the basic laws of contract and to endorse an unconstitutional ex post facto approach to the law. Chase's dissent in *Osborn* took the highest possible moral ground. Because state laws upholding slavery and slave sales ran afoul of "original principles of liberty, justice, and right," Chase argued, they never had legitimate standing. Therefore, treating the Thirteenth Amendment as nullifying those laws was not an ex post facto action. When Chase asserted that slavery had always been "against sound morals and natural justice" and protected only by "positive law," he echoed the natural-law arguments that he and other antislavery lawyers had sometimes made in the antebellum era. "Freedom national, slavery local" had been the slogan of Chase's Free-Soil party. Now he tried to write it into the Constitution.

Although the Republicans on the Court rarely espoused the radical position that Chase returned to in his final years, they did at least share a portion of Chase's commitment to antislavery and "equality before the law" for African Americans. That commitment was crucial to Reconstruction, especially as some of the Southern states sought to subvert federal Reconstruction legislation and the new constitutional amendments. After the Civil War, all the Southern states passed "black codes," which restricted the freedom guaranteed to former slaves under the Thirteenth Amendment. Southern state courts often looked the other way when unreconstructed white Southerners used newly created organizations, such as the Ku Klux Klan, to harass, terrorize, and kill African Americans — actions that often represented attempts to inhibit blacks from exercising their new voting rights. Federal remedies to such actions were provided mainly by the lower federal courts and by Congress, which adopted not only the Civil Rights Act of 1866 and the Reconstruction Act of 1867 but also a set of acts in 1870 and 1871, generally known as the "Ku Klux Klan Acts," which lent new powers to the U.S. military in order to destroy such organizations as the Klan and to enforce the Fourteenth and Fifteenth Amendments.

During Chase's term, the Supreme Court only occasionally voiced its position on the scope of rights created by Reconstruction legislation and the Reconstruction amendments. Most of the major Court decisions on these matters came after Chase's death in May 1873. On the few occasions that the Chase Court did speak on Reconstruction, at least at first, the Republican justices seemed as unequivocal as Chase in their commitment to African American rights. In 1866, for example, Justice Swayne argued for a broad conception of black freedom in *United States v. Rhodes,* an opinion, delivered on circuit, that struck down a Kentucky law barring black testimony in cases involving whites. Reconstruction was "an act of great national grace," Swayne argued, and the new national laws provided federal "protection over everyone."

Five years later, the Republicans had secured a majority on the Court. Ironically, it was precisely at this moment that they began to narrow the expansive boundaries of freedom suggested in *Rhodes.* A hint of things to come appeared in *Blyew v. United States* (1871), which again took up the question of black testimony in Kentucky. Despite Swayne's ruling in *Rhodes,* a Kentucky statute still prevented African American witnesses from testifying in certain cases involving white defendants. As a result, African American witnesses had been prohibited from testifying in a case in which whites had murdered an African American woman. Given the decision in *Rhodes,* one might have expected the Court to invalidate the statute. But William Strong, who wrote the majority opinion, saw a crucial distinction in *Blyew:* The aggrieved party, the murdered woman, was dead, and because dead people had no rights, the Kentucky law had caused no harm and hence did not violate the Constitution. The majority's bizarre reasoning unwittingly sent the message that, if Southern states were going to deprive African Americans of their rights, they had better deprive them of their lives, too. As the dissenting Justice Bradley, joined by Swayne, put it, the majority's construction put "a premium on murder." Moreover, argued Bradley, "to deprive a whole class of the community of this right, to refuse their evidence and their sworn complaints, is to brand them with a badge of slavery; is to expose them to wanton insults and fiendish assaults; is to leave their lives, their families, and their property unprotected by law." Bradley's reasoning seemed a logical extension of Swayne's in *Rhodes* and Chase's in *Turner,* but his notion that the Thirteenth Amendment and the Civil Rights Act of 1866 outlawed not only slavery but also every "badge" of slavery was no longer popular with his colleagues. Indeed, it would not gain favor with the Court again until the 1960s. Already in 1871, the Court had begun to turn its back on Reconstruction.

Bradwell and *Slaughterhouse*

By 1873, the Court was in full retreat. In that year, the Court issued decisions on two of the most famous cases of the Chase era, both landmark interpretations of the Fourteenth Amendment. In *Bradwell v. Illinois,* Myra Bradwell (Plate A.10) claimed that the Illinois bar had violated her Fourteenth Amendment rights when it denied her petition to practice law, even though she had studied law, had qualified for the bar, and would have been admitted to the bar if she had been a man. None of the justices took Bradwell's side except Chase, who dissented from the majority but issued no opinion, perhaps because he was too infirm to draft one (he died three weeks later). The majority opinion, authored by Samuel Miller, claimed that practicing law was not a right but a privilege, one that could be regulated by the states. In a concurring opinion, Bradley, whose *Blyew* opinion had offered an expansive vision of freedom, at least for African Americans, and had made no distinction between black men and black women, explained that women's "natural and proper timidity and delicacy" made them unsuitable for law and other professions; they belonged where they had always been, in "the domestic sphere." Because Congress and the lower courts had already made it clear that women as a group were not to enjoy the benefits of Reconstruction, the Court's decision in *Bradwell* was predictable.

That could not be said of the *Slaughterhouse* decision, which the Court issued the day before *Bradwell.* On its surface, the case had nothing to do with African Americans or the Reconstruction amendments. To the extent that it involved civil rights, it concerned merely the right of slaughterhouse butchers to dump toxic substances — specifically, the carcasses and guts of slaughtered animals — into the Mississippi River in and around New Orleans. For many years, Louisiana lawmakers had recognized the health hazards of the slaughterhouses. A health official in 1866 reported that "when the river is low, it is not uncommon to see intestines and portions of putrefied animal matter lodged immediately around the pipes" of the New Orleans water works. In response, Louisiana lawmakers regulated the slaughtering trade by prohibiting the landing and butchering of animals at all locations in New Orleans except the Crescent City Slaughterhouse, a private facility to be overseen by state officials. To health officials, this was a modern solution to an age-old problem. To independent butchers, it was a corrupt, state-sanctioned monopoly. They sued the Crescent City Slaughterhouse, claiming that the monopoly violated the Thirteenth Amendment — the butchers were forced into "servitude" by having to work for the business or give up their trade — and also the Fourteenth Amendment, the first section of which prohibited states from adopting laws that abridged the "privileges and immunities" of U.S. citizens or deprived them of "life, liberty, or property, without due process of law." The case offered the Court an unprecedented opportunity to render an interpretation of the Reconstruction amendments.

Miller, the author of the *Bradwell* opinion, also wrote the opinion of the slim 5–4 majority in the *Slaughterhouse Cases,* which upheld the monopoly. Had the matter come before the Court prior to Reconstruction, the monopoly could easily have been justified as the fair exercise of the traditional state "police power," the powers retained by a state to maintain the health, safety, and welfare of its citizens. But the plaintiffs' use of the Reconstruction amendments forced Miller and the majority to find a different way to reach the same result. Their solution, which forever shaped the jurisprudence of the amendments, involved developing a new argument and recycling an old one.

The new argument was straightforward enough: The Thirteenth and Fourteenth Amendments were designed for African Americans only and could not be used to demand a federal guarantee of "privileges and immunities" for nonblacks or, in this case, a group of tradesmen. Chase and Swayne dissented from the majority, but they had themselves set the stage for Miller's opinion, inadvertently, by focusing exclusively on black emancipation and racial equality in their own earlier arguments concerning the Reconstruction amendments in such cases as *Rhodes* and *Turner.*

Although the majority opinion, limited as it was, might seem to have been at least a victory for African Americans, the phrasing provided a basis for narrowing the scope of the Reconstruction amendments even further. To the extent that the Fourteenth Amendment conferred "additional power" to the nation, the opinion suggested, it was a power only "to impose additional limitations on the States." Here was the germ of the "state action" doctrine that would come to dominate Fourteenth Amendment jurisprudence. The nation could intervene on behalf of African Americans only when a *state* law or action violated the amendment. If a *private* citizen deprived the rights of African Americans, the hands of the federal government were tied.

The old argument that Miller recycled was the contention of a distinction between state and national citizenship, an argument similar to that made by Taney in *Dred Scott*. According to the majority, the Fourteenth Amendment applied only to cases in which states abridged the privileges and immunities of people who were *national* citizens exclusively. The butchers did not belong to that category, because they were *state* citizens of Louisiana first; their national citizenship flowed only from their state citizenship. Although the opinion was clear about the status of the butchers, it was obscure about the status of others. Who was a citizen by virtue of the nation — only the foreign-born who held dual citizenship, perhaps? — and who was a citizen by virtue of a state? What made this aspect of the opinion especially pernicious, however, was that it interpreted the Fourteenth Amendment as Taney might have, even though one of the purposes of the amendment had been to overturn what Taney had done in *Dred Scott*. It could just as well have been Taney instead of Miller expressing shock that "the whole theory of the relations of the State and Federal governments to each other and of both these governments to the people" had changed. Taney was dead, and the Civil War had been fought and won by those who believed that such a change indeed had been one of the fruits of Union victory. Reading the majority opinion, however, it was possible to imagine that the war had been but a trifle.

Slaughterhouse's Dissenters and the New Fourteenth Amendment

As pivotal a decision as Miller's was, *Slaughterhouse* would become better known for its dissenting opinions, both of which, like the majority opinion, had strains that harkened back to Taney, although in significantly different ways. Justice Field's dissent, which was joined by Chase, Bradley, and Swayne, began with a more salutary view of the Fourteenth Amendment than Miller's majority opinion. Like Miller, Field agreed that no new rights were granted by the amendment's "privileges and immunities" clause. But the amendment nonetheless did modify federalism, Field argued, because it overturned the idea that state citizenship could somehow limit someone's basic privileges and immunities, "which of right belong to the citizens of all free governments." In enshrining "the right of free labor," and by extension the right of contract, as "one of the most sacred and imprescriptible rights of man," Field echoed Taney's landmark 1837 opinion in *Charles River Bridge*.

In addition to signing on to Field's dissent, Bradley issued a further dissent of his own, which went even further than Field's in highlighting the transformative quality of the Fourteenth Amendment. He made explicit what Field had implied, that the amendment was not limited to African Americans and that "the mischief to be remedied was not merely slavery and its incidents . . . but that spirit of insubordination and disloyalty to the National government which had troubled the country for so many years." However, like Field and Miller, Bradley echoed Taney — ironically, the Taney of the *Dred Scott* decision, which Bradley despised. Part of that decision had claimed that Congress had violated the Fifth Amendment's "due process" guarantee when it denied slaveholders' property rights by prohibiting slavery from the northern territories in the Missouri Compromise. Bradley took a similar view of "due process," arguing that a government could abridge "due process" only by laws that were "necessary or proper for the mutual good of all." Were Bradley's vision to be realized — and, eventually, it was — the standard for deeming a regulation constitutional would become impossibly high. Courts would have unprecedented power to strike down any law deemed threatening to the right of any citizen, organization, or corporation to "life, liberty, and property."

Although Field and Bradley were in the minority in *Slaughterhouse*, the doctrines they espoused, later to be termed "liberty of contract" (Field) and "substantive due process" (Bradley), would come to control the Court's view of the Fourteenth Amendment by the end of the century. Taken together, the majority and minority opinions in *Slaughterhouse* transformed the Fourteenth Amendment from a weapon for the dispossessed against discriminatory laws to a tool for corporations against well-intentioned regulations.

The Chase Court's Achievements

Regardless of the merits of *Slaughterhouse* or of any of the Court's individual decisions in the nine years that preceded it, the Court under Chase's leadership had done much to regain the legitimacy so badly damaged during Taney's last years. By the time of Chase's death, partisanship no longer dominated the Court as it had during the last years of Taney's term and the first years of Chase's. In *Slaughterhouse*, for example, the majority was composed of four Republicans and one Democrat; the minority, two Republicans, a Democrat, and an Independent. Nor did the Court follow a clear sectional agenda, as it had under Taney. Although no new Southerner had joined the Court under Chase, the Court, at least until *Slaughterhouse,* had followed a balanced course in reuniting the nation. The Court had clarified and delineated laws carefully, neither yielding control of Reconstruction to anti-Southern Republicans nor rejecting radical Reconstruction out of hand in favor of a purely Southern, states' rights agenda. Finally, the Chase Court steered a course away from the judicial supremacy attempted by Taney in *Dred Scott.* In that decision, Taney had taken aim at Congress; he would have taken aim at the presidency as well had that office not already been diminished by decades of ineffectual leadership. In contrast, the Court by the end of the Chase era was more restrained, maintaining a coequal relationship with Congress and the president. To be sure, the Court had not been timid under Chase. It had overturned ten congressional acts, eight more than the total overturned by all previous Courts, although most of those acts were relatively insignificant. In the midst of the volatile circumstances of Reconstruction, a time when Congress gained unprecedented power and the presidency was tested as never before — by a war, an assassination, and an impeachment — the Court moved forward with caution and judiciousness.

Under Chase, the Court regained much of the respectability that it had lost under Taney. A number of the Court's rulings, most notably *Milligan,* the Second Legal Tender Cases, and *Slaughterhouse,* eventually came to represent guidelines taken seriously by military and civilian authorities. During the last three decades of the nineteenth century, as the United States grew into a modern, industrial nation, Americans looked confidently to the Court to set the boundaries between government power and individual rights. The renewed faith in the Supreme Court was, in large part, the product of Chase's success in restoring luster to the tribunal. In 1868, the chief justice allowed his presidential ambitions to distract him from his main duties. But when he died on May 7, 1873, he left the Court in better shape than he had found it.

—MICHAEL VORENBERG

FOR FURTHER READING AND RESEARCH

On the Supreme Court during the Civil War and Reconstruction, see David M. Silver, *Lincoln's Supreme Court* (Urbana, Ill., 1956); and Charles Fairman, *Reconstruction and Reunion, 1864–1888, Part One* (New York, 1971), volume 6 of the *History of the Supreme Court of the United States* (the Oliver Wendell Holmes Devise). For general legal and constitutional developments during this period, see

Harold M. Hyman and William Wiecek, *Equal Justice Under Law: Constitutional Development, 1835–1875* (New York, 1982); Harold M. Hyman, *A More Perfect Union: The Impact of the Civil War and Reconstruction on the Constitution* (New York, 1974); and Stanley I. Kutler, *Judicial Power and Reconstruction Politics* (Chicago, 1968). The most recent comprehensive biography of the chief justice is John Niven, *Salmon P. Chase: A Biography* (New York, 1995). On civil liberties, see Mark E. Neely, Jr., *The Fate of Liberty: Abraham Lincoln and Civil Liberties* (New York, 1991). On currency, see Irwin Unger, *The Greenback Era: A Social and Political History of American Finance, 1865–1879* (Princeton, N.J., 1964). On civil rights, see Robert J. Kaczorowski, *The Politics of Judicial Interpretation: The Federal Courts, Department of Justice, and Civil Rights, 1866–1876* (New York, 1985).

The Civil Rights Act of 1866

Aside from abolishing slavery and involuntary servitude, the Thirteenth Amendment, ratified in December 1865, declared that "Congress shall have power to enforce this article by appropriate legislation." The need for such legislation became apparent even before the amendment had been ratified. In a number of states of the Deep South, legislatures passed laws restricting African Americans' basic rights, such as the right to assemble, to carry arms, and to rent or purchase land. Most Republicans regarded these measures, which they termed "black codes," as violations of the Thirteenth Amendment. Republicans in the Thirty-ninth Congress, which assembled in December 1865, steered through Congress a civil rights act that would overturn not only the black codes but also the 1857 *Dred Scott* decision's declaration that African Americans were not citizens. Congress adopted the act in 1866. By far the fullest definition of citizenship and the broadest guarantee of African American rights ever written into federal law, the act was regarded as an overreach of congressional power by many, including President Andrew Johnson. Johnson vetoed the act, but Congress overrode the veto with a two-thirds vote. In order to give the act firmer constitutional footing, Congress incorporated much of the wording of the measure into the first section of the Fourteenth Amendment. Congress passed the resolution for that amendment in 1866, and it was ratified by the states in 1868. The Civil Rights Act of 1866 has withstood a number of constitutional challenges, and although the act was eventually broken up, with different parts being incorporated into different sections of the federal code, most of the act's crucial elements remain in effect.

According to the Civil Rights Act of 1866, Section 1:

All persons born in the United States and not subject to any foreign power, excluding Indians not taxed, are hereby declared to be citizens of the United States; and such citizens, of every race and color, without regard to any previous condition of slavery or involuntary servitude, except as a punishment for crime whereof the party shall have been duly convicted, shall have the same right, in every State and Territory in the United States, to make and enforce contracts, to sue, be parties, and give evidence, to inherit, purchase, lease, sell, hold, and convey real and personal property, and to full and equal benefit of all laws and proceedings for the security of person and property, as is enjoyed by white citizens, and shall be subject to like punishment, pains, and penalties, and to none other, any law, statute, ordinance, regulation, or custom, to the contrary notwithstanding.

6

The Waite Court   1874–1888

The Collapse of Reconstruction and the Transition to Conservative Constitutionalism

C HIEF JUSTICE SALMON CHASE died in May 1873. It seemed as if President Grant would never find a replacement. Rarely in American history had the office of chief justice been vacant longer than two or three months. Grant deliberated for more than half a year, then announced that he was offering the position to one of his most stalwart Senate allies: New York Senator Roscoe Conkling, a powerful man of supremely injudicious temperament. Surprisingly, Conkling had not been consulted on the offer, and the forty-four-year-old declined. In short succession, two other senators and the president's secretary of state also turned down the offer.

Realizing that he might do better to start with someone who was willing to take the job, Grant nominated Attorney General George H. Williams. Unfortunately, many in the legal community considered him unfit in terms of both talent and character, despite his high office. His nomination collapsed when the Senate Judiciary Committee discovered that Williams had used the Justice Department's contingent fund for personal purchases.

Grant then sent Caleb Cushing's name to the Senate. Cushing had served as chief U.S. counsel before the Geneva Tribunal, which arbitrated the Civil War–era *Alabama* claims dispute between the United States and Great Britain. But his nomination was doomed after opponents made public a March 1861 letter Cushing had written in which he introduced a government clerk to Jefferson Davis. The Republican Party might have been leaving the war behind but was not yet prepared to elevate to chief justice a man who was willing to give advice to traitors. After the *New York Times* described the search for a new chief justice as "humiliating" and "scandalous," the president began to look for a candidate with a reputation for honesty and party loyalty, someone who would also be a relative political unknown unburdened by a potentially controversial public record. He found his man in Ohio.

The Chief Justice and the Court

Morrison Remick Waite was the enterprising son of the former chief justice of the supreme court of Connecticut. He left for Ohio soon after graduating from Yale and by the 1850s was a respected lawyer and a partner in a prosperous law firm. As a former Whig, he helped organize the Republican Party in Ohio. He first came to the attention of President Grant in 1871 when appointed one of three U.S. counsel at the Geneva Arbitration Tribunal, created to settle differences with Britain arising from British aid to Confederate warships during the Civil War. During his service, he earned a reputation as hard working and well prepared. Almost all the arguments before the tribunal were conducted by the senior members of the team — Cushing and William Evarts — but Waite did a fine job when a hot dispute arose over the meaning of "base of naval operations." When the tribunal awarded the United States a generous $15.5 million in damages, it was one of the Grant administration's few triumphs, as well as the greatest achievement of Waite's professional career. At a Toledo dinner celebrating his return, Waite was moved to quote Milton's affirmation: "Peace hath her victories no less renowned than those of war." One year later, Waite was elected to the Ohio constitutional convention and became the convention's presiding officer.

Waite's record was certainly respectable, but it was far from notable. Ohio Senator John Sherman had to contact the congressman from Toledo to get information on Grant's nominee. (He was told: "M. R. Waite age 57 — Born at Lyme, Conn't. Graduated at Yale 1837. Commenced practice law Toledo 1839.") Waite's nomination was so unexpected that on receiving the telegram, his first instinct was to assume that it was a practical joke. This was not simply self-effacement. The previous holders of the office of chief justice had all been former senators, senior cabinet officials, or members of the Constitutional Convention.

The selection of a provincial lawyer from Toledo, Ohio, for chief justice of the United States might have shocked the political establishment under most circumstances, but given the record of the previous eight months, the decision was received mostly with relief. In the words of The Nation: "The President has, with remarkable skill, avoided choosing any first-rate man. . . . [But], considering what the President might have done, and tried to do, we ought to be very thankful." On news of the nomination, the New York Tribune predicted that the Senate "will not venture to consider whether Mr. Waite is precisely the man for Chief Justice, but will look only to his respectable standing as a lawyer, as a citizen, and as a Republican, and gladly vote him into a seat where we had hoped never to see any one of less heroic stature than Marshall and Chase." The Senate agreed. Dispensing with hearings, it confirmed the nation's seventh chief justice by a vote of 63–0.

The contrast between the relative obscurity of the new chief justice and the reputations of his new colleagues was striking. Among the luminaries sitting on the Court were Lincoln-appointed Samuel F. Miller, who would become known for his support of personal liberties and his opposition to concentrations of corporate and financial wealth; Stephen J. Field, who had been appointed by Lincoln and would establish himself as the Court's most impassioned advocate of constitutional protections for economic liberty and personal property; and Grant-appointed Joseph P. Bradley, a former railroad lawyer who ended up providing the Waite Court with some of its best arguments for supporting economic regulation and the powers of the national government. These justices were part of the select group responsible for the post–*Dred Scott* rebuilding of the Court's power, striking down an unprecedented ten congressional statutes in the decade after the Civil War. Just a few years after Waite became chief justice, President Rutherford B. Hayes appointed John Marshall Harlan to replace David Davis, who had quit the Court to take a seat in the Senate. Harlan, a six-foot-three Kentuckian, would earn a reputation as one of the Court's great dissenters.

Bradley and Harlan ended up befriending the chief. Miller, who was a bit resentful that he had been passed over for the position, wrote to a friend that Waite was "pleasant, a good presiding officer, *mediocre*, with fair amount of professional learning." The cantankerous Field was less tolerant of Waite's shortcomings, writing that he was a man who "would never have been thought of for the position by any person except President Grant." It was a testament to Waite's character and work habits that he was able to move past the hostility and condescension that some of his new brethren felt toward him to become relatively well regarded as a Court manager, if not as a legal thinker or writer. By temperament, he was a conciliator, which was quite useful given the Court's strong personalities. He was also able to maintain one of the most important internal norms of the nineteenth-century Court, whereby the justices would strive whenever possible to avoid writing concurring or dissenting opinions, even when they disagreed with the majority opinion. According to Waite's private docket book, only 9 percent of decisions had one or more dissenting votes when published, whereas 40 percent included dissenting votes when the case was first discussed in conference. Thus, under Waite's leadership, these justices, unlike their modern counterparts, often managed to keep silent about their views so as to convey to the country an image of consensus.

Establishing himself among these powerful and confident national figures was not the only challenge facing a relatively unknown Ohio lawyer. Waite was preparing to oversee a Court whose workload was exploding (Plate A.12). In 1875, one year after Waite became chief justice, a lame-duck Republican Congress intent on channeling more economic litigation into corporate-friendly federal courts dramatically expanded the jurisdiction of the federal judiciary. In 1870, the justices began their term with 636 cases waiting to be settled; by 1880, the figure was up to 1,202. Ten years later, in 1890, the justices started the year with 1,816 cases on their docket — almost a tripling of the workload over two decades. By the end of Waite's tenure, the Court was almost four years behind in its work, a condition that led him to urge Congress to provide "relief for the Supreme Court" by creating an intermediate system of appellate courts for the federal system — something that another lame-duck Republican Congress would authorize in 1891, just a few short years after his death.

Along with this avalanche of everyday appeals, the Supreme Court was asked to address questions of great national importance. Waite was chief justice from the time of Grant's second administration through the administrations of Rutherford B. Hayes, James A. Garfield, Chester Arthur, and Grover Cleveland. These years represented a transition from the immediate post–Civil War preoccupations with Reconstruction and the fate of the former slaves to late-nineteenth-century concerns about the impact of industrialization on American life. There were already enormous pressures for a return to so-called normalcy, which meant ending federal control of Southern politics and federal protection for blacks. By 1873, President Grant had halted civil rights enforcement, extended patronage to "respectable" Southern Democrats, pardoned convicted Klansmen, and prepared for the end of "carpetbag rule" in the South. Yet alongside these emerging sentiments lay the continuing legal legacy of Reconstruction — not only in the Thirteenth, Fourteenth, and Fifteenth Amendments but also in various enforcement acts passed by Congress. It would be up to the justices to decide how far to reconcile the inherited spirit of these laws with the prevailing spirit of the times.

The Gilded Age

It was not a good sign for the cause of civil rights when even former radical Republicans, such as Horace Greeley and Edward L. Godkin, began to argue for reconciliation and for a new Republican political agenda that focused on alliances between Northern and Southern commercial interests. Capital investment in the United States would increase nineteenfold between 1850 and 1900. The postwar expansion of manufacturing and the developing capacity of the railroads to distribute goods across state lines meant that owners, producers, workers, and consumers were relating to one another on a national scale rather than as relatively autonomous segments of a localized economy. The Republican Party of the 1870s wanted to promote all these developments. The Supreme Court, with its constitutional supervision over state and federal regulation of interstate commerce, would have a significant role to play in these plans, especially in determining how much to accommodate the pressures for innovative federal regulation and how much to tolerate potentially disruptive state regulation.

Alongside the center-stage battles of black civil rights and industrialization were other important national questions, including constitutional protections for women and the application of the Bill of Rights to the states through the newly passed Fourteenth Amendment. Not surprisingly, the Waite Court responded to most of these issues in a way that reflected the preferences of the post-Reconstruction Republican Party. Although the Democratic Party was able to win a majority in the House of Representatives during the 1874 midterm elections, the Republican Party was able to maintain control of the two institutions that controlled appointments to the federal judiciary—the presidency and the Senate—throughout most of the 1870s and 1880s. Both in 1876 and 1888, Republican presidents won in the Electoral College despite loss of the popular vote. In 1880, the Republican presidential candidate won the popular vote as well but by fewer than 10,000 votes (out of almost 9,000,000 cast nationwide). It proved to be an important victory, given that three new appointments to the Supreme Court were made in 1881 and 1882.

These highly competitive and tumultuous times in American politics saw the Crédit Mobilier Affair, in which a number of national figures, including Vice President Schuyler Colfax and Congressmen Blaine and Garfield, accepted lucrative stock in the Union Pacific's construction company; a bitterly disputed presidential election, the resolution of which involved the appointment of five of the justices to a fifteen-member Electoral Commission that voted on party lines to give the presidency to Hayes over Samuel J. Tilden; and the assassination of James A. Garfield by a disgruntled office seeker. The corruption of the political system and the failure of democracy itself were depicted in the cartoons of Thomas Nast and in popular political satires, such as *The Gilded Age* (1873) by Mark Twain and Charles Dudley Warner. Notably, the Supreme Court remained relatively unscathed by the most serious criticisms of Gilded Age politics.

In 1881, right in the middle of Waite's tenure, future Supreme Court Justice Oliver Wendell Holmes published his famous book, *The Common Law*, with its famous opening statement: "The life of the law has not been logic:

it has been experience. The felt necessities of the time, the prevalent moral and political theories, intuitions of public policy, avowed or unconscious, even the prejudices which judges share with their fellow-men, have a good deal more to do than the syllogism in determining the rules by which men should be governed." It is a little too facile to claim that the Waite Court remained unscathed merely because the justices reflected "the felt necessities of the time." Still, Holmes's lesson about the life of the law is as good a starting point as any for an understanding of the Waite Court's decision making.

The Reconstruction Amendments

The Supreme Court got its first opportunity to interpret the Fourteenth Amendment in the *Slaughterhouse Cases* (1873), not long before Chief Justice Chase's death. The issue was the state of Louisiana's creation of a slaughterhouse monopoly in the city of New Orleans. In a 5–4 decision written by Justice Miller, the majority ruled that the Fourteenth Amendment did not prohibit Louisiana from establishing the monopoly. In other words, it was not one of the "privileges or immunities" of national citizenship to practice the profession of being a butcher; it was not a violation of equal protection to create this sort of monopoly, especially in light of the public health considerations; and it was not a deprivation of liberty or property to tell some former butchers that they could no longer practice their profession in the manner in which they were accustomed. The minority — Field, Bradley, Chase, and Swayne — argued that the monopoly violated a person's "right to pursue the ordinary avocations of life without other restraint than such as affects all others," which they believed was protected by the new addition to the Constitution.

The Chase Court may have had the first opportunity to interpret the Fourteenth Amendment, but it was the responsibility of the Waite Court to clarify the scope of its protections. In one area of the law, the justices simply took their cue from another 1873 Chase Court decision, *Bradwell v. Illinois* (1873), which held that it was not unconstitutional for Illinois to prevent women from practicing law (Plate A.10). Two years later, Mrs. Virginia Minor asked the Waite Court to strike down Missouri's law prohibiting women from voting, arguing that she was a U.S. citizen entitled to all the "privileges and immunities" guaranteed by the Fourteenth Amendment (Plate A.11). In *Minor v. Happersett* (1875), Chief Justice Waite declared for a unanimous Court that voting was not a privilege of national citizenship. Under the Constitution, states had the authority to regulate suffrage, and no one had ever previously suggested that states were required to give the vote to every person who was a citizen of the United States. The only change in this understanding brought about by the Civil War amendments was that states could no longer deny the vote based on race. Future expansions of suffrage would have to come through a liberalization of state laws or the passage of additional constitutional amendments.

At the time of the Fourteenth Amendment's ratification, it might have been reasonable to assume that the most likely, and most deserving, beneficiaries of its protections would be black Americans. As Miller had put it in the *Slaughterhouse Cases*, "the one pervading purpose" behind the Civil War amendments was to secure the freedom of blacks. Around the same time that the Supreme Court announced its decision in *Minor v. Happersett*, a lame-duck Republican Congress passed a law that would come to represent the last gasp of Reconstruction, the Civil Rights Act of 1875, which prohibited discrimination in so-called public accommodations, such as inns, theaters, and railroads. Within a year of the Civil Rights Act's passage, however, two decisions were handed down that signaled the end of direct federal intervention to protect former slaves. In *U.S. v. Reese* (1876), a unanimous Court declared unconstitutional sections 3 and 4 of the Civil Rights, or Enforcement, Act of 1870, which made it a federal offense for state election inspectors to refuse to receive or count votes or to obstruct any citizen from voting. In his opinion for the Court, Chief Justice Waite emphasized that under the Fifteenth Amendment, Congress had the authority to pass a law that addressed racial discrimination in voting but not to protect voting rights more generally, as the language of the statute seemed to do. Even though the prosecution alleged that the denial of voting rights was based on discrimination on account of race, the justices concluded that the foundation of this prosecution was a statute whose terms were overly broad. It was a fatal blow to federal protection of black voting rights.

The outcome in *U.S. v. Cruikshank* (1876) was similar. This case involved a series of federal indictments alleging conspiracy "to injure, oppress, threaten or intimidate any citizen, with intent to prevent or hinder his free exercise and enjoyment of any right or privilege granted or secured to him by the Constitution or laws of the United States." A Negro posse that was attempting to occupy a courthouse under the authority of a sheriff who had been commissioned by the state's Republican governor was attacked by a mob of whites. Between sixty and a hundred blacks were killed in what became known as the Colfax Massacre. Almost one hundred whites were indicted for violating section 6 of the Enforcement Act of 1870, but only a handful were eventually arrested and tried. In *U.S. v. Hall* (1871), a precedent allowing such indictments had been established by Circuit Judge William B. Woods, but the political climate had so changed by 1876 that a unanimous Supreme Court was ready to put a stop to federal prosecutions.

In his opinion for the Court, the chief justice held that the rights at issue were protected against infringement by state and federal authorities, not against infringement by private individuals. Because there was no indication that the defendants were acting as agents of the state, the federal government had no authority to intervene under the Civil War amendments; instead, the state governments had the responsibility of responding to acts of private individuals. Language in the indictment also alleged that some of the defendants prevented certain individual from voting, but it was not alleged that they did so because of the race of the defendants, and without such an allegation, that indictment could not be sustained as an enforcement of rights under the Fifteenth Amendment. Other counts were likewise dismissed as being too vague and general to be the basis of an acceptable indictment.

From a later vantage point, this decision might seem to represent a reactionary obstruction of an important feature of the agenda of the postbellum Republican Party. In fact, very few contemporaneous commentators — Northern or Southern, Democrat or Republican — objected to the outcome. Only a few Republican papers warned that the gutting of the Enforcement statutes meant a new "opportunity for serious abuses, and perhaps terrorism in the South."

There is no question that an intensification of such violence was one of the most important and predictable results of the decision. A year after these two decisions, President Hayes followed through on the agreement reached with Democratic Party leaders during the election crisis and withdrew the army from Louisiana and South Carolina. Within a few years, congressional Democrats were able to pass a law prohibiting U.S. marshals from using military forces in the execution of election laws. In the South, black voting, which had been robust in the decade following the end of the Civil War, plummeted in the wake of these decisions by a Court dominated by loyal Republicans adjusting to the new normalcy.

In the post-Reconstruction regime, federal enforcement power was apparently acceptable only in cases not involving black voting rights. In *Ex parte Siebold* (1880), for example, the Court upheld those parts of the Enforcement Acts that made it a federal offense for state officials at a congressional election to neglect to perform a duty under federal law. In this case, the neglect of duty took the form of ballot stuffing at elections in Baltimore and Cincinnati. But in *U.S. v. Harris* (1883), which arose from prosecutions under the Ku Klux Klan Act of 1871, the Court once again relied on *Reese* and *Cruikshank* to declare unconstitutional the federal prosecution of private vigilantes.

The Waite Court was not uniformly hostile to black civil rights. However, the justices tended to speak out against only the most undeniable violations of equal protection. In *Strauder v. West Virginia* (1880), the Supreme Court, over dissents by Justices Field and Clifford, struck down a state statute that explicitly limited jury service to whites. Justice Strong noted that the Court had said in *Slaughterhouse Cases* that the Fourteenth Amendment "was designed to assure to the colored race the enjoyment of all the civil rights that under the law are enjoyed by white persons," and this meant "that no discrimination shall be made against them by law because of their color." Similarly, in *Ex parte Virginia* (1880), the justices, over another dissent by Field, upheld federal prosecution of a state judge for explicitly excluding blacks from juries.

However, even these rare victories for the cause of black civil rights led to a legal dead end. In another 1880 Virginia case, *Virginia v. Rives,* the Court ruled that discrimination could not be assumed simply because no black jurors had ever been chosen in a particular county. As long as states were smart enough to enact formally neutral laws and judges smart enough not to declare that they were discriminating against blacks, the mere fact that no blacks were ever selected for juries would not be treated as a violation of the Fourteenth Amendment. Future generations might be forgiven if the sum of these decisions seemed to add up to advice on how to perpetuate discrimination rather than serious efforts to prevent it.

From the beginning, the Waite Court had embraced a limited view of the power of the federal government to promote civil rights under the Civil War amendments. In many respects, then, the Court's infamous decision in the *Civil Rights Cases* (1883) merely represented a predictable culmination rather than an unexpected or dramatic departure. Still, the outcome carried with it the weight of history. In an opinion written by Justice Bradley, the Court declared unconstitutional the Civil Rights Act of 1875. The reasoning was entirely predictable, based on the results in *Reese* and *Cruikshank:* In the view of the majority, the Fourteenth Amendment was not designed to weed out discrimination by private individuals or businesses. Bradley added a lecture on how the time had come for the country to realize that there was no longer a need to legislate for the special protections of blacks: "When a man has emerged from slavery, and by the aid of beneficent legislation has shaken off the inseparable concomitants of that State, there must be some stage in the progress of his elevation when he takes the rank of a mere citizen, and ceases to be the special favorite of the laws, and when his rights as a citizen, or a man, are to be protected in the ordinary modes by which other men's rights are protected."

The difference this time around, besides the sheer magnitude of the putative federal protection that was being stripped away, was the dissenting voice. It was in this case that Justice Harlan, a Southern Republican and former slaveholder, began to establish his reputation as one of the Court's great dissenters. At the time of his appointment, some concern was expressed about the wisdom of placing a Southerner on the Court so soon after the end of the Civil War. But once Harlan spoke, it became clear that there was a higher price to be paid by a Court whose members had no firsthand experience with Southern race relations and who took too easy comfort in lectures that celebrated how blacks had joined the ranks of mere citizen. Harlan knew better. "I cannot resist the conclusion that the substance and spirit of the recent amendments of the Constitution have been sacrificed by a subtle and ingenious verbal criticism." The majority's interpretation of the Fourteenth Amendment had reduced it to "splendid baubles, thrown in to delude those who deserved fair and generous treatment at the hands of the nation." Harlan believed that a federal law against private discrimination was authorized by the Thirteenth Amendment's prohibition against slavery or involuntary servitude, whose provisions were not limited to state action. Anticipating an argument that would be used eighty years later in support of a resurrected version of this civil rights act, Harlan also suggested that this law could be upheld "as applicable at least to commerce between the States." Whatever the specific rationale, the fundamental principle at stake was that "there cannot be, in this republic, any class of human beings in practical subjection to another class, with power in the latter to dole out to the former just such privileges as they may choose to grant."

Just as the majority had tried, at every opportunity, to find a reason why the federal government had no direct authority over civil rights enforcement, Harlan offered reasons why such authority could be found, if the eyes were willing. Although this would never be known from the official report of the decision, Harlan's intensely personal motivation was amply demonstrated by his decision to write out his blistering dissent with the same pen and inkwell that Chief Justice Taney had used when composing the infamous *Dred Scott* decision. Still, despite Harlan's eloquence and the noble sentiments underlying his dissent, the Supreme Court has continued—to this day—to follow Bradley's more cramped understanding of Congress's power under the Fourteenth Amendment.

The same year the Court handed down the *Civil Rights Cases*, it decided *Pace v. Alabama* (1883), upholding a statute imposing more severe penalties for living "in adultery or fornication" when the parties were of different races. Field conceded that it would be unconstitutional for the state to impose harsher penalties on blacks than on whites. But in this case, there was technically no difference in the ways blacks and whites were treated: Both blacks and whites who violated the statute were punished more harshly than would be the case if they cohabited with members of their own race. "The punishment of each offending person, whether white or black, is the same." This time, the decision was unanimous. Even Harlan was not willing to invest his eloquence in a decision that sanctioned interracial adultery or fornication.

The Waite Court did establish one relatively important precedent relating to state discrimination. In *Yick Wo v. Hopkins* (1886), a unanimous Court, in an opinion by Justice Matthews, ruled that it was unconstitutional for government to take a general law (in this case, requiring laundry operators to have a license) and apply it in a blatantly discriminatory manner (by denying people of Chinese ancestry a license while granting non-Chinese applicants a license). "The fact of this discrimination is admitted. No reason for it is shown, and the conclusion cannot be resisted, that no reason for it exists except hostility to the race and nationality to which the petitioners belong." In the canon of constitutional law, *Yick Wo* has come to stand for the important principle that government may violate equal protection not only through the passage of discriminatory legislation but also through the discriminatory administration of facially valid laws. It was an important precedent, but it would take quite some time before the case would do real work for individuals who believed that they were being victimized by biased administrators.

The Reinvention of the Fourteenth Amendment

The most important work that would be done by the Fourteenth Amendment over the next half century would involve not civil rights for blacks or other victims of racial discrimination but precisely those categories of cases that were dismissed as irrelevant when the Chase Court first interpreted the amendment — namely, cases involving state regulation of business. In this regard, one of the Waite Court's most canonical decisions came in *Munn v. Illinois* (1877).

In the early 1870s, a movement known as the Patrons of Husbandry (less flamboyantly, the Grange) began to develop in the Midwest in opposition to the economic power of railroads, corporations, and other property owners in a position to take advantage of farmers. Farmers were especially upset at the rates set by railroads for hauling crops to market and by owners of grain elevators for storing the waiting crops. In Illinois, Iowa, Minnesota, and Wisconsin, state legislatures responded by regulating the maximum prices that railroads and grain elevators could charge. The grain elevator law at issue in *Munn*, for example, was passed under the authority of the Illinois state constitution, which required that the legislature pass laws "for the protection of producers, shippers, and receivers of grain and produce."

Not surprisingly, the Granger movement's success caused great concern to investors. The use of political power to prevent property owners from charging what the market would bear for the use of their property was characterized as confiscatory, communistic, and just plain bad economics — a threat to investment. To win in court, however, it was also necessary to have a legal argument. The law was challenged on the ground that, by preventing property owners from setting their own prices, the legislature had in effect deprived them of property without due process of law, in violation of the Fourteenth Amendment.

The Court handed down its decision on March 1, 1877, the day before President Hayes was declared elected by the Hayes-Tilden Election Commission. In a decision written during the election crisis by the chief justice, with substantial help from Bradley, the Court ruled that property that is "clothed with a public interest"— in the sense that it is "used in a manner to make it of public consequence, and affect the community at large"— could be regulated "by the public for the common good." At this early stage in the interpretation of the Fourteenth Amendment, the chief justice went out of his way to signal that federal courts should be deferential to state legislatures, writing: "For protection against abuses by legislatures the people must resort to the polls, not to the courts." Field filed a lone dissent, complaining that the Court's decision amounted to the ridiculous proposition that "property loses something of its private character when employed in such a way as to be generally useful." He argued that the charging of rates that some considered "unreasonable" did not present the sort of "harm" or "nuisance" that justified state prohibition of the practice. In his dissent in the companion cases involving railroad rates, Field insisted that, by emphasizing the importance of deference to state legislatures, the decision "practically destroys all the guaranties of the Constitution and of the common law."

Thankfully for Field's beleaguered railroad tycoons, the Granger movement did not significantly repel investment in railroads. In fact, by the time the decision was handed down, little was left of the Grangers as a political force. By 1878, many of the Granger laws had been repealed, often at the behest of the same legislators who had initially advocated their adoption; they had learned that they could impose price controls but that they could not guarantee that property owners would maintain service, quality, or investment in their states. Still, even though the judiciary was no longer needed to deal with the Granger "threat," many conservatives were extremely disappointed at the majority in *Munn*. At one point, Field became so frustrated with his brethren's apparent disregard for property rights that he explored a run for the presidency in 1884 as a way to "have placed on the Bench able and conservative men and thus have brought back the decisions of the Court to that line from which they should not have departed." Field also arranged for well-known conservative lawyers, such as John Norton Pomeroy, to write for prominent legal journals articles criticizing such decisions as *Munn v. Illinois* for striking "at the stability of private property," a right that represented "the very foundation of modern society and civilization." The conservative American Bar Association was also formed in the wake of *Munn* to organize elite commercial bar advocacy for more sympathetic judicial decision making.

Such opposition notwithstanding, the Court at this point was not prepared to act against any state law that might have an impact on a person's property. A year after *Munn*, Justice Miller attempted to deflect additional efforts to use the Fourteenth Amendment to assault state regulation. At issue in *Davidson v. New Orleans* (1878) was whether the due process clause was violated when the government assessed land in order to raise funds for swamp drainage. Miller noted that, in recent years, the Court's docket had become "crowded with cases in which we are asked to hold that State Courts and State Legislatures have deprived their own citizens of life, liberty or property without due process of law." Apparently, the clause was now looked on "as a means of bringing to the test of the decision of this court the abstract opinions of every unsuccessful litigant in a State court of the justice of the decision against him, and of the merits of the legislation on which such a decision may be founded."

Miller implied that the central point of the due process clause was to require that, when it acted against a person's life, liberty, or property, states provide an adequate "process." This, however, was not to say that state legislatures could get away with all interferences with property rights. If a state acted arbitrarily or unreasonably against someone's vested rights, it could be found in violation of the Fourteenth Amendment.

As it turned out, this was all the opening needed to keep due process litigation thriving. In the fifteen years after 1873, fewer than seventy cases were decided under the Fourteenth Amendment; in the thirty years from 1888 to 1918, more than seven hundred would be decided. Principles established in these nominally deferential Waite Court opinions became the basis for more aggressive judicial supervision of state regulation. Even the *Munn v. Illinois* central holding — declaring that property affected with a public interest could be regulated — contained within itself a negative corollary: Namely, property not affected with a public interest deserved protection from overzealous state legislatures.

After the Granger laws were repealed, many state politicians and railroad owners eventually agreed to replace them with a system whereby special railroad commissions would determine reasonable rates after due investigation and consultation with all interested parties. This regulatory system would be upheld by the Supreme Court in *Stone v. Farmers Loan & Trust Co.* (1886). This time, however, the justices issued a warning to state officials: "This power to regulate is not a power to destroy, and limitation is not the equivalent of confiscation. Under pretense of regulating fares and freights, the State cannot require a railroad corporation to carry persons or property without reward; neither can it do that which in law amounts to a taking of private property for public use without just compensation, or without due process of law." That same year, the Waite Court confirmed what previously had been assumed: that corporations would be considered "persons" for purposes of asserting constitutional protections under the Fourteenth Amendment. It would take only a few more years for the Court, led by a new chief justice — and over the dissents of Bradley, Gray, and Lamar — to declare in *Chicago, M. & St. P. Ry. v. Minnesota* (1890) that judges were obligated under the due process clause to protect the property rights of investors or corporations by reviewing the reasonableness of any rates set by state authorities, thus essentially overruling *Munn v. Illinois.* Increasingly, "for protection against abuses by legislatures," the people were being allowed to bypass the polls and resort to the courts.

That point was not reached by the Waite Court, which preferred to uphold business regulation while issuing warnings to legislators against overreaching. In 1887, for example, the Court upheld a state prohibition against the manufacture of beer, even for private consumption, on the ground that the use of property could be regulated if the law promoted public health, safety, and morality. On this point, even Justice Field agreed. However, as in *Stone* the previous year, the justices made it clear that they would not be "misled by mere pretences." Legislation "purporting to have been enacted to protect the public health, the public morals, or the public safety" but having "no real or substantial relation to those objects" would be overruled. This language of promoting "public health, safety, and morality" was used to characterize the so-called police powers, the general authority of state legislatures to promote the well-being of their citizens. There is no doubt that the Waite Court was extremely accommodating of these traditional state powers. However, by the late 1880s, the justices were prepared to say that it was the "duty of the courts" to evaluate whether a law restricting liberty or property has "a real or substantial relation" to the advancement of public health, safety, or morality. This principle of late-nineteenth-century constitutional law, established by the Waite Court, would subsequently become extremely important as conservative judges encountered "social legislation" for which they had little patience.

The Commerce Clause

The Waite Court's review of commercial regulation involved more than the Fourteenth Amendment and the police powers. Conservatives preferred courts to strike down any property regulation they did not like, but during this period, Republican Party leaders were more interested in facilitating the development of a national economy than in having federal judges act as strict overseers of all exercises of state police powers. Those who cared about the creation of a legal framework for a fully national economy were more concerned about litigation arising under the Constitution's clause that gave Congress the authority to regulate "commerce among the states"—that is, interstate commerce. Throughout the century, the Supreme Court had used the commerce clause to articulate the scope of Congress's authority and to determine when state regulations interfered with the national goal of promoting the flow of commerce around the country. The Taney Court had established a loose framework for evaluating state regulation that might have an impact on interstate commerce, holding that states could regulate when the subject matter would benefit from different local regulations rather than one uniform national rule. It became the responsibility of the Waite Court to elaborate the principle in the context of rapid industrialization.

In one of its first commerce clause decisions, the Waite Court took advantage of an opportunity to reiterate and fortify one of the keystones of this jurisprudence. In *Welton v. Missouri* (1876), the justices struck down as inconsistent with the commerce clause a state tax that discriminated against sellers of out-of-state goods. Justice Field explained that interstate "transportation and exchange of commodities . . . requires uniformity of regulation." To this day, the nondiscrimination principle at the heart of *Welton* remains one of the core principles of the commerce clause.

That same year, in *Henderson v. Mayor of New York* (1876), the justices also declared that New York had no authority to demand that ship owners help the state guard against an immigrant passenger's becoming a public charge by requiring them to pay either a bond or a passenger tax. As Miller put it, the Taney Court had established that Congress's power to regulate commerce was exclusive with respect to "whatever subjects of this power are in their nature national or admit of one uniform system or plan of regulation." Any "regulation which imposes onerous, perhaps impossible, conditions on those engaged in active commerce with foreign nations . . . must of necessity be national in its character." One of the major results of *Henderson* was that Congress felt compelled to pass its first general immigration law in August 1882, as well as the Chinese Exclusion Acts of 1882, 1884, and 1888.

The Court demonstrated the same concern with state burdens on interstate commerce when Missouri attempted to exclude Texan, Mexican, or Indian cattle from entering the state during eight months of the year. In *Hannibal & St. Joseph R. R. v. Husen* (1878), the justices acknowledged that the state was free, under its police powers, to protect its people by excluding diseased animals or convicts or paupers, but because it prevented the entry of any out-of-state cattle, this law violated the presumption under the commerce clause that goods be allowed to flow freely across state lines. The general principle, as announced by the chief justice in *Hall v. DeCuir* (1878), was that "state legislation which seeks to impose a direct burden upon interstate commerce, or to interfere directly with its freedom, does encroach upon the exclusive power of Congress."

What made *Hall* more noteworthy than many of these other cases was its sensitive subject matter: The law being struck down prohibited racial segregation in public conveyances. In its decision, the Court refused to allow the law to be applied to a steamship traveling between Louisiana and Mississippi. "No carrier of passengers can conduct his business with satisfaction to himself, or comfort to those employing him, if on one side of a State line his passengers, both white and colored, must be permitted to occupy the same cabin, and on the other be kept separate." Implicit in this passage is the conclusion that a state law requiring segregation would not violate the equal protection clause. After all, if segregation laws were inherently unconstitutional, it would not burden interstate commerce for states to require integrated facilities. Between 1881 and 1891, nine Southern states passed Jim Crow laws requiring segregation in transportation. Two years after Waite's death, the Court inconsistently ruled in *Louisville, New Orleans & Texas Railway Co. v. Mississippi* (1890) that it did not violate the commerce clause for states to require railroads to provide "equal, but separate, accommodation for the white and colored races." The constitutionality of segregation would not be confirmed until it was addressed by the Fuller Court in *Plessy v. Ferguson* (1896), but once again, the Waite Court had laid the groundwork for the more infamous decisions of a later Court.

While it worked to prevent states from interfering with the flow of interstate commerce, the Court also rearticulated a principle, first suggested by John Marshall, that states were free to regulate the manufacturing or production of goods because these activities occurred, as a definitional matter, before the flow of commerce had begun. In *McCready v. Virginia*

(1877), the Court upheld a Virginia law that limited the planting and harvesting of oysters to in-state residents. Commerce, Chief Justice Waite declared, had "nothing to do with land while producing, but only with the product after it has become the subject of trade." On this view — standard at the time — the mere act of producing an item did not make it a piece of interstate commerce, because one might choose to consume it, destroy it, sell it to a neighbor, or do any number of things that would keep it forever out of interstate commerce. At the time, *McCready* was constitutional common sense, but it would later become controversial, especially when Congress began contemplating the passage of national regulations on producers and manufacturers and the Fuller Court drew on this Waite Court precedent to explain why the Sherman Anti-Trust Act could not be applied to sugar refineries.

In *Wabash, St. L. & Pac. Ry. v. Illinois* (1886), one of the Waite Court's most important assaults on state regulation, the justices held that states had no authority to outlaw discriminatory rates for the intrastate portion of an interstate journey. The majority relied on *Hall* for support. If each state established its own rate regulation and applied it to journeys across state lines, the "embarrassments upon interstate transportation . . . might be too oppressive to be submitted to." The effect of *Wabash* was to further undercut the influence of state railroad commissions, which had emerged in the wake of the collapse of Granger legislation, and force Congress to take action. Prior to *Wabash*, Congress had left it to the states to cope with the political conflicts surrounding railroad rates. Soon after the decision, Congress enacted the Interstate Commerce Commission Act of 1887, and President Cleveland appointed conservative treatise writer and judge Thomas M. Cooley as its first chairman.

The flip side of this Republican Court's hostility to disruptive state regulation of interstate commerce was its support for most exercises of federal power under the commerce clause. For example, in *Pensacola Tel. Co. v. Western Union Tel. Co.* (1878), the Court, through Waite, held that Congress's commerce power included the power to authorize the operation of an interstate telegraph. On the other hand, in the *Trade-Mark Cases* (1879), Miller led the Court in voiding a federal law regulating trademarks, on the ground that the law was not limited to articles used in interstate or international commerce. The justices were inclined to be accommodating of federal power, but they still insisted that Congress link its authority to its constitutional source.

That same year, the Court handed down a decision that supported federal power but angered corporate elites. In the *Sinking Fund Cases* (1879), the Court upheld a congressional statute that amended the charter of the Union Pacific Railroad by requiring it to establish a sinking fund with the

United States Treasury for the redemption of a government loan. The law was passed after railroads stalled on making required interest payments on government bonds while continuing to distribute substantial earnings to stockholders and private bondholders. By the end of the century, the debt owed to the government would be close to $116 million, with no assets dedicated to meeting it. The sinking-fund law required the railroads to pay 25 percent of their annual net earnings into the federal treasury. The law was resisted by railroad-friendly senators, such as Ohio's Stanley Matthews, but in the wake of the Crédit Mobilier Affair, it passed what would otherwise have been a more corporate-friendly Congress.

The act was challenged on the ground that it amounted to a deprivation of property without due process of law and thus violated the Fifth Amendment. (The contract clause was not relevant to the case, because its prohibitions applied only to state governments.) In an opinion by the chief justice, the Court acknowledged that both state governments and the federal government were constitutionally required to honor their contracts. However, in the original agreement, Congress had expressly reserved the power to amend federal charters, which meant that it was not a violation of the original agreement to make changes so long as the terms of the amendment were prospective. Field, Strong, and Bradley dissented, arguing that the decision left vested rights of contract with less protection against federal action. In Bradley's words, "it sets the example of repudiation of Government obligations" and "asserts the principle that might makes right."

The decision in the *Sinking Fund* cases, coming just two years after *Munn*, so infuriated corporate and financial elites that some of them vowed to do something about it. During the election of 1880, New York's business aristocracy, led by financier Jay Gould, expressed "real anxiety" over "the course of the Supreme Court in the Granger cases and in the Pacific R. R. case," and noted that "the next President will almost certainly have the appointment of three new Judges." (Ward Hunt was paralyzed, Nathan Clifford was ailing, and Swayne, seventy-six years old, had made it known that he intended to resign.) A letter was sent to prospective Republican nominee Garfield by Whitelaw Reid of the *Tribune*, indicating that "monied men" and "corporations" were "unwilling to elect a President unless they are sure that he disapproves what they call the revolutionary course of the majority of the court. If they could be satisfied on this point, I know we could make a big demonstration at once"—that is, a demonstration in the form of a significant campaign contribution. Garfield would not allow himself to make an overt promise on particular appointments, but he did respond in writing that "I have stated to you, fully, my well considered views of the constitution in reference to the sanctity of Contracts and of vested rights — Under no circumstances would I entrust the high functions of a Justice to the Supreme Court, to any person whom I did not believe to be entirely sound on these questions." Garfield received a reported $150,000 from Gould; along with financial support from John D. Rockefeller, he was able to squeeze out a 10,000-vote victory over his Democratic presidential opponent.

Garfield's first nomination came less than two weeks after his inauguration. He named Ohio Senator Stanley Matthews — formerly Jay Gould's chief Midwestern counsel and vigorous opponent of the Sinking Fund legislation — to fill the vacancy created by Swayne's retirement. Matthews had originally been nominated by the outgoing President Hayes but was resisted by senators who opposed his position during the Sinking Fund debates. The deference afforded a new president, however, allowed Matthews to win Senate approval by a 24–23 vote, despite complaints in the press that the appointment was the result of "powerful corporations with a view to their own purposes." Given all the efforts of the captains of industry, it seems a shame to point out that, while on the Court, Matthews was moderately conservative but did not join Field's more extreme positions on judicial protection for vested rights.

Gould's efforts to pack the Court suffered a more serious blow with Garfield's assassination. Chester Arthur, who had no "understanding" with Gould and his associates, appointed Samuel Blatchford and Horace Gray, who aligned themselves with Waite on most of the economic issues facing the Court. The push to make a conservative Court even more conservative would have to wait until after the end of the Waite Court.

The Bill of Rights

Although of little interest to those who sought to influence Supreme Court appointments, the justices also were forced to address a series of unprecedented questions relating to the meaning of the Bill of Rights in the postwar period. In *Reynolds v. U.S.* (1879), one of the most important precedents set by any Court, the justices upheld Congress's authority to outlaw polygamy. It was the first time that the Supreme Court had addressed the meaning of the First Amendment's protection for the "free exercise" of religion. The campaign to wipe out Mormon polygamy in the Utah territories had been initiated by President Grant. In order to set up a test case for the law, the Mormon Church hierarchy used the secretary to Brigham Young, George Reynolds. Chief Justice Waite's opinion emphasized that, under the First Amendment, "Congress was deprived of all legislative power over mere opinion, but was left free to reach actions which were in violation of social duties or subversive of good order." This distinction between protection for religious opinion but not religious conduct was arguably at odds with the language of the Constitution, which emphasizes the "free exercise" of religion and not merely freedom of belief, but the distinction has served the Court well over the years and has not prevented later Courts from extending constitutional protections to some religious practices.

A few years later, the Court handed down another landmark case, *Hurtado v. California* (1884), which raised the interesting and persistent question of whether the "due process" clause of the Fourteenth Amendment "incorporated" the specific guarantees of the Bill of Rights and thus applied them against the states. Under the original Constitution, it was well established that the guarantees of the Bill of Rights applied against the federal government but not state governments. When Hurtado was tried for murder in California and eventually sentenced to death, he complained about having to face trial without having first been indicted by a grand jury. California law allowed for trials to proceed based only on the filing of information by a district attorney, but Hurtado pointed out that the Fourteenth Amendment now required states to follow "due process of law," and he argued that the "process" he was "due" involved the exemplary protections of the federal Bill of Rights, including the protection of a grand jury.

The Court, in an opinion by Justice Matthews, concluded that indictment by a grand jury was not a necessary feature of "due process of law," despite the existence of that guarantee in the Bill of Rights. Due process "must be held to guarantee not particular forms of procedure, but the very substance of individual rights to life, liberty, and property." This meant that states were free to choose other procedures in criminal trials—such as commencing a murder prosecution by information rather than by grand jury indictment—as long as those procedures remained "within the limits of those fundamental principles of liberty and justice which lie at the base of all our civil and political institutions." To hold otherwise would be to prevent new processes from being developed and reconciled with due process. To avoid such a stifling, the Court held that "any legal proceeding enforced by public authority, whether sanctioned by age and custom or newly devised in the discretion of the Legislative power, in furtherance of the general public good, which regards and preserves these principles of liberty and justice, must be held to be due process of law." Once again Harlan dissented, arguing that the Framers of the Constitution believed that indictment by a grand jury was an essential safeguard against prosecutorial oppression and thus qualified as a core feature of "due process" under our constitutional system.

The opposing positions in *Hurtado* established for the next century the major terms for debating the meaning of the Fourteenth Amendment's due process clause in the area of state criminal procedure. Matthews's opinion was designed to give the states as much leeway as possible so long as the Court believed that "fundamental principles of liberty and justice" were being followed. Later, in the twentieth century, this would become known as the "fundamental fairness" approach to due process and would be the basis for refusing to impose the specific requirements of the federal Bill of Rights on all states. Justice Harlan's dissenting position later became associated with the so-called incorporation movement, which advocated using the due process clause of the Fourteenth Amendment as the basis for requiring the states to abide by the provisions of the Bill of Rights, just like the national government. It would take more than eighty years before the Supreme Court would gravitate toward Harlan's position. For the foreseeable future, a majority of Waite Court justices were content to interpret the Fourteenth Amendment in such a way as to prevent overly intrusive federal court supervision of state practices.

Assessment of the Waite Court

To maintain proper perspective on the power of the justices, it helps to realize that they were not always able to prod the political landscape to conform to their vision of American politics. In *Trist v. Child* (1875), toward the very beginning of Waite's tenure as chief, the Court ruled that courts could not enforce contracts made with a lobbyist based on a promise to obtain passage of an act of Congress. "In our jurisprudence," wrote Justice Swayne, "a contract may be illegal and void because it is contrary to a constitution or statute, or inconsistent with sound policy and good morals." He continued: "The theory of our government is, that all public stations are trusts, and that those clothed with them are to be animated in the discharge of their duties solely by considerations of right, justice, and the public good. . . . No people can have any higher public interest, except the preservation of their liberties, than integrity in the administration of their government in all its departments." Needless to say, despite the power of this vision and the unquestioned respectability of its advocates, there is no evidence that the justices had any effect whatsoever on the degree of integrity exhibited in the high offices of American politics during the 1870s and 1880s.

Still, the Waite Court was not without its accomplishments. It was the first Court to elaborate on the meaning of the Fourteenth Amendment, and the precedents this Court established would shape constitutional law in the

United States for at least a half century. In some cases, the precedents remained good law through the twenty-first century. With respect to the protection of property against state laws, the justices acted cautiously and with an eye toward long-standing constitutional practices, by accommodating many regulatory impulses. However, along with the practice of restraint came the establishment of certain constitutional principles that paved the way for the more active use of judicial power in the decades to come. The justices helped ensure the creation of a national economy by using the commerce clause to sweep away disruptive state regulation. They also encouraged and supported the expansion of federal power to promote and regulate commerce, immigration, Mormon religious practices, and Native Americans. At the same time, the justices identified limits on federal power that would be used by later Supreme Courts all the way through to the great battles of the New Deal era. The justices articulated positions on the role of the Bill of Rights in our reconstructed constitutional system that structured constitutional arguments for the next century. Most tragically, they took the lead in facilitating the deconstruction of Reconstruction, making direct federal protection of blacks virtually impossible and inviting hostile state legislation, including the imposition of Jim Crow. The best that can be said for these efforts is that the Court was taking its cue from other national power holders and was playing its role as a partner in a national governing coalition.

Chief Justice Waite died in 1888. Always a tireless worker, he had labored for months on the Court's opinion in the *Bell Telephone Cases,* which involved the validity of patents owned by the American Bell Telephone Company. The extensive opinion, which would eventually take up an entire volume of the *U.S. Reports,* was completed on March 5 and scheduled for public announcement two weeks later. In the interim, the chief justice became ill. Poor health notwithstanding, he walked to and from a senator's evening reception and the next day came down with a chill. The following day, he insisted on attending the Court's announcement of the decision that he had worked so hard to complete, but once in the Court's chambers, he found himself too weak to make the announcement himself. Attorney General Garland later said, "It was evident to the observer that death had almost placed its hands upon him." Within hours, he was diagnosed with pneumonia and passed away three days later, on March 23.

Waite's death was followed by other significant changes in the Court's personnel. By the time Stephen J. Field retired from the Court in 1897, seven new justices had been appointed. The Court constructed by Republican and conservative Democratic presidents in the late 1880s and 1890s was less inclined to caution and moderation when it came to reviewing state and federal regulations of commerce. Nevertheless, in exercising its power more aggressively, the new Supreme Court found plenty of support in the transitional yet trend-setting decisions of the Waite Court.

—HOWARD GILLMAN

FOR FURTHER READING AND RESEARCH

To learn more about the Waite Court, start with C. Peter Magrath's thoughtful and well-written biography *Morrison R. Waite: The Triumph of Character* (New York, 1963). The Court's decision making during this era is more comprehensively, albeit exhaustively, covered in Charles Fairman's *Reconstruction and Reunion, 1864–1888, Part Two* (New York, 1987), volume 7 of the *History of the Supreme Court of the United States* (the Oliver Wendell Holmes Devise). Charles Warren's *The Supreme Court in United States History* (Boston, 1926) is still a classic source of information and political analysis.

Among the more readable recent histories of the Court are Bernard Schwartz's A *History of the Supreme Court* (New York, 1993); and Melvin I. Urofsky and Paul Finkelman's *A March of Liberty: A Constitutional History of the United States, Volume I: From the Founding to 1890* (New York, 2002). David P. Currie, in *The Constitution in the Supreme Court: The First Hundred Years, 1789–1888* (Chicago, 1985), summarizes many decisions that are not reviewed in the standard Court histories. Gustavus Myers's *History of the Supreme Court of the United States* (Chicago, 1918) usefully, and provocatively, interprets these events from a more socialistic perspective, emphasizing the class connections and biases of the justices of the Gilded Age. For a more general overview of American politics and public life during this period, the best place to start is with Morton Keller's *Affairs of State: Public Life in Late Nineteenth Century America* (Cambridge, Mass., 1977).

Plate A-1 John Jay, first chief justice of the United States, 1789–1795, portrayed here in the Court's original judicial robes.

Plate A-2 The Old Royal Exchange Building (Merchants Exchange), New York City, site of the first term of the Supreme Court.

View of the State-House at Philadelphia.

Plate A-3 A view of the State House at Philadelphia, 1798, by Joseph Bowes.

Plate A-4 The Mayor's courtroom from the balcony, Old City Hall, Philadelphia, shared by the United States Supreme Court, 1791–1800.

Plate A-5 William Marbury, ardent Maryland Federalist, financier, and one of twenty-three names sent by President Adams to the Senate as justices of the peace for Washington County, District of Columbia, on the eve of his departure from office.

Plate A-6 The Old Supreme Court Chamber in the Capitol basement, restored to the style of the mid-nineteenth century. After ten years of sharing a Capitol committee room, the Court obtained use of the basement chamber in 1810 and remained there until 1861, interrupted only by four years of renovation (1815–1819).

Plate A-7 The Old Senate Chamber, ca. 1900, home of the Supreme Court from 1861 until 1935.

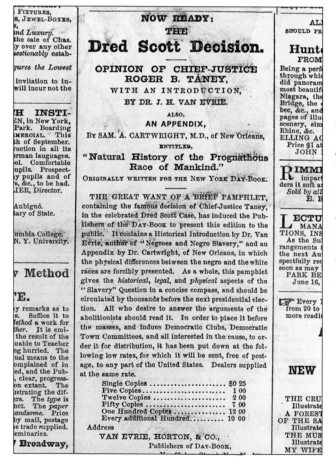

Plate A-8 The political importance of the *Dred Scott* decision is underlined in this admiring advertisement for a pamphlet version of Chief Justice Taney's opinion, produced for maximum circulation among Northern Democrats and antiabolitionists.

Plate A-9 Lambden Milligan and other Indiana civilians, arrested in 1864 for conspiracy to free and arm Confederate prisoners. Milligan was sentenced to hang by a military tribunal. The constitutionality of his arrest, trial, and conviction was addressed by the Supreme Court in *Ex parte Milligan* (1866).

Plate A-10 Qualified to practice law in Illinois, Myra Bradwell was refused admission to the state bar by the Illinois Supreme Court because of her gender. The U.S. Supreme Court found that the court's decision did not violate the Fourteenth Amendment.

Plate A-11 An officer in the National Woman Suffrage Association, Virginia Minor of St. Louis, Missouri, was denied an opportunity to register to vote in the 1872 presidential election. Minor's suit (prosecuted through her husband) reached the U.S. Supreme Court in 1874. The Court affirmed the Missouri Supreme Court's earlier decision upholding the right of states to deny suffrage to women.

Plate A-12 The satirical magazine *Puck* portrays the litigation crisis besieging the Supreme Court by the mid-1870s.

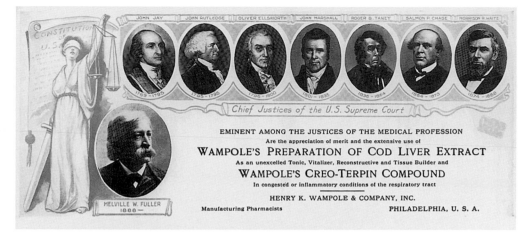

Plate A-13 This pharmaceutical company advertising blotter, ca. 1890, uses images of the nation's chief justices to affirm the honesty of its claims, an example of the heightened profile of the Supreme Court in late-nineteenth-century popular culture.

Plate A-14 The Waite Court listening to oral argument in session in the Old Senate Chamber (1888).

Plate A-15 William Jennings Bryan's 1896 presidential campaign attacks on the Supreme Court provoked *Harper's* to depict the bench under a "Popocratic" administration. Populist governors Pennoyer of Oregon and Waite of Colorado join Jacob Coxey, Eugene Debs, "Pitchfork" Ben Tillman, Illinois Governor John Peter Altgeld, Nevada Senator William M. Stewart, and 1892 Populist presidential candidate James Baird Weaver. The Constitution lies in tatters.

7

The Fuller Court   1888–1910

Property and Liberty

J USTICE MELVILLE WESTON FULLER presided over a Court that has been accused of multiple failings. No less illustrious a member than Oliver Wendell Holmes, Jr., criticized it for reading Social Darwinism into the Constitution in 1905. No less a legal scholar than Roscoe Pound condemned the Fuller Court for practicing a mechanistic formalism in 1909. To its critics, the Fuller Court was a heartless, mindless body that spouted a laissez-faire philosophy and devoted itself to protecting corporate property interests above all else: not a pretty picture and not an accurate one.

To be sure, the members of the Fuller Court hailed from backgrounds that would have tended to encourage conservatism. Chief Justice Fuller, who settled in Chicago, was originally a New Englander and college educated at a time when that was a rare privilege. So were his colleagues: Stephen J. Field, David J. Brewer (who was Field's nephew), Horace Gray, and Henry Billings Brown. But then so too was Holmes — a Boston Brahmin and a Harvard man. Their fathers were often professionals: Fuller, John Marshall Harlan, and Rufus W. Peckham came from lawyering families; Field and Brewer were ministers' sons; Holmes, Sr., was a physician and a writer. Many of them had been political partisans prior to their elevation to the bench: Party loyalties often brought them to the attention of the president who appointed them.

To replace Morrison Waite in 1888, President Grover Cleveland chose Fuller because he was a strong Democrat from the West. Fuller had hesitated before accepting the position (he made $30,000 a year as a lawyer but would earn only $10,500 on the bench), but he turned out to be a gifted chief justice and a skillful administrator of the Court's business. Fuller's charm enabled him to form friendships easily, and he worked to prevent his colleagues' disagreements from poisoning the atmosphere of their conferences.

He assigned the writing of decisions by specialty and ability and preferred to give important cases to others. This usually made his brethren happy, but they could not keep up with the increasing number of appellate cases: 1,800 were on the docket for 1890, and three years' worth of cases were waiting to be scheduled. In response to the justices' complaints, Congress in 1891 passed the Evarts Act, which established nine circuit courts of appeal and allowed the justices welcome discretion in hearing certain types of cases.

Although the Court's decision-making processes were efficient, the results remained controversial. The populace was sharply divided over how well the Fuller Court decided many of the important cases that it heard. Public opinion tended to be influenced most by outcomes in prominent cases, which were not necessarily representative of the Court's overall tenor. After all, if the Fuller Court had been dogmatically wedded to laissez-faire philosophy, it would presumably have opposed most economic regulation. Instead, it sustained the overwhelming majority of exercises of the police power — the power of the state to protect the health, safety, and welfare of its people — that came before it. Most of the laws that regulated railroads, quarantined cattle, inspected meat, prohibited lotteries, and controlled public utilities were upheld.

Similarly, rather than practicing a uniform and simplistic formalism, the members of the Fuller Court wrote opinions in a range of styles. Justice Gray loved legal research and would start with precedents as far back as Magna Carta, but he preferred to defer to legislatures just as much as Holmes, whose own opinions were startlingly short. Justice Peckham usually reasoned through a case on his own and regularly issued challenges to legislatures. Social Darwinist notions of "survival of the fittest" were far from the minds of justices like Harlan of Kentucky, who served as an elder in the Presbyterian Church, or the deeply religious Brewer, whose calling cards read, "Right is Might." In fact, the only justice who showed any admiration for Charles Darwin or his follower Herbert Spencer was Holmes himself, who also lauded Thomas Malthus's dire theories of overpopulation. Still, if the brethren were not, after all, running dogs for the capitalist class, several important decisions on economic issues did attract an enormous amount of popular complaint. For the justices were generally supporters of the legal status quo during an era that witnessed enormous economic growth and accompanying social disaster that many Americans believed to require government action.

The Fuller Court Era

The Civil War had boosted technology, mass production, and new managerial models. Refrigeration allowed year-round production of meat, which became centralized in the Midwest under such names as Swift and Armour. The Bessemer process revolutionized the steel industry and dropped the cost of constructing railroads and buildings. In 1901, Andrew Carnegie's mills alone were producing more steel than the entire nation of Britain. Oil production shot up, and John D. Rockefeller's Standard Oil Company managed to gain control of 90 percent of it. Economic growth brought on legal conflict: The Supreme Court had passed on the interstate commerce clause in only 5 cases before 1840; by 1898, the justices had pored over the clause in 213 cases. Justice Samuel F. Miller, who had been a commercial lawyer before coming to the bench in 1862, told his law students in 1889 that "the time has come when the Constitution and laws of the United States are not the mere theoretical object of the thoughts of the statesman, the lawyer, or the man of affairs: For the operations of its Government now reach to the recesses of every man's business, and force themselves upon every man's thoughts."

The Fuller Court helped along corporate growth and the accumulation of immense fortunes by extending legal protections to the national marketplace. The Court did this for two reasons: One was its institutional guardianship over interstate commerce and private property, and the other was its members' commitment to a continuing economic and political recovery from the Civil War. The Court's willingness in *Minnesota v. Barber* (1890) to strike down a state tax law that discriminated against out-of-state products is an example of the first impulse, as were the justices' slightly confused attempts to prevent double taxation of the same property by two different states; compare *Steamship Co. v. Pennsylvania* (1887), *Maine v. Grand Trunk Railway Co.* (1891), and *Galveston, Harrisburg, & San Antonio Railway Co. v. Texas* (1908). Individual states might prefer to favor their own residents and gouge outsiders through their tax laws, but the Court stopped them with the interstate commerce clause and the rules of tax residency. In an analogous way, the Fuller Court's opposition to municipal bond repudiation created a truly national market in local bonds through its application of the law merchant. The blunt-spoken Justice Miller denounced the bond decisions as "a farce" that favored the haves over the have-nots. Westerners who were grappling with local cases of fraud resented having to pay off bonds for railroads that had never been built. But without the Court's support, bonds from one part of the country would not have found buyers elsewhere. A national marketplace of investment bound the regions of the nation together and allowed railroads, waterworks, and other local improvement projects to flourish.

The economic growth of the period was spectacular and the standard of living increased. But the costs were great. Twelve-hour workdays were typical in factories, and even with long hours, a man's wages were not enough to support a family. Workers fought back in union campaigns that sometimes ended in bloodshed. A strike in 1892 at Andrew Carnegie's Homestead, Pennsylvania, steel mill left sixteen dead, all the union men fired, and wages cut by 50 percent. And work could not always be found. The failure of a Pennsylvania railroad company early in 1893 provoked a stock market crash that caused 500 banks and 15,000 businesses to go under. Thousands of men and women found themselves out of work during the worst depression of the century. In the West and the South, farmers complained throughout the period that railroad monopolies overcharged, discriminated among shippers, and bought up the state legislators who elected U.S. senators. Frank Norris captured the power of the railroads when he dubbed the Southern Pacific Railroad *The Octopus* in his 1901 novel. The farmers organized themselves and by 1892 had reached out to labor leaders in order to form the Populist Party, which called for shorter industrial workdays and a graduated income tax. The Populists also wanted to alter the political economy of the United States; as one explained in 1895, "The way to avoid railroad ownership of the government is to have government ownership of the railroads."

Popular demands for action produced new state and national regulations that were in turn challenged before the Fuller Court. The justices found themselves most divided, and most hated, in their efforts to cope with regulations that obviously redistributed wealth or interfered with contractual relations. Opposition to such legislation reflected uneasiness with new governmental forms, such as the railroad commission, and with new understandings of the economy. Despite the growth of corporations and unions, the individual male remained the primary actor in the economy for the older justices. A man's freedom to act in the marketplace remained valuable as an expression of human capacity, as a source of personal wealth, and as an engine of social good. Justice Joseph P. Bradley, who ended his long career on the Court in 1892, once explained that *political* equality was what the founding fathers were referring to in the Declaration of Independence. *Economic* equality was a bad idea for two reasons. First, because God-given human faculties varied naturally, "there are many species of luxury"—such as art, literature, and music—"which the great mass of mankind are incapable of enjoying." Second, the redistribution of wealth was counterproductive, for it "would smother enterprise, produce listlessness," and make one man dependent on others. The older justices generally agreed that capitalism suited human nature and benefited society.

So when it intervened in the economy, government needed to take care that it did not unconstitutionally impinge on the rights of the individual. The judges all insisted that they were passing on the constitutionality of legislation, not its wisdom—they were judges, not legislators—but some of them clearly thought the more aggressive tendencies in economic regulation to be unwise. Justice Harlan explained in a speech from 1908 of the need to counter "the pernicious doctrines of the present day that are called socialism and paternalism." What was merely a reasonable exercise of the state police power and what crossed the line into paternalism divided the judges. Justice Brewer uttered one of his best-known lines in 1892 — "The paternal theory of government is to me odious"— in his dissent in *Budd v. New York*, in which Justices Field and Brown joined. The majority upheld a New York law that set a maximum rate for storage at privately owned grain elevators. Justice Samuel Blatchford explained that the legislature might regulate natural monopolies on which farmers and dealers were forced to depend. He relied on the rule formulated in *Munn v. Illinois* (1877), in which the Waite Court had approved a so-called Granger law (sympathetic to farmer interests and named after the Granges, farmers' organizations) on the ground that a grain elevator was a business affected with a public interest. Rufus W. Peckham, who would be appointed to the Supreme Court three years later, had dissented when New York's highest court upheld the law in 1889. He denounced it as vicious, communistic, and inefficient. Justice Harlan, however, had been a member of the majority. It is unlikely that he would have voted to uphold a "communistic" law.

If these issues divided the Court, much more did they attract criticism. One legal journal sputtered in response to Justice Brewer's announcement that he found paternalism odious, "What if it is? He was not put there to decide constitutional questions according to what was or was not odious to him personally." Popular hostility peaked in 1895 in response to three decisions that seemed completely inconsistent for their declarations of the scope of government power: *U.S. v. E. C. Knight Co.*, the *Income Tax Cases*, and *In re Debs*. Not since its 1857 decision in *Dred Scott* had the Supreme Court encountered such a hail of abuse.

The Scope of Government Power

E. C. Knight

By 1890, each of twenty-one states had its own antitrust statute designed to prevent the corporations it had chartered from combining their assets to form monopolies, but the statutes' effectiveness depended crucially on the maintenance of the prohibition by all states. In 1889, the New Jersey legislature allowed its corporations to take control of companies chartered by other states (called foreign corporations) through an exchange of stock. Some 280 corporations rechartered in New Jersey, which collected a lucrative tax in exchange. Public outcry against the trusts intensified, and in 1890, Congress passed the Sherman Anti-Trust Act with only one vote opposed. The act prohibited "every contract, combination in the form of trust or otherwise, or conspiracy, in restraint of trade or commerce among the several States, or with foreign nations." The United States brought suit against the E. C. Knight Company and three other Pennsylvania-chartered companies, all of which had swapped stock with the giant American Sugar Refining Company of New Jersey that now controlled 98 percent of the business of refining sugar in the country. Speaking for eight of the justices, Chief Justice Fuller found for the companies on the ground that they were engaged in manufacturing, which was a local activity controlled by state law, not in interstate commerce, which would have fallen under congressional authority and the Sherman Act. "Commerce succeeds to manufacture, and is not a part of it."

This distinction seemed pointless to the lone dissenter, Justice Harlan. Although he nodded to the importance of preserving federalism, he was distressed at the power of the trusts, which he doubted the states could control. "Suppose another combination, organized for private gain and to control prices, should obtain possession of all the large flour mills in the United States; another, of all the grain elevators; another, of all the oil territory; another, of all the salt-producing regions. . . . What power is competent to protect the people of the United States against such dangers except national power?" The *Northwestern Law Review* chimed in: "It looks doubtful if the government would ever be able to control such powerful, shrewd and rich monopolies or trusts." Many Americans felt as though the country had been left without protection.

Fuller had not created a legal no man's land where neither nation nor state could act. Pennsylvania, in this instance, could still go after its own corporations for joining in a trust. But state prosecutors had too much to do to prosecute each business, and state officials feared losing important manufacturing concerns to states with more indulgent attitudes toward trusts. Cooperation among the states proved unsuccessful: Too many were tempted "toward the lowest level of law regulation," as the U.S. commissioner on corporations reported in 1904. Practically, it would fall to the nation to act.

Income Tax Cases

The second controversy of 1895 also involved a federal law that was struck down by the Court. This time, the Court was closely divided and its reasoning specious.

The Wilson-Gorman Tariff Act of 1894 was designed to shift the burden of federal taxation. Until its passage, federal taxes had largely been tariffs, falling most heavily on consumption and thus disproportionately on poorer Americans who had to consume most of what they earned. The new plan was to lay a 2 percent tax on incomes over $4,000, with exemptions for charitable, religious, and educational corporations, as well as mutual insurance companies and mutual banks. Two percent might seem a marvelously low rate today, but at the time, the tax appeared to wealthy Americans and conservative newspapers to be the thin end of a communist wedge. The debate in Congress was bitter, with western and southern Democrats in favor of the law and northeastern Republicans opposed. Congress stipulated that no court could hear a suit to restrain collection of the tax, but a canny New York lawyer with the help of a sympathetic U.S. solicitor general (who would be fired for his trouble) found a way. The lawyer brought suit against Farmer's Loan and Trust Company in the name of one Charles Pollock of Massachusetts on behalf of Pollock and other shareholders who complained that the company intended to pay the tax, which was allegedly unconstitutional, and so would lessen the value of the shares they held. The case, heard twice by the Court, in March and April, turned on the question whether a tax on income from personal property and real estate was a direct tax under the Constitution. Direct taxes had to be apportioned among the states according to the size of their populations. Precedents held that an income tax was not a direct tax (one had been levied during the Civil War). Apportioning an income tax in any case made very little sense.

The lawyers for Pollock emphasized the radical implications of the law. One warned, "The act of Congress which we are impugning before you is communistic in its purposes and tendencies." Another fumed, "I have thought that one of the fundamental objects of all civilized government was the preservation of the rights of private property." The opposing attorney for the trust company gave a different warning to the justices: "Nothing could be more unwise and dangerous — nothing more foreign to the spirit of the Constitution — than an attempt to baffle and defeat a popular determination by a judgment in a lawsuit." But the majority of the Court, speaking through Chief Justice Fuller in both instances, held that the tax was direct under the Constitution and so had to be apportioned according to each state's population — a questionable interpretation at best. Only Justices White and Harlan dissented in the first instance. Brown and Jackson joined them in the second.

The justices' arguments over the decision mirrored the division of the American people over the value of an income tax. Justice Field, who seems to have been unhappily impressed by the Paris Commune of 1871, concurred in the first decision and predicted: "The present assault upon capital is but the beginning. It will be but the stepping-stone to others, larger and more sweeping, till our political contests will become a war of the poor against the rich; a war constantly growing in intensity and bitterness." Justice Brown also feared for the future of the country, but his concerns were the opposite of Field's. He hoped that the decision "may not prove the first step toward the submergence of the liberties of the people in a sordid despotism of wealth." The impassioned and sometimes sarcastic manner in which Harlan delivered his dissent (Field further provoked him by muttering under his breath all the while) attracted the scorn of conservative papers, which accused him of acting like a Populist politician. A Brooklyn paper praised the majority: "May God long spare the lives of the judges and keep them on duty who have smitten down this monstrous wrong in the temple of human law." But the monster would not stay smitten. In its platform for the 1896 presidential election, the Democratic Party called for Congress to find some way to institute an income tax. And so began the effort that would culminate in passage of the Sixteenth Amendment to the Constitution, proposed in Congress in 1909 and ratified by the states in 1913, giving Congress the "power to lay and collect taxes on incomes, from whatever source derived, without apportionment among the several States." The income tax became the chief source of revenue during World War I.

In re Debs

The last controversy of 1895 made the apparent helplessness of the national government implied by the majority in the two prior cases especially vexing to onlookers. It began in a place originally designed to harmonize the interests of labor and capital: the town of Pullman near Chicago. George Pullman, inventor of the Pullman railroad car, built a model town to free his workers from the dark, unhealthy tenements typical of big cities. The town offered its residents broad avenues and brick housing with gas and water, a shopping arcade, a theater, a library, and parks. A committee of the Illinois Bureau of Labor Statistics visited in 1884 and was impressed. George Pullman had always insisted that he was simply an enlightened businessman who knew that what was good for his workers was good for him, but the committee praised the town's plan as "conceived and executed in a spirit of broad and unostentatious philanthropy." The Pullman Company made the most of its good press, and visitors came from all over the world to see for themselves.

The trouble that destroyed the town's image began when the depression hit in 1893 and the Pullman Company cut wages up to 30 percent. The workers complained that they could not cover the fixed rents charged for company housing, but George Pullman refused to drop them. The workers decided to strike, and their plight caught the eye of the American Railway Union (ARU), which voted not to handle Pullman railroad cars until the disagreement had been resolved.

The ARU's president, Eugene V. Debs, put out the call. By the end of June, workers on all the railroads in the Midwest were refusing to switch or haul Pullman cars. The General Managers Association (GMA), made up of the twenty-four railroads that ran out of Chicago, called for an end to the boycott. Businessmen and middle-class Americans feared that a nation-wide strike would cause economic chaos. There was frightened talk in the newspapers of possible food shortages, of children crying for milk. Illinois Governor John Peter Altgeld, who had long been allied with labor, refused to send in state officers to break up the strike. But the GMA had more luck with the U.S. attorney general, who deputized 3,400 men to run the trains. The deputies clashed with the workers and their supporters, and the violence increased the fears of the federal authorities. President Grover Cleveland sent in federal troops to put down the strike, and the attorney general obtained an injunction in early July from the federal circuit court to prevent Debs and other union men from leading the strike. When Debs refused to obey the injunction, he was arrested for contempt of court. With the union leaders jailed, the strike collapsed. The first local attorney Debs asked to defend him was one of Justice Harlan's sons, who refused for fear of being identified with a radical cause. Justice Harlan would later remark that Governor Altgeld was "not worth the powder it would take to blow him up." Nevertheless, he urged his son to reconsider because the case was so important. By then, however, Clarence Darrow, a railroad attorney, had quit his job in order to defend Debs.

Darrow petitioned the Supreme Court for a writ of habeas corpus, but a unanimous bench denied it. Justice Brewer declared in *In re Debs* on May 27, 1895, that the national government had the power to ensure the free flow of interstate commerce and the mails against such forcible ob-struction as organized by the conspiring union leaders. Debs and his men had actually offered to handle trains with mail cars so long as no Pullman cars were attached, but the GMA had refused the compromise in order to bring down the wrath of the federal government on the union. Brewer took pleasure in the majestic power of the nation: "If the emergency arises, the army of the Nation, and all its militia, are at the service of the Nation to compel obedience to its laws." Brewer stressed that the injunction was a perfectly proper remedy. The federal government did not have to stand around waiting for the machinery of criminal procedure to gear up in order to take on marauding strikers.

But an injunction meant sidestepping many of the protections built into the criminal law. An injunction could be so broad that it need not even name the individuals to whom it applied; the judge who issued it also had the power to punish all those whom he thought had violated its terms; there was no jury of one's peers where one might find more sympathy for labor. When Debs was released after serving six months in jail, he told the crowd welcoming him home that an injunction "is not a law in and by the representatives of the people; it is not a law signed by a President or by a governor. It is simply the wish and will of the judge." Populist politicians asked for Congress to limit the power of the courts to issue injunctions. The Democratic Party platform of 1896 denounced the practice as well. Railroad managers and other businessmen, meanwhile, learned to ask routinely for injunctions in order to cripple strikes. The willingness of state and federal courts at all levels to issue labor injunctions provoked labor leaders and their supporters to write bitterly of "Government by Injunction."

Consequences of the 1895 Decisions

As a result of its 1895 decisions, the Supreme Court came to be seen by many Americans as an enemy of the people, an institution captured by the wealthy. It was defended by many others, who complained that the Democratic platform was an attack on constitutional government. In 1896, the Populists endorsed the Democratic candidate for president, William Jennings Bryan, a renowned orator from Nebraska, but some Democrats broke from the party and ran their own candidate. The Republican Party ran William McKinley, governor of Ohio, as a responsible alternative to Bryan, whom they branded an anarchist and a revolutionary. Other issues played a part in the election of McKinley to the presidency, but the Democratic attack on the Court had frightened voters who feared the Constitution was itself at stake (Plate A.15). As the economic situation improved, class tensions eased, but criticisms of the Court continued through the end of Chief Justice Fuller's term in 1910.

The controversial decisions of 1895 raised issues that repeatedly divided the Court, the legal community, and the American people: the power of the courts, the power of the legislatures, and the nature and direction of the economy. These issues came up as the brethren under Chief Justice Fuller tried to distinguish between legitimate exercises of governmental power and illegitimate abuses of power that took property from one group of citizens and handed it over to another.

Three areas show the difficulties the Court faced. Rate regulation involved public carriers, such as railroads, and posed the problem of how to be fair to both the public and the owners. Antitrust laws were invoked against unions as well as corporations. And labor laws designed to improve the conditions of industrial workers raised the question of just how far the state could go to protect the individual. The English legal scholar James Bryce pointed out that federal judges with life tenure were immune to political pressures, so their virtue was rarely tempted. But he added, "It is true that a virtue is compatible with a certain bias of the mind, and compatible also with the desire to extend the power and jurisdiction of the court." Particularly as the Fuller Court's older members ceded place to younger men, such as Justice McKenna, who replaced Justice Field in 1897, and Justice Day, who came to the Court in 1903, such biases became more apparent in deepening differences among the Court's members over assumptions about political economy.

Rate Regulation

Because the states could not control interstate commerce, rate regulation by federal bodies was the only constitutional way to control shipping rates set by the railroads. Efforts had been made since the 1870s to create a federal commission to control interstate commerce and especially to police the abuses of the railroads. The House of Representatives twice approved a law, but the more conservative Senate struck it down. Then in 1887, after extensive public hearings, Congress passed the Interstate Commerce Act. The act prohibited pools, discriminatory rates and rebates, and higher rates on short hauls than on long hauls over the same line but did not authorize the commission to fix rates. The act provided only that rates be reasonable and just. Historians now argue that the act set the commission up for failure.

The brethren were uneasy about administrative commissions for another reason. They were governmental hybrids — part executive, part judicial, and part legislative in character — and this made them appear illegitimately powerful as well. Hence, in *I.C.C. v. Alabama Midland Railway Company* (1897), the Court refused to allow the Interstate Commerce Commission (ICC) to set rates. The commission had ordered the railroad to stop charging higher rates on freight shipped between eastern cities and Troy, Alabama, than it charged on freight shipped between those cities and Montgomery, some fifty miles farther west. The railroad appealed the order on the grounds that the two cities were not in similar circumstances; several railroads converged on Montgomery, which meant that it had to compete by offering shippers lower rates, but Alabama Midland faced no competition in Troy. The Court agreed, but Justice Harlan, who thought that monopolies threatened the nation with a new form of slavery, complained in dissent that the ICC "has been shorn, by judicial interpretation, of authority to do anything of an effective character." And indeed, after 1898, the ICC devoted itself almost exclusively to the collection of information and publication of statistics. Rates continued to rise, and farmers and other small shippers continued to lobby for protection from the railroads.

In 1906, President Theodore Roosevelt's efforts to revive the ICC resulted in the passage of the Hepburn Act, which gave the commission clear authority to fix "just and reasonable" rates and expanded its jurisdiction. In *I.C.C. v. Illinois Central Railroad Company* (1910), Justice White, a Louisiana Catholic who had come to the Court in 1894 and was usually opposed to economic regulation, showed an awareness of the complaints that had arisen about the Court's hostility toward the commission. "Power to make the order and not the mere expediency or wisdom of having made it, is the question," White wrote in upholding the power of the commission to tell a railroad how to distribute coal cars during a car shortage. But earlier, in *Harriman v. I.C.C.* (1908), the Court had limited the commission's investigatory powers to those matters about which complaints had been made. Edward Henry Harriman, a railroad tycoon, had been called before the commission to testify on consolidation schemes among the railroads but refused to answer certain questions put to him. Justice Holmes held for the Court that the commission had exceeded its authority, but Justices Day, Harlan, and McKenna protested in dissent that "the act should not be construed so narrowly as to defeat its purposes." Once more, they complained, the Court was unnecessarily restricting the commission's reach.

Years earlier, the states had made their own efforts to regulate the rates on commerce within their borders through commissions or statutes, but the Court had been as suspicious of the willingness of the states to safeguard the interests of the owners of railroads as it would later be of the ICC's. Eventually, the Court set itself up as the final arbiter of the reasonableness of rates. As Justice Bradley pointed out in his dissent in *Chicago, Milwaukee and St. Paul Railway Co. v. Minnesota* (1890), this meant breaking from the rule laid down in *Munn* that the states could determine how to regulate the rates charged by businesses affected with a public interest. In this case, the Court struck down a Minnesota law as a violation of the Fourteenth Amendment because the law did not provide for judicial review of the rates set by the state's Railroad and Warehouse Commission. Justice Blatchford argued that the law was unconstitutional because "it deprives the company of its right to a judicial investigation, by due process of law, under the forms and with the machinery provided by the wisdom of successive ages for the investigation judicially of the truth of a matter in controversy." It was up to the judiciary to decide whether the rates set were in fact reasonable. Rates that were set so low as to deprive the railroad of its property without compensation violated due process of law.

Justice Bradley was correct in pointing out that the Court was setting aside *Munn*, but in so doing, it was simultaneously invoking a different kind of precedent. Justice Brewer made this clear in *Reagan v. Farmers' Loan and Trust Co.* (1894), when he analogized the power of rate setting with the power of eminent domain. In both exercises of power, the government was taking private property: In each, it was the Court's job to determine whether the compensation offered was adequate. Justice Brewer, who liked to use rhetorical questions to make his strongest points, asked:

> If the State were to seek to acquire the title to these roads, under its power of eminent domain, is there any doubt that constitutional provisions would require the payment to the corporation of just compensation, that compensation being the value of the property as it stood in the markets of the world, and not as prescribed by an act of the legislature? Is it any less a departure from the obligations of justice to seek to take not the title but the use for the public benefit at less than its market value?

Fear of the government's capacity to redistribute wealth was clear.

If the Court were to pass on the reasonableness of rates, it would have to take on the work of a railroad commission itself. In fact, it busied itself in trying to do precisely that. In *Reagan v. Farmers' Loan and Trust Co.*, for example, the unanimous Court not only considered the rates set by the Texas commission but also reviewed the railroad's construction and operating costs and its financial situation. The high point of this effort came in *Smyth v. Ames* (1898), an opinion written by Justice Harlan. In considering the rate schedule set by the Populist-controlled Nebraska legislature, Harlan articulated what came to be called the fair-value rule. According to the rule, the judiciary was to play a key role in determining whether a state's rates were so low that they prevented a railroad "from earning such compensation as under all the circumstances is just to it and to the public." The Court felt no need to guarantee a road its operating expenses or the dividends on its stock, as it might be run inefficiently or corruptly. The corporation's interests *and* the public interests had to be considered. "How such compensation may be ascertained, and what are the necessary elements in such an inquiry, will always be an embarrassing question," Harlan admitted. Then he suggested that construction costs, improvement costs, the present costs of construction, earning capacity, and operating expenses might all be factored into the equation.

State legislatures were not pleased with this line of decisions; nor have historians been particularly complimentary in their assessment of the fair-value formula. They point out that the federal courts had neither the time nor the expertise to act as a supercommission and, potentially, were usurping the powers of the legislative branch. Economists charge that the Fuller Court simply created a circular formula—rates charged would determine the value of the railroad, which would determine the rates charged, and so forth. But the Court's effort in *Smyth* also reflected a general belief that a monopoly, which many railroads were in most of the counties through which they ran, must be limited to a morally justifiable level of profit. The contemporaneous reform movement for a limit of 5 percent profit on tenement housing is an example from outside the courtroom of a belief in the need for a moral limit on profits. The same principle was to be applied in the rate cases: The public should not gouge the railroad, but neither should the railroad gouge the public.

Antitrust Decisions

Obviously, the Court's decision in *E. C. Knight* (1895) had left many Americans afraid that the Court was opposed to antitrust legislation and would allow monopolies to gouge the public. Their fears were exaggerated. In fact, the commitment of the older justices to the economic ideal of individuals working out their own destinies in the marketplace made them suspicious of large combinations. For example, Justice Peckham, who had denounced as communism state regulation of grain elevators, also delivered the opinion in *United States v. Trans-Missouri Freight Association* (1897), which held that the Sherman Act applied to a freight association, one of whose objects was the private setting of rates. Peckham's support for these prosecutions was based on the legal precedents in which restraints of trade had been held illegal and on his conception, drawn from political economy, that the country would suffer if every independent dealer were reduced to being a "mere servant or agent of a corporation." Justice Peckham also delivered *U.S. v. Joint Traffic Association* in 1898, which upheld the prosecution of an association formed by railroads for the purpose of jointly agreeing what rates to charge their customers. Without oversight, declared the Court, even if the rates that the railroads had currently agreed to abide by were reasonable, the railroads in association might increase them arbitrarily at any time. "It is the combination of these large and powerful corporations, covering vast sections of territory and influencing trade through out the whole extent thereof . . . that constitutes the alleged evil."

The evil of combinations in restraint of trade was spectacularly exposed the next year in another decision delivered by Peckham: *Addyston Pipe and Steel Company v. U.S.* A disgruntled employee had handed over to the federal government damning evidence of an agreement among companies manufacturing pipe to set prices in collaboration and to avoid competing in each other's markets. Thus, Addyston Pipe and Steel had control over the Cincinnati area, another corporation was handed control of Louisville, the next got Atlanta, and so forth. The scheme allowed the companies control of their own prices. Even though these were manufacturing companies, as in *E. C. Knight,* the Court did not hesitate to condemn the combination as an attempt to restrain trade. It was clear that the combination's whole purpose was to interfere with the normal course of interstate commerce and competition. A similar decision came in *Swift and Co. v. U.S.* (1905), the federal prosecution of the Beef Trust. The government charged that, in order to regulate prices and shipments, a large number of companies in the meatpacking industry had agreed not to bid competitively against one another. The defendants claimed that they were engaged only in intrastate commerce and production and cited *E. C. Knight* repeatedly. But the Court would not entertain the defense. Justice Holmes set out what came to be called his stream-of-commerce doctrine. "When cattle are sent for sale from a place in one State, with the expectation that they will end their transit, after purchase, in another, and when in effect they do so, with only the interruption necessary to find a purchaser at the stock yards, and when this is a typical, constantly recurring course, the current thus existing is a current of commerce among the States." When the meatpackers restrained this stream of commerce, they violated the Sherman Act.

Whereas *Addyston Pipe* and *Swift* were obvious violations of the Sherman Act, according to the unanimous opinion of the justices, *Northern Securities Co. v. U.S.* (1904) raised the question whether a stock-swapping scheme would also fall afoul of the act. Encouraged by President Theodore Roosevelt, who boasted of his trust-busting ambitions, federal prosecutors had taken on two of the best-known robber barons — J. P. Morgan and James J. Hill — who had created the Northern Securities Company to hold the stock of three railroads. Justice Harlan held that the company was designed to restrain trade by ending competition among the three roads. *Northern Securities* popularized the antitrust movement as never before, but it also signaled a division within the Court. The dissenters, who included Justices White and Holmes, objected to such a broad construction of the commerce clause. They also objected that the Sherman Act applied only to unreasonable restraints of trade, not to every restraint of trade. Arguably, every contract in existence had the necessary effect of restraining trade. The question whether a distinction should be recognized between reasonable and unreasonable restraints had also produced dissenters in

Trans-Missouri Freight and *Joint Traffic*. It would eventually produce a bitter argument between Justice Harlan and a new majority headed by White, by then the new chief justice, in the Great Trust Cases of 1911.

Convinced on the whole that corporate combinations had organized in order to violate the natural laws of competition, the justices were equally of the opinion that unions did the same and so applied the Sherman Act to them as well. *Loewe v. Lawlor* (1908), popularly known as the Danbury hatters' case, began when the hatters' union tried to organize a national boycott against hats made in Dietrich Loewe's nonunionized factory in Danbury, Connecticut. Loewe and his partner brought suit under the Sherman Act against Martin Lawlor, national secretary of the United Hatters, and other union men. The United Hatters argued that the secondary boycott that they had organized did not amount to a conspiracy in restraint of trade. It was true that antitrust legislation grew out of a popular concern with domineering corporations, but the language of the act did not exclude labor unions, although efforts had been made to have it do so. In 1908, the Court unanimously declared in *Loewe v. Lawlor* that the act prohibited all combinations in restraint of trade, including union boycotts. Speaking through Justice Fuller, the Court remanded the case to the federal district court for trial. The jury awarded Loewe $74,000, which under the Sherman Act's triple-damages provision became $222,000. The hatters won an appeal but then lost on retrial in 1912. The unions turned for help to Congress, which in 1914 passed the Clayton Anti-Trust Act, which declared that "the labor of a human being is not a commodity or article of commerce." Though hailed as "Labor's Magna Carta," it is debatable whether this amounted to much in the way of concrete assistance.

Labor Laws

Concern about the power of both the state and corporations to undermine a man's freedom (it was agreed that a woman, being of the weaker sex, had less contractual freedom) to contract provoked the last set of cases in which the Fuller Court wrestled with a new vision of the economy. *Allgeyer v. Louisiana* (1897) was the first decision in which the Court held that the due process clause of the Fourteenth Amendment barred the states from violating an individual's liberty of contract unless the state could show a reasonable justification for so doing.

The law at issue in *Allgeyer* involved an out-of-state insurance policy, but the decision's ultimate impact was on labor regulation. Louisiana, like many other states, allowed "foreign" corporations (those chartered in other states) to do business within its borders only if they met certain conditions, and it prohibited its residents from doing business with corporations that had not complied with the law. E. Allgeyer & Company had contracted with a non-compliant New York firm for a policy to cover the shipment of one hundred bales of cotton and was fined $3,000 by the state of Louisiana. Speaking for a unanimous Court, Justice Rufus W. Peckham held that the liberty protected by the Fourteenth Amendment was broad, embracing "the right of the citizen to be free in the enjoyment of all his faculties; to be free to use them in all lawful ways; to live and work where he will; to earn his livelihood by any lawful calling; to pursue any livelihood or avocation, and for that purpose to enter into all contracts which may be proper, necessary and essential to his carrying out to a successful conclusion the purposes above mentioned." Louisiana could not prohibit its residents from making valid contracts outside the state. *Allgeyer* clearly freed insurance companies to sell policies in the national marketplace and so expressed the Court's commitment to the encouragement of interstate commerce. But the case did more than that. It placed the burden on the state to justify the reasonableness of *any* restraint it placed on liberty of contract that affected any kind of otherwise lawful economic activity. Although the law at issue in *Allgeyer* involved an insurance policy, the decision's ultimate impact was on labor regulation.

Justice Peckham had long felt that economic regulation by the state overreached legitimate governmental powers. While he sat on the New York Court of Appeals from 1887 until 1895, he championed the argument made in Justice Stephen J. Field's dissent from *Munn v. Illinois* (1877) that the liberty guaranteed by the Fourteenth Amendment included freedom to make use of one's property without undue interference by the government. In *People v. Gillson* (1888), for example, Peckham struck down the rather silly application of an antilottery law to a promotional scheme hatched by the Atlantic & Pacific Tea Company to give away a teacup and saucer with the purchase of coffee. As he would in *Allgeyer,* Peckham explained here that "the term 'liberty' as used in the Constitution is not dwarfed into mere freedom from physical restraint of the person as by incarceration, but is deemed to embrace the right of man to be free in the enjoyment of the faculties with which he has been endowed by his creator, subject only to such restraints as are necessary for the common welfare."

Once seated on the country's highest bench, Peckham could set national precedents that severely limited state regulation of economic matters. It was no surprise, then, that Justice Peckham dissented along with Justice Brewer from the decision in *Holden v. Hardy* (1898). Here, the Court decided that the state of Utah was justified in enacting a law limiting the employment of underground miners to eight hours a day. Albert F. Holden had been fined for employing one man for ten hours a day at an underground mine and another for twelve at a mill for reducing ores. He protested that the statute was class legislation that violated his and their liberty to contract freely. Justice Brown was unimpressed. He noted that "the law is, to a certain extent, a progressive science" and that the states had altered their views of what were proper exercises of their police power over the health, safety, and welfare of their citizens. Indeed, mining was the most dangerous industrial work at the time; according to some estimates, three miners were killed every two days. Brown explained that "classes of persons, particularly those engaged in dangerous or unhealthful employments, have been found to be in need of additional protection." The majority in *Holden* found that men working in mines could reasonably be placed among such classes.

Men working in bakeries, on the other hand, could not, at least according to the majority in *Lochner v. New York* (1905), in which the Court struck down a state law that barred bakers from working a sixty-hour week as an unconstitutional infringement on an individual male's right to liberty of contract. Women were another matter altogether, as the owner of Grand Laundry in Portland, Oregon, learned when he was prosecuted for violating a state law that set ten hours as the maximum that women could be allowed to work in laundries or factories. Curt Muller was fined $10 but appealed the conviction all the way to the Supreme Court. At the request of the National Consumer's League and with its help, Louis D. Brandeis, known as the People's Lawyer before he joined the Court in 1916, took up the state's argument in *Muller v. Oregon*. If the Court needed to be persuaded that the law was a legitimate exercise of the state's police power over the health, safety, and welfare of its citizens, he would do it. Brandeis spent only two pages of his brief on the legal precedents. The remaining ninety-five pages quoted from European and American reports on factory conditions and medical data in order to prove that such long hours took an inevitable toll on women's health. The Court was convinced. Justice Brewer, the man who found governmental paternalism odious, spoke for all his brethren in expressing their agreement that the statute passed constitutional muster. The vast evidence — everything from a report of factory inspectors for imperial Germany to the testimony of a Massachusetts physician — proved that arduous work at excessive hours harmed women physically and "as healthy mothers are essential to vigorous offspring, the physical well-being of woman becomes an object of public interest and care in order to preserve the strength and vigor of the race." Brewer took care to note that the biological differences "properly placed" woman in a class by herself "and legislation designed for her protection may be sustained, even when like legislation is not necessary for men and could not be sustained." Brewer may have thought so, but legal progressives were buoyed by the success of the Brandeis Brief and learned to copy its approach. It taught them that given sufficient statistical, sociological, and economic information, the Court could be convinced that a state had sufficient reason to exercise its police power in labor issues.

Despite *Muller,* liberty of contract remained a legitimate concept in the eyes of most of the members of the Fuller Court. The Civil War might have increased its legitimacy in the eyes of some, as the right to contract had been denied to free slaves and was treasured by freedmen and women. This was especially true of Justice Harlan, the only consistent advocate of black civil rights. A former slaveholder who embraced the Republican Party, Harlan dissented in the *Civil Rights Cases* (1883) and *Plessy v. Ferguson* (1896) in ringing words that condemned any judicial approval of the legacy of slavery. In *Hodges v. U.S.* (1906), he argued in dissent that white terrorists who drove black men from their jobs had effectively denied their right to contract to work. Harlan carried this understanding of liberty into the industrial setting. So it was Harlan who struck down the Erdman Act of 1898 that Congress had passed in order to avoid a repeat of the paralysis of the railroads that accompanied the Pullman Strike of 1894. One of its provisions prohibited employers from requiring workers involved in interstate commerce to sign contracts in which they promised not to join unions, from firing workers for joining unions, and from compiling blacklists of unionized workers to circulate among employers. This first provision banned what were called "yellow dog contracts" after the slang of the day for a low-down or no-account thing or person.

Justice Harlan insisted in *Adair v. U.S.* (1908), despite the split vote in *Lochner v. New York* three years earlier, that the brethren were all agreed that there was such a thing as liberty of contract and here applied it to the federal government through the Fifth Amendment. The contract provisions of the Erdman Act exceeded Congress's constitutional power over interstate commerce. "What possible legal or logical connection is there between an employee's membership in a labor organization and the carrying on of interstate commerce?" Harlan asked rhetorically. The Erdman Act's contract provisions were several steps more remote from interstate commerce than was the Oregon labor statute in *Muller* from its concern for the health of its female citizens, but Justice Joseph McKenna answered Harlan's question in his dissent: Dismissals of union members could provoke strikes that could shut down the nation's commerce. Holmes, as in *Lochner,* insisted that so long as the legislature had power over a particular subject, it should be allowed to make policy decisions — even to the point of encouraging labor unions — even though the justices disagreed with their wisdom.

The wisdom of encouraging labor unions divided Americans of the period, but what really irked legal progressives was Justice Harlan's emphasis in *Adair* on the equality of rights between employer and employee, the one to fire and the other to quit: "the employer and the employee have equality of right, and any legislation that disturbs that equality is an arbitrary interference with the liberty of contract which no government can legally justify in a free land." To assert that corporate employers of hundreds or thousands stood on an equal legal footing with each one of those employees seemed to progressives less important than the obvious imbalance of power between them. In this instance, William Adair represented the Louisville Nashville Railroad Company, which hardly seemed to have been reduced to an equality in bargaining powers with the worker it fired for joining the Brotherhood of Locomotive Firemen.

Law professor Roscoe Pound, then of the University of Chicago, condemned *Adair* in "Liberty of Contract," a famous article in the *Yale Law Journal*. Pound complained that the justices' minds were stuck in an eighteenth-century "individualist conception of justice" that was originally designed to destroy feudal and mercantilist restrictions on the economy in order to free all to compete equally in the marketplace. But the new threats to economic freedom were the powerful corporations that dictated terms of employment to thousands of powerless workers. When the Court assumed that both worker and employer were equal bargainers, it revealed an outdated laissez-faire preference and a "mechanical jurisprudence in which conceptions are developed logically at the expense of practical results." Instead of artificial, formalist reasoning, Pound demanded a sociological jurisprudence that used the evidence of the social sciences to examine the harsh realities of industrial capitalism.

Adair may have signaled the backwardness of the Court to Professor Pound, but the justices remained more open to accepting the reasonableness of new economic regulation than their historical reputation would imply. This was made evident the same month in the *Employer's Liability Cases* (1908), in which the majority of the Court allowed Congress to set aside a traditional common-law rule according to which an employer could not be held liable for the injury done to one worker through the negligence of another. Industrial accidents were frighteningly common at the turn of the century. More than 35,000 deaths and 536,000 injuries occurred on the job each year between 1880 and 1900. Under the fellow-servant rule, a servant or his or her heirs could sue only another (presumably poor) servant for negligence, not the master who had hired them both. The widows of two railroad workers sued the railroads and then appealed to the Supreme Court. The Court split into five separate, concurring, or dissenting opinions over whether Congress had the power to pass the law and whether the law dealt only with interstate commerce. Justice White delivered the majority opinion, which held that Congress had the power as far as interstate commerce was concerned but that the act as written so blended together interstate with intrastate commerce that it violated the

Constitution. Congress corrected the language that same year in the second Employer's Liability Act, so that there was no question that it applied only to workers engaged in interstate commerce.

Even that would not have satisfied the concurring justices — Peckham, Brewer, and Fuller — who opposed the idea that Congress could touch the fellow-servant rule in the first place. For them, as for other Fuller Court justices in other instances, regulation of the economy should be restricted to traditional forms and concerns. The new relations of corporate employer and industrial worker make the very vocabulary of the fellow-servant rule seem archaic to our ears, but to the dissenters, the constitutional job of the courts was to prevent wayward legislatures from undermining traditional rights and duties.

The Fuller Court and Economic Change

The battles within and surrounding the Fuller Court demonstrate the difficulty of holding this particular line during an era of unprecedented economic change. Most members of the Fuller Court conceived of the economy in terms that had become remote from the realities of the marketplace. The primary economic actor remained in their minds the individual male, endowed by God with the faculties that allowed him to work and profit himself. This traditional vision could make for popular decisions or unpopular ones. When they upheld antitrust prosecutions under the Sherman Act, the justices reflected the widespread belief that only underhanded dealings could explain the enormous combinations that had come to dominate the economic landscape. If the natural laws of supply and demand were allowed free play, surely this would not have happened. Economists argued to no avail that some industries are naturally prone to bigness. Congress had come to believe that something untoward was going on, and the courts helped them try to stop it. On the other hand, the justices on the Fuller Court also worried about abuses of government power that would victimize individuals trying to make the most of what they had. The justices did not oppose the regulation of natural monopolies, such as railroads, so much as they were concerned with how it was done. Private interests were not to be sacrificed to public ones, and vice versa. Similarly, the justices saw themselves as protectors of men's liberty of contract as against the overreaching powers of government. The justices of the Fuller Court took a certain pride in being the men who were to make sure of balancing private right against public good, but their vision of both right and good has become increasingly remote to succeeding generations.

—LINDA PRZYBYSZEWSKI

FOR FURTHER READING AND RESEARCH

The only full-length biography of Chief Justice Fuller is Willard L. King, *Melville Weston Fuller: Chief Justice of the United States, 1880–1910* (New York, 1950), in which Fuller appears as charming as his historical reputation would suggest. More controversial figures on the Fuller Court have garnered more attention. Carl Brent Swisher, a scholar of progressive tendencies, cast a critical eye in *Stephen J. Field: Craftsman of the Law* (Washington, D.C., 1930), but no understanding of Field can be complete without reading Charles W. McCurdy's defense of the coherence of his doctrinal record in "Justice Field and the Jurisprudence of Government-Business Relations: Some Parameters of Laissez-Faire Constitutionalism, 1863–1897," *Journal of American History* 61 (1975), 970–1005.

The importance of religion and training in moral philosophy to conservative jurisprudence is stressed in Linda Przybyszewski, "The Secularization of the Law and the Persistence of Religious Faith: The Case of Justice David J. Brewer," *Journal of American History* 91 (September 2004), 471–496; and Joseph Gordon Hylton, "David Josiah Brewer and the Christian Constitution," *Marquette Law Review* 81 (1998), 417. Works on Justice Holmes are numerous, but start with G. Edward White, *Justice Oliver Wendell Holmes: Law and the Inner Self* (New York, 1993). Justice John Marshall Harlan's unusual record is explained by his allegiance to constitutional nationalism, white paternalism, and religious faith in Linda Przybyszewski's *The Republic According to John Marshall Harlan* (Chapel Hill, N.C., 1999).

The Fuller Court as a whole was roundly criticized from the progressive perspective in Arnold Paul, *Conservative Crisis and the Rule of Law: Attitudes of Bar and Bench, 1887–1895* (Ithaca, N.Y., 1960). More nuanced works corrected the Court's bad reputation. Owen M. Fiss discards the class-bias explanation in favor of the influence of social-contract tradition in *Troubled Beginnings of the Modern State, 1888–1910* (New York, 1993), volume 8 of the *History of the Supreme Court of the United States* (the Oliver Wendell Holmes Devise). James W. Ely, Jr., describes Fuller's responsibilities as chief justice but broadens his focus to explain the brethren's commitment to federalism in *The Chief Justiceship of Melville W. Fuller, 1888–1910* (Columbia, S.C., 1995). John E. Semonche offered a useful term-by-term account of the work of the Fuller Court in *Charting the Future: The Supreme Court Responds to a Changing Society, 1890–1920* (Westport, Conn., 1978). The significance and reality of legal formalism are debated in two important articles: William E. Nelson, "The Impact of the Antislavery Movement upon Styles of Judicial Reasoning in Nineteenth Century America," *Harvard Law Review* 87 (1974), 513; and Walter F. Pratt's quantitative analysis "Rhetorical Styles on the Fuller Court," *American Journal of Legal History* 24 (1980), 189.

The Fuller Court and Race After Slavery

Because the school desegregation decision of *Brown v. Board of Education* (1954) overturned *Plessy v. Ferguson* (1896), many think of *Plessy* as *the* segregation decision of the nineteenth century. In fact, the case attracted little attention. White Americans thought that the *Civil Rights Cases,* which found private discrimination perfectly consistent with the Fourteenth Amendment, had already settled the question of segregation in 1883. At that time, Justice Joseph Bradley's opinion for the Court had left open the possibility that approval of segregation by individuals would not extend to segregation ordered by the state. A group of black men from New Orleans decided to test a Louisiana law that required "equal but separate accommodations" in a suit brought by Homer Plessy, a man of mixed racial heritage. But Justice Henry Brown's majority opinion found that segregation laws violated neither the Thirteenth nor the Fourteenth Amendment and reflected only the social, not the civil or political, inferiority of blacks. In his most famous dissent in favor of civil rights, John Marshall Harlan declared, "Our Constitution is color-blind." The Supreme Court had been more generous in protecting the political right of jury duty for black men — *Strauder v. West Virginia* (1880)— but in *Gibson v. Mississippi* (1896), the Fuller Court permitted whites to reinstitute lily-white juries by cloaking their racism in neutral language. *Williams v. Mississippi* (1898) also permitted literacy tests that were tacitly designed to strip black men of their Fifteenth Amendment voting rights. Black litigants did convince the Court to condemn debt peonage in *Bailey v. State of Alabama* (1910), but by then, Southern whites had succeeded in reestablishing their racial supremacy.

The *Lochner* Era

When scholars refer to the period beginning at the turn of the twentieth
century as the *Lochner* era, they mean that the Court's decision in *Lochner
v. New York* (1905) typified a period when the Court became so committed
to a position in opposition to state regulation of the economy that its decisions amounted to judicial legislation. In fact, the Fuller Court often upheld
economic regulation, and the brethren were closely divided in *Lochner*. But
both the disappointment voiced by organized labor at the decision and
a memorable dissent by Oliver Wendell Holmes magnified the decision's
prominence. Speaking for a 5–4 majority, Justice Rufus Peckham struck
down a New York law that prohibited bakery workers from working more
than ten hours a day, six days a week. Justice Holmes responded with
his famous complaint, "The Fourteenth Amendment does not enact
Mr. Herbert Spencer's *Social Statics*." Holmes effectively accused the majority of embracing Spencer's Social Darwinist theories. To be fair, the majority did not; nor did most Americans who eyed economic regulation with
suspicion. Protective regulation had been allowed in dangerous industries,
such as deep-shaft mining — *Holden v. Hardy* (1898). But baking was not
a dangerous occupation, and Peckham held that in such cases, laws
"limiting the hours in which grown and intelligent men may labor to
earn their living, are mere meddlesome interference with the rights of
the individual."

The dissenters disagreed. Justice Harlan was convinced that the state
had reason to act in light of the poor working conditions, ill health, and
early mortality of bakers. This kind of statistical and medical evidence
would eventually convince the Fuller Court to permit state laws limiting
the hours of women workers — *Muller v. Oregon* (1908). In *Bunting v. Oregon* (1917), the White Court would allow similar limits to be placed on
men's working hours.

The *Insular Cases* (1901): Law for the Empire

Although they turned on a seemingly arcane topic — tariff rates — the *Insular Cases** (1901) involved the essential question of the extent of governmental power over conquered territory. The Spanish-American War of 1898 can be described either as a Republican crusade to free the oppressed people of the Spanish Empire or a cynical effort to obtain American coaling stations across the globe. In any case, the United States gained control over Puerto Rico and the Philippines. But many whites were opposed to incorporating more dark-skinned people into the American citizenry, whereas others opposed imperialism on principle. In the first *Insular Cases* decision, *DeLima v. Bidwell,* Justice Brown held for the Court that Puerto Rico was not a foreign country. In the second, *Downes v. Bidwell,* Brown's opinion approved the Foraker Act, which placed tariffs on Puerto Rican goods anyway and organized the island's government (tariffs would pay for the administration of the island). Brown reassured the minority that no one need fear for the rights of inhabitants of "unincorporated territories" because "There are certain principles of natural justice inherent in the Anglo-Saxon character."

In dissent, Justices Harlan, Fuller, Brewer, and Peckham insisted that the Constitution must apply to all territory under American control. They dissented again in subsequent "insular" decisions involving the Bill of Rights. Thus, in *Dorr v. United States* (1904), Harlan sarcastically observed that the majority had effectively amended the Constitution to guarantee a jury trial in federal cases "*except where Filipinos are concerned.*" But the majority reflected the government's view that the islanders would need decades of training before taking on the privileges and duties of citizenship.

* Scholars have differed over which cases to include under the rubric of the *Insular Cases.* Some limit the title to the tariff cases decided in 1901. Others recognize these as the original *Insular Cases* but include several others decided between 1901 and 1904. Others treat the title as including yet others stretching to 1922 and beyond as the "progeny" of the original *Insular Cases.*

8

The White Court 1910–1921

A Progressive Court?

HE SECOND DECADE of the twentieth century covered both the life span of the White Court (1910–1921) and the salad days of the sprawling and enormously influential reform movement known as progressivism. Their histories are entwined. Progressivism first emerged in the early 1900s, and its leaders often defined the movement in terms of opposition to Chief Justice Fuller's *"Lochner"* Court, so called after the notorious 1905 case of that name and the laissez-faire individualism that seemed to animate its hostility to reform legislation. In contrast to the Fuller Court but in time-honored conservative fashion, the White Court accommodated the reform impulse while carrying much of the past into the present, tempered but not deeply changed. Discontent with the nation's judiciary and with the Constitution itself was never more sharply expressed than during the Progressive Era, but the Supreme Court managed to cultivate a reputation for "progressiveness," even as it kept old doctrines and practices alive.

Choices for the White Court

In May 1910, Chief Justice Fuller spoke at the Court's memorial service for Justice David Brewer, one of the principal judicial architects of laissez-faire. "As our brother Brewer joins the great procession, there pass before me the forms of Mathews and Miller, of Field and Bradley and Lamar and Blatchford, of Jackson and Gray and of Peckham, whose works follow them now that they rest from their labors." These were virtually Fuller's last words from the bench. He died on Independence Day 1910. Rufus Peckham, author of *Lochner v. New York* (1905), had died less than a year earlier. William Moody would soon retire, and John Marshall Harlan, the great dissenter, had only one year left of his thirty-four on the Court. By 1912, five new justices were on the Court: a new majority under a new chief. Amidst the birth of the Progressive Party and a three-way race for the presidency that included two of progressivism's leading standard-bearers, Theodore Roosevelt and Woodrow Wilson, the curtain seemed to have fallen on the *Lochner* era.

The incumbent president, Taft, also bent to progressivism's influence. Without abandoning deeply conservative commitments, political and constitutional, Taft emerged as something of a business- and good-government-minded progressive. More important, Taft had been a distinguished federal court of appeals judge and in 1921 would succeed Edward White as chief justice. A sophisticated lawyer, politician, and statesman, Taft loved the Court and prized his opportunity as president to rehabilitate it.

In choosing nominees, Taft sought men like himself. When Peckham died in 1909, Taft nominated his friend and erstwhile colleague on the Sixth Circuit, Horace Lurton. His second nominee, to replace Brewer, was more daring: Charles Evans Hughes, progressive governor of New York and already a nationally prominent reform politician.

Taft's choice for chief justice to follow Fuller was something of a surprise. Edward D. White was a Confederate veteran from Louisiana and a leader of that state's efforts to "redeem" itself from Republicans, Reconstruction, and black suffrage. Appointed to the Court in 1894 by Democrat Grover Cleveland, White had established a record as a thoughtful and able jurist. Although part of the *Lochner* majority, he had dissented forcefully from the wildly unpopular *Pollock v. Farmers' Loan & Trust Co.* (1895), invalidating the federal income tax, and his antitrust dissents in *U.S. v. Trans-Missouri Freight Association* (1897) and *Northern Securities Company v. U.S.* (1904) embodied the views of forward-looking conservatives, such as Taft. White was a man of great personal warmth, and although, according to Justice Holmes, his writing left much to be desired, "his thinking is profound, especially in the legislative direction which we don't recognize as a judicial requirement but which is so, especially in our Court." By choosing the first chief justice from the Deep South, Taft won praise for bipartisanship and for binding the nation's sectional wounds.

With White's nomination, Taft also sent the names of Willis Van Devanter of Wyoming and Joseph Lamar of Georgia for associate justices. Van Devanter would grow increasingly conservative during his twenty-seven years on the bench, and he proved one of laissez-faire's most able defenders. Lamar lasted only five years. His death in early 1916, along with Lurton's death in 1914 and Hughes's resignation in 1916 to run for the presidency on the Republican ticket, opened the second important round of appointments to the White Court. But Harlan's death in 1911 had already given Taft his sixth appointment, the most in one presidential term since George Washington. Taft chose Mahlon Pitney, the chancellor of New Jersey. Pitney's experience as an equity judge would decisively influence the White Court's notorious opinions bearing on the labor injunction.

"If ever in the history of the Supreme Court successive appointments by one President have seemed to embrace dialectical opposites," Benno Schmidt has observed, "Woodrow Wilson's appointments of James C. McReynolds in 1914 and Louis D. Brandeis in 1916 are the ones." McReynolds, replacing Lurton, proved a crude anti-Semite; Brandeis, replacing Lamar, was the first Jew to sit on the Supreme Court. McReynolds became the most doctrinaire proponent of laissez-faire in the Court's history; Brandeis was the greatest progressive of his day, on or off the bench. Both, however, were antitrust stalwarts, and this was the issue on which Wilson most wanted to nudge the Court. Wilson's third nominee, replacing Hughes, was John Clark of Ohio, another progressive.

These newcomers to the Court during White's reign joined Joseph McKenna, appointed by President McKinley in 1898, and William Day, appointed by Roosevelt in 1903. And, of course, they joined Oliver Wendell Holmes, the most original thinker in the history of American judging, who brought the great — many say the only truly American — school of philosophy, pragmatism, into legal thought. Holmes was a pioneer in the intellectual assault on classical legal thought, setting out many of the key elements of progressive jurisprudence. But Holmes shared none of Brandeis's faith in ordinary citizens' capacity for intelligent self-government and social reconstruction. It was the intellectual incoherence and dogmatism of laissez-faire constitutionalism that demanded that judges defer to reformist lawmakers.

Progressivism and the Constitution

Canvassing the work of the new Court for the *New Republic,* the leading journal of progressive opinion, Harvard's Felix Frankfurter detected the end of an era when "the quality of the Court was exemplified in the sturdy personalities of Justices like Brewer and Peckham." In a much-noted 1913 *Columbia Law Review* article, "The Progressiveness of the Supreme Court," Charles Warren counted up recent instances in which the Court had struck down social and economic legislation and found them few. A year later, more popular journals were reaching the same conclusion: The Supreme Court "has caught the present-day infection. It is progressive."

Progressivism was a many-sided response to the staggering new scale and patterns of modern life that were overturning familiar, local ways of doing business, producing goods, building communities, and participating in politics. Above all loomed the "trust" and "the main question" of the day: "the regulation by law of corporate activity in its relations to the country at large." With the "trust" came other "social problems" that preoccupied progressives, primarily the "labor question." Republican self-government required citizens with a measure of independence and authority in their work lives. Yet the bulk of the nation's producers now were permanent wage earners, dependent on the industrial labor market, enduring low wages and long hours; lacking public or private provision against the hazards of injury, unemployment, and old age; and remaining without voice or choice at work. Progressives differed over what was to be done about either the "trust" or the "labor question," but all agreed that a vastly greater measure of public authority, regulation, and "social control" was needed.

Beyond the world of industry lay more social problems: the "great cities," teeming with millions of "new immigrants" from southern and eastern Europe; and the disintegrating patriarchal family, undermined by migration and by the massive entry of women into the wage labor force.

Progressivism's concerns were diverse. So were its constituents. At the movement's core was a resolve to reinvigorate values of dignity and independence in the modern urban world. Progressivism united the old middle class — shopkeepers, business proprietors, and skilled workers — with legions from the new professions with their penchant for bringing scientific, managerial, and professional "expertise" to bear on social problems. Progressivism was also a women's movement. Excluded from the suffrage and from party politics, women entered public life through the movement's countless reform organizations, from urban settlement houses to such national associations as the Consumers' League, which drafted child labor, wage and hour, and worker and consumer safety laws and lobbied and litigated on their behalf. Enlightened leaders of big business and the corporate bar were also prominent. Who better to design the new administrative state that would tame the giant new private corporations than the men who constructed them?

No wonder progressivism's reform vocabulary was varied. The old antimonopoly outlook, linking progressives to the Populist and Jacksonian generations of American reform, stood alongside modern reformers' emphasis on expertise. Faith in expertise infused the progressives' administrative-state-building ambitions and their efforts to curtail the abstract, rigid, and formalistic habits of late-nineteenth-century legal thinking in governing social and economic life.

Equally pervasive in progressive thought was the rejection of a dogmatically individualistic liberal "legal" understanding of justice for a truer and deeper "social" understanding. When progressives spoke of social versus legal justice, they meant a conception of fairness and right that looked beyond legal forms and legal equality to address the "actualities" of wealth and poverty, along with power and powerlessness. Many leading progressives, such as Louis Brandeis, held that the Constitution's guarantees of liberty and equality of rights *demanded* that social problems be addressed in order that a politically and economically independent citizenry be sustained. All Americans "must have a reasonable income" and regular employment; "they must have health and leisure," decent "working conditions," and "some system of social insurance." Merely satisfying material needs did not suffice. There could be no "political democracy" without "industrial democracy," without workers' participation in decisions determining "how the business shall be run." No more than his grittier counterparts in the labor movement did Brandeis expect the courts to enact this vision, but that took nothing from its constitutional essence: wise restraint on the judiciary's part and affirmative reform obligations on the other branches of government to restore constitutional democracy in industrialized America. Brandeis thus concurred with Theodore Roosevelt that governing in the twentieth century meant a change of focus from the creation of wealth to its distribution. Roosevelt agreed with Brandeis that courts and lawyers needed a jurisprudence that was more attentive to social facts and social consequences. Both held that courts and judicial authority needed to yield far more often to the greater fact-finding capacities and democratic accountability of lawmakers and to the ongoing expertise of administrative regulation and the humane interventions of social agencies.

Claiming authority for "We, the People" to decide what the Constitution meant, Roosevelt made constitutional reform a centerpiece of his progressivism. He was hardly alone. No other period in the nation's history saw such a burgeoning of proposals for constitutional change. Roosevelt favored restoring "the people's" authority through the device of the referendum, enabling citizens to review and overturn state (but not federal) supreme court decisions that invalidated state laws. Other progressives championed more radical measures: recall of state judges, congressional supermajorities to overturn federal judicial decisions invalidating acts of Congress, and outright abolition of judicial review. Almost every prominent progressive agreed that the national Constitution had to be changed and the power of the federal courts diminished. To some extent, progressive politicians wanted simply to "scare the hell out of judges," to push them toward more generous views of legislative and executive power and more modest and "modern" views of judicial authority. But the progressive commitment to a more fully democratic form of constitutionalism was often genuine.

The White Court, then, addressed the legitimate bounds of corporate activity and of government regulation and reform at a moment of great constitutional ferment. Some powerful voices held that the Constitution abhorred redistribution; others, that it demanded it. The Court's authority to decide such questions was itself contested. How did the Court navigate these shoals, what did it preserve, and what did it change? And because this Court, in sharp contrast to its predecessor, acquired a reputation for "progressiveness," how well did the nation's underdogs fare before it?

The "Trust Question"

From the 1880s until the beginning of World War I, the legitimacy of the large-scale corporation was hotly contested. The antitrust decisions of the White Court generated as much public attention and controversy as the Warren Court's civil rights decisions. The Court's decisions spoke to the future of the nation's political economy and the legitimate bounds of corporate size and power when these were the leading issues of the day.

Trusts and giant corporations threatened the classical liberal model of a competitive marketplace and the venerable principle that a democratic republic required economically "independent" citizens and a broad distribution of productive property. The antimonopoly movement indicted big business for destroying small and middle-sized firms, enslaving labor, engaging in immoral business practices, bilking consumers, and corrupting the nation's legislatures. The depth of feeling prompted Congress to enact the 1890 Sherman Antitrust Act, which condemned "every contract, combination in the form of trust or otherwise, or conspiracy in restraint of trade or commerce," and outlawed monopolization of any part of interstate commerce. These provisions have gone virtually unchanged and remain the basis for nearly all federal antitrust prosecutions today.

Congress left it to the courts to determine what specific forms of business conduct and structure violated the act, but for two decades, neither the courts nor commentators could agree whether the act simply codified common-law norms or enacted stricter prohibitions. The common law distinguished between "reasonable" and "unreasonable" restraints on trade, condemning only the latter, but the statute contained no such distinction. Congress had preferred ambiguous statutory language so that it could please competing constituencies: the agrarian and populist public demanding the restoration of proprietary capitalism; the metropolitan business interests favoring the continued development of the new giant corporations under enhanced oversight. This tension between a vision of antitrust that condemned "bigness" on broad social and political grounds and one focused more narrowly on the prevention of overwhelming and ill-gotten market domination and abusive competitive practices would continue to run through the law and politics of antitrust for decades.

The Supreme Court pursued a jarring course. From 1897, when it decided the *Trans-Missouri* case, through the end of Chief Justice Fuller's tenure in 1910, a majority of the Court, led by Justices Peckham and Harlan, insisted that the Sherman Act went beyond the common law to condemn *all* restraints of trade. To fold the word "reasonable" into the statute would be the worst kind of "judicial legislation." This view met ridicule and alarm in powerful dissents by Justices Holmes and White, in lower-court opinions, and in speeches by political leaders, including Roosevelt. Holmes accused the majority of enacting a literal ban on combination and with it "a universal disintegration of society." White was more measured, but the stakes were high for him too. The majority, he feared, by assailing such a broad swath of combinations and agreements among firms, imperiled not only the common law's reasonable limits on the rule of free competition but also the Constitution's protections of property rights and freedom of contract, all in disregard of modern technology and business conditions that entailed a substantial measure of consolidation. Paradoxically, Harlan and Peckham had departed common-law jurisprudence to reinstate a proprietary capitalist's vision of "natural laws of competition," whereas White and Holmes invoked the old common-law tradition to vindicate a new economic theory (the inevitability of corporate consolidation) and a legal outlook that they thought better suited to mature industrial capitalism.

As president, Roosevelt was persuaded that consolidation and giant corporations were inevitable. However, he did initiate proceedings against two of the most notorious trusts, James M. Duke's American Tobacco Company and John D. Rockefeller's Standard Oil Company. The government prevailed against both in the lower courts, but in the Supreme Court, deaths and retirements meant delay, and both cases were reargued in January 1911.

Antitrust seemed to stand at a crossroads. The doctrinal question — whether the common-law "rule of reason" was a feature of the Sherman Act — translated in public discourse into the broader question of whether the nation's antitrust law would condemn all trusts or only "bad" ones. If the Fuller Court's doctrine of unrestricted competition persisted under White, every corporate consolidation would be vulnerable to the charge of diminishing the free play of competition and depriving the country of independent dealers. The corporate reorganization of the nation's economy would continue but beyond the pale of the law.

The new chief justice marshaled a majority of eight behind an opinion that largely upheld the lower courts' dissolution order but also declared that the common law's "rule of reason" was the "guide" to interpreting the Sherman Act. The dissenting views of Justice White had become the prevailing views of Chief Justice White's new eight-member majority. In lonely dissent, Harlan assailed the Court for betraying what he saw as Congress's populist purpose in 1890: abolition of "the slavery that would result from aggregations of capital." By abandoning its initial reading of the Sherman Act, the Court was indulging in "judicial legislation" in the interests of the rich and powerful.

President Taft stood by his chief justice and declined to call for any amendment to the Sherman Act. Indeed, doctrinally, Taft read the decisions as foreclosing little and in their wake pursued the most active policy of antitrust prosecutions against major corporations that the nation had ever seen. Progressives in Congress and in state legislatures, however, heeded Harlan's call and denounced the Court for reading into the Sherman Act just the phrase that the trusts wanted to see in it. Public confidence in the nation's antitrust law virtually vanished.

Roosevelt had no more use than Chief Justice White for the old Fuller Court's vision of "competition, free and unrestricted." His own outlook heretofore had called for something very much like the "rule of reason" to allow "good" trusts to flourish and "bad" ones to be hectored by a vigorous executive (Plate B.1). But in 1912, Roosevelt challenged Taft for the Republican nomination, based on the proposition that Taft had drifted toward stand-pat conservatism. Exhibit A was Taft's defense of the federal judiciary, contrasted with Roosevelt's advocacy of a modern regulatory state.

Losing the Republican nomination, Roosevelt helped create and then ran on the Progressive Party platform, which promised national corporation law and national regulation of industry and big business through a powerful federal commission. Woodrow Wilson also demanded antitrust reform, although his rhetoric ran to restoring competition. Together, Roosevelt and Wilson garnered three votes to every one for Taft. Greater legislative and administrative intervention in the corporate economy seemed inevitable. In 1914, President Wilson signed into law two new antitrust measures: the Federal Trade Commission (FTC) and the Clayton Acts. The first created a regulatory commission with power to identify and proscribe "unfair methods of competition" and "deceptive business practices." The second outlawed particular unfair business methods, price discrimination, tying contracts, and some kinds of interlocking directorates. But the language was sufficiently qualified and ambiguous to leave room for the more conservative Court of the 1920s to construe most of the acts' provisions as no more than codifications of inherited judge-made rules.

A conservative outcome also attended the era's last great Sherman Act prosecution, against U.S. Steel. Launched by President Taft in 1912, the government's case was meant to affirm the continued robustness of the Sherman Act after the "rule-of-reason" decisions. The government's complaint described the rapid integration of the steel industry in the last years of the nineteenth century, culminating in consolidation of erstwhile competitors into U.S. Steel in 1901 and the numerous other corporate boards (Standard Oil, International Harvester, Pullman, and so on) on which directors of U.S. Steel sat. The complaint charged that the extent of the corporation's "power and control" was "incompatible with the healthy commercial life of the Nation" and sought its dissolution.

The case took five years to reach the Supreme Court, and the Court held it over to be decided in peacetime. In 1920, the Court ruled against the government, with a distinctly pro-bigness reading of the *Standard Oil* and *American Tobacco* precedents. "Size" was no "offense," even if merger and consolidation resulted in a corporation's controlling all or most of an industry. Nor was power an offense, as long as it was not used to harass or oppress rivals or exclude others from entering the industry. The outcome was a defeat for those who still hoped to find in the Sherman Act a stout weapon against the "curse of Bigness," and it drew down the curtain on the trust-busting era.

The "rule-of-reason" decisions had gone far toward settling the "trust question" and pushed it from the center of national politics. Congress had chosen modest reform, embodied in the 1914 statutes, spurning Roosevelt's statist vision of a national commission with power to issue and revoke national corporate charters and to supervise corporate pricing, accounting, and capitalization and investment policy. Combined with Congress's modesty, the Court's common-law-inspired handiwork helped guarantee both the continuing centrality of the judiciary and the high degree of autonomy from party politics and state command that private elites and organizations would enjoy in the corporate economy of the twentieth century.

The Commerce Power

The "trust question" went further than antitrust law. To address corporate size and power was also to ask how far Congress's power extended in its efforts to confront the social problems that attended the new corporate economy.

Until the late nineteenth century, Congress had acted to promote economic growth and only rarely to regulate commerce among the states. However, the construction of nation-spanning railroads, the growth of big industry, and the emergence of national markets in countless goods produced a new sense of an interconnected national economy whose governance demanded national lawmaking. The Interstate Commerce Commission Act of

1887 and the Sherman Act marked a new era in national regulation, and the Progressive Era brought many more excursions by Congress into regulatory realms once occupied only by the states. Congress acted under the commerce clause to address such quintessential progressive causes as consumer safety, worker safety and accidents on the railways, child labor, and the interstate and international "traffic in women." And because regulation almost always burdens one group or another, there was never a want of litigants to raise the banner of states' rights and claim that any given exercise of the commerce power invaded lawmaking authority that the Constitution reserved to the states.

The Fuller Court had left a mixed legacy of commerce clause doctrines. *E. C. Knight* (1895) drew a bright and categorical line between the states' police powers and the nation's authority over interstate commerce, declaring whole realms of economic activity, including manufacturing, off-limits for Congress. Yet bright lines were blurred by *Champion v. Ames* (1903), in which the Fuller Court upheld a statute forbidding interstate transportation of foreign lottery tickets. The tender spot here was that Congress's purpose in outlawing the shipment of lottery tickets was not a "commercial" one; Congress was using its commerce power to promote a social goal, outlawing an article it deemed injurious to public safety or morals — much as if, in fact, it possessed a plenary police power.

Congress acted thus when it passed the Pure Food and Drug Act of 1906. A celebrated and hard-won reform, the act was opposed by manufacturers and by Southern Democrats on the ground that Congress had no national police power to exercise. But in 1911, a unanimous Court upheld the act in *Hipolite Egg Co. v. United States*, a case involving a shipment of preserved eggs. Defendants argued that the eggs had passed into the general mass of property in the state and were thus beyond Congress's power to regulate under the commerce clause. It would be sufficient answer, said the Court, to point out that the eggs here were still in their original packages and so had not passed into the internal commerce of the state. But the Court went further, holding that "articles which are outlaws of commerce may be seized wherever found."

What, however, was an outlaw of commerce? And was Congress free to decide, so that if Congress excluded an article from commerce, rather than merely regulating its movement, the article thereby became an outlaw? If so, the power was a plenary one, like the states'. The Court gave no clear answer. But in the next important case testing the reach of this incipient national police power, the Court again upheld its exercise. The Mann Act, or White-Slave Traffic Act, as it dubbed itself in its section 8, was enacted in 1910 and upheld by the Court three years later in *Hoke v. United States*. Section 8 punished the transportation in interstate or foreign commerce of "any woman or girl for the purpose of prostitution or debauchery, or for any other immoral purpose." The impoverished single woman from the countryside, adrift in a European or American city and lured into prostitution by a "procurer" who sent her to business partners in New York or Chicago, was the paradigmatic "white slave." In her dependency and exploitability, she symbolized the extremities of single women's urban vulnerability and the moral dangers and degradation of urban life.

The Court's decision once more was unanimous. To be sure, Justice McKenna reasoned, the states enjoyed primary authority over morals but only within their own borders. Beyond the borders of each state was "a domain which the States cannot reach and over which Congress alone has power; and if such power be exerted to control what the States cannot it is an argument for — not against — its legality." Progressive public opinion was rhapsodic, reading *Hoke* as an endorsement of the new nationalism and the most progressive opinion ever. No longer would there be a twilight zone between state and federal authority where social ills lay beyond the reach of government action. Conservatives read the opinion with foreboding, as a substantial "extension of federal power over states" and an opening for Congress to "assert whatever moral view it sees fit and give it vigor in commerce legislation." What would confine Congress to moral issues? Why could it not "reach out and promote everything it wishes under a general welfare policy"?

In 1913 and 1914, the Court handed down two more important commerce clause decisions upholding governmental power, both in the traditional domain of railroad regulation — the *Minnesota Rate Cases* (1913) and the *Shreveport Rate Case* (1914). From the Marshall Court onward, the Supreme Court had always regarded the commerce clause as not only a source of national power but also a restraint that might operate on state regulation even in the absence of any federal legislative action whenever the Court concluded that a challenged state measure encroached on the principle of a common national market. In the absence of federal legislation, a ruling against state encroachment created a regulatory no man's land, either because the Court would turn around and also strike down or foreclose congressional action or because the subject did not lend itself to national regulation.

Against this backdrop, the *Minnesota* and *Shreveport* decisions suggested that the White Court was markedly more hospitable than its predecessors to the exercise of both state and federal regulatory power. The *Minnesota* decision upheld the power of the states to regulate railroad rates for intrastate hauls even when that regulation would force down interstate rates, so long as there had been no federal regulation of those rates. The *Shreveport* decision extended federal authority by upholding the

Interstate Commerce Commission's power to set the rates of railroad hauls entirely within the state of Texas, overriding the rates set by the state commission, because the intrastate rates competed against traffic between Texas and Louisiana. *Shreveport* was a victory for national regulatory authority and celebrated by nationalist-minded progressives as such. It was also, of course, a victory for the railroads, for it freed them, in like circumstances, from rates set by the generally more aggressive state-level rate commissions.

Child Labor

At the turn of the century, one child in six between the ages of ten and fifteen was a wage earner. Most labored in industry, under grim conditions. Federal regulation and prohibition of child labor were central goals of all progressives. Many states embraced reform initiatives, but regulation was neither universal nor uniform. States willing to abolish child labor found themselves not only disadvantaged in national markets but also unable, under the commerce clause, to exclude other states' cheaper child labor products from their own market. In 1912, the Department of Labor established the Children's Bureau to investigate and report. In 1913, the Court's decision in *Hoke* encouraged child labor reform advocates by appearing to recognize a national police power in the domain of interstate commerce. In 1916, the first federal measure aimed at child labor was passed.

Writing for a 5–4 majority in *Hammer v. Dagenhart* (1918), Justice Day stunned Congress and most of the nation by invalidating the Child Labor Act. Day distinguished such cases as *Champion, Hipolite Egg,* and *Hoke* by reasoning that Congress's regulatory power in those cases hinged on "the character of the particular subjects dealt with." Here, in contrast, the goods produced by child labor were in themselves harmless; nor did interstate transportation itself accomplish any harm.

Justice Day's reasoning was flatly question-begging, as Holmes pointed out in a classic dissent. In view of the power of Congress etched by the Court in those earlier cases, "it is enough that in the opinion of Congress the transportation encourages the evil."

The feebleness of the *Hammer* majority's efforts to evade recent precedents suggested a growing uneasiness with the implications of decisions like *Hoke* for the notion of a limited central government. Plainly, too, the majority was determined to preserve the realms of manufacturing, mining, and agricultural employment for the individual states to regulate. Not for the last time, the Court's majority chose public opprobrium rather than condone overreaching by either federal or state lawmakers. *Hammer* took progressives particularly by surprise, so persuaded had they become by their own sanguine pronouncements that the *Lochner* Court was long gone.

Due Process and State Legislation

Some progressive optimism had been warranted, especially during the first half of the decade. Scores of state reforms were upheld against due process and equal protection challenges. State regulators of railroad rates, insurance, and banks all found their work more generously overseen by the White Court than by its predecessors. Occasionally, the Court spoke through Justice Holmes and alarmed the more nervous members of the corporate bar with broad characterizations of the police power. Thus, in *Noble State Bank v. Haskell* (1911), the Court upheld a depositors' guaranty fund, which levied assessments on average daily deposits of all Oklahoma's banks. The bank claimed that requiring solvent banks to bail out insolvent competitors was a taking of property in violation of due process. For a unanimous Court, Holmes warned against "pressing the broad words of the Fourteenth Amendment to a dryly logical extreme." Admittedly, taking one bank's property to pay the debts of another was "in its immediate purpose" a private use. But so were many other schemes of mutual protection undertaken by state law. The police power extended "to all the great public needs."

Such broad assurances confirmed the "Progressiveness of the United States Supreme Court" in many progressives' eyes and prompted conservative laments that "the door is now open wide to all manner of socialistic suggestions." Yet those closer to the trenches noted that even such modest measures as these had required decades of struggle. In *Bunting v. Oregon* (1917), for example, the White Court unceremoniously interred the *Lochner* decision by upholding a maximum-hours law for both men and women. For the majority, it was by then well established that maximum-hours laws were valid in their general application as health measures. But other industrial nations had long since moved on to minimum-wage and workmen's compensation schemes and broader protections for workers against the hazards of industrial life. In the United States, such schemes remained in constitutional limbo. The White Court upheld a handful of relatively narrow and voluntary workmen's compensation schemes as well as one that included a compulsory insurance fund. But the Court pointedly reserved to itself the judgment whether particular schemes provided employers a "reasonably just" alternative to common-law adjudication, and even this was not enough for White, Van Devanter, McReynolds, or McKenna. For McReynolds, workmen's compensation "experiments" fell outside the judge-made common law of the labor contract. Their strict liability standards and their cost-spreading insurance-style rationales all seemed "revolutionary," productive of "discontent, strife, idleness and pauperism" and "leading straight toward destruction of our well-tried and successful system of government."

Minimum-wage laws came before the Court in *Stettler v. O'Hara* and *Simpson v. O'Hara* (both 1917). Their survival was even more uncertain than workmen's compensation, for the laws were upheld not 5–4 but by an evenly divided White Court. About a dozen states had enacted minimum-wage laws during the Progressive Era. All were restricted to women and so seemed eminently defensible as health measures following the gendered perspective of such precedents as *Muller v. Oregon* (1908). Still, in the eyes of White, Van Devanter, McReynolds, and McKenna, minimum-wage laws looked more like "class legislation," the unconstitutional taking from A and giving to B. Brandeis, meanwhile, recused himself: He had argued the cases to the White Court two years earlier, before his appointment to the bench in 1916. Thus, when Felix Frankfurter reargued the cases, the Court divided 4–4. Had the lower-court decision invalidated the Oregon law, the four who deemed the law unconstitutional would have been the four voting to affirm and thus the four who prevailed. Invalidation of a women's minimum-wage law, eventually to come in 1923 (*Adkins v. Children's Hospital*), would have occurred in 1917, at the hands of the "progressive" Court.

As it was, minimum-wage laws for women squeaked by. *Coppage v. Kansas* (1915) became the case that coldly reminded reformers of the continued force of laissez-faire constitutionalism. *Coppage* declared that due process forbade a state from outlawing the "yellow dog" employment contract, under which workers had to promise their employers not to join a union. Some fifteen states had enacted anti–yellow dog contract laws. As well as reminding workers that continued employment depended on shunning unions, the yellow dog–contract was deemed to endow employers with a "property interest" in the nonunion status of their workers. Confronted by union organizers, the employer could invoke the contract and a federal or state court would enjoin all organizing efforts as interferences with the employer's "property" in the workers' agreements.

To organized labor and its progressive supporters, outlawing the yellow-dog contract would make it a bit more difficult for employers to use their economic power to prevent or intimidate workers from organizing. For Justice Pitney, who authored *Coppage*, that was exactly the problem. The statute at issue was not a legitimate exercise of the state's police power, for it did not address the public health, safety, or welfare. Instead, it simply interfered with the employer's freedom of contract in order to promote "the upbuilding of the labor organizations." Of course, as Justices Day and

Hughes argued in dissent, this begged the question why states could not decide that the public welfare required just such a constraint on employers. Liberty of contract was infringed by countless legal restraints, many restricting freedom to exploit economic advantage. As for Holmes, "In present conditions a workman not unnaturally may believe that only by belonging to a union can he secure a contract that shall be fair to him. If that belief, whether right or wrong, may be held by a reasonable man, it seems to me that it may be enforced by law in order to establish the equality of position between the parties in which liberty of contract begins."

Two decades would pass before Holmes's pragmatic assessment of the legal conditions of liberty in employment contracts found favor on the Court. In the meantime, *Coppage* — combined with robust conservative dissent in the workmen's compensation and minimum-wage cases — demonstrated that the laissez-faire Constitution of Peckham and Brewer lived on amid the seemingly dominant doctrinal strain of judicial deference toward the states' expanding uses of regulatory power.

Organized Labor

Coppage encourages us to think of the judiciary's approach to labor as one of laissez-faire. Courts invalidated reforms that appeared to infringe on rights of property and contract but otherwise left the employment relationship austerely alone. But this view is misleading, for the common law of employment was as much one of enforced status as free contract. As the United States developed into an industrial nation, courts infused free-contract principles with the old and hierarchical doctrines of master and servant, which emphasized relations of obedience, discipline, and control.

To early-twentieth-century judges contemplating the need for authority in the industrial workplace — for means to discipline an unruly workforce, often recent migrants from peasant countrysides overseas, and to subdue a trade union movement intent on challenging employers and setting its own work rules — the common law of master and servant resonated with modern times. Courts recognized an employer's property interests in the employees' labor, as well as, in many contexts, their loyalty and obedience. (*Coppage*'s yellow dog contracts were but one of several legal bases for antistrike and antiboycott injunctions.) Hundreds of judicial decrees forbade "whomsoever" from doing "whatsoever" to carry out a strike or boycott that the courts had condemned. The decrees resembled custom-made criminal codes, outlawing quitting "in concert," picketing, holding meetings, singing union songs, supplying funds or food or other support to striking workers, and publishing the names of "unfair" employers. Punishment for defying labor injunctions was meted out by the injunction judge himself, in a contempt proceeding without a jury.

Nowhere were the yellow-dog contract and the antiunion injunction more common than in the nation's mining regions. One could not work in a West Virginia mine without signing a yellow-dog contract. Wherever United Mine Workers (UMW) organizers went, federal and state courts followed, enjoining organizing efforts as infringements on the operators' property right in nonunion employees. The White Court entered these bitter battles in the coal fields in *Hitchman Coal & Coke Co. v. Mitchell* (1917). Pitney, author of *Coppage*, also wrote the Court's opinion in *Hitchman*, sustaining the practice in the lower courts. Pitney condemned efforts to unionize the contract-bound miners as a new incarnation of an ancient wrong, enticing away a rival's servants. In his view, "any court of equity would grant an injunction to restrain this as unfair competition." *Hitchman* helped legitimate the savagery with which mine operators policed their company towns. In *Hitchman*'s wake, scores of yellow-dog injunctions against the UMW blanketed West Virginia's coal counties.

The Sherman Act stood as another legal foundation for labor injunctions. Beginning in the 1890s, firms whose products moved in interstate commerce found some lower federal courts prepared to grant decrees condemning strikes and boycotts as conspiracies and combinations in restraint of trade, in violation of the new federal antitrust law. Other lower courts disagreed, but not the Supreme Court, which ruled in *Loewe v. Lawlor* (1908) that the Sherman Act covered union activities.

In 1912, the election of Woodrow Wilson and of a Democratic majority in the House combined with the revolt of reform-minded Republicans in Congress to open the way to change. When Wilson signed the Clayton Act into law in 1914, complete with its declaration that labor was not an article of commerce, American Federation of Labor (AFL) chief Samuel Gompers hailed it as organized labor's "Magna Carta." Indeed, the act did declare that "nothing contained in the anti-trust laws . . . forbid[s] the existence and operation of labor . . . organizations" and listed ten "peaceful" and "lawful" labor activities, including strikes and boycotts, that injunctions could not forbid. But others insisted that the statute fell far short of granting labor immunity from antitrust law or of repealing "government by injunction." To William Howard Taft, at the time in private practice and president of the American Bar Association, the labor provisions did nothing more than state "what would be law without the statute." Certainly, the language of the Clayton Act's labor provisions was ambiguous, and most historians agree that the ambiguities were deliberate. Congress had chosen largely to leave power to determine the fate of the unions where it had been — with the courts.

Duplex Printing Press Co. v. Deering (1921) offered the Supreme Court's first interpretation of the Clayton Act's labor provisions. Members of a machinists' union had refused to set up printing presses built by the one manufacturer that would not recognize their union. This was not, then, a broad sympathy strike or general boycott — the kind of action courts condemned as class-based animosity lacking any basis in economic self-interest — but rested squarely on the defendants' interest in maintaining their union contracts. Justices Brandeis, Holmes, and Clarke agreed that this was precisely the kind of peaceful boycott that the Clayton Act was meant to safeguard. But the majority read the act as Taft had predicted. Nothing that the federal courts had previously outlawed had become legal.

Duplex contrasted starkly with antitrust decisions involving corporate conduct. The White Court's "rule of reason" had legitimated vast combinations, such as U.S. Steel. Yet federal antitrust law deemed the machinist union's Lilliputian attempt to combine the efforts of workers at a handful of printing press makers an illegal restraint of trade. The majority that modernized antitrust law to accommodate the giant corporation remained wedded to an old and deeply authoritarian view of the rights of employers and their "servants." Only in the changed climate of the 1930s would organized labor find relief from the judicial regime of "government by injunction" and antitrust liability.

War Powers and Free Speech

"War," Randolph Bourne wrote in 1918, "is the health of the State." America's preparation for and entry into World War I brought a vast expansion of national authority and federal bureaucracy. The national government became a pervasive and powerful presence in everyday life, claiming unprecedented powers over private property and local affairs. The national government ran the railways and the avenues of communication, directed industry and regulated the price of foodstuffs, and operated a vast propaganda and censorship machine. All this called forth constitutional challenges, but the Court spurned them, upholding national authority with greater consensus than fifty years before, during the last great wartime expansion.

Congressional "preparedness" in 1916 authorized the president to take over the nation's railways in event of war. Takeover included rate setting for all classes of service, intra- as well as interstate, denying state regulatory commissions power over any government-operated line. North Dakota disagreed, and when its case reached the Court, thirty-seven states filed an amicus brief. Speaking through Chief Justice White, the Court upheld the government in *Northern Pacific Railway Co. v. North Dakota* (1919). The president, said White, had not acted under the commerce clause but under the government's war power, which was "complete and undivided" and reached what ordinarily were local and state affairs as far as necessary to meet the emergency. Similar decisions upheld the national government's takeover of telephone and telegraph lines, its power to conscript citizens to serve in the military overseas, and to control agricultural prices. War gave Americans' their first, temporary experience living under a modern national regulatory and administrative state. War demonstrated the capacities of government to mobilize and invigorate resources and citizenry in the face of crisis, setting valuable precedents for the New Deal's administrative and regulatory state building.

A more dismal precedent, happily never repeated on the same scale, was that of wartime and postwar political repression unleashed by the national government—the worst invasion of civil liberties in the nation's history. Progressives rarely protested; nor did the White Court. But when wartime repression was followed by the 1919–1920 "Red Scare" and more deportations, prosecutions, and jailing of political radicals, progressive lawyers and judges began to rethink. Perhaps one could continue assailing courts that struck down social reforms while championing those that struck down laws repressing freedom of expression. By the end of Chief Justice White's tenure, his Court's great dissenters, Brandeis and Holmes, had laid the foundations of modern free-speech law.

The Espionage Act of 1917 outlawed not only treason but also attempts to cause disobedience in the armed services or obstruction of recruitment or enlistment in the armed forces. The 1918 Sedition Act made it a crime to "utter, print, write or publish any disloyal, profane, scurrilous, or abusive language" against the government. Other wartime legislation authorized exclusion of foreign-language publications from the mails and deportation of anyone who believed in the forceful overthrow of government. Thousands were convicted under these and kindred state laws. Half a dozen cases reached the Supreme Court in the spring of 1919, in the thick of the postwar Red Scare.

In the first case, *Schenck v. United States* (1919), the secretary of the Socialist Party's Philadelphia branch had been indicted for sending antidraft circulars to men accepted for military service. Schenck's conduct may have amounted to a violation of the Espionage Act, but did the Constitution's guarantee of free speech protect him? According to Holmes, for a unanimous Court, it did not. For justification, Holmes looked to traditional principles of responsibility for attempted crimes. At common law, unsuccessful attempts could be punished if they came dangerously close to success but not otherwise. Hence the test in every case was whether the words used were of a nature, and in such circumstances, "as to create a clear and present danger that they will bring about the substantive evils that Congress has a right to prevent."

Schenck brought the phrase "clear and present danger" into discussion, but Holmes's reasoning used the venerable "bad-tendency" test, derived from Blackstone: The right of free speech precluded prior restraint (prior censorship), but the law could punish speech that had any tendency to harm the public welfare. In *Schenck,* it was enough that, in time of war, circulars like the defendant's had some tendency to obstruct the draft. In a companion case, the Court unanimously affirmed the conviction of Eugene Debs, the famous labor leader and Socialist candidate for president, for a speech criticizing the war and praising men imprisoned for draft resistance. Although citing *Schenck* as dispositive, Holmes's opinion nowhere mentioned "clear and present danger"; nor would it have been easy to show that the danger of obstructing the draft was either clear or present.

Holmes's decisions upholding the Espionage Act convictions dismayed his liberal admirers. Zechariah Chafee, a young law professor at Harvard, wrote a widely noted law review article asserting that the Framers' First Amendment was intended not simply to outlaw prior restraints of speech but also to curtail the common law of sedition. Chafee then seized on Holmes's "clear and present danger" language in *Schenck* and claimed disingenuously that Holmes had intended to craft a test that would make "the punishment of words for their bad tendency impossible."

Along with the excesses of the Red Scare, the criticisms of Chafee and others helped prompt Holmes and Brandeis to reconsider the significance and purposes of free speech. Chafee's creative reconstruction of "clear and present danger" gave them a means to set out changed views without repudiating their prior decisions. When in the next term, the Court affirmed another Espionage Act conviction in *Abrams v. United States* (1919), Holmes and Brandeis dissented and began to elaborate "clear and present danger" in ways that transformed it into a First Amendment test providing substantial protection for dissident speech. Most important, their reading of the test precluded punishment of speech unless it imminently threatened an illegal act. Unlike his opinions the previous term, Holmes's *Abrams* dissent gave enduring expression to the values of free speech and political toleration in a liberal democratic society. "When men have realized that time has come to upset many fighting faiths, they may come to believe even more than they believe the very foundations of their own conduct that the ultimate good desired is better reached by free trade in ideas."

In time, the dissents of Holmes and Brandeis would become authoritative statements of the meaning of the free-speech clause, quoted in hundreds of decisions down to the present day. That Holmes chose the metaphor of free trade to evoke the value of free exchange of ideas speaks volumes of the grip of laissez-faire liberalism on the constitutional imagination of the White Court. But if they used the metaphor of the market, the dissenters reminded the Court and the nation that, as Brandeis put it, many Americans could not "believe that the liberty guaranteed by the Fourteenth Amendment" safeguarded "only liberty to acquire and to enjoy property."

Race Relations

The White Court's decisions on race relations were among its most notable and most surprising. Racism in America grew worse during the Progressive Era. Segregation and black disenfranchisement were consolidated in the South, lynching flourished, Woodrow Wilson welcomed Jim Crow to Washington, and racist "science" poured out of the nation's great universities, filling respectable white public opinion with notions of blacks' innate inferiority. Almost all leading white progressives agreed with, or at least acquiesced in, the conclusion reached by the soured Georgia Populist Tom Watson. Social reform for white Southerners required black disenfranchisement and segregation. Blacks were a "backward people"; disenfranchisement, a "necessary reform." Progressives' responsibility lay in persuading Southern whites of the virtues of benign segregation over "brutality." Gradual uplift in "separate and special" institutions would lead the "Negro" toward "industrial efficiency" without endangering the betterment of white farmers and workers.

Although race relations hit rock bottom in almost every quarter, advocates for racial equality found a measure of support on the Supreme Court for the first time. The White Court not only refused to support the forces of racial oppression but also resisted them at some critical points. The Court, famously, "follows the election returns." Why not here? The cases fall into four main areas.

"Separate but Equal"

First came the doctrine of separate but equal, originating in *Plessy v. Ferguson* (1896). *Plessy* did not find that the Constitution required racially separated railway facilities to be equal; the Louisiana statute at issue included an equality requirement, and the Court merely held that the statute satisfied the Constitution. *Plessy,* then, provided no occasion for the Court to decide whether separate and *un*equal could be constitutional, although language in the opinion and in other 1890s race cases suggested that the

Constitution required only reasonableness. In 1914, in *McCabe v. Atchison, Topeka & Santa Fe Railway Company,* a majority of the Court decided to confront the question.

McCabe involved an Oklahoma law permitting railroads to provide first-class accommodations only to white passengers. The case was decided in the defendants' favor on narrow procedural grounds, but a majority of the justices spoke on the merits in an opinion authored by future Chief Justice Charles Evan Hughes. The railroad and the Oklahoma attorney general argued for a "reasonable" inequality: To require first-class accommodations for blacks was unreasonable, as there was little demand. Hughes rejected this out of hand: "the essence of the constitutional right is that it is a personal one." It was the individual "who is entitled to equal protection of the laws."

The logic of *McCabe* spelled Jim Crow's doom in many important Southern institutions. But the Court's readiness to press that logic remained unrealized until *Missouri ex rel. Gaines v. Canada* (1938), decades away, and on its face, *McCabe* did not threaten the constitutionality of segregation per se. The typical Jim Crow statute required that separate be equal, and federal courts would continue to wink at actual inequalities as long as legal formalities were observed. Still, the Supreme Court's condemnation of express inequalities in public transportation was a signal event, particularly at a moment when Southern lawmakers were creating an increasingly oppressive regime of racial apartheid, and the other two branches of the federal government were only encouraging them.

Residential Segregation

The White Court also made new law in the area of residential segregation — the only context in which the Court rejected "separate but equal." *Buchanan v. Warley* (1917) involved a Fourteenth Amendment challenge to a residential segregation ordinance in Louisville, Kentucky. The ordinance required that houses sold on city blocks that were majority white (or black) could be occupied only by whites (or blacks). The occupancy rights of existing owners were left undisturbed, and there was an exception for servants. Such ordinances originated in 1910 in Baltimore and spread to dozens of Southern cities, especially in the border states. Virginia authorized its cities to divide whole areas, even entire towns or cities, into "segregation districts," where only one race could live.

Residential segregation laws spurred challenges from local chapters of the newly formed National Association for the Advancement of Colored People (NAACP). Moorfield Storey, the NAACP's first president, argued the Louisville case in the Supreme Court. Storey denounced Louisville's claim that the law operated equally on black and white; the city's own brief proclaimed that "only the most degraded and vicious element among the white would be willing to live in a normally negro section." No less centrally, Storey argued that the ordinance injured the rights of property prized by laissez-faire constitutionalism.

The Court adopted both aspects of Storey's argument, recalling that the core purpose of the Reconstruction amendments was to ensure "equality of civil rights" for blacks and also that the "fundamental law" of the Fourteenth Amendment prevented "state interference with property rights." The Court thereby finally, and unanimously, drew a constitutional limit to Jim Crow. It was the least any Supreme Court sternly committed to property rights and economic liberty could do, and its practical impact on racial segregation was tiny. But it was more than most Court watchers, white or black, expected. After all, "separate but equal" neighborhoods could be defended as "reasonable" social policy on much the same ground as "separate but equal" railway cars and schools: social peace, custom, the inability of law to change racial feelings.

Perhaps a Court less deeply committed to policing legislative interference with property rights would have done less on behalf of African Americans. A more "progressive" court might have exercised greater deference toward the policy objectives of the city of Louisville. It is among the great ironies of laissez-faire constitutionalism that an ideology notorious for its callous indifference to the plight of the economic underdog could on some critical occasions lend assistance to the racially oppressed.

Laissez-Faire and Economic Liberty

The Court's third major foray into race relations was also bound up with laissez-faire and economic liberty. The irony was even more pointed, for the cases involved labor relations and liberty of contract. In *Coppage* and the like, the Court's devotion to liberty of contract and hostility toward "class legislation" led it to strike down laws that *attacked* the economic coercion and exploitation of workers in the nation's industries. But in *Bailey v. Alabama* (1911) and later cases, this same devotion prompted the invalidation of laws that *intensified* exploitation and coercion of black workers in Southern agriculture.

From the end of slavery onward, Southern lawmakers sought ways to "make serfs of the blacks," and by the early twentieth century, they had fashioned an infernal web of laws and institutions: slavery-like convict labor, convict leasing, criminal surety laws whose fodder was supplied by broad and harsh vagrancy and petty-theft statutes, contract enforcement laws, false-pretense laws, and a host of others. The law at issue in *Bailey* was a false-pretense statute, criminalizing entry into a labor contract with the "fraudulent intent" to breach it after obtaining an advance on wages. The typical agricultural labor contract was usually for one year and included some advance pay. The Alabama statute in question was typical in making the fact of breach presumptive proof of the required "intent." Alabama also barred defendants from testifying in refutation of the presumption. Thus, criminal conviction followed from mere breach of contract and failure to pay a debt.

The Justice Department's amicus brief on Bailey's behalf pointed out that the statute gave Alabama planters "absolute dominion over the negro laborer." In one of his first opinions for the Court, however, Justice Hughes divorced the case from the South. "No question of a sectional character" was involved. The case was purely one of liberty of labor; the statute might hence be viewed "as if it had been enacted in New York." Its "natural operation and effect" was to punish mere breach of contract, creating a species of peonage in violation of the Thirteenth Amendment (intended "to make labor free") and of the antipeonage statute that the Reconstruction Congress had enacted in 1867 under that amendment.

No doubt it gratified Hughes, as well as the Court's most laissez-faire-minded members, to invoke "freedom of labor" on behalf of a downtrodden laborer. Liberty of contract had not previously been invoked by the Court to protect employees from their employers. The decision was hailed by Northern and Southern progressives alike. Peonage, unlike segregation, was seen as an unwholesome and embarrassing vestige of the old, slave South. Thus, *Bailey* became a reassuring symbol of the progressive tendencies of constitutional law. In one of its first opinions under its new, ex-Confederate chief, the Court had risen above sectional recriminations and the bitter dilemmas of race to extend federal protection to the "least among us" in the name of free labor.

In fact, freedom to sell one's labor to whom one pleased and to quit without fear of violence and legal compulsion remained far off for African Americans in much of the rural South. Private violence and intimidation, a lily-white officialdom devoted to "holding the negro down," and the ever-present threat of the chain gang combined with continual debt to keep countless black laborers in semibondage. These forces would never be fully routed while Southern blacks lacked the power to vote.

Black Suffrage

The promise of the Fifteenth Amendment had been that with suffrage, the freedmen would be enabled to safeguard their freedom themselves. But the federal government had long since abandoned its commitment to the black man's right to vote. Early-twentieth-century Republican leaders, such as Taft, more interested in sectional reconciliation and Southern votes, publicly declared that black suffrage had been a failure. Progressive Democrats, such as Woodrow Wilson, emphatically agreed. The Fuller Court had put none of its moral capital into black suffrage, upholding literacy tests and the like, and bluntly refusing relief to black citizens denied opportunity to register as voters.

Improbably, however, a case came that mitigated the Court's abandonment of the Fifteenth Amendment. *Guinn v. Oklahoma* (1915) involved that particularly blatant disenfranchising device, the grandfather clause, which exempted from Oklahoma's literacy test all persons qualified to vote in 1866 (before the Fifteenth Amendment's enactment) and lineal descendants of such persons. The clause insulated illiterate whites from the literacy requirement.

Guinn would never have reached the Court had it not been for a U.S. attorney prepared to press criminal charges against state election officials in defiance of instructions from the attorney general to drop the matter. Had it involved some measure more central to the machinery of disenfranchisement than the grandfather clause, the Justice Department might well have dismissed the suit, even as it got under way. But few Southern states still relied on the grandfather clause. Perhaps, too, the Justice Department expected the Oklahoma jury to acquit. In any event, the lower federal court found the clause a violation of the Fifteenth Amendment; the jury found on careful instructions that the defendants had deprived blacks of their constitutional rights; and the court of appeals certified the question of validity, and nothing else, to the Supreme Court. And there, the ex-Confederate chief mustered a unanimous Court behind condemnation of the clause.

For the first time, the Court struck down a state law disenfranchising black people and breathed a bit of life into the battered Fifteenth Amendment. It was no more than that. The decision left the literacy test alone and any other disenfranchising measure that could be read as neutral rather than a racial ruse "on its face." Few Southern newspapers failed to point out that grandfather clauses had "merely helped to disarm any opposition from the illiterate whites." For many conservative Southern whites, "neutral" measures, such as the poll tax and property qualifications that could be used against poor white Populists as well as poor blacks, were more appealing.

Southern white supremacy enjoyed sympathy and support in white public opinion throughout the country. Black disenfranchisement remained durable after *Guinn*, just as segregation on the railways did after *McCabe*. Both cases involved outlier statutes that were racially exclusionary and unequal on their face. Invalidating them nevertheless implied a principle. The Court would not allow the Reconstruction amendments to become entirely dead letters. Statutes that flouted the promise of equality in their very terms would be struck down. Separate but equal was acceptable, but openly mandated racial exclusion was not.

In *Buchanan,* and in *Bailey* and the other peonage cases, the Court went slightly farther, drawing a constitutional limit to the reign of "separate but equal" and striking down laws central to black serfdom. It was no coincidence that these two more robust decisions spoke less of racial equality than of property rights and freedom of contract. The laissez-faire constitutionalism bequeathed by the Fuller Court — the federal judiciary as fearless, countermajoritarian guardian of economic liberty — remained, a vital aspect of the White Court's identity and arsenal. What better way to affirm the ideal's evenhandedness than to wield it not only on business's behalf but also for the "least among us"?

Nevertheless, no important political constituency had demanded such progress or evenhandedness on black America's behalf. The elected branches of the federal government did far less. Almost all white standard-bearers of progressivism embraced the callous and bigoted notion of the "backward black race's" slow, evolutionary progress, into which segregation and disenfranchisement fit snugly and smugly. The Court acted because the momentum of racism had produced laws that were blatantly unconstitutional, and a straight-faced commitment to constitutionalism and vigorous judicial guardianship demanded standing behind the Reconstruction amendments. Doing so boosted the morale of the newly founded NAACP, sustained its faith in the nation's judiciary, and established precedents that would bear more ample fruit in a better season, decades away.

Progressivism and the White Court

In hindsight, the most "progressive" impulse of the White Court lay in its modest assault on Jim Crow and in the great dissenting opinions by Holmes and Brandeis interpreting the First Amendment. Both presaged the role of the federal judiciary as an important champion of the rights of racial minorities and political dissidents against executive and legislative oppression and indifference. At the time, however, the benchmarks of "progressiveness" were different. Theodore Roosevelt posed the day's "vital questions" best: "proper control" of large corporations, securing the rights of industrial workers, and resisting judicial constraint on the powers of "the people themselves" — and of lawmakers and new administrative agencies — to address such matters.

Here, the White Court gained its reputation for "progressiveness" by up-holding many more social and economic reforms than it struck down. Not infrequently, it mustered a majority behind an opinion by Holmes or Brandeis reminding the lower courts that property rights and liberty of contract were not absolutes and could not restrain government from ad-dressing "all the great public needs." But liberty of contract and the rights of property retained real potency—in *Coppage* and the labor injunction cases and in many dissents by the chief justice, Van Devanter, McReynolds, and McKenna. Alongside the progressive currents of doctrinal develop-ment continued to flow a conservative one.

Indeed, the *Lochner* Constitution still defined the terms of argument. Even though White Court judicial review most often reaffirmed the state police power, the Court continued to entertain the most extravagant claims of liberty of contract, encouraging the predominantly conservative, Re-publican lower federal bench routinely to grant decrees against the en-forcement of hundreds of state laws. Even when overturned, these decrees delayed for years the implementation of the social reform at issue.

Just as the Court's more conservative members drew back from bold so-cial reforms emanating from the states, so too they resisted Congress's ef-forts. After upholding the federal police power in early cases, the Court hes-itated at the implications for their vision of a limited central government. Child labor was the bridge too far. The conservative majority was deter-mined to preserve manufacturing, mining, and agricultural employment for the individual states to regulate, leaving in place the contradiction of a national government constitutionally barred from regulating core ele-ments of national economic life. And the Court left intact its own final au-thority over trade unionism, corporate expansion, and corporate conduct too, interpreting the era's new antitrust laws to reaffirm the judiciary's common-law governance over the nation's political economy. In all these ways, the federal judiciary under the White Court's stewardship remained a profoundly conservative institution in a progressive age.

—WILLIAM E. FORBATH

FOR FURTHER READING AND RESEARCH

The single most insightful general study of the White Court is Alexander M. Bickel and Benno C. Schmidt's *The Judiciary and Responsible Government, 1910–1921* (New York, 1984), volume 9 of the *History of the Supreme Court of the United States* (the Oliver Wendell Holmes Devise). Before his untimely death, Bickel wrote the still unrivaled chapters dealing with the politics of judicial appointments, the inner workings of the Court, and judicial review of federal and state social and economic legislation. No less valuable are the chapters by Schmidt, which offer a detailed account of the White Court's race-relations cases and their historical context and significance. Progressivism, the protean movement that defined so much of the White Court's agenda, is the subject of a whole library's worth of studies; among the best overviews are Robert H. Wiebe, *The Search for Order, 1877–1920* (New York, 1967); Arthur Link and Richard L. McCormick, *Progressivism* (Arlington Heights, Ill., 1983); and Morton Keller, *Regulating a New Society: Public Policy and Social Change in America, 1900–1933* (Cambridge, Mass., 1994). On the Court's all-important antitrust cases and the broader legal and political contests over corporate consolidation, the key work is Martin J. Sklar, *The Corporate Reconstruction of American Capitalism, 1890–1916* (Cambridge and New York, 1988). On the Court's controversial role as architect of the law of industrial relations and industrial conflict, see William E. Forbath, *Law and the Shaping of the American Labor Movement* (Cambridge, Mass., 1991). And, finally, on the Court's postwar encounters with wartime repression of free speech and political liberty and, especially, on the emergence of modern First Amendment jurisprudence in the Holmes and Brandeis dissents, see David M. Rabban, *Free Speech in Its Forgotten Years* (Cambridge and New York, 1994).

9

The Taft Court 1921–1930

Groping for Modernity

WILLIAM HOWARD TAFT fulfilled a lifelong dream on October 3, 1921, when he became chief justice of the United States. Although his years in the executive branch — as commissioner of the Philippines and then secretary of war under President Theodore Roosevelt, followed by four years (1909–1913) as president himself — had not been unrewarding, Taft above all else loved the bench. He had, he believed, a judicial temperament, and he venerated the law. "I love judges and I love courts," he once wrote. "They are my ideals, that typify on earth what we shall meet hereafter in heaven under a just God." The nine years that he headed the nation's high court, however, proved to be difficult, and the accomplishments of his tenure owed as much to the executive ability he brought to the position as to his love of the law. The difficulties resulted from historic changes in the nation's social, economic, and political fabric. The Court responded to these changes much as the nation did — with some resolution and a great deal of confusion.

Taft's Management of the Judiciary

Taft presided over a Court made up primarily of legal conservatives who subscribed to what William Wiecek has termed "legal classicism." Taft the administrator believed that the lessons he had learned in the executive branch could be applied to the courts as well. With his wealth of contacts in Congress and in the Republican administrations of Harding and then Coolidge, Taft had the knowledge, the experience, and the political network to undertake a complete reform of the federal judiciary. He did so successfully and well deserves the title of father of modern judicial management.

Taft achieved his first victory in this campaign when Congress passed a 1922 act establishing a conference of each circuit's senior judges, who would meet on a regular basis with the chief justice to identify problems in the system, and empowering the chief justice to reassign district court judges on a temporary basis to help reduce backlogs. During hearings on the bill, Taft became the first chief justice to testify before a Senate committee. He believed it to be "one of the most important acts in the history of the judiciary." The act not only set up the conference, the predecessor of today's Judicial Conference, but also required an annual report on the judiciary, analogous to the State of the Union. Perhaps most important, the act recognized the federal courts as a single administrative unit and established the basic tools through which this system could be properly managed.

Three years later, Congress gave Taft the second tool he needed in the Judiciary Act of 1925, also known as the Judges' Bill. A committee consisting of Justices Sutherland, McReynolds, and Van Devanter had drawn up the bill. Taft had begun lobbying for it immediately after passage of the 1922 measure.

The Judges' Bill granted the Supreme Court control of its docket. Before 1925, the Court had relatively little direct control over its docket and had to hear on appeal a variety of cases, the majority of which had nothing to do with constitutional issues and in many cases not even with federal law. The workload of the Court had increased to the point that it took nearly two years for a case to be heard after its initial filing. Taft believed that the Supreme Court should be primarily a constitutional court, its chief task to interpret that document so "as to furnish precedents for the inferior courts in future litigation and for the executive officers in the construction of statutes and the performance of their legal duties." The Judges' Bill reduced the mandatory jurisdiction of the high court and gave it the power to pick and choose which cases it would hear through the discretionary writ of certiorari. The provisions of the bill implemented Taft's belief that the main business of the Supreme Court should be the development of federal law, a task that required broad managerial discretion.

Taft also took it on himself to find the Court more dignified quarters. In the 1920s, the Court still met in the Old Senate Chamber in the Capitol (Plates A.7 and A.14). The justices had no privacy (after robing in one room, they had to parade down a corridor to the courtroom), lacked private offices, and made do with a single cramped room in the basement for a library. In 1925, Taft began lobbying vigorously for a separate building that would not only be totally under the Court's control but also give the Court the public stature appropriate to a branch of government coequal with the

Congress and the presidency. Congress responded favorably and approved the site he recommended on East Capitol Street next to the Library of Congress and facing the Capitol. Taft involved himself in all aspects of the building's architecture and design (Plates B.3 and B.4) but, sadly, did not live to see completion of his Marble Palace in 1935.

The chief justice fought for measures he believed necessary to the Court's management and opposed bills he believed would harm the judiciary. Southern champions of states' rights and some Midwestern insurgents opposed federal diversity jurisdiction; in 1928, George Norris of Nebraska and Thomas Walsh of Montana sponsored S.3151 to strip federal courts of both federal question and diversity jurisdiction. Norris, who headed the Senate Judiciary Committee, managed to get the bill reported favorably to the floor. Although Taft could not openly oppose the measure, he displayed a deft political touch as he rounded up influential lawyers and bar association heads to speak against the bill, which ultimately failed.

Taft's efforts to impose managerial uniformity on the federal courts faltered in only one area, when Congress refused to accede to his request that it authorize judicial promulgation of uniform rules of civil procedure, merging both law and equity, which would be binding in all federal courts. The Conformity Act of 1872 had in theory called for the same procedure in state and federal courts. But by the 1920s, state procedural reforms had changed state rules greatly, whereas federal rules had become riddled with exceptions. But even though Taft failed in his attempt, he had squarely recognized the problem. Within a few years, so too would Congress. The Rules Enabling Act authorizing the Court to prepare and implement the Federal Rules of Civil Procedure passed in 1934 and went into effect in September 1938. In many ways, the rules are also a legacy of Taft's efforts to impose proper managerial practices on the judicial system.

Finally, Taft believed that in order for its pronouncements to be as authoritative as possible, the Court should speak with one voice, a view held by Taft's judicial idol, John Marshall. Within the Court, he promoted teamwork and tried to "mass" the Court in order to give greater credence to its rulings. He worked well with both the conservatives and the liberals (Brandeis thought Taft's management of the Court, if not his personal jurisprudence, superb), assigned opinions fairly and carefully, and made conferences far more pleasant than they had been under White. During his term as chief, 84 percent of all written opinions were unanimous, compared to fewer than 20 percent today. Few of Taft's own opinions have withstood the test of time, but his abilities as chief justice in the administration of the federal judiciary are widely recognized. It is ironic in many ways that the man who had been such a poor politician and administrator as president performed so brilliantly in these areas as chief justice.

Protection of Property Rights

In dealing with the jurisprudential legacy of the Taft Court, one is struck by great incongruities. On the one hand, the conservative nature of the Court's majority tended to favor business, the status quo, and property rights and to oppose government regulation and labor unions. On the other hand, the Court sustained national power, restricted property rights to accommodate the new idea of zoning, took a broad view of interstate commerce, and began the revolution in civil liberties through the process of incorporation.

Conservative opposition to federal regulatory agencies was clearly manifested in *Federal Trade Commission v. Gratz* (1920) and found even stronger expression in *Federal Trade Commission v. Curtis Publishing Company* (1923), which in essence dismissed any fact-finding done by the agency and gave federal courts the power to investigate the evidence anew. If the Court agreed with the FTC's conclusions, they would be binding; if not, the Court would make its own determination. As a result, corporations could tie up the FTC for years by challenging every ruling in federal court and then going through a process of introducing evidence that the FTC supposedly had overlooked. The Court cannot be held solely responsible for the emasculation of the FTC and other federal regulatory agencies. Both the Harding and Coolidge administrations did their best to pack commissions with men sympathetic to the very business interests they were supposed to regulate. In 1925, for example, Coolidge named lumber attorney William E. Humphreys to head the FTC, and Humphreys immediately denounced the agency as "an instrument of oppression and disturbance and injury instead of help to business."

The Court also dealt with a rash of rate cases, stemming from its earlier insistence in *Smyth v. Ames* (1898) that the judiciary had to be the final arbiter of the fairness of administratively set rates for public utilities. Only two members of the Court fully understood the economic intricacies of rate making — Pierce Butler, a former railroad lawyer, and Louis Brandeis, who had served as shippers' attorney in numerous rate-making hearings before the Interstate Commerce Commission. Nevertheless, in *State of Missouri ex rel. Southwestern Bell Telephone Company v. Public Service Commission of Missouri* (1922), Justice McReynolds charged that the commission had not allowed for a fair return on invested capital because it had been negligent in assessing the current value of the property. The case showed how a determined company could eviscerate state rate-making agencies by continual appeals to sympathetic courts, claiming that the evaluation had been unfair.

Brandeis entered a separate opinion attacking the whole notion that courts should be involved in rate making. Although he agreed in this case that the rates had in fact been too low, Brandeis noted that prices of property and equipment fluctuated from year to year, so that it would never be possible to set a reliable rate schedule if every determination by a state agency could be attacked in federal courts. Brandeis's proposal for the Court to establish basic principles of rate making and then leave their implementation to state agencies and state courts received little encouragement from either the brethren or business interests, but eventually his argument against federal judicial involvement in state rate making won out. The courts withdrew from the rate-making business in the 1930s.

Support of Federal Power

If it seemed intent on destroying the effectiveness of the FTC, the Court nonetheless upheld a strong federal regulatory power in *Railroad Commission of Wisconsin v. Chicago, Burlington & Quincy Railroad* (1922). The Transportation Act of 1920 had expanded the authority of the Interstate Commerce Commission over not only interstate rates but also intrastate rates. In 1921, the commission had issued a new rate schedule that in many areas was higher than rates set by state agencies. Wisconsin and twenty other states attacked the law as exceeding the federal government's power. The Court unanimously upheld the ICC. The law "imposed an affirmative duty," Taft explained, to "fix rates and to take other important steps to maintain adequate railway service for the people of the United States." This reasoning reappeared when the Court upheld the recapture provisions of the 1920 law in *Dayton-Goose Creek Railway Company v. United States* (1924) and emphasized the need to see the railroads as a national system in *Colorado v. United States* (1926).

Perhaps because of his experience in the executive branch, Taft himself took a broad view of the federal commerce power. In 1928, he told Harlan Fiske Stone that the power of Congress over interstate commerce is "exactly what it would be in a government without states." In *Stafford v. Wallace* (1922) and *Board of Trade of the City of Chicago v. Olsen* (1923), Taft reiterated his view that "it is primarily for Congress to consider and decide the fact of the danger [to commerce] and meet it. This court will certainly not substitute its judgment for that of Congress in such a matter unless the relation of the subject to interstate commerce and its effect upon it are clearly non-existent." The Taft Court also took a strongly nationalistic view of the dormant commerce power, which it used in the 1920s to strike down state legislation that "unduly burdened" interstate commerce. In *Compania General de Tabacos de Filipinas v. Collector of Internal Revenue* (1927), the chief justice, speaking for a unanimous Court, made clear that the Court would sustain and protect a national common market.

The chief justice's former experience as president also strongly influenced the Court's decision in *Myers v. United States* (1926), which finally brought the Reconstruction-era Tenure of Office Act (1867) before the judiciary. In 1920, President Wilson had fired Frank S. Myers, the postmaster of Oregon, without Senate approval. Myers died shortly afterward, and his estate sued for damages and lost wages. Taft's opinion for the Court declared unconstitutional the congressional limitation on the president's power to remove appointed officers, and his comments gave the chief executive broad discretion in both appointments and removals. Brandeis entered a strong dissent, which became the law nine years later when the Court reversed *Myers* in *Humphrey's Executor v. United States* (1935).

The Court also sustained federal power in the first cases testing the new device of federal grants-in-aid, sums of money given by the national government to the states to be used for specified purposes. In 1921, Congress passed the Sheppard-Towner Act to promote state infant and maternity care programs. States did not have to participate in the program, but if they did, the grants-in-aid had to be expended under conditions set forth by Congress. The reactionary mood of the 1920s had little use for social frills, such as maternity care, and critics charged Congress with having extended federal power into areas specifically reserved to state authority.

In 1923, the Court had the opportunity to rule on this issue in *Massachusetts v. Mellon,* when the state attacked the constitutionality of the Sheppard-Towner Act. The decision, by Justice Sutherland, sustained the act indirectly by denying that the Court had jurisdiction. Massachusetts had presented "no justiciable controversy either in its own behalf or as the representative of its citizens." A state could not act for its citizens against the United States, because they were citizens of the United States as well. As to the issue of the federal government's invading state power, the Court declared it a political question and therefore not amenable to judicial resolution. In his comments, however, Sutherland clearly implied the constitutionality of noncoercive grants. If the state did not wish to engage in the program and thus accept federal oversight, it could simply refuse to participate. But if it accepted federal funds, it had no power to question the use of legally collected tax monies.

Retreat on Social Issues

Labor

The label *conservative* or indeed even *reactionary* often applied to the Taft Court stems in large measure from its treatment of labor and of state reform legislation. There is no question that the majority of the Taft Court justices held definite antilabor prejudices.

Labor leaders thought that they had won a major victory in the Clayton Act of 1914. Section 6 explicitly declared that labor did not constitute a commodity or an article of commerce and that, consequently, the antitrust laws should not be interpreted to forbid unions from seeking their legitimate objectives. Section 20 prohibited federal courts from issuing injunctions or restraining orders in labor disputes unless necessary to prevent damage to property and also forbade injunctions against peaceful picketing or primary boycotts.

The Supreme Court ruled on these sections in *Duplex Printing Press Company v. Deering* (1921). The case had arisen when unions boycotted a manufacturer's products in New York to enforce a strike in Michigan. Justice Mahlon Pitney ruled that the law had not legitimized such secondary boycotts and that section 6 had not provided a blanket exemption from the antitrust laws. The law's wording protected unions only in lawfully carrying out their legitimate objectives. Because secondary boycotts were unlawful, neither section 6 nor section 20 applied. Moreover, Pitney interpreted section 20 to mean that injunctions could be issued not only against the immediate parties — the employer and the striking workers — but also to restrain another union from supporting the strikers.

The *Duplex* case came down immediately after *Truax v. Corrigan*, in which the Court struck down a state anti-injunction statute. In this case, an Arizona restaurant owner had sought an injunction in state court against peaceful pickets, claiming that the state law denying him an injunction had deprived him of his property rights without due process of law. Taft agreed and declared the law unconstitutional as an arbitrary and capricious exercise of power and as a highly injurious invasion of property rights. Even Pitney found this too much. In his dissent, he argued that states had considerable latitude to determine "each for itself, their respective conditions of law and order, and what kind of civilization they shall have as a result."

Brandeis dissented in both cases. In *Truax*, he saw the anti-injunction statute as a positive good; whenever he could, especially in his powerful dissents, which bore a striking resemblance to the "Brandeis briefs," he explored the social needs that had called forth the legislative response.

In *Duplex,* he explained how Congress, in the Clayton Act, had determined that abuses of the injunction had gone too far in limiting labor's legitimate activities and had set up a standard that it considered fair to both parties. Judges did not have the prerogative to undo congressional policy because they disagreed with it or because their own economic and social views ran counter to those of the legislative branch. As with so many of his dissents in the 1920s, Brandeis's reasoning in *Truax* would eventually be adopted by a later Court as constitutionally correct.

The two decisions are also important in illuminating how the Taft Court used principles of federalism to create a gray area that precluded both state and federal restrictions on the injunction. Whenever unions threatened to strike, employers could go into court and get an injunction, a court order barring workers from going out on strike. As a result, the rest of the decade saw government by injunction quite as extensive as before the Clayton Act; more than two hundred injunctions were issued during the 1920s Railway Shopmen's strike alone. By the end of the decade, one commentator after another had joined in the general condemnation of the use of injunctions. The American Civil Liberties Union's annual report for 1928–1929 declared that "the most extreme restrictions on free speech and assemblage are caused by injunctions in industrial conflicts. It is the weapon of repression most difficult to combat." But not until the Depression undermined the dominance of business interests did reformers finally get the Norris-LaGuardia Anti-Injunction Act through Congress in March 1932; a number of states then followed with similar measures of their own.

Labor's supposed protection under the Clayton Act suffered further erosion in the two *Coronado Coal Company* cases in 1925. The United Mine Workers had been trying to unionize Southern coalfields to prevent the ruination of Northern mines by the cheaper Southern coal. Following the standard established in *E. C. Knight* (1895), Chief Justice Taft ruled that coal mining itself did not constitute interstate commerce. A strike, as the simple withholding of labor, could not be enjoined under the Clayton Act. But a strike that aimed at stopping the interstate shipment of nonunion coal certainly fell within the proscriptions of the Sherman Act. Therefore, any labor activity that had the intent, and not simply an incidental result, of interfering with interstate commerce violated the antitrust laws.

Two years later, in *Bedford Cut Stone Company v. Journeymen Stone Cutters Association,* the Court again showed how it could manipulate definitions to restrict labor. In conformity with their union's constitution, a handful of peaceful stonecutters refused to work on limestone cut by nonunion workers in the unorganized Bedford Cut Stone Company. The firm sought an injunction, but in order to enjoin the strikers, the lower court had to rely on the Sherman Act's restriction on secondary boycotts.

The Supreme Court agreed with this approach and then justified it by turning a very local and limited strike into a burden on the stream of interstate commerce. Under the rule of reason, the Court would tolerate reasonable restrictions on trade caused by industry but would disregard its own rule when asked to apply it to the clearly reasonable activities of a labor union.

Women

Protective legislation also fell on judicial hard times. Even some conservatives protested when the Supreme Court's majority resurrected the *Lochner* (1905) doctrine in *Adkins v. Children's Hospital* (1923). In striking down a federal statute establishing minimum wages for women in the District of Columbia, Justice Sutherland reaffirmed the paramount position of freedom of contract in economic affairs. Freedom, he declared, "is the general rule and restraint the exception; and the exercise of legislative authority to abridge it can be justified only by the existence of exceptional circumstances." Emancipated by the Nineteenth Amendment, women no longer had need for protective laws. They could work for whatever amount they freely chose to contract for, just like men.

The ruling and the reasoning behind it shocked the nation. Most people had assumed that after *Muller v. Oregon* (1908) and *Bunting v. Oregon* (1917), the Court had accepted the need to protect certain classes of society through the state's police power. Sutherland ignored a decade of cases and went back to *Lochner;* even in the conservative 1920s, his opinion seemed overly reactionary. He launched into a vigorous attack on minimum-wage legislation of any sort. Wages constituted the "heart of the contract" and could never be fixed by legislative fiat. Human necessities could never take precedence over economic rights, for "the good of society as a whole cannot be better served than by the preservation of the liberties of its constituent members."

Even Chief Justice Taft, who could hardly be described as liberal, could not swallow Sutherland's opinion and registered one of only twenty dissents he filed during his decade on the Court. Taft conceded that people differed over the efficacy of minimum-wage legislation, but in as strong a statement of judicial restraint as Holmes or Brandeis ever delivered, Taft argued that "it is not the function of the Court to hold congressional acts invalid simply because they are passed to carry out economic views which the Court believes to be unwise or unsound." Holmes agreed with Taft and added a few pithy comments in a dissent of his own. He deplored the fact that liberty of contract, which had started out as an "innocuous generality," had now become dogma. As for Sutherland's fatuous claim that women's suffrage had ended the need for special legislation, Holmes simply observed that "it will need more than the Nineteenth Amendment to convince me that there is no difference between women and men." (Brandeis took no part in the 5–3 decision, because his daughter Elizabeth served on the District of Columbia Minimum Wage Board.)

The year after *Adkins*, the Court, again speaking through Sutherland, upheld a state statute prohibiting the employment of women between the hours of 10 PM and 6 AM in restaurants in large cities. In *Radice v. New York* (1924), Sutherland declared that facts existed to justify such regulation, even though he had dismissed the extensive facts supplied in *Adkins*. Sounding more like Holmes and Brandeis, he indicated that courts should defer to factual findings reached by a legislature. Sutherland apparently believed that a significant difference existed between the very limited police powers of the federal government and the more extensive authority enjoyed by the states. Working conditions could be subject to state regulation, but the courts would determine the reasonableness of the regulations.

Adkins influenced protective-legislation cases that came before the high court throughout the decade. Sutherland had conceded four well-delineated areas in which courts would accept restraints on contractual freedom: (1) work on public projects; (2) the character, time, and method of wage payments; (3) fixing the hours of labor; and (4) rates charged by businesses affected with the public interest. Reformers saw very little flexibility in the first three categories but hoped that an expansive view of the fourth would permit some experimentation by the states. They soon learned differently. Between 1920 and 1930, the Court found approximately 140 state laws unconstitutional, a large majority on the ground that they violated the liberties of property and contract guaranteed by the Fourteenth Amendment's due process clause.

The "Public Interest" Defined

The lesson was not long in coming. In late 1923, in *Wolff Packing Company v. Court of Industrial Relations*, the conservative majority adopted a narrow view of business affected with a public interest. After World War I, Kansas had embarked on a major experiment in molding law to meet current needs. In 1920, the state passed the Industrial Relations Act, requiring arbitration of all disputes in key industries, such as food, clothing, and shelter, and created a special Industrial Court to handle the arbitration. The act also gave the court powers to enforce its decisions, including the authority to set wages and control working conditions. In the *Wolff* case, Taft destroyed the Industrial Court by ruling the act unconstitutional.

Merely because a state declared a business affected with a public interest did not make it so, and the state could not use that rationalization to interfere with property rights.

Taft listed the only businesses that could be so characterized: public utilities, carried on by a public license; traditional businesses long recognized as subject to regulation, such as inns and gristmills; and businesses in which natural economic laws did not operate, such as monopolies, or whose nature had changed so as to warrant some governmental regulation. For all practical purposes, Taft had apparently negated a half-century of legal development since *Munn v. Illinois* (1877) and put nearly all businesses outside the reach of state regulation. The distinction between public and private, a key element of classic thought, might have faded in stream-of-commerce cases, but in *Wolff*, Taft and the conservatives reminded the nation that they intended to view that as an exception rather than as the rule.

The consequences of the new doctrine appeared quickly. For example, New York had declared theater ticket prices to be a matter of public concern and enacted legislation regulating the resale price of tickets from agencies. In *Tyson v. Banton* (1927), Sutherland simply pointed out that a ticket agency did not fall into any of the three categories that Taft had listed in *Wolff*, and he invalidated the law. In *Ribnik v. McBride* (1928), the Court struck down a New Jersey statute regulating the fees of employment agencies. Sutherland insisted that an employment agency "is essentially a private business," and he declared that "it is no longer fairly open to question that the fixing of prices for food, clothing, house rental, wages to be paid, whether minimum or maximum, is beyond the legislative power." The following year, the Court reemphasized this point when it struck down a Tennessee law that authorized a state official to fix gas prices within the state (*Williams v. Standard Oil Company*).

But if the key to determining the constitutionality of regulatory legislation lay in whether the subject of the regulation fell within the public or the private sphere, how should one explain the landmark ruling in *Euclid v. Ambler Realty* (1926)? Among conservatives, property had always held a near sacred status, and the core of substantive due process had been the almost unlimited right of an owner to use and dispose of property. In *Buchanan v. Warley* (1917), the Court had struck down a local ordinance prohibiting blacks from living in certain areas but had done so not on equal protection grounds but because the rule deprived people of their right to buy and sell property.

During the first quarter of the twentieth century, many municipalities enacted comprehensive land-use, or zoning, plans in an effort to manage growth and sustain the aesthetic nature of the community. The codes varied, but nearly all included some limits on land use in certain areas and placed limits on the type and size of buildings that could be erected. A commercial establishment, for example, could not be built in an area designated for residential use. Landowners and developers challenged these codes on a variety of constitutional grounds, but state courts disagreed on their legitimacy. Eventually, in 1926, the challenge to the zoning ordinance of Euclid, Ohio, reached the Court.

The author of the 6–3 majority opinion upholding the zoning ordinance was George Sutherland, the same justice who had written *Adkins*. In an effort to explain this vote, Sutherland's biographer suggests that the outcome was strongly influenced by the ideas of Thomas Cooley, the influential nineteenth-century judge and legal writer who had written extensively on property rights and their limitations under common law. Sutherland's opinion described the zoning act not as a deprivation of property but as an enhancement. Common law had long allowed for the abatement of nuisances even if doing so restricted property rights, as the end result would be the enhancement of value in all adjoining property. The fact that Euclid was undergoing rapid expansion could not be denied, and overcrowding as well as chaotic development would be harmful to all property owners. Sutherland may also have been influenced by the fact that when Ambler had bought the property, the zoning ordinance had already been in effect, and this undermined the company's claim that its property had been taken without due process; he might have thought differently had the ordinance been passed *after* Ambler had purchased the land.

But if the state could regulate private property in order to ensure rational growth, what remained of the old distinction between public and private? If one's land could be said to be affected with a public interest, what limits, if any, could be imposed on state regulation? This question could not be easily answered by the tenets of the older legal classicism, and *Euclid*, as much as any case, played a major role in its downfall.

The Bill of Rights and the States

Ever since *Barron v. Baltimore* (1833), the Bill of Rights had been held to apply only to the federal government. Although some people argued that the Fourteenth Amendment had extended those guarantees to the states, that view had not yet gained Court approval. In 1922, in *Prudential Insurance Company v. Cheek*, the Court reaffirmed that state infringement of civil liberties remained beyond the control of the federal government or its courts. The Fourteenth Amendment, according to Justice Pitney, had not extended the Bill of Rights to the states. He thus denied Brandeis's argument, made two years earlier in his dissent in *Gilbert v. Minnesota*, that the liberty guaranteed by the Fourteenth Amendment went beyond property rights to include personal freedoms as well.

The first fruits of that dissent appeared in 1923, when the Court struck down a state statute that forbade the teaching of foreign languages in elementary schools. In *Meyer v. Nebraska,* Justice McReynolds applied the *Lochner* doctrine, declaring that liberty denotes

> not merely freedom from bodily restraint but also the right of the individual to contract, to engage in any of the common occupations of life, to acquire useful knowledge, to marry, to establish a home and bring up children, to worship God according to the dictates of his own conscience, and generally to enjoy those privileges long recognized at common law as essential to the orderly pursuit of happiness by free men.

To be sure, McReynolds found property rights involved in the case, as the Nebraska law "materially" interfered "with the calling of modern language teachers." But he also found the measure a violation of free speech. The goal of the legislature to foster "a homogeneous people with American ideals" was understandable in light of the recent war, but now "peace and domestic tranquility" reigned, and he could find no adequate justification for the restraints on liberty. Without using the exact words, McReynolds in effect applied the clear-and-present-danger test and found the statute lacking.

Two years later, McReynolds spoke for a unanimous Court in *Pierce v. Society of Sisters* (1925). The Ku Klux Klan had pushed through a law in Oregon requiring children to attend public schools, with the clear intent of driving the Catholic schools out of existence. Again, McReynolds found "no peculiar circumstances or present emergencies" to justify such an extraordinary measure. The law interfered with both personal and property rights. "The child is not the mere creature of the State," he wrote; "those who nurture him and direct his destiny have the right, coupled with the high duty, to prepare him for additional obligations." Moreover, the law directly attacked the vested property rights of private and parochial schools. McReynolds had only hinted at the constitutional foundation for parochial education in *Meyer;* he firmly established it in *Pierce.*

McReynolds found the justification for both *Meyer* and *Pierce* totally within the due process clause of the Fourteenth Amendment; he applied the *Lochner* doctrine but intimated that other than property rights might be protected as well. American Civil Liberties Union attorneys picked up on McReynolds's two school opinions and Brandeis's *Gilbert* dissent and decided to challenge directly the traditional doctrine that the Bill of Rights did not apply to the states. Their opportunity came in *Gitlow v. New York* (1925).

The *Gitlow* case posed a challenge to New York's 1902 Criminal Anarchy Act. Benjamin Gitlow, a leading figure in the American Communist Party, had been convicted for publishing a radical newspaper, a "left-wing manifesto," and other allegedly subversive materials. If Fourteenth Amendment liberty reached as far as McReynolds had suggested, his lawyer argued, surely it would include the protection of the press and speech. Although the Court affirmed the conviction, Justice Sanford noted: "For present purposes we may and do assume that freedom of speech and of the press — which are protected by the First Amendment from abridgement by Congress — are among the fundamental personal rights protected by the due process clause of the Fourteenth Amendment from impairment by the States." So, for the first time, the Supreme Court put forward what came to be known as the doctrine of incorporation, by which the Fourteenth Amendment "incorporated" the liberties protected in the Bill of Rights and applied them to the states.

Ever since the ratification of the Fourteenth Amendment, debate has continued over whether its framers intended the amendment to extend the Bill of Rights to the states. Historical evidence exists on both sides of the argument. The weight of the evidence supports the claim that the drafters wanted to extend and protect the rights of the freedmen by applying the Bill of Rights to the states as well as to the federal government. But the "original intent" argument is somewhat sterile, given the subsequent perversion of the Civil War amendments in the retreat from Reconstruction. Brandeis was certainly right in his claim that due process had to include more than protection of property, and he could refer to the older English idea of the "law of the land," which went far beyond the rights of property.

If the constitutional system provides certain minimal procedural and substantive guarantees, they must be derived from either explicit or implicit clauses of the Constitution. Since the 1920s, the Court has ruled that the Fourteenth Amendment's due process clause means that the states cannot infringe on fundamental rights. Defining those fundamental rights, however, has been a continuing Court task, one that has engendered much controversy. The process is still not complete, because a developing society is continually reexamining and redefining its values.

Free Speech and the *Whitney* Opinion

Even after agreeing that the First Amendment applied to the states as well, the Taft Court, in its dealings with free speech, nonetheless continued to use the "clear and present danger" test that Holmes had enunciated in *Schenck v. United States* (1919). Holmes had tried, in his dissent in

Abrams v. United States later that year, to make the test more speech protective, but a majority of the Court always managed to find danger lurking in political speech, particularly in the writings and speech of those on the left. It remained for Louis Brandeis, in *Whitney v. California* (1927), to express what has become the bedrock principle of First Amendment jurisprudence, that freedom of speech is a necessary component of democratic society.

Charlotte Anita Whitney, a niece of Justice Stephen J. Field and "a woman nearing sixty, a Wellesley graduate long distinguished in philanthropic work," had been convicted under the California Criminal Syndicalism Act of 1919 for helping to organize the Communist Labor Party there. The law made it a felony to organize or knowingly become a member of an organization founded to advocate the commission of crimes, sabotage, or acts of violence as a means of bringing about political or industrial change. Miss Whitney denied that it had ever been intended that the Communist Labor Party become an instrument of crime or violence; nor was there any proof that it had ever engaged in violent acts. Nevertheless, the conservative majority, led by Justice Sanford, upheld the act as a legitimate decision by the California legislature to prevent the violent overthrow of society. The due process clause did not protect one's liberty to destroy the social and political order.

For technical reasons, Brandeis chose not to dissent, but in his concurring opinion, joined by Holmes, he provided a defense of intellectual freedom unmatched for its powerful reasoning in the annals of the Court. Not only here but in other speech cases, Brandeis claimed, the majority was operating on a totally inappropriate set of assumptions by measuring the limits of free speech against potential danger to property and ignoring the benefits that the free exchange of ideas in itself conferred on society as a whole. Brandeis agreed that, under certain circumstances, a legislature could limit speech, but the proper test for exercising that power would be whether the words posed a clear and imminent danger to *society,* not only to property interests. Suppression of ideas worked a great hardship on society. Before that could be allowed, the Court had a responsibility to develop objective standards, a responsibility that it had thus far failed to meet. Brandeis made it quite clear that, like Holmes, he did not fear ideas and that Americans should not, either.

Brandeis's eloquent opinion set out what would become the basis for First Amendment jurisprudence. Holmes had rested his First Amendment views on what has been termed the marketplace of ideas. Because we cannot know immediately which ideas are good and true and useful and which are not, we must let them vie against one another in the faith that after full exposure and discussion, the truth will win out. This is to some extent a "negative" view of the First Amendment and reflected Holmes's famed skepticism. He saw nothing particularly good or bad in free speech other than the forum it allowed for intellectual competition.

Brandeis, on the other hand, saw free speech as an essential aspect of citizenship. Men and women had the duty in a democracy to be good citizens, which meant being informed on the issues confronting them. How could individuals make intelligent decisions about those issues without having basic information about them? How could citizens judge which side had the better argument unless they could hear both sides and then join in the debate? The fact that some viewpoints ran against the grain or disturbed popular sensibilities made no difference; history was replete with examples of unpopular ideas that had eventually gained public acceptance. Brandeis thus provided a positive justification for protection of speech — the necessity for the citizenry to be fully informed about issues and to be aware of all viewpoints. But Brandeis would not limit First Amendment protection to political speech alone; his opinion in *Whitney* clearly valued speech as a cultural, social, and educational, as well as a political, value in a free society.

The Fourth Amendment

The criminal-law provisions of the Bill of Rights, found in the Fourth through Eighth Amendments, had also never been applied to the states, although many states had written some of these guarantees into their own constitutions. In the 1920s, the Court for the most part preferred to leave the control of criminal justice in the hands of the states, although it showed itself willing to extend federal standards and authority in cases of outright abuse of fair procedures.

The decade had started with the *Silverthorne Lumber* decision, in which an outraged Holmes had chastised the Department of Justice for seizing books and papers from the suspects' office "without a shadow of authority." Six other members of the Court had joined in his expansion of the exclusionary rule, ensuring that the government could not benefit from illegally secured evidence. But in state and federal courts, the flood of cases growing out of efforts to enforce the Eighteenth (Prohibition) Amendment brought some retreat from this position, and in *Byars v. United States* and *Gambino v. United States,* both in 1927, the Court developed what came to be known as the "silver platter" doctrine: Evidence obtained in an illegal state search would be admissible in a federal court so long as there had been no federal participation. The doctrine invited the abuses that followed; state law enforcement officials blatantly violated fair procedures (often in violation of their own state laws) and then turned the evidence over to federal officers, who secretly knew about, and had often instigated, the illegal search. Not until 1960 did the Court abolish the silver-platter doctrine, in *Elkins v. United States.*

Prohibition, in fact, became a law enforcement nightmare. Many Americans deliberately violated the law, and bootleggers applied the latest technology to their efforts to give a thirsty citizenry what it wanted. They used a relatively new invention, the automobile, to run illegal liquor into the country from Canada or from country stills into the cities. In December 1921, federal agents stopped a car outside Detroit (which because of its proximity to Ontario, Canada, had become a major focal point for imported liquor). The agents searched the car without a warrant and found 68 quarts of whiskey and gin behind the upholstery. After conviction for violation of the Volstead Act of 1920 (which implemented the Eighteenth Amendment), the defendants appealed to the Supreme Court, claiming that their Fourth Amendment rights had been violated.

In *Carroll v. United States* (1925), by a 7–2 vote, the Court upheld the conviction. Chief Justice Taft found the search reasonable because the agents had had probable cause; the defendants, all suspected of previous bootlegging operations, had been traveling on a road frequently used by smugglers. Because of time constraints, the officers had been unable to get a warrant; had they waited to apply for one, the car would have been gone by the time it arrived. So the Court carved the automobile exception out of the Fourth Amendment's requirement that no search or seizure take place without a warrant. Where a warrant could reasonably be secured, Taft urged, it should be; otherwise, police did not need warrants to stop and search automobiles. The decision generated much criticism from legal scholars, but the *Carroll* doctrine is still the law.

Technology also gave the government new means to prosecute its fight against crime, notably the ability to pry into the private affairs of a suspect without entering the premises. In *Olmstead v. United States* (1928), the Court gave its blessing, by a bare majority, to telephone wiretapping. Chief Justice Taft's formalistic view of wiretapping completely ignored the Fourth Amendment's intent. There had been no entry, he claimed, but only the use of an enhanced sense of hearing. To pay too much attention to "nice ethical conduct by government officials would make society suffer and give criminals greater immunity than has been known heretofore."

The Taft opinion elicited dissents from Butler, Holmes, and Brandeis. In a well-reasoned historical analysis, the generally conservative Butler repudiated Taft's sterile interpretation of what the Fourth Amendment meant. Holmes, in a comment that soon caught the liberal imagination, condemned wiretapping as "a dirty business." But the most impressive opinion came from Brandeis, who forthrightly declared that he considered it "less evil that some criminals should escape than that the government should play an ignoble part. . . . If government becomes a lawbreaker, it breeds contempt for law."

The most noted and influential part of Brandeis's dissent dealt with the question of privacy. The Framers of the Constitution, Brandeis wrote, "sought to protect Americans in their beliefs, their thoughts, their emotions and their sensations. They conferred, as against the Government, the right to be let alone — the most comprehensive of rights, and the right most valued by civilized man." That passage would be picked up and elaborated on until finally, in *Griswold v. Connecticut* (1965), the Court recognized privacy as a constitutionally protected liberty.

Wiretapping itself remained legally permissible for many years, although Congress in 1934 prohibited admitting wiretapping evidence in federal courts. Not until 1967, in *Berger v. New York*, did the Court finally bring wiretapping within the reach of the Fourth Amendment.

Although the Taft Court preferred to leave criminal matters to the states, it did interfere occasionally. One case is notable because it affected race relations, an area that the Court considered wholly within state authority. The racial tensions following World War I had led to a series of urban riots in the North and triggered a wave of lynchings in Southern states. Lynching offended the Court in a way that nonviolent forms of discrimination did not. In *Moore v. Dempsey* (1923), Justice Holmes ruled that a federal court should hear the appeal of five Negroes convicted of first-degree murder by an Arkansas state court, where the constant threat of mob violence had dominated the proceedings. Such an atmosphere, he held, amounted to little more than judicially sanctioned lynching, and when state courts could not provide minimal procedural fairness, the federal courts had a clear duty to "secure to the petitioners their constitutional rights."

Race

The Court's expansion of constitutional protection in criminal procedure happened to have come in a case involving Negro defendants, but the Court generally showed very little concern over issues of racial prejudice. A typical case was *Corrigan v. Buckley* (1926), in which a unanimous Court refused to declare restrictive covenants — used to prevent the sale or lease of property to blacks — as violative of due process. The following year, in one of the few civil rights victories for blacks, the Court in *Nixon v. Herndon* (1927) struck down a Texas law excluding Negroes from voting in the Democratic primary as a violation of the equal protection clause of the Fourteenth Amendment. But the decision had little lasting impact, for party leaders soon developed informal but effective ways to exclude blacks.

The Taft Court, including its liberal faction, showed no great concern for other racial minorities, either, or for aliens. Asian immigrants had been considered eligible for citizenship under the first naturalization law of 1790 only because the statute had not explicitly excluded them. In 1870, however, Congress had formally limited naturalization to whites, and in *Ozawa v. United States* (1923), the Court, through Justice Sutherland, unanimously interpreted the act as excluding Japanese. The Court interpreted the 1870 statute, which had made Negroes eligible for citizenship, as limiting other eligible immigrants to Caucasians. The Court then extended the ban to East Indians in *United States v. Bhagat Singh Thind* (1923), even though the defendant claimed that Asian Indians had pure Aryan blood. A year later, Filipinos came under the ban in a dictum in *Toyota v. United States*, a case denying citizenship to a Japanese member of the armed services even though Congress in 1918 and 1919 had provided that "any alien" serving in the nation's military could file for naturalization. According to the Court, Congress had not meant to expand the idea beyond the limits of the 1790 and 1870 statues.

Nor did the Court have any problem upholding various western state laws prohibiting land ownership by aliens who had not declared their intention to become citizens, laws specifically aimed at Asians ineligible for naturalization. In *Terrace v. Thompson* (1923), Justice Butler sustained a Washington State law on the ground that, although Congress had exclusive control over immigration and naturalization, a state retained full power to deny aliens economic rights within its borders in the absence of legislation or a treaty.

The superpatriotism of the decade manifested itself in the Court's denial of citizenship to aliens who, despite many exemplary qualities, happened to be pacifists. In a noted case, *United States v. Schwimmer* (1929), an older Quaker woman of unblemished character had refused to promise to bear arms in defense of the country and had been denied naturalization as a result. The Court upheld the ruling and drew from Holmes one of his most eloquent dissents. "If there is any principle of the Constitution," he declared, "that more imperatively calls for attachment than any other it is the principle of free thought — not free thought for those who agree with us but freedom for the thought we hate." He failed to see how the country would suffer by taking as citizens those people "who believe more than some of us do in the teachings of the Sermon on the Mount."

The indifference to the lack of fair procedure for aliens reflected in part the Taft Court's general attitude toward civil liberties and in part the growing public animus toward aliens and all things foreign. Few voices protested the Court decisions, for even the liberals of the time recognized a distinction between the *rights* of an American citizen and the *privileges* accorded to an alien. Civil liberties jurisprudence, as well as popular ideas on this subject, had not yet fully developed. It is not so surprising, then, that the Supreme Court showed minimal concern in this area.

Buck v. Bell

One case from this time that displays in full the Taft Court's indifference to individual liberties dealt not with people of color or aliens or pacifists but with a white Southern girl, Carrie Buck. The eugenics movement that spread across the United States in the early twentieth century led a number of states to enact involuntary sterilization laws in efforts to "improve" the race. Virginia enacted such a law, but it remained unclear whether it would pass constitutional muster. The superintendent of the State Colony for Epileptics and Feeble-Minded at Lynchburg, Albert Priddy, decided to test the validity of the law, and the person he chose for his test case was eighteen-year-old Carrie Buck (Plate B.2).

A victim of rape, Carrie had become pregnant, and the family with which she was living had her committed to the Lynchburg institution, where a relatively primitive I.Q. test showed her to have the intelligence of a nine-year-old. Carrie's mother, Emma, also confined to the colony, tested out at eight years. After Carrie gave birth to her daughter, Vivien, Priddy recommended that she be sterilized, began the administrative process, and hired lawyers to test the law in the courts. At the trial, the state presented witnesses to prove Carrie's feeblemindedness, and one described the Buck family as part of the "shiftless, ignorant, and worthless class of anti-social whites." Young Vivien was described as "not quite normal."

Carrie Buck's attorney, paid for by the institution, put on a weak defense. He admitted, for example, that he agreed with the sterilization policy. Nonetheless, he carried an appeal to the Supreme Court and there offered an equal protection argument; the law, he claimed, discriminated against people confined to institutions and denied them their "full bodily integrity." Holmes, speaking for an 8–1 Court in *Buck v. Bell* (1927), dismissed all these arguments in a short, five-paragraph opinion. Three paragraphs described the facts of the case. The remainder dismissed the equal protection claim as "the usual last resort of constitutional arguments" and declared that "three generations of imbeciles are enough." Paying his usual deference to the legislature, Holmes affirmed the judgment. Only Pierce Butler dissented without opinion.

The case has had a bad odor about it ever since, but the worst aspect is that years later, it became clear that Carrie Buck had not been feebleminded at all. She had advanced with her class grade by grade in public school until taken out to work in her foster home. Her final report card rated her as "very good — deportment and lessons." In her later years, she had been active in reading groups and dramatics, and a social worker described her as an "alert and pleasant lady," despite a very hard life. There were no imbeciles at all among the three generations of Buck women.

The Taft Court's Legacy

The Court over which William Howard Taft presided from 1921 until 1930 left a decidedly mixed legacy. Its probusiness, antilabor decisions have been for the most part discredited, with the exception of the broad stream-of-commerce interpretation it gave to congressional power under the commerce clause. The theories of substantive due process and freedom of contract that it used to justify those decisions led to a popular perception that the Court, like the other branches of government in the 1920s, favored big business above all other interests. Following the onset of the Depression, liberal groups won control of the Congress and the White House, but the Four Horsemen (see the sidebar on page 246) clung to their outmoded legal classicism. Eventually, their stubbornness would lead to the constitutional crisis of 1937.

Yet even while protecting business interests, the Court slowly began the process of incorporation, by which the Fourteenth Amendment "incorporated" the protections of the Bill of Rights and applied them to the states. Although the process did not progress very far in the 1920s, the Taft Court had laid the foundation for the great revolution in civil liberties that would culminate during the Warren Court era (1953–1969). Concern for individual liberties became a major part of the Court's docket in part because the Taft Court took the first necessary steps.

Finally, the administrative changes in the Court and its procedures, often overlooked when examining cases, changed the way the Supreme Court of the United States, and indeed the entire federal judiciary, did business. Under Taft's guidance, the federal judiciary became what the Framers had intended it to be: a coequal branch of government. It acted as such owing to the reforms that Taft managed to secure from Congress. The erection of the Supreme Court building, taking the nation's high court from a basement room in the Capitol to a place of its own on "the Hill," had great symbolic importance in this transformation.

Perhaps most important, Taft took over a Court bogged down in myriad and often mundane issues because of older laws that let people carry almost any sort of case up through the appeals process and made the Court what it is today: a constitutional tribunal hearing only issues of constitutional significance and of federal law. The Judges' Bill of 1925 is one of a number of reasons why the legacy of the Taft Court is far greater than the credit given to it by many scholars.

—MELVIN I. UROFSKY

FOR FURTHER READING AND RESEARCH

One cannot understand the jurisprudence of the Taft Court without William M. Wiecek, *The Lost World of Classical Legal Thought: Law and Ideology in America, 1886–1937* (New York, 1998). Robert Post's forthcoming volume on the Taft Court, volume 10 of the *History of the Supreme Court of the United States* (the Oliver Wendell Holmes Devise) will be the definitive work on the subject, and several pieces of it have already appeared. See "Federalism in the Taft Court Era: Can It Be 'Revived'?" *Duke Law Journal* 51 (2002), 1513; "Defending the Lifeworld: Substantive Due Process in the Taft Court Era," *Boston University Law Review* 78 (1998), 1489; and "Judicial Management and Judicial Disinterest: The Achievements and Perils of Chief Justice William Howard Taft," *Journal of Supreme Court History* 1998 (1998), 50.

For some of the issues involving business, see Carl McFarland, *Judicial Control of the Federal Trade Commission and the Interstate Commerce Commission, 1920–1930* (Cambridge, Mass., 1933); and Robert E. Cushman, *Independent Regulatory Commissions* (New York, 1941). For labor, see Daniel R. Ernst, *Lawyers against Labor* (Urbana, Ill., 1995); and Christopher L. Tomlins, *The State and the Unions: Labor Relations, Law, and the Organized Labor Movement in America, 1880–1960* (New York and Cambridge, 1985). A biting critique of the Taft Court's bias against reform legislation is Thomas Reed Powell, "The Supreme Court and the State Police Power, 1922–1930," *Virginia Law Review* 17 and 18 (1931–1932), 529.

For the incorporation debate, see Richard C. Cortner, *The Supreme Court and the Second Bill of Rights* (Madison, Wisc., 1981); John Hart Ely, *Democracy and Distrust: A Theory of Judicial Review* (Cambridge, Mass., 1980); William E. Nelson, *The Fourteenth Amendment: From Political Principle to Judicial Doctrine* (Cambridge, Mass., 1988); and Akhil Reed Amar, *The Bill of Rights: Creation and Reconstruction* (New Haven, Conn., 1998). For the *Olmstead* case, see Walter F. Murphy, *Wiretapping on Trial* (New York, 1965). Criminal law in general is explored in David J. Bodenhamer, *Fair Trial: Rights of the Accused in American History* (New York, 1992).

The two school cases are discussed in William G. Ross, *Forging New Freedoms: Nativism, Education and the Constitution, 1921–1927* (Lincoln, Neb., 1994). The best exegesis of the Brandeis opinion is Vincent Blasi, "The First Amendment and the Ideal of Civil Courage: The Brandeis Opinion in *Whitney v. California*," *William & Mary Law Review* 29 (1988), 653. Holmes's opinion in the sterilization case is completely demolished in William E. Leuchtenburg, "Three Generations of Imbeciles," in his *The Supreme Court Reborn* (New York, 1995).

Part III

THE THIRD SEVENTY YEARS

★ ★ ★

There and Back Again

THE THIRD, MODERN PHASE OF SUPREME COURT HISTORY HAS been the most momentous, studded with controversial decisions, partisan critiques, and political struggle. Emerging from the Taft years equipped to be a powerful force in American governance, the Court became enmeshed in a confrontation with the other branches of government over the social and economic policies crafted by the Roosevelt Administration in response to the Great Depression, and to the inequalities of wealth and resources pervasive in American life. Climaxing dramatically in 1937's tense "court-packing" crisis, the confrontation did not sideline the Court in a repeat of *Dred Scott's* near-death experience. But the Court did adjust its constitutional role, leaving executive and legislative government far greater latitude in economic policy.

During the era that followed, the Court steered toward an enhanced emphasis on the guardianship of personal liberties. First on display during the fractious Stone and Vinson years, this orientation achieved decisive ascendancy during the Warren Court, particularly during the activist era of "History's Warren Court" after 1962. Nor did the ostensibly conservative Burger Court decisively retrench. Thus, a quasi-liberal consensus on the proper role for the Supreme Court lingered from the early 1940s into the early 1980s. Retrenchments—or, rather, dramatic, even revolutionary, change in the Court's approach to American constitutional law—began only with the Rehnquist years. The result in some minds has been a complete repudiation of understandings received from the previous forty years of the extent of government's regulatory capacity, of citizens' freedoms and protections, of voting rights, and of the Court's own role in processes of governance. To its critics, the Rehnquist Court has returned American constitutional law to the state of the early 1930s, virtually wiping clean the modern cycle of Supreme Court history.

Yet now, in the final days of the Rehnquist era, the Court under an ailing and often absent chief justice gives the impression less of unity and determination than of division. Appointment of a new chief justice may dissipate the current moment's aura of uncertainty, yet the process of nomination and approval may well become a further new occasion for deep division over the direction of American constitutional law. Already, early in the second George W. Bush administration, judicial appointments and indeed the very autonomy of the federal judiciary have become subjects for bitter political conflict. Nomination and appointment of a new chief justice are likely to bring only additional acrimony. For a fragmented Supreme Court, for a federal judiciary already exposed to political pressure, indeed for the country as a whole, the stakes are high.

10

The Hughes Court 1930–1941

Evolution and Revolution

CHARLES EVANS HUGHES presided over the Supreme Court during a critical period of transition, one in which the Court abandoned its longtime function as the arbiter of economic regulatory legislation and pioneered its modern role as a guardian of personal liberties. Spanning a period (1930–1941) that matched almost precisely the duration of the Great Depression, the Hughes Court was forced to consider the full constitutional implications of the administrative state in cases arising out of an unprecedented torrent of federal and state legislation designed to restore and sustain economic stability. The Court's initial resistance to the New Deal provoked President Roosevelt's famous proposal to "pack" the Court with additional justices. The Court parried the threat of Roosevelt's plan by sustaining the constitutionality of his reform legislation.

The so-called Judicial Revolution of 1937 initiated a long period of deference on the part of the Court to congressional and state legislation on economic issues. During the same period, however, the Court steadily increased its scrutiny of legislation affecting racial minorities, access to the political process, and the liberties prescribed by the Bill of Rights.

The Shape of the Hughes Court

A man of vast experience in public affairs and possessed of a stable temperament and moderate opinions, Charles Evans Hughes was ideally suited to lead the Court during a time of political and judicial crisis. No one ever has ascended the nation's highest bench with a more distinguished record of service in both public office and the legal profession. Born in upstate New York in 1862, Hughes was the only child of a Baptist minister and an erudite mother who instilled in him a rigorous education and high moral standards. Hughes attended Brown and in 1884 graduated from Columbia Law School. He practiced law for the next twenty years in New York City, except for two years when he taught law at Cornell.

From an early age, Hughes demonstrated an intensity of purpose and self-control that often drove him to the point of nervous exhaustion. Hughes's outward self-confidence, his reserved public personality, and his insatiable appetite for hard work inspired barbs that he was a "bearded icicle." In private, however, Hughes was a gifted raconteur and charming conversationalist. Unabashed in providing legal services for wealthy individuals and corporations, Hughes moved comfortably in the salons of the upper classes even while he retained the physical and moral discipline he had learned in the Baptist parsonage.

Hughes first came to public attention during 1905–1906, when he chaired state legislative investigations that exposed corruption in the New York utilities and insurance industry and generated reductions in rates and premiums for consumers. Elected governor in 1906 on the Republican ticket, Hughes successfully promoted significant progressive legislation, including the enactment of the nation's first compulsory workers' compensation law, an eight-hour day for railway workers, and railroad safety regulations. When conservatives frustrated his plans for more extensive progressive legislation after his reelection in 1908, Hughes gladly accepted his first appointment to the Supreme Court, where he served from 1910 to 1916. Hughes's reputation as a progressive grew during his tenure on the Court, for he generally voted to uphold social and regulatory legislation.

Hughes resigned from the Court in 1916 when Republicans drafted him to run for president in the hope that he could reunite a party deeply divided between its progressive and conservative wings. Hughes was defeated by Woodrow Wilson, although the election was so close that the shift of a few thousand votes in California would have reversed the result. Following his defeat, Hughes established a lucrative law practice in New York City but remained active in public causes. From 1921 to 1925, he served with great distinction as secretary of state, promoting the cause of world peace and kindling goodwill for America abroad. After three more years of law practice, Hughes became judge of the World Court in 1928. He resigned in February 1930 to become chief justice of the United States.

So stellar were Hughes's qualifications for the chief justiceship that President Hoover claimed that he had never considered anyone else. In fact, there is some evidence that Hoover also contemplated the elevation of Associate Justice Harlan Fiske Stone, a personal friend of Hoover's, but rejected him as too liberal. The outgoing chief justice, William Howard Taft (who, when president, had offered Hughes his first appointment to the Court) strongly supported Hughes as his successor, fearing that Stone was not sufficiently conservative. Because Hughes's credentials and his reputation as a moderate progressive seemed completely sound, neither Hughes nor the Hoover administration was prepared when both progressive Republicans and Southern Democrats vigorously opposed his confirmation.

Hughes's nomination quickly became a lightning rod for liberal and populist resentment against the northeastern social and economic elite that Hughes seemed to epitomize. As Senate Judiciary Committee Chairman George W. Norris of Nebraska complained, a man "who has lived in luxury, is not fit to sit in judgment in a contest between organized wealth and those who toil." Liberals and progressives also used Hughes's nomination as an occasion to express frustration at the Court's frequent invalidation during the past four decades of federal and state social and economic regulatory statutes. These critics did not agree that the due process clauses of the Fourteenth and Fifth Amendments permitted the Court to scrutinize closely the substantive content of state and federal regulatory legislation to ensure that businesses were not deprived of property without "due process of law." To progressives, this doctrine of "substantive due process" stifled democracy by permitting unelected judges to read their own social and economic biases into the Constitution and by allowing them to substitute their own policies for those of elected lawmakers. Progressives also complained that the federal courts had hobbled Congress with decisions that too narrowly interpreted the scope of congressional power to regulate interstate commerce and impose taxes. Correctly foreseeing that the worsening economic depression would produce increased demand for controversial economic legislation, liberals claimed that the Court needed a more progressive chief justice to counterbalance the conservatives, who had so often dominated the Court during the 1920s.

While progressives claimed that Hughes was but a tool of corporate business interests, Southern states' rights advocates condemned his broad vision of federal power. Hughes's critics also complained about his age: At sixty-seven, he would be the oldest person ever appointed chief justice. Senate opposition toward the nomination may have been particularly robust, as it was the first Supreme Court nomination that the Senate had considered since changing its rules in 1929 to permit open debates on judicial appointments, previously discussed only in closed session. Attacks on Hughes enabled senators to score political points that their constituents would notice. After several tumultuous days, the Senate confirmed Hughes by a 52–26 vote, with eighteen senators not voting — one of the narrower confirmations in the Court's history.

New Justices

Controversy over the Court flared up again two months later, when President Hoover nominated John J. Parker, a federal appellate judge from North Carolina, to succeed Edward T. Sanford, who had died on the same day as Taft. Like the attacks on Hughes, opposition to Parker was prophetic of the pressures that would roil and transform the Court during the coming decade. Parker's nomination encountered intense opposition from organized labor, which objected to an earlier decision of his restricting the activities of trade unions. The NAACP also conducted a highly organized campaign against the nomination, complaining that Parker had advocated curtailment of African American participation in politics. In its first rejection of a Supreme Court nominee in thirty years, the Senate defeated Parker's nomination 41–39.

After Parker's defeat, the Senate quickly and without controversy confirmed Hoover's replacement nominee, Owen J. Roberts, a Philadelphia attorney. Although Roberts had devoted most of his career to the representation of business interests, particularly railroads, liberals trusted him because he had helped to prosecute miscreants in the Harding administration's Teapot Dome scandal and had sometimes represented labor unions for nominal fees.

With one exception, Roberts's confirmation in 1930 was the last change to the composition of the Court until 1937. Early in 1932, Benjamin N. Cardozo replaced Oliver Wendell Holmes, who had resigned at age ninety-one after Hughes visited him at his home on a Sunday afternoon to suggest gently that the time had come for him to relinquish the burden of his judicial duties. The meeting may have been more painful for Hughes than for Holmes, who with good grace immediately wrote a letter of resignation. Cardozo, a brilliant legal thinker who had modernized the common law in his innovative and nationally influential decisions as chief judge of New York's highest court, was a logical choice to succeed so distinguished a justice as Holmes. Hoover, however, had reservations about Cardozo's liberalism and was reluctant to appoint him because another New Yorker (Stone) and another Jew (Brandeis) were already on the Court. After prodding from progressive Republicans, Hoover decided that competence and integrity were more important considerations than ideology, geography, ethnicity, or religion. Hoover also recognized that his selection of the widely popular Cardozo would avoid repetition of the controversies provoked by the Hughes and Parker appointments. At a time when his administration was reeling from the political fallout of the Great Depression, Hoover could ill afford more controversy.

Like Holmes, Cardozo was an advocate of restraint in judicial review of economic legislation. But he was much more willing to scrutinize laws that interfered with personal liberties. He therefore often voted with Brandeis and Stone, forming a reliable bloc of three "liberal" justices. Meanwhile, Justices Van Devanter, McReynolds, Sutherland, and Butler constituted a "conservative" alliance that more carefully scrutinized economic legislation and tended, with important exceptions, to be less solicitous of civil liberties. The stubborn conviction of these justices that their conservative interpretation of the Constitution was needed to prevent political and economic chaos earned them the title "the Four Horsemen of the Apocalypse." Hughes and Roberts were swing voters on economic regulatory legislation but generally voted with the liberal bloc on issues of personal liberty.

Even though the Court was deeply divided between liberals and conservatives in many critical cases, there was little personal animosity among the justices. Hughes encouraged amicable relations among the brethren and was on cordial terms with all of his colleagues, particularly Brandeis and Van Devanter, even though these justices were very different from each other in judicial philosophy and temperament. Occasional flares of tension arose on the Court when Hughes's votes with the conservatives exasperated the liberals, especially Stone. The ever-irascible McReynolds meanwhile grew even ruder toward his liberal colleagues as the Court ruled on the constitutionality of a mounting quantity of regulatory legislation that he regarded as a threat to the Republic's very foundations.

Administrative Skills

Hughes's formidable intellect and personality served him well as chief justice. Professor Paul Freund of Harvard remarked that "his Jovian figure seemed to occupy the central seat by natural right" and that Hughes's questions to attorneys "showed a remarkable capacity to bring an argument into focus, to go for the jugular." Similarly, Robert H. Jackson observed that Hughes "did not exert authority; he radiated it."

Hughes was similarly commanding in the Court's weekly conferences. Felix Frankfurter recalled that Hughes "never checked free debate, but the atmosphere which he created, the moral authority he exerted, inhibited irrelevance, repetition, and fruitless discussion." Frankfurter also praised Hughes for showing "uncommon resourcefulness in drawing elements of agreement out of differences and thereby narrowing, if not always escaping, conflicts." Hughes's consummate thoroughness in studying cases awed numerous observers and encouraged a high level of preparation by his colleagues. As a former clerk recalled, "seated at the head of the conference table with records, briefs, and law books (all with innumerable bookmarks) piled high about him, he somehow exuded complete preparation and conveyed the impression that anyone who disagreed with him had better know *all* the facts and know them well."

Like other chief justices, Hughes used his power to assign the writing of opinions to particular justices as a means to influence the content of decisions. When Hughes voted with the Court's conservatives in divided opinions, he often assigned the opinion to Sutherland, who was the most articulate and moderate of the Court's Four Horsemen. Hughes's critics claimed, with some fairness, that Hughes attempted to curry admiration among liberals by regularly writing opinions when he voted with the liberals but rarely when he sided with the conservatives in a decision or a dissent.

Hughes's efficient administration helped the Court stay abreast of its workload, which averaged approximately one thousand cases per term. The Court also was able to keep up with its work because the Judiciary Act of 1925 had given it much more control over its docket. Every justice personally reviewed every certiorari petition, and the Court sometimes bent the "Rule of Four" to grant certiorari when fewer than four justices strongly favored review of a case. In order to permit more time at conference for discussion of important cases, Hughes limited certiorari discussions to an average of three and a half minutes.

Although no major changes occurred in Supreme Court procedure during Hughes's chief justiceship, the Court helped to bring about important reforms in the procedure of the lower federal courts. In 1934, the Court developed rules for criminal appeals in order to help expedite an appellate process that had been rife with delays. After Congress in 1934 authorized the Court to adopt rules for civil procedure, the Court spent several years working with lower federal courts to develop the Federal Rules of Civil Procedure, which the Court promulgated in 1938. The rules, which with various revisions remain in effect today, have helped to standardize procedure and expedite the disposition of cases.

A Liberal Dawn

With low expectations of the Hughes Court, liberals were relieved and gratified during its first few years when the Court seemed to be moving in a more moderate direction. In *O'Gorman & Young v. Hartford Fire Insurance Co.* (1931), for example, the Court in a 5–4 decision joined by Hughes upheld a New Jersey statute that regulated fire insurance rates by prohibiting companies from allowing their agents to collect more than "a reasonable amount" as a commission on sales of policies. Finding that the statute affected the public interest because the compensation of agents directly affected the size of insurance premiums, the Court rejected the insurance industry's argument that the law violated the Fourteenth Amendment by taking property without due process of law. In another 5–4 decision in May 1931, *State Board of Tax Commissioners of Indiana v. Jackson,* the Court sustained an Indiana law that imposed higher tax rates on grocery store chains than on stores owned by a single individual. Meanwhile, the Court demonstrated a high degree of solicitude for personal freedom in decisions involving personal liberties.

In *New State Ice Company v. Liebmann* (1932), however, the Court reverted to stricter scrutiny of economic regulation, striking down an Oklahoma statute that prohibited the manufacture, sale, or distribution of ice without a license from a state agency. The Court concluded that the ice business was not sufficiently infused with a "public interest" to warrant such regulation. Distinguishing decisions in which the Court had upheld regulation of agricultural and mining activities, the Court explained that "here we are dealing with an ordinary business, not with a paramount industry upon which the prosperity of the entire state in large measure depends." In a strong dissent joined by two other justices, Brandeis urged the Court to defer to the legislature.

The Oklahoma statute was enacted before the Depression. Nevertheless, the Court's decision portended badly for measures designed to restore prosperity. As the Great Depression grew ever more severe, the federal government and the states increasingly attempted to stabilize the economy by enacting precisely the type of regulatory legislation that the Court had invalidated in such decisions as *Liebmann.* Intervening in the private economy more than any other peacetime government in the nation's history, the Hoover administration created innovative programs, such as the Reconstruction Finance Corporation, which provided federal loans to troubled commercial and financial institutions.

The pace of legislation vastly accelerated after the Democratic landslide in the 1932 elections, which swept Franklin D. Roosevelt into the White House and produced large Democratic majorities in both houses of Congress. Taking office at a time when 25 percent of heads of households were unemployed, bank failures had reached epidemic proportions, and stock market valuations had fallen nearly 90 percent since 1929, Roosevelt understood that unprecedented action was needed. At his behest, Congress enacted a spate of legislation — a "New Deal"— to promote short-term relief of suffering, intermediate-term recovery of the economy, and long-term reform designed to prevent the occurrence of another depression. Both proponents and opponents of these controversial New Deal measures and their state counterparts anxiously awaited the Supreme Court's evaluation of their constitutionality.

The Court's first major decision affecting legislative efforts to fight the Depression came in January 1934 in *Home Building & Loan Association v. Blaisdell*. The decision sustained the constitutionality of a Minnesota statute that permitted courts to allow distressed farmers additional time to make mortgage payments. The Court held that the law did not violate the Constitution's prohibition of a state's impairment of contracts, because all contracts included an implicit reservation of power by the state to protect the public interest. The Court found that the growth of farm foreclosures in Minnesota, which threatened the state with economic chaos, justified the enactment of a statute that merely postponed mortgage payments and did not alter the ultimate obligation of farmers to repay fully their mortgage obligations with accrued interest.

The pragmatism of the Court's decision perhaps reflected fear of growing anarchy in the face of economic hardship. During the months before *Blaisdell*, Iowa farmers had disrupted judicial foreclosure proceedings and had nearly lynched a county judge who refused to postpone farm foreclosures. Circumstances, however, did not deter the Four Horsemen. In a vigorous dissent joined by Van Devanter, McReynolds, and Butler, Justice Sutherland urged a literal reading of the contracts clause, which would permit no state interference with the terms of private contracts, even in the face of economic emergency.

Early in 1935, the New Deal won a major judicial victory in three closely divided decisions — *Norman v. Baltimore & Ohio Railway Co., Nortz v. United States,* and *Perry v. United States* — upholding Congress's 1933 repudiation of the gold standard in both private and public contracts, a measure that was intended to conserve the nation's gold reserves, discourage hoarding of bullion, and prevent bank failures. In sustaining the prohibition on repayment in gold in private contracts, the Court explained that Congress had broad power to regulate the nation's monetary system in order to facilitate the national interest. The Court ruled that Congress lacked power to repudiate gold clauses in public contracts, as this would impugn the integrity of the federal government. But the Court held that the bondholder who challenged the statute had suffered only nominal damages, because the fall in prices during the Depression had wiped out most of the difference between the value of repayment in gold and repayment in currency. In an acrimonious dissent joined by the other three Horsemen, McReynolds expressed "abhorrence" of the government's "repudiation and spoliation" of contractual obligations. Racked with anger, McReynolds delivered an even more sizzling condemnation of the opinion in oral remarks from the bench. "This is Nero at his worst," he exclaimed. "The Constitution is gone."

Hostility Toward New Deal Legislation

The Four Horsemen were more successful in other cases in protecting the Constitution from the legislation they feared would destroy it. The *Gold Clause* cases were among the few Court victories that the New Deal won during Roosevelt's first term in office. In the first test of major New Deal legislation, the Court in January 1935 struck down National Industrial Recovery Act (NIRA) provisions permitting the president to prohibit interstate shipment of so-called hot oil — oil produced in excess of limits set by oil-producing states to raise prices. Although the Court did not deny that Congress could delegate power to the president to regulate interstate commerce, the Court explained in its 8–1 decision that the statute failed to provide the president with sufficient guidelines for the exercise of such authority.

The "hot oil" decision foreshadowed the Court's unanimous invalidation of most of the remainder of the NIRA four months later in *Schechter Poultry v. United States*, in which the Court dismissed the government's case against a Brooklyn poultry producer charged with selling sick chickens and violating the poultry code's provisions on wages and hours. The decision had little practical importance: The NIRA was due to expire the following month and had proved so ineffective that Congress seemed disinclined to renew it.

But the Court's reasoning threatened other New Deal measures. First, the Court declared that the economic emergency could not alone justify the statute, as "extraordinary conditions do not create or enlarge constitutional power," a conclusion that seemed inconsistent with the Court's broader interpretation of the Constitution in *Blaisdell*. Second, the Court amplified its objections to the "hot oil" section of NIRA and held that Congress had unconstitutionally delegated legislative power to the president. The legislation's grant of authority to establish industry codes was too sweeping and the guidelines too broad and too vague. As Cardozo remarked in a concurring opinion, this was "delegation running riot." Finally, the Court construed Congress's power to regulate interstate commerce restrictively, holding that the Schechter poultry business was so local that it had only an "indirect" effect on interstate commerce and therefore was beyond congressional regulation.

The Court dealt further blows to the New Deal in two other decisions announced on the same day as *Schechter*. In *Louisville Joint Stock Land Bank v. Radford*, the Court invalidated a 1933 federal statute that denied banks the power to foreclose on bankrupt farms until five years after adjudication of bankruptcy. The Court held that the statute contravened the Fifth Amendment's due process clause, which limited congressional power to regulate private economic transactions, and constituted a taking of the property of the mortgage holders without due process of law. In the second decision, *Humphrey's Executor v. United States*, the Court limited the president's power to dismiss members of independent federal regulatory commissions. Holding that Roosevelt had improperly removed a Federal Trade Commission member who had openly opposed New Deal measures, the Court explained that the president could remove commissioners only for good cause, not for political reasons.

As a result of this triad of decisions, May 27, 1935, became known as "Black Monday" to New Dealers. Roosevelt and many of his supporters despaired at these decisions, for they indicated that the Court was not prepared to interpret the Constitution expansively enough to permit the president and Congress to reshape the economy. In his first public criticism of the Court, Roosevelt complained at a press conference that these decisions belonged to the "horse-and-buggy age," and he privately began to explore options for curbing the Court. Meanwhile, liberal members of Congress introduced a spate of bills to limit judicial power, including measures to permit Congress to override Supreme Court decisions and constitutional amendments to redefine the commerce power.

The Court renewed its onslaught against New Deal legislation early in 1936, when, in *United States v. Butler*, it narrowly construed the congressional taxing power to invalidate the Agricultural Adjustment Act. In *Butler*, the Court held that a tax on processors of agricultural products, used to fund price supports for farmers who limited production, was not a proper tax, because it was used as an instrument of economic and social policy rather than to raise revenue for general federal purposes. In a dissent joined by Cardozo and Brandeis, Justice Stone vigorously articulated a broader vision of the taxing power.

Four months later, in *Carter v. Carter Coal Company* (1936), the Court struck down another important New Deal measure, the Bituminous Coal Conservation Act, which had established a commission to assist the hardhit coal industry by regulating production, prices, and the working conditions of miners. Ignoring evidence that the devastation of the coal industry greatly exacerbated the national depression, the Court held that coal mines were local operations and therefore beyond the power of Congress to regulate under the Constitution's interstate commerce clause. A week later, in *Ashton v. Cameron County Water Improvement District*, the Court nullified the Municipal Bankruptcy Act of 1934 on the ground that Congress had invaded state sovereignty by permitting local governments to declare bankruptcy. The four dissenters — Cardozo, Hughes, Brandeis, and Stone — contended that the statute did not trample on state power, because the statute permitted the states to disapprove the bankruptcy of their municipalities.

Aside from its decisions in the *Gold Clause* cases, the only significant victory that the Court gave to the Roosevelt administration during its first term was approval of one limited feature of the Tennessee Valley Authority Act. In February 1936, *Ashwander v. Tennessee Valley Authority* upheld the validity of a contract between the federal Tennessee Valley Authority (TVA) and a private power company for the sale of excess power generated by a TVA dam. The Court reasoned that the TVA had built the dam in order to provide power for national defense and to improve the navigability of interstate waterways, both of which were within the undisputed power of Congress, and that the federal government likewise had power to dispose of property it had legally acquired. The Court, however, did not rule on the constitutionality of the TVA's massive program of soil reclamation, flood control, electric power development, and other activities designed to transform the depressed economy of the Tennessee Valley, encompassing much of the state of Tennessee as well as parts of several other states.

The Court did not have occasion to rule on the constitutionality of a number of other important New Deal programs, because there was little doubt that Congress had power to appropriate funds for the general welfare. Hence, the Public Works Administration and the Works Progress Administration (WPA), which provided jobs for millions of people in a vast array of activities ranging from the construction of public buildings to the preparation of oral histories, survived without significant challenges. So did the Civilian Conservation Corps (CCC), which put hundreds of thousands of youths to work on soil conservation projects, and the Home Owners Loan Corporation, which helped to refinance home mortgages.

Nevertheless, by the end of 1936, it seemed inevitable that the Court would eventually hear serious challenges to the constitutionality of such foundational New Deal measures as the Social Security Act of 1935, the securities acts of 1933 and 1934, and the 1935 National Labor Relations Act (NLRA). These statutes were more important than such programs as the WPA and the CCC because they were intended to accomplish lasting reforms rather than alleviate temporary distress. The Social Security Act, with its far-reaching system of unemployment compensation and old-age pensions, was designed to prevent poverty among the millions of unemployed and elderly. The securities acts were supposed to prevent future stock market crashes by regulating the securities industry. The NLRA, which the Roosevelt administration in many ways came to regard as the most important New Deal statute, was intended to prevent labor unrest by creating a National Labor Relations Board to define bargaining units, supervise labor elections, certify labor representatives, and adjudicate complaints against employers. The Court's various decisions restricting congressional power, particularly the commerce power, were bad portents for these and other laws.

The Social Security Act seemed especially vulnerable, particularly because the Court in May 1935 had invalidated an analogous statute that required railroads and their employees to contribute to a government-administered pension plan. In *Railroad Retirement Board v. Alton,* the Court's five-member majority contended that the railroad pension statute took property without due process of law, in violation of the Fifth Amendment, and exceeded Congress's power under the commerce clause. Similarly, the new Securities and Exchange Commission (SEC) suffered a setback during the spring of 1936, when the Court held in *Jones v. SEC* that the commission could not compel an applicant for registration of a stock to testify about his stock plan after he had withdrawn his application. In a dissent joined by Stone and Brandeis, Cardozo argued that the Court's ruling encouraged stock fraud because it permitted stock manipulators to escape SEC exposure of fraud by withdrawing their registration applications. The Court did not address the constitutionality of the SEC as such, but its decision did not bode well for a future test.

Meanwhile, the Court continued to demonstrate quite directly its aversion toward economic regulation. In the most dramatic of these decisions, *Morehead v. New York ex rel. Tipaldo,* the Court in June 1936 struck down a New York minimum-wage law for women and children on the ground that it deprived employers and employees of the liberty of contract that the Court found to be implied in the Fourteenth Amendment's due process clause. The 5–4 split in this decision, Roberts joining the Four Horsemen, highlighted once more the Court's deep divisions. In a blistering dissent, Stone declared, "there is grim irony in speaking of the freedom of contract of those who, because of their economic necessities, give their service for less than is needed to keep body and soul together." The *Tipaldo* decision even offended many conservatives, particularly as it interfered with the rights of the states; the Republican national platform in the upcoming presidential election expressed support for minimum-wage laws, although it stopped short of calling for an amendment to overturn *Tipaldo.*

The Court-Packing Plan

Even though the New Deal clearly appeared on a collision course with the Court, Roosevelt generally refrained from attacking the Court during his reelection campaign. Mindful of the near reverence many Americans had for the Court, Roosevelt was careful not to play into the hands of Republican charges that the Roosevelt administration had dictatorial tendencies that threatened American traditions of self-government. Some form of

Court-curbing measure seemed inevitable, however, after a Democratic landslide in which Roosevelt won 61 percent of the popular vote and carried all but two states, and the Democrats obtained majorities of more than three-quarters in both houses of Congress. The worst of the Depression had ended during Roosevelt's first term, but unemployment remained high, and Roosevelt aptly observed in his second inaugural address that one-third of the nation lacked proper nourishment, housing, and clothing. Making plain that such poverty in a land of plenty was politically unacceptable, Roosevelt clearly indicated that he was not willing to permit the Court to strangle more of the New Deal programs enacted during his first term or to impede the new reform programs that he intended to champion during his second term.

Many of Roosevelt's advisors and supporters recommended enactment of a constitutional amendment that would permanently curtail the Court's power. Roosevelt, however, feared that the cumbersome amendment process — approval of two-thirds of the members of both houses of Congress and three-quarters of the state legislatures — would take too long and encounter fierce opposition from well-financed business interests. He preferred ordinary legislation that would not directly curb judicial review. Thus, on February 5, 1937, Roosevelt announced a proposal to permit the president to appoint as many as fifty new federal judges, including six U.S. Supreme Court justices, to supplement the services of any judge who had served for ten years and had failed to resign within six months of his seventieth birthday (Plate B.7). Roosevelt at first contended that the legislation was needed because so many of the justices were elderly and could not keep up with their work, an argument so disingenuous that it cost the proposal much support. Only a month later did he admit that the additional justices were needed to ensure the success of New Deal legislation.

Roosevelt's proposal provoked widespread opposition. Conservatives wisely stayed largely in the background, permitting liberals to lead the assault. Some of the most vehement opponents were old-line progressives, mostly Republicans, who for decades had attacked the Court for its opposition to social and regulatory legislation and had proposed countless measures to curb its powers. Progressives correctly pointed out that the plan did not curtail the Court's institutional powers and that it aggrandized the power of a president who was dependent on the urban political machines that progressives loathed. Some liberals who favored New Deal programs feared that the assault on the Court would upset the delicate balance of powers among the three branches of government and erode the Court's ability to safeguard personal freedom. Recent decisions protecting personal liberties and racial and ethnic minorities, such as *Near v. Minnesota* (1931) and *Powell v. Alabama* (1932), provided critical reminders that the

Court's power was used not just to protect powerful economic interests. The proposal encountered opposition not only from many intellectuals but also from ethnic Americans who had not forgotten that the Court had protected the integrity of parochial schools in *Meyer v. Nebraska* (1923) and *Pierce v. Society of Sisters* (1925).

Roosevelt's contention that more justices were needed because a geriatric Court was staggering under its workload was belied by Hughes himself in a March 22 letter to Senator Burton K. Wheeler, the chair of the Senate Judiciary Committee. Declaring that the Court was "fully abreast of its work," Hughes contended that increasing the number of justices would impair the Court's efficiency. Hughes also dismissed as "impracticable" the argument that an increase in justices would permit the Court to divide itself into groups to hear particular types of cases. Hughes explained that issues coming before the Court were so important that all justices needed to consider them and that any division of work might violate the Constitution's provision for the creation of "one supreme Court." Hughes noted in the letter that, for lack of time, he had not consulted any of his colleagues except Brandeis and Van Devanter. He expressed the belief that all nevertheless would concur with him. As all the justices were in Washington at the time that Hughes wrote the letter, however, there is no clear reason why he could not have consulted more widely. Stone, for one, was irked by the chief justice's secrecy. Hughes may have feared that in fact, not all the justices would concur in his reasoning or agree with his decision to oppose the plan publicly.

The Judicial Revolution of 1937

Even more important than Hughes's letter in the defeat of the Court-packing plan, however, was a significant series of spring 1937 decisions that signaled a transformation of the Court's attitude toward economic regulatory legislation. Thus, one week after Hughes presented his letter, the Court sustained the constitutionality of three federal and two state economic regulatory statutes. In the decision that most clearly signaled a break with the past, *West Coast Hotel v. Parrish*, a 5–4 Court sustained a Washington State minimum-wage statute virtually indistinguishable from the New York minimum-wage law the Court had struck down the previous June in *Tipaldo*. Hailed as the "switch in time that saved the Nine," the Court's decision in *Parrish* marked the Court's permanent rejection of substantive due process in economic regulatory cases. Roberts, the justice who switched, always claimed that Roosevelt's Court-curbing plan did not influence him, because he had cast his vote in December 1936, two months before Roosevelt announced the Court-packing plan. Roberts contended that he changed his vote because counsel for Washington State, unlike New York's lawyers, had explicitly asked the Court to reject the Court's liberty-of-contract precedents. As some sort of attack on the Court seemed inevitable after Roosevelt's landslide reelection in November, however, Roberts's explanation is not altogether convincing.

In other opinions offered on the same day, the Court also appeared to re-verse itself in unanimously sustaining the constitutionality of the second Lemke-Frazier Farm Bankruptcy Act, which was nearly identical to the legislation that the Court had unanimously struck down two years earlier on Black Monday in *Radford*. The Court reasoned that the Court's objec-tions in *Radford* had been met, insofar as the new statute made clear that creditors retained their right to future settlement of claims.

Two weeks later, the Court further underscored the transformation of its attitude toward regulatory legislation, sustaining the constitutionality of the National Labor Relations Act (NLRA), one of the cornerstones of the New Deal. In *NLRB v. Jones & Laughlin Steel Corp.*, a 5–4 decision, the Court interpreted the Constitution's commerce and general-welfare clauses in an expansive manner that permitted Congress to regulate labor relations in the steel industry. Rejecting its old distinction between "direct" and "in-direct" effects on commerce, the Court found that the regulation was constitutional because steel production was part of a "stream of commerce" insofar as it obtained raw materials through interstate commerce and shipped its finished products by interstate commerce. Hughes declared in his opinion that Congress had the power to "protect interstate commerce from the paralyzing consequences of industrial war" by regulating labor re-lations in industries that "organize themselves on a national scale, making their relation to interstate commerce the dominant factor in their activi-ties." The Court adopted an even more expansive vision of the commerce power in a companion case, *NLRB v. Friedman-Harry Marks Clothing Co.*, which approved the NLRA's application to a small clothing manufacturer. Even a highly localized business, apparently, could be found to have a detectable impact on interstate commerce.

Six weeks after its NLRA decisions, the Court handed the Roosevelt administration yet another major victory, upholding in two decisions the major provisions of the Social Security Act, the most far-reaching of all the New Deal statutes. *Steward Machine Company v. Davis* held that Con-gress's power to levy taxes was broad enough to permit Congress to impose a tax on employers in order to fund an unemployment-compensation pro-gram to protect unemployed workers from poverty. In *Helvering v. Davis*, which sustained the old-age provisions of the Social Security Act, the Court similarly upheld congressional power to tax employers for the benefit of workers and to spend money in aid of the general welfare.

The prospects for Roosevelt's Court-packing plan were further diminished when Justice Van Devanter resigned in May 1937 in order to take advantage of a new statute permitting federal judges to retire at full pay after age seventy. Because most of the cases in which the Court had expressed its new-found receptivity toward economic regulation had been decided by bare 5–4 majorities, Van Devanter's resignation provided Roosevelt with the opportunity to appoint a justice who could stabilize the new liberal majority by providing an additional vote. To fill the vacant seat, Roosevelt nominated Senator Hugo L. Black of Alabama, one of the most reliable champions of New Deal legislation. In light of waning support, and need, for the Court-packing bill, the Senate Judiciary Committee in June reported it unfavorably, alleging that it undermined judicial independence "in direct violation of the spirit of the American Constitution." A compromise bill, which would have permitted the president to make one supplemental appointment each year, quietly died on July 22, when the Senate voted to return it to committee.

The Court's abandonment of substantive due process and reinterpretation of congressional powers during the spring of 1937 was so sudden, so sweeping, and so permanent that its decisions have come to be known as "the judicial revolution of 1937." In recent years, however, some scholars have correctly pointed out that the Court's break with the past was not so abrupt as has generally been supposed. The Court had always scrutinized state and federal economic regulatory statutes closely, but invalidation had been fairly rare. Even in its early years, the Hughes Court had sustained more regulatory legislation than it had ever struck down, and most of its decisions had been unanimous. Still, it is difficult to deny that the Court's 1937 decisions were a watershed, for the Court has never again so closely scrutinized the constitutionality of state or federal economic regulation. Even though the decades before the judicial revolution of 1937 saw the Court generally uphold regulatory legislation, the Court had nevertheless invalidated many high-profile statutes. Moreover, the specter of judicial nullification cast a constant pall over efforts to enact federal and state regulatory legislation. After 1937, the state and federal governments for the first time faced no such judicial threats.

The Court Remade

The Judicial Revolution of 1937 was consolidated because Black's appointment was only the first of eight that Roosevelt was able to make during the remainder of his tenure. Four more of these occurred during the Hughes Court era, enabling Roosevelt to "pack" the Court seriatim without any legislated increase in the number of justices. Sutherland's resignation early in 1938 reduced the conservative bloc to two. Roosevelt replaced Sutherland with Solicitor General Stanley F. Reed, who supported the Court's new-found deference to social and economic regulatory legislation but would prove less liberal on civil liberties issues than most other Roosevelt nominees. Cardozo, who died in July 1938, and Brandeis, who resigned in January 1939, were succeeded by justices of similarly liberal politics and powerful intellect. Cardozo's seat was filled by Roosevelt's trusted advisor Harvard Law Professor Felix Frankfurter, the architect of many New Deal programs. Brandeis was succeeded by William O. Douglas, formerly chairman of the Securities and Exchange Commission. Finally, after Pierce Butler died in November 1939, Roosevelt appointed his attorney general, Frank Murphy, who would compile a highly liberal record during his decade on the Court. At the end of the Hughes era, the only remaining Horseman on the Court was James C. McReynolds, who did not resign until Roosevelt's election to a third term destroyed his hopes of depriving Roosevelt of the opportunity to name his successor.

In contrast to the controversies over Hoover's nominations of Hughes and Parker, none of Roosevelt's nominations to the Court encountered significant opposition, in part because Democrats commanded large majorities in the Senate. Black's nomination originally was controversial because Black was an ardent populist on economic issues. The controversy grew when rumors spread that he had once belonged to the Ku Klux Klan. But Black's membership in the Senate ensured swift confirmation by his colleagues. Shortly after Black's confirmation, a journalist proved that Black had been a Klan member briefly during the 1920s, and there were widespread calls for his resignation. Black defused the scandal by delivering a terse radio address in which he explained that he had severed all ties with the Klan. Black's judicial commitment to racial justice and the preservation of civil liberties quickly dispelled anxiety about his racial and social attitudes.

The Revolution in Civil Liberties

Black's commitment to the protection of civil liberties was shared by most of his colleagues on the Court. At the very time that it was abandoning careful scrutiny of economic legislation, the Court was beginning to undertake more intense scrutiny of legislation that impeded personal liberties. The shift was signaled by Justice Stone in 1938 in *United States v. Carolene Products*. After reiterating the Court's deference to economic legislation by holding that a statutory definition of adulterated food was not a denial of due process, Stone wrote a footnote indicating that the Court might exercise a more rigorous review of noneconomic legislation. In particular,

Stone explained that the Court might adopt a "narrower scope for operation of the presumption of constitutionality" for legislation impinging on the protections of the Bill of Rights. He also hinted that the Court might apply "more exacting judicial scrutiny" under the general provisions of the Fourteenth Amendment to legislation "which restricts those political processes which can ordinarily be expected to bring about repeal of undesirable legislation." Finally, he indicated that the Court might in the future conduct a "more searching judiciary inquiry" into the constitutionality of legislation "directed at particular religious, national, or racial minorities" insofar as "prejudice against discrete and insular minorities" might tend "to curtail the operation of those political processes ordinarily to be relied upon to protect minorities."

Although couched only in hypothetical terms, Stone's famous "Footnote Four" provided a blueprint for the Court's activism on behalf of personal and political liberties during the remainder of the twentieth century. It has aptly been described as a "revolution in a footnote." Judges, lawyers, and scholars today generally agree that the so-called countermajoritarian role of the Court envisioned in Stone's footnote is appropriate because the interests and rights of political, racial, and religious minorities may be vulnerable to the executive and legislative branches of government, which tend to be controlled by majority interests. In contrast, there is less need for special scrutiny of economic regulatory legislation, because persons who are aggrieved by such regulation generally have greater recourse to the political process.

In cases involving personal liberties, however, the civil liberties revolution had begun even before the "Judicial Revolution of 1937." The Hughes Court had established a liberal record in civil liberties from the beginning. During Hughes's chief justiceship, the Court took significant steps in incorporating into state law various key provisions of the Bill of Rights, particularly freedom of speech, freedom of the press, and the right to counsel. The Taft Court had first suggested that the First Amendment's guarantee of free speech was incorporated into state law through the due process clause of the Fourteenth Amendment, but the Court did not formally endorse the application of the free-speech clause to state cases until its 1931 decision in *Stromberg v. California*, overturning California's criminal conviction of the left-wing supervisor of a children's summer camp for displaying the Soviet flag. Two weeks later, the Court incorporated the First Amendment's clause on freedom of the press into state law in *Near v. Minnesota*, which invalidated a "gag law" under which a court had enjoined a newspaper from publishing articles accusing Minneapolis officials of corruption. The Court held that the ancient common-law doctrine that prohibited governments from issuing prior restraints against publication was constitutionalized by the First Amendment and was binding on the states. In dissent, Butler, Van Devanter, McReynolds, and Sutherland argued against imposing the First Amendment on the states. The Court protected freedom of the press again in 1936, this time unanimously, when it struck down a Louisiana law, enacted at the behest of Huey Long, that imposed an advertising tax on the state's largest newspapers.

The court in *Powell v. Alabama* (1932), a year after its decision in *Near*, held that the Fourteenth Amendment's due process clause required states to provide lawyers at no cost to criminal defendants who faced the death penalty. This decision practically, although perhaps not technically, incorporated into state law the Sixth Amendment's guarantee of a right to counsel, at least in capital cases. Accordingly, the Court ordered new trials for the "Scottsboro Boys," nine African American youths who had been accused of raping a white woman. A few years later, in *DeJonge v. Oregon* (1937), the Court incorporated the First Amendment's guarantee of peaceable assembly into state law. In *DeJonge*, the Court invoked the freedom of assembly and free-speech clauses in overturning the conviction of a Communist under an Oregon statute that imposed criminal penalties for conducting meetings of persons who advocated the overthrow of the government. The Court continued the incorporation process in 1940 in *Cantwell v. Connecticut*, applying the First Amendment's guarantee of the free exercise of religion to the states in a decision that overturned the conviction of a Jehovah's Witness who had been convicted of disseminating religious literature without a license.

The Hughes Court made clear, however, that there were limits to its willingness to incorporate the Bill of Rights into state law. In refusing to incorporate the Sixth Amendment's prohibition against double jeopardy, the Court in *Palko v. Connecticut* (1938) explained that the Fourteenth Amendment required incorporation only of those rights, particularly freedom of speech and the press, that are "of the very essence of a scheme of ordered liberty" and "so rooted in the traditions and conscience of our people as to be ranked fundamental." It remained for the Warren Court during the 1960s to take a more expansive view of incorporation and to subsume most of the remaining provisions of the Bill of Rights into state law.

Because most states already had their own bills of rights similar to the federal Bill of Rights, incorporation of federal rights into state law was significant not so much because it introduced new rights into state law but because it enabled the federal judiciary to interpret the scope of such rights. For example, Alabama's constitution included a right to counsel clause that was even broader than the Sixth Amendment's, but Alabama courts had interpreted the provision so narrowly as to permit the state on the eve of trial to assign inexperienced lawyers to represent the Scottsboro defendants. In *Powell,* the Court held that the Sixth Amendment entitled defendants who are accused of a capital crime to more meaningful representation.

The Hughes Court and Race

The Hughes Court also made significant progress in protecting African Americans, in whose rights the Court had shown little interest since Reconstruction. The Court's decisions reflected the growing economic and political power of blacks. The migration of four million blacks to Northern states during the first three decades of the twentieth century enabled many to escape from farm tenancy and obtain higher-paying industrial jobs. Moreover, the absence of racial restrictions on voting in Northern elections enhanced the political clout of blacks, who became pivotal voters for whose ballots both parties competed. Meanwhile, the NAACP escalated its political and legal challenges to racial discrimination.

In a 1931 decision, *Aldridge v. United States,* the Court held that a black charged with murder of a white could raise the issue of racial prejudice in the examination of prospective jurors. In its second decision involving the Scottsboro case, in 1935, the Court overturned the conviction of one of the defendants because blacks were systematically excluded from the jury. Even in cases that did not directly involve racial discrimination, the Court began to consider the racial implications of state actions. In *Powell,* for example, the Court did not shrink from acknowledging the racial context of the Scottsboro case. Similarly, the Court's 1936 decision in *Brown v. Mississippi,* which nullified confessions produced by torture, recognized that the victims were African Americans, even though the fact was not critical to Hughes's conclusion that "the torture chamber may not be substituted for the witness stand."

The Court began to shake the legal foundations of school segregation in its 1938 decision in *Missouri ex rel. Gaines v. Canada,* in which the Court ordered the state of Missouri to admit a black to its all-white law school. The Court held that Missouri's offer to pay his tuition at an out-of-state law school did not satisfy the commands of the Fourteenth Amendment's equal protection clause, because the state denied blacks the privilege of attending law school in their home state solely by reason of race. By establishing a more rigorous standard for application of the so-called separate-but-equal doctrine on which the Court evaluated the constitutionality of segregation, *Gaines* began to establish the doctrinal foundation for the Warren Court's ultimate invalidation of school segregation in *Brown v. Board of Education* (1954).

The Court's decisions on voting by African Americans were more mixed.

During the period of the Hughes Court, black disenfranchisement was rife throughout the South. As a state's denial of the right to vote in general elections clearly violated the Fifteenth Amendment, black disenfranchisement generally was accomplished through racially discriminatory poll taxes and literacy tests and by exclusion of blacks from Democratic primary elections conducted ostensibly by the party rather than by the states. Inasmuch as nomination by the Democratic Party was tantamount to election in most Southern states, black exclusion from Democratic primaries was the equivalent of almost complete disenfranchisement.

Although the Hughes Court did not address the constitutional implications of poll taxes and literacy tests, several of its decisions did address the constitutionality of racial discrimination in primary elections. In *Nixon v. Condon* (1932), the Court overturned a Texas statute authorizing the Democratic Party's executive committee to prohibit blacks from voting in the party's primary elections, a law that Texas had enacted in response to the Court's 1927 ruling (*Nixon v. Herndon*) that the state itself could not bar blacks from voting in the primary. In both decisions, the Court concluded that the laws violated the Fourteenth Amendment's prohibition against denial of equal protection by a state. In *Grovey v. Townsend* (1935), however, the Court unanimously held that the Texas Democratic Party could exclude blacks from its primary when it did so without the benefit of state legislation, even though the state was deeply involved in the regulation of primary elections.

The Court took a more expansive view of state action in *U.S. v. Classic* (1941), holding that state officials who altered and falsely counted ballots in a congressional primary election were subject to prosecution by federal authorities. Although this decision did not involve race, the Court's recognition that primaries were integral to the electoral process paved the way for its decision in *Smith v. Allwright* (1944), which overruled *Grovey* in holding that a state could not permit a political party to exclude blacks from voting in primary elections.

Hughes's Resignation

The reelection of Franklin D. Roosevelt in 1940 to an unprecedented third term helped to ensure the continued appointment of justices who would protect civil liberties against state and federal intrusions and who would defer to Congress and the states in cases involving economic regulation. Hughes, now seventy-nine, remained mentally acute but was beginning to suffer from physical infirmity. When Roosevelt sought Hughes's advice about a successor, Hughes recommended Associate Justice Harlan Stone, whom Hoover had considered for chief justice eleven years earlier and whom Roosevelt now nominated. Hughes was able to retire from the chief justiceship in July 1941 with confidence that the Court would continue on the new course established during his term.

The Impact of the Hughes Court

Although the Hughes Court clearly changed the nation's constitutional landscape, the causes and extent of this transformation remain a subject of controversy. At a minimum, the Judicial Revolution of 1937 produced the Court's permanent abandonment of restrictive interpretations of due process and the commerce and taxing powers that sometimes had strangled state and federal social and economic regulatory legislation during the previous half century. As the Court during those decades had upheld far more such legislation than it had nullified, the Hughes Court did not so much craft new doctrines as apply old ones more expansively and consistently. The 1937 "revolution" may seem more dramatic than it actually was insofar as it followed two years during which the Court became unusually hostile toward regulatory legislation as it reviewed the constitutionality of a plethora of often hastily enacted laws that enhanced federal power, particularly presidential power, to an unprecedented degree. Moreover, the "revolution" did not represent a wholesale shift in opinion by the entire Court but mostly only a partial alteration of the stances of two justices, Roberts and Hughes. The results of this "revolution" may have been permanent only because Roosevelt was able subsequently to nominate so many justices who were sympathetic toward economic regulatory legislation.

Because the Hughes Court's deference toward economic regulatory legislation may have represented more of an evolution than a revolution in legal theory, some scholars have maintained that the Hughes Court was influenced more by its own reexamination of constitutional doctrines than by the external pressures of Court packing and widespread popular support for New Deal legislation. Although it is possible that the Court's greater receptivity toward reform legislation beginning in 1937 reflected fears that the Court would lose some of its power or legitimacy, it is more likely that the ravages of the Great Depression helped to convince Roberts and Hughes, like millions of other Americans, that there was a compelling need for more state and federal economic regulation and that the Constitution did not impede such laws.

Although the Hughes Court marked the end of the Court's activism in scrutinizing state and federal economic legislation, the Court during the 1930s commenced a new era of activism that has continued to the present day on behalf of personal liberties. Here again, the Court did not significantly alter constitutional doctrine, as the Taft Court had handed down pioneering decisions on personal liberties and had begun the process of incorporating the Bill of Rights into state law. The Hughes Court, however, expanded this process both quantitatively and qualitatively in its decisions protecting freedoms of speech, press, and religion from intrusions by the states. The Hughes Court also breathed new life into the equal protection clause in its decisions protecting African Americans from racial discrimination, helping to lay some of the groundwork for the much more sweeping decisions of the following decades. In its deference toward economic legislation and its vigorous guardianship of personal liberties, the Hughes Court may be described as the first "modern" Court.

—WILLIAM G. ROSS

FOR FURTHER READING AND RESEARCH

Although there is not yet any comprehensive study of the Hughes Court, various aspects of the Court during the 1930s have received exhaustive attention and debate. In particular, the Court-packing plan and its significance remain the subject of much controversy. William E. Leuchtenburg's *The Supreme Court Reborn: The Constitutional Revolution in the Age of Roosevelt* (New York, 1995) presents a thorough overview of the Court-packing episode and accepts the traditional theory that the Court's 1937 decisions represented a "judicial revolution." Laura Kalman's *The Strange Career of Legal Liberalism* (New Haven, Conn., 1995) likewise regards the New Deal Court as a break with the past, which Kalman attributes in large measure to the external influence of the Court-packing plan. In contrast, Barry Cushman's *Rethinking the New Deal Court: The Structure of a Constitutional Revolution* (New York, 1998) argues that the Court's decisions in 1937 were grounded in well-established doctrines and constituted an evolution rather than a revolution. Similarly, G. Edward White's *The Constitution and the New Deal* (Cambridge, Mass., 2000) emphasizes judicial continuity, as does Richard D. Friedman's "Switching Time and Other Thought Experiments: The Hughes Court and Constitutional Transformation," *University of Pennsylvania Law Review* 142 (1994), 1891. For a solid historical study of the incorporation process, see Richard C. Cortner, *The Supreme Court and the Second Bill of Rights* (Madison, Wisc., 1981). The most comprehensive biography of Hughes remains Merlo J. Pusey's *Charles Evans Hughes*, 2v. (New York, 1951). Alpheus Thomas Mason's *Harlan Fiske Stone: Pillar of the Law* (New York, 1956), the only major Stone biography, is a rich source of information on the inner workings of the Hughes Court.

The Four Horsemen

Willis Van Devanter, James C. McReynolds, George Sutherland, and Pierce Butler — the four Supreme Court justices who staunchly opposed New Deal legislation both before and after the so-called Judicial Revolution of 1937 — were derided by their contemporary critics as the "Four Horsemen of the Apocalypse" because their strident warnings about the dangers of governmental economic regulations seemed to prophesy the imminent demise of capitalism and democracy. The mocking label has remained forever attached to names that consistently appear near the bottom of lists ranking Supreme Court justices by reputation, a symbol of their losing constitutional struggle against economic regulatory legislation.

The Horsemen's low repute is understandable insofar as their theories of constitutional limitations on state and federal power have been more or less obsolete since 1937; their apocalyptic prophecies proved equally unfounded. Nor was any, with the exception of Sutherland, a particularly articulate or prolific author of judicial opinions. Indeed, Van Devanter's reluctance to write opinions frustrated three successive chief justices. Historians who might desire to spare the Horsemen from unfavorable stereotyping have little to work with — the personal papers of Butler and McReynolds have been destroyed, and those of Van Devanter and Sutherland are scant compared with the collections of many other twentieth-century justices. If all that were not enough, the collective reputation of the Horsemen also suffers from the justices' individual quirks: Butler was relentlessly pugnacious; McReynolds, legendarily misanthropic and eccentric, a bully of his judicial colleagues and staff, and stridently contemptuous of Jews, African Americans, and women's rights.

The Four Horsemen tend to be lumped together in the lore of constitutional history because they indeed had much in common and even met privately as a group to formulate strategy during the years when consideration of New Deal legislation divided the Court into bitter factions. All four were hardheaded, practical men whose antiregulatory predilections reflected their roots in rural and frontier societies that valued "rugged individualism." Reared in a small Indiana town, Van Devanter at age twenty-five established a law practice in the politically and economically chaotic Wyoming Territory, where he litigated cattle-rustling cases and land disputes and prepared the territory for statehood by codifying its statutes. Sutherland, another Westerner, was raised and practiced law in territorial Utah, where suspicion of the federal government was deeply ingrained in the culture. Butler grew up on a hardscrabble Minnesota farm. McReynolds was the son of a wealthy Tennessee plantation owner who opposed public education along with other egalitarian innovations.

As practicing attorneys, the Horsemen shared the political outlook of their clients, mostly corporations opposed to state and federal regulation. Railroads were major clients of all but McReynolds. Before joining the Court, three of the Horsemen were closely associated with the conservative wing of the Republican Party. McReynolds was a conservative Democrat. All, however, displayed occasional streaks of liberalism. As a U.S. senator from Utah, Sutherland advocated women's suffrage and a federal workers' compensation law; McReynolds vigorously enforced the Sherman Antitrust Act during his tenure as a Justice Department attorney and later as attorney general.

Although the Horsemen are usually dismissed as irrelevant curiosities, each had a long and influential tenure on the Court. Van Devanter (1911–1937) and McReynolds (1914–1941) served more than a quarter of a century; Sutherland (1922–1938) and Butler (1923–1939) each had tenures of sixteen years. Even though the Court in economic regulatory decisions since 1937 has rejected their restrictive interpretations of due process, the commerce clause, and the taxing power, the Horsemen often articulated powerful arguments for their positions and succeeded for many years in stemming the tide of state and federal economic regulation. Moreover, they voted to uphold far more regulatory legislation than they voted to strike down, opposing federal and state regulation mostly in "cutting edge" cases.

At least two of the Horsemen left a more lasting legacy in civil liberties laws, for Sutherland and McReynolds wrote landmark opinions striking down governmental regulations that restricted personal liberties. Striking down restrictions on parochial school education in *Meyer v. Nebraska* (1923) and *Pierce v. Society of Sisters* (1925), McReynolds articulated a broad vision of personal liberty that presaged incorporation of the Bill of Rights into state law and laid the foundations for a constitutional right of privacy. Sutherland wrote the Court's opinions in *Powell v. Alabama* (1932), incorporating into state law the Sixth Amendment's right to counsel in capital cases; and *Grosjean v. American Press Co.* (1936), invalidating a newspaper tax. In cases in which the Court prohibited discrimination against African Americans, Sutherland and Van Devanter tended to vote with the majority. Sometimes, as in *Grosjean*, all four Horsemen voted in favor of civil liberties. In *Brown v. Mississippi* (1936), all supported invalidating the coerced confession of an African American. In *DeJonge v. Oregon* (1937), they supported striking down Oregon's syndicalism statute.

Far from being anomalous, the Horsemen's decisions opposing governmental restrictions on personal liberties were consistent with their misgivings about the power of the state to regulate economic activity. Still, the Horsemen's libertarianism should not be overestimated. All four dissented in *Near v. Minnesota* (1931), which incorporated into state law the First Amendment's guarantee of freedom of the press.

11

The Stone and Vinson Courts   1941–1953

Transition and Transformation

L IKE THE SOCIETY in which they were embedded, both the Supreme Court and its interpretation of the Constitution underwent transition and transformation at midcentury. Most important, the Court after 1937 abandoned an older way of thinking about law and its role in a democratic society and set off in search for new validations of the legitimacy of judicial review, a quest that has continued ever since. The era of chief justices Stone and Vinson also saw First Amendment doctrine assume much of its modern content, although the influence of domestic anticommunism distorted the trajectory of that development for a time. The era saw the ice of segregation begin to crack and the nascent civil rights movement score significant victories over racist institutions. Finally, the Court during this time began to grapple with the national-security state that developed during World War II and the cold war and with the seemingly permanent accretion of presidential power and of the national power over the states that the imperatives of the new order dictated.

The era was one of rapid turnover in the Court's membership. President Franklin D. Roosevelt made eight appointments after 1937 and moved Harlan Fiske Stone to the center seat. President Harry S. Truman made an additional four, including Stone's successor, Fred M. Vinson. Although this extraordinary makeover was all the work of Democratic presidents, it did not in any sense create an ideological monolith. Interpersonal animosities caused and complicated by difficult personalities among the justices, divergent ideologies, and the very frequency of new appointments made the Court unstable and fractious throughout the midcentury years. Yet the Court's stance on the issues it faced — First Amendment rights of speech and religion, equal protection, federalism, separation of powers — and its struggles to find a new legitimacy in turbulent times displayed sufficient coherence and continuity in this decade and a half to justify treating the

Courts of Stone and Vinson as a unitary body. In a real sense, it was one Court that happened to be presided over by two short-term chief justices.

A Beginning and an End

Harlan Fiske Stone, associate justice of the U.S. Supreme Court, was vacationing in a cabin near Estes Park, Colorado, in July 1941 when he learned that the U.S. Senate had just confirmed him as the chief justice of the United States, to replace the recently retired Charles Evans Hughes. Stone, the most unpretentious of men, summoned a nearby National Park Service commissioner who had authority to administer oaths and, in these rustic surroundings, was sworn into exalted office.

So incongruous a beginning marked a fitting transition from the previous half-century of the Court's history, an era dominated by a judicial outlook that was formal and classical. It fell to Stone and his colleagues to shepherd American public law out of the thicket of classical legal thought and onto the broad plains of modernity. They only half succeeded: Classicism was abandoned, but the midcentury Court forged no clear alternative around which to unite, giving its work an air of temporizing expediency.

This failure is attributable largely to the inability of the strong, contentious personalities that comprised the Court to achieve any lasting consensus: Felix Frankfurter, at his worst, hectoring, petty, arrogant; his nemesis, William O. Douglas, brilliant, slapdash, abrasive; Hugo L. Black, courtly but unyielding in his embrace of a fundamentalist originalism; Robert H. Jackson, a wordsmith with no peer in the history of the Court, idiosyncratic yet yoked (sometimes) with Frankfurter in resisting judicial activism; Frank Murphy and Wiley Rutledge, the Castor and Pollux of a passionate, results-oriented commitment to civil liberties and racial equality. Each of these men in his own way heralded modern public law. They set its agenda and exalted its goals: protecting individual freedom and enabling democratic self-governance. Inadvertently, they also disclosed its vulnerabilities.

Classical legal thought, in ascendancy after 1890, had conjured a vision of law that assumed the existence of immutable principles that defined right and wrong, justice and injustice. From these principles, lawyers derived rules of law that could be marshaled into a system by the techniques of legal science. The foremost of these techniques was logic, which produced the formal but sterile internal coherence that Oliver Wendell Holmes, Jr., called the *elegantia juris*. Embodied in legal norms, these abstract rules of supposed universal applicability would ensure justice, denying judges a discretion that might be improperly swayed by political preference or personal sympathy. These legal rules were above politics, neither produced by the democratic compromises necessary to legislation nor amenable to them.

In this view, judges were what Sir Edward Coke had called them centuries earlier: the oracles of the law. They discovered law; they did not make it. They had first to discern the norms and then apply them impartially. In the American system, they enjoyed the boon of written constitutions established originally by the supreme authority, the sovereign people. The Constitution provided norms that were expressed in words and phrases to be interpreted as the sovereign's commands. No liberty was to be infringed but by due process of law; the states could not impair the obligation of contracts; no government could take property except for public uses and only on payment of just compensation. Thus, judges found ready at hand explicit, written guides to the meaning and effect of the people's sovereign will.

Legal classicism sought to place property, contracts, and unregulated markets beyond the reach of legislative meddling. Classical law treated the relationship between worker and employer as basically a contract, in which the freedom of both parties was protected from legislative interference. The eponymous case of the classical era, *Lochner v. New York* (1905), embedded that ideological stance in constitutional law. Nor could legislatures frustrate expectations of profit-making opportunity by hedging entrepreneurial liberty with regulations. Liberty was best secured by judges who tightly confined and policed legislative authority.

This powerful, persuasive ideology encountered challenges almost as soon as it began to emerge. The labor struggles and social unrest of the 1880s and 1890s troubled the certitudes of classical thought, especially after critics pointed out that the outcomes such thought generated tended to mirror the political preferences of the judges and lawyers who advanced them.

Classical legal thought was also vulnerable to the intellectual critique posed by modernism and its philosophical expression, pragmatism, largely because it did not occur to its exponents to doubt the possibility of attaining objective truth or objective justice. When John Dewey asserted that truth was a function of results, not of a priori premises, and when scientific inquiry shifted to probabilistic reasoning, edging aside Euclidean and Newtonian absolutes, the epistemological foundations of legal classicism began to tremble. Yet classical judges clung ever more resolutely to their disintegrating certitudes as the only permissible legal response to social unrest and economic dislocation.

Around the turn of the century, eminent judges and legal thinkers joined the assault on classicism. Future Supreme Court Justice Oliver Wendell Holmes, Jr., and Roscoe Pound of the Harvard Law School were two of the most penetrating. Holmes's "Path of the Law" (1897) and Pound's law-review articles on "sociological jurisprudence" undermined classicism's legitimacy. In the 1920s, a loosely affiliated group of legal academics known as the Legal Realists carried the assault further, exposing the fictions of classical thought as rationalizations for results arrived at on the basis of unrecognized or unadmitted political agendas.

The renewal of social conflict ignited by the onset of the Great Depression in 1931 made these questions of more than academic concern. After wavering in the Depression's early years, a majority of the Supreme Court determined to block state and federal efforts to regulate economic relationships. This ensured a confrontation with Franklin D. Roosevelt's New Deal and its state counterparts, which produced a constitutional crisis. This struggle, lasting from 1934 through 1937, ended with the complete repudiation of classical premises. From 1937 through 1942, the Court scrapped almost all the hitherto-dominant structure of legal thought. In the political arena, the New Deal confirmed the permanence of the regulatory state, discarding absolute conceptions of property and contract rights in favor of legislative authority to regulate for the common welfare. Judges would no longer second-guess economic policy.

The Court of the 1940s was the first to carry on its work in this changed era. The demise of classical thought, however, had created an intellectual and jurisprudential vacuum capable of threatening the legitimacy of judicial review and the role of courts in a democratic society. The issue was of more than abstract significance, for in *United States v. Carolene Products* (1938), the Court affirmed its abandonment of economic oversight but indicated that it would redirect its activism to counter intrusions on the liberties enshrined in the Bill of Rights, to obstructions of the democratic political process, and to the oppression of minorities.

The nine justices who sat together for the first time in October 1941 constituted a remarkably new Court. Seven had been nominated by FDR, leading observers to predict, half correctly, that they would comprise a "New Deal Court," meaning a Court indulgent toward Roosevelt's initiatives and regulatory innovations. That was true insofar as the post-1941 Court continued to uphold all New Deal regulatory measures: the National Labor Relations (Wagner) Act, the Social Security Act, and the Fair Labor Standards Act. But the idea of a "New Deal Court" was misleading if it suggested a monolithic body of judicial Roosevelt clones. Cohesion among them began to unravel immediately.

Only Chief Justice Stone and Justice Owen Roberts predated the New Deal. The new chief had come onto the Court in 1925 after serving as dean of the Columbia Law School and briefly as attorney general of the United States. Burly, genial, and tolerant, Stone seemed well suited to lead the heterogeneous and largely unknown group of jurists gathered in

October 1941. His dissents in *Di Santo v. Pennsylvania* (1927) and *United States v. Butler* (1936) presaged an outlook that would pose no unreasonable barriers to state and federal economic regulation. As a former academic, however, Stone proved overly indulgent of his colleagues in his management of debate in conference, in striking contrast to his predecessor, who ran the daylong Saturday sessions fairly but with brisk efficiency.

The senior justice and only other holdover from the pre-1937 era was Owen Roberts, appointed in 1930. Roberts's response to the challenges posed by state and federal New Deal legislation had been erratic; the man himself remains an enigma to those who seek a coherent thread in his thought. He was the author of the fatuous *Butler* opinion that provoked Stone's influential dissent, describing the Court's authority in exercising judicial review in simplistic classicist terms that were repudiated the next year. His was the supposed "switch in time" that swung the Court in 1937 from a 5–4 majority hostile to regulatory authority to a 5–4 majority supporting it. Contemporaries rightly regarded his views as unpredictable.

The Roosevelt nominees had not yet had much opportunity to impress their views on public law. First among them was Hugo L. Black, former U.S. senator from Alabama, dedicated New Dealer, and backer of FDR's misconceived court-packing plan. An astonishing autodidact, Black wrote in simple, direct prose that spoke clearly to ordinary men and women. Over time, he lapsed into a fundamentalist originalism, claiming absolute authority for text and the Framers' intent that he thought he found in the Constitution and Bill of Rights. Stanley Reed of Kentucky, the next nominee, left much less of a mark on the Court's work despite a cosmopolitan education and nineteen years of service as a justice.

Felix Frankfurter, who soon became Black's nemesis, was a striking contrast to the bland, colorless Reed. Boundlessly energetic, possessed of a forceful but narrow intellect, political, and prone to behaviors that were obnoxious, hypocritical, and petty, Frankfurter was the most difficult of the Stone Court's personalities. Appointed just after him was *his* nemesis, William O. Douglas, brilliant legal academic and former chair of the Securities and Exchange Commission. A fluent though facile writer, Douglas was politically ambitious and easily distracted from Court responsibilities (not least by vigorous outdoors hiking and equally vigorous extramarital liaisons). His opinions were slapdash and sometimes as erratic as Roberts's.

Frank Murphy, former Michigan governor and Philippines high commissioner, was a fervent exponent of civil rights and civil liberties. Rightly criticized for subordinating legal constraints to liberal political ends, Murphy was a passionate clarion of legal protection for human dignity. James F. Byrnes, at the opposite pole from Murphy ideologically, served only one year on the Court and left no impress on its work. Robert H. Jackson, former U.S. solicitor general and attorney general, was another New Deal alumnus. Usually joining Frankfurter in resisting judicial activism, Jackson was the most memorable prose stylist ever to have sat on the Court, filling his opinions with aphorisms and *bon mots* that still sparkle a half-century later. The last FDR appointment, Wiley Rutledge, was another legal academic and the only member of the Roosevelt Court who had experience as a judge on a lower federal court. He joined Murphy as a fervent patron of civil liberties and rights. Their deaths in 1949 left the Court bereft of its leading human-rights consciences and ensured a rightward lurch in the Court's ideological orientation.

The First Amendment

The Stone and Vinson Courts were responsible for an extensive range of precedents construing the speech and religion clauses of the First Amendment. These Courts wrote on a virtually clean slate for the free-exercise and establishment clauses, and their speech decisions both advanced and retarded the cause of personal liberties.

The 1941 Court inherited a well-developed and dynamic line of precedent construing that provision of the First Amendment stating that "Congress shall make no law . . . abridging the freedom of speech, or of the press. . . ." World War I–era cases had to give content to the speech clause through the clear-and-present-danger test, which held that governments could inhibit political speech only if that speech posed an imminent threat to important government interests, such as keeping the peace or waging war. But for the first decade after the First World War, the Court permitted suppression of speech that had only a remote or doubtful tendency to threaten interests of the state. After 1931, however, the Hughes Court broadened the clear-and-present-danger test to protect the freedom of political discourse by insisting that the danger had to be truly threatening and immediate. By 1941, this test had produced a speech-protective doctrinal atmosphere.

The principal contribution of the Stone and Vinson Courts to the development of the speech clause was an alternative test, categorization, which was much less protective of political speech. In *Chaplinsky v. New Hampshire* (1942), a unanimous Court held that the state could place whole categories of speech — obscenity, profanity, libel, and fighting words — entirely outside the ambit of First Amendment protection. Justice Frank Murphy explained that such speech threatened the social order and did not promote the search for truth.

Chaplinsky's categorization strategy proved dynamic and fecund: It immediately spawned a fifth category, commercial speech (*Valentine v. Chrestensen* [1942]); over time, other categories cloned, expanded, or simply faded away. As an alternative to clear-and-present-danger today, categorization retains a sinister potential that permits judges to declare whole kinds of communication, including symbolic expression, unprotected by the First Amendment. Did the fighting-words component of categorization apply to a speaker stirring up a mob hostile to his ideas? In *Terminiello v. Chicago* (1949), the Court applied it to protect a speaker whose speech provoked a hostile mob. Two years later, in *Feiner v. New York*, the Court applied this hostile-audience offshoot of fighting words in precisely the opposite fashion, to uphold a conviction for rabble-rousing.

Categorization also produced offspring—the doctrine of group libel. In *Beauharnais v. Illinois* (1952), a 5–4 majority of the Court sustained a state statute prohibiting slanderous or libelous statements about any "class of citizens" defined by race or religion. Justice Frankfurter held that, if a state could punish libelous statements directed toward an individual, by a parity of reasoning and with greater force, it could prohibit unflattering comments about entire groups. The *Beauharnais* group-libel doctrine is probably defunct today, but in its time, it confirmed categorization's speech-suppressive tendencies. Yet at the same time, in *Winters v. New York* (1948), the Vinson Court pioneered obscenity doctrine by striking down on vagueness grounds a statute that permitted censorship of "stories of deeds of bloodshed, lust, or crime." And in *Joseph Burstyn, Inc. v. Wilson* (1952), the Court overturned a blasphemy statute as applied to a movie that the censor thought was "sacrilegious."

The midcentury Court extended the First Amendment's reach to a problem that Justice Frankfurter characterized as "speech-plus": picketing in the context of a labor dispute. The Court at first seemed to protect such a form of communication in *Thornhill v. Alabama* (1940). But after World War II, the scope of the First Amendment shrank in this area, and the Court tolerated ever-greater intrusions on labor's foremost way of publicizing its views in struggles with management.

The postwar Court confronted constitutional issues surrounding content-neutral restrictions on speech for the first time. The First Amendment speaks most clearly to the problem of a state's suppression of the substantive content of speech, as, for example, in a statute restricting political discussion by criminalizing "seditious" speech. But what of laws that do not refer to the content of speech as such but instead only regulate the time, manner, or place of speech? This problem arrived at the Court on the roofs of "sound trucks," motor vehicles with sound-amplification devices mounted on them. Between 1948 and 1952, the Court resolved these sound-truck cases inconclusively, but in doing so, it began to explore issues taken up by later Courts: the problem of the captive audience, the reciprocal rights of speaker and auditor, the impact of technology on the First Amendment, and the time-place-manner formula for resolving content-neutral cases.

Free Exercise

The Court's work in the religion clauses of the First Amendment was more momentous. With one major exception, no cases decided by the Court before World War II had construed either of these clauses. When the justices encountered them for the first time in 1940, therefore, they wrote on a clean slate. Moreover, within a decade, they had established for both clauses precedents that have endured to the present, although not without challenge. The Stone and Vinson Courts laid the foundations of all First Amendment religion clause law.

The Supreme Court had provided content to the free-exercise clause for the first time in 1878, when a Mormon convicted of violating a federal statute prohibiting polygamous marriage in the territories appealed his conviction on the ground that the law interfered with the practice of his religion. (Mormons at that time believed that polygamy was divinely ordained.) In *Reynolds v. United States,* the Court upheld the law and in doing so articulated the basic test that has shaped free-exercise litigation ever since: Must a state make an exception to a neutral law of general applicability for practices mandated by religious belief? If it banned polygamy, did Congress nevertheless have to permit Mormons to practice it because they considered it part of their religious obligation? The Court's answer was a resounding no, and that settled the issue for more than half a century.

The religious practices of the Jehovah's Witnesses in the 1930s provoked countless constitutional confrontations. Believing that the streets were their church, the Witnesses took to them to proselytize confrontationally, provocatively condemning Roman Catholicism and other organized religions as "a fraud and a racket." But the practice that most offended non-Witnesses was their refusal to salute the American flag, which they considered a "graven image." In the climate of heightened anxiety and patriotism of 1940, this ensured their prosecution. After determining that the First Amendment's religion clauses were as binding on the states as they were on Congress (*Cantwell v. Connecticut* [1940]), the Court heard an appeal from Witness parents whose children had been expelled from school in Pennsylvania for refusing to salute the flag. Applying the

Reynolds rule, Justice Frankfurter upheld the school board's action in *Minersville School District v. Gobitis* (1941), over a lone and prophetic dissent by Justice Stone.*

Frankfurter's patriotic rhetoric in *Gobitis* inadvertently encouraged violent and pervasive persecution of Witnesses. This led some members of the Court to doubt the wisdom of the holding. In 1943, the Court jettisoned it in *West Virginia Board of Education v. Barnette*. Treating the issue as one of freedom of speech rather than as a free-exercise problem, Jackson overturned the action of the school board in ringing libertarian terms. More effective as rhetoric than as doctrine, Jackson's opinion vindicated First Amendment liberties in the midst of war: "One's right to life, liberty, and property, and other fundamental rights may not be submitted to vote; they depend on the outcome of no elections." Jackson extolled "the majestic generalities of the Bill of Rights" and warned that imposed conformity of opinion "achieves only the unanimity of the graveyard." He concluded with a ringing peroration: "If there is any fixed star in our constitutional constellation, it is that no official, high or petty, can prescribe what shall be orthodox in politics, nationalism, religion, or other matters of opinion or force citizens to confess by words or act their faith therein." In an embittered dissent, Frankfurter defended his *Gobitis* reasoning and called for judicial self-restraint.

Barnette not only terminated the official prosecution and mob persecution of Jehovah's Witnesses but also redirected free-exercise doctrine for a time. In place of *Reynolds*'s permissive stance, states were now obligated to demonstrate that their goals in restricting religious exercise were compelling and their means for achieving those goals narrowly tailored. (This was the strict-scrutiny test, adapted from the equal-protection area.) This doctrinal posture was protective of religious freedom. It would endure through the 1970s (*Sherbert v. Verner* [1963] and *Wisconsin v. Yoder* [1972]), but a more conservative Court, indifferent to suppression of religions practiced by racial minorities, would return to the *Reynolds* rule in 1992 in *Employment Division v. Smith*.

The 1940s Court also extended protection to door-to-door proselytizing (*Murdock v. Pennsylvania* [1943] and companion cases) but upheld state power to prohibit the use of children in the Witnesses' street ministry (*Prince v. Massachusetts* [1944]). Overall, the climate of religious freedom was more expansive at the end of World War II than it had been at the beginning, and for this the Court may claim much of the credit.

---

* The Gobitas family surname was rendered Gobitis in the Supreme Court decision as a result of a printer's error. The case has been known as *Minersville School District v. Gobitis* ever since.

The Establishment Clause

Both the text and the Framers' intentions that produced the text are more opaque for the establishment clause than for its free-exercise sibling. The text merely states that Congress "shall make no law respecting an establishment of religion." What the Framers intended remains unclear today, except for one point in eclipse now: The House repeatedly rejected every proposal to authorize nonpreferential aid to all religions. In subsequent religious controversies before World War II, judges and political leaders ignored the establishment clause as irrelevant in constitutional debates. Disputes about religion flared repeatedly over control of church property after schisms, state-mandated prayer in public schools, or state financial aid to parochial schools. But the disputants almost never invoked the clause or even seemed to notice it. Thus, when the U.S. Supreme Court was confronted with religious controversies after the war and turned to the clause for the first time for guidance in resolving them, the justices found the words of the clause devoid of any meaning that could be found in the Framers' intentions, historical experience, or judicial precedent. The Vinson Court again wrote on a clean slate.

When New Jersey taxpayers in 1947 challenged a state law subsidizing all school children, including those attending parochial schools, for bus fare incurred by those who rode public transportation, the Court had to give meaning to the establishment clause for the first time. In *Everson v. Board of Education,* the Court unanimously endorsed a doctrine of strict separation between church and state and clothed that doctrine in a compelling metaphor: "the wall of separation." The justices did split among themselves, 5–4, but only over the application of the newly minted doctrine, not its content. If anything, Wiley Rutledge's and Robert Jackson's dissents espoused strict separation even more fervently than Justice Black's majority opinion.

Having no authentic history to work with, Black fabricated a synthetic history of establishment struggles in America. He used Enlightenment ideals of tolerance and reason to give meaning to European religious experience, a long struggle against intolerance and repression caused by churches' wielding state power in such things as the Inquisitions. The attempted transplantation of such practices to the New World "shock[ed] the freedom-loving colonials into a feeling of abhorrence [and] aroused their indignation," Black wrote. Invoking Thomas Jefferson's Act for Religious Freedom (1785), Black adopted Jefferson's metaphor, the wall of separation, as canonical for the meaning of the establishment clause, even though Jefferson had penned the phrase two decades later. Church and state must be strictly separated, neither being permitted to control the other.

The justices returned to the establishment clause in two cases involving "released time," a practice whereby public schools excused children from classes to attend religious instruction. In *McCollum v. Board of Education* (1948), the Court held the practice unconstitutional when the religious teaching was done in the public school but sustained it in *Zorach v. Clauson* (1952) when the children went off school grounds to be catechized in churches and synagogues. Douglas's opinion in *Zorach* declared that "we are a religious people whose institutions presuppose a Supreme Being" and stated that government cannot be hostile to religion, two ideas that later proved to be incompatible with *Everson's* strict separation. Out of the loose dicta in all these cases emerged polar-opposite doctrinal positions on strict separation. By the late twentieth century, a majority of the Supreme Court would come around to the idea that states might provide financial aid to religious programs and might host seasonal religious displays in the name of nonpreference and "accommodation."

World War II and Civil Liberties

In American experience, war has usually had a direct but short-lived effect on political freedom and civil liberties. During the War for American Independence, some of the states harassed Loyalists, confiscated their property without compensation, and resisted restitution afterward. The Lincoln administration curbed political opposition during the Civil War, though to a lesser extent than contemporary critics charged. World War I saw drastic inroads on political freedom, and a complaisant Court acquiesced. Until World War II, presidential power had always grown in wartime but like a balloon, deflated after the war. After World War II, war-induced expansion of national authority proved irreversible.

Generally speaking, though, American experience in World War II did not validate Cicero's dictum that "in the clash of arms, the laws are mute." On the contrary, public law proved to be a surprisingly effective aegis of political liberty during the war. The Court was protective of political speech during World War II, in contrast to its performance a quarter-century earlier. In the midst of the war, in a case reversing the conviction of a Nazi propagandist for failing to report his activities, Chief Justice Stone cautioned that "men are not subjected to criminal punishment because their conduct offends our patriotic emotions" (*Viereck v. United States* [1943]). In contrast to the earlier cases, decided under the Espionage Act of 1917, the Stone Court construed the statute narrowly and protected political publications, even those that were racist, anti-Semitic Nazi rants (*Hartzel v. United States* [1944]).

Immigration, naturalization, and deportation produced some of the Court's leading war-related decisions. In a major advance for First Amendment speech liberties, the Court intervened when the federal government attempted to denaturalize and deport William Schneiderman because he had been an active member of the Communist Party. In *Schneiderman v. United States* (1943), a majority of the justices forestalled this attempt. Justice Murphy extolled "the spirit of freedom and tolerance in which our nation was founded" in pointing out that Schneiderman was being harassed for his beliefs; he was not charged with any wrongdoing but only for the incompatibility of his ideology with more conventional views of American traditions. The Court evenhandedly extended the same protection to a naturalized member of the pro-Nazi Bund (*Baumgartner v. United States* [1944]).

After the war, the justices continued to frustrate a decade-long politically motivated effort to deport the West Coast leftist labor leader Harry Bridges because of his radical associations (*Bridges v. Wixon* [1945], *Bridges v. United States* [1953]). In all these decisions, a majority of the justices construed the clear-and-present-danger test stringently, requiring a clear showing of illegal conduct before an individual could be punished or deported for radical beliefs and associations.

Conscientious objectors posed challenges for civil liberties in wartime. Here, the Court's record was mixed. In *In re Summers* (1945), the justices permitted Illinois to deny admission to the bar of a qualified conscientious objector who would not take an oath to serve in the state militia. But in *Estep v. United States,* decided the next year, the justices permitted a Jehovah's Witness conscientious objector to appeal his draft classification in federal courts after he had exhausted his administrative remedies. And in *Girouard v. United States* (1946), the Court reversed two harsh antiobjector precedents of the 1930s to permit naturalization of a Seventh-day Adventist objector who would not "take up arms" (the words of the naturalization oath at the time) but would serve in a noncombatant capacity. These decisions left the position of the conscientious objector constitutionally tenuous and vulnerable to legislative whim. Not until the 1970s did constitutional law ground the right to conscientious objection on a firmer basis.

Not surprisingly, the role of the military in American society expanded dramatically during the war in such areas as the powers of military courts, the permissible scope of martial law, the jurisdiction of war crimes tribunals, and the law of treason. In 1942, the FBI apprehended eight German saboteurs who had landed on beaches in Florida and New York and blended into American society in civilian attire (a crucial fact that denied them conventional POW status). President Roosevelt authorized a special military commission (a court of seven army general officers) to try them for offenses against the international and unwritten laws of war, principally sabotage and espionage (Plate B.9). The scope of powers accorded the military commission by presidential order were constitutionally vulnerable on several counts, but the military commission went ahead anyway, tried the saboteurs, and sentenced them to death. The Supreme Court rejected their appeal in *Ex parte Quirin* (1942), and six of them were promptly executed.

The leading precedent that shaped and confined all governmental actions in this area was *Ex parte Milligan* (1866), in which a unanimous Court reversed the conviction and death sentence of a Confederate irregular by a military commission for acts committed in Indiana during the Civil War (Plate A.9). The Court held that neither the suspension of habeas corpus nor military commissions can displace the authority of civilian courts if they are open and functioning, outside a theater of actual military operations. *Milligan* stands as a permanent bar to wartime expansion of martial law and military tribunals, but its authority was severely tested in the saboteurs' case.

In *Quirin*, Chief Justice Stone evaded *Milligan* and upheld the authority of the commission against all challenges. He disingenuously confined *Milligan* by holding that it did not apply to "enemy belligerents." This created a sweeping, indefinitely expandable power in military courts to try civilians under the unwritten laws of war and minimized protections that might have been afforded by the Bill of Rights, the stringent constitutional definition and procedural protections in treason prosecutions, and the writ of habeas corpus. *Quirin* would reach far into the future to authorize military custody of civilians of a different sort after the terrorist attacks in the United States in 2001.

Actual treason prosecutions during and after World War II were more encouraging for the cause of civil liberties. The most important of these cases was *Cramer v. United States* (1945), a treason prosecution of a friend of one of the *Quirin* saboteurs who was resident in the United States and who had met with one of them. In *Cramer*, the Court reaffirmed the stringent substantive evidentiary standards mandated for treason by the Constitution and enhanced by Chief Justice John Marshall's Burr trial opinions in 1807.

The Court was determined not to interfere with war crimes trials held in Germany and Japan, principally because a majority of the justices believed that they lacked jurisdiction to hear appeals from military trials, which is what the war crimes tribunals were (*In re Yamashita* [1946], *Hirota v. MacArthur* [1948]). But a different result emerged when military courts displaced civilian tribunals in Hawaii, an American territory.

Martial Law in Hawaii

Immediately after Pearl Harbor, the army imposed martial law there, for a time entirely replacing both civilian courts and civil administration with direct military rule. Although it gave back some of this authority within a year, the army retained extensive control over all aspects of life in the islands, controlling the minutiae of government regulation and civilian behavior. Army provost courts replaced civilian territorial courts for all but nonjury civil cases. Military judges presided over the trial of all criminal offenses, and their proceedings were lax even by military standards, including the abrogation of jury trial. Civilian observers in the islands and in Washington denounced this system of military administration as "lawless" and "totalitarian."

This problem made its way to the Court after war's end in *Duncan v. Kahanamoku* (1946), in which the Court held military trials of civilians illegal. Skirting constitutional issues, the majority held that the Organic Act that had constituted the territory did not authorize displacement of civil courts by military authority.

Japanese Internment

The Japanese attack on Pearl Harbor brought to the fore a problem that had been worsening over the previous half-century: white envy and resentment of the Japanese on the West Coast. Fearing competition from the industrious Japanese in agriculture, fisheries, and retail trade, white farming organizations formed racist pressure groups to limit Japanese immigration and prohibit ownership of land by Japanese. After December 7, 1941, these pressure groups found a powerful ally in the army, which demanded evacuation of all Japanese from coastal areas on the ground that they (or some unspecified number of them) were actually or potentially disloyal and might commit acts of sabotage or provide assistance to the Japanese navy.

This confluence of interests produced the policy of Japanese internment, a three-step process that first imposed a curfew on all Japanese (non-naturalized, naturalized, and native-born), then forced them to evacuate their homes and report to "relocation centers," and finally relocated all of them to twelve internment sites in interior locations stretching from northern California to Arkansas. There they were held in detention in bleak, spartan barracks housing behind barbed wire, under the eye of armed military sentries.

This deprivation of liberty and property was challenged in three separate cases corresponding to each of the steps of the internment process. In these decisions, the Supreme Court comprehensively sustained Japanese internment but planted important doctrinal seeds that were to germinate two decades later in ways much more favorable to civil liberties.

The first case was *Hirabayashi v. United States* (1943), in which the Court unanimously sustained the curfew phase of the program but only by papering over deep divisions among the justices over the racist impetus behind internment. These divisions burst out when the next phase, exclusion, came before the Court in 1944 in *Korematsu v. United States*. Justice Black, writing for a six-member majority, again sustained the government's program but only by insisting that relocation could somehow be considered apart from detention in the camps. With that artificial distinction unnaturally propped up, he then justified exclusion on the basis of military necessity as determined by the president and the army, whose decisions were ratified by Congress. Black implausibly denied the racial motivations behind the measure and bristled at the suggestion that the evacuees were being herded into "concentration camps," one of the few times in Black's career when his composure, at least in print, became ruffled. In fervid dissents, Jackson, Roberts (a surprise), and Murphy refuted Black's disingenuous positions and warned of the dangers latent in his dangerous concession to executive and military power. *Korematsu*, Murphy charged, was a "legalization of racism."

Finally, in *Ex parte Endo* (1944), the Court made an empty concession to the rights of the Japanese internees by holding that a person whose loyalty was unchallenged could not be held in the detention camps unwillingly. But by that time, the government was dismantling the program, so the holding had no practical impact or value.

The internment cases had three long-range impacts. The first, and so far the most lasting, was found in dicta in Black's *Korematsu* majority opinion, which stated that "all legal restrictions which curtail the civil rights of a single racial group are immediately suspect . . . courts must subject them to the most rigid scrutiny." This passage became the source of later strict-scrutiny doctrine in the area of equal protection, in which suspect classifications, such as race, come to the courts inherently suspect. To sustain racial categorization, the government must demonstrate that its ends are "compelling" and its means to achieve those ends "narrowly tailored."

The second impact derived from the first: Such strict scrutiny has proved fatal to a government racial classification — with the sole and invidious exception of *Korematsu*. That case stands, therefore, as a caution that not even stringent strict-scrutiny review will necessarily void a race-motivated governmental act.

The third impact derived from later and near-universal acknowledgment of the injustice of the Japanese internment, reflected in several presidential apologies, authorization of minimal reparations to the victims, and erection of a monument in Washington, D.C., to the Japanese wartime experience. In the federal courts, attorneys exposed the falsity of the government's claims, resting on suppression of evidence, that the Japanese posed a threat of subversion or sabotage, and the *Hirabayashi* and *Korematsu* convictions were vacated.

National Power in War and Cold War

If the results of decisions impinging on civil liberties were mixed, the Supreme Court's handling of cases involving national power was not. "War expands the nation's power," Justice Rutledge conceded in his dissent in *Yakus v. United States* (1944). This view had long-lasting implications for both the separation of powers and federalism. Presidential power and the powers of the national government vis-à-vis the states grew dramatically during the war, and the Court ratified every accretion.

The modern "national security constitution," as Harold Koh has termed it, emerged out of FDR's vigorous response to totalitarian aggression after 1940. At first on his own initiative, FDR used the instruments known as the executive order and the executive agreement to an extent unprecedented and even unimaginable to his predecessors. By executive agreement, an instrument primarily of foreign affairs, he committed the nation to crypto-belligerent status in 1940 and to a quasi-alliance with Great Britain in 1941. The Court upheld this immense expansion of presidential authority first in *United States v. Belmont* (1937) and then during the war in *United States v. Pink* (1942). FDR used the executive order, an instrument used principally in domestic matters, to impose on the entire nation a structure of economic regulation more comprehensive than anything Americans had ever before experienced. The Court sustained this regime of economic control first in *Lockerty v. Phillips* (1943) and then in *Yakus v. United States* (1944). Congress acquiesced in all FDR's actions and ratified many of them by statute, so the Court was not alone in affirming these beginnings of the imperial presidency.

Although presidential authority did not recede after the war, it experienced in 1952 a check that has provided, at least potentially, a valuable constraint on executive power. In 1952, President Harry S. Truman ordered federal seizure of the nation's steel mills to prevent a threatened strike that he feared would set back steel production in the Korean conflict. To his dismay, the Court rebuffed this overture in *Youngstown Sheet and Tube Co. v. Sawyer* (1952). Although the justices diverged widely among themselves, producing six opinions in a 6–3 division, the majority concluded that there was neither constitutional nor statutory support for Truman's actions (Plate B.10). Justice Jackson's concurrence has proved to be the most long-lived in its influence. He laid out a scale that located exercises of presidential power in relation to congressional actions. The president's power is highest where Congress has provided positive support for it, whether express or implicit. It is weaker when Congress has not acted at all one way or the other and is at its lowest ebb when the chief executive acts in defiance of Congress's stated or implied intent.

Congress too enhanced its regulatory authority during the war, and the Court again proved supportive. This expansion occurred principally in the ways that Congress regulates interstate and foreign commerce. Problems arise in the area of federalism when congressional initiatives conflict with state regulation. Where Congress has acted explicitly, its policy prevails over any inconsistent state policies under the authority of the supremacy clause of the Constitution's Article VI. This is known as "preemption," and the Court reaffirmed it in *Hines v. Davidowitz* (1941) and *Rice v. Santa Fe Elevator Corp.* (1947). The justices also sustained an implicit federal authority in the so-called tidelands controversy in *United States v. California* (1947) and in *United States v. Texas* (1950), upholding federal control over subsurface coastal lands and their mineral riches, such as oil, the prize of the entire struggle, against a state grab for resources. In 1953, though, Congress ceded title to the states.

The more difficult problem arises when Congress has not spoken and states have acted in a realm reserved to Congress, such as the regulation of commerce. Constitutional scholars speak of a "dormant commerce power," by which they mean a doctrine that attempts to infer congressional intent when Congress has not spoken. Unfortunately, the doctrine is ambivalent, sometimes reading congressional silence as permission for the states to regulate as they wish until Congress steps in. At other times, though, the Court applies the doctrine to infer that Congress by its silence has expressed its intent that the states not intrude at all, leaving private actors free of potentially conflicting state regulations.

After the war, the Court consistently resolved this ambivalence against state regulatory interference with the national market. In *Southern Pacific Co. v. Arizona* (1945), the Court struck down a state attempt to regulate the length of trains passing through the state. The Court balanced federal interests in an unimpeded national market or transportation system against state police power interests and came out resoundingly in favor of federal authority. Another prong of dormant-commerce-power doctrine struck down state protectionism. In *H. P. Hood & Sons v. DuMond* (1949), the Court, in a ringing opinion by Justice Jackson, extolled the national market and condemned state interference by isolationist or protectionist measures. He insisted that states could not use their police power authority to stifle interstate competition or to impede the free flow of goods in the national market.

Postwar Jurisprudential Issues

The war may have been a distraction for the justices, its urgent priorities diverting their attention from a problem unresolved for almost a decade: how to justify the role of courts in a democracy after the specious assumptions of classical thought had been abandoned. This issue had three major components. First, was objectivity possible for judges? Could they demonstrate convincingly that the results of adjudication were produced by something more detached than the judges' political and ideological preferences? Such objectivity was a precondition to the second component: the rule of law. Although no one had succeeded in providing a definitive formulation of the rule of law ideal since Albert Venn Dicey had formulated the problem in the 1880s, Americans, including the justices of the Supreme Court, remained dedicated to it. Judging that reflected only a judge's political biases would be a travesty of the ideal.

The third component was a reaction against the legal-realist-induced skepticism that had haunted American public law since the 1920s. The Nazi experience suggested that a purely amoral positivist approach to law could end in the horrors of totalitarianism, where law became the perverted and debased instrument of party or dictator. The only alternative that was obvious to Americans was democracy, but what was law's place in a democratic society? Was there any role for judicial review in majoritarian government?

During the war, two members of the Court had given this problem occasional attention. Felix Frankfurter's experience since his elevation to the Court in 1939 confirmed a conviction he had formed long before: Courts should not overturn the results of legislative judgment for any reason short of obvious conflict with a clear constitutional prohibition. Judicial deference was as necessary in the 1940s and 1950s toward legislation affecting civil liberties as it had been through the classical era with respect to economic regulations.

Hugo L. Black provided a contrasting solution to the objectivity problem. He believed that the Framers of the Constitution in 1787, 1789, and 1868 had bequeathed to later generations a definitive text, particularly in the Bill of Rights, that had an objective and determinate meaning accessible to judges, who were thereby bound to apply its terms literally, with no fudging permitted by balancing legislative ends against individual interests.

In response to challenges by interviewers to a position he advocated, Black was fond of pulling out from his coat a pocket-sized copy of the Constitution and proclaiming that the answers to all constitutional issues were to be found there. Anything not answered by the Constitution was beyond judicial power.

These two contrasting judicial philosophies were bound to clash, and that collision was sure to be spectacular, given the personalities and aptitudes of the two men. Through the 1940s, the incipient conflict came to focus on the problem of "incorporation": To what extent, if at all, were the restraints of the Bill of Rights binding on the states through ratification of the Fourteenth Amendment in 1868? By 1947, Black came to the position that the Bill of Rights was completely binding on the states. Frankfurter, on the other hand, rejected incorporation altogether, insisting that judges must determine which of the liberties mentioned in the Bill of Rights were binding on the states, based on judicial understandings of the values of the American people. Black and Frankfurter accused each other of allowing too much scope to judicial discretion, and each insisted that only his own position accorded with the true nature of the Constitution.

The issue came to a head in the 1947 case of *Adamson v. California:* Did a state statute that permitted the prosecution to comment on prior convictions if a criminal defendant chose to testify fall afoul of the Fifth Amendment's prohibition on self-incrimination, as incorporated against the states by the Fourteenth Amendment? Frankfurter insisted that it did not, because nothing in the Bill of Rights was incorporated. Rather, if a state procedure was void, it was only because it was incompatible with local community standards of decency. Black rejected that idea. "I fear to see the consequences of the Court's practice of substituting its own concepts of decency and fundamental justice for the language of the Bill of Rights," he wrote in dissent. Frankfurter, in a rebuttal concurrence, claimed that the due process clause imposes on the Court the duty of "an exercise of judgment" to determine whether the state procedure "offend[s] those canons of decency and fairness" of "English-speaking peoples."

Although Frankfurter was with the majority in *Adamson,* he sensed that he had not adequately responded to the objectivity problem. He returned to the project in *Rochin v. California* (1952), a case presenting the question whether the guarantee of due process of law was violated by pumping the stomach of a criminal defendant suspected of having swallowed capsules of an illegal drug. The Court unanimously held that it was, and Frankfurter took the occasion to demonstrate that vague, unspecific notions of due process could be objectively applied. He insisted that judges do not apply their "merely personal and private notions." The meaning of due process is ascertained by "reason" and fixed by "the compelling traditions of the legal profession." These assured "the requisite detachment and . . . sufficient objectivity." Black derided this confidence in the judgment of a judicial elite.

The *Adamson* and *Rochin* debates settled nothing. Though the incorporation controversy faded, its substantive question remains contested today. Although rejecting Black's total-incorporation position, the Court nevertheless has incorporated nearly all the Bill of Rights piecemeal. The larger issue behind the incorporation controversy, finding a jurisprudential replacement for classical legal thought, continues unresolved. That, in turn, cast a cloud over the legitimacy of the midcentury Court's work.

The Court in Transition

Justice Roberts, disenchanted with the Court's direction since 1940 and increasingly alienated from his colleagues, resigned in 1945. President Truman, distracted by the momentous issues that he had confronted since his accession to office on the death of President Roosevelt, quickly appointed Harold H. Burton to the vacant seat. Burton, a moderate, respected Republican senator from Ohio, had worked closely with Truman during the war. In his thirteen years' service, he supported the nascent civil rights movement but held to a more orthodox and conservative Republican line on economic issues, especially those involving labor unions.

Chief Justice Stone's death in 1946 precipitated a controversy that temporarily besmirched the reputation of the Court. Justice Jackson, serving as chief prosecutor of Nazi war criminals in the war crimes trials in Nuremberg, hoped to be nominated to succeed Stone. At the same time, he harbored a growing animosity toward Justice Black. Believing that Black had counseled Truman not to appoint him, Jackson publicly aired intra-Court controversies over Black's role in deciding several cases involving labor unions. The scandal blew over quickly, after Truman nominated Fred M. Vinson to the center seat. Vinson, another congressional friend of Truman's, had served with distinction in all three branches of government: in the House of Representatives, on the United States Court of Appeals for the D. C. Circuit and as Chief Judge of the Emergency Court of Appeals, and in various administrative and executive positions during the war, including such hot-seat positions as director of economic stabilization. After the war, Vinson served briefly as secretary of the Treasury at Truman's behest.

The deaths of Justices Murphy and Rutledge within months of each other in the summer of 1949 created two more vacancies on the Court. Truman's nominations to fill them gave the Court a decidedly more conservative cast, so that the remainder of Vinson's tenure saw the justices more supportive of governmental power over the noneconomic liberties of citizens. The justices did not retreat, however, from their growing commitment to the cause of civil rights. Tom C. Clark, Truman's third appointment, had served as Truman's attorney general and, in that role, had vigorously pursued suspected subversives. Contemporaries underestimated both his abilities and his support for the causes that fired the passions of the man whose seat he took, Justice Murphy. Truman's last appointment proved far less distinguished, however. Sherman Minton, yet another Senate colleague of the president who had also sat on the court of appeals with Vinson, served for seven years on the Court but wrote no significant opinions.

The Cold War

The change in the ideological complexion of the Court occurred at a time when the anti-Communist crusade that had been building for half a century crested and triumphed. Distilled from a witches' brew of xenophobia, racial segregation, and business hostility to labor unions, anticommunism was propelled by apprehension over Soviet expansionist ambitions and a well-founded revulsion at the enormities of Stalinist oppression. The Soviet Union provided a focus for these complementary fears in the deepening climate of anxiety over foreign relations after 1946. But anti-Communist energies turned more readily to the enemy at hand, domestic leftist radicals, including but not limited to members of the American Communist Party. In this climate, defined by the momentary triumph of the anti-Communist worldview, protection for First Amendment liberties of speech, press, and assembly retreated for a decade.

The two-year period 1949–1950 was a particularly grim moment for Americans in the rapidly escalating cold war. The Soviet Union first established its control over the Eastern European bloc countries, then exploded an atomic bomb. Many Americans, including the president, wanted to believe that this feat was possible only by the treachery of "atomic spies" in the United States who had passed the "secrets" of nuclear fission to Soviet agents. When North Korea invaded South Korea in June 1950, seemingly at the direction of the USSR and Red China, which had been "lost" to Communist control the previous year, a nuclear Armageddon seemed at hand. The times were propitious for crushing domestic subversion, and the Supreme Court stood by, ready to lend a hand.

The Court found its first opportunity when officers of a leftist union refused to sign the non-Communist affidavit mandated by the Taft-Hartley Act of 1947. In *American Communications Association v. Douds* (1950), a divided Court upheld the constitutionality of these provisions against a First Amendment challenge but only by ignoring the political-speech implications of the statute and treating it more safely as a regulation of commerce, a subject by then concededly within the ambit of Congress's powers. In doing so, however, the justices, with the lonely exceptions of Black and Douglas, endorsed the image of all Communists as subversive traitors. The Court accepted Congress's declaration that Communists sought "the overthrow of the Government of the United States by force and violence," a formula derived from state criminal syndicalism statutes of the late nineteenth century. In *Douds,* Chief Justice Vinson held that courts must balance claimed First Amendment liberties against the imperatives of national security and survival. In such a contest, if the political climate is heated enough, national security always wins.

Douds set the stage for the major cold war decision of the Vinson years: *Dennis v. United States* (1951). In 1948, Attorney General Tom Clark, now on the Court, had begun prosecution of the top leadership of the American Communist Party under the Smith Act (1940) for conspiring to organize the Communist Party and to teach and advocate doctrines calling for overthrow of the government of the United States by force and violence. Each of the three stages of this prosecution (trial, appeal, ultimate appeal) was significant. In the U.S. district court, a combination of disastrous trial tactics by the defendants and their counsel, together with Judge Harold Medina's obvious hostility toward them, ensured their conviction. For good measure, Medina sentenced defense counsel for contempt of court for their overly aggressive trial tactics.

The U.S. court of appeals affirmed the convictions in an influential opinion by Judge Learned Hand. Hand reinterpreted the clear-and-present-danger test by a pseudomathematical sliding scale: "whether the gravity of the evil, discounted by its improbability, justifies such invasion of free speech as is necessary to avoid the danger." On appeal to the U.S. Supreme Court, a 6–2 majority (Justice Clark having to recuse himself) upheld the conviction and, in an opinion by Chief Justice Vinson, adopted Hand's sliding-scale test. Accepting uncritically the demonized image of the Communist Party as a dangerous conspiracy, Vinson balanced speech freedoms against national security and came out solidly for security. Vinson's opinion, not one of his best, was internally incoherent and at times almost self-contradictory, but its conclusion was clear: Governments could prosecute Communists for advocating ideas.

In dissent, Black expressed the hope that "in calmer times, when present pressure, passions, and fears subside," the Court would "restore" First Amendment liberties to the preferred position they had occupied in the previous two decades. That did eventually happen, but in its remaining three years, the Vinson Court upheld the federal loyalty program (*Bailey v.*

Richardson [1951]); tolerated sweeping naturalization and deportation powers (*Knauff v. Shaughnessy* [1950], *Harisiades v. Shaughnessy* [1952], *Shaughnessy v. United States, ex rel. Mezei* [1953]); and sustained parallel state antisubversive activities (*Adler v. Board of Education* [1952]). It did, however, also extend some protections for freedom of association to groups that appeared on the attorney general's list of suspected subversive organizations.

The Vinson Court's last encounter with cold war issues was also its least admirable. In affirming the death sentences of Julius and Ethel Rosenberg for espionage, the justices, imprisoned in a cold war anti-Communist mentality, were blind to the numerous failures of the judicial process in the trial and appeals of this high-profile case.

Controversy continues half a century later over what exactly the Rosenbergs did in their espionage activities on behalf of the Soviet Union. Ethel was a passive participant: She knew of her husband's activities but did not actively engage in spying. Julius spied, but his contributions were principally in the area of conventional weapons. How significant his indirect involvement with atomic espionage was remains in dispute.

The trial judge, Irving Kaufman, was obviously biased in his handling of the trial. The evidence introduced at trial was corrupted by perjury. Judge Kaufman conferred improperly with the prosecution before sentencing and did everything he could behind the scenes to forestall any successful appeal from the death sentence he imposed. (He was not alone in this improper judicial behavior: Chief Justice Vinson and Justice Jackson conferred with the attorney general during the Court's conference debates.) On appeal to the Supreme Court, Justice Douglas vacillated erratically in his certiorari votes, leaving the impression that he was inattentive or indifferent to the legal and constitutional issues raised. His last-minute interventions on behalf of the defendants appeared cynically opportunistic.

The Court heard six separate appeals from affirmation of the death sentences, each of them raising serious questions about the fairness of Judge Kaufman's conduct of the trial or about legal and constitutional issues raised by the indictment and sentencing. The most important of these issues was whether the defendants had been convicted under the proper statute. Their conviction was based on the Espionage Act of 1917, which provided for punishment by death; the other contender, the Atomic Energy Act of 1946, did not authorize the death penalty.

In the end, the Court shut its eyes both to the problems at trial and to the legal and constitutional questions posed, and the Rosenbergs went to the electric chair. "No discussion of merits!" lamented Justice Frankfurter, "only a rush to judgment." Their trial and execution were, in the opinion of the foremost scholarly authorities on the topic, "a grave miscarriage of justice."

Civil Rights

The longest-lasting and most positive achievements of the midcentury Court lay in the field of civil rights, an accomplishment obscured by the Warren Court's better-known advances, which began with *Brown v. Board of Education* (1954). The equal protection clause of the Fourteenth Amendment had been a dead letter since 1875, sunk into a coma by the poisoned apple of the *Slaughterhouse Cases* (1873) and the *Civil Rights Cases* (1883). Part of the problem was that the value of interpersonal equality was entirely new when it was inserted into the Constitution in 1868 and more or less unacceptable to most white Americans if fully implemented across racial lines. Earlier visions of equality, such as those promoted by Thomas Jefferson and later Jacksonian Democrats, were for white men only.

The intentions of the framers of the Fourteenth Amendment, including its equal protection clause, have been widely misunderstood and misinterpreted. Section 1 of the amendment was meant to accomplish all the following goals in the area of racial equality: first, to make national and state citizens of all people born in the United States and thereby to confer all the privileges, powers, and immunities of citizenship on them; second, to extend the protections of the Constitution to all people, to endow them with full and equal status as members of the polity and to empower them to call on the state for protection; and third, to validate the Civil Rights Act of 1866, which conferred on the freedpeople the capacity to enter into contracts, hold property, enjoy legally recognized family relationships, have access to courts as parties and witnesses, and be subject to the same laws as whites "and no other." The framers also intended to confer on Congress all powers necessary to enforce the provisions: citizenship, privileges and immunities, due process, and equal protection.

When civil rights issues came up before the Stone Court, they were not structured in equal protection terms, because the equal protection clause had not yet emerged from its post-*Slaughterhouse* drugged sleep. Instead, civil rights problems were framed in terms of federalism: To what extent could federal authority extend into what had been traditionally the prerogatives of state police power? This appeared first in struggles over the white primary. The Court had successively held that states could not exclude blacks from voting in primary elections (*Nixon v. Herndon* [1927]), that states could not permit parties to dictate racial voter qualifications for primary voting (*Nixon v. Condon* [1932]), but that party conventions acting without direct state involvement could limit voting in their primary elections to "white citizens" (*Grovey v. Townsend* [1936]). Then, in a case that did not directly implicate racial discrimination in voting, *United States v. Classic* (1941), the Court sustained the Justice Department's use of the 1866 Civil Rights Act and the 1870 Enforcement Act to suppress voting frauds in primary elections.

Classic suggested that state-sovereignty arguments might prove unavailing if black voters again challenged the white primary. That is what happened in *Smith v. Allwright* (1944), when the Court sustained federal authority to prohibit the white primary under the Fifteenth Amendment. The Court extended this salient in 1953 in *Terry v. Adams* to strike down a local state party committee's action denying blacks access to local primaries. Ridding the South of the white primary did not do much in the short run to overcome racial disfranchisement, but it marked the beginning of a drive to realize finally the promise of the Reconstruction amendments in the area of voting.

Police brutality emerged as the other civil rights issue in the Stone and Vinson era. White supremacy maintained its power through violence, both by private actors (lynchings) and by police. Could federal power punish racial violence when perpetrated by a police officer or a sheriff? The dilemma here was that such violence, by definition, violated state laws. Could it nevertheless be "under color of" state law, as required by the Reconstruction-era Enforcement Acts? This conundrum split the Court in *Screws v. United States* (1945), with a bare majority, speaking through Justice Douglas, holding that it could. Justice Frankfurter, never a friend to the legal regime of Reconstruction at any time, condemned the hairsplitting necessary to achieve the majority's result. But had his view prevailed, the federal government would have been powerless to prevent racist police violence. As with the white primary, *Screws* marked only the beginning of effective federal response to the problem. But it did at least save that potential from the fastidious legalisms and unthinking animosity of the judicial-restraint bloc.

Civil rights issues accelerated after the war, as the NAACP litigated school segregation and employment discrimination more persistently and as African American communities throughout the nation organized to resist Jim Crow's injustices. The White House, for the first time ever, threw its weight behind such efforts in President Truman's 1947 civil rights program. Legal academics called their practicing colleagues' attention to the long-dormant potential of the equal protection clause as an engine for challenging segregation. All these efforts began to pay off in a series of heartening victories for civil rights plaintiffs.

The Supreme Court weakened segregation in interstate transportation by first striking down a state Jim Crow law as it applied to interstate bus and rail transportation (*Morgan v. Virginia* [1946]), then by sustaining a state's power to prohibit discrimination in transportation even where the carrier was interstate or international (*Bob-Lo Excursion Co. v. Michigan* [1948]). Finally, in *Henderson v. United States* (1950), the Court hinted broadly that the day of *Plessy v. Ferguson* (1896) (which was, after all, a transportation case) was passing.

When confronted with an NAACP challenge to racial covenants, the Court returned to the problem of state action that had been injected into constitutional interpretation in the *Civil Rights Cases* (1883). Racial covenants prohibited the sale or rental of residential property to specified racial or religious groups. In *Shelley v. Kraemer* (1948), the Court unanimously stated that such provisions were not per se illegal or unconstitutional but that their enforcement by state courts would be, as judicial involvement constituted state action. *Shelley* did not put an end to racial discrimination in housing by any means, but it did affirm a doctrinal climate far more hospitable to the cause of civil rights than the nation had previously known.

Although the transportation and racial-covenant cases were important to the day-to-day lives of black communities, the foremost civil rights agenda item was education. Here too, the Court blazed a path through the tangle of racism in public life, first taking up cases involving professional and graduate schools. The Court had spoken to this issue before the war in *Missouri ex rel. Gaines v. Canada* (1938), striking down a state scheme to keep Missouri's state university law school segregated by meeting tuition expenses of black Missourians who wanted to attend law school, as long as they went out of state. After the war, the NAACP contested *Plessy*'s separate-but-equal doctrine in higher education more forcefully than ever and was rewarded with a string of doctrinal victories. The Court struck down exclusion and segregation in state university law and graduate schools in *Sipuel v. Board of Regents* (1948), *McLaurin v. Oklahoma State Regents* (1950), and *Sweatt v. Painter* (1950).

These cases were the Vinson Court's principal legacy to the cause of desegregation. But they did not reach the touchiest issue of all: segregation in grade schools and high schools. The Court heard arguments in 1952 in a case raising that issue, *Brown v. Board of Education,* but the Justices were deadlocked among themselves, and Chief Justice Vinson was unable to marshal them into any sort of coherent and unified response. He was himself uncertain about the unconstitutionality of segregation, as was his fellow Kentuckian, Stanley Reed. So too was Robert H. Jackson, principally because he could not formulate purely legal arguments demonstrating the unconstitutionality of state-mandated segregation. Owing to the divisions on the Court, the issue was held over, awaiting the advent of a chief who could dissipate the justices' confusion and irresolution.

Summary of the Stone and Vinson Courts

The era of Chief Justices Stone and Vinson, 1941–1953, remains a little-explored period in the history of the Supreme Court. These years may not continue to languish in relative obscurity, however, for they offer important portents for the constitutional law of the early-twenty-first-century state. The justices of the Stone and Vinson period confronted numerous war-related issues that have, lamentably, recurred: military tribunals, detention without trial, and deportation of immigrants. The leading cold war precedents lapsed as U.S.-Soviet tensions began to ease, but they too show signs of revival in the twenty-first century as Americans redefine the threat to their security from communism to terrorism. As part of that same response to the challenge of war and international tension, the Court sanctioned a growth in federal and executive power that has never receded.

The great irony of the Stone and Vinson Courts lay in the fact that their most lasting contributions were in the fields of civil rights and civil liberties. Although only Justices Murphy and Rutledge were fervently committed to the cause of racial justice, a majority of their colleagues came around, until even holdouts Reed and Jackson capitulated. So important were the precedents in the civil rights area that, after 1953, Warren Court advances were only the realization of doctrinal salients in place before Earl Warren took his seat.

The Court's record in matters of civil liberties was more mixed, in part because the Stone Court had to deal with unprecedented issues posed by total war and in part because its successor succumbed to the anti-Communist fervor of the cold war. Yet in civil liberties issues not complicated by cold war tensions, the justices established long-lived First Amendment benchmarks in press freedom and political speech. Its religion clause precedents laid the groundwork for modern establishment and free-exercise clause doctrine.

None of this should be surprising. No fifteen-year period in the Court's history has been insignificant, and this particular period saw more pressures on the Constitution than most. War, cold war, desegregation, and the rise of civil liberties in the modern state ensured that the work of the Supreme Court would reverberate through its time down to ours.

—WILLIAM M. WIECEK

FOR FURTHER READING AND RESEARCH

The reader seeking to inquire more deeply into the 1941–1953 era should begin with Melvin I. Urofsky's *Division and Discord: The Supreme Court Under Stone and Vinson, 1941–1953* (Columbia, S.C., 1997), which is the finest single-volume treatment of the Stone and Vinson Courts available. Urofsky's volume will be joined by William M. Wiecek's *The Birth of the Modern Constitution: The United States Supreme Court, 1941–1953* (New York, 2005), volume 12 of the *History of the Supreme Court of the United States* (the Oliver Wendell Holmes Devise). Through his path-breaking use of the papers of the justices, Alpheus T. Mason created a portrait of the workings of the Court of unprecedented intimacy in his *Harlan Fiske Stone: Pillar of the Law* (New York, 1956). Although dated and uncritical of its subject, it remains a model of judicial biography. Peter G. Renstrom has compiled a useful collection of documents, essays, and other reference materials in *The Stone Court: Justices, Rulings, and Legacy* (Santa Barbara, Calif., 2001). It is to be followed by a similar collection in the same ABC Clio series by Michal R. Belknap for the Vinson Court. In *The Supreme Court in Conference (1940–1985)* (New York, 2001), Del Dickson has edited the papers of the justices to recreate the conference debates on the major cases of that momentous period. The edited materials must be used with care because the editor has taken liberties with the notes in an effort to make them conversational and more conformable to what he imagines they must have sounded like. Finally, Mark Silverstein has written one of the most perceptive of several books comparing the Court's principal antagonists of the period: *Constitutional Faiths: Felix Frankfurter, Hugo Black, and the Process of Judicial Decision-making* (Ithaca, N.Y., 1984).

12

The Warren Court 1954–1968

Procedural Liberalism and Personal Freedom

ELIX FRANKFURTER, always ready to dramatize, recalled that his reaction on learning of Fred Vinson's death in September 1953 was that it was his first real indication that there was a God. Frankfurter was anticipating the reargument of the school desegregation cases in the October 1953 term. The cases had been put over, Frankfurter wanted history to believe, because Vinson had been unable to lead the Court to a conclusive resolution of the question of segregation's constitutionality. In reality, the cases had been put over because Frankfurter and Robert Jackson had been unable to find the path to voting that segregation was unconstitutional without making what they themselves regarded as political rather than legal judgments.

Vinson's replacement, Earl Warren, had no such difficulties. Warren was a progressive Republican who had been a crusading district attorney before his election in 1942 as governor of California. In a decision he never entirely repudiated, Warren supported the wartime removal of Japanese Americans from the West Coast. Enormously popular, he once received the endorsements of both major parties for reelection. In 1948, he was the Republican candidate for vice president; during the 1952 campaign season, he was a realistic favorite-son candidate of the California delegation, holding its votes to see whether the leading contenders, Dwight Eisenhower and Robert Taft, would cancel each other out. Richard Nixon, recently elected to the Senate, maneuvered the California delegation toward Eisenhower. In a crucial preliminary vote, Warren freed the California delegation to vote in a way that pushed Eisenhower ahead. In the end, Warren held on to California's votes, but the state's role in ensuring Eisenhower's nomination made the candidate grateful to Nixon, winning him a place on the ticket, and to Warren. Warren took away from the Republican convention an enduring dislike for Richard Nixon, who, he thought, had manipulated the

California delegation and effectively denied Warren his chance for the presidential nomination.

After the election, Eisenhower promised Warren appointment to the Supreme Court at the first available opportunity and also asked that, meanwhile, Warren come to Washington immediately as solicitor general. After considering the financial implications, Warren agreed. Before he had a chance even to be nominated as solicitor general, however, Vinson died. Warren expected to be named as Vinson's replacement, but Eisenhower initially wanted to put Warren off, saying that he had meant to give Warren a seat as associate justice. Warren held Eisenhower to his word and got the nomination. He took his seat in time to open the Court's 1953 term.

In an important sense, there were two Warren Courts. The first, lasting from Warren's appointment to 1962, was dominated by *Brown v. Board of Education* (1956), national security cases, and the political reaction to the Court's actions. The first Warren Court did not retreat under the pressure, but it advanced rather cautiously, with some stops along the way. Its central organizing principle was that the Constitution required procedural fairness in the process of government. The second Warren Court lasted from 1962 until Warren's retirement in 1969. Called "history's Warren Court" by Scot Powe, that Court's most astute historian, the second Warren Court was firmly in liberal hands and began to develop a constitutional law centered on individual freedom to supplement the first Warren Court's procedural concerns (Plate B.12). History's Warren Court faced serious opposition too, but its vision would dominate constitutional law for decades after Warren's retirement.

The First Warren Court

Desegregation

The four desegregation cases combined under the name *Brown v. Board of Education* were plainly the most important cases before the Court. For a generation, the NAACP had been pursuing a sustained challenge to segregation. The NAACP's first plans were developed by a young lawyer named Nathan Margold and then, because Margold's plan was unrealistic in light of conditions in the South and the NAACP's resources, modified by Charles Hamilton Houston, dean of the Howard Law School. Houston had a star pupil, Thurgood Marshall, who eventually took charge of the litigation. After the Supreme Court ruled in *Sweatt v. Painter* (1950) that the University of Texas had to desegregate its law school, Marshall concluded that the time had come to take on segregation in its central feature: the separation of white and African American children in the South's elementary and secondary schools.

The NAACP developed five cases. Two involved the border states of Kansas (*Brown* itself) and Delaware; two involved the heartland of segregation, South Carolina and the most segregated part of Virginia; the fifth involved the District of Columbia. The challenge in the four state cases rested on the Fourteenth Amendment's equal protection clause; the challenge in the District of Columbia case relied on the due process clause of the Fifth Amendment, which raised the difficult question of how an amendment adopted in 1791 when slavery existed could somehow be interpreted to make racial segregation, apparently a smaller violation of human rights, unconstitutional.

The Supreme Court had temporized over segregation long enough, and the justices knew when they decided the Texas law school case that they would soon have to decide whether segregation in the elementary and secondary schools was unconstitutional. Indeed, they were so eager to take the issue on that they pushed the attorney general of Kansas to make an appearance in defense of the state's limited segregation statute, which allowed larger school districts to operate segregated schools. Instead, the attorney general sent an assistant, Paul Wilson, who in his short career had never argued a case in any appellate court, much less appeared in the U.S. Supreme Court. The Supreme Court also took hold of the District of Columbia case, which was awaiting full briefing and argument in the local court of appeals and put *it* on the Supreme Court's docket as well.

The cases were argued for the first time in December 1952, when Vinson was still chief justice. Vinson, a Kentuckian by birth, was a weak leader on the Court and was uncertain about whether the Court could find segregation unconstitutional. Although no formal votes were ever taken, the records of the justices' discussions suggest that a narrow majority was ready to do so. Frankfurter and Jackson remained unsure, however. The justices also knew that a decision against segregation would be enormously controversial in the Deep South. They preferred to avoid dissents that would give segregation's supporters ammunition in the inevitable challenges to the Court's authority.

Frankfurter proposed that the cases be reargued. The Court's practices discouraged rearguments for no reason, so Frankfurter developed five questions that the advocates would be asked to address during the reargument. Some dealt with the original understanding of the Fourteenth Amendment; others, with the form of remedial order the Court might adopt if it held segregation unconstitutional. Before the reargument occurred, Frankfurter had resolved his ambivalence about whether overturning segregation could be justified by legal rather than policy arguments, and Warren had replaced Vinson. These two events made the reargument something of a charade, with the advocates addressing questions that no longer mattered much to the justices.

Warren, drawing on his political experience, wanted a Court opinion that was both unanimous and easy for the public to read. His opinion was indeed simple. After briefly recounting the facts, the opinion described as "inconclusive" the historical evidence about whether the drafters of the Fourteenth Amendment thought that the amendment itself made segregation unconstitutional or authorized the courts to declare it unconstitutional. Warren wrote that the Court could not "turn the clock back to 1868, when the Fourteenth Amendment was adopted," or to 1896, when the Court upheld segregation in *Plessy v. Ferguson*, a case involving railroads. Instead, the Court had to consider the constitutionality of segregated education in light of the place public schools had taken in American society. Education was, Warren continued, "perhaps the most important function" of modern governments, essential preparation for a successful career and for participation as a citizen in the nation's public life.

Warren then turned to the Court's recent cases, showing, he said, that equality required more than equivalence in the physical plants at segregated schools. "Intangible" factors affected the effectiveness of schooling, and they too had to be equalized. But, the Court concluded, they could not be. Quoting from the lower court's findings in *Brown*, Warren described the ways in which segregation impaired the motivation of African American children to learn. This part of the discussion included a footnote identifying "modern authorities" that "amply supported" this psychological conclusion. "In the field of education," the Court concluded, "the doctrine of 'separate but equal' has no place. Separate educational facilities are inherently unequal." Warren then finessed the doctrinal difficulties in the District of Columbia case with the simple observation that it was "unthinkable" that the national government would be held to a lower standard of equality than state governments were.

Frankfurter had concluded that the Court could declare segregation unconstitutional but only if it acknowledged difficulties in implementing a decision striking the practice down. Warren accepted Frankfurter's suggestion that the Court find segregation unconstitutional and then order a third argument, this one directed solely at the question of the appropriate remedy. With Frankfurter's vote in hand, Warren persuaded Jackson to go along. Then he approached Stanley Reed, a Kentuckian like Vinson whom scholars have presumed was firmly committed to segregation. Warren told Reed that a dissent in the segregation cases would be particularly bad for the Court and for the country because it would only fuel resistance to a decision a solid majority of the Court was going to render. Reed readily concurred. Warren had a unanimous Court (Plate B.11).

After the argument on remedy, Warren wrote a short opinion again incorporating a key provision from Frankfurter. The Court's difficulty was that long-standing legal tradition had it that constitutional rights were "present and personal," meaning that successful plaintiffs were entitled to a remedy that would immediately give them the rights they had been denied. In *Brown*, this implied that the remedial order should direct immediate desegregation of segregated schools. Everyone agreed that there might be minor administrative problems associated with the transition to a desegregated system but that those would take no more than a summer to resolve. Slightly more difficult was the question of whether the desegregation order itself should require the admission of all Africans Americans to previously white schools or simply the particular plaintiffs, with other African Americans benefiting from *Brown*'s precedential effect only when they brought their own lawsuits.

These difficulties could have been resolved, but the justices were acutely aware that the question of remedy in the desegregation cases was at least as much political as legal. The justices knew that Southern states would resist desegregation and that resistance would increase in intensity from the border states to the Deep South. From his contacts with liberal white Southerners, Frankfurter mistakenly believed that they could lead their states to accept desegregation if they were given enough time to prepare the ground. He proposed that the Court say that desegregation should occur "with all deliberate speed," a phrase intended to give Southern states time to develop gradual plans for desegregation in the face of anticipated resistance. Yet the Court could not openly acknowledge the reasons for refusing to order desegregation immediately, and Warren's opinion said explicitly that it "should go without saying that the vitality" of the principles of equality *Brown* announced "cannot be allowed to yield simply from disagreement with them." Yet that was precisely what the "all deliberate speed" formulation encouraged — and indeed the prospect of disagreement was what motivated the Court to adopt that formulation in the first place.

As the justices anticipated, the white South rejected *Brown*. Border states did begin the desegregation process, usually assigning students to the school nearest them. In rural areas, this resulted in substantial integration of schools, but in urban areas, characterized by widespread residential segregation by race, neighborhood schools would remain substantially segregated. To ensure that they would, some school boards even tinkered with assignment boundaries.

The Deep South was different. There, school boards and legislatures erected enormous barriers to even modest desegregation. Some required

African American children seeking admission to previously white schools to go through a rigorous screening process that few or none successfully completed. Others redrew the boundaries of neighborhood school districts to ensure that schools would remain segregated even after the boards started to assign children to their neighborhood schools. And, when these programs failed, some Southern legislatures adopted programs of "massive resistance," culminating in school closures when desegregation was imminent.

These maneuvers within the law to avoid desegregation accompanied legal arguments against *Brown*. The Virginia editor James Jackson Kilpatrick revived a theory called "interposition," developed before the Civil War by South Carolina Senator John C. Calhoun to protect slavery. According to Kilpatrick, the Constitution allowed each state's legislature and governor to stand between the national government and the state's citizens when the national government itself breached the Constitution, as it did, Kilpatrick said, in invalidating segregation.

Southern politicians in Congress who rejected *Brown* published a "Southern Manifesto" in 1956, explaining why they believed the Supreme Court's decisions were themselves unconstitutional. Signed by every member of Congress from the Deep South, Virginia, and Arkansas, with others making the total number of signatories 101 of the 128 members from the region, the Southern Manifesto promised that its signers would "use all lawful means to bring about a reversal of this decision which is contrary to the Constitution."

More substantial as a legal matter were questions, raised by respectable legal academics as well as by Southern segregationists, about Warren's reliance on psychology and about the social science footnote in the *Brown* opinion. Constitutional law could not be law, critics said, if it rested on so slim a foundation as the opinions of "modern authorities" about the psychological effects of segregation. Warren himself later observed that he never regarded the footnote as particularly important. What mattered, he believed, was the evident reality of segregation in the South, something apparent to any person who took a serious look at segregation. The footnote, according to Warren, was designed simply to dress up what common sense revealed.

The Supreme Court avoided direct involvement in enforcing the desegregation decisions, except in 1958 when Arkansas governor Orval Faubus capitalized on the desegregation crisis to advance his political career. When the Little Rock school board reluctantly agreed to a court order requiring the integration of one of the city's high schools, Faubus took the stump to encourage violent resistance by whites. Faubus deployed the state's National Guard to Central High School, nominally to facilitate desegregation but actually to interfere with it. Violence erupted when Faubus withdrew the National Guard after a meeting with Eisenhower. Eisenhower, upset at the state's defiance of national authority, placed the state's National Guard under federal control and deployed troops to protect the African American students at the high school. Claiming that the violence *and* the troops used to eliminate it disrupted education, the Little Rock school board asked the federal courts for permission to suspend its desegregation order. The case rapidly reached the Supreme Court, which held an extraordinary summer session to ensure that its decision requiring the board to continue its efforts would come down before school reopened in the fall of 1958. In an equally extraordinary gesture, the Court's opinion, *Cooper v. Aaron* (1958), was published under the names of all nine of the justices and specifically noted that the three justices who had joined the Court after *Brown* agreed fully with that decision.

The Court also dealt with some collateral aspects of the South's resistance to *Brown*. Purporting to believe that desegregation litigation was stirred up by "outsiders" from the NAACP, several states mounted substantial legal attacks on the NAACP's ability to operate. They tried to force the organization to disclose its membership lists, in the hope that fears of retaliation by whites would lead African Americans to shun the organization. They invoked traditional legal proscriptions against stirring up litigation against the NAACP's lawyers, seeking to disqualify them from appearing in court because of their supposed unethical actions. The Supreme Court batted down each of these efforts, sometimes on procedural grounds, which led to additional delays before the NAACP was able to operate, and sometimes finding the NAACP's activities protected by the First Amendment.

National Security and Criminal Justice

The Warren Court dealt with more than segregation, of course. Warren brought his skills as a politician to the task of managing the Court's often quarrelsome members. For years, Frankfurter, Douglas, and Black had been nearly at each other's throats. With Warren at the head of the Court, their personality conflicts had little effect on the Court's work, although their disagreements over constitutional interpretation continued. Warren was what political scientists call the Court's social leader, whose personality made it possible for people with quite different views to work easily together. The justices described Hugo Black as the Court's "task" leader, whose ideas provided the center around which the Court's solutions revolved. As the second Warren Court emerged, William Brennan took over the Court's intellectual leadership.

In the mid-1950s, the Warren Court cautiously took on the public response to what some politicians described as the threat that domestic communism posed to the nation's security. The Court imposed procedural requirements on the national government's program for screening its employees to determine their loyalty. In *Quinn v. United States* (1955), the Court allowed witnesses before legislative investigating committees to invoke their Fifth Amendment guarantee against self-incrimination, on the theory that statements made at such hearings might subsequently be used against the witnesses in criminal prosecutions for unlawfully advocating the use of violence to overthrow the government. The Court relied on the First Amendment indirectly, as a reason for interpreting narrowly the scope of investigating committees' authority. In *Pennsylvania v. Nelson* (1956), a case in which a leading member of the Communist Party had been sentenced in a Pennsylvania prosecution to fifty years' imprisonment, the Court also held that the federal statute making it a crime to advocate the use of violence to overthrow the government precluded states from enforcing their own laws dealing with the same subject.

In the 1956–1957 term, the government lost every national security case the Court decided. The Court's decision in *Jencks v. United States* (1957), for example, required the government to inform criminal defendants of statements made to government agents in interviews before trial, so that the defendant's lawyers could cross-examine the witness effectively. *Jencks* was a national security case in which the government had relied on testimony from a witness who turned out to be a perjurer, but its implications reached into every federal criminal prosecution.

In *Yates v. United States* (1957), the Court also gutted the Smith Act's ban on advocacy of forcible overthrow of the government by interpreting the statute, in light of the First Amendment, to require that the government show that each individual it prosecuted did more than simply teach the abstract desirability of forcible overthrow but indeed urged listeners to be ready to engage in forcible overthrow at some time in the indefinite future when the conditions were right. The Court had upheld the Smith Act convictions of front-rank leaders of the Communist Party in *Dennis v. United States* (1951). *Yates* overturned the convictions of second-rank party leaders. In the end, only one second-rank leader ever served time for violating the Smith Act.

The Warren Court also began to examine more closely the administration of criminal justice. The Court had entered the field earlier, provoked in large measure by the persistence of abusive police tactics, including beatings of suspects, and the prevalence of such abuses as part of the South's system to keep African Americans in the place white Southerners believed they should hold. The Warren Court began to extend its prior holdings to address troublesome practices that were not, however, quite as repulsive as the physical beatings the Court had already addressed. In *Irvine v. California* (1954), it found that breaking into a house to plant a recording device violated the Fourth Amendment but not the Fourteenth Amendment's due process clause, which applied to state prosecutions. In *Mallory v. United States* (1957), the Court overturned a rape conviction because the police had not taken the suspect before a judge for processing quickly enough, and the prosecution had relied on a statement taken from the suspect before the court appearance. In the same year, the Court invalidated an unusual Illinois procedure that allowed convicted defendants to appeal only if they paid for a trial transcript. Developing a doctrine that could have been used to challenge a wide range of practices that effectively limited the legal rights of the poor, the Court held in *Griffin v. Illinois* (1957) that the Illinois procedure violated the right of poor defendants to equal protection of the laws. Hugo Black's opinion said, "There can be no equal justice where the kind of trial a man gets depends on the amount of money he has." Black certainly did not intend — immediately — to insist that poor defendants have access to lawyers who were as able as those the most affluent defendants could hire, but his opinion certainly opened up wide vistas for a new jurisprudence of equality.

The Warren Court's Critics

The Court's decisions on national security and criminal procedure fed into the existing political controversy over *Brown* and its aftermath. Academic critics suggested that the Court's decisions were "unprincipled," a term they used to describe decisions that purported to rely on principles that the critics believed would not be applied in similar cases. The critics argued, for example, that some of the Court's First Amendment decisions resulted from sympathy for the NAACP and would not be applied in cases involving other litigants, that the Court's decision invoking the equal protection clause to assist indigent defendants cast doubt on the constitutionality of all sorts of other government programs in which the scope of the available benefits turned on an individual's ability to pay for the benefits, and — most pressingly — that the Court had invoked the special characteristics of modern education to justify *Brown* and then disingenuously and without extended discussion held segregation of parks, beaches, and golf courses unconstitutional as well. The Court's defenders replied, in essence, that the Court's desegregation decisions were plainly justified by the injustice of segregation in all its forms and suggested that the Court's other controversial decisions might well be defended on the ground of justice too, although they did not work out a full account of the demands of justice except in the context of segregation.

The Southerners who opposed *Brown* were joined in their discomfort with the Court by Republican conservatives, who believed that the Court's national security and criminal-procedure decisions weakened the nation's ability to defend against the Communist threat and against criminals more generally. The politicians who criticized the Court invoked the academics' criticisms as well, often to the discomfort of the academics, who were by and large liberal in their political predispositions and reasonably sympathetic to the outcomes the Court reached. Proposals in Congress to limit the Supreme Court's power to hear national security cases won extensive support, although none was enacted. Congress did enact a statute in response to the Court's decision in *Jencks* that accepted the witness-disclosure requirement and then provided a sensible procedural framework for managing it.

Apparently responding to the congressional reaction, the Court retreated from its national security holdings. Read carefully, the Court's initial decisions had relied on the Constitution to provide background for holdings that in fact did not enforce constitutional rights. When cases in which *only* the Constitution was available returned to the Court, it held that congressional investigations could go forward without violating the Constitution. Witnesses might have a Fifth Amendment right not to testify, but they did not have a First Amendment right to avoid answering altogether. Assessing the records in two Smith Act cases in this new light, the Court now upheld one conviction in *Scales v. United States* (1961) but was still ready to overturn the conviction in a companion case, *Noto v. United States* (1961).

History's Warren Court

By 1962, the Warren Court had become a cautiously liberal Court. The attacks on the Court in the late 1950s had led it to retreat from the most advanced positions that some of its opinions suggested. Three new members joined the Court during the controversies over *Brown* and national security law. John Marshall Harlan, a prominent New York corporate lawyer who was the grandson of an earlier justice, John Marshall Harlan, and Potter Stewart, a member of a prominent political family in Ohio, were moderate Republicans, more conservative than Warren in their instincts but fully committed to *Brown*. Harlan eventually became the conservative conscience of the Warren Court, insisting that its decisions conform to some recognizable principle and adhering to those decisions when, in his view, they did.

Eisenhower appointed William J. Brennan, Jr., to the Court in 1956. Brennan, a Catholic and a Democrat, had been a management-side labor lawyer prior to his appointment to the New Jersey Supreme Court. Brennan came to the attention of Attorney General Herbert Brownell when Brennan stood in for New Jersey's much more prominent chief justice, Arthur Vanderbilt, at a conference on procedural reform. Eisenhower used the Supreme Court vacancy to shore up his reelection campaign by nominating a northeastern Catholic. Although Eisenhower later reportedly called Brennan's nomination a mistake because Brennan turned out to be the leading liberal on the Supreme Court, Eisenhower in fact had cared about Brennan's demographic characteristics, not his ideology, when the appointment was made.

The Court's greater caution in some of its cases was misleading. The Court's more conservative members could sometimes pull out a victory when the political conditions were right and the doctrines available. But these justices were clearly on the defensive. The Court's liberals, in contrast, could regularly try out an advanced position to see what would happen. More often than not, the liberals could preserve the core of their position even as they abandoned some of its more extreme applications, leaving them ready to move forward when the nation was ready for it — meaning, in effect, when they obtained a more solid majority on the Supreme Court.

That came about in 1962. Charles Whittaker, appointed by Eisenhower in 1957, suffered a nervous breakdown because he found himself unable to decide what to do in the Court's difficult cases. President John F. Kennedy selected his old friend Byron White to replace Whittaker. White, a Rhodes scholar, former Supreme Court law clerk, and professional football player, ran part of Kennedy's campaign for the presidency, heading the effort to get Republicans and independents to support Kennedy, and then became deputy attorney general, administering the Justice Department. White was a legal technician, committed to national power and generally sympathetic to the claims made by lawyers associated with the Democratic coalition.

Felix Frankfurter's retirement was more important than Whittaker's in creating history's Warren Court. Frankfurter suffered a series of debilitating strokes, tried to soldier on, but eventually decided that he was unable to continue his work. Frankfurter's replacement was Arthur Goldberg, Kennedy's secretary of labor. Goldberg was the consummate New Deal liberal. The most prominent labor movement lawyer of the 1950s, he had been the architect of the 1955 merger of the American Federation of Labor and the Congress of Industrial Organizations, becoming the AFL-CIO's first general counsel. With Goldberg on the Court, there were five reliable votes for nearly every position that establishment liberals believed to be required by the Constitution.

Two cases from 1962–1963 demonstrate the effect of the new appointments. Both involved the Southern attack on the NAACP. *Gibson v. Florida Legislative Investigation Committee* (1963) revisited arguments over the actions of a committee created by the Florida legislature in 1959 to inquire into the activities of "subversive organizations." Purporting to investigate Communist influence on the NAACP, the committee had demanded that NAACP officials confirm or deny that particular people were NAACP members. The officials had refused, citing the First Amendment. When the case was first argued, Frankfurter was on the Court, and a five-justice majority voted to allow the inquiry to proceed, on the theory that the committee could not decide whether a legislative response to Communist influence was necessary unless it found out whether there was such influence. Reargument reversed the outcome after Frankfurter left the Court. Goldberg wrote the Court's opinion upholding the NAACP's First Amendment claim. The second case, *NAACP v. Button* (1963), involved Virginia's attempt to stop the NAACP's lawyers from soliciting clients for desegregation lawsuits, invoking long-standing rules of professional ethics against solicitation of and support for litigants by their lawyers. Again the Court with Frankfurter voted to allow Virginia to invoke its rules in the face of the NAACP's claim that its activities were an essential part of its program of challenging segregation in the courts, a program, the organization said, that was protected by the First Amendment. Once again, after Goldberg replaced Frankfurter, the Court voted to halt Virginia's efforts.

The newly fashioned Warren Court majority confronted new issues, and some old ones, raised by the civil rights movement. The movement had shifted from the courtroom to the streets, as civil rights protestors marched against practices of segregation by public authorities and private companies. The Court had no difficulty dealing with statutes that required segregation but struggled over the proper response to the new civil rights activism. The difficulty was that the demonstrations and, more important, the tactic of sit-ins, with protestors occupying seats in restaurants where they were refused service, were aimed at racial discrimination practiced by private parties. The Fourteenth Amendment had been interpreted since 1883 to make only discriminatory "state action" unconstitutional. Private discrimination, most of the justices continued to believe, was untouched by the Constitution.

The sit-in cases reached the Court in the form of prosecutions of demonstrators for trespassing on private property by remaining at the restaurants after the owners had asked them to leave. In case after case, the Court managed to avoid directly confronting the state action problem by finding some subtle indications that the restaurant owners were complying with orders from state officials or by holding that the demonstrators could not fairly be found to have been violating the breach-of-the-peace statutes that were the basis of their convictions.

The Court came closest to addressing the fundamental issue in 1964, when Congress was debating the proposal that became the Civil Rights Act of 1964. In *Bell v. Maryland* (1964), a majority voted to uphold the convictions of demonstrators in Maryland. Brennan was desperate to avoid a Court decision that he knew would be taken as a rebuke to the civil rights movement when crucial votes in Congress were about to take place. He struggled to find reasons for getting rid of the cases. After several unsuccessful efforts, Brennan managed to persuade enough of the majority inclined to uphold the convictions that a recently adopted Maryland statute might be construed to cast doubt on the validity of the convictions under Maryland law. The Court vacated the convictions and sent the case back to the Maryland courts, thereby avoiding the difficult state-action question once again.

Then the issue disappeared from the Court. The reason was that Congress joined the civil rights struggle by enacting the Civil Rights Act of 1964, which prohibited discrimination in employment and at places of public accommodation, such as restaurants and hotels; and the Voting Rights Act of 1965, which put in place an intrusive set of measures aimed at eliminating practices that Southern voting officials had used to keep African Americans from voting, such as discriminatorily administered literacy tests. Congress feared that the state-action doctrine would prevent a constitutional defense of the Civil Rights Act as a measure aimed at promoting the equal protection of the laws and so rested the act on the federal power to regulate interstate commerce. The Court, dominated by nationalists who interpreted the Constitution to give the national government power over essentially any topic on which a legislative majority could be mustered, upheld both statutes. Civil rights then became a matter of legislative and administrative concern rather than a central topic of constitutional adjudication.

Nevertheless, the civil rights movement continued to put cases on the Court's docket. Many of the Warren Court's important free-speech cases came out of the civil rights movement. Some involved applications of doctrine dating from the 1940s, under which the Constitution was held to entitle protestors to access public streets and parks to conduct demonstrations. Innovative uses of new "public forums" pushed existing doctrine forward. Thus, in *Brown v. Louisiana* (1966), the Court upheld the right of demonstrators to conduct silent sit-ins at a segregated public library. The Court balked, however, in *Adderley v. Florida* (1966), when asked to hold that the Constitution required city officials to allow a demonstration on the grounds of a courthouse (which happened to house the local jail, the demonstration's real target).

Free Speech

Probably the most important First Amendment case the civil rights movement produced was *New York Times v. Sullivan* (1964), which helped transform constitutional doctrine generally. In *Chaplinsky v. New Hampshire* (1942), decided at the time it had begun to develop modern First Amendment doctrine, the Court had held that certain well-defined categories of expression were outside the First Amendment's coverage. These categories, the Court said, included libel, obscenity, and commercial speech. *Sullivan* was a libel case. The *New York Times* had published an advertisement about civil rights demonstrations in Montgomery, Alabama, under the heading "Heed Their Rising Voices." L. B. Sullivan, in charge of the Montgomery police, claimed that statements in the advertisement were false and injurious and hence libelous in that they misrepresented the facts in a way that damaged his reputation in Alabama. There were indeed minor factual inaccuracies in the advertisement, but the claim that they harmed Sullivan's reputation was hardly credible. Obviously aiming to damage the *New York Times,* the Alabama jury awarded Sullivan $500,000 in damages, and the Alabama Supreme Court, applying traditional standards for libel cases, affirmed the award.

Justice Brennan's opinion for the Court repudiated the idea that libel as a general category was outside the First Amendment. The *Sullivan* case itself illustrated the underlying problem. The traditional standards for libel allowed juries to award damages in cases involving matters of real public concern, based on trivial factual misstatements. Such damage awards would deter newspapers from publishing stories that might be inaccurate on some details but nonetheless be valuable contributions to public understanding. Brennan's solution was to hold that the Constitution limited the occasions on which juries could award damages for harm to reputation based on factual misstatements. Libel awards were permissible, he wrote for the Court, only when the publisher acted with "malice," which the Court defined as knowledge that the statements were false or willful disregard of inquiry into whether the statements were true or false.

Eventually, *Sullivan* would generate an increasingly arcane body of constitutionalized libel law, with the Court considering whether the rules should differ depending on whether the person criticized was a public figure, a limited-purpose public figure, or a purely private figure; whether the statements dealt with matters of public concern or merely of private concern; whether the statements were factual or mere opinions; and much more. Libel law rapidly became disconnected from its origins in a controversy arising out of the civil rights movement.

The *Sullivan* case's enduring importance lay in its confirmation that the 1942 statement about the First Amendment's scope was no longer good law. In 1958, the Court, again led by Brennan, began to erode the statement by holding that the First Amendment limited the kinds of material that governments could suppress as obscene. In *Roth v. United States* and a companion case, *Alberts v. California,* affirming convictions for federal and state obscenity offenses, Brennan wrote that obscenity convictions were permissible only if the material lacked redeeming social value.

As the society grew increasingly tolerant of sexually explicit materials, the Court became correspondingly uncomfortable with what seemed to its liberal majority an indefensible Puritanism reflected in obscenity convictions. Using a variety of techniques, the Court managed to vacate nearly every obscenity conviction that came to it, although a majority never settled on the standard that should govern obscenity cases. In practice, the effective standard was described by Potter Stewart as allowing suppression of "hard core pornography." Stewart acknowledged that he could not define what he meant by that term, but in *Jacobellis v. Ohio* (1964), he offered his famous test: "I know it when I see it." As a legal standard, this was not entirely satisfactory, but the Warren Court was unable to improve on it.

Criminal Justice

The civil rights movement affected the Warren Court's consideration of the constitutional law of criminal procedure, because of the way the criminal justice system affected African Americans. Police officers questioned, searched, and arrested many African Americans and often displayed indifference to even fundamental constitutional prohibitions. And, just as important parts of the Warren Court's free-speech doctrine began in concern for the rights of African Americans and then expanded on to broader terrain, so too with the constitutional revolution in criminal procedure.

The second Warren Court moved quickly to reform the administration of criminal justice. The first thing it had to do was make sure that defendants had lawyers who could bring constitutional violations to the courts' attention. In 1942, the Court held that the Constitution required states to provide lawyers to defendants facing serious charges but only if the cases presented special difficulties. Over the years, the Court struggled with the application of this "special circumstances" test; by 1963, the justices had had enough. Warren directed his law clerks to be on the lookout for a petition for review that squarely raised the claim that *every* defendant should get a lawyer. From a Florida prison came Clarence Earl Gideon's handwritten petition for review in his case, a fairly routine burglary, saying that his constitutional rights had been violated because he did not have a lawyer (Plate B.13). Warren seized on Gideon's petition. The Court appointed Abe Fortas to argue Gideon's case, and twenty-two states filed amicus briefs supporting Gideon. The outcome was never in doubt. Hugo Black, who had dissented in 1942, wrote the Court's opinion finding in Gideon's favor.

With lawyers at their side, defendants were able to raise many constitutional claims. The Warren Court was most concerned about two areas: searches and police interrogations. *Wolf v. Colorado* (1949) had held that the Constitution limited states' power to conduct searches but that the Constitution did not require that the states exclude evidence found as a result of an unlawful search. Critics of the exclusionary rule often quoted Benjamin Cardozo's critical observation that the rule meant that the criminal was to go free because the constable blundered. *Wolf* meant that the courts would repeatedly say that constables had blundered but that there was nothing they could do about it. This was not a stable outcome, and eventually, in *Mapp v. Ohio* (1961), the Court overruled *Wolf.*

The prospect of excluding evidence that hurt their clients gave defense lawyers new incentives to challenge police practices. The Warren Court began to explore the circumstances under which searches violated the Fourth Amendment's ban on unreasonable searches. The Court said that the amendment stated a preference for judicial supervision of the search process by referring to search warrants and that many searches without warrants were presumptively unconstitutional. The presumption could not be too strong, though, because police officers often confronted fairly urgent situations in which evidence might disappear if they waited for a judge to give them a warrant. The Warren Court started to delineate the circumstances under which the police could conduct searches without warrants, but the law's full development awaited Warren's retirement.

The Supreme Court's original confrontation with the administration of criminal justice had come in the 1930s and 1940s, in a series of cases, such as *Brown v. Mississippi* (1936), in which Southern sheriffs beat confessions out of African American suspects. At first, the Court focused on the outrageous police conduct, calling it a violation of the due process of law required by the Fourteenth Amendment. Gradually, the doctrinal basis of the Court's supervision of interrogations shifted from the Fourteenth Amendment to the Fifth Amendment's ban on self-incrimination. The Court began to ask whether confessions were coerced, engaging in close factual inquiries to determine whether the police conduct overrode the suspect's will. This approach proved to be as unsatisfactory as the special-circumstances test had been for providing lawyers, and for the same reasons.

The Court searched for an alternative approach. The justices first thought that the Sixth Amendment might work, suggesting that police questioning of suspects who had lawyers interfered with the suspects' constitutionally guaranteed right to counsel. *Gideon* increased the number of represented suspects, but many suspects were not defendants, of course, and did not have lawyers when the police questioned them and, often, obtained the evidence needed to turn them into defendants and eventually convicts. The Court's solution came in the famous — and notorious — case of *Miranda v. Arizona* (1966), the source of the warnings that have become embedded in American culture. *Miranda* addressed the problem of coercive police practices by requiring the police to inform those they questioned of their right to halt the interrogation at any time.

Police officials were initially outraged at the *Miranda* decision, asserting that it would surely interfere with their ability to lock criminals up. Congress responded by enacting a statute directing federal courts to admit all voluntary confessions. The statute made failure to give the *Miranda* warning relevant, but not dispositive, to the determination of voluntariness. The Department of Justice regarded this statute as unconstitutional from the moment of its enactment and never relied on it in federal prosecutions. The question of the statute's constitutionality did not reach the Supreme Court until 2000, when in *Dickerson v. United States*, the Court agreed with the Justice Department and held the statute unconstitutional.

Police officials and prosecutors quickly discovered that the *Miranda* decision did not limit their conduct much. Police departments instructed their officers on how to comply with the decision, and police behavior adjusted to the new rules. Suspects, perhaps out of bravado, perhaps out of ignorance, continued to talk with the police after getting the *Miranda* warnings.

Whatever police officials ended up thinking, though, the public was in no mood to tolerate Court decisions that seemed to impede law enforcement. A new "law and order" constituency opposing the Warren Court began to develop.

Politics and Religion

Opposition arose, too, when the Court began to reform state legislatures. The problem the Court faced was malapportionment, the practice of awarding legislative seats in ways that led to gross overrepresentation of rural areas and underrepresentation of cities and, more important in the long run, of the nation's growing suburbs. In 1946, Justice Frankfurter had cautioned the Court to stay out of what he called a "political thicket," arguing that apportionment questions were so bound up with ordinary politics that the courts would inevitably suffer if they tried to use legal rules to discipline the apportionment process.

The Warren Court disagreed. Its first move was to place apportionment on the judicial agenda. *Baker v. Carr* (1962) involved a Tennessee legislature that had not been reapportioned since the early 1900s, despite a state law requiring regular reapportionments. In what Warren later described as "the most important case" of his tenure, Justice Brennan rejected the argument that appointment questions were inherently political. The courts could apply ordinary principles of equal protection law to determine whether an apportionment treated all voters equally.

Justices Stewart and Tom Clark suggested that the decision's reach might be limited to cases like Tennessee's, where the decades-long failure to reallocate seats meant that the existing distribution of seats reflected no policy whatever. But the Warren Court's ambitions were broader. The Court rapidly adopted the famous "one person, one vote" rule, first in a case involving a peculiar Georgia system for electing the state's governor and then in cases involving ordinary legislative districts. Warren wrote the Court's opinion in *Reynolds v. Sims* (1964), capturing the rationale for the rule with his usual common sense: "Legislators represent people, not trees or acres. Legislators are elected by voters, not farms or cities or economic interests."

Legal academics went after the homespun simplicity of Warren's reasoning, pointing out that he had chosen one of many possible theories of legislative representation. Incumbent legislators too opposed the Warren Court's reapportionment decisions, which threatened their sinecures. A movement to restrict the Court's jurisdiction or to amend the Constitution flared up. Its proponents, mostly elected officials, soon discovered that their constituents agreed with Warren, and the reapportionment decisions turned out to be among the Warren Court's most popular.

The same cannot be said about the Warren Court's initiatives in the constitutional law of religion. The Court upheld Sunday closing laws in *McGowan v. Maryland* (1961), saying that social change had leached out any religious content from state requirements that retail stores close on Sundays and that the impact of such laws on religious people who observed Saturday as their Sabbath did not mean that the laws violated the constitutional ban on laws that interfered with the free exercise of religion. In *Sherbert v. Verner* (1963), the Court did find a free-exercise violation in an unusual state law that was interpreted to deny unemployment assistance to a woman who had to turn down all the jobs she was offered because every one would have required her to work on her Sabbath.

Some of the Warren Court's establishment clause holdings were also uncontroversial, such as its decision upholding a state law that provided

books to children attending schools in New York, including schools affiliated with religious organizations. Controversy exploded, however, when
the Court struck down the widespread practice of opening school sessions
with short readings from the Bible. The Court's first decision on prayers in
schools was relatively modest. New York's governing board for public
schools wanted to start the school day with a prayer but did not want to offend the state's largest denominations by choosing an existing prayer. Instead, the board drafted its own, seemingly inoffensive prayer: "Almighty
God, we acknowledge our dependence upon Thee, and we beg Thy blessings upon us, our parents, our teachers and our country." In *Engle v. Vitale*
(1962), the Court held the prayer unconstitutional. The decision was mildly
controversial, although the underlying proposition — that if the establishment clause meant anything, it meant that the government could nôt write
prayers people had to say — should not have been. A year later, though, the
controversy intensified when in *Abington School District v. Schempp*
(1963), the Court struck down state laws requiring readings from the Bible
to open the school day.

Jews and members of some traditional Protestant denominations
favored a strict separation between church and state and approved the
Court's decisions. Catholics and a large number of Protestants did not. The
Court's decision was widely ignored, as school districts persisted in using
prayers. Still, *Schempp* fed a growing sense, emerging from the Court's
criminal-procedure decisions as well, that the Court had been captured by
an elite that was out of touch with the concerns of ordinary people.

The Two Warren Courts

The political reaction to the second Warren Court was predictable. It had
accumulated too many enemies. The popular reapportionment decisions
fit into a jurisprudence that *supported* what the majority believed, but
many of its other decisions rested on a substantive vision of the importance
of personal autonomy that fit well with elite understandings but not with
the views of a populace that retained stronger commitments to families
and neighborhoods than the more mobile liberal elites.

From Warren's appointment to 1962, the first Warren Court comple-
mented the politics of the New Deal in Congress and the presidency. New
Deal political programs were invulnerable to serious challenge, as shown by
their acceptance by the Eisenhower administration. The political base for
those programs was less secure, however, particularly when Republicans
and conservative Southern Democrats abandoned their attack on the New
Deal and were able to turn their energies to politically more promising

targets. Fitfully and never entirely securely, the first Warren Court acted to protect the interests of important components of the New Deal coalition, including African Americans and political liberals facing McCarthyite attacks. The first Warren Court articulated a constitutional jurisprudence that corresponded to the pluralist politics characteristic of the New Deal. The Court was interested in ensuring that all interest groups had a fair chance to bargain in the political process.

History's Warren Court retained this concern for fair procedures in politics, as the reapportionment cases showed. But the altered political context of the 1960s freed the Warren Court to expand its scope to a substantive liberalism as well. The second Warren Court dealt with two presidents and a Congress that had no qualms about the New Deal and indeed sought to expand its reach, particularly through Johnson's Great Society programs. That Warren Court collaborated with the political branches in the Great Society. The Warren Court's decision in *Gideon* signaled to the political branches that expanded legal services programs for the poor, even if not mandated by the Constitution, were nonetheless fitting complements to the Court's interpretations of the Constitution's requirements.

The Great Society's substantive concern for equality may have derived from its attention to the plight of the African American community, but the defense of equality became embedded in a more general substantive account of liberalism's requirements. The Warren Court's participation in the sexual revolution, for example, can best be explained not by any account of a procedurally oriented liberalism but rather by liberalism understood as the vehicle for achieving personal autonomy. The Court's obscenity decisions may have been its most visible contribution to the sexual revolution, but its decision in *Griswold v. Connecticut* (1965) was its most symbolic; the Court held unconstitutional a statute making it a crime to *use* contraceptives. Connecticut never enforced its statute directly against people who did use contraceptives, but the statute effectively deterred doctors from prescribing and pharmacists from selling contraceptives. As a practical matter, the *Griswold* decision had little effect; only Connecticut and Massachusetts had such stringent anticontraceptive statutes on the books by 1965. Yet *Griswold* was an important articulation of an autonomy-oriented liberalism quite different from the procedural liberalism of pluralist political bargaining. It set the stage for not only the Burger Court's abortion decisions but also the Supreme Court's endorsement of an agenda of women's equality—which, however, the Warren Court itself never promoted directly.

Griswold and the Warren Court's decisions about criminal procedure shared another characteristic, creating some tension with autonomy-oriented liberalism. The second Warren Court took guidance from the views articulated by professionals who, the Warren Court's justices believed, were the paradigmatic leaders of modern welfare state bureaucracies. Connecticut's anticontraceptive statute was troublesome in part because it was patently inconsistent with the medical profession's views. Decisions like *Miranda* sought to bring police professionals' "best practices" to all police departments, as was shown by Warren's interest in determining what warnings the Federal Bureau of Investigation gave suspects. The *Miranda* warnings themselves went beyond what the FBI did but only with respect to their treatment of what had to be said about the availability of lawyers — another group of professionals, of course.

The coexistence on the Warren Court of procedural and autonomy-oriented liberalism explains one controversy that arose in the decades after Warren's retirement. The question historians addressed was whether the Court should be called the Warren Court or the Brennan Court. The case made for the latter designation generally relied on the observations that Brennan's opinions formed the basis for more post-1968 developments than Warren's did and that Brennan managed to sustain liberalism on — and obtain liberal decisions from — a Court staffed by conservative justices. In reality, the Court was both Warren's and Brennan's. Warren's opinions encapsulated the Court's liberal proceduralism, whereas Brennan's foreshadowed the more robust autonomy-oriented liberalism that emerged after Warren's departure.

The End of the Warren Court

The Warren Court's growing cadre of enemies opposed the Court's collaboration with the Great Society and its articulation of an autonomy-oriented liberalism. Southern segregationists never reconciled themselves to *Brown*. Religious conservatives, centered in the South but represented throughout the country, correctly saw the school prayer decisions as a challenge not only to their practices but also to the very idea, embedded deep in their religious views, that personal autonomy ought to be subordinated to the requirements of revealed religion. Probably most important, the Warren Court's revolution in criminal procedure happened to coincide with a sharp rise in the crime rate, which the Court's opponents were happy to attribute to the Court's decisions.

Beginning with Barry Goldwater's presidential campaign in 1964, Republicans saw the possibilities of a "Southern strategy" that would detach white Southerners from the Democratic Party in national elections. Richard Nixon's successful 1968 presidential campaign capitalized on the increase in crime by taking Earl Warren and his Court as one of its primary targets. Nixon promised to use Supreme Court appointments to strengthen what he called the "peace forces" on the Court.

Warren had an enduring antipathy to Nixon, born in what Warren regarded as Nixon's betrayal of the Warren favorite-son presidential candidacy in 1952. Warren tendered his resignation in the spring of 1968, anticipating the possibility that Nixon would win that year's election. The retirement, Warren said, would be effective at the president's pleasure — a formulation designed to ensure that Warren would leave only if the Senate approved a successor Johnson nominated.

Johnson put forward Abe Fortas, his old friend and political adviser, to be chief justice, and an old political friend from Texas, court of appeals judge Homer Thornberry, to take the associate justice seat Fortas would vacate. Like Warren, Republicans calculated that Nixon's prospects for election were good and filibustered Fortas's nomination. Senator Strom Thurmond of South Carolina asked Fortas about the Court's 1957 *Mallory* decision; when Fortas evaded answering, Thurmond thundered, "Mallory, Mallory, Mallory, I want that word to ring in your ears — Mallory. A man who raped a woman, admitted his guilt, and the Supreme Court turned him loose on a technicality." Fortas was also damaged by the charge that he was Johnson's crony, a charge supported by disclosures that Fortas had continued to advise Johnson while Fortas sat on the Court — even to the point of drafting speeches for Johnson — and only strengthened by Thornberry's nomination. The final blow was the disclosure that a former law partner had guaranteed that Fortas would receive $15,000 every year for giving a summer course at American University (when his salary as a justice was $39,000 a year). An effort to break the filibuster failed, and Fortas asked that his nomination be withdrawn.

Warren did retire, a year later. In the meantime, Nixon's Department of Justice developed evidence that Fortas had a questionable relationship with Louis Wolfson, who had been convicted of securities law violations. Fortas had pushed ethical constraints on judges to a point near, and perhaps beyond, their limits. He might not have committed a criminal offense, but Attorney General John Mitchell made it clear that he was prepared to hand the department's evidence over to Congress, which certainly would begin an impeachment proceeding. Warren himself was outraged at Fortas's relation with Wolfson and urged Fortas to resign, in the interests of the Court. Fortas did, eliminating the possibility of his impeachment.

Nixon nominated Warren Burger to succeed Earl Warren. The symbolism of Warren's last days on the Court was inescapable. In an opinion by Warren that invoked the people's right to choose those who would govern them, the Court reversed a judgment of a court of appeals upholding the decision by the House of Representatives to deny a seat to Adam Clayton

Powell, Jr., a flamboyant and corrupt representative from New York's Harlem district. The court of appeals decision had been written by Warren Burger.

—MARK TUSHNET

FOR FURTHER READING AND RESEARCH

Lucas A. Powe, Jr., *The Warren Court and American Politics* (Cambridge, Mass., 2000), is an essential, comprehensive overview of the Warren Court, proceeding chronologically. A short, thematic study is Morton J. Horwitz, *The Warren Court and the Pursuit of Justice* (New York, 1998). A useful collection, organized around essays focusing on individual justices, is Mark Tushnet, ed., *The Warren Court in Historical and Political Perspective* (Charlottesville, Va., 1993).

Biographies of the justices provide the best pathway into understanding the Warren Court, although some important members of the Court lack good biographies. Bernard Schwartz, *Super Chief: Earl Warren and his Supreme Court* (New York, 1983), is a pedestrian account that has the advantage of providing a great deal of information about the Supreme Court's internal workings and discussions. Ed Cray, *Chief Justice: A Biography of Earl Warren* (New York, 1997), is a journalist's account, with good insights into Warren's background and personality. Roger Newman, *Hugo Black: A Biography* (New York, 1994), examines Black's entire career, beginning well before the Warren Court. Tinsley Yarbrough, *John Marshall Harlan: Great Dissenter of the Warren Court* (New York, 1992), is competent but no more than that. Laura Kalman, *Abe Fortas: A Biography* (New Haven, Conn., 1990); and David Stebenne, *Arthur J. Goldberg: New Deal Liberal* (New York, 1996), are excellent works on their subjects' lives, in which the Supreme Court years were only a small part.

Studies of the Court's important cases are also valuable. On the NAACP's litigation before and after *Brown*, see Mark Tushnet, *Making Civil Rights Law: Thurgood Marshall and the Supreme Court, 1936–1961* (New York, 1994); on *Gideon v. Wainwright*, see the classic, Anthony Lewis, *Gideon's Trumpet* (New York, 1964); and on *New York Times v. Sullivan*, see Anthony Lewis, *Make No Law: The Sullivan Case and the First Amendment* (New York, 1991).

13

The Burger Court   1969–1986

Once More in Transition

THE WARREN COURT ended in controversy. In 1968, Republican Party presidential nominee Richard Nixon ran as much against the Warren Court as against his Democratic opponent. "Law and order" became Nixon's central campaign theme, bringing a traditionally local political issue onto the national political stage. Urban riots had recently captured the nation's attention, reported crime rates had jumped over the course of the 1960s, and public opinion polls identified crime as an increasingly important issue to the electorate. Nixon focused on this generalized unease over public safety and argued not only that the federal government had failed to do enough to stop crime but also that it had actively hampered effective law enforcement. Topping Nixon's list of culprits who had contributed to the "shocking crime and disorder in American life today" were judges who had "gone too far in weakening the peace forces as against the criminal forces."

Chief Justice Earl Warren had already tried to secure his legacy against a likely Nixon electoral victory but had failed. Warren was convinced that Robert Kennedy would win the presidency in 1968. When Kennedy was killed while campaigning for the Democratic nomination, Warren, along with many others, thought that the Democrats' chance of holding the White House passed with him. Days later, Warren informed lame-duck President Lyndon Johnson that he was retiring from the Supreme Court. At the age of seventy-seven, Warren knew that his health could not hold out indefinitely, and he explained to Johnson that he wanted a successor who shared Warren's vision of the Court and the Constitution. On June 11, 1968, Warren wrote a formal note to the president, declaring his "intention to retire as Chief Justice of the United States, effective at your pleasure." As Warren wished, the president's response was to accept the retirement "effective at such time as a successor is qualified." Warren and Johnson agreed that Associate Justice Abe Fortas would be the best choice to be the next chief justice.

Fortas had long been a formidable legal presence in Washington, D.C., was a close associate of Johnson's, and was a staunch liberal. Although Johnson had the benefit of a Democratic majority in the Senate, there was little enthusiasm for Fortas. Unsurprisingly, the Republicans were particularly unhappy with Warren's strategic resignation, and Nixon himself argued that the selection of new justices should be left to the next president. Fortas, perhaps unwisely, agreed to testify at the hastily scheduled confirmation hearings of the Senate Judiciary Committee. The hearings did not go well for Fortas. The justice was questioned closely about the extent of his continuing relationship with President Johnson after Fortas had joined the Court. More fundamentally, Southern Democrats and Republican senators used the hearings to pillory the Warren Court itself. Senator Strom Thurmond, in particular, denounced the Warren Court for putting criminals back on the streets. By the time the hearings were over, it was evident to many observers that the Fortas nomination was doomed. A subsequent disclosure of the justice's questionable financial entanglements and a brief Senate filibuster finally led the president to admit defeat and withdraw the nomination in early October. The next president would choose Earl Warren's successor.

The "Nixon Court"

Republican presidential nominee Richard Nixon and independent candidate George Wallace kept up the pressure on the Court throughout the summer and fall. Although the federal judiciary was criticized for its decisions on "busing"—active measures to achieve racial integration in individual schools—school prayer, and obscenity, the Court's decisions expanding the rights of criminal defendants received the greatest attention during the campaign. Wallace was the more strident of the two, contending that the Court was "destroying constitutional government," but Nixon was equally focused on the issue, arguing that the Court had "encouraged criminals." The public was responsive. Large majorities believed that the courts were not harsh enough with criminals, and opinion polls showed the Supreme Court's ratings with the public taking a sharp dive in 1968. Nixon pledged that he would appoint to the Court "strict constructionists" who would refrain from imposing their "social and political viewpoints on the American people." Nixon promised to look for individuals with "experience or great knowledge in the field of criminal justice" and a "deep and abiding concern for these forgotten rights" of crime victims.

Nixon drew some of the material for his campaign criticisms of the Warren Court from a widely publicized 1967 speech by Warren Burger. Burger was then serving as the chief judge on the prestigious U.S. Court of Appeals for the D.C. Circuit. He had emerged as the most prominent critic of the Warren Court in the federal judiciary, and it was no surprise when he proved to be Nixon's choice to be chief justice. Burger had attended college and law school at night while working as an insurance salesman. He graduated in 1931. A Minnesota Republican, he had been active in gubernatorial and presidential politics in the late 1940s and early 1950s. He was rewarded for his work on behalf of Dwight Eisenhower in the 1952 Republican convention with a post in the Department of Justice. Eisenhower later nominated him for the circuit court, and he was confirmed in 1956. Burger was a leading conservative on the court of appeals and took a particular interest in criminal justice issues.

When Nixon won the election, he and Warren agreed that the chief justice should remain on the Supreme Court through the end of the 1968 term. The nomination of the sixty-one-year-old Warren Burger was quickly ratified by the Senate with only three dissenting votes, and he was sworn in as the fourteenth chief justice on June 23, 1969. Burger served on the Court for seventeen years.

As chief justice of the United States, Burger had a keen interest in judicial administration. During his tenure, he increased the number and improved the training of court administrators and even took an interest in improving the training of state judges and the quality of prisons. Burger also lobbied Congress for more judges to deal with the increasing federal caseload. The Supreme Court's own docket had grown dramatically in the Warren era, from fewer than 1,700 cases when Warren took the bench to more than 4,000 when he left, and Burger sought ways to bring the caseload under control. Although Congress did reduce the number of mandatory appeals that the Court was required to hear, Burger was unsuccessful in convincing Congress to create another appellate court to screen the filings that would otherwise have gone to the Supreme Court. Although the Court's docket still grew over the course of Burger's tenure, to more than 5,000 cases, the rate of increase did slow substantially.

The legal skills of the new chief justice were less well regarded. In terms of the number of opinions he authored, Burger was among the least productive justices on the Court. Burger often frustrated his colleagues with his relatively weak understanding of the cases, and his opinions rarely won praise for either their reasoning or their style. He also bred suspicions that he abused the prerogatives of the chief justice by claiming the right to assign the task of writing the opinion for the Court when Burger seemed to have initially voted with the dissenters.

Warren Burger was the first of four appointments that Richard Nixon would make to the Court during his first term of office. In fact, by the time Nixon had settled on Burger as his choice to be chief justice, a second vacancy had already opened on the Court. Abe Fortas announced his resignation from the Court on May 15, 1969. His failed nomination to be chief justice had attracted media interest in his finances, and the story broke in May 1969 that, weeks after becoming an associate justice in 1965, Fortas had entered into a lifetime consulting contract with a family foundation controlled by financier Louis Wolfson, who then was under investigation for securities fraud. Although Justice William O. Douglas urged Fortas to fight through the controversy, he had little support among the other justices or in the Capitol. In the aftermath of the controversy and lesser revelations about Douglas's own finances, Warren pushed ethics reforms through the Judicial Conference, limiting outside income for federal lower court judges. Warren was unable to convince the justices of the Supreme Court to adopt similar rules for themselves, however, and after Warren's retirement, the Judicial Conference suspended the rules for the lower-court judges as well.

Nixon had decided to wait until after Burger was confirmed before nominating someone to fill Fortas's seat. The administration did not want to continue the tradition, followed since Louis Brandeis's appointment in 1916, of preserving a "Jewish seat" on the Court and instead saw the vacancy as an opportunity to build on Nixon's electoral strategy by appointing a young, conservative, Southern Republican. But the plan proved difficult to implement. In August 1969, Nixon nominated South Carolinian Clement Haynsworth, Jr., of the U.S. Court of Appeals for the Fourth Circuit. Labor unions and civil rights organizations mounted fierce opposition to the nomination, and charges of ethical improprieties contributed to a narrow defeat in the Senate in November. The administration quickly tried again with Georgian G. Harrold Carswell, who had been confirmed for a seat on the Fifth Circuit just months earlier. Carswell's legal qualifications were soon criticized as weaker than Haynsworth's, and it came to light that Carswell had given some aid to segregationist efforts in the 1940s and 1950s. Although one erstwhile senator famously opined that even mediocre people needed representation on the Supreme Court, the Senate, for the first time in American history, turned down a second consecutive presidential nomination for the Supreme Court, in April 1970.

Complaining that the Senate would not confirm a nominee from the South, Nixon sought to avoid further confirmation fights by nominating Harry Blackmun. Blackmun was a sixty-one-year-old childhood friend of Warren Burger's and was then serving on the Eighth Circuit. Unlike Burger's hardscrabble beginning, however, Blackmun had attended Harvard for college and law school before returning to private practice in Minnesota. In 1950, Blackmun became general counsel for the Mayo Clinic before being appointed to the federal circuit court by Eisenhower in 1959. Amassing a distinctly conservative judicial record in criminal cases and a moderate record in civil rights cases, Blackmun won praise from across the political spectrum. His confirmation by the Senate was swift and unanimous, and he assumed his seat on June 9, 1970. He would serve on the Court for twenty-four years.

Then, on September 17, 1971, Justice Hugo Black, hospitalized after suffering a stroke, informed the president that he was immediately retiring from the Court. Black died eight days later. Black had been a prominent U.S. senator from Alabama when he became President Franklin Roosevelt's first appointment to the Supreme Court in 1937. In his years on the bench, Black had been a forceful advocate for judicial restraint, arguing that judges should strictly adhere to the constitutional text and not go beyond it. Black's particular approach to constitutional interpretation led him to take an absolutist position on First Amendment protections against government, but he was more accommodating of government power in the context of other civil liberties. His skepticism about the constitutional foundations of some of the Warren Court's more activist decisions had led him to frequently side with Chief Justice Burger during their two years together on the Court.

Just three days after Black's retirement, Chief Justice Burger informed the administration that Justice John Marshall Harlan also would be retiring from the bench, and he died of cancer in December 1971. Grandson and namesake of an earlier Supreme Court justice, Harlan had been a successful Wall Street litigator before being chosen by Eisenhower for a seat on the Second Circuit Court of Appeals and then, soon thereafter, the Supreme Court. On the bench, Harlan had joined Justice Felix Frankfurter as a strong advocate for judicial deference to legislative majorities. Harlan's departure left Nixon with two vacancies to fill but with little opportunity to tilt the balance of the Court, given that Black and Harlan had both been Warren-era dissenters.

Black's retirement left the Court without a justice from the South, but the administration was wary after its difficulty filling Fortas's seat. Amid a welter of media scrutiny, the administration sifted through several candidates, including a number of women, before finally turning to Lewis Powell and William H. Rehnquist, who were nominated together. At sixty-four, Powell was older than Nixon preferred for a nominee but had the virtue of being an easily confirmable Southerner. Powell was a descendant of the first settlers of Virginia and had received his law degree from Washington and Lee as well as a master's degree in law from Harvard. A Democrat, Powell was a partner in a leading Richmond law firm and had been active in local public affairs, including service as chairman of the Richmond school board that had overseen peaceful racial integration of its schools. He was also a national leader of the legal profession, having served as the president of the American Bar Association, among other organizations. Powell's selection was widely hailed, and the Senate confirmed him with only one dissenting vote on December 6, 1971. Powell served on the Court for fifteen years.

The forty-seven-year-old Rehnquist was the more surprising, and controversial, choice. Powell had been discussed by the administration as a potential nominee since the Warren vacancy, but Rehnquist was not under active consideration until the day before his public nomination. A Wisconsin native, Rehnquist received master's degrees in political science from Harvard and Stanford before graduating first in his class in law at Stanford. After serving as a clerk for Justice Robert Jackson, Rehnquist settled in Phoenix, Arizona, where he practiced law and was active in state and national politics. When Nixon won the White House, Rehnquist became an assistant attorney general in charge of the prestigious Office of Legal Counsel, where he was often called on to defend the president's policies. As a staunch conservative, Rehnquist's nomination drew fire from a number of organized interests, especially civil rights groups. After a contentious Senate debate, he was confirmed on December 10, 1971, by a 68–26 vote, the largest number of "no" votes received by a successful Supreme Court nominee up to that time. In 1986, Rehnquist would succeed Burger as chief justice.

Within three years of assuming office, then, Nixon had been able to name four new justices to the Supreme Court, including the chief justice. The necessity of winning support from a Democratic Senate and the happenstance of the pattern of vacancies, however, prevented Nixon from turning the Court in a dramatically new direction. Initially known as the "Minnesota Twin" for his close alignment with his old friend Burger, Blackmun soon developed an independent voice and moved steadily to the left over the course of his tenure on the Court. As the strictest conservative on the Burger Court, Rehnquist became known as "The Lone Ranger" for his vigorous solo dissents. After these four appointments, the Court proved to be closely balanced, with five holdover justices from the Warren Court remaining on the bench.

William Douglas, William Brennan, and Thurgood Marshall formed the reliable core of the liberal wing of the Court. After Black's retirement, Douglas was the last remaining Roosevelt appointee. A flamboyant Westerner and committed civil libertarian, Douglas infuriated conservatives, who more than once threatened his impeachment. Brennan had joined the Court as the result of Eisenhower's election-year decision to seek a young

Catholic Democrat from the state judiciary to fill a Supreme Court vacancy. He had quickly become the intellectual and tactical leader of the liberals on the Court and a key architect of the Warren Court's accomplishments. Thurgood Marshall had been the founder and leader of the NAACP's Legal Defense Fund during its years of greatest success, winning historic judicial victories against racial segregation. He had been named to the Second Circuit by John F. Kennedy and then to the Supreme Court by Lyndon Johnson.

The two other Warren-era justices on the Burger Court, Potter Stewart and Byron White, became known as possible swing justices, who would sometimes join with some of the Nixon justices to issue more conservative decisions. Placed on the Court by Eisenhower in 1958, Stewart was a classic moderate who often found himself in the minority during the Warren Court's most activist phase but who played a pivotal role in the Burger Court's decision making in the 1970s. John F. Kennedy had placed White on the Court in 1962. A close friend and political associate of Kennedy, he had developed a distinctly mixed voting record that proved to be moderately conservative on civil liberty issues.

The "Peace Forces"

After Nixon's law-and-order campaign and four appointments, many people expected that the Burger Court would mount a counterrevolution against the Warren legacy. Those expectations generally went unfulfilled. Perhaps unsurprisingly, the Court's clearest course change came in the area of criminal justice, where Nixon and his justices were most in agreement. The Burger Court, more sympathetic to law enforcement than the Warren Court had been, reined in the more liberal precedents laid down in the 1960s. Even here, however, the Burger Court primarily prepared the way for the more conservative Rehnquist Court rather than cut a bold new path of its own. The Burger Court did not abandon, for example, even the most controversial of the Warren Court innovations, such as the 1966 *Miranda* protections against involuntary confessions or the 1961 expansion of the exclusionary rule barring illegally obtained evidence from trial. Instead, the Court worked to limit their applicability.

Generally speaking, the Burger Court sought to alleviate the constraints that had been placed on police investigations of crime. In the 1971 case of *Harris v. New York*, Burger and Blackmun joined original *Miranda* dissenters Harlan, Stewart, and White to hold that defendant confessions excluded under *Miranda* could nonetheless be used to impeach a defendant's trial testimony. *Miranda* warnings were understood to be practical safeguards against coerced confessions rather than constitutional rights themselves. Following this view, the Burger Court carved out exceptions to *Miranda* in grand jury proceedings, when confessions were to be used only to gather other evidence against a defendant, when police questioning advanced immediate public safety, and when police questioned suspects who were not yet under arrest. The Court also held that defense counsel did not have to be present for line-ups and other out-of-court identification of suspects who had not yet been indicted.

The Burger Court took a similar approach to the exclusionary rule. Most notably, in the 1984 case of *United States v. Leon,* White wrote the majority opinion for the Court, creating a "good-faith" exception for evidence seized by police under a search warrant that was only later ruled invalid. The Court also recognized a variety of contexts in which police could conduct searches without first obtaining a warrant, including full-body searches of anyone placed under arrest, weapon pat-downs of suspects on the mere basis of a tip from an informer, searches of impounded vehicles and closed containers in vehicles, aerial photography of fenced land, and in a broad range of cases in which consent is granted.

The Burger Court also limited the availability of appellate review of the conduct of criminal trials. In one majority opinion, Rehnquist emphasized that the trial should be the "main event." Involvement of appellate courts was warranted only in "exceptional cases." If state courts provided full and fair opportunity for constitutional objections to the admission of evidence, for example, the justices were willing to preclude federal appellate courts from intervening. The Court was also willing to accept state rules creating a legal presumption that defendants had waived constitutional objections if they were not raised at trial, and it broadened the "harmless error" rule, instructing appellate courts to uphold the results of trials at which only relatively minor procedural errors had been made.

Even in the area of criminal justice, however, the Burger Court could render surprisingly liberal decisions. Perhaps the most notable criminal justice case decided by the Burger Court was the 1972 judgment in *Furman v. Georgia* striking down the death penalty as unconstitutional. Over the dissents of all four Nixon appointees, the majority concluded in *Furman* that the death penalty was applied arbitrarily and as a consequence violated the Eighth Amendment's guarantee against cruel and unusual punishment. With shifting and narrow majorities, however, the Court in 1976 upheld some revised death penalty statutes that sought to reduce jury discretion in applying capital punishment, while striking down others that imposed a mandatory death penalty that left no room for jury deliberation. Over the remaining decade of the Burger Court, the justices continued to struggle with the details of a constitutionally acceptable procedure for imposing the death penalty. Likewise, the Court concluded that the Eighth Amendment prohibited criminal penalties that were significantly disproportionate to the crime committed, such as a life sentence for a nonviolent offense.

The 1972 *Furman* decision is reflective of the ways in which the Burger Court, especially in its early years, could match and sometimes exceed the record of the Warren Court. The Supreme Court struck down state and federal laws as unconstitutional at about the same rate under Chief Justice Burger as it did in the 1960s during the Warren Court's most activist phase. The number of invalidations of state and local policies actually peaked in 1972, during Burger's tenure. Numbers alone do not suggest the importance of the laws that were being rejected by the Court, but in several instances, the Burger Court's actions were as bold as anything that the Warren Court did.

Social Issues

Sexual Liberties

No case illustrates this point better than *Roe v. Wade* in 1973. The 1965 Warren Court decision in *Griswold v. Connecticut* struck down a state prohibition on the use of contraceptives as a violation of a constitutionally protected right to marital privacy. Although the Connecticut law at issue was unique in the nation and widely condemned, the decision was controversial, as it turned on a generalized right to privacy that was not explicit in the Constitution and had not previously been recognized by the Court. In 1972, Brennan wrote the majority opinion in *Eisenstadt v. Baird,* extending that protection to unmarried couples as well. In *Roe,* Blackmun wrote the opinion for a seven-person majority bringing abortion within this protected zone of privacy. Blackmun's opinion made little effort to explain the constitutional basis for the right itself but instead concentrated on the permissible scope of state regulation of abortion.

Roe was politically dramatic. Unlike the idiosyncratic contraceptive ban at issue in *Griswold,* legislative restrictions on abortion were widespread and were already the subject of political controversy. In the 1960s, the rise of an organized abortion rights movement linked medical and legal professionals, civil libertarians, and women's rights activists. By the early 1970s, a majority of state legislatures had actively considered repeal or reform of their abortion laws. At the same time, however, an active pro-life movement had started to organize in response to these reform efforts, and only a handful of states had adopted reforms. Public opinion had become more sympathetic to reform over the course of the 1960s, but a majority remained against abortion on demand by the time of *Roe.* The Court's decision in *Roe,* striking down all limitations on abortion prior to fetus viability, went far beyond prior legislative reforms and helped catalyze the pro-life movement to mount strident political resistance to the decision.

Roe was also doctrinally striking. The opinion in *Roe* made little effort to explain the constitutional basis or scope of this broad right to privacy, leaving many questions about its future applications unanswered. The Court was forced to return to the abortion issue repeatedly over the course of Burger's tenure, and it remained steadfastly hostile to restrictions on abortion, with the exception of the question of public funding of abortions. The Court proved unwilling, however, to extend the right to privacy much beyond abortion. The Court let stand, for example, a zoning ordinance barring more than two unrelated persons from living in the same housing unit, although it later struck down an ordinance limiting housing units to members of a single nuclear family. The Court also allowed states to maintain a centralized record of prescriptions issued for certain specified drugs.

The Burger Court's most notable privacy case outside the abortion context came in *Bowers v. Hardwick* in 1986. In that case, Georgia's criminal ban on sodomy was challenged as violating a right to privacy that included the right of two gay men to engage in consensual sexual activity. In a 5–4 decision, the Court rejected the challenge. White's majority opinion argued that states retained a broad power to regulate sexual activity, including homosexual sodomy. Joining the majority composed of Burger, Rehnquist, White, and the Court's newest member, Sandra Day O'Connor, Powell cast the decisive vote. In his concurring opinion, Powell doubted that "conduct condemned for hundreds of years has now become a fundamental right," but he also questioned whether a criminal conviction for engaging in such conduct could survive Eighth Amendment scrutiny. By contrast, writing a dissent for Brennan, Marshall, Stevens, and himself, Blackmun contended that the states could not enforce any particular view of morality and that individuals had a broad "right of intimate association."

Gender Discrimination

Abortion rights were not the only victory that the women's movement achieved in the Burger Court. The Court also broke new ground in casting constitutional doubt on gender-based distinctions in government policy. The Court had previously determined that government classifications based on race or ethnicity were "suspect" and required strict judicial scrutiny to ensure compliance with the equal protection clause of the Fourteenth Amendment. Such strict scrutiny, which has also been applied by the Court when fundamental rights have been burdened and which policies rarely survive, requires that the government demonstrate a compelling interest that justified the policy at issue and that the means for achieving that interest were narrowly tailored to minimize the intrusion on the constitutional value. The Burger Court extended heightened scrutiny to classifications based on gender as well. In 1971, the chief justice wrote for a unanimous Court in striking down as without any rational basis a state law favoring the appointment of men over women to administer estates. In 1973, eight members of the Court voted to strike down the military's practice of distinguishing between male and female dependents of military personnel when awarding such benefits as larger housing and medical care. Brennan was able to muster four votes in that case to declare gender a suspect category, but the other five justices refused to take that step, with Powell observing that in doing so, the Court would be preempting the equal rights amendment then awaiting ratification.

The momentum behind the ERA came to a halt, however, even as the Court remained hostile to laws discriminating against women. In the 1976 case of *Craig v. Boren,* Brennan spoke for a majority in applying what has become known as "heightened," but not "strict," scrutiny to gender classification, in which government must demonstrate that the policy serves "important governmental objectives" and is "substantially related to the achievement of those objectives." Over the course of the 1970s and early 1980s, the Burger Court struck down a number of government policies that treated men and women differently. The Court was somewhat more accommodating of policies that seemed primarily to burden men, however, with Powell, Blackmun, and John Paul Stevens holding the swing votes in such cases. Most notably, the Court in 1981 upheld male-only registration for the military draft. How to characterize the policies at issue in such cases was often far from obvious. Apparent burdens on men could often be framed as hurting women. In the draft registration case, for example, feminists argued that the exclusion of women reinforced gender stereotypes. The very next year, the newly confirmed O'Connor wrote the opinion for a narrow majority striking down Mississippi's single-sex nursing school provisions as perpetuating gender stereotypes.

Two More Justices

The gender-equality cases were among those affected by the final two appointments to the Burger Court. On New Year's Eve in 1974, Douglas suffered a severe stroke. Although he tried to return to the bench, he finally left office on November 12, 1975, leaving Gerald Ford to choose his successor. Ford was hardly working from a position of strength. He had gained the Oval Office only through the resignations of Vice President Spiro Agnew and President Nixon, and the Republicans, already a minority in Congress, had suffered devastating losses in the post-Watergate 1974 midterm elections. Seeking to avoid a confrontation with the Senate, the president left the selection of a nominee largely to his relatively apolitical attorney general, Edward H. Levi, the former president of the University of Chicago. Levi and Ford eventually settled on John Paul Stevens, a fifty-five-year-old federal appeals court judge on the Seventh Circuit.

Stevens had been born into a prominent Chicago family. He had attended the University of Chicago and was a standout student at Northwestern University School of Law. After clerking for Justice Wiley Rutledge for a year, he entered private practice in Chicago, specializing in antitrust law and litigation, interrupted by stints in the 1950s with the House Judiciary Committee and the Department of Justice, working on antitrust issues. Nixon appointed him in 1970 to the circuit court, where he solidified his reputation as a legally skilled moderate. He was quickly and unanimously confirmed by the Senate and assumed the bench on December 19, 1975.

No appointments were made during the single-term Carter presidency. In 1981, Ronald Reagan entered the White House committed to remaking the courts, and the administration immediately began the search for conservative judicial candidates. Speculation on the possibility of a female nominee had circulated around the last two vacancies to the Court, and although in the 1970s, few conservative women had the requisite credentials, Reagan had announced during his campaign that, if elected, he would name a woman to the Supreme Court. When Potter Stewart informed Vice President George Bush in February 1981 that he planned to retire from the Court at the end of its term, the administration soon focused on Sandra Day O'Connor as his potential successor. Then serving on the Arizona Court of Appeals, the fifty-one-year-old O'Connor had the support of Burger, who had recently met her at a judicial conference, and Rehnquist, her former Stanford Law School classmate. O'Connor's tough-on-crime record in the Arizona legislature and courts were enough to overcome doubts about her stance on abortion. O'Connor's nomination encountered some resistance from conservatives, but in the end, she was unanimously confirmed by the Senate on September 21, 1981.

Equal Protection and Race

The Burger Court addressed the implications of the equal protection clause outside the context of gender as well. In 1971, the Court declared that alienage was a suspect category requiring strict judicial scrutiny. Although the

Court struck down a number of laws denying various government benefits and jobs to resident aliens, including illegal aliens, it did allow states to favor citizens for positions carrying out important government functions. The Court also took a critical view of laws discriminating against illegitimate children, holding such policies to a heightened standard of scrutiny. It declined, however, to make age or wealth constitutionally suspect categories. In a narrow 1973 decision in *San Antonio School District v. Rodriguez*, the Court refused to find a federal constitutional violation in the unequal funding of school districts, a decision that had the effect of shifting such disputes into the state courts for resolution under the state constitutions.

Race was the central concern for equal protection clause jurisprudence. Here, the Burger Court was left with a number of difficult racial issues generated by the civil rights activism of the 1950s and 1960s. At the end of the Warren era, the Supreme Court had instructed lower courts and school officials to develop workable plans for achieving the immediate racial integration of public schools, and in Burger's first term, the Court reaffirmed the need for immediate integration. The expansive orders of the trial judges attempting to accomplish these goals were already the subject of controversy by the time of Nixon's first presidential campaign, especially as they tackled urban school districts in the North as well as in the South and moved beyond the legally mandated (de jure) segregation at issue in *Brown v. Board of Education* to deal with the de facto school segregation that resulted from combining neighborhood schools with patterns of residential segregation.

The Burger Court was soon faced with evaluating these plans. The first arrived in 1971, in *Swann v. Charlotte-Mecklenburg Board of Education*. Although Burger was quite hostile to the busing plan adopted by the trial judge, the Court wanted to maintain the unanimity it had achieved in the earlier desegregation cases. As a result, a unanimous opinion, issued in Burger's name, upheld a broad power on the part of the trial courts to remedy past school segregation but insisted that schools should eventually be freed from judicial oversight and that the Constitution did not require that schools have any particular racial balance. In 1973, the Court fractured over an expansive busing plan imposed on the Denver schools after a finding of relatively limited de jure segregation. The next year, in a 5–4 decision on a Detroit busing case, the Court imposed limits on the remedial powers of the lower courts to reach across school district boundaries in order to achieve a better racial balance. The overall result was the Court's acceptance of continuing judicial oversight of schools to encourage integration.

The Burger Court also confronted a broader set of racial issues beyond desegregation. One such issue was the legal significance of apparently nondiscriminatory policies that nonetheless had a disparate, and negative, impact on blacks as compared with whites. In *Griggs v. Duke Power Co.* (1971), a unanimous Court focused on "the *consequences* of employment practices, not simply the motivation" and concluded that the Civil Rights Act of 1964 barred "practices that are fair in form, but discriminatory in operation" unless they could be justified by business necessity. The Court declined to carry disparate-impact analysis into the constitutional arena, however, where it could have been used to launch strict judicial scrutiny of government policy decisions. In 1980, Stewart spoke for a five-person majority in arguing that multimember electoral districts were constitutionally acceptable unless they were adopted with specific discriminatory intent. In 1982, however, O'Connor, Stewart's successor, swung the Court the other way, concluding that the objective effect of diluting minority voting power was presumptive evidence of discriminatory intent in maintaining an at-large electoral system.

A divided Court gave its approval to the affirmative action policies that were getting under way during Burger's tenure. The Nixon administration had been a supporter of affirmative action programs, and they spread rapidly through both the public and private sectors. Programs targeting racial minorities for benefits, however, raised constitutional concerns when adopted by government institutions and statutory concerns when adopted by private businesses. The statutory problem under the Civil Rights Act, the text and legislative history of which seemed to bar depriving any employee of opportunities or benefits on the basis of race, was addressed in the 1979 case *United Steelworkers of America v. Weber,* which involved a training program that had openings set aside for black employees. In a 5–2 decision, Brennan concluded for the majority that programs designed to "break down old patterns of segregation and hierarchy" were consistent with the broad mission of the Civil Rights Act.

Affirmative action had also been addressed the previous year in *Regents of University of California v. Bakke,* which involved the admission policy of a medical school that had set aside openings for racial minorities. The medical school at the University of California at Davis was constrained by both the constitutional equal protection clause and the Civil Rights Act's prohibition of racial discrimination in programs receiving federal funding, and *Bakke* touched on both sets of legal constraints. Casting the decisive fifth vote, Powell argued that California's admission plan was unconstitutionally rigid but that a more flexible plan that took race into account could be justified on the basis of a desire to achieve a diverse student body. The other eight justices split into two equal groups. One group, led by Brennan, would have upheld the admission policy at issue in the case under both the Constitution and the Civil Rights Act and more generally argued that affirmative action plans should be held to a lower level of judicial scrutiny than other race-conscious policies. Another group, led by Stevens, argued that any race-conscious plan violated the terms of the Civil Rights Act. Powell's opinion in *Bakke* became the road map for many institutions designing affirmative action programs, but subsequent Burger Court cases resulted in similarly fractured majorities that did little to clarify the legal status of affirmative action.

Religion

As with criminal justice and racial desegregation, the Warren Court had also launched the federal judiciary into new conflicts over religious liberty that the Burger Court inherited. The Burger Court justices, with the primary exception of Rehnquist, largely followed the Warren Court's lead on the free-exercise clause. Brennan had written the key Warren-era opinion in *Sherbert v. Verner* (1963), which applied strict scrutiny to government policies that burdened religious beliefs and practices. In 1972, Burger embraced the *Sherbert* approach when mandating that Amish children beyond the eighth grade be provided an exemption from compulsory-schooling laws. Nonetheless, the Burger Court did find limits to this constitutional protection. The Court concluded, for example, that the federal government did not have to accommodate the racial policies of the religious Bob Jones University by preserving the school's tax-exempt status, and a divided Court deferred to the military's decision not to exempt yarmulkes from its dress code.

The establishment clause proved somewhat more difficult for the Burger Court, as it had for earlier Courts. Soon after joining the Court, Burger, while upholding tax exemptions for religious property, called for a "benevolent neutrality" that could accommodate but not sponsor religion. In striking down direct public payment of teacher salaries in parochial schools in *Lemon v. Kurtzman* (1971), Burger formulated a three-part test for determining violations of the establishment clause, focusing on whether the policy had a secular purpose, neither advanced nor inhibited religion, and avoided excessive government entanglement with religion. *Lemon* proved influential but difficult to apply.

In practice, a more liberal wing of the Court, including Brennan, Marshall, Douglas, and Stevens, favored a stricter separation of church and state. A more conservative wing, including Burger, Rehnquist, and White, favored greater accommodation of religion. The results in individual cases often depended on such swing justices as O'Connor and Powell. In the context of primary and secondary education, a majority of the justices tended to favor greater separation, striking down, among other things, state reimbursement for parochial school tuition, public funding of classroom equipment for religious schools, and a required moment for silent prayer. In other contexts, a majority could be more accommodating, upholding, among other things, funding of academic buildings at religious colleges, opening prayers at legislative sessions, and some city-sponsored Christmas holiday displays.

Freedom of Speech and Press

Similarly, the Burger Court moderated but did not reverse the Warren Court's expansion of a broad freedom of expression. The Warren Court had struggled with the question of how to distinguish obscene materials that did not enjoy constitutional protections from other materials that were protected by the First Amendment. The Burger Court laid down more concrete standards that invited state legislatures to specify prohibited obscene content and allowed juries to determine whether materials violated local community standards. Concerned about the effect on third parties, the Court likewise allowed zoning restrictions on adult movie theaters and broadcast regulations on "indecent" programming.

The Burger Court also struck out on its own in the area of speech protections, particularly at the intersection of money and speech. Commercial speech had traditionally received little protection from the Court, but in 1975, the Court extended greater constitutional protection to such speech. The Court acted first in a case involving a state ban on the advertisement of abortion services, emphasizing that the interest of consumers in commercial speech justifies its inclusion within the First Amendment. Soon thereafter, the Burger Court struck down, among other things, state bans on the advertisement of prescription drug prices, of routine lawyer services, and of casino gambling.

As the advertising of abortion services suggests, there can be a close relationship between politics and profits. That relationship was central to the issue of campaign finance regulation, which gained newfound significance in the aftermath of Watergate. In 1974, Congress amended the Federal Election Campaign Act to restrict the amount of money that could be donated or spent on electoral campaigns. Two years later, in *Buckley v. Valeo*, a deeply divided Court imposed significant constitutional restrictions on government regulation of campaign finance. Led by Brennan, Powell, and Stewart, the Court upheld public financing of campaigns, public-disclosure requirements for campaign contributions, and limits on private contributions to candidates and campaigns, given the government's strong interest in protecting against the corruption of elected officials. But the Court struck down other important aspects of the reforms as unconstitutionally limiting political speech. Notably, a majority held that the government might not limit how much money individuals and organizations themselves spent on behalf of favored candidates, how much of their own money candidates might spend in their campaigns, or the total amount spent in a political campaign. The government's interest in regulating campaign expenditures was not sufficient in the Court's eyes to justify reducing the "quantity of political speech." A majority of the justices later held that the independent campaign expenditures of corporations and political action committees were likewise constitutionally protected.

Although less innovative than the decisions on commercial speech and campaign finance, one of the best-known Burger-era free-speech decisions came in the 1971 Pentagon Papers case. The Department of Justice had sought an injunction against the *New York Times,* and subsequently the *Washington Post,* barring publication of reports based on a leaked classified Pentagon study of the origins of the Vietnam War. The lower federal courts had issued temporary restraining orders against the papers while they heard the case to determine whether the release of the materials posed an immediate danger to national security. The Supreme Court quickly took the case and issued a decision four days later. In 1931, the Court had ruled that the First Amendment clearly prohibited the prior restraint of publication in peacetime. A crucial question in 1971 was whether the same constitutional prohibition held in time of war. Although six justices could agree that the courts should not restrain the press from publishing the reports, the justices could not agree on an answer to the more general question of prior restraint in wartime. Douglas, Black, and Brennan favored broad freedom for the press in such circumstances; Burger, Harlan, and Blackmun thought national security justified the suppression of the reports. Stewart and White, however, found insufficient statutory authority for imposing prior restraints in such cases, despite the likely damage to national security, although criminal sanctions after publication might still be available.

Separation of Powers

As the opinions of Stewart and White in the Pentagon Papers case indicate, separation-of-powers issues were also a point of concern for the Burger Court. In that particular case, the Nixon administration was taking action on its own without clear authorization from Congress and relying on the president's intrinsic authority over national security. For Stewart and White, presidential authority alone was not enough to justify judicial suppression of the press. The campaign finance case also raised separation-of-powers issues, as the president, the Senate, and the House of Representatives each chose two members of the original Federal Elections Commission. As part of the decision in *Buckley v. Valeo*, the Court held that the Constitution required that the commissioners all be appointed by the president and confirmed by the Senate.

Other cases were more centrally concerned with such structural questions. Undoubtedly, the most prominent of these was *United States v. Nixon* in 1974. Representing the United States, Watergate special prosecutor Archibald Cox sought the enforcement of a subpoena that had been issued against President Nixon ordering the release of the secret White House tapes of discussions that had taken place in the Oval Office. Claiming executive privilege, the administration refused to turn over the tapes and fired Cox. His successor, Leon Jaworski, continued to press the case, and an eight-member Supreme Court issued a unanimous opinion ordering the president to turn over the tapes. Although the Court admitted that such materials were privileged, the courts, not the president, were to have the final say over whether the materials were relevant to a criminal prosecution and had to be released.

The Burger Court tended to emphasize the importance of the role of the judiciary in the constitutional structure in other cases as well. It held, for example, that low-level executive-branch officials could be held liable in court for civil rights violations, despite the lack of statutory foundation for such lawsuits, and that high-level officials had only qualified personal immunity from lawsuits arising from their official actions. Similarly, because "the judiciary is clearly discernible as the primary means through which . . . rights may be enforced," individual congressmen were liable in court for employment discrimination despite a lack of statutory authorization for such claims. A narrowly divided Court did, however, recognize a president's immunity from lawsuits derived from his official actions. The Court also refused to become involved in a dispute, which it characterized as a nonjusticiable political question, between Congress and the president over President Jimmy Carter's abrogation of the mutual defense treaty with Taiwan.

Many of these cases focused directly on the relative power of the courts in the constitutional system, but the Burger Court also rendered important separation-of-powers decisions that did not implicate judicial power. In a bid to impose fiscal discipline on the federal government in an era of persistent deficits, the Gramm-Rudman-Hollings Act of 1985 designated that the comptroller general would identify spending cuts that would be necessary to bring the budget in line with statutory targets that the president would then implement. The comptroller general, however, was an officer removable by joint resolution of the House and Senate. In *Bowsher v. Synar*

(1986), five of the justices held that this provision of the deficit-reduction act unconstitutionally delegated executive powers to a legislative agent. Two other justices thought the provision was unconstitutional because the policy decisions being delegated to the comptroller general were essentially legislative in character but were not subject to the normal legislative process. Following the majority opinion, Congress responded by shifting the duties in question from the comptroller general to the Office of Management and Budget in the executive branch.

The decision in *Immigration and Naturalization Service v. Chadha* (1983) was of somewhat greater practical significance. Over the course of the twentieth century, many decisions involving both general policy and particular individuals that were once made in Congress had been shifted to the executive branch. One way in which Congress sought to retain influence over these decisions was through the "legislative veto." Such statutory provisions would give executive-branch officials the authority to render some particular decisions with the proviso that such decisions would be suspended if, within a designated time frame, one or both chambers of Congress voted to override them. Jagdish Chadha overstayed his student visa and faced deportation. The attorney general granted Chadha a hardship exemption that allowed him to remain in the United States as a permanent resident, but the House of Representatives exercised its legislative veto to override that decision, subjecting Chadha to a new deportation order. Writing for a seven-justice majority, Burger concluded that legislative vetoes were unconstitutional. The Court determined that congressional decisions to alter the policies being implemented by the executive branch were "essentially legislative in purpose and effect." As such, they could be legally binding only if they passed through the normal legislative process, which meant passage through both chambers of Congress and the president's signature.

Chadha had the effect of freeing administrative agencies from some of the formal constraints on their decision making. The Burger Court also acted to limit judicial oversight of administrative agencies. The Administrative Procedures Act of 1946 provided for judicial review of administrative decisions. The Burger Court determined that the courts should be deferential in exercising this power of review, however, asking only whether there had been an "abuse of discretion" by executive-branch officials. Even on questions of statutory interpretation, the Court favored judicial deference to "reasonable" administrative decisions. At the same time, however, the Burger Court imposed new procedural requirements on government decision makers not covered by the Administrative Procedures Act. The Court held, for example, that individuals were constitutionally entitled to formal hearings before administrators could terminate their benefits under the Aid to Families with Dependent Children program and to notification and hearing before public utilities could discontinue service. The Court, however, was deeply split over the due process requirements for terminating public employees.

The Burger Court issued a number of significant decisions affecting the range of disputes that could be brought before the federal judiciary. In the absence of specific statutory authority, the Court was unwilling to allow groups or individuals to sue simply on the basis of generalized concern for the environment or police misconduct. The Court also required that any statutory right to sue be explicit before the Court would recognize it. But when statutes granted standing to sue to parties affected by government action, the Court was willing to read those entitlements broadly. It also proved to be fairly open to federal civil lawsuits for rights violations by the states, allowing such suits against municipalities, including violations of statutory as well as constitutional rights, and allowing an award of attorney fees against the states, but it did exclude federal courts from intervening in ongoing state prosecutions.

Federalism

The Burger Court made a notable but brief effort to protect state and local governments from federal encroachment. Since the New Deal, the Supreme Court had given the federal government a largely free hand to take action without concern for the constitutional boundaries between state and federal powers. The Burger Court broke from that pattern of deference in *National League of Cities v. Usery* (1976). A narrow majority led by Rehnquist overturned a Warren-era decision to hold that federal labor regulation could not be applied to state and city employees. Such federal regulations, Rehnquist concluded, "impermissibly interfere with the integral governmental functions" of the states. The Court was unable to find another instance of impermissible federal regulation, however, and eventually abandoned the effort. In 1985, Blackmun, who had provided the fifth vote for the majority in 1976, switched sides and wrote the opinion overturning *Usery* as "unsound in principle and unworkable in practice." States should look to Congress, not the courts, to protect their interests. In a brief dissent, Rehnquist expressed confidence that the principles he had advocated in *Usery* would "in time again command the support of a majority of this Court." That confidence was vindicated after Rehnquist's own elevation to chief justice.

Narrow majorities on the Burger Court were solicitous of the states in other cases as well. In *Oregon v. Mitchell* (1970), the Court struck down a federal statute lowering the voting age to eighteen. Although a majority of the justices agreed that the federal government could set the voting age for federal elections, five justices believed that the legal voting age for state elections was beyond federal control. The next year, the Twenty-sixth Amendment created a uniform voting age of eighteen. A narrow majority also expanded the protection offered to the states by the Eleventh Amendment. The Eleventh Amendment made explicit the immunity of states from lawsuits in federal courts filed by citizens of other states, which supplemented the long-understood state immunity from federal suits by their own citizens. Since the late nineteenth century, however, the Court had allowed federal suits against individual state officials to stop violations of constitutional rights. A five-justice majority of the Burger Court limited that principle, holding that federal courts could enjoin state officials from violating rights but could not order the state governments to pay monetary damages in such cases. Although it subsequently allowed the federal government to abrogate state sovereign immunity when it was acting to enforce the Fourteenth Amendment, the Burger Court also required that Congress must express its intent to do so "in unmistakable language."

A Court in Transition

Clearly, the Burger Court did not launch the conservative counterrevolution that some observers expected. Although appointed by Republican presidents, the new members of the Burger Court were ideologically diverse, reflecting the political goals and contexts of the presidents who nominated them. Moreover, the new justices replaced Warren-era dissenters as well as members of the activist Warren Court majority. The balance of power on the Burger Court was not held by solid conservative majorities but by the swing votes of idiosyncratic justices, such as Powell, Stewart, and White. These newly powerful justices changed the tone of the Court, for they were not given to the grand theorizing and rhetorical flourish of important Warren-era figures. Brennan and Rehnquist often did verbal battle from the wings, but the key opinions were more usually written by one of the centrists. Not only did the Burger Court set new records for the number of dissenting opinions it produced, but it also produced twice as many plurality opinions than had been produced in the entire history of the Court. Additionally, far more Burger Court decisions were made by one-vote majorities than by any previous Court. Although sometimes characterized as moderate or pragmatic, the Burger Court was capable of taking wild ideological swings from term to term and issue to issue, depending on the inclination and composition of the shifting majorities.

The one area of fairly clear conservative movement came in the area of greatest concern to the Nixon administration: criminal justice. That rightward movement was characterized by a gradual pulling back from the full implications of Warren-era decisions expanding the rights of criminal suspects and defendants rather than simply overturning those decisions. In other areas of law, such as religious liberty, free speech, and federalism, conservative decisions were more sporadic and less stable. Rather than orchestrating a reversal, the Burger Court looked for ways by which conservatives could live with what the Warren Court had wrought.

The Burger Court was also capable of carrying forward the liberal activism of its predecessor: Many of its most remarkable decisions fell into this category. Although it had taken the bold step of striking down Jim Crow, the Warren Court had left to the lower courts and to its successor many of the most difficult issues of how best to remedy past discrimination. The Burger Court proved willing to embrace broad judicial power to remedy de jure segregation and gave its approval to such controversial policies as racial busing and affirmative action. In step with its times, the Burger Court joined in the women's rights movement with dramatic decisions on abortion and gender discrimination. The Burger Court's ban on the implementation of the death penalty, though short-lived, was as boldly progressive as any of the Warren Court's criminal justice decisions.

In hindsight, the Burger era seems to show a Court in transition: no longer the Warren Court but certainly not yet the Rehnquist Court. The justices of the Burger era accepted the enhanced role for the courts that Warren and his colleagues had carved out, but they no longer agreed among themselves as to how the Court should use its power or what the best solution to the nation's social problems might be. Like the country more broadly, the Burger Court turned somewhat more conservative as it struggled to digest the social and political changes of the 1960s and early 1970s, but although sometimes nostalgic about the past, it made little effort to go back to the ways things once were.

—KEITH E. WHITTINGTON

FOR FURTHER READING AND RESEARCH

Two useful overviews of the Burger Court are Bernard Schwartz, *The Ascent of Pragmatism: The Burger Court in Action* (Reading, Mass., 1990); and Earl M. Maltz, *The Chief Justiceship of Warren Burger, 1969–1986* (Columbia, S.C., 2000). Collections of essays examining various aspects of the Burger Court include Bernard Schwartz, ed., *The Burger Court: Counter-Revolution or Confirmation?* (New York, 1998); and Vincent Blasi, ed., *The Burger Court: The Counter-Revolution That Wasn't* (New Haven, Conn., 1983). Charles M. Lamb and

Stephen C. Halpern, eds., *The Burger Court: Political and Judicial Profiles* (Champaign, Ill., 1991) includes essays focusing on each of the justices who served on the Burger Court.

More intensive studies of particular aspects of the Burger Court's work include Barbara H. Craig, *Chadha: The Story of an Epic Constitutional Struggle* (New York, 1988); Lee Epstein and Joseph Kobylka, *The Supreme Court and Legal Change: Abortion and the Death Penalty* (Chapel Hill, N.C., 1992); David J. Garrow, *Liberty and Sexuality: The Right to Privacy and the Making of Roe v. Wade* (New York, 1994); Nancy Maveety, *Representation Rights and the Burger Years* (Ann Arbor, Mich., 1991); Leo Pfeffer, *Religion, State, and the Burger Court* (Buffalo, N.Y., 1984); and J. Harvie Wilkinson, *From Brown to Bakke: The Supreme Court and School Integration, 1954–1978* (New York, 1979). The inner workings of the early Burger Court were also the subject of a notorious journalistic account in Bob Woodward and Scott Armstrong, *The Brethren: Inside the Supreme Court* (New York, 1979).

The Court and Abortion: *Roe* and Its Progeny

In 1973, abortion was an increasingly hot political issue. The feminist movement was burgeoning, the Equal Rights Amendment was awaiting ratification in the states, and a coalition of feminists, civil libertarians, and medical and legal professionals had succeeded in placing abortion reform on the legislative agenda in states across the country. After a period of success in legislatures, state and federal courts, and public opinion, however, the momentum for reform seemed to have stalled in the face of an organizing pro-life movement.

Abortion had not yet become a contentious national issue when *Roe v. Wade* and its companion case, *Doe v. Bolton,* first reached the Supreme Court in 1971. They were among a large number of abortion-related cases that had been filed in the courts in the late 1960s and early 1970s, many, such as *Doe,* tied to the American Civil Liberties Union. *Roe* addressed an older Texas statute that prohibited abortion except to save the life of the mother. *Doe* challenged a modern Georgia "reform" statute that allowed abortion only in the case of a fetal defect or of a pregnancy endangering the mother or resulting from a rape. After oral arguments, a majority of a seven-member Court voted to strike down both laws as unconstitutional.

Justice Harry Blackmun was assigned to write the opinion for the Court. By the time it was completed, however, new appointees Lewis Powell and William Rehnquist had been confirmed, and five of the justices decided to have the case reargued. On January 22, 1973, the Court finally issued a 7–2 decision, with Rehnquist and Byron White dissenting.

Blackmun grounded the case in the constitutional right to privacy previously recognized in *Griswold v. Connecticut.* Given the significant consequence of pregnancy to a woman, he argued, the state could restrict access to abortion only when it had a compelling interest. In the first trimester of pregnancy, the Court was unwilling to recognize any such interest. In the second, states could regulate abortion as necessary to protect the mother's health. In the third, they could prohibit abortion entirely except when the mother's health was in danger. The decision had the effect of striking down the existing abortion laws in every state.

Over the next two decades, hundreds of laws attempting to restrict the right to abortion were passed in nearly every state. Abortion became a sharply polarized, and increasingly partisan, national political issue. Opponents of *Roe* maintained a steady legislative and legal campaign to resist, weaken, and, preferably, overturn the decision, and the Court has been faced with a steady stream of abortion-related cases.

Abortion measures able to pass Congress have generally fared well in the Court. In *Harris v. McRae* (1980), the Court ruled that the government might refuse to provide public funding for abortion services, expanding an earlier such decision regarding state funding. In *Bowen v. Kendrick* (1988), the Court held that religious organizations providing pro-life family planning services were constitutionally eligible for federal grants. In *Rust v. Sullivan* (1991), the Court upheld executive-branch regulations restricting funding to clinics that performed or encouraged abortions. As Congress passed legislation barring the obstruction of abortion clinics in 1994, the Supreme Court upheld judicial injunctions to the same effect.

Measures more at odds with *Roe* that have been passed by state legislatures have had less success. The Burger Court emphatically struck down a ban on advertisements for abortion services, parental-consent requirements for minors, spousal- and prospective-father-consent require-ments, waiting periods, burdensome informed-consent requirements, and restrictions on how doctors could perform abortions, including standards of care for the treatment of postviability fetuses. A turning point of a sort came in 1989, in *Webster v. Reproductive Health Services,* when Rehnquist wrote for a five-justice majority allowing a requirement of second-trimester testing for fetal viability and a legislative preamble recognizing conception as the beginning of human life. More significantly, *Webster* seemed to signal the existence of a majority willing to reconsider *Roe.* In the 1992 decision *Planned Parenthood v. Casey,* however, a 5–4 Court reaffirmed the existence of a constitutional right to abortion, with Sandra Day O'Connor, Anthony Kennedy, and David Souter writing the plurality opinion. In *Casey,* the Court abandoned *Roe's* trimester framework in favor of an "undue burden" standard for evaluating restrictions on abortion in light of "a substantial state interest in potential life throughout pregnancy." In doing so, the Court struck down a spousal-notification requirement but upheld waiting periods, informed-consent requirements, and judicial-bypass procedures for minors seeking abortions without parental consent. *Casey* stabilized the Court's doctrine on abortion and reduced its caseload on this issue. In 2000, however, the Court struck down a ban on so-called partial-birth abortions, reaffirming that the government may not regulate the method of abortion in a manner that does not promote the health of the mother.

U.S. v. Nixon

In June 1972, five men were arrested for breaking into the headquarters of the Democratic National Committee in the Watergate Hotel in Washington, D.C. It was soon reported that they were part of a "dirty tricks" operation linked to the Committee to Reelect the President, but the White House denied any specific involvement with those activities. That fall, Nixon won reelection in a landslide, although the Democrats retained firm control of the House and Senate.

In the spring of 1973, a combination of press reports, Senate investigations, and judicial proceedings resulted in the resignation of high-level administration officials, including the attorney general, and allegations that Nixon was involved in the effort to cover up White House links to the Watergate burglary. The new attorney general, Elliot Richardson, appointed Archibald Cox to serve as a special prosecutor to investigate the Watergate affair. In July, a presidential aide informed the Senate investigating committee that presidential conversations were taped. The committee issued a subpoena ordering the president to turn over related tapes and documents, and the special prosecutor likewise obtained a judicial subpoena for the same material. The president refused to obey either order, arguing that internal White House deliberations had absolute executive privilege from outside scrutiny.

Judge John Sirica, who was overseeing the Watergate prosecutions, rejected the claim of executive privilege and ordered that the materials be made available for his inspection. On appeal, a circuit court panel agreed with the trial judge. After Cox rejected a proposed compromise, Nixon ordered his attorney general to fire him. In what became known as the Saturday Night Massacre, Richardson resigned rather than dismiss Cox, as did the deputy attorney general. Robert Bork, the solicitor general and next in line at the Justice Department, finally carried out Nixon's order. In the face of subsequent public protest, some of the tapes were released, and a new special prosecutor, Leon Jaworski, was appointed. In May 1974, he too obtained a subpoena for the tapes. After the administration appealed again to the circuit court to have the subpoena quashed, Jaworksi petitioned the Supreme Court for an immediate hearing, which the justices granted.

U.S. v. Nixon was the first case in which the Supreme Court was squarely faced with the question of the existence and scope of executive privilege. Although all the justices agreed that the subpoena should be enforced and that some form of executive privilege existed, they disagreed on the related legal issues. Nonetheless, the justices were committed to producing a unanimous opinion on such an important issue and in such a high-stakes confrontation between the Supreme Court and the president. Although the White House had so far adhered to the legal process and fully participated in judicial hearings, the possibility existed that Nixon would in the end deny that any judicial decision was binding on this critical constitutional question of presidential power.

Justice William Brennan had suggested that the Court issue a joint opinion, signed by all members of the Court, as it had done in the Little Rock desegregation case, *Cooper v. Aaron* (1958). Burger refused that suggestion, viewing the drafting of an opinion for the Court as his responsibility. Burger's draft, however, was not acceptable to the other justices, and it was substantially revised by the others before a final opinion was issued.

On July 24, 1974, the Supreme Court issued its unanimous opinion upholding the subpoena. The Court first concluded that the Court had a genuine case to hear and that the circumstances surrounding the case justified an expedited review. Although the special prosecutor was a subordinate executive-branch official, he operated under Justice Department regulations that included the specific authority to contest claims of executive privilege. This was not merely a dispute within the executive branch but a case that could be resolved by the judiciary. On the substance of the case, the Supreme Court asserted that it was the "ultimate interpreter" of the Constitution and could alone determine the existence of an executive privilege. Although it rejected Nixon's claim of an absolute privilege, the Court seemed to admit the existence of a constitutionally grounded, but qualified, executive privilege for confidential presidential communications. At least outside the context of national security, the "legitimate needs of the judicial process may outweigh Presidential privilege." In such rare circumstances as when specific presidential communications are relevant to the conduct of a criminal trial, judges may require the president to turn over confidential materials for judicial scrutiny.

Later that day, the president announced that he would "comply with that decision in all respects." Within a week, the House Judiciary Committee had adopted articles of impeachment against the president. Soon thereafter, the White House released the tapes showing Nixon's involvement in the cover-up. On August 8, Nixon resigned from office.

14

The Rehnquist Court 1986–

Radical Revision of American Constitutional Law

T HE REHNQUIST COURT began its life with members appointed by no fewer than six presidents, from Eisenhower through Reagan. Perhaps inevitably, diversity in background was matched by deep division in ideology. Changes in personnel notwithstanding, division of opinion has continued to be the Court's most recognizable characteristic. But division has not prevented the Court from engineering dramatic changes across the gamut of American constitutional law, changes that have undone much of the work of liberal reform undertaken in the decades after World War II and tilted the law quite firmly in the direction espoused by the rising conservative movement of the 1990s. Whether the subject has been civil rights or property rights, crime or punishment, legislative authority or the nature of federalism, the Rehnquist Court's majority has been zealous in its commitment not simply to break sharply from the constitutional patterns that have predominated since the early 1950s but also to build a new and radically different structure of judicial authority to guard against their recurrence.

Development of the Rehnquist Court

William Rehnquist was sworn in as chief justice on September 26, 1986, nearly fifteen years after he had first been nominated an associate justice by Richard Nixon. The original Rehnquist Court's senior associate justice was William J. Brennan, an Eisenhower appointee who had served since 1956. Byron White, next in seniority, had served since 1962 and was the lone remaining Kennedy appointee. Thurgood Marshall, appointed by Johnson and perhaps the Court's most famous justice at the moment of Rehnquist's appointment as chief, had served since 1967. Harry Blackmun had been appointed by President Nixon in 1970. Two years later, Nixon added Lewis Powell and Rehnquist himself. President Ford nominated John Paul Stevens in 1975, and Ronald Reagan added Sandra Day O'Connor in 1981. Reagan nominated Antonin Scalia to be an associate justice in 1986 at the same time that he nominated Rehnquist for the chief's position, vacated by the retiring Warren Burger.

In one of his first innovations as chief justice, Rehnquist subtly altered the dynamics of decision making on the Court. Prior to the Rehnquist Court, the Court's senior associate justice would speak at the end of the conference, a tradition that encouraged junior justices to take part. Rehnquist reversed the practice. Now Brennan would follow the chief at the beginning of the conference.

More obvious changes were to come about through retirements and replacements. The first occurred early in 1988, when, in the wake of the Bork nomination battle, Anthony Kennedy replaced Powell. Kennedy's arrival had little immediate impact, but when David Souter replaced Brennan in 1990, the Court began to tilt more sharply to the right. The replacement of Thurgood Marshall by Clarence Thomas in late 1991 radically accentuated the makeover. The dominant group on the Court now consisted of five members: Rehnquist, O'Connor, Scalia, Kennedy, and Thomas. The appointments of Ruth Bader Ginsburg in 1993 and Stephen Breyer in 1994, replacing White and Blackmun, completed the lineup that would remain stable for at least the next decade (Plate B.14) without doing much to alter the Court's new dynamic. In 1986, Justices Brennan and Marshall had been liberal in ways that the Court's current minority is not. Harry Blackmun, although appointed as a conservative, had often made common cause with Brennan and Marshall. White and Powell, both conservatives, nevertheless saw the law in a very different way than Rehnquist, Scalia, and Thomas, the Court's most radical conservatives. Today, Ginsburg and Breyer, together with Stevens and Souter, are often to be found in opposition to the dominant conservatives, but none are liberals as that term would have been understood by Marshall and Brennan. They lack the passion of the Court's one-time left, and their opposition has focused largely on matters of detail and certain "hot-button" issues.

Opening Salvos: The Court and the Constitution

"Strict" Interpretation

A decade before his elevation to the center seat, Rehnquist had already laid down his marker in an article in the 1976 *Texas Law Review*, challenging the idea of a "living Constitution." When interpreting the Constitu tion, Rehnquist insisted, the Court should confine itself to the words of the Constitution and, when necessary, the historical record. Admittedly, the Constitution included many "general phrases," and "any particular Justice's decision when a question arises under one of these general phrases will depend to some extent on his own philosophy of constitutional law." But Rehnquist insisted that the Constitution should not be interpreted to cover new problems, even though that conclusion was not itself mandated by the Constitution's language. Specifically, Rehnquist denied that the men who wrote the Thirteenth, Fourteenth, and Fifteenth Amendments "would have thought any portion of the Civil War Amendments, except section five of the fourteenth amendment, was designed to solve problems that society might confront a century later." Section 5 gave Congress the power to enforce the Fourteenth Amendment. Rehnquist, that is, was denying that courts had any business applying the Reconstruction amendments to problems in contemporary America. Such was the job of Congress, not of the courts. In fact, Rehnquist would subsequently lead the Court in denying that section 5 gave Congress any more power than the Court to enforce the Fourteenth Amendment. Beneath an argument that interpretation of the Constitution should be restricted to its language lurked the more significant argument that the language of the Reconstruction amendments should be interpreted very narrowly with respect to both the Court's powers *and* those of Congress.

Rehnquist's article left unspecified the limitations he thought appropriate to impose on the Fourteenth Amendment, except the general implication that the equal protection and due process clauses — surely among the most general of the Constitution's phrases — were being used far beyond their intended meanings. Simultaneously, however, Rehnquist was arguing more specifically in numerous opinions that the Fourteenth Amendment did not incorporate the Bill of Rights. To Rehnquist, the absence of express language in the Fourteenth Amendment referring to the Bill of Rights meant that the Bill of Rights did not apply to the states.

In 1985, Justice Brennan responded to Rehnquist in a widely republished talk delivered at Georgetown, addressing what Brennan called "contemporary ratification." Brennan had little regard for the view that text or original intent could solve the problem of interpretation. Interpretation was necessary because the Constitution's "majestic generalities and ennobling pronouncements are both luminous and obscure." The words were the beginning of the process, not the end. Principles of freedom and democracy had to be examined under contemporary circumstances to discover meanings that the Founders could never have contemplated. For Brennan, the "position that upholds constitutional claims only if they were within the specific contemplation of the Framers" in 1787, 1791, or 1868 had a strong "political underpinning." It "establishes a presumption of resolving textual ambiguities against the claim of constitutional right."

Brennan saw the same political objective behind the assertion that the Court should avoid deciding constitutional issues and leave it to the legislatures. "It is the very purpose of a Constitution — and particularly of the Bill of Rights — to declare certain values transcendent, beyond the reach of temporary political majorities." That those who drafted the Constitution did not write specifically about the proper resolution of disputes occurring one or two centuries after they had completed their work did not mean that their work had become irrelevant. They "had no desire to enshrine the status quo. Their goal was to make over their world."

Thurgood Marshall offered his own unique retort to strict interpretation two years later, on the bicentennial of the Constitution:

> I do not believe that the meaning of the Constitution was forever "fixed" at the Philadelphia Convention. Nor do I find the wisdom, foresight, and sense of justice exhibited by the Framers particularly profound. To the contrary, the government they devised was defective from the start, requiring several amendments, a civil war, and momentous social transformation to attain the system of constitutional government, and its respect for the individual freedoms and human rights, we hold as fundamental today. When contemporary Americans cite "The Constitution," they invoke a concept that is vastly different from what the Framers barely began to construct two centuries ago.

Marshall could not be satisfied by ways of trying to understand what the men intended in 1787 or what the male citizenry might have understood it to mean at that time:

> The men who gathered in Philadelphia in 1787 . . . could not have imagined, nor would they have accepted, that the document they were drafting would one day be construed by a Supreme Court to which had been appointed a woman and the descendent of an African slave. "We the People" no longer enslave, but the credit does not belong to the Framers. It belongs to those who refused to acquiesce in outdated notions of "liberty," "justice," and "equality," and who strived to better them.

Subsequently, Justice Scalia weighed in with his own stinging attack on Brennan's and Marshall's notion of a living constitution that should change as circumstances change. For Scalia, new problems may arise, but the Constitution is unchanging, its meaning fixed in 1787.

On the Rehnquist Court, the chief justice and Justice Scalia, joined later by Clarence Thomas, have become advocates of what is now known as "originalism" in interpretation. They have not heeded Israeli Chief Justice Aharon Barak's observation that judges who limit themselves to the words of controlling texts enjoy "more discretion than the judge who will seek guidance from every reliable source" because in their view "original" means a narrow, not a broad or liberal, interpretation. Thus, in *Michael H. v. Gerald D.* (1989), Scalia criticized reliance on "general traditions [which] provide such imprecise guidance, they permit judges to dictate rather than discern the society's views" and argued for "the need, if arbitrary decision-making is to be avoided, to adopt the most specific tradition as the point of reference."

Rehnquist, Scalia, and Thomas oppose attempts to explore the principles at work in constitutional provisions; each provision embodies only so much of any applicable principle as the Founders themselves would have thought appropriate. Principles are dangerous because they are expansive. Antiquated practices are much narrower and much less likely to challenge contemporary legislative behavior.

Although only Rehnquist, Scalia, and Thomas have fully subscribed to this position, it has been at the core of much of the Rehnquist Court's explanation of decisions taken by Court majorities, usually including, in addition to Rehnquist, Scalia, and Thomas, the votes of Justices O'Connor and Kennedy. As a result, throughout the Rehnquist era, the pages of Supreme Court opinions have burned with the flames of the debate over originalism. On the Court, justices have freely charged one another with infidelity to the Constitution. Farther afield, academic meetings and journals have devoted many hours and many pages to the method of constitutional interpretation. And senators questioning candidates for the Court have repeatedly asked whether they would "follow the Constitution" and precedent, even though no consensus has existed as to what "following the Constitution" means.

All this sound and fury notwithstanding, the real issues on the Rehnquist Court have had little to do with methods of reading constitutional or statutory language. Observers and commentators eventually began to notice this about a decade after the debates got fully under way. The argument over originalism merely hid the politics of Supreme Court decision making behind a fig leaf of rival interpretive claims. Judged by their own standards, Rehnquist, Scalia, and Thomas have been no more faithful to the text and original understanding of the Constitution than those they attacked. Once the new majority had been assembled and solidified, a number of decisions began to show that the justices weren't always doing what they professed.

Words Mean What the Justices Say

Words do not constrain on the Rehnquist Court. Consider the case of St. Clair Adams, who went to work as a salesman in a Circuit City store in California. The store's standard employment contract included an arbitration clause. At issue in Adams's case was a 1925 statute. In section 2, Congress had written that in any "transaction involving commerce," people could contract to have all disputes settled via arbitration. In section 1 of the same statute, however, Congress had written that the arbitration provision did not apply to disputes between employers and "workers engaged in foreign or interstate commerce." In 1925, the two provisions were coextensive: Congress was not requiring employees to give up their right to take their disputes to court, whatever might be written in the employment contract. But in *Circuit City Stores, Inc. v. Adams* (2001), the Rehnquist Court held that the two provisions were not coextensive. Since 1925, the Supreme Court had come to read congressional power over interstate commerce very broadly. Hence, the arbitration clause should apply to all commerce over which Congress had gained power. But the Court decided that the exception for employment disputes should be read as narrowly as Congress's power over commerce was read in 1925. Hence, a statute that did not send employment disputes to arbitration when it was written sends those disputes to arbitration now because the statute has been "interpreted" by the Rehnquist Court to do so, based on a decision to read the word *commerce* in two different ways in two adjacent sections of the same statute. Claiming that it was merely looking at the words of the statute, the Court decided that the meaning of the word *commerce* in the phrase "transaction involving commerce" was different from and broader than in the phrase "workers engaged in foreign or interstate commerce."

The Rehnquist Court's approach to the Eleventh Amendment provides another example of broad reinterpretation at work. The amendment directs that federal courts may not hear cases brought against a state by citizens of "another" state. Beginning with *Seminole Tribe v. Florida* (1996), however, the Rehnquist Court decided that "another State" also meant "the same" state. The Court has since invoked "Eleventh Amendment immunity" to limit the reach of federal statutes dealing with discrimination, labor, patents, and trademarks, among others. Such decisions fly in the face of the very language that originalism venerates.

History—When Convenient

When the text is not clear, originalists argue, history, however narrowly interpreted, should control. That proposition, however, has also proven dispensable.

In 1986, at the beginning of the Rehnquist era, one David Lucas bought some property on the South Carolina coast. Two years later, a state government agency adopted regulations for building on the coast. By then, Lucas had built and sold one lot but not the other, intending it for himself. Lucas felt that the new regulations imposed a burden on his lot that had not been imposed on his neighbors, and he sued.

The takings, or "just compensation," clause of the Fifth Amendment requires that the government pay the owner the value of property taken for a public use. When the clause was written, the Founders were thinking about takings as physical appropriations of property by government for the purpose, for example, of erecting a public building or building a road. The founders did not contemplate application of the clause to regulations that would impose general limitations on all property or on property of a certain type, such as all property in cities or towns or other built-up neighborhoods.

The Rehnquist Court, however, adopted the position that regulations as such could constitute a taking of property for which the Constitution requires compensation. Despite their philosophy of interpretation, the Court's conservatives frankly admitted that neither the text nor the history of the clause supported their contention. When it heard *Lucas v. South Carolina Coastal Council* in 1992, the Court did not ask whether the property in question was being singled out for treatment different from that of all the other property in the area. Instead, the Court applied a new doctrine under which regulations applied to property across the board could be considered a taking that required compensation. The majority claimed that its position was in general accord with what it termed "the historical compact recorded in the Takings Clause that has become part of our constitutional culture." But as Blackmun put it in dissent, no clear and accepted historical compact justifying the Court's new takings doctrine existed. "Instead, the Court seems to treat history as a grab bag of principles, to be adopted where they support the Court's theory, and ignored where they do not."

A number of conservative academics and lawyers had been urging the Court to use the takings clause to force government to compensate owners whenever it regulated property in ways that depressed its value or imposed new obligations. The potential impact of that idea is enormous. Every regulation has an impact on private property. If compensation were required for every variation in values, government action could be rendered impossible. The Court didn't follow this track but instead crafted a set of rules to distinguish regulatory takings that would be allowed from those that would require compensation. In Lucas's case, the rules would allow South Carolina's courts to decide whether the activity that Lucas wanted to engage in — building on the dunes — was a nuisance. If so, he never had possessed a right to build there; it was not part of the property rights he could legally buy or own. If not, the Court was to ask whether the regulation would entirely wipe out Lucas's ability to use the property. If so, compensation was required.

Economists can debate whether the outcome crafted by the Court was appropriate. The point being made here is a different one: Whether meritorious or not, the outcome belied the principles — fundamental regard for the text or the history of the Constitution — that the Court had identified as its lodestar in American constitutional law.

Deference to Democratic Branches

In 1977, Associate Justice Rehnquist argued that the idea of a "living Constitution . . . is a formula for an end run around popular government." An essay, "Common-Law Courts in a Civil-Law System," that Antonin Scalia published in 1997 made the same point: Respecting popular government should lead to "the elimination of restrictions upon democratic government." Yet from its inception in 1986 through 2002, the Rehnquist Court has found more acts of Congress unconstitutional than did any other Court in the nation's history. Moreover, the Rehnquist Court has done so while deciding far fewer cases than the preceding Warren and Burger Courts — a few more than 80 cases per term for about the last decade, down from about 166 decisions per term of the Burger Court. The Court's pace was fairly slow during its first eight years, from 1986 through 1993. But in the eight years from 1994 through 2002, the Rehnquist Court picked up speed, overruling federal statutes at a faster rate than the Court had in any other similar period. In that eight-year period, the Rehnquist Court overruled more congressional statutes than had any Court in the history of the Supreme Court, with the single exception of the entire seventeen-year span of its immediate predecessor, the Burger Court. This does not appear to be the record of a "restrained" Court, deferential to democratically elected branches.

Federalism and the Discovery of Constitutional Spirits

Examination of one final realm of adjudication will complete this analysis of the Rehnquist Court's record in sticking strictly to the text. When the text has not been helpful, the Court's conservative majority has done precisely what it argues justices should not do: abandon text and history and resort to the "spirit" of the Constitution. This course has become clearest in cases dealing with "federalism," or the relationship between the states and the federal government.

The first cases were relatively minor. In *United States v. Lopez* (1995), the Court held that Congress could not prohibit guns from schools, because that sphere of regulation belonged to the states. Observers and commentators concluded that *Lopez* portended nothing dramatic. The Court, it seemed, was simply warning Congress to be aware that there were limits to its powers over the states.

But a trio of cases in June 1999 forced Court watchers to take notice. In two cases between the state of Florida and the College Savings Bank located in New Jersey, *College Savings Bank v. Florida Prepaid Postsecondary Educ. Expense Bd.* (1999) and *Florida Prepaid Postsecondary Educ. Expense Bd. v. College Savings Bank* (1999), the Court held that Congress could not protect a patent and a trademark against infringement by the Florida state government. The Constitution is very specific about patents and copyrights, giving Congress the power to provide "Authors and Inventors the exclusive Right to their respective Writings and Discoveries." In another clause, the Constitution makes federal statutes "supreme" over state law in their sphere of jurisdiction and binds both state and federal judges to follow applicable federal law. Nothing in the text of the Constitution, then, supported the Court's conclusion that Congress could not require Florida to respect the rights of patent owners. Rather, the terms of the Constitution foreclosed Florida from denying patent owners their national granted patent rights. This notwithstanding, the Court majority held that the state of Florida enjoyed a prior "sovereign immunity" against congressional enforcement of federal patent and trademark law that had been neither validly abrogated nor voluntarily waived.

Nor do the terms of the Constitution explain how the Court could conclude in the third 1999 case, *Alden v. Maine*, that Congress cannot require states to obey national rules in areas clearly and unmistakably within the competence of Congress. In *Alden*, state employees had complained in state court that they were not paid overtime owed under the 1938 Fair Labor Standards Act. The Court had previously held on several occasions that the act was within the powers of Congress under the commerce clause. The Eleventh Amendment applies only to actions in federal courts. State judges are bound by the supremacy clause to apply federal law and give it precedence over state law wherever Congress has the constitutional power to regulate. Nevertheless, the Court held in *Alden* that this federal statute could not be enforced against the states in state courts, either. The Court relied on general claims about the spirit of the Constitution and, once more, on the states' "sovereign immunity." Sovereign immunity is not mentioned anywhere in the Constitution, let alone preserved by it as a shield for the states against compliance with federal law. Nevertheless, Justice Kennedy wrote for the Court: "We have . . . sometimes referred to the States' immunity from suit as 'Eleventh Amendment immunity.' The phrase is convenient shorthand but something of a misnomer, for the sovereign immunity of the States neither derives from nor is limited by the terms of the Eleventh Amendment." The Court found sovereign immunity implied in the "structure" of the Constitution and in some of the ratification debates. However, it had little to say about the text itself.

The Rehnquist Court's decisions in these federalism disputes were a major surprise for the legal community. These decisions were not minor shots across the bow, as in *Lopez*, but direct strikes on the powers of Congress. What the Court's decisions meant was that federal law was unenforceable if the states chose to disregard them. None of these decisions owed anything to the Rehnquist Court's self-proclaimed interpretive principles. Their correctness, or error, stands on grounds independent of any consistently applied set of interpretive principles.

"Preconceptions About the Law"

Defending his refusal to recuse himself from hearing a case in the U.S. Supreme Court on which he had worked while in the Nixon administration, the newly appointed Justice Rehnquist wrote in a 1972 memorandum in *Laird v. Tatum* that "it is virtually impossible to find a judge who does not have preconceptions about the law." Examining the Rehnquist Court, one could be forgiven for concluding that preconceptions have gained ascendancy over law.

Voting Rights

As associate justices on the Burger Court, Rehnquist and O'Connor took part in such decisions as *Salyer Land Co. v. Tulare Lake Basin Water Storage Dist.* (1973) and *Ball v. James* (1981), which restricted to property owners voting rights for water storage district and school district elections. Rehnquist and O'Connor also voted in apportionment cases, such as *Brown v. Thompson* (1983), to allow a difference of as much as three to one in population between legislative districts. Finally, in *Davis v. Bandemer* (1986), a gerrymandering case before the Burger Court, Rehnquist and O'Connor voted that the Court should not deal with gerrymandering, which affects which political party gets what percentage of the legislature.

Positions adopted in these Burger Court election cases previewed Rehnquist-era outcomes. In *Presley v. Etowah County Commission* (1992), lame-duck commissioners defeated by two black challengers in Etowah County, Alabama, changed the powers of the county commissioners so that the new commissioners would be deprived of the authority to supervise various county government functions that commissioners had formerly enjoyed. Under the Voting Rights Act of 1965, Etowah County could not put changes in election practices or rules into effect without the approval of the attorney general of the United States. The county had not bothered to seek that approval, so the incoming black commissioners sued. The Rehnquist Court held that the lame-duck commissioners were entitled to act as they had.

A year later, a second battle went to the heart of the Voting Rights Act. The issue was representation in the legislature. Under section 2 of the act, no state or political subdivision could deny or abridge the right to vote "on account of race or color." In addition, states that had historically denied voting rights to minorities — mostly but not exclusively the former slave states of the old Confederacy — were barred by section 5 of the act from making any change that had "the purpose [or] effect of denying or abridging the right to vote on account of race or color." The latter provision has been interpreted as prohibiting any retrogression in the voting rights of minorities. The provision also required approval of either the attorney general or a federal court before any change in the election laws of covered jurisdictions could go into effect.

The Rehnquist Court has decided that the attorney general does not have the right to examine compliance with section 2 before approving a change under section 5. The result has been a multisided conflict. Blacks have argued that states are discriminating and cutting back on their rights. Whites have argued that in the effort to meet the requirements of section 2, states and localities are intentionally making racially discriminatory decisions in favor of blacks. The Court writes as if both of these contrary arguments can be true — that states may be out of compliance with the statute because they are discriminating *against* blacks and yet simultaneously be out of compliance with the Constitution because they are discriminating *in favor of* blacks. The alchemy that makes this sound plausible is the rule that discrimination is defined by the intentions of the government. The Court holds that the government may not discriminate against blacks but also that it cannot correct its misbehavior by consciously fixing it.

"First past the post" is the form of election for legislators most familiar in the United States. Single legislative seats are allocated to single electoral districts; whoever gets the greatest number of votes in the district wins the seat. In drawing lines for the districts, however, the parties regularly engage in gerrymandering; that is, they shape districts to favor one of the political parties and specific incumbents. The party in power packs as many supporters of its rival into a single district, thereby "wasting" all votes over 50.1 percent. The remaining opposition voters are then spread among as many districts as possible to dilute their impact. There are many examples. Gerrymandering has split the New York legislature into a Democratic Assembly and a Republican Senate, because of the way the district lines group and waste Republican votes for the Assembly and Democratic votes for the Senate. Similarly, in 1994, a majority of voters in Texas voted Republican, but political gerrymandering ensured that Democrats won two-thirds of all legislative seats.

One can design districts to favor either party, or one can design districts to be relatively competitive, so that swings among the voters will affect many seats. One can also design districts to be roughly proportional to the strength of the political parties in the state, county, or other jurisdiction for which the entire legislature is elected. In amendments to the Voting Rights Act, Congress in 1982 directed courts evaluating districts to apply an effects test partially determined by the numbers. Congress added, however, that proportional representation was not required. The Burger Court tried to steer a middle course between those two provisions. The Rehnquist Court, on the other hand, has ignored the effects test almost entirely.

For twenty-eight years after the Voting Rights Act was passed, the Court consistently approved efforts to provide representation, mostly in the states of the old Confederacy, to blacks, who had been discriminated against in the voting systems of those states. But in *Shaw v. Reno* (1993), the Court held that the creation of a black-majority district in North Carolina by a process that segregated black and white voters would violate the equal protection clause. Thus, *Shaw* put at issue the basic weapon of the Voting Rights Act. In later redistricting controversies, the Court largely abandoned the segregation rationale, partly because all the districts in question had racially mixed populations, and turned instead to the question of intent. In a series of cases over the course of a decade, the Court overturned every effort to provide districting plans that reduced but did not eliminate the underrepresentation of blacks.

In *Easley v. Cromartie* (2001), the original North Carolina litigation came back to the Court for a third time. The result was a 5–4 decision finally approving the twice-revised North Carolina redistricting plan. For the first time since the census of 1990, the Court found that a state had been able to devise a defensible districting plan that provided some representation for blacks but not so much that it was clearly designed along racial lines. Justice O'Connor joined Stevens, Souter, Ginsburg, and Breyer in support. Clarence Thomas wrote a dissent, joined by Rehnquist, Scalia, and Kennedy.

Three years after *Shaw v. Reno,* the Court dropped another bombshell. In *Bush v. Vera* (1996), the issue was the reapportionment of the Texas legislature after the 1990 census. The Texas legislature had responded to the growth of population in south Texas by creating a new majority–African American district and a new majority-Hispanic district and redrawing another majority–African American district. Plaintiffs claimed that the plan was a racial gerrymander. Defendants said that it was a political gerrymander to protect Texas Democrats. The Court agreed with the plaintiffs that the redistricting was racially motivated. But the Court also made it clear for the first time that in its view, protecting incumbents was permissible and an acceptable defense against claims that redistricting had been undertaken for racial reasons. Redistricting, according to the Court, was a means by which politicians might properly protect themselves from the public. Protecting incumbents, according to O'Connor's majority opinion, was "a legitimate districting consideration."

The Court's treatment of the Voting Rights Act and of political gerrymandering, along with Rehnquist and O'Connor's earlier handling of right-to-vote and one-person-per-vote cases, provide the crucial backdrop to the momentous case of *Bush v. Gore* (2000). On the night of the 2000 presidential election, the outcome came to depend on voting in the state of Florida. Counting in Florida put George Bush ahead, but the outcome was inconclusive, turning on just a few hundred votes. A recount was called for. But the paper ballots used in several counties posed some difficulties in determining the choices that voters had made. The ballots were marked by punching out holes. In some cases, the punch did not completely sever the "chad" (waste paper) from the ballot. Some chads hung by a single point; others, by two or three; some were merely dimpled.

Florida law required that "no vote shall be declared invalid or void if there is a clear indication of the intent of the voter." Accordingly, the Florida Supreme Court ordered a trial court judge to administer a recount of disputed ballots and to determine the intent of the voters where it could be determined from the ballot. But on Saturday, December 9, 2000, on petition from the Bush campaign, the U.S. Supreme Court ordered a stay of the count until it could hear arguments for and against the recount.

In a concurring opinion, Justice Scalia addressed petitioner Bush's application for injunctive relief from the "irreparable harm" that the recount threatened. (Under the rules, courts are not supposed to issue an injunction unless failure to do so would result in irreparable harm.) "The issue is not, as the dissent puts it, whether '[c]ounting every legally cast vote can constitute irreparable harm,'" Scalia wrote. "One of the principal issues in the appeal we have accepted is precisely whether the votes that have been ordered to be counted are, under a reasonable interpretation of Florida law, 'legally cast vote[s].'" Scalia then described the irreparable harm that would result from allowing the count to continue. "The counting of votes that are of questionable legality does in my view threaten irreparable harm to petitioner [Bush], and to the country, by casting a cloud upon what he claims to be the legitimacy of his election."

This suggested that failing to count votes was less harmful than counting them because the result of a recount could cast doubt on the claim of George Bush that he had been properly elected. The reaction was strong on both sides. The Bush campaign claimed vindication. The Gore campaign was outraged.

Three days later, the Supreme Court stopped the official count permanently. The Court found the recount flawed because disputed ballots would be counted under different rules in different counties. In fact, votes throughout Florida had been counted according to varying standards, and the results certified had contributed to Bush's narrow lead in the first count. In Florida, as in the rest of the country, elections were organized locally, by county boards using different types of ballot and handling the ballots in their own ways. If there was inequality, in other words, it was rampant all over Florida, not merely in the counties in dispute (principally Miami-Dade and Palm Beach Counties). And in fact, the Court did not conclude that there was anything wrong with a multitude of jurisdictions counting ballots in different ways — there was no single state rule regarding the counting of ballots, and the Court did not require one. Rather than send the case back again with an order to establish a single standard and count the ballots according to that standard, the Court ordered an end to all recounting.

In prior decisions dealing with neutral rules, the Supreme Court had defined denial of equal protection as the intention to discriminate. With respect to ballots, that meant that different counties or registrars or other officials doing the counting did not deny equal protection merely by counting ballots differently. An intent to discriminate also had to be shown. No intent to discriminate was shown in *Bush v. Gore*. Nevertheless, the Court was silent on the omission. It neither required nor discussed the centrality of the intentional discrimination standard to the definition of denial of equal protection. Only by ignoring its own rule that equal protection is defined by intent and by ignoring the existence of different voting boards and practices all over Florida — indeed, all over the United States — all counting votes in different ways was the Court able to conclude that there was a violation of equal protection across voting boards in this single regard.

Capital Punishment

The Rehnquist Court has been vigorous in its efforts to erect procedural barriers to block postconviction efforts to obtain federal court review of state criminal convictions. In a series of cases, however, the Court decided that it would permit review of state convictions if an error "caused the conviction of an innocent person." Innocence would be more important than bare objections to police procedures. In *Herrera v. Collins* (1993), a capital case, the Rehnquist Court was presented with just such a claim. Convicted of murder, Leonel Herrera argued that he had been the victim of a feud among drug dealers and had been framed to protect others involved. After years of effort, counsel had found a good deal of exculpatory evidence. But Texas law deprived its courts of power to reopen a case to examine newly discovered evidence. In addition to the new evidence they attempted to present to the state courts, counsel also produced affidavits in the federal courts by an eyewitness and a judge. The witness identified his own father as the killer. The judge swore that the actual killer had admitted the killing to him while the judge, then an attorney, was representing the killer on another matter. No court, however, had ordered a hearing to examine whether there was sufficient cause to call a new trial. The federal district court stayed Herrera's execution, but the Court of Appeals concluded that it did not have the authority to do so. The Supreme Court held that new evidence of actual innocence was insufficient basis for federal intervention where the original trial was procedurally sound. Herrera had been the beneficiary of all the process to which he was entitled. Eleven weeks later, he was executed.

In recent years, many death-row inmates have been released because other courts and state governors have taken seriously the possibility that an innocent person might mistakenly be executed. To date, the Rehnquist Court has not been part of that movement.

Discrimination and Civil Rights

In *Adarand Constructors v. Pena* (1995), the Court outlined rules that would govern its review of cases arising from policies intended to relieve racial discrimination. First came skepticism: "Any preference based on racial or ethnic criteria must necessarily receive a most searching examination." Second came consistency: "The standard of review under the Equal Protection Clause is not dependent on the race of those burdened or benefited by a particular classification." Third came congruence: "Equal protection analysis in the Fifth Amendment area is the same as that under the Fourteenth Amendment."

Taken together, these three propositions lead to the conclusion that any person, of whatever race, has the right to demand that any governmental actor subject to the Constitution justify any racial classification subjecting that person to unequal treatment under the strictest judicial scrutiny. In other words, the Court was insisting on an essentially colorblind Constitution; any deviation in any direction would be "strictly scrutinized" and found wanting except in the most exceptional circumstances. The impact of these rules has been particularly noticeable in "affirmative action" cases. With the single exception of *Grutter v. Bollinger* (2003), which sustained a University of Michigan Law School affirmative action plan that avoided all use of numbers, the Rehnquist Court has repeatedly ruled that affirmative action violates the equal protection clause because it is not colorblind.

The Court's statement of rules, however, has puzzled many commentators. One scholar, Jed Rubenfeld of Yale, argues that the Court acts so consistently against laws designed to prohibit discrimination that its position is best described as "anti-anti-discrimination." In each case alleging discrimination against a minority, the Court has found some explanation other than discrimination that, in its view, has caused the disparate treatment at issue. In *Wards Cove v. Atonio* (1989), for example, the Court was presented with a complaint that the Wards Cove Packing Company had systematically segregated its workforce. All the company's cannery operations took place in Alaska, but white-collar staff were recruited exclusively from the lower U.S. West Coast and housed in a building separate and apart from the cannery workers. The latter were exclusively native Alaskan and Inuit, recruited locally. Job openings in each department were available only to those employed in the department and were not posted in the other building. Questioned, one of the supervisors responded that the Caucasian staff from the West Coast would not mix with the Alaskan and Inuit workers. The Rehnquist Court held that there was no discrimination and proceeded to promulgate rules that terminated further antidiscrimination litigation under the federal Equal Employment Opportunity Act.

Another prominent discrimination case, *Hernandez v. New York* (1991), arose from jury-selection procedures. The case involved a prosecutor who had excluded jurors who could speak and understand Spanish as well as English, on the ground that they could therefore understand witnesses in the case who would speak in Spanish independently of translation. The Court decided that the exclusion of the jurors was not discriminatory: Prosecutors could justifiably seek jurors who would be reliant solely on the translation of testimony that would be provided. Most Americans serving on juries, of course, do not have to rely on translators — they simply listen to testimony as it is given. Jurors who cannot speak English would undoubtedly be excluded from sitting on most juries in the United States. Nevertheless, the Court accepted the prosecutor's explanation.

Congress responded to the Court's discrimination jurisprudence with the Civil Rights Act of 1991, which restored much of what the Supreme Court had changed. In the process, Congress countermanded rulings on the meaning of the Civil Rights Act handed down in no less than nine separate Supreme Court decisions. Following passage of the act, however, the Court began chipping away at the capacity of Congress to legislate in the civil rights arena. One step was to deny that Congress had power to make state government live up to the requirements of federal civil rights laws. *Board of Trustees of the University of Alabama v. Garrett* (2001), for example, eliminated claims that states had discriminated against the disabled. Patricia Garrett had worked for the University of Alabama for seventeen years and received several promotions. When she was diagnosed with breast cancer and demoted, the Court ruled that she had no remedy in federal courts. The Americans with Disabilities Act (1990) no longer offered her protection. Nor had she any remedy in state courts, because the Court held that the act prohibited only intentionally discriminatory behavior, not behavior that merely discriminated without justification. Thus, the state courts could not rely on what had previously been the controlling interpretation of the federal statute.

A second step was to deny that Congress had the power to legislate under the commerce clause unless the activity involved a commercial transaction. That eliminated one of the jurisdictional foundations for the federal Violence Against Women Act. Christy Brzonkala was allegedly repeatedly raped by two students at Virginia Polytechnic Institute. Despite crucial admissions by one of the accused students, the school found him guilty only of abusive language and allowed him to return to class. Congress had determined that state enforcement was insufficient to protect women and provided for a federal remedy. But in *United States v. Morrison* (2000), the Rehnquist Court decided that Brzonkala had no remedy in federal courts.

The same case removed the Violence Against Women Act's other foundation — the Fourteenth Amendment — by denying that Congress had power to legislate under the amendment unless there was a record indicating that the states were unwilling to protect civil rights. On the record before it, the Court held that there was no such record to support the Violence Against Women Act. Denied both possible constitutional foundations, the act became unenforceable. *Morrison* also drove home a general restraint on congressional resort to the Fourteenth Amendment already established in *City of Boerne v. Flores* (1997). In that case, the Court had found that Congress had no power to legislate under the Fourteenth Amendment against practices that the Court would not treat as unconstitutional unless pursuant to a record demonstrating a pattern of abuse that required broader legislation in order to stop the narrower unconstitutional behavior.

The historic Civil Rights Act of 1964, comprehensively prohibiting discrimination in public accommodations (stores, hotels, theaters), public facilities, public education, federally assisted programs, and employment, was based largely on Congress's constitutional power over "commerce . . . among the several states" and was sustained as such in *Katzenbach v. McClung* (1964). The Fourteenth Amendment prohibits any state from denying anyone due process or the equal protection of the laws. In 1964, that would have seemed a completely appropriate constitutional foundation for the statute. In the later nineteenth century, to be sure, the Supreme Court had severely narrowed Congress's antidiscrimination powers under the Fourteenth Amendment. However, during the 1960s, the Warren Court had overruled several of those nineteenth-century precedents and had authored decisions — see, for example, *Katzenbach v. Morgan* (1966) and *Jones v. Alfred H. Mayer Co.* (1968) — that referred to Congress's powers under the Thirteenth and Fourteenth Amendments to support both the Civil Rights Acts of the Reconstruction Congress and the 1965 Voting Rights Act.

The cases of the last decade discussed previously have now comprehensively undermined the constitutional basis for Congress's fundamental civil rights legislation. The Court is well aware of this. Justice Kennedy's opinion for the Court in *Boerne* explicitly compared the Voting Rights Act to another statute the Court had found unconstitutional. The only difference, said Kennedy, was that the incidents in the record in front of Congress were newer in the case of the Voting Rights Act. It is not yet clear what is left of the Civil Rights Acts of 1964 and 1965 and their many amendments and cousins.

The Court's position on discrimination issues relating to sexuality has been less consistent. In *Boy Scouts of America v. Dale* (2000), the Court found that New Jersey's antidiscrimination law had to give way to the right of association. In that case, a gay scout leader had been fired from his position because of his views about gay rights, not because of anything he did as scoutmaster (Plate B.15). New Jersey banned discrimination by legislative act. The right of association is a nontextual inference from the First Amendment — the kind of right the Rehnquist Court claims to disfavor. Nevertheless, in *Dale,* the Court held that it trumped New Jersey's antidiscrimination law. Rehnquist and O'Connor had both joined the majority in *Bowers v. Hardwick* (1986), decided at the very end of the Burger Court, holding that Georgia could punish consensual and private homosexual acts. But O'Connor has joined in two more recent opinions written by Justice Kennedy that have moved the Court firmly in the other direction,

Romer v. Evans (1996) held that a Colorado constitutional amendment denying gays and lesbians access to protection "across the board" was "unprecedented in our jurisprudence." A class of persons had been identified "not to further a proper legislative end but to make them unequal to everyone else." And in *Lawrence v. Texas* (2003), the Court overruled *Bowers* and held that a Texas statute that criminalized intimate sexual conduct between two people of the same sex violated the due process clause.

Why has the Rehnquist Court not only opposed affirmative action but also argued over laws that prohibit discrimination? There are at least two answers, each related to different positions held by different members of the Court.

For Scalia, Rehnquist, and Thomas, the answer is most clearly set out in Scalia's dissent in *Romer v. Evans* (1996). There, Scalia, joined by Rehnquist and Thomas, described antidiscrimination law as "special protection" and "special treatment" for homosexuals. At another point in his dissent, he described antidiscrimination law as "preferential treatment" and "favored status for homosexuality." Scalia elaborated by describing other prejudices that might be encountered in the course of a job interview but would not qualify the interviewee to seek protection:

> The interviewer may refuse to offer a job because the applicant is a Republican; because he is an adulterer; because he went to the wrong prep school or belongs to the wrong country club; because he eats snails; because he is a womanizer; because she wears real-animal fur; or even because he hates the Chicago Cubs. But if the interviewer should wish not to be an associate or partner of an applicant because he disapproves of the applicant's homosexuality, then he will have violated the pledge which the Association of American Law Schools requires all its member schools to exact from job interviewers: "assurance of the employer's willingness" to hire homosexuals.

Scalia's argument is that we all are subject to or victims of a variety of prejudices. He might as easily have made his point by referring to prejudices about weight or hair or accent. For Scalia, to be exempted from such prejudices is to be accorded special treatment. Thus, antidiscrimination law discriminates.

But for the other six members of the Court, discriminatory treatment is treatment that considers such characteristics as race, national origin, religion, sex and sexual preference, or disability, which should be irrelevant except where there are important reasons why the distinction is truly significant. That is, people have a right to be considered on their merits irrespective of such matters. Discrimination means to be subjected to such prejudice. Antidiscrimination law promises equal treatment. Curiously, in affirmative action cases, Scalia agrees that people, including white people, have a right to be considered on their merits free from such generally irrelevant considerations as race and so forth and that equal treatment forbids such discrimination. But when the agenda turns to discrimination laws, he changes tack.

Justices O'Connor and Kennedy have added their own refinements. They, like their colleagues, have repeatedly quoted the language of *Personnel Administrator of Mass. v. Feeney*, a 1979 Burger Court decision that the equal protection clause was implicated only when "a state legislature selected or reaffirmed a particular course of action at least in part 'because of,' not merely 'in spite of,' its adverse effects upon an identifiable group." In other words, they seek conscious and deliberate intentions. They are not looking merely for carelessness, which might be action "'in spite of' its adverse effects." Instead, to be found discriminatory, action must be deliberate, "'because of' . . . its adverse effects upon an identifiable group."

Given their demand for conscious and deliberate intentions, O'Connor's and Kennedy's assumptions about people's motives determine the results. Where minorities have claimed discrimination, O'Connor and Kennedy, invoking the deliberate-intent test, have consistently insisted that there was some other nondiscriminatory reason. So in *Wards Cove*, they saw no deliberate segregation, and in *Hernandez*, they saw no discrimination against bilingual jurors. Where whites have claimed discrimination, however, O'Connor and Kennedy have given no credit to nondiscriminatory reasons and concluded that the white claimants had in fact been discriminated against. They are so consistent that, despite the employment of reasoning very different from Scalia's, it is difficult to distinguish their decisions from his.

In a recent and particularly interesting remark that shows considerable self-consciousness, Kennedy, concurring in *Board of Trustees of the University of Alabama v. Garrett* (2001) and joined by Justice O'Connor, wrote: "Prejudice, we are beginning to understand, rises not from malice or hostile animus alone. It may result as well from insensitivity caused by simple want of careful, rational reflection or from some instinctive mechanism to guard against people who appear to be different in some respects from ourselves."

Such a formulation should be much more protective than the stress on conscious and deliberate intentions on which Kennedy and O'Conner have relied heretofore. It also seems much more in line with congressional decisions regarding the civil rights acts. Perhaps those remarks, particularly the tantalizing "we are beginning to understand," indicate that Kennedy and O'Conner will begin to see discrimination in those situations in which white Americans systematically disadvantage dark-skinned fellow Americans but self-servingly protest that they had no such intention. To date, however, they are yet to see such discrimination. They have provided relief in cases that come prepackaged as discriminatory conduct but not in those cases in which the issue is whether the lower courts properly found that there was or was not discriminatory conduct.

A case from the Court's 2002 term, *Miller-el v. Cockrell,* illustrates both the promise of evolution in Court members' ability to see discrimination and their continued limitations. A defendant in a criminal trial in Texas complained that the jury-selection procedures discriminated against the possibility of putting black jurors in the box. The evidence included a federal magistrate's report that described blatant and deliberate manipulation of the jury pool, using techniques included in training manuals that instructed prosecutors on how to exclude blacks, and the testimony of several witnesses who had worked inside the district attorney's office. But the lower court felt constrained to reject all that evidence because it was, barely, possible to look at the prosecutor's reasons for rejecting black jurors in the particular case and, if one gave him the benefit of the doubt, imagine that there were nondiscriminatory reasons. The Court sent the case back, saying that the courts below had used the wrong standard. They were entitled to look at the history of abuse in determining the prosecutor's motives. At this point, O'Connor had been on the Court more than two decades; Kennedy, a decade and a half. This was the first occasion on which, on the proof, they sided with a minority complainant in a discrimination case. Scalia, meanwhile, filed a concurring opinion in which he stressed the reasons why the lower courts could and should still find that there had been no discrimination. Thomas dissented.

The Rehnquist Court: "Fair-Weather Federalists"?

In 1999, R. Shep Melnick published in the *Wilson Quarterly* an article that labeled the Rehnquist Court "Fair-Weather Federalists." According to Melnick, the Rehnquist Court had revived the concept of federalism from a half-century of slumber. From 1937 to 1990, federalism had played only a minor role in Supreme Court opinions. But then the Court had veered sharply. National laws would not be interpreted to bind state governments unless Congress clearly stated that intention. When Congress did state its intention to control state practice, the Court decided that Congress had no right to "commandeer" states to enforce federal laws. When Congress clearly had the constitutional power, the Court held, the Eleventh Amendment and unwritten principles of federalism prohibited Congress from enforcing those laws in either state or federal courts.

The Rehnquist Court certainly speaks like a Court committed to a revival of federalism. The question remains, however, whether federalism explains the Court's decisions. Between 1986 and 2002, the Rehnquist Court found state constitutional provisions, statutes, and ordinances unconstitutional in 104 cases. That is approximately one-third the number in the record of the Burger Court and two-thirds of the Warren Court's tally. Conversely, as we have seen, the Rehnquist Court has held more federal statutes unconstitutional than has any other Supreme Court in the history of the country. This suggests a record very favorable to the states.

Patterns in the Court's decision making, however, complicate the story. As we have just seen, many of the Court's rules restricting national power in favor of the states have concentrated on disabling federal antidiscrimination law. The Court has also acted in some cases to disable state antidiscrimination law, as it did in *Boy Scouts of America v. Dale*. One may ask whether the Rehnquist Court's primary concern is to protect federalism or to disable antidiscrimination laws in general.

Other patterns call into question the federalist tag altogether. In a number of cases, the Court has held that federal law preempts state law, thus forbidding states to regulate in areas where ambiguous federal statutes are read to "occupy the field." Those decisions sound nationalist, not federalist, or pro-state. In other instances, the Rehnquist Court has alternated between nationalist and federalist stances, depending on the position that Congress, the states, or localities have taken on issues that the Court has adopted as matters of particular concern. For example, the Court has often sounded federalist in criminal cases in which the states have wanted to give their police more leeway than the federal rules would allow. When states have turned to measures more protective of individual rights and the protections of due process, however, the Rehnquist Court has switched ground and overruled the states. In both instances, outcomes have seemed driven more by the Court's hostility to criminal defendants per se, even when what is at issue are substantial questions of the innocence of the person in prison or on death row, than its concern for federal relationships.

Trends on the Rehnquist Court: First Amendment Dissensus

In 1984, Gregory Lee Johnson set fire to an American flag outside the Republican National Convention in Dallas. He was arrested and convicted of violating Texas law, which prohibited desecrating an American flag. Five years later, the U.S. Supreme Court overturned his conviction as a violation of the right of free speech guaranteed by the First Amendment. For those who follow the Supreme Court closely, *Texas v. Johnson* should not have been a surprise. The Court had made it clear in many cases that condemning behavior because of its expressive conduct is a violation of the

First Amendment. And the Court had also frequently made it clear that the government could not dictate the particular use made of the flag as a symbol, whether to defend the policies of the country or to attack them. What was stunning about the decision, then, was not the result—any other conclusion would have forced major changes in Supreme Court doctrine—but the lineup of the justices.

The Court's opinion was written by Justice William Brennan, who had served more than three decades and would soon retire. He was joined by Thurgood Marshall and Harry Blackmun, justices who often sided with Brennan in cases that divided the Court. He was also joined by two of the Court's conservative justices—Antonin Scalia and Anthony Kennedy—both of whom usually opposed Brennan. Chief Justice Rehnquist wrote a dissent that was joined by Byron White, a Democrat appointed by Kennedy; John Paul Stevens, a liberal Republican appointed by Ford; and Sandra Day O'Connor, a conservative Republican. Such a mix of liberal and conservative justices on the same sides of speech controversies would become increasingly common on the Rehnquist Court.

In a well-known 2001 article that examined the Rehnquist Court's voting patterns in free-speech cases, Eugene Volokh concluded that Justice Kennedy was the Court's most consistent vote for the free-speech position, followed, in order, by David Souter, Clarence Thomas, Ruth Bader Ginsburg, John Paul Stevens, Antonin Scalia, William Rehnquist, Sandra Day O'Connor, and Stephen Breyer. The alignment bears little resemblance to liberal/conservative splits in other areas of law. The only justices appointed by any Democratic president, for example, are Ginsburg and Breyer. Ginsburg shares with Stevens a position near the middle of the Court on free-speech issues, although both are often relatively liberal on other issues. Breyer, also relatively liberal on most issues, is least likely to vote in favor of free speech. Of the conservatives, in addition to Kennedy, Thomas votes quite often in favor of free speech. The three other conservatives—Scalia, Rehnquist, and O'Connor—are relatively unsupportive of free-speech claims. Overall, positions on speech issues on the Rehnquist Court no longer seem to correlate with positions on other issues.

Part of the explanation lies in the controversies that have given rise to free-speech issues presented to the Court. Some of the conservative justices have argued for stronger protection for the speech rights of abortion protesters and have also argued for stronger protection for commercial speech. These justices have been less moved to ban hate speech than some of the liberal justices. At the same time, the core liberal support for free speech has been taxed by campaign finance reform and by hate speech. Several relatively liberal members of the Court have argued that hate speech should not be protected and that there are important reasons to ban it. And they have warmed to campaign finance restrictions. Again, although conservatives on the Court have argued that nudity and pornography are quite harmful to the public, several of them have united with their more liberal colleagues in insisting that statutes limiting public expression, including nudity, and including expression over the Internet, be carefully constructed and meet high standards for specificity and avoidance of chilling protected speech.

None of this, however, fully explains the ringing pro-free-speech feelings that drive the pen of Anthony Kennedy or the split, in some speech cases, between Thomas and Scalia. With respect to First Amendment speech doctrine, a great deal of rethinking is going on in the Rehnquist Court.

In the case of the First Amendment religion clauses, by contrast, the Rehnquist Court has engineered major changes in American law. Some of the most basic notions about the religion clauses were established by the Vinson Court, which erected a "wall of separation" between church and state. The wall was defended both as a protection for individual freedom of conscience and for religious institutions from government intrusion in their activities.

The Rehnquist Court has overthrown the wall. In *Zelman v. Simmons-Harris* (2002), the Court held that legislation establishing public subsidies to enable children to move from public to private or parochial schools (vouchers) was permissible so long as the choice was given to the parents and the legislation was written to cover individuals and schools without explicit reference to religion. The case arose in Cleveland amid considerable sentiment that the city's public schools ill-served their constituency. Vouchers seemed to some a way out of the problem. The voucher program was limited to those planning to attend schools that charged no more than $2,500. The justices argued over whether that cap kept private nonreligious schools, which charged more, from participating. Apparently, private nonreligious schools had chosen to participate in the program but had admitted only a few students. The Court responded that, given all the choices available to the parents, including choices within the public schools, the program did not favor religious schools.

Zelman made it clear that vouchers were permitted, even where the terms of the enabling statute had a tendency to eliminate all but religious schools from the voucher program itself. The Court counseled that one must look beyond the voucher program to all the alternatives available to parents.

What else the decision might mean depends on how one understands what it means for the government to be neutral toward religion. For prior generations, a secular education was neutral; it provided a floor of education in subjects that were not inherently religious, on top of which everyone was free to add the teachings of their own faith in their own time. For many Americans, the response was Sunday school or after-school classes. In public school, children of all faiths would be educated together.

If neutrality means that we must compare all the options, public schools included, and if a public secular education is treated not as a common neutral floor but as one education among others, with its own religious point of view, the Rehnquist Court has put the country on the road to routinely requiring vouchers, ending American public education as we have known it in favor of an educational system much more like those of Europe and other parts of the world, where children are divided by faith early in their lives. For the moment, a divided 2004 decision resisted that inference.

The Legacy of the Rehnquist Court

To survey the activities of the Rehnquist Court since 1986 is to discover that, in many respects, the Court has returned the law to the way it stood some seventy years ago, in the early years of the Roosevelt administration, a remarkable departure from trends followed by the Court's predecessors for the past seven decades. Both Congress and the states are now variously required by the Court to keep their hands off matters that the Court has decided are unfit for regulation. Federal constitutional law regarding the freedoms of Americans has largely been moved back toward the position it occupied when the Court was making its first tentative steps toward applying the first ten amendments. The Court is revisiting the period when the idea that persons accused of crimes had rights was still largely in the dreams of lawyers committed to truth and justice, when the religion clauses posed no barrier to interdenominational rivalry over which Bible should be used in school classes, and to the period in which protesters were troublemakers to be handled with the full force of law. To be sure, one may note glimmerings of new, potentially enlightened, understandings of discrimination. One can also observe that the Court's dissensus on free-speech issues points up the inadequacies of a straightforward liberal/conservative analysis in explaining every twist and turn of the justices' decision making. Yet judged as a whole, the impact of the Rehnquist Court on American constitutional law has been profoundly conservative. The years since 1986, and particularly since the early 1990s, have been witness to one of the most radical upheavals in received understandings in the history of the U.S. Supreme Court.

—STEPHEN E. GOTTLIEB

FOR FURTHER READING AND RESEARCH

On the Rehnquist Court, see Stephen E. Gottlieb, *Morality Imposed: The Rehnquist Court and Liberty in America* (New York, 2000). Lee Epstein, Jeffrey A. Segal, Harold J. Spaeth, and Thomas G. Walker, *The Supreme Court Compendium: Data, Decisions, and Developments* (Washington, 2003), is a gold mine of data. On the inside workings of the Rehnquist Court, see James F. Simon, *The Center Holds: The Power Struggle Inside the Rehnquist Court* (New York, 1995); David G. Savage, *Turning Right: The Making of the Rehnquist Supreme Court* (New York, 1992); and Bernard Schwartz, *The Unpublished Opinions of the Rehnquist Court* (New York, 1996).

For the justices' own views, see especially William H. Rehnquist, "The Notion of a Living Constitution," *Texas Law Review* 54 (1976), 693; William J. Brennan, Jr., "The Constitution of the United States: Contemporary Ratification," *National Lawyers Guild Practitioner* 43 (1986), 1; Stephen Breyer, "On the Uses of Legislative History in Interpreting Statutes," *Southern California Law Review* 65 (1992), 845; Thurgood Marshall, "The Constitution's Bicentennial: Commemorating the Wrong Document?" *Vanderbilt Law Review* 40 (1987), 1337; and Antonin Scalia, *A Matter of Interpretation: Federal Courts and the Law: An Essay by Antonin Scalia with Commentary by Amy Gutmann, Editor . . . [et al.]* (Princeton, N.J., 1997).

Jeffrey Rosen has written a very readable series on the justices. See, for example, "The Leader of the Opposition," *New Republic* (Jan. 18, 1993), 20, on Scalia; "A Majority of One," *New York Times Magazine* (June 3, 2001), 32, on O'Connor; and "Ruth Bader Ginsburg: The New Look of Liberalism on the Court," *New York Times Magazine* (October 5, 1997), 60.

Bush v. Gore

On the night of the 2000 presidential election, November 7, major television networks announced that Democratic candidate Al Gore had won the state of Florida and predicted that Gore would be the national winner. Later that evening, they quoted Republican candidate George Bush saying the networks had been too hasty. By the next morning, all was confusion. The Florida Division of Elections reported that in fact, Bush had a margin of 1,784 votes over Gore, comprising less than 0.5 percent of the popular vote in the state, requiring an automatic machine recount. The machine recount showed Bush ahead but by an even smaller margin. The Gore campaign then sought manual recounts in Volusia, Palm Beach, Broward, and Miami-Dade Counties under Florida election procedures. The national vote total, meanwhile, favored Gore over Bush by approximately a half million voters.

With the recounts in process, Florida Secretary of State Katherine Harris refused to waive the statutory November 14 deadline for reporting vote totals. The Florida Supreme Court postponed the deadline to November 26. That day, the Florida Elections Canvassing Commission declared Governor Bush the winner of Florida's twenty-five electoral votes and hence winner of the Electoral College.

On November 27, pursuant to Florida's contest provisions, Gore filed a complaint in Leon County Circuit Court, contesting the result. The Florida Supreme Court rejected some of Gore's challenges to the results in Nassau County and Palm Beach County. But the Court upheld Gore's claim that nine thousand ballots on which the machines had failed to detect a vote for president ("undervotes") should be tabulated manually. According to the language of the Florida statute as embodied in the order of the Florida Supreme Court, a "legal vote" is a ballot on "which there is a 'clear indication of the intent of the voter.'" The court therefore authorized the circuit court to order "the Supervisor of Elections and the Canvassing Boards, as well as the necessary public officials, in all counties that have not conducted a manual recount or tabulation of the undervotes . . . to do so forthwith." The court also determined that both Palm Beach County and Miami-Dade County, in their earlier manual recounts, had properly identified net gains of 215 and 168 legal votes for Gore.

The U.S. Supreme Court granted certiorari, vacated the Florida Supreme Court's decision on December 4, and sent it back for clarification about the source of its decision. On December 8, the Florida Supreme Court ordered the Leon County Circuit Court to tabulate by hand the nine thousand Miami-Dade County ballots that appeared to have been marked but that the machine had not counted, to include certain votes in the certified vote totals for Gore and his running mate, to determine the proper number of votes to be reassigned in Palm Beach County, and to conduct manual recounts in all Florida counties where so-called undervotes had not been subject to manual tabulation. The next day, the U.S. Supreme Court granted the application of the Bush campaign for a stay of the recount and granted certiorari. Three days later (December 12), the U.S. Supreme Court halted the recount on the ground of an absence of clear rules uniformly applied and declared Bush the winner.

Rumors in Washington suggested that both Chief Justice Rehnquist and Justice O'Connor wanted to retire and hoped to retire under a Republican president. Neither did. Family members of two other members of the Court, Scalia and Thomas, worked for the law firms that represented Bush in the controversy over the elections or worked on the campaign itself.

On July 15, 2001, the *New York Times* reported that the election of President Bush might have turned on the counting of a number of illegal ballots, the acceptability of which had been determined "by markedly different standards, depending on where they were counted." This conflicted with the grounds of opposition to a manual recount stated by Florida Secretary of State Katherine Harris and eventually by the U.S. Supreme Court. The *Times* and a consortium of newspapers that examined the ballots in Florida would later conclude that had the ballots been counted in the manner that Vice President Gore sought, they would have confirmed Bush as the winner but that the result would have favored Vice President Gore had all rejected ballots been examined statewide. Correcting for illegal absentee ballots that had been counted would have confirmed Mr. Gore's victory.

Part IV

ACROSS TWO CENTURIES

★ ★ ★

The Supreme Court and
the Life of the Law

THE FINAL PART OF THIS BOOK CAPS THE CHRONOLOGICAL AC-
count of the Court's history by inquiring into the full sweep of the Court's
place in American culture and politics. First, we concentrate on the Court
itself as an institution deeply engaged in the shaping of American legal culture. How does the Supreme Court represent itself as an institution in
American life, to the legal profession, and to the public at large? This question takes us back to the very beginnings of the Republic, to the moment
when the various institutions of the federal government were first given
physical form in the buildings that they occupied and in the ceremonies
and forms of self-presentation that they adopted to show themselves off as
the authoritative institutions they claimed to be. Dress, deportment, and
the design of specialized spaces all convey information about the relative
standing of a person or an institution. All have been crucial in establishing
in the public mind a sense of the place of the Supreme Court in the web of
federal power.

Just as important are the forms and procedures adopted by the Court itself to control the performance of law before it, none more important than
the rules the Court formulates to govern how information is presented to
it. Needless to say, both the practices of advocacy and the rules that the
Court uses to govern it have changed hugely over time. Nonetheless,
throughout its history, the conventions and rituals of oral argument have
been central to not only the Court's methods of decision making but also its
public personality, its image.

For two hundred years, the Court has also played a significant role in the
greater expanse of American popular culture, both as an institution to be
observed and as a creative force in itself. It does its best to control its image there too, although with mixed results, for the proliferation of media
limits the Court's capacity to influence representation of itself outside its
own immediate precincts. Capacity to control how the Court is perceived
at any given moment is also rendered uncertain by the pervasive influence
of politics. The Court inevitably is judged politically, for so much of its imprint on American life and culture is indeed political. We conclude, therefore, by examining the question of how much political impact the Court has
and how much of that impact is intentional. Does the Supreme Court "follow the election returns"? Has it in the past? Will it in the future? In light
of the most recent events shaping perceptions of the Supreme Court's place
and influence in American life and culture, this subject seems to be the
most appropriate one on which to close.

15

First Appearances

*The Material Setting and Culture
of the Early Supreme Court*

IN ARCHITECTURAL AND CEREMONIAL TERMS, as well as in practice, parity among the three powers of government came late to the United States. One of the most startling facts of the Supreme Court's history is that it had no home of its own until 1935, some 145 years after its founding. Until President — subsequently Chief Justice — William Howard Taft took on the construction of a Supreme Court building as a personal crusade, the legislative and executive branches did not worry much about what kind of setting the Court deserved, whether in its first temporary locations in New York (1790) and Philadelphia (1791–1800) or in its ultimate destination, the new federal city of Washington, D.C., where the government moved into unfinished quarters late in 1800. Although Congress and the president had their own distinct accommodations, the Supreme Court made do with borrowed space for fourteen decades. In New York, it shared a market hall (Plate A.2); in Philadelphia, a city hall (Plate A.4). On arriving in Washington, the Court had to beg the legislature for marginal space in the Capitol building — a committee room. Eventually, rather than construct the anticipated courthouse on Judiciary Square, Congress simply handed down the Senate's cast-off chambers. In 1810, when the Senate moved upstairs to a grander new chamber, its original ground-floor room was redesigned as a vaulted, single-story courtroom inside the Senate's original, roughly semicircular walls (Plate A.6). In 1860, the Court moved to the chamber directly above, when it too was abandoned by an expanding Senate (Plate A.7).

Second-hand quarters were in some ways appropriate to the Court's modest beginnings. Historians habitually note the negligible caseloads of its first full sessions and point out that the Court did not take its irrevocable step toward claiming what would become its most important role, judicial review, until its decision in *Marbury v. Madison* (1803), thirteen years after the first call to order. Only gradually did the Court develop coequal power in a government based on the separation of powers — a conception of the judiciary that was quite unlike that of its British parent or of France, its near contemporary in political revolution. The Court's early quarters and material habits confirm its beginnings as a poor sibling of the legislative and executive branches of government, far from the institution that would settle the winner of the presidency in 2000 from its own freestanding temple on Capitol Hill.

Yet the Court's potential stature was ceremonially evident from the outset. Take, for example, the assumption, unstated in the Constitution or in statute, that the highest justice of the nation, or in an emergency, of the highest court at hand, would administer the oath of office at the president's inauguration. That the head of the executive power would take the oath before a judge was a significant departure from the practices of the constitutional monarchy and parliamentary government of Britain or of the experimental republican governments of the French Revolution of 1789.

In England, according to the authoritative eighteenth-century jurist Sir William Blackstone, the source of justice resided in the people. By long tradition, the people conferred the right to administer justice on their monarch, but because the monarch also functioned as nominal plaintiff in criminal trials, he or she could not personally decide cases. For this reason as well as practicality, the monarch appointed delegates, judges who served by royal authority and pronounced judgments in the king's or queen's name. It would have been inconceivable for a dynastic ruler to be sworn in by his own judges; the Crown did not require legitimation from a judiciary.

In France, revulsion against the personal identification of the absolutist king as the nation's source of justice made the legislatures of the revolutionary decade famously chary of granting the reformed judicial power any parity with or checks on the legislative and executive authorities, with enduring effects on the status of its post-Revolutionary courts. In the United States, by contrast, a ceremony in which the chief judge swore in the president indicated that in a governmental system based on a written constitution stipulating a high court, the judiciary possessed a unique governmental stature, the relative modesty of its material culture in the early decades notwithstanding.

With the implementation of the American separation of powers in constitutional government, the relations among the legislative, executive, and judicial branches were implicitly materialized in the physical relationships among their sites in the early federal capital cities and in the relative grandeur of their buildings. These formed what we may call a topography of power. Expedient in the established cities of New York and Philadelphia, this topography was formalized in the layout of the new federal city of

Washington. Its urban and architectural features were shaped by the major political issues consuming the Republic in its earliest years — notably, the battle between centralizing Federalists and opponents who worried that federalism might lead to the mutation of the presidency into a monarchy — and by the related ethos of republican simplicity, widely embraced to exemplify democratic practice and allay Anti-Federalist fears. Simplicity was expressed in buildings through the adoption of a chaste neoclassical style newly fashionable in Europe and associated with aesthetic restraint conjoined with social grandeur for public institutions. It inspired columnar porticos and pediments grander than the entrances to previous, domestically modeled public buildings but nonetheless simple in form and decoration. Federal authority and ceremony had to appear superior to that of its failed predecessor, the Confederation Congress. But it also had to avoid the taint of tyranny, associated with displays of luxury.

Of the primary institutions of the federal government, the legislature secured the grandest setting for its law-making responsibilities, and the executive maintained a dignified domestic profile suitable for receiving dignitaries and citizens. The judiciary was left to construct a distinctive institutional character and material presence for itself from whatever mandates it could locate in the Constitution and the Judiciary Acts of Congress. Here, we trace the initial steps in that process in order to explore, through the example of the Court's first decade, the role of material culture in its institutional life and character.

New York's Topography of Power

New York City had the privilege of inaugurating the three branches of federal government in 1789–1790 and the attendant problem of accommodating them on short order in the existing cityscape, still concentrated in lower Manhattan. The Court convened in a building facing that of Congress, each at opposite ends of the five-block-long Broad Street. A de facto hierarchy between the legislative and judicial branches of government is suggested by the marked difference in grandeur between the Exchange Building, where the Court met, at the south end of Broad Street next to Fraunces Tavern, and Federal Hall, made over for Congress from the New York City Hall, where Broad dead-ended in Wall Street. A private house was rented for the president at some remove from the public buildings.

Built by the city in 1754, the Exchange was one of several market buildings in New York (Plate A.2). It resembled the multipurpose town houses built in continental Europe from the Middle Ages, popular in English towns from the sixteenth century, and common in many of the American colonies: a two-story rectangular building signaled on the skyline by a small cupola serving as a belfry centered on its prominent roof, whose ground floor was open to its surroundings through arcaded walls and served as a market or a site for business transactions among merchants, and whose enclosed upstairs hall housed government meetings of all types, including law courts. New York's Exchange sheltered a food market on the ground floor, including butchers; the city rented out the meeting room for such commercial purposes as a coffee house and exhibitions of imported goods. Only sporadically was the upper hall reclaimed for governmental meetings, as in 1786, when it was assigned to the court of appeals for maritime cases, the only federal court established under the Confederate Congress, while the latter met at City Hall.

In 1788, in preparation for the arrival of the new federal government, the city renovated the Exchange's meeting room for government use, where the new hierarchy of federal courts would share it with the state legislature and the city's common council. Part of the job entailed expelling the most odoriferous commerce to a new market building nearby and chaining off the street to bar noisy merchants' carts during sessions.

This specialization of buildings and urban districts for single uses was part of a nationwide and European trend that contributed to a growing sense of dignity among the new federal institutions. By the beginning of the nineteenth century, law courts in Northern states were abandoning town houses in favor of specialized courthouses sited away from market districts and new city and state halls for legislative and executive use similarly excluded market use. The rise of a professionalized bar and its importance in court brought an increased formality to courtrooms and their proceedings, prompting the separation of courthouses from other agencies of government. It became common to segregate law courts from city halls and mixed-use town houses, although state capitol buildings, the local analogue to federal capitol buildings, generally continued to house all three branches of government. In 1799, New York would demolish the Exchange as obsolete, both as a market and as a public hall.

The legislators' quarters in Federal Hall were far more elegant. Completed as the New York City Hall in 1701 solely for colonial government use, combining assemblies, law courts, and offices, the building also had housed meetings of the Continental Congress and Confederation Congress, which decided that the new federal government would first convene in New York City. Hoping to wrest permanent status as the federal capital away from Philadelphia, its major competitor, the city commissioned a monumental remodeling of the building for the exclusive use of the new Congress from Pierre Charles L'Enfant, the French military engineer and architect who had cemented a close friendship with George Washington and other Federalists while a volunteer in the Revolutionary War. L'Enfant had settled in New York as an architect and would soon design the plan for a permanent federal capital agreed on by Congress in 1790 as a compromise between North and South: the central seaboard location of the new city of Washington in the federal District of Columbia.

Compared to the roughly $500 (in period currency) spent on renovating the Exchange, City Hall's renovation consumed over $50,000. The building L'Enfant inherited was a variant on the town house type represented by the Exchange: a two-story structure with large upstairs windows, an arcade at ground level, and a belfry centered on the roof. In this case, the formula had originally been adapted to strictly governmental use by reducing the usual arcade to a welcoming entranceway and flanking it by two solid, projecting wings containing assembly rooms on both floors. L'Enfant rearranged the building's interior around a Senate chamber facing south toward Broad Street and a House chamber facing north. He also aggrandized its appearance, bringing a French tradition of palacelike buildings for royal government purposes to bear on the more modest traditions of the British colonies, whose motherland had long favored domestic over institutional architecture. Most important, he filled in the central section with an evocation of a classical temple front: a pedimented two-story portico that culminated the vista up Broad and incorporated a balcony where President Washington took his oath in view of the public as well as the then nonpublic Senate. This façade competed with the most ambitious of the new statehouses, particularly Thomas Jefferson's templelike Virginia State House still being completed at Richmond, and architecturally eclipsed Philadelphia's more historically significant Independence Hall, officially the Pennsylvania State House (Plate A.3)—the early-eighteenth-century centerpiece of a new range of government buildings that would soon capture the honor of hosting the federal government until the permanent federal capital city was ready. The *Gazette of the United States,* for instance, established Federal Hall as a benchmark for American government buildings by declaring its façade "truly august" and the building "on the whole superior to any building in America."

By contrast to the Court and Congress, the executive branch was accommodated separately and less extravagantly in a house that explicitly looked like the president's home rather than an institutional headquarters. The rented dwelling doubled as presidential office and reception suite, adapting the tradition by which Europeans ruled from palace residences to a more ordinary, if decorous, residential standard. This launched the tradition of a domestic character for the White House, which incorporates but is not dominated by the president's Oval Office. What Washington's first New York quarters lacked in architectural grandeur, however, was compensated for by the exceptional pomp of his inauguration on the balcony of Federal Hall. And because no Supreme Court yet existed, no chief justice of the United States administered the presidential oath of office and affirmed the Court's presence alongside the other branches. Instead, Chancellor Robert Livingston, chief justice of the state of New York, did the honors, as he had already done for the House of Representatives. Associate Justice Cushing rather than Chief Justice John Jay would administer the oath to Washington for his second term in 1793. Only at John Adams's inauguration did the full Supreme Court first attend the ceremony as the chief justice administered the oath.

Rituals of Appearance

How a new governmental institution takes possession of its quarters offers insight into its early institutional character and standing in the balance of powers. When the Supreme Court itself first convened in February 1790, down the street, it did so with little fanfare compared to the festivities of the presidential inauguration or the bells and cannon fire that announced the first day of Congress. Chief Justice John Jay of New York was present on the day appointed in the Federal Judiciary Act of 1789, the first Monday of February, but the associate justices, convened from five other states, straggled in late, although not nearly so late as Congress at its inaugural session the previous spring. (The hardships of travel in the late eighteenth century inevitably dented all federal calendars and consequently all attempts at federal formality.) By the next day, four of the original panel of six justices had arrived, enough to constitute a quorum and permit the Court's inauguration. Because no cases were brought to the Court until its second year, however, the business before the justices was simply to launch proceedings by establishing basic rules of procedure, appointing a staff, and constituting the beginnings of a Supreme Court bar from among the applicants in attendance, followed in short order by adjournment and departure for the other obligation of the early justices: itinerant duty on federal circuit courts.

For courtroom procedure and customs, the new Court leaned on the norms immediately available, those of the states' superior and county courts, which had been variously adapted from English precedent during the colonial period and scarcely needed modification to accord with the new state constitutions. As to the appointment of a staff, here too the Court's beginnings were simple: In addition to the two officials authorized from the outset by Congress in the Judiciary Act of 1789 — a clerk of court to keep records and receive and issue court documents and a federal district marshal to keep order in the courtroom — only a crier is mentioned, and his job of proclaiming the orders of the Court soon devolved on the marshal and clerk. A reporter of the Court's decisions appeared in Philadelphia in the 1790s but not as a Court appointment. Reporting was initially a profitable publishing enterprise for the journalist who pioneered a compilation of the Court's major opinions. The office of reporter was not approved by Congress as an additional staff position until 1816, indicating the slow development of a convenient mode of reference to Court jurisprudence for those who could not attend its sessions in person.

Although substantively accurate, however, so brief and functional a description of the Court's first moments is a little deceptive. Resort to ceremony, though unostentatious, demonstrated that the Court was taking possession of a place in the topography of federal power, albeit one clearly lower in the hierarchy than Congress and the presidency. In the absence of surviving descriptions, tradition suggests that the justices would have been met by an escort of the local bar and other dignitaries at the lodgings rented for them or after they had first gathered at John Jay's house. A procession would have formed, led by the already appointed federal marshal of the New York State district (the equivalent of a sheriff at the state level or in England), whose job included serving the Supreme and Circuit Courts whenever they met in his district. With his tipstaves wielding their staves, or emblems of office, the marshal would have escorted the justices through the city streets to the courtroom, with the bell in the Exchange's cupola announcing their arrival. Such an adaptation of the more elaborate English tradition used in county courts to greet royal judges on circuit and to open the Crown court in Westminster is recorded for the opening of the Supreme Court's second year in Philadelphia and was already observed by some state courts.

In such processions, judges were normally identifiable by their archaic garb, based on traditions adopted in the distant European past, with only modest periodic updates and emblematic of the inherently conservative role of justice. Legislators and presidents simply wore the formal long coats and knee breeches, preferably homespun, with the fashionable wigs or natural hair-dressing styles of the day. American judges, like their English counterparts, wore robes over their civilian clothing. But as this Court had not yet acquired its own distinctive costume, the justices are reported to have appeared in civilian black coats. Not until its 1792 term in Philadelphia did the Court's own custom-ordered robes finally arrive.

As debate over the extent of new federal prerogatives encompassed judicial clothing, the delay may have been just as well. The justices' European counterparts were bound by rules of dress, but Congress left it to the Court to determine its own costume, limited only by the inherent conservatism of the judiciary. What the Court chose — probably a black robe aggrandized by a broad red facing exposed along the opening and voluminous red sleeves, originally trimmed in ermine — was well received on first appearance by Philadelphia observers who praised its "elegance, gravity and neatness" (see Plate A.1). But it came under fire from others for a gaudiness redolent of inappropriate authority. Perhaps in consequence, the original robes (of which John Jay's survives in the Smithsonian Institution and both Jay's and Paterson's were represented in portraits dated to about 1794–1795) were replaced prior to 1802 with plain black robes.

Multiple meanings had accreted around judicial costume and its colors. The black Supreme Court robe adopted by 1802 had deep roots, probably derived from clerical vestments and expressing a similar withdrawal from worldly interests, as required for fair judgment. Some British commentators have linked the color to mourning, attributing the black robes of royal barristers to the costume they were ordered to wear to the funeral of James II in 1685 and never relinquished. Americans, on the other hand, deemed black suitable for republican judges because it repudiated the Redcoats, their monarch, and the pomp of monarchy. Red was generally traditional for European high-court judges on ceremonial occasions and was associated with the monarch, who originally bestowed royal clothing on his judicial delegates. The taint of livery informed criticism of the first U.S. Supreme Court robes, as well as of state supreme court benches choosing something even worse: entirely red robes. The Pennsylvania Supreme Court was severely criticized in Philadelphia in 1785 for doing just that.

Nonetheless, compared to the British Lord Chancellor's ceremonial garb of ermine-edged crimson robe, hood, and mantle, abundantly trimmed in gold braid, his American counterpart, Jay, certainly displayed republican simplicity. And the justices eschewed from the outset the cumbersome, shoulder-length full-bottomed wigs English judges have worn for formal appearances ever since such appurtenances came into general fashion in the late seventeenth century. William Cushing, the most sartorially minded justice, preemptively abandoned the wig he had worn in his previous position as chief of the Supreme Judicial Court of Massachusetts for an ordinary fashionable wig of the day, probably with short side curls and a queue, after being mocked in the street when he wore it into town on first arrival. He did not need the prompt of Jefferson's remarks about "monstrous wigs" that made judges "look like rats peeping through bunches of oakum."

The First Courtroom

The procession affected the justices as well as the public, ritually transporting them from the shared public realm into the judicially policed zone of the courtroom, open to the public yet set apart, like a secular counterpart to a church, from everyday space, time, and rules of behavior. Its destination, the Exchange, stood like an island at the south end of Broad Street, a freestanding building with a gable end facing Federal Hall.

No records of the layout survive, but period habits provide a basis for a speculative reconstruction. The upstairs courtroom filled the building's width and much of its length but left fifteen feet for a stair hall and entrance at one end. Descriptions record a roomy rectangle, thirty feet by sixty feet, with a vaulted ceiling ballooning up under the gambrel roof. A high ceiling would have helped ventilate a crowded room, but the vault hindered acoustics; preference eventually settled on high but level ceilings in later, purpose-built courtrooms. Inside the courtroom, the procession would have moved through a hierarchical sequence of increasingly restricted zones, in a ritual of assuming possession and control. Entering through the public door likely centered in one end wall, the justices would have processed through the area open to public visitors to the "bar," or railing, that sequestered the well of the courtroom, an area coming to be restricted to lawyers, officers, and other actors in court proceedings. Leaving the public behind as they penetrated the bar by one of two side gates, the justices and lawyers then parted company. The latter found seating in the well, on long benches or in Windsor chairs around a single table; the justices mounted the steps at one end of a tall platform or bench lining the back wall. Behind a shared paneled desk, they would have taken seats in order of precedence. In a typical courtroom, these layers of social space were additionally signified by the gradation of finishes from homely, plastered white walls at the public end to carved wainscoting inside the bar and carved paneling for the bench and for the wall that formed the judges' backdrop.

The elevated bench facing the entrance gave the justices both honorific visibility and practical visual control of the assembly and maintained the ancient monarchical and feudal custom that underlies the practice of a high table for dignitaries in a banquet hall. Given a maximum of six justices for the courts meeting here, the bench was probably straight, whereas platforms and benches for Virginia courts, for instance, designed for as many as two dozen judges, would extend partway down the hall's side walls in a U-shape, following either the older, plainer tradition of squared-off corners or the more fashionable curvilinear tradition established in English county courts in the latter seventeenth century and adopted in some of the colonies. The semicircular bench, regardless of its length, was the more honorific form because it evoked associations with the similar apsidal shapes of church sanctuaries and ancient Roman law courts in secular basilicas. But this part-time courtroom was likely installed on the cheap. We do not know whether the justices enjoyed the distinction of individual, cushioned armchairs rather than sharing a single, continuous bench — both were current in American state courts — but a common platform would have indicated their corporate character.

Chief Justice Jay's seat could have followed the protocol for the presiding judge in the grander colonial courts: a "great chair" occupying the center of the platform, generally raised a step above the other chairs or flanking benches for associate judges, furnished with an honorific canopy or pediment and crowned with a coat of arms, which traditionally specified the royal authority in whose name the court ruled. The judicial great chair had come about as a substitute for the throne, as befitted the king's judicial delegate, and it shared in the throne's relationship with the religious tradition of bishops' seating, expressing the king's consecration at his coronation. It had counterparts in the presiding officers' seating in the British Parliament's Houses of Lords and Commons, in the elected assembly and governor's council of the colonial governments, and in the reformulated bicameral legislatures in the states and federal government, where it proved far more enduring than in courtrooms. In Federal Hall, for instance, both the octagonal House of Representatives' chamber and the smaller, rectangular Senate chamber enthroned the presiding officer on a platform (crowned in the Senate by a canopy as well as the national arms) set against the end wall of the room facing the members, who sat at desks on a level floor below him. Because New York's provisory courtroom doubled as a legislative chamber, a special chair seems likely, additionally singled out by the insignia that would have been attached to the chair, or more likely hung on the wall directly above: the new national coat of arms featuring the eagle that is still emblazoned on U.S. passport covers. The economical assimilation of the symbolism of the great chair into the decoration of the courtroom's rear wall seems to have rapidly become standard in American courtrooms, as shall be seen in the Philadelphia courtrooms to which the Supreme Court next moved.

Authority and Asymmetry

The question of precisely whose authority underlay the Court's verdicts was contentious. Was authority vested in the Court itself, the president, Congress, or in the name of the American people? As the Judiciary and Process Acts of 1789 left the matter vague, Jay determined, with the consent of his associates, that the Court would issue writs in the name of the U.S. president. The decision was announced as one of the rules of procedure established by the Court in its first session and immediately stirred anxiety among Anti-Federalists, such as the young lawyer DeWitt Clinton, nephew of New York's governor. Clinton wrote his brother: "tho' apparently unimportant, [it] smells strongly of monarchy. . . . A federal process beginning with 'George Washington by the grace of God &c.['] will make the American President as important in Law forms as the British King." Nevertheless, the Jay Court decision endured: The Court still holds that "all process of this Court issues in the name of the President of the United States."

The chief justice's own status relative to his associates was signified by his central position as well as by his rightful title in the Constitution as "Chief Justice of the United States." The title was the lesser of these markers, for President Washington simply commissioned Jay as Chief Justice of the Supreme Court, setting a precedent in practice. Only after the Civil War did Chief Justice Chase obtain a reaffirmation of the Constitutional title in statute, arguing that the Constitution's wording made the chief justice the leading justice of the entire judiciary at federal and state levels, not merely of the unique Supreme Court. The order of seating, however, placed Jay clearly at the head of the Supreme Court. As they do today, and as their British counterparts had long done, the associate justices sat to the chief justice's right and left, alternating sides in order of seniority, defined by the date of their commissions and, in case of overlapping date, by seniority in age. Thus, a portrait of the complete bench, including Justice Rutledge, who never attended a Supreme Court session, and the late appointee Justice Iredell, would have shown, from left to right: Iredell, Wilson, Rutledge, Jay, Cushing, and Blair.

From an architectural perspective, the total number of six justices was a ceremonial handicap. It meant that the chief justice could not dominate the bench from a central seat, even though it was desirable for him visibly to culminate the bench at its center and to terminate the view down the courtroom's central axis from the public entrance. Nor could he function visually as the figure who gave the Court an odd number of votes, thus capable of breaking a tie in a court that handed down its decisions in individual, or seriatim, form for its first decade. Such symmetry was a centuries-old mainstay of the classical aesthetic tradition. Just as he would give a building's portico an even number of columns in order to frame a central opening that constitutes the building's main entrance and processional axis, a classically trained architect might well have expected to provide an odd number of seats in order to align the visual and processional axes of the courtroom with its furnishings and enhance its grandeur. Federalist politicians, however, expediently adapted the colonnaded temple as an architectural metaphor for stability and unity in their need for persuasive symbols. Despite their inconveniently odd number, the original group of states was widely represented as thirteen columns gradually coalescing into a single colonnade, breaking the classical principle but dominating federal iconography, which favored thirteen of many emblems, such as the arrows clutched in the eagle's talons on the national coat of arms. In his letter of appointment to each justice, Washington famously likened the new federal court to the single "chief pillar on which our national government must rest," replacing the architectural ensemble of the temple with the single element of the column.

The number of justices derived, of course, from a geographical rather than an architectural sensibility: the assignment of two Supreme Court justices to double as itinerant judges staffing each of the three federal circuits into which the original state territories were organized. This provision of the Judiciary Act of 1789 formed the basis for the eventual growth of the Supreme Court to a visually more satisfactory bench of nine in 1837, when each justice was assigned to one of the new total of circuit courts, reflecting the growing expanse of the Union and its member states. Although that number has never been considered significant in itself and the total has fluctuated (for political as well as geographical reasons) between even and odd numbers over time, nine ultimately became the norm, as seen today, even after the justices were relieved of circuit court duty in 1911.

The Role of Layout

Courts and Legislatures

The physical layout of most American courtrooms diverged significantly from that of legislative chambers. In a legislative chamber, members sat at desks arrayed in semicircular rows centered on the rostrum, usually on a level floor, although the Senate's and House of Representatives' chambers in Washington were given stepped floors and seating. To this day, an elevated rostrum crowned with governmental symbols facing the members arrayed in radial arcs of desks remains the norm for the layout of American legislative chambers at state and national levels, whatever the room's shape or ceiling type. Derived from the ancient Greek and Roman theater with stepped seating, this layout was adapted for the new revolutionary legislatures in France at the same period, under the watchful eyes of such American statesmen as Jefferson, always attentive to architectural arrangements. Charles Goodsell's recent survey of American state legislatures shows that Americans generally favor level seating in segmental arcs of desks instead of the semicircular stepped seating of the French chambers, and often locates them within a rectangular room rather than a semicircular one, deflating the theatricality but not the democratic rationale of the French model. In its partial emulation of the French model, the American legislative chamber deliberately eschewed Britain's parliamentary layout, in which stepped benches for opposing parties face one another across a largely empty aisle that runs the length of a rectangular chamber and culminates in a great chair for the presiding officer at one end. Although the British parliamentary layout was obviously inappropriate for a court-room, the American and French legislative layout, derived from the theater, more closely approximated courtroom traditions, in which both parties ap-peared side by side to face the bench.

An American can generally expect to find two major differences be-tween a legislative chamber and a courtroom — that is, between the major public theaters of activity for the two government branches meeting in reg-ular public sessions. Both emerged in the late eighteenth century. The first depends on the orientation of a usually rectangular room. When intended for a legislature, it is normally laid out along its short axis, which forms a central aisle from public entrance to the rostrum, with the members' seats arrayed in wide arcs stretched along the length of the room to either side of the aisle. When a courtroom, it is normally laid out along the long center-line, which forms an extended, ceremonial axis of vision from the public entrance to the bench, punctuated by the series of spatial zones already de-scribed for New York, sequenced from the most public to the most official and limited type of access: the first for public spectators; the next limited to the parties, attorneys, and witnesses, who in a trial court are flanked along one side wall by the box for the trial jury; a narrow but deferential void; and finally the bench, with the clerk close at hand. Separating the public from the well of the court is a railing or bar that shares its name with the members of the bar who dominate its benches or pairs of tables and chairs. Restricted access to the well is afforded by a central gate, or, during the interval when the central spot along the inside of the bar was occupied by a prisoners' dock, two gates at either end. Undersheriffs or constables guard these entrances, while a marshal (in federal courts) or sheriff (in state courts) may guard the steps to the bench. The clerk once sat at a table directly below the bench on the central axis but now occupies a desk to one side of the bench at a lower level.

The second difference is in shape: A legislature's furniture typically forms a semiellipse, with the members' seats arrayed in shallowly curved lines facing the rostrum set against a flat wall. When a pre-1960s court-room uses a semicircular form, it is for the bench (with or without an apse-shaped wall behind it), which faces furniture arranged in generally straight rows for the parties and the public. Curiously, the distinction between the two institutional layouts was disregarded for the U.S. Supreme Court dur-ing its long stay in the Capitol building, in the interests of economically tucking it into the shells of former Senate chambers (Plates A.6 and A.7). In the courtrooms at the Capitol, the bench, like the legislative rostrum, occu-pied the flat side of a semicircular chamber. Only in the purpose-built courthouse opened in 1935 did the courtroom regain an explicitly judicial character.

Courts and Courts

After 1790, although still early in the Supreme Court's history, a distinction began to emerge between two types of courtrooms adapted to different procedures. One is the appellate courtroom (the primary role of the Supreme Court), which considers appeals based on briefs or oral arguments by the parties' attorneys together with the written record from the trial court, ruling on problems of law rather than factual evidence. This type of courtroom does not need equipment for presenting factual evidence in court, such as provision for witnesses and their cross-examination, and for the citizen jury charged with judging that oral evidence. In the other type, the trial courtroom more familiar to courthouse visitors and watchers of film and television, the symmetry of the room is distorted to accommodate a jury box along one side wall at right angles to the bench and a witness stand next to the bench, where judge, jurors, and parties can all observe the speaker. The distortion leads attorneys to skew the ceremonial direction of their speech in order to address simultaneously the jury to one side and the judge at the end: Their focus is diffused. By contrast, in a bench trial in a trial court and in appellate courts hearing arguments, the symmetry of the room and its proceedings are maintained since opposing attorneys take turns speaking directly to the bench from a centrally placed lectern.

Because in New York and Philadelphia the early Supreme Court shared its provisory meeting places with lower courts, and because the Supreme Court and its state counterparts expected to hear occasional cases under original jurisdiction in jury trials, its early courtrooms used a trial layout, ignoring the distinction between trial and appellate court layout that later became significant. Eventually, however, the Court would delegate its rare cases of first instance to a commissioner (now a special master) to collect evidence. By the time the Court received its own custom-designed building in 1935, its courtroom layout could not be mistaken for a trial court's. The room was unequivocally designed for the bench to hear oral arguments and announce decisions. The enhanced hierarchy and longitudinal orientation of the courtroom as compared to the legislative chamber, and the symmetry of the appellate court's organization around a long, central axis stretching from the citizens' entrance to the chief justice, rather than the trial court's complexity, gives the supreme theater of judicial authority a uniquely formal character among the governmental powers.

At the Supreme Court's inauguration in 1790, the multipurpose American courtroom was on the cusp of developing the more specialized, pro-

Plate B-1 "The President's Dream of a Successful Hunt," by Clifford Berryman, captures the distinction between "good" and "bad" trusts embraced by Theodore Roosevelt and implicit in the Supreme Court's 1911 adoption of the "rule of reason" (whether corporations became large through fair or unfair competition) to guide antitrust adjudication.

Plate B-2 Carrie Buck, unsuccessful plaintiff in the compulsory-sterilization case *Buck v. Bell* (1927), with her mother. The case is notorious for Justice Holmes's curt majority opinion endorsing eugenics.

Plate B-3 Justices Brandeis, Van Devanter, Taft, Holmes, Butler, Sanford, and Stone view a model of Cass Gilbert's design for the new Supreme Court building, ca. 1929.

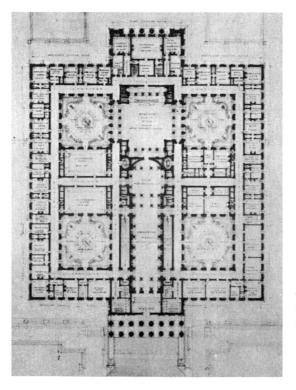

Plate B-4 The floor plan for the Cass Gilbert Supreme Court.

Plate B-5 Presentation drawing of the Cass Gilbert design for the court-room of the new Supreme Court building, by J. Floyd Yewall, 1931.

Plate B-6 Franklin Delano Roosevelt, played by George M. Cohan, addresses the nation as the Supreme Court listens, in a scene from *I'd Rather Be Right* (1937).

Plate B-7 Planning a greatly enlarged Supreme Court, FDR seeks a Public Works Administration grant from Harold Ickes, Secretary of the Interior.

Plate B-8 Leopold Dilg (Cary Grant), Supreme Court nominee Michael Lightcap (Ronald Coleman), and Nora Shelley (Jean Arthur) at breakfast together in a scene from *Talk of the Town*.

Playe B-9 Accused Nazi saboteur Richard Quirin on trial before a special military commission (November 1942).

Plate B-10 The Supreme Court reacts adversely to the Truman Administration's assertions regarding presidential powers in the *Steel Seizure* case.

Plate B-11 In front of the U.S. Supreme Court building after the announcement of the decision in *Brown v. Board of Education*, May 17, 1954. From the left: George E. C. Hayes, Thurgood Marshall, and James Nabrit, Jr.

Plate B-12 The Warren Court, 1962–1965 ("History's Warren Court"). From the left: Tom C. Clark, Bryon R. White, Hugo L. Black, William J. Brennan, Jr., Chief Justice Earl Warren, Potter Stewart, William O. Douglas, Arthur Goldberg, John Marshall Harlan. Goldberg was succeeded by Abe Fortas in 1965.

DIVISION OF CORRECTIONS

CORRESPONDENCE REGULATIONS

MAIL WILL NOT BE DELIVERED WHICH DOES NOT CONFORM WITH THESE RULES

No. 1 -- Only 2 letters each week, not to exceed 2 sheets letter-size 8 1/2 x 11" and written *on one side only*, and if ruled paper, do not write between lines. *Your complete name* must be signed at the close of your letter. *Clippings, stamps, letters* from other people, *stationery* or *cash must not be enclosed* in your letters.

No. 2 -- All *letters* must be addressed in the *complete prison name* of the inmate. *Cell number*, where applicable, and *prison number* must be placed in lower left corner of envelope, with your complete name and address in the upper left corner.

No. 3 -- *Do not send any packages without a Package Permit.* Unauthorized *packages* will be destroyed.

No. 4 -- *Letters* must be written in English only.

No. 5 -- *Books, magazines, pamphlets,* and *newspapers* of reputable character will be delivered *only if* mailed direct from the publisher.

No. 6 -- *Money* must be sent in the form of *Postal Money Orders* only, in the inmate's complete prison name and prison number.

INSTITUTION ____ CELL NUMBER ____

NAME ____ NUMBER ____

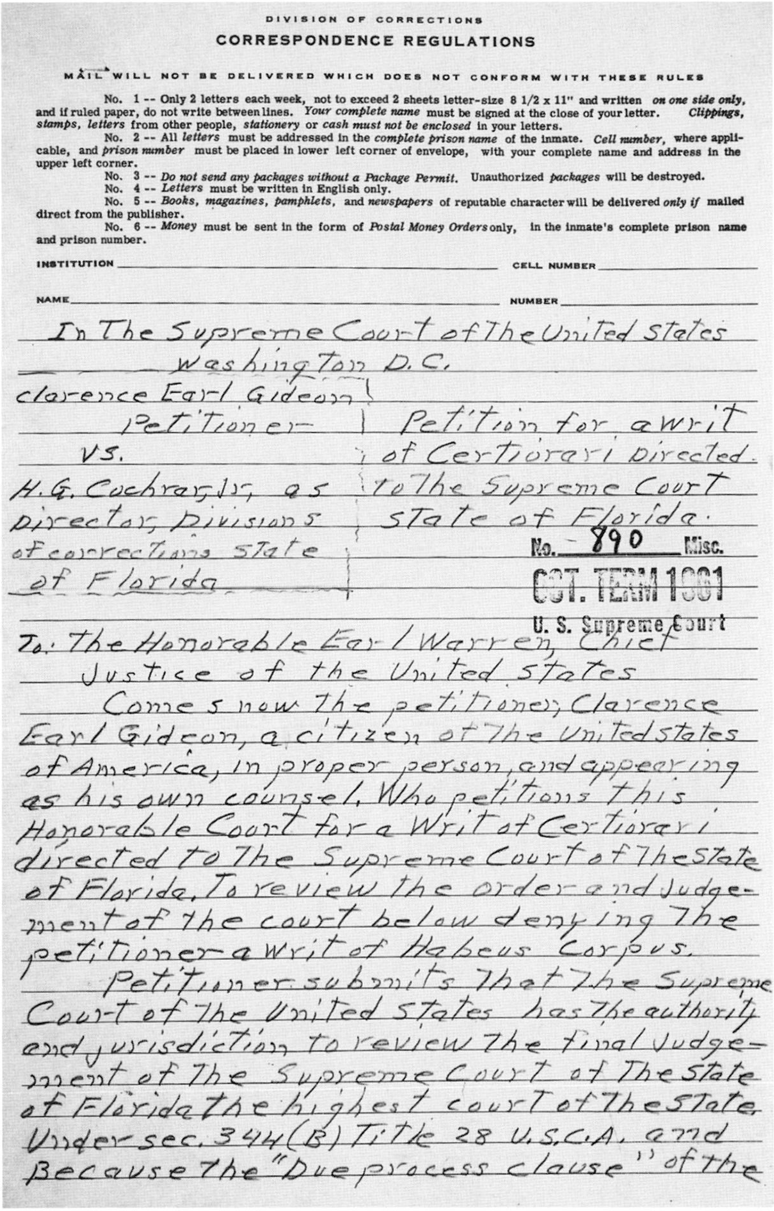

In The Supreme Court of The United States
washington D.C.

clarence Earl Gideon
Petitioner
VS.
H.G. Cochran, Jr, as
director, divisions
of corrections state
of Florida

Petition for a writ
of Certiorari Directed
to The Supreme Court
state of Florida.

No. 890 Misc.

OCT. TERM 1961

U. S. Supreme Court

To: The Honorable Earl Warren, Chief
Justice of the United States

Comes now the petitioner, Clarence Earl Gideon, a citizen of The United states of America, in proper person, and appearing as his own counsel. Who petitions this Honorable Court for a Writ of Certiorari directed to The Supreme Court of The State of Florida, To review the order and Judgement of the court below denying The petitioner a writ of Habeus Corpus.

Petitioner submits That The Supreme Court of The United States has The authority and jurisdiction to review The final Judgement of The Supreme Court of The State of Florida the highest court of The State Under sec. 344(B) Title 28 U.S.C.A. and Because The "Due process clause" of the

Plate B-13 The first page of Clarence Earl Gideon's handwritten four-page petition to the Supreme Court for a writ of certiorari, beginning the case that would become *Gideon v. Wainwright* (1963).

Plate B-14 The "classic" Rehnquist Court, 1994–2004. From the left: Antonin Scalia, Ruth Bader Ginsburg, John Paul Stevens, David H. Souter, Chief Justice William H. Rehnquist, Clarence Thomas, Sandra Day O'Connor, Stephen Breyer, and Anthony M. Kennedy.

Plate B-15 James Dale (center) and his attorneys, Ruth Harlow and Evan Wolfson, hold a press conference following the Supreme Court's decision in *Boy Scouts of America v. Dale* (2000).

fessional layout outlined above. Two major factors encouraged formality. First, the growing influence of proficient attorneys representing parties in court led to the sequestration of the well for the bar from the public benches at the back of the room. Taken over by a bar jealous of newly claimed prerogatives, the well was off-limits to lay citizens except for those sitting on grand and trial juries, in boxes sized to their unequal numbers at either side of the well. Eventually, grand juries would abandon the courtroom for special chambers of their own, leaving only one jury box along one side of the well. The second factor was the late adoption of the familiar adversarial trial procedure entailing cross-examination of witnesses by opposing counsel in criminal and civil matters. A development of the later eighteenth century in England, adversarial process permeated U.S. courts in the decades leading up to the Civil War. Only in the early nineteenth century did courtrooms begin to acquire specially designated witness stands and docks from which witnesses and defendants in custody would speak, often placed at the back of the well.

Eighteenth-century courts had few specialized spaces. Witnesses, litigants, and even defendants in custody would simply make their way as needed through the crowd in the well to stand before the clerk's table to be questioned directly by the judges on the bench looming above them. In colonial and rural state courts, public spectators gathered in a crowd at the back of the courtroom but also invaded the benches in the well and sometimes even availed themselves of seating on the bench. By the early nineteenth century, however, the shift to greater formality was under way. Strict policing of the gates of the bar created a hard line of authority, which in turn led to the provision of bench seating for the public near the public entrance, sometimes supplemented by a public balcony above.

Whereas in trial proceedings an often boisterous public began to submit to the professional demands of the law around the turn of the century, appellate hearings were inherently more decorous, attracting fewer visitors because their more technical business was tedious to laymen. Those drawn by curiosity to the first Supreme Court sessions would likely have been associated with government office or its reportage, apart from the occasional crowd drawn by a magnetic attorney such as Daniel Webster.

It was probably not until the late nineteenth or early twentieth century that the space of the court again changed decisively, the dock disappearing in favor of presenting defendants in custody unfettered in the courtroom and the witness stand moving to a position adjoining the bench. By the second quarter of the nineteenth century, however, the shift from judicial examination to cross-examination by counsel had brought about an additional change of furnishing in the well, from long rows of benches, or seating around three sides of one large table, to the pairs of tables we see today, which visibly separate the two sides and render obvious to all just which side is examining a witness. The design for a state trial courthouse in the widely used pattern book of the Massachusetts builder Asher Benjamin, first issued in 1806, shows the early courtroom layout with long benches for the bar flanked by a pair of jury boxes and the new features of a dock against the enclosing bar and a pair of witness stands located between the bar and the dock. In contrast, the now classic American trial court layout familiar to aficionados of courtroom dramas is exemplified at the Cook County Criminal Courthouse in Chicago (1929), used as the set for the trial in the film *The Fugitive* (1993). It shows the subsequent shift to a single box for trial jury (the grand jury having moved to its own quarters); the built-in witness stand and clerk's desk flanking the judge's bench; two tables for the two parties, with the defendant seated with defense counsel whether in custody or free; and a bar separating the public seating area from the well with a central opening that aligns with and intensifies the central longitudinal axis of vision from the public entrance to the bench. Further, it includes two features eventually also adopted by appellate courts, including the Supreme Court: the paired tables for the parties, the lack of adversarial process notwithstanding, and, by the time of the 1935 Court building, the proliferation of professional doorways from a private zone of offices at the judicial end of the courtroom, enabling justices to wait for the courtroom to fill before magically appearing from behind the bench, in lieu of the old procession through a shared entrance.

Of these developing features, the well of the New York Exchange's courtroom, which also served the inferior federal circuit court for hearing cases under original jurisdiction, was probably equipped with long benches or a single table with peripheral seating for the bar, flanked by jury seating. Yet because the room was simultaneously used for morning legislative sessions of the State House of Assembly and afternoon sessions of the Court, we can surmise that, apart from a combination bench/rostrum against the end wall and a railing to sequester the public at both kinds of sessions, the furnishings may have lacked such fixed features as jury boxes.

The Oath of Office

Like British royal judges at the time, the justices arrived having already taken their oaths of office privately, in this case, before a single inferior judge. That meant that they strode into court with the authority to assume the bench immediately, although they carried the proof in their letters of commission from President Washington, on whose versos the judge administering their oaths had recorded completion of those acts. The clerk of the New York Supreme Court of Judicature, standing in for a day until a Supreme Court clerk could be appointed, began proceedings by reading aloud their commissions so as to publish their appointments and enter them into the Court's minutes. By contrast, the judges of the national system of trial courts newly established in France in 1791 were sworn in publicly in their courtrooms by the city council, which sat at the judicial bench to administer the oaths to the judges in the well, then exchanged places with them and vowed in turn to obey the court's verdicts, a reciprocity recorded in a pair of paintings depicting the Judicial Oath and the Vow of the People and subsequently hung in the courtroom. Similarly, France's new national high court took its inaugural oaths of the same year collectively in open court from delegates of the legislature and the constitutional king.

What permitted the judicially autonomous, private installation of the American Court was apparently the Senate ratification of the president's nominations, coupled with the premise of loyalty to a stable, written constitution. Greater public formality developed after 1850: a public ceremony to swear in each new justice in the Supreme Court chamber and then welcome him to his seat on the bench, following a complementary oath of loyalty to the Constitution administered privately by the chief justice or in a public ceremony by the president at the White House, as the president prefers. But the president rarely attends the Supreme Court's ceremony or opening session, for he is liable to be ignored in the name of judicial autonomy and impartiality, as President Kennedy discovered to his dismay when he attended Justice Arthur Goldberg's installation in 1962.

Despite his closeness to John Jay, Washington did not attend the first session in 1790; rather, he hosted a state dinner for the justices two nights later. Nonetheless, the press reported the courtroom as "uncommonly crowded" at its first session, drawing federal legislators (including aspirants to the Court's new bar), the mayor and other city officials, the federal district judge who would work with the Supreme Court on circuit duty, the new federal attorney general, the state supreme court and its grand jury, members of the state bar, and "a number of respectable citizens."

Beginning the Docket in Philadelphia

The federal government's move to Philadelphia for the interim of December 6, 1790, to November 1800 required adapting procedures tentatively embraced in New York to a different set of buildings in a different city — the largest in the nation with the greatest political standing as the leading host of the confederation assemblies. These buildings comprised a symmetrical, coordinated row of state, county, and municipal headquarters facing

Chestnut Street between 5th and 6th Streets (Plate A.3). Their drawback for federal government was that the complex was dominated by the State House, in whose ground-floor Assembly Hall the Declaration of Independence had been proclaimed and the U.S. Constitution drafted, but which Pennsylvania, whose government had grown to comprise the characteristic bicameral state legislature, would not yield to Congress. Instead, the federal legislature and judiciary were relegated to two smaller, symmetrical buildings intended to frame the State House ever since its completion in 1735 but not built until the city needed to accommodate its federal guests. These were the City Hall (1789–1791) — today called Old City Hall — situated to the east of the State House (on the left in Plate A.3) and the County Courthouse (1790–1791, extended 1793) to the west of the State House, presently called Congress Hall in honor of its first occupants (on the right in Plate A.3). The row of legislative and judicial headquarters was appropriately out of view of the typically Georgian brick house rented for Presidents Washington and Adams, facing Market Street a block away (now demolished), preserving the decorum of the separation of federal powers in its fragile first decade. In hopes of persuading the federal government to renounce construction of its new capital city and remain in Philadelphia, Pennsylvania extended Congress Hall in 1793 and began a grander executive mansion. But those modest efforts hardly compared with the plans being laid for Washington, D.C.

The early-eighteenth-century State House set the character for the complex. A two-story rectangular brick building crowned with a central feature (a cupola, replaced by a rear stair tower capped in the 1790s by a temporary low belfry and steeple), it was linked on either side by arcades to small wings for public records and offices. Its lack of an arcaded ground-floor market was consistent with the government's decision to move from the central commercial district to the quieter fringe of town. A grand version of a fashionable house of the time, its design was based on the English Georgian style disseminated through the pattern books of English architect James Gibbs. The similarity of the 1730s State House and the house rented for the president typified the relative lack of differentiation between public and domestic buildings in the colonial period.

The original layout of the State House expressed the hierarchy of colonial government. As customary, the governor's council met in a chamber on the upper level, expressing its superior power in the colony — a balance of powers reconceived at independence. Downstairs, on either side of a central hall beyond the main entrance, were two parlorlike chambers roughly forty feet square, the eastern one for the colony's highest court and the western for the unicameral colonial legislature. Apparently symmetrical, these rooms embodied a fundamental difference in public accessibility, comfort, and implicit status for the two institutions. The courtroom, much frequented by the public, was ever open to the hallway through a broad triple arcade, and no effort was made to heat the unenclosed room, whereas the assembly, which probably met in closed session, boasted the privacy and warmth afforded by doors and two fireplaces.

In the 1770s and 1780s, the Pennsylvania government made the Assembly Hall available for continental and constitutional meetings, moving its legislature to smaller quarters upstairs, and giving the courtroom to the state's new Supreme Court. Only in 1789, after considerable pleading, was the courtroom also enclosed, with stove heating added in 1791 (although today the arches have been reopened in a reconstruction of the room's appearance from 1778 to 1789). Of the federal branches, only the judiciary ever occupied the State House, using the newly enclosed State Supreme courtroom for its February 1791 term pending completion of City Hall.

The matched pair of brick buildings intended for the framing corner lots, rectangular structures with pitched roofs that were eventually built after 1789, necessarily defer to the State House but also boast some of the new honorific features associated with public buildings by the end of the century: the round-headed, or compass, windows that had come to be favored over the century for churches and courthouses; and projecting, central sections crowned with pediments to frame the main entrances — modest, columnless variants on the temple façade L'Enfant had given New York's Federal Hall and the full-blown versions Jefferson was popularizing through his Virginia Capitol.

Most interesting of all are their floor plans. The major chambers on each level fill the rear of the buildings, where, unlike the State Supreme Court, the south end walls open out into polygonal two-story bays, under arches constituting honorific frames for the judges and the mayor and Senate president who presided over their respective courts and assemblies. This feature is consonant with the semicircular apse that terminated many Virginia courtrooms and had come into wider use by 1789, although the use of an architectural frame (the arch spanning the bay), in lieu of the customary decorative markers of authority such as the canopy or the tabernacle frame and coat of arms on the rear wall, is a variation later used to frame the Supreme Court bench (and the presiding officer in the legislatures) in vaulted chambers at the Capitol in Washington, D.C. The ground-floor courtroom at City Hall, roughly fifty feet wide by forty feet long, excluding the bay, nominally belonged to the Mayor's Court (a criminal jurisdiction presided over by the mayor with two aldermen) but has been reconstructed to represent the period from August 1791 through 1800 when it was shared with the federal Supreme Court, circuit, and district courts. The end bays were a novelty compared to the flat walls of the Assembly Hall and the

Supreme Court at the State House, whose fancy pilasters and paneling centered on a tabernacle frame that formed the honorific backdrop for the presiding figures seated at an elevated judicial bench and desk, respectively. In effect, the federal legislature and judiciary both adapted their habits to Philadelphia quarters based on a judicial rather than a legislative norm — the opposite of what happened in Washington, D.C., where both moved into the Capitol Building designed for the legislative branch, and the Supreme Court made do with essentially legislative layouts for its next 135 years. The comparison of the Court's quarters in Philadelphia and Washington thus offers the opportunity to see what difference this circumstance made for the Court's capacity to establish an architectural character and ceremonial ambience specific to its unique role as the nation's high court.

In both its Philadelphia locations, the State Supreme courtroom and the Mayor's courtroom, the U.S. Supreme Court shared quarters with lower trial courts. The windows behind the bench, especially in the south-oriented Mayor's courtroom, would have had Venetian blinds to moderate the sunlight on which the courts depended, in combination with candlelight, for reading documents. The benches themselves had to be adapted to accommodate six individual chairs for the Court's large number of judges relative to the state supreme court and other courts of the region (Plate A.4).

It was here in the Mayor's courtroom that the Supreme Court launched its substantive appellate work. Simultaneously, however, the Court began to exercise its range of original jurisdiction as set out in the Constitution. Most of the latter cases were handled by equity procedure, entailing bench decisions. But three — *Georgia v. Brailsford et al.* (1794), *Oswald v. New York* (1795), and *Cutting v. South Carolina* (1797) — followed common-law procedure requiring jury trials, creating a mixed profile for the nascent institution. Inconceivable in today's Court, jury trials technically remain an option for the few original-jurisdiction cases still in the Court's purview. The major reason they have been abandoned is that the cases tried by jury in the 1790s fell into a category that so offended the vanity of the newly sovereign states — suits between a state and citizens or subjects of other states or foreign powers — that the first Court decision of this type, *Chisholm v. Georgia* (1793), in which the Court found against the state, precipitated the first amendment after the Bill of Rights, which revised the Constitution to eliminate that category of suits. Once adopted, in 1798, the Eleventh Amendment was immediately and formally accepted by the Court, putting an end to the likelihood of further jury trials presided over by the bench. By the time of its move to Washington, the Supreme Court assumed the character of a rarified appellate court and, once the federal district court moved to separate quarters in 1822, shed its trial furnishings.

The early trials in Philadelphia contrast with the only public trial of original jurisdiction ever held in the present-day Supreme Court building, in preparation for the Court's decision of *New Jersey v. New York* (1998), concerning rights to Ellis Island. It was organized as a bench trial presided over by a special master delegated to conduct the fact-finding and make a recommendation to the Court regarding a decision; it was scheduled during the Court recess; and it was pointedly located in one of the Court's two reception rooms, *not* in the Supreme courtroom itself. Since at least the early twentieth century, special masters have managed the trial aspects of the few surviving categories of original jurisdiction (usually disputes between states) outside the walls of the Court. The modern Supreme Court takes care to project a unified character based on its unique power of judicial review.

It is intriguing to imagine the character of the Court as originally established, with inflammatory jury trials making use of the early trial furnishings now reconstructed in both Philadelphia courtrooms. Appellate and bench trials as well as jury trials needed some of the furnishings seen here: the clerk's desk below the bench and to one side, and the marshal's or sheriff's desk nearby; the single table shared by the opposing parties' counsel positioned in the center of the well, suggesting that cross-examination had not yet come into use; and the bar, which normally limited the public to the area near the entrance, a zone expanded in the Mayor's courtroom by an upstairs balcony, from which its photograph was taken. Jury trials, by virtue of requiring the jury to be able to determine fact from oral testimony in court, required jury seating sequestered from the public and with a good view of the attorneys and witnesses, provided in the box to one side of the well. According to the reconstruction, the jury benefited from an early instance of an elevated witness stand set below the bench and to one side of it, hypothetically reconstructed on the basis of English models. If indeed originally present, it probably faced the jury box in the Mayor's courtroom as it does in the State Supreme courtroom so that, in *Oswald v. New York*, the jury would have been able to observe the faces of the two witnesses. In the case of the Pennsylvania Supreme Court, the well is flanked by a pair of boxes with stepped seating set toward the public end of the courtroom and used both for grand juries and for the public, since this courtroom lacked a balcony. Finally, both reconstructed courtrooms include a freestanding dock for defendants in custody at the public end of the well, also modeled on English precedent; more recent research indicates that American docks were usually attached to the center of the bar, as in Benjamin's model plan.

When the justices were not assembled at the brief biannual terms in their official locale, circuit duty brought them into contact with still ruder sites for dispensing justice — the full variety of ordinary trial courthouses, of course, but also more basic substitutes, such as tavern and boarding house parlors. An efficient use of judges, circuit duty more importantly exposed the justices to the nation to which they were responsible — particularly, from the perspective of this essay, its material circumstances.

Republican purpose was served by the modesty of accommodations for circuit courts and their justices, much as the variety of quarters in the early capital cities had offered the Court multiple potential incarnations as the ultimate dispenser of justice. But circuit duty was arduous. Lengthy periods of travel far from family deterred a number of potential appointees, and justices viewed the very crudeness of accommodations as compromising their prestige and dignity. Circuit riding's hardships enhanced the attraction of other political positions, contributing to instability in the early bench (in the shape of Jay's and other defections) and its low prestige relative to the other branches.

The Supreme Court would coalesce only after it moved to Washington, D.C., when the public began to see the institution headed by Chief Justice Marshall as dignified, corporate, and cohesive — the character that has been so carefully nurtured ever since. Marshall took this cohesiveness to its greatest extreme, leading a British visitor to observe that Marshall personally delivered the opinions for his Court with "the three judges on either side gazing at him more like learners than associates." It was the simplicity of accommodations in early Washington, not unlike those of circuit riding, that, ironically, helped establish that corporate identity. Marshall persuaded his associates to board together without their families, creating a hothouse climate of negotiation that generated a new custom of largely unanimous decisions, replacing the seriatim decisions that had publicly exhibited the individualism marking most American judicial practice. Here began the unusually intense cult of secret deliberation that has come to characterize the Court's unique role of constitutional judicial review, one that the more recent phenomenon of multiple dissents and concurrences has not dislodged.

Conclusion

Throughout its early years, we have seen, the Court's position in the topography of federal power was marginal. It would remain so even though the move to Washington inaugurated a more coherent construction of institutional character. In location and form, the Court's quarters in the Capitol belied its autonomy and its development toward parity with the other powers, architecturally compromising its image and work. This predicament was replicated on the larger stage of the federal city. Initial plans postponed provision for the judiciary, presuming an eventual building on Judiciary Square, to one side of the monumental district delimited by the Capitol and the President's House. Not until the early twentieth century, when the City Beautiful movement's McMillan Commission plan (1902) attempted to reinstate and expand L'Enfant's neoclassical vision for the Mall and its frame of public buildings, was the Supreme Court's absence from the city plan reconsidered and a scheme hatched for a separate new building, distinct from the lower courts at the Old City Hall on Judiciary Square. In 1910, President Taft appointed Cass Gilbert a charter member of the Commission of Fine Arts, which still guides the development of Washington's public buildings and grounds. In the late 1920s, Gilbert and Taft together conjured the final appearance of the Court in its own building, completed in 1935.

The building's design was unabashedly traditionalist and monumental for its time, a decade when debate was just heating up over bringing to the Mall the avant-garde International Style of architecture vigorously promoted by New York's Museum of Modern Art. Monumentality in the mode of the Capitol and White House was Gilbert's means to atone for more than a century of neglect and to cope with a site that denied the Court the role of third partner triangulating the balance of powers in Washington's map. For that reason, President Hoover urged the site ultimately given to the Jefferson Memorial, but Chief Justice Taft insisted on the block just east of the Capitol's Senate wing, next to the Library of Congress. Although Gilbert failed to interest his clients in an alternate site that lay several blocks further east on a direct processional axis with the Capitol (thereby escaping both architectural competition with the enormous library building and a subordinate topographic relationship to the Capitol), the architect nonetheless managed to endow the relatively small Court with the impressive visual scale due a coequal government power. Not only does the building look larger than it is, but its interior was lavishly spacious for its limited staff— just in time to accommodate a burgeoning bureaucracy and, at a moment of stressful debate over the Court's proper role, to awe increasing numbers of tourists with the long processional and visual axis from the building's temple portico through a sequence of vast, imposing spaces to the center of the bench that dominated the courtroom at the building's heart (Plate B.4). So superhuman was the building's scale that one of the justices reputedly declared that the black-robed brethren would resemble nine beetles in the Egyptian temple of Karnak (Plate B.5). Conceptually, however, the courtroom resembles less the sanctuary of a temple than a reliquary—a preciously wrought, openwork case, framed on all four sides by open colonnades in which the relics, constitutional rights, remain alive in the interpretations of the justices. This combination of public permeability with sequestration from the everyday realm has set a model for high courts regardless of architectural style, as evidenced by the modernist High Court of Australia (1980).

As it happened, the culmination of the initiative to enshrine the Court in an imposing locale of its own in Washington's topography of federal power coincided with one of the sharpest conflicts in the nation's history over appropriate relations among the institutions in that landscape. We are given to political explanations for the Court-packing crisis of 1936–1937, but why not consider the influence of material culture on politics? Perhaps the cranes slowly stacking blocks of marble on Capitol Hill throughout the first half of the 1930s were a daily reminder that an institution hitherto accommodated under the legislative dome was about to graduate, spurring an impulse to define the Court's new "place" before geographic and architectural autonomy led the Court to settle on its own definition. Defying the commonplace that institutions acquire grand buildings only in their dotage, the material settings of the federal branches have, sometimes counterintuitively, weighed into the balance of powers throughout the nation's history.

—Katherine Fischer Taylor

FOR FURTHER READING AND RESEARCH

Our understanding of the material culture of the Court's first decade depends on R. P. Reeder, "The First Homes of the Supreme Court of the United States," *Proceedings of the American Philosophical Society* 76 (1936), 543–596; and the research of the Independence National Historic Park staff in restoring the government buildings at Philadelphia, particularly Daniel Sharp, *Supreme Court Chamber of Independence Hall: Furnishings Plan* (Philadelphia, 1979); and Lee Nelson, *Old City Hall, Independence National Historical Park, Pennsylvania: Historic Structure Report, Architectural Data Section* (Washington, D.C., 1970). It will be reshaped by the new books by Carl Lounsbury, *The Courthouses of Early Virginia* (Charlottesville, Va., 2005); and Martha McNamara, *From Tavern to Courthouse: Architecture and Ritual in American Law, 1658–1860* (Baltimore, 2004), in combination with Clare Graham, *Ordering Law: The Architectural and Social History of the English Law Court to 1914* (Aldershot, England, 2003). William C. Allen, *History of the United States Capitol: A Chronicle of Design, Construction, and Politics* (Washington, D.C., 2001), is an authoritative, up-to-date account of the Capitol building, including the Supreme Court's quarters, by a staff member of the Office of the Architect of the Capitol.

For the Supreme Court Building of 1935, there is as yet no full-scale study. The Supreme Court Curator's office has mounted well-researched exhibitions in the building. The most helpful publications are Cass Gilbert, Jr., "The United States Supreme Court Building," *Architecture* 72 (December 1935): 301–327; Allan

Greenberg and Stephen Kieran, "The United States Supreme Court Building, Washington, D.C.," *Antiques* 128 (October 1985), 760–769; the photographic monograph by Fred J. Maroon with historical text by Suzy Maroon, *The Supreme Court of the United States* (New York, 1996); and the astute architectural appreciation by Paul Byard, "Representing American Justice," in Barbara Christen and Steven Flanders, eds., *Cass Gilbert, Life and Work: Architect of the Public Domain* (New York, 2001). Geoffrey Blodgett, "The Politics of Public Architecture," also in *Cass Gilbert, Life and Work*, offers an account of Gilbert's appointment as the new building's architect. On the institutional and ceremonial functioning of the Court, which shapes its material culture history, see Joan Biskupic and Elder Witt, *The Supreme Court at Work* (Washington, D.C., 1997); and Robert Schnayerson, *The Illustrated History of the Supreme Court of the United States* (New York, 1986). A starting point for the Court's share in the changing balance of powers is Biskupic and Witt, *The Supreme Court and the Powers of the American Government* (Washington, D.C., 1997). The major histories cited in other chapters contain pertinent anecdotal references to the Court's material culture, but a synthetic, analytic history of the relationship between its architectural accommodation and its work and representation remains to be written.

16

Advocacy Before the Supreme Court

1791 to the Present

O RAL ADVOCACY has always been a critical component of the Supreme Court's process for deciding cases (Plate A.4). The cry of the marshal to open a session of the Court is a modern reminder of centuries-old traditions: "Oyez, oyez, oyez, all persons having business before this Honorable Court shall draw nigh and give their attention, for the Court is now sitting. God Save the United States and this Honorable Court." Since the Court's inception, advocacy has changed dramatically in style and content but in one aspect has remained constant. Of the three great branches of American government, the Supreme Court is the only one in which, on a regular basis, an ordinary citizen can stand directly before leaders of government and publicly plead a case. Unlike the modern presidency, in which even press conferences have become relatively infrequent occurrences, or joint sessions of Congress, which are reserved for rare occasions, the Supreme Court sits in open, public session fourteen weeks out of every year, three days per week, one hour per case, except in rare circumstances in which the time for argument is lengthened.

Early Practices

It was not always that way. At the outset, the Court's process for deciding cases was rather haphazard. Not long after the Court's first session, uncertainty over the rules of practice led the attorney general to make a formal request of the justices for guidance as to procedures the bar should follow. In 1791, the Court responded with a set of rules advising that counsel should generally adhere to the practices of the King's Bench in England. In retrospect, this early accommodation reflected expediency rather than considered judgment. By longstanding tradition, advocates at the King's

Bench presented their material orally to the court. Advocates in England routinely read aloud to the members of the court even the opinions from which appeal was taken, before proceeding into the relevant facts, points of law, and authorities on which their cases were built. Judges had little or nothing to prepare in advance but would sit listening patiently for days as advocates presented the two sides of a case. The rationale, still largely in place in England today, was that proceedings should be open for all to see. If a judge knew nothing about a case save what the advocates said about it, the parties and public alike could be assured that no furtive influences had infiltrated the process.

By formally embracing King's Bench practices, the Supreme Court of the United States set itself on an early course in which arguments could — and did — last for days on end. Very little is known about the course of arguments in the 1790s, but notes available from a few cases indicate that, although they occasionally asked questions of counsel, the justices mostly listened to the advocates' presentations for hours without interruption. When the parties made clear that they had said all they wanted on the case, the Court ended the argument. In some celebrated cases, such as the Marshall era's *McCulloch v. Maryland* (1819) and *Gibbons v. Ogden* (1821), advocates' oral arguments lasted for a week or more.

The golden era in Supreme Court advocacy began after John Marshall became chief justice. Under Marshall's leadership, the Supreme Court took on much greater importance in American life. As a result, the most talented lawyers in the country were drawn to practice before the Court. Some of the greatest lawyers in American history — Thomas Addis Emmet, William Pinkney, William Wirt, Daniel Webster, and a series of attorneys general, including Caesar Rodney and Roger Brooke Taney — earned distinction at the Supreme Court bar. In the most important cases of the 1810s and 1820s, those advocates routinely were involved. Even among that list, Daniel Webster stood out as perhaps the Court's most skilled and successful practitioner. Webster argued a number of landmark cases in the Court's history, notably *Dartmouth College v. Woodward* (1819), *McCulloch v. Maryland* (1819), *Gibbons v. Ogden* (1821), *Cohens v. Virginia* (1821), and *Osborn v. Bank of the United States* (1824). His only loss in a major constitutional case during that era was *Ogden v. Saunders* (1827). These cases represented the high-water mark of the Supreme Court under the leadership of Chief Justice John Marshall. In them, the Court announced a series of principles that have governed the constitutional structure of our system of government ever since. During the period of the Marshall Court, the Supreme Court's rulings ensured the primacy of the Court in construing the Constitution and of the national government with respect to the states.

Because these issues were so critically important to the new nation and because there were so few precedents on which to rely in making arguments, advocates drew on whatever resources and inspirations they could muster in framing their presentations. An advocate might invoke history, Roman law, the Bible, or legal developments in the colonial period in attempting to persuade the justices. That kind of advocacy obviously required a considerable breadth of knowledge, even if some of the information conveyed by the advocate was only partially germane to the issues before the Court.

It was not uncommon for the premier Supreme Court advocates also to hold prominent positions in public life. Daniel Webster, for example, represented Massachusetts in the U.S. House of Representatives from 1823 to 1827 and in the Senate from 1827 to 1841 and 1845 to 1850. Although he argued some of his greatest cases in the short interval between his service as a U.S. representative from New Hampshire from 1813 to 1817 and his assumption of a congressional seat from Massachusetts in 1823, he also argued significant cases while serving in Congress, such as *Mason v. Haile* (1827) and *Charles River Bridge v. Warren Bridge* (1837). Webster's legal causes established him as a proponent of a strong national government, a position he espoused in numerous public orations as well. Webster often took ideas he had developed in his Supreme Court arguments and used them in his public speeches. Those speeches, in turn, identified him as a proponent of points of view that he was then retained to argue in Supreme Court cases.

The eloquence of such advocates as Webster and Pinkney made the Supreme Court a popular forum for the entertainment of Washingtonians. The great advocates drew large audiences to the Court. For hours, an audience would sit in rapt and appreciative attention as a lawyer argued his cause. There is even some evidence that advocates played to the crowds, particularly when the justices themselves were not asking many questions.

By the 1830s, however, the Court was tiring of extended orations and likely resented advocates' using arguments before the Court as a forum for their own personal aggrandizement. Chief Justice John Marshall observed that the "acme of judicial distinction" was "the ability to look a lawyer straight in the eyes for two hours and not hear a damned word he says." In 1833, the Court issued a rule calling for the submission of cases on "printed arguments" where counsel thought it could accommodate the parties and save expenses. Thus began the process of filing written briefs in the Court. The practice was not observed consistently until 1850, when a new rule required that printed briefs be submitted before the Court would hear argument in a case. A rule adopted the previous year, meanwhile, limited counsel to two hours for making an argument without the special leave of

Court. In combination, the two rules augured a significant change from the English oral tradition of legal advocacy. Henceforth, the Supreme Court would begin to develop the process that it uses today, with increasing emphasis on the written submissions of the parties.

Practice in the Court was slow to adapt to those changes in the rules, as the *Dred Scott* case illustrated. Argued first in February 1856 and again the following December, the case involved some of the most important members of the Taney Court bar: Reverdy Johnson, Montgomery Blair, Henry S. Geyer, and George T. Curtis. Notwithstanding the reputation of the advocates and the importance of the issues — but perhaps reflecting the style of advocacy in the times — the briefs submitted in the case were not especially comprehensive. Blair's initial brief for *Scott* ran to only eleven printed pages. After the case was set for reargument, Blair filed two more briefs, one of only eight pages and the other of forty.

As the bar was adjusting to this evolution in the way cases were argued to the Court, the government's advocacy was also changing in a fundamental way. From the moment of the Court's creation, the attorney general had been not only the titular head of the Supreme Court bar but also one of its most frequent advocates. Even though the first attorney general, Edmund Randolph, was lured to the office by George Washington with the promise that he could practice law in his spare time (he was paid only half of what other cabinet officers were paid), the reality was that attorneys general soon were overworked.

The Creation of the Office of Solicitor General

By the Civil War, the federal government's litigation in the Supreme Court was so extensive that the government was paying outside counsel thousands of dollars each year to argue its cases in the Supreme Court. Such advocates, even if skilled private practitioners, could not be expected to keep the government's institutional interests always at heart, particularly when such interests might conflict with the arguments most likely to prevail in the particular case. Nor were all the advocates particularly skilled in representing the United States in the country's highest court.

Moreover, some executive departments with extensive litigation, such as Treasury, tended to take litigation positions that were not always consistent with positions developed by the attorney general for other parts of the government. The endemic fractiousness of such a state of affairs came into full public view in 1867, when the attorney general and the secretary of the Treasury appeared on opposite sides in a case known as *The Gray Jacket* (1867). The Court expressed its dislike of the situation in stark terms, holding that when the United States is a party represented by the attorney general, no other officers for the federal government can take an opposing view. Henceforth, the attorney general would hold the authority to determine the government's litigation position in the Supreme Court.

The Court's decision in *The Gray Jacket* underscored the need to provide the attorney general with assistance in representing the government in litigation. In 1870, after literally decades of pleading by successive presidents and attorneys general of all parties, Congress finally enacted a law that created the Department of Justice. As part of that enactment, Congress provided for the establishment of "an officer learned in the law, to be called the solicitor-general."

To an important extent, the creation of the Office of the Solicitor General was one of the most profound developments for advocacy and practice in the Supreme Court's history. Unlike many countries that do not centralize the government's advocacy function before their highest court, the solicitor general is able to formalize a position on behalf of the federal government in a way that maximizes consistency and the government's broader interests. As a frequent and repeat player, the solicitor general can also build credibility and respect among the justices. And because of the experience gained from frequent appearances before the Court, the solicitor general and the lawyers in the office develop skills that are appreciated by the justices and advantageous to the government.

The first solicitor general, Benjamin Bristow, set a high standard for excellence as an advocate. In his first two Supreme Court terms as solicitor general, Bristow argued forty cases, either alone or in tandem with another attorney from the Department of Justice (including, in a number of cases, the attorney general himself). Bristow worked assiduously to prepare for oral arguments and presented them in an unadorned style, stripped of rhetoric and honed to the particular issue directly presented. His successor, Samuel Phillips, earned a similar reputation during his long tenure as solicitor general. The directness with which Bristow and Phillips argued on behalf of the government made their arguments more efficient; their success as advocates led the way for a change in advocacy style away from the more dramatic rhetorical presentations of earlier times.

Early on, the attorney general designated the solicitor general to be the principal officer in charge of formulating the government's position in the Supreme Court. That power has bred enormous respect throughout the government but a respect earned through the skill and dedication of the lawyers in the office. It is routine for lawyers from interested departments and agencies to convene in the solicitor general's office to discuss a case of widespread importance to the government, with the solicitor general acting sometimes as referee between conflicting positions that other officials might wish for the government to take.

In 1879, during the period when Bristow and Phillips were acknowledged leaders of the Supreme Court bar, the Court admitted its first female member, Belva Lockwood, to practice before the court. In 1880, Lockwood became the first woman to argue a case in the Supreme Court. Notwithstanding her trailblazing role, few female advocates appeared before the Court again until the twentieth century, when female government lawyers began to appear before the Court with regularity. Those lawyers played a critical role in breaking down gender stereotypes that until then had made Supreme Court advocacy an almost exclusively white-male club. Beatrice Rosenberg, for example, argued approximately thirty criminal cases before the Supreme Court in the middle of the twentieth century. Helen Carloss earned plaudits from Justice William O. Douglas for her skill as an advocate for the government in tax cases from the 1920s to the 1940s. Those attorneys helped to pave the way for Ruth Bader Ginsburg's historic efforts as a private counsel in six landmark gender-equality cases in the 1970s.

Twentieth-Century Developments

Increasing diversity among advocates in the Supreme Court was not the only important development affecting oral argument in the twentieth century. By 1911, the rules of the Court provided that each side would have one and a half hours for oral argument (down from two hours per side), with the petitioner granted the opportunity to open and close the argument. This further compression of time in which to present arguments reflected structural changes occurring in the federal court system. In 1891, Congress had enacted the Evarts Act, which created the circuit courts of appeals as an intermediate tier of courts between the district courts and the Supreme Court. The expectation, since fulfilled, was that those courts would siphon off a large number of cases from Supreme Court review. Prior to the enactment of the Evarts Act, the Supreme Court had a backlog of 1,190 cases, meaning that oral arguments sometimes occurred years after cases had been docketed and the parties had submitted their briefs to the Court.

The creation of intermediate appellate courts helped the Supreme Court to redress that backlog and also enabled the parties to further refine their presentations so that the Supreme Court could address fewer, and more discretely focused, issues in the case. Although those dynamics might have encouraged the Court to keep the time for oral argument at two hours per side, the decrease in time allowed the Court to exert greater control over its docket. In some cases, the Court used that flexibility to increase the time allotted for argument; in others, in which the circuit court of appeals had already comprehensively addressed the issues, the Court further decreased the time for argument to forty-five minutes per side.

For a decade, the Court followed the practice of deciding somewhat ad hoc how much time to set aside for oral arguments. In the 1920s, the Court formalized its process by assigning cases to either a "regular" or a "summary" docket. Cases on the "regular" docket were allotted one hour per side for argument, with no more than two counsel per side being allowed to argue. Cases on the "summary" docket were given thirty minutes per side, with only one counsel per side presenting argument. Interestingly, the rules still allowed — as they had in the 1830s — that if one party chose to rest its submission on the briefs, the opposing side could nonetheless present oral argument. Such occurrences, however, were rare.

By the New Deal era, with the Court sharply divided on many issues of great constitutional importance, oral argument was changing in a more profound way, beginning to resemble the style of today. Although it occasionally expanded time for argument, the Court increasingly used the limited time available to ask questions of counsel. Over the eight decades since 1850, the practice of filing written briefs had slowly taken hold, with the result that justices could read voluminous submissions in preparation for arguments.

The transformation of oral argument from extended prepared speech to question and answer was by no means complete in the 1930s, but the trend was well-enough established to be clear in some of the most important constitutional cases of the era. In *Helvering v. Davis* (1937), for example, the Court addressed the constitutionality of the Social Security Act's imposition of a tax on employers and employees so that funds would be available for the payment of old-age benefits by the government. Although he was in charge of the Department of Justice's Antitrust Division, which had no formal interest in the case, Robert H. Jackson was selected to defend the government's position because of his reputation within the government as a skilled advocate. Those qualities were necessary, as the justices peppered Jackson with question after question. Justice Douglas would later describe Jackson's "piercing look over his spectacles" as he argued with "greater intensity, precision, and force" than any other advocate of his time.

Unfortunately, few mid-twentieth-century advocates could match Jackson's skill. Justices continued to complain — sometimes publicly — about the quality of the advocacy before the Court. Part of the difficulty was of their own doing. As the justices became more active in questioning advocates, the arguments themselves became much more difficult to deliver coherently. The skill set of the advocate had to evolve to stay abreast of the changing dynamics of oral argument. Instead of simply preparing a set speech, the advocate had to master the case to be able to answer questions with tact and insight. The mental agility necessary for justices and advocates alike made the oral argument a much more interactive exercise.

In addition to the compressed time, the composition of the Supreme Court had a great deal to do with the changed dynamics of oral argument. In *Helvering*, for example, Justice Harlan Fiske Stone virtually cross-examined Robert Jackson. Justice Felix Frankfurter was also renowned for his frequent questions, a function, perhaps, of his ease with teaching in the Socratic style as a professor at the Harvard Law School. Frankfurter's relentlessness drew criticism from within the Court itself. Justice Douglas wrote in his memoirs, published after Frankfurter's death, that "some of us would often squirm at Frankfurter's seemingly endless questions that took the advocate round and round and round." Indeed, a sign of the other justices' views of Frankfurter's tendencies may be gleaned from the celebrated *Youngstown Sheet & Tube Co. v. Sawyer* (1952) — the *Steel Seizure Case*. Even though Justice Frankfurter was in the middle of a question to the government's counsel as the time reached 4:00 PM, the normal hour for adjournment, the other justices are reported to have simply exited the bench.

As the justices became more active in their questioning, the purposes of oral argument began to shift appreciably. That dynamic proceeded apace into the last third of the twentieth century, when questioning from the bench completely dominated oral arguments. Rather than preparing set speeches that a lawyer could hope to deliver with little interruption, the advocate had to be nimble, quick of mind, and totally immersed in the details of the case.

There were important exceptions to the trend. Proceedings in the *Steel Seizure Case*, for example, bear more resemblance to arguments in the nineteenth and early twentieth centuries than to the later era. The case was argued in 1952, in the midst of the Korean War, and involved a question of surpassing constitutional importance: whether the president could order the government to seize steel mills and keep them open in the face of a labor strike, on the ground that the steel was needed to support the war effort. Although allotted three hours for argument by a special order reflecting the importance of the case, John W. Davis made an opening presentation that consumed less than half of that time. Only Justice Frankfurter asked Davis a question, to which Davis replied that he would defer until a more convenient time in his argument. As it turned out, Davis never did answer Frankfurter's question. (By contrast, only in rare circumstances in the past twenty-five years have advocates requested — and been granted — an opportunity to defer answering a question. The justice would insist on an answer, and the advocate would be well advised to provide it.)

When Solicitor General Philip Perlman rose to defend President Truman's seizure of the steel mills, the justices were quite active in asking questions for more than two and a half of his three hours allotted for argument. Whereas Davis's argument resembled the set-piece oratorical style of arguments of old, Perlman's reflected the newer tendency of the justices to ask multiple questions. Unfortunately for him, and the government, those questions were highly skeptical of the president's authority to exert control over the nation's steel mills at issue in the case (Plate B.10).

The Court also actively questioned counsel in the series of five cases, argued seriatim, that became famous as *Brown v. Board of Education* (1954). In *Brown*, the Court took the opportunity of hearing cases from various states and the District of Columbia to assess the constitutionality of segregation from a far more comprehensive standpoint than would have been possible in a single case. All those cases, in fact, had been brought by plaintiffs represented by the NAACP's Legal Defense Fund, whose general counsel was Thurgood Marshall. Marshall had orchestrated a litigation strategy that focused on convincing the Supreme Court to strike down racial barriers by bringing before the Court factual situations that would best illustrate the various principles counsel would urge the Court to establish. Marshall's organized advocacy strategy enabled him and his colleagues to press those cases with the facts and circumstances best suited to obtain rulings that would optimize the desegregation struggle. He wished to avoid pushing in the lower courts cases that were less likely to provide the compelling circumstances that would maximize the chance for victory on appeal. The *Brown* cases also, of course, provided a rare opportunity to showcase the skill of attorneys of color (Plate B.11).

The success of Marshall's litigation struggle caused other groups to emulate the Legal Defense Fund's tactics. Litigation campaigns emerged to promote gender and other racial equality, to advance fair housing, and to attack the constitutionality of the death penalty.

Further Restrictions on Time Allotted to Oral Argument

All these developments were occurring at a time of increasing pressure on the Supreme Court's docket. The Court addressed the crisis by formalizing a further reduction in the amount of time allotted to argument. By the last third of the twentieth century, arguments of thirty minutes per side had long become the norm in more than 80 percent of the cases argued in the Supreme Court. The Court achieved that outcome by designating more and more cases for its "summary calendar." Because the designation became so common, the Court changed the rules in 1970 to conform to the practical reality it was creating through management of its docket. Each case would now be allotted thirty minutes per side for argument. In exceptional cases, a party could request additional time. That schedule has continued to the present day.

The compression of time in Supreme Court arguments has invariably heightened the pressure on counsel to make their points succinctly and precisely. Since the 1970s, argument has become dominated by the quick thrust and parry of question and answer. The triumph of that dynamic marks the fundamental change in the nature of advocacy in the Supreme Court from days-long orations that could fill hundreds of printed pages. In the vast majority of cases today, a Supreme Court advocate is fortunate to be able to utter three sentences before being interrupted with a question.

A product of the compression of time over the years has been to place even greater importance on the written briefs. Under the rules, each party may submit a written brief of up to fifty pages, with petitioner getting the opportunity to file a twenty-page reply brief. The justices study those briefs carefully before the oral argument, taking notes, noting questions, and discussing the case with their law clerks. The justices also review the judicial opinions being appealed, the pertinent precedents in the area, and other authorities that can inform the Court's decision.

The written briefs set out the basic information about the case, such as the basis of the Court's jurisdiction, the facts that have given rise to the lawsuit, a statement of the case, and the arguments in support of the party's position. Depending on the nature of the case, those arguments can focus on the text and structure of a statute, a description and recitation of key precedents, and the policy reasons why that party should prevail. The best briefs tend to be tightly structured, closely measured analyses that offer the Court a substantial wealth of information from which to decide the case. Briefs should give a cogent but balanced statement of the facts, legal context, and procedural history of the case. Briefs should then address the merits by offering a theory of the case that first explains why that party should prevail and by then addressing why the Court should reject the other side's position.

The arguments themselves can be quite difficult to formulate. A case may turn on a very fine textual distinction, such as the difference in statutory provisions governing robbery and larceny between one containing only the word *takes* and another using the phrase "takes and carries away." Advancing arguments about those differences may take the advocate into the history behind the use of particular language at common law, the intent of Congress in incorporating certain words into the statute, the structure of the statute as a whole, and the intent of Congress as reflected in committee reports, hearings, and floor statements. The Court also will be sensitive, in varying degrees, to the policy rationale behind the rule adopted by Congress.

Many constitutional cases pose special challenges because of the rich history of the development of constitutional law in the United States and the many possible points of comparison among various situations that might instruct the Court on what the proper rule should be. In briefing and arguing a constitutional case, the advocate is ever mindful of analogies. Not only are analogies helpful because the precise question at issue does not contain an on-point precedent (if it did, there would of course be no need for the Supreme Court to review the case) but also because the justices are reassured when a rule being advocated is like one in a closely comparable situation they have already decided.

Cases involving the Fourth Amendment, for example, provide especially fertile ground for arguments drawn from analogies. That amendment, which protects the people from illegal searches and seizures, is implicated in encounters between law enforcement officials and members of the public every day throughout the country. Practical problems give rise to litigation. Can the police order a driver out of the car at a routine traffic stop? The Court has held the practice permissible, on the ground that the officer's interests in guarding against possible harm outweighs the privacy interests of the driver in staying in the car. What about passengers? Over a dissent arguing that the Constitution requires passengers to be treated differently, the Court has held that passengers may also be ordered out of the car during a routine traffic stop, on a similar rationale: The safety of the officer(s) at the scene outweighs the privacy interests of the passenger. But myriad practical issues arise from those holdings. If the passenger wants to walk away, would it be constitutional under the Fourth Amendment for the officer to say that the passenger must stay at the scene? What if the officer wanted to force the occupants of the car to lie spread-eagled on the ground? Would that be constitutional?

Those kinds of hypothetical situations are relatively easy to avoid answering in a brief, but they become the fodder for many Supreme Court arguments, as the justices seek to understand the logical extensions and outer limits of a party's position. Even the best briefs cannot answer all the questions that naturally will arise in the Court's consideration of the issues. Sometimes an advocate writes a brief deliberately to avoid taking a position on a particularly difficult point.

Oral argument provides an opportunity for the Court to address such issues. The justices pose hypothetical questions probing whether certain situations are analogous to better understand how the rule being advocated may properly be cabined. The justices also detect when a brief seeks to avoid addressing an issue that may be of interest when the Court is considering how to write the opinion in the case. They can put the advocate on the spot during the oral argument to provide an answer intentionally omitted from the briefs. The most powerful briefs tend to minimize intentional avoidance of difficult issues by offering a scholarly treatment of the issues (and logical corollaries) posed by the case.

The use of oral argument as a means of ferreting out answers to difficult questions about the case necessarily has altered the importance of oral argument for the Court and the objectives the advocate tries to achieve. The best advocates appreciate that a persuasive presentation in the briefs will more often than not be the determining factor in the case. In those situations, oral arguments involve fewer questions about the facts or record and more questions about the logical implications of the rule being advocated. If persuaded that the party's argument is correct in the situation presented in the briefs but otherwise is objectionable outside that context, the Court may issue an opinion expressly limiting the reach of the holding to simply the situation presented by those facts. Conversely, if the justices are satisfied that the principle underlying the proposed holding is sound, they may feel less constrained in issuing a more expansively worded opinion.

Rarely do the justices discuss the cases among themselves prior to oral argument. Rather, the argument itself becomes the first opportunity for the justices to glean what each thinks about the case, their questions signaling their views and areas of possible concern. Because the justices will meet in conference within days of the argument to make a preliminary vote on the case, the argument becomes a kind of preconference for the justices.

That tendency increased after William H. Rehnquist became chief justice in 1987. During Warren E. Burger's term as chief justice, justices were said to complain about the long, unfocused conference discussions on cases. Although only the justices themselves attend the conference and are scrupulous about maintaining confidences, word has filtered out that Rehnquist maintains such a tight control on the conferences that the justices do not produce real dialogue in the sense of exchanging views and debating the nuances of a case. Rather, conferences in the Rehnquist era provide each justice with an opportunity to state views about a case, without substantial give and take. Because the conferences provide few opportunities for real debate, justices now ask questions not only to learn the responses from counsel but also to elicit responses (through other questions from their colleagues on the bench) that may shape the views of another member of the Court. When that dialogue occurs in its most extreme form, a justice will pose a question to obtain a particular response from counsel. If, in providing that response, the advocate gives an answer another justice finds objectionable, that justice in turn will pose a question to obtain a clarification that may cause counsel to retract an earlier answer. The unprepared attorney can get batted back and forth between several justices and completely lose control over the argument.

To be helpful to the justices, counsel must be attentive and flexible in presenting argument. Justices can and do ask questions about a range of matters: the record, precedent, the party's positions. Supreme Court justices also frequently ask hypothetical questions that explore the outer limits of the party's theory of the case. Those types of questions test the implications of the legal principles by probing how that principle would be applied in other factual contexts. Those questions often come at a rapid clip — in some cases, as frequently as an average of three per minute during a thirty-minute argument. As Justice Ruth Bader Ginsburg has written, "oral argument, at its best, is an exchange of ideas about the case, a dialogue or discussion between court and counsel." But that exchange can become an intense experience for the advocate, who must find a way to allay the justices' concerns in just a sentence or two.

Preparation for Oral Argument

In preparing to argue in the Supreme Court, the best advocates heed the wisdom of Robert Jackson, himself one of the finest Supreme Court advocates of the mid-twentieth century and a Supreme Court justice: "When the day arrives, shut out every influence that might distract your mind. . . . Friends who bear bad news may unintentionally distract your poise. Hear nothing but your case, see nothing but your case, talk nothing but your case. If making an argument is not a great day in your life, don't make it; and if it is, give it everything in you."

Preparation for a thirty-minute argument in the Supreme Court may take weeks. The advocate will engage in quiet study of the briefs and master the record. Case upon case must be read and learned, statutes analyzed, and a vast array of other materials mastered. Because the advocate knows going in that questions will be at the forefront of the argument, preparing answers becomes a principal focus of preparation. The best advocates anticipate the vast majority of the questions the justices ask, diligently prepare answers, and deliver them seamlessly while simultaneously developing an argument that contains a broad theme that is reiterated and emphasized during the course of the argument. The best advocates also know and stress the key points that develop their case affirmatively, as well as the most persuasive responses to the other side's arguments. As Justice Ginsburg has noted, an advocate should remain "alert to opportunities to use a question to advance a key point." Thus, in the hands of a skilled advocate, a question that poses a criticism of the advocate's position can be turned into an opportunity to make an affirmative point.

To develop that kind of skill requires not only assiduous preparation but also practice. Because the ability to field difficult questions has become such a focal point of modern Supreme Court argument, most advocates now appearing before the Court conduct at least one moot court or practice session prior to the argument. In that moot court, other attorneys or former judges prepare the case as would a justice, reading the briefs and cases and formulating questions of counsel. The moot court is conducted in the same fashion as the argument itself, with the advocate delivering a short prepared opening and then taking questions from the "bench." Some moot courts can last for hours — even for a short argument — if the panelists are experienced questioners and have prepared well. The idea behind the moot court is to raise as many questions as possible that a justice might ask, so that the advocate can practice articulating answers. If done well, the advocate will not hear a single question in the Supreme Court for the first time and will have thought through an answer before having to deliver it.

Descriptions of preparation may give the impression that argument has become a "canned" recitation of predicted questions and memorized answers. In fact, the intensity of the experience and the speed with which the justices pose their questions virtually ensure that oral argument will be a spontaneous exchange between counsel and the members of the Court. No advocate can anticipate the order in which the justices will interrupt the advocate's argument with their questions or even the precise way they will word them. Sometimes a justice will ask a question that is sufficiently off-kilter that only the advocate can recognize it as such, but answering such questions becomes a difficult balance of tact and resolve, as the advocate has to make the point clearly without offending the justice.

Participants in moot courts often include lawyers who have filed briefs as amicus curiae, or friends of the court. The role of amicus curiae has played an increasingly important part of advocacy before the Supreme Court in the last third of the twentieth century and beyond. In cases of great national importance, briefs from dozens of amicus groups may be filed. In the 2003 case involving the admissions criteria used at the University of Michigan, for example, more than sixty amicus briefs were filed in support of Michigan. Those briefs ran the gamut of every walk of life in the country and included submissions from corporations, labor groups, students, private and public universities, veterans groups, and a group of retired military leaders, including former chairmen of the Joint Chiefs of Staff.

Unlike some district courts and courts of appeals, which can be sparing in granting leave for amicus groups to file a brief, the Supreme Court is typically quite liberal in allowing amicus participation. If the amicus has an interest in the case, most parties routinely consent to the filing of a brief, even knowing that it will be contrary to their position. And if a party fails to give consent, the court typically grants a motion to file a brief if it is timely.

In the vast run of cases, amicus participation extends only to the written briefs. Only rarely will the Supreme Court grant motions for amici to participate in the oral argument. The one exception to that generalization is the solicitor general, in cases in which the United States or a federal agency is not a party to the lawsuit but the government has an interest in the case. Over the past decade, the Office of the Solicitor General as an amicus curiae has participated in the oral argument of approximately one-third of all argued cases. That participation can be critical, offering the Court a broader focus than the parties can provide, as well as the skill and experience of advocates who regularly appear before the Court. As the Court's docket has shrunk from approximately 125 cases in the early 1990s to approximately 80 cases in the early 2000s, the percentage of cases in which the solicitor general participates as an amicus in oral argument has increased. The cases in which the federal government tends not to participate involve questions of law applying uniquely to states and disputes of a private nature that do not implicate any discernible or important federal interest.

Because a decision in a Supreme Court case can have long-lasting and significant effects, the pressure on an advocate to perform at the highest level can be enormous. For in the truest sense, the advocate has not only the client's interests at stake but also all those similarly situated throughout the country. Hundreds of active lawsuits throughout the country may be affected by a Supreme Court decision, and a conscientious advocate will prepare scrupulously to ensure that those interests are also represented in the best possible fashion. Even the most insignificant Supreme Court cases can rightly be viewed as the pinnacle of a lawyer's career, for the opportunity to argue in the Court comes rarely to those outside a select few in the private bar and the Solicitor General's Office.

The opportunity for any lawyer to argue before the highest court in the land, no matter how rare, reflects a majestic egalitarianism in the Court's process for selecting cases. The predominant factor in determining which cases the Court will hear is whether divisions have arisen in the courts of appeals in resolving the issue presented. Thus, even the most momentous of cases may be argued by a little-known advocate arguing for the first time in the Supreme Court, if the case presents an issue that the Court has decided requires resolution.

At the filing of a lawsuit, even the litigants themselves may have little inkling that the case will work its way up to the Supreme Court or will raise issues of national and historic importance. Unlike countries in which only select members of the bar are permitted to appear before their highest court, a lawyer who has worked on a case from its earliest stages may live the dream of "arguing the case all the way to the Supreme Court." When that happens, the advocate will stand face to face with the leaders of one of the three branches of American government, who will display for all to see their dedication, inquisitiveness, and intellect in resolving issues great and small in the continuing development of the nation.

—DAVID C. FREDERICK

FOR FURTHER READING AND RESEARCH

The place of advocacy in Supreme Court practice has, curiously, attracted little scholarly attention. The most comprehensive treatment is to be found in David C. Frederick, *Supreme Court and Appellate Advocacy* (St. Paul, Minn., 2003). Scattered earlier studies have focused largely on the practical, but within these limits are certainly informative. See John W. Davis, "The Argument of an Appeal," *American Bar Association Journal* 26 (December 1940), 895; Frederick Bernays Wiener, "Oral Advocacy," *Harvard Law Review* 62 (1948), 56; Robert H. Jackson, "Advocacy Before the Supreme Court: Suggestions for Effective Oral Presentations," *American Bar Association Journal* 37 (November 1951), 801; and E. Barrett Prettyman, Jr., "Supreme Court Advocacy: Random Thoughts in a Day of Time Restrictions," *Litigation* 4 (1978), 16. For pertinent recent observations, see Ruth Bader Ginsburg, "Remarks on Appellate Advocacy," *Southern California Law Review* 50 (1999), 567. For a guide to contemporary practice, see Robert Stern, Eugene Gressman, Stephen Shapiro, and Kenneth S. Geller, *Supreme Court Practice*, 8th ed. (Washington, D.C., 2002), 569–609.

17

The Supreme Court and Popular Culture

Image and Projection

T HE U.S. SUPREME COURT has left its imprint on every area of American life. This imprint has included those shared products and practices to which people look when seeking meaning and context for their own daily activities: in short, *culture*. Popular culture's images of the Court have historically taken shape within two contexts: the ongoing dispute over the Court's relationship to partisan politics and an ever-changing media environment that has become dominated by visual imagery.

Popular Images of the Supreme Court

Both those hoping to maximize and those desiring to minimize the Court's influence — along with those struggling to understand its role — have always carried their debates beyond the cozy confines of the legal establishment to nonlegal realms, including that of commercial popular culture. Even before there was a Supreme Court, people able to participate in public discussion were already fighting over what such a tribunal might mean for popular political culture. Opponents of the Constitution of 1787 saw the proposed Supreme Court as a powerful, potentially antidemocratic force. In contrast, proponents of the new charter, most famously Alexander Hamilton writing in *Federalist* No. 89, described a Court unable to enforce its own decisions as the "weakest branch" of the government created by the Constitution. From the very beginning, its friends recognized (in the later words of Justice Felix Frankfurter) that the Court "possessed . . . neither the purse nor the sword" and so depended, more than other governmental institutions, "on sustained public confidence in its moral sanction."

Victorious in the presidential election of 1800, Thomas Jefferson cast himself as the champion of a popular political culture that understood the Constitution far better than the Federalist establishment. To Jefferson and his supporters, any representation that ignored Federalist justices' partisan role and spotlighted only constitutional arguments seemed badly focused. The nation's first popular medium, the Jeffersonian newspapers of the early nineteenth century, presented Supreme Court justices as politicians, like members of Congress and the executive branch, and hence open to ordinary political criticism.

Champions of the Court sketched a different portrait, emphasizing the justices' unique role in American life as "teachers to the citizenry." Acknowledging the high court's broad impact, including on national culture, its supporters insisted that the justices conduct themselves in a manner that guaranteed their independence from political influence, guard the Court's autonomy, and preserve the nation's constitutional republic — while imparting republican principles to the masses through educative example. The ideal of a judicial body shielded from partisan politics emerged concretely during the Supreme Court's first popular test in 1804–1805. As a way of derailing what they saw as a nationalist assault on state authority by Federalist justices, members of one Jeffersonian faction looked to the impeachment process. Led by John Randolph of Roanoke, they targeted Associate Justice Samuel Chase, an outspoken Federalist. The Chase impeachment attempted to tear down any distinction between Jeffersonianism's popular politics and the workings of the Supreme Court and seemed the prelude to ousting Chief Justice John Marshall and perhaps other Federalists. But the effort failed. Some Jeffersonians, estranged from Randolph and willing to insulate the high court from this kind of political threat, voted with the Federalists to acquit Chase.

The idea of an independent Supreme Court retained a tenacious, although always contested, hold on the popular imagination. Seen from this perspective, the Supreme Court has historically enjoyed a place and responsibilities in American popular culture distinct from those of other governmental institutions. The dominant image is of a group of specially trained jurists pondering public issues from somewhere above the popular political fray. The justices rule only on genuine *legal* controversies that require concrete, vital choices over the meaning of the Constitution, the supreme law of the land. (Supreme Court justices, for example, never meet as an advisory body on prospective constitutional questions.) Before issuing any opinion, the Court must reason its way through an actual case, whatever its political origins and ramifications. It must act according to a uniquely informed view of the meaning of the Constitution itself, a recognized body of legal-constitutional doctrines and procedures, and, ultimately, the ideal of the "rule of law."

Disputes about the Court's relationship to popular politics intertwine with the media environment in which political and legal representations appear. The discussion that follows traces the nature of changing media practices, but one constant in the Court's popular image should be highlighted at the outset. No one who is not physically present during oral arguments or the announcement of decisions can *see* the Court at work. Hence, at the beginning of the twenty-first century, the presence of the Supreme Court is registered visually in much the same ways as during the early nineteenth — through cartoons, illustrations, or fictional dramatizations. Most state courts now allow, and sometimes welcome, televised coverage of their proceedings. Not the U.S. Supreme Court. The Court has released audiotapes of oral arguments, but these representations remain entirely within the aural and archival realm: They have yet to be broadcast "live," in real time. Nor has the Court even used an "in-house" photographer to snap still pictures of the justices and their staffs at work. In an age in which the practice and performance of governance have become inseparable from the art of visual imagery, the Supreme Court has continued to find shelter behind its red velvet curtain.

The Supreme Court in the "Age of Letters," 1801–1835

During the early nineteenth century, most leaders of the American bar, particularly those with allegiances to the Federalist Party, extolled the Supreme Court and Chief Justice John Marshall. Meanwhile, Marshall and his younger Federalist colleague, Justice Joseph Story, also cultivated the Court's cultural reputation.

Custodians of American culture in the earliest years of the Republic generally made no sharp distinction between legal-constitutional and other forms of discourse. Nineteenth-century literary collections sometimes included legal-constitutional arguments alongside poetry and prose. Prominent lawyers and judges, including Marshall and Story, qualified as "men of letters," writers whose literary efforts off the bench drew as much attention as the opinions written for the Supreme Court itself.

Early in the nineteenth century, for example, Marshall penned a five-volume *Life of George Washington* (1804–1807). His account, more a history of the formation of the American union than a conventional biography, offered a Federalist view of past and present issues. It so enraged Jefferson that he vainly urged Joel Barlow, a prominent Jeffersonian writer and poet, to author a corrective.

Marshall began his Washington project with dreams of turning a substantial profit but had to settle for a comfortable financial return and considerable literary acclaim, especially from pro-Federalist reviewers. Later, the chief justice produced a two-volume abridgement, in the hope of competing with Mason Weems's wildly popular one-volume biography of Washington for the allegiance of younger readers.

Story, considered both a better constitutional technician and a more felicitous legal writer than the chief justice, enjoyed a more celebrated literary career. Oliver Wendell Holmes, Jr., who would himself win fame as a Supreme Court justice and an author, credited Story with doing more than any other writer to make Anglo-American law "luminous and easy to understand." But besides his nine works of legal commentary, Story also produced a book of poetry and a text on American government; he also gave numerous public addresses, often on literary topics.

Legal knowledge thus went hand in hand with cultural erudition during the Supreme Court's earliest days. Styling themselves more than mere lawyers, the new nation's prominent attorneys, such as Daniel Webster, William Pinkney, and William Wirt (author of a celebrated 1817 biography of Patrick Henry), enjoyed reputations as exciting cultural performers. The high court became their most prestigious stage.

Oratorical fashions of the day demanded an ornate, lengthy address. Counsel appearing before the high court could speak without being interrupted by questions from the bench for as long as they wished. Webster's oration/argument in *Dartmouth College v. Woodward* (1819) lasted more than two hours and, according to Federalist legend, left Chief Justice Marshall in tears. Justice Story claimed that the Supreme Court — graced by orators who could match, if not surpass, Webster's skills at imagery and pacing — attracted an audience that displayed "the taste, the beauty, the wit, and learning that adorned the city" of Washington, D.C. The Supreme Court's chambers, then located in the basement of the U.S. Capitol building, were regularly filled with spectators.

Supreme Court judges of the Marshall and Story era did more than hear cases in Washington and participate in that city's high cultural life. In pairs, the justices, including the chief, presided over the several U.S. circuit courts. Twice a year in that capacity, Marshall returned to his hometown of Richmond, where he tried to assume a different popular image: an ordinary son of the Virginia soil. According to one tale, a carelessly dressed Marshall was even mistaken for the kind of down-at-the-heels "character" who would accept a quarter — as the nation's chief justice did! — to deliver turkeys from the market. When not on the circuit bench or hauling poultry, Marshall might be found enjoying Richmond's male-centered tavern culture. While winning national recognition for presiding over the

Supreme Court, he gained local fame for his tenure as chief judge of the Richmond Quoits Club, a position that involved making independent, professionally astute judgments about the placement of the rings.

The austere Story cultivated a very different off-Court image. Already acclaimed as a writer, Story in 1829 began supplementing his judicial duties with a professorship at Harvard Law School. There, his task became nothing less than the remolding of legal education and, more broadly, of liberal arts learning. The study of law, Story insisted, would enable a graduate of Harvard Law "to build his reputation upon the soundest of morals, the deepest principles, and the most exalted purity of life and character." Story helped make Harvard the nation's best-known law school, a center for both legal learning and cultural display. A number of graduates, including Richard Henry Dana, Jr., and James Russell Lowell, launched literary rather than legal careers from the cultural foundation that Harvard Law School had provided.

Some of Harvard Law's products also became journalists, a profession just beginning to scrutinize the Supreme Court's performance. G. Edward White, the foremost historian of the Court during the Marshall and Story era, has noted that a steadily growing body of journalistic commentary signaled the Court's success in establishing its presence in American cultural life. The press portrayed the Court as not merely a political force "but also as an agent in the less discernable but more profound transformation of American culture in its entirety."

Not every journalist saw the Court changing the country — and its culture — for the better. Even though the Chase episode had removed impeachment from their arsenal, Jeffersonian critics still viewed the Court as a thoroughly political body, the judicial arm of the Federalist Party. Chief Justice Marshall faced fierce criticism from popular Jeffersonian orators and newspapers. The chief justice's opinions on behalf of a broad interpretation of national power, such as that authorizing creation of a national bank in *McCulloch v. Maryland* (1819), rekindled the states' rights ire of John Randolph and brought others from Virginia, including that commonwealth's leading jurist, Spencer Roane, into the fray. Marshall, writing under a pseudonym (as did his opponents), stepped down from the bench and confronted his critics in a newspaper debate marked as much by personal vituperation as by legal learning.

Early-nineteenth-century popular journalism about the Supreme Court established patterns that have remained largely intact. Newspapers did not "cover" the Court on any sustained basis but generally noticed only those cases that had stirred popular passions. Meanwhile, the journals of the day, particularly the *North American Review*, invented a journalistic tradition that paralleled the celebratory, insider perspective being created by such jurists as Story and Webster. Whereas newspapers aligned with Andrew Jackson were joining their president in assailing the Court for decisions in conflict with Democratic Party positions, the *Review* was lauding the justices for elevating the tone of American culture and purifying its politics. "What an immense range of discussion any inquiry has been explored by this learned and diligent tribunal! What mighty questions have been agitated and settled! What incalculable benefits" have flowed from its legal-cultural work! The entire nation was "daily enjoying the invaluable benefits of their learning and diligence."

President Jackson easily matched Jefferson in his dislike for the work of the chief justice. Buoyed by a popular political swell that far surpassed that of the Jeffersonian era, Jackson advanced a claim to see the Constitution more acutely than any Supreme Court justice could. Committed to what one contemporary constitutional theorist has called a "state-centered vision of white male democracy," Jackson simply defied Supreme Court rulings in favor of Native American treaty rights. In addition, he implicitly overruled *McCulloch v. Maryland* by vetoing a congressional measure that would have rechartered the national bank and, later, by withdrawing governmental funds, thus killing an institution that Jacksonians viewed as a legacy of John Marshall's old Federalist Party. Between 1835, the year of Marshall's death, and 1837, Jackson also remade the Court in his own image with five new appointments, including two that resulted from Congress's decision to expand the Court's membership from seven to nine.

The Supreme Court and a Changing Cultural Dynamics, 1835–1880s

The revamped Court—headed after 1836 by Roger B. Taney, who had led Jackson's attack on the national bank—never possessed the cultural cachet of the Marshall era. This was understandable in light of broader cultural changes occurring in American life. New cultural forms burst into view during the 1830s and 1840s. Heralded by later historians as a "communication-information explosion," the "democratization of American culture," or a "graphic revolution," a series of interrelated developments transformed how every type of discourse—including those of the law and the Supreme Court—was produced, circulated, and consumed.

The sheer volume of print and visual imagery alone remade American culture. Steam-driven presses doomed the print-for-subscription culture of the early nineteenth century just as steam-powered locomotives speeded newspapers, books, and journals across a growing country. Inexpensive daily papers, the "penny press," and pulp books flooded the journalistic and literary marketplace. As a permanent two-party political system emerged during the mid-1830s, pitting Jackson's Democrats against his Whig opponents, journalists began choosing up sides and making their papers into mouthpieces for one of the two major parties or for their minor-party rivals.

In this new cultural milieu, the nineteenth-century Supreme Court justices who succeeded Marshall and Story failed to qualify as "men of letters," and the oratorical style of the Marshall Court era fell from favor. Popular audiences expected speakers, including lawyers and politicians, such as young Abraham Lincoln, to display what the historian Kenneth Cmiel has called a "middling style." Platform performers began mixing language and imagery once considered "vulgar" with words and images that displayed a considerable degree of learning but not the old-style elegance. Simultaneously, other popular orators, particularly antislavery stalwarts, such as John P. Hale and Cassius Marcellus Clay, thrilled younger cultural critics, such as Walt Whitman, by their ability to spark dialogic, personalized exchanges with audiences.

Most broadly, the old "Republic of Letters" slowly faded away. During the 1840s and 1850s, the guardians of a culture that later students of this "American Renaissance" would dub "romanticism" saw venerable lawyer-statesmen, such as Webster, as hopelessly old-fashioned rhetoricians. Webster and the other lawyers who had graced the Marshall Court had tried to articulate broadly imagined, supposedly widely shared legal-constitutional principles — expounded in a florid rhetorical style — that could hold together the law, American culture, and the nation itself. Celebrants of the Court had credited its justices with bringing a sense of cultural coherence and stability to law and politics by incorporating those principles into their judicial opinions. But the cultural elite of the American Renaissance, headed by devoutly antislavery Northerners, such as Ralph Waldo Emerson, viewed the world very differently. Even if informed about legal matters, cultural figures, such as Emerson, Walt Whitman, and Henry David Thoreau, judged Webster's stolid legal-constitutional tropes out of step with the rapidly moving, morally charged spirit of the age. In 1830, Emerson could still praise Webster for standing up to the secessionist gestures of Southern slaveholders, represented by John C. Calhoun and Robert Hayne of South Carolina. Ten years later, as Webster turned to devising a constitutional formula for holding together the Union while safeguarding slavery, Emerson claimed that he could no longer even read Webster's legalistic rhetoric. A further decade later, as Webster struggled in Congress to frame what would become the Compromise of 1850, Thoreau condemned "lawyer's truth" as "not Truth, but consistency or a consistent expediency."

Simultaneously, Webster found his beloved Supreme Court abandoning the culture he had once helped to exemplify. Webster's style of legal-constitutional performance had always rested on oratory that appealed to general principles rather than specific doctrines and depended more on rhetorical flourishes than on case-law citations. By 1840, an increasing emphasis on narrowly professional skills — such as parsing judicial precedents and juggling doctrinal subtleties — was pushing aside the generalist discourse of the Marshall era. The Supreme Court still heard lengthy oral arguments, but their content became more technical in nature. The Court also began looking to the written briefs submitted by opposing counsel. These texts supposedly helped the justices identify the legal doctrines and case-law precedents that were becoming more important to the Court's work. Uncomfortable with these changes, Webster spent less and less time on his law practice and rarely appeared in the Court chamber where he had earlier been a star.

Scott v. Sandford (1857; known as the *Dred Scott* case) serves as an important symbol of the post-Marshall era in Supreme Court history. After lengthy oral arguments and much political maneuvering, Chief Justice Taney tried to use the Supreme Court to limit popular discussion over the future of slavery in the territories. He held that Congress lacked constitutional authority to halt slavery's expansion, a ruling that invalidated the Missouri Compromise of 1820. And he flatly declared that persons of African descent, "even when free," enjoyed their legal "privileges" as a result of "kindness and benevolence rather than right." Members of this "degraded class," even when not enslaved, could never become U.S. citizens.

Taney's image of a proslavery republic, along with the views offered in various concurring and dissenting opinions, entered a political culture in which the tropes of melodrama increasingly structured popular debate. Antislavery publications cast Taney as a villainous character, the judicial counterpart to Harriet Beecher Stowe's fictional Simon Legree. Several years later, a newspaper gleefully greeted Taney's 1864 death by proclaiming that "the ancient High Priest" of the "temple of the man-stealers" now lay "cold at the altar." Congress had routinely appropriated funds for a marble bust of every other deceased chief justice. But Senator Charles Sumner successfully protested that any popular honor to Taney would dishonor the country. "If a man has done evil during his life he must not be complimented in marble," Sumner proclaimed. Only after Taney's successor, Salmon P. Chase, died in 1873 did Congress quietly fund memorial statuary for both departed chief justices.

Did *Scott v. Sandford* affect the image of the Supreme Court to the same degree? Yes, according to the "standard story" of the Taney Court.

In this cautionary tale, *whenever* the justices have followed Taney and stepped down from their pedestal to make ordinary political or cultural judgments, they have wounded themselves, the institution they served, and the very ideal of constitutional government. In contrast, *Dred Scott's* foremost historian, Don Fehrenbacher, insisted that the opprobrium heaped on Taney left the popular image of the Court itself relatively untouched. Antislavery (and later "Radical") Republicans did spar with the Court during the Civil War and early Reconstruction years, but these clashes remained limited to the world of high politics, not that of popular culture.

If the impact of *Scott v. Sandford* on the Court's image remains a contested issue, the case clearly demonstrated how the relationship between popular culture and law had changed since Marshall's day. His opinion in *McCulloch* (1819) had prompted a fierce newspaper war but one that remained largely limited to Virginia; by 1857, the changing cultural dynamics meant that the popular clamor over *Dred Scott* rapidly spread throughout the nation and into various media (Plate A.8). The Court's official reporter, who had hoped to profit by selling his own pamphlet edition of the various opinions, found himself competing against instantaneous versions of *Scott v. Sandford*. With so many different texts in print so quickly, Associate Justice John Catron worried about his own rather slim concurrence getting lost in the cascade.

Popular interest rested not only on the particular issues at stake but also on the broader cultural forces that had, by the 1850s, made the coverage of legal cases into a recognizable pop-cultural genre. Images of law could now be found almost anywhere in the vast realm of commercial popular culture (Plate A.13). A never-ending parade of popular accounts of "notorious cases"—legal disputes in which the media spotlight could easily accent deeply held, seemingly intractable cultural tensions—could entertain a steadily growing audience. Thus, at the same time that legal performances at the U.S. Supreme Court were becoming more narrowly "professional," new forms of legal storytelling were flourishing in the popular media and in the nation's far-flung courtrooms. Almost any local courtroom, it seemed, could offer a stage for a drama that might eventually play, nationally, in every media form. The popular press, to take only one example, regularly spotlighted trials involving charges of adultery. Notorious cases of this kind, such as the 1875 adultery and seduction trial of the celebrated minister Henry Ward Beecher, became an important form of popular, commercialized entertainment.

Few of these dramas, however, were staged in the U.S. Supreme Court. As an entertainment-generating venue, it lacked the ready supply of colorful cases, direct testimony from witnesses, and gallery-playing attorneys —

elements that were to be found in lesser legal forums. The nation's highest appellate court generally remained aloof from the kind of controversies that could engage a wide popular audience.

The "Mormon cases" of the late nineteenth century provided one of the few exceptions. Here, in contrast to earlier antislavery cases, such as *Dred Scott,* the Court became the hero of the melodrama. The constitutional issues, which involved such questions as the very nature of a federal system and the First Amendment's guarantee of religious liberty, became entangled with the vivid popular imagery surrounding the Mormon practice of polygamous marriage. The antipolygamy campaign, long associated with the crusade against chattel slavery, had gained momentum after 1862, when Congress declared bigamy a federal crime. In 1873, Ann Eliza Young abandoned her polygamous relationship with Brigham Young and, as "The Rebel of the Harem," embarked on a spectacularly successful lecture tour; it attracted members of Congress and even President Ulysses S. Grant and his wife. The popular clamor helped to propel a political effort to use federal authority against the "polygamic theocracy" in Utah, a campaign whose constitutional implications eventually reached the Supreme Court in *Reynolds v. U.S.* (1878).

Mormon elders initially welcomed, very wrongly, it turned out, the case. Their lawyers argued that Congress lacked authority to legislate on local marriage relationships or religious practices. Charles Devens, the attorney handling the appeal for the federal government, would have none of this. His legal brief to the Court and well-publicized oral argument drew on popular images of how polygamy corrupted the virtue of not only respectable women but also that of the larger body politic. The Court's 1879 opinion, upholding congressional power, invoked constitutional doctrine, but at the same time, it invoked the images of polygamy found in popular iconography. Polygamous relationships, in this widely disseminated view, opened the door to all manner of "barbarous" practices, including miscegenation. By drawing on nonlegal images of polygamy to bolster its opinion in *Reynolds,* the Court encouraged numerous pictures, particularly in the fertile field of political cartooning, of the justices heroically vanquishing the scourge of plural marriage.

The Supreme Court and the Rise of Mass, Commercial Culture, 1880s–1935

The cartoonist's art, an important part of the popular culture surrounding *Reynolds v. U.S.,* soon became the only window through which ordinary citizens could "see" the Supreme Court at work. In 1886, a photographer snapped a still picture of Justice Horace Gray dozing during an oral argument. A contemporary piece of popular doggerel told of

> . . . an old Justice named Gray
> Who slept & who snored every day—
> His lunch he would eat
> Then nap on his seat
> And wake up "with did you say?"

Considerably less amused, the Court excluded all cameras from its chambers.

As in the Mormon cases, though, controversial litigation encouraged cartoonists and popular writers to ratchet up the volume of editorial opinion about the Court. A series of controversial rulings by the Court, including *Pollock v. Farmers Loan and Trust Co.* (1895)—a 5-4 decision that declared a federal income tax unconstitutional—prompted a broad-based, popular, and often visual response. The income tax decision provided an immediate opening for at least one enterprising patent-medicine entrepreneur, who placed this advertisement adjacent to coverage of the Supreme Court's ruling:

> THE INCOME TAX
> Didn't Yield half so easily as the most
> Stubborn COUGH OR COLD will if
> Tackled at once with
> RIKER'S EXPECTORANT

According to the historian Michael Kammen, the Supreme Court encountered nearly as much popular controversy around the turn of the twentieth century as during the era of *Scott v. Sandford*. During this period, the Chicago humorist-editorialist Finley Peter Dunne, whose dialect-inflected columns appeared under the name of "Mr. Dooley," issued his famous verdict on the relationship between the Court and popular politics. When facing controversial issues, Dunne's alter ego wryly opined in 1901: "th' Supreme Court follows th' iliction returns."

Popular accounts of the time elaborated Mr. Dooley's perspective. Utopian novels, such as *Waiting for the Signal* (1897) by Henry O. Morris and Edward Bellamy's *Looking Backward* (1888), speculated about how a very different kind of Supreme Court could play a much more constructive role in a reimagined American Republic. In the wake of *Plessy v. Ferguson* (1896), novels by African American writers cast the late-nineteenth-century Court as every bit a bastion of white supremacy as it had been during the days of Roger B. Taney.

In his *History of the Supreme Court of the United States* (1912), Gustavus Myers collected a generation's worth of popular, critical writing. A veteran of muckraking journalism, Myers transferred the familiar story of elite domination of political life to the realm of constitutional law. In every age, as this popular history saw constitutional politics, the Supreme Court promoted the economic interests of the ruling class. The book also tried to create a new image for the justices themselves. No justice, it claimed, had ruled against ordinary people more consistently than Stephen J. Field. Yet Justice Field, after serving on the Court from 1863 to 1897, "left less of an estate than many a petty merchant or even a half-way successful shyster lawyer." His "corruption was that of a purely mental subservience induced by his class views, attachments, and obligations." Similarly, the image of a plain-living John Marshall provided a cover for his judicial machinations in favor of land speculators. The chief justice's "air of democratic simplicity"—the slovenly dressed, tavern-crawling, quoits-throwing everyman—cleverly concealed how his Court's decisions were "laying the bulwarked foundations of an era of unrestricted capitalist development." In Myers's view, then, the justices themselves were largely pawns in a much larger game than constitutional law, one played by the nation's most powerful interests.

The critics hardly went unchallenged. Professors of constitutional law and leaders of the bar dismissed popular criticism as the uninformed drivel of rank amateurs. At the same time, the Court's less-credentialed partisans mounted a complementary, popular defense. Using a variety of media, they memorialized the Court's historical contributions and lauded its ongoing role in preserving constitutional government from deranged enemies. A lead cartoon in a September 1896 issue of *Harpers Weekly*, for example, showed a nightmarish vision of what could befall the nation if the Populist Party were able to place its jurists, such as John Peter Altgeld, on the Supreme Court (Plate A.15).

Defenders of the Court also mobilized their historical capital, beginning with the imposing figure of John Marshall. "Marshall-mania" would be too strong a term, but the last years of the nineteenth century and early years of the twentieth century certainly witnessed a "Marshall revival" across a wide range of popular media. Statues and portraits were ceremoniously unveiled; Marshall's former home in Richmond, Virginia, became a protected antiquity; the American Bar Association sponsored, in 1901, a multistate celebration of the hundredth anniversary of the beginning of his tenure as chief justice; and new biographies appeared. In 1919, a multivolume hagiography by former Senator Albert Beveridge was published, as well as a more scholarly, one-volume contribution by political scientist Edward S. Corwin, the unofficial chief justice of constitutional studies.

By 1919, though, Marshall had a contemporary rival whose image in popular culture would soon outshine even his: Associate Supreme Court Justice Oliver Wendell Holmes, Jr.

At the beginning of the Marshall revival, in the 1880s, Holmes was an
ambitious but little-noticed lawyer who was nearly fifty years old. When
Theodore Roosevelt appointed him to the U.S. Supreme Court in 1903,
Holmes was not even the best-known person with the surname of Holmes.
His own author-father and the fictional detective hero of Sir Arthur Conan
Doyle had attracted considerably more notice than this still-obscure jurist
from Boston. By the 1930s, though, the fame of Justice Holmes challenged
even that of Marshall.

What might explain popular culture's embrace of this Brahmin jurist?
Holmes, of course, looked like a Supreme Court justice, at least in popular
imagery. Tall, with ramrod posture, he continued to wear a luxurious, old-
style mustache that recalled the Civil War era in which he had matured.
The justice himself also assiduously cultivated his popular image. He gave
frequent popular addresses, including stirring memorials on the Civil War.
At the same time, he formed close ties with a group of much younger,
largely Jewish intellectuals, particularly the Harvard Law School professor
Felix Frankfurter, who also tended to the Holmes mystique. Looking beyond specialized law publications, they used popular journals, such as the
New Republic, to laud Holmes as the author of sparkling Supreme Court
opinions, often in dissent, on behalf of the constitutionality of social-
welfare legislation and the protection of civil liberties. Holmes willingly,
and effectively, played the role in which he was cast.

The popular media also embraced the justice. In 1922, he graced the
cover of *Time* magazine. At the same time, his admirers began marking his
birthday with a public celebration; for his ninetieth, in 1931, they sponsored a radio broadcast that featured a tribute from the new chief justice,
Charles Evans Hughes, and well-practiced remarks from the honoree himself. The *New York Times* declared that the aging justice, "perhaps the
greatest of living judges," had used the relatively new medium perfectly. After his death in 1935, Holmes remained the subject of numerous legal publications, a best-selling biography entitled *Yankee from Olympus,* a stage
play, and even a Hollywood "biopic." Had television been in the picture
during Holmes's tenure on the Supreme Court, it takes little imagination
to see him sitting for the type of avuncular interview that justices of the TV
era, such as Hugo Black and William O. Douglas, later gave.

Justice Holmes raised the bar for every subsequent member of the Supreme Court. Although dissenting historians have tried to redraw the image of Holmes as a progressive and civil libertarian, the contemporary picture has persisted. To the bafflement of his critics, Holmes has continued

to symbolize the highest traditions of legal scholarship, literary craftsman-
ship, and socially informed constitutionalism.

Appearances also remained important to other members of the Court.
Although the justices had no desire to see cameras in their chambers, they
did want to improve the quality of their surroundings. Since 1860, when it
finally left the Capitol basement, the Court had met in upgraded but still
second-hand surroundings: the old Senate chamber located near the Capitol Rotunda (Plates A.6 and A.7). After much discussion during the 1920s
about the need for a place that better represented the Court's lofty image,
Congress finally approved a separate Court building and authorized famed
architect Cass Gilbert to design it (Plates B.3, B.4, and B.5). Popularly
called the "Marble Temple," the new building opened in the fall of 1935
amid minimal internal pomp but maximum external controversy.

The New Deal and the Popular Look of a
New Supreme Court, 1935–1950

The controversy had boiled up over how a majority of the Court viewed
Franklin Roosevelt's New Deal. By 1935, as Scot Powe has noted, there was
little doubt that it "opposed not only the particulars of New Deal legislation
but the premises as well." The Court struck down as unconstitutional
much of the legislation that Roosevelt considered crucial to fighting the
Depression. Soon, sharp differences over the role that nine nonelected
judges should play in public policymaking returned the Court to the popular spotlight.

As earlier in the century, leaders of the legal establishment and popular
writers weighed in — both for and against the Court. Following in the
muckraking tradition of Gustavus Myers, journalists Drew Pearson and
Robert Allen in 1936 published the best-selling *Nine Old Men*, one of several book-length attacks on the Court. So far as it was possible to gauge political behavior, most Americans appeared to be discussing the Supreme
Court. The *New York Times* imagined a citizenry so engrossed in debating
the Court's work that animated talk of constitutional law often dominated
discussion at the breakfast table. Certainly, the volume of print publications, easier to measure than the pitch of private conversations in the typical American home, increased dramatically.

Popular satirists found the Supreme Court a convenient target. *Duck
Soup* (1933), a movie starring the Marx Brothers, merrily assaulted every
possible political institution, including the Court. "His Excellency" Rufus T.
Firefly (Groucho Marx), the errant force in this political farce, whimsi-
cally assumes any governmental post, including that of the chief justice of

Freedonia. While presiding over a pun-filled treason trial, he suddenly leaves the bench to serve as defense counsel for the accused (Chico Marx). The musical-comedy play, *I'd Rather Be Right* (1937), written by George S. Kaufman and Moss Hart, abandoned the indirection strategy of *Duck Soup* and openly lampooned the Court as a group of loony old men bent on invalidating any law proposed by Roosevelt (Plate B.6).

Utopian speculation, both fiction and nonfiction, also enlivened popular discourse. Not content simply to reinvent the Court, these works sketched a panoramic view of how a new constitutional structure might look — and then operate. *A New Day Dawns: A Brief History of the Altruistic Era (1930-2162 AD)*, by Charles Elton Blanchard, foresaw a unicameral legislature, a single-term presidency, frequent popular referenda, and a constitution that changed frequently. As the female president who occupied the White House in the 1960s explains, any congressional statute that was approved in a nationwide referendum "should automatically amend the constitution and repeal any existing statutes it contradicts. The Supreme Court will be no longer needed to thwart the will of the people expressed through Congress."

Hollywood picked up one of the most popular books in this genre, *Gabriel over the White House* (1933). Both the print and filmic versions of *Gabriel* foresaw a presidential dictatorship as a likely response to economic disarray. Produced by William Randolph Hearst's Cosmopolitan Studio, the movie seemed a one-dimensional appeal for virtually unlimited presidential authority. Images of constitutional experimentation, then, provided the popular backdrop to that well-known constitutional battle: FDR versus the Supreme Court of the United States.

On his reelection in 1936, Roosevelt, the first president to have served a full term without appointing a single justice, faced the oldest Court in U.S. history. Although Roosevelt obviously wanted justices who saw constitutional matters his way, he disingenuously claimed that the Court lacked the physical and mental stamina to handle its caseload. Consequently, he proposed a law that would have allowed him to "pack" the Court by appointing an additional justice, up to a total of fifteen, for every member of the Court who had reached the age of seventy (Plate B.7). The idea resembled one from *Gabriel over the White House*, a work that FDR admired. Commenting on FDR's plan, *I'd Rather Be Right* has its Roosevelt character quip that the sitting justices would likely have been more supportive "if I'd suggested putting six new *girls* on the bench."

When the battle ended, the traditional nine-person Supreme Court remained, but the new justices that Roosevelt eventually appointed (eight by 1941) appeared to take a very different view of the Constitution than those they replaced. The Roosevelt justices never met a piece of social-economic legislation they didn't like. In *Wickard v. Filburn* (1942), for example, the Court unanimously ruled that Washington could limit agricultural production intended for solely private use, on the theory that such a farming practice inevitably affected the total volume of agricultural commodities that would ultimately be sold in the interstate marketplace and, therefore, justified governmental regulation. According to the Court's legal supporters, the decision showed that the postpacking justices could clearly discern the proper relationship between legal principles and real-life experiences.

Relatively few people likely read *Wickard v. Filburn,* but many millions watched *Talk of the Town,* a successful motion picture that offered a very similar message, to a very different audience, that very same year of 1942. One of the few Hollywood movies to feature the character of a Supreme Court Justice, *Talk of the Town* warrants some attention, for it highlights the "segmented" nature of twentieth-century representations of the Constitution and the Supreme Court.

Karl Llewellyn, the Columbia law professor and legal realist, once suggested that there were at least three major levels at which legal imagery circulated. First, there was "jurisprudence for the hundreds," for those learned specialists who could appreciate the doctrinal twists in such decisions as *Wickard.* Then, there was "jurisprudence for the hundred thousand," representations intended for members of the bar and laypeople interested in how the Court approached more general legal-constitutional issues, such as the battle over economic regulation. Finally, the popular-culture industry produced works, such as *Talk of the Town,* that could be seen as jurisprudence for the millions. Commercial products in this category did aim to show how legal-constitutional work unfolded, but the primary goal of their producers was to use images to fashion texts that promised to provide pleasure for the largest possible audiences.

Talk of the Town begins in a small New England town, Lochester. After burning down his own mill and causing the death of one of his workers, a corrupt factory owner manipulates the town's legal system to pin the deed on Leopold Dilg (Cary Grant), the town's resident anarchist. Fearing that the corrupt legal establishment will railroad him, Dilg hides out in Nora Shelley's (Jean Arthur's) bed and breakfast, the very same place where Michael Lightcap (Ronald Colman), a law school dean who is a candidate for the U.S. Supreme Court, has taken a different kind of refuge. Anxious to avoid the popular tumult that his expected nomination will spark and to pursue scholarly endeavors, Dean Lightcap seeks only solitude. Instead, this Ivy League academic, who bears a vague resemblance to Oliver Wendell Holmes, Jr., finds himself adrift in romantic and legal complications that vastly exceed his limited real-world experience. The movie's love-triangle plot asks Nora Shelley to choose between the anarchist and the lawyer. It also, though, poses another question: What qualifies a lawyer — indeed, a highly distinguished jurist — to join the post-1937 Supreme Court?

Written by Sidney Buchman, a Communist Party member who had earlier scripted *Mr. Smith Goes to Washington* (1939), *Talk of the Town* provides a full answer to this second question. It first shows the professor debating juridical theory with the unlettered anarchist, in a Hollywood parody of the *New York Times* claim that people were chewing on constitutional matters during breakfast (Plate B.8). Lightcap, hitherto concerned only with "the philosophy" of the law, next gains first-hand experience in how legal power *really* operates. Eventually, he performs a series of heroic deeds. He faces down a mob intent on lynching Dilg, unravels the plot hatched by the industrialist, and, most important, explores the gulf between high-blown legal theory and on-the-ground experience. Properly reeducated in legal realism (and the reality of emotion), Professor Lightcap now possesses the proper qualifications for the nation's highest court. The final sequences show him donning his judicial robes and taking his seat on the bench.

Talk of the Town, as with any Hollywood movie, gives viewers multiple paths through its narrative. For people interested in seeing an unstable love triangle reduced to a stable marriage, the movie's producers tested several possible endings before pairing Nora with Leopold rather than with Michael Lightcap. (The studio press kit highlighted this romantic theme; in contrast, reviewers for popular magazines generally focused on how *Talk* portrayed the Court and its justices.) Viewers seeking a "political" movie, in the mode of *Mr. Smith,* could concentrate on the final sequences, shot in a faithful reproduction of the Supreme Court's new chambers, which celebrate the tribunal and glamorize its newest recruit. They could also align their gaze with that of Leopold Dilg, who renounces his anarchist politics and decides he can leave social-constitutional issues to professionals, such as Mr. Justice Lightcap. After traveling to Washington to watch the new justice join the Court, Dilg tells Nora that he's seen enough of the Supreme Court's workings. "The rest is about law; very boring," he tells Nora. Lightcap "looks fine up there . . . The country's in good hands."

This linkage between the *look* of the Supreme Court's newest member and the fate of the country, then, implicitly endorses the importance of visual imagery to "jurisprudence for the millions." More important, it also suggests that people can forego constitutional law with breakfast and remain confident that the New Deal Court — staffed by justices adept at handling both legal principles and real-life problems — sees constitutional matters from a perspective informed by practical, popular knowledge. In contrast to *Mr. Smith,* with its critical imagery of an easily manipulated

Senate, *Talk of the Town*, which garnered seven Academy Award nominations, reverentially portrays the Supreme Court and its new justice.

Several years later, the real-life story of Oliver Wendell Holmes, Jr., which contains almost as many plot twists as the fictional tale of Michael Lightcap, also became a motion picture. Despite some obvious differences, Hollywood's *Magnificent Yankee* (1950) offers much the same view of the ideal(ized) Supreme Court justice as *Talk of the Town*. Without invoking its imaginative license to show Justice Holmes (Louis Calhern) doing anything as exciting as tracking down a murderer or romancing the owner of a B&B, *Magnificent Yankee* pictures a Brahmin-like jurist who sees the necessity to bridge the gap between legal theory and practical experience. The movie, for example, shows Holmes formulating his famous clear-and-present-danger test for legally protected speech while walking with his fellow justice, Louis Brandeis, through the Washington Zoo!

The Supreme Court and American Popular Culture, 1950–Present

During the second half of the twentieth century, the Supreme Court's place in popular culture differed from that of other political and legal bodies. During this period, the boundary between the commercial culture industry and virtually all other governmental institutions, including most legal tribunals, appeared increasingly blurred. More than ever before, the realm of the law seemed to overlap with that of popular culture. There was an increasing "vanishing line," according to Richard Sherwin, between popular media and a law that was "going pop." A "feedback loop" was coming to connect legal and popular imagery, more quickly and tightly than ever before.

Most Americans, as well as citizens of other countries, took their view of the U.S. legal system, however sketchy or badly informed it might be, from popular culture. Familiar with TV shows from the United States, a majority of Canadians mistakenly assumed that their nation's constitutional law included the "Miranda rights" found in the United States. At the same time, popular interest in the drama — as well as the tragedy and comedy — of law mushroomed. Representations proliferated in virtually every media. The entertainment industry made courtroom-centered fare a regular (and highly profitable) part of its offerings, from dramas, such as *Anatomy of a Murder* (1959) and *Matlock*, to comedies, such as *Jury Duty* (1995) and *Night Court* (1984–1992). "Real-life law" became the raw material for mass-mediated products. The true-crime genre, a visit to any mass-market bookstore would confirm, burgeoned into a major literary form. Similarly, tell-all biographies and memoirs — part of the larger tell-all genre that writer Joyce Carol Oates once labeled "pathography"— flourished. Legal celebrities of any magnitude could become the object, or the author, of such works.

In a related vein, the number of "notorious" cases appeared to expand exponentially. By the end of the twentieth century, local- and state-level courts provided a seemingly inexhaustible supply of cases, the most evocative of which might qualify as the next "trial of the century." The presence of TV cameras in most state courts and the rise of 24/7 cable TV outlets, especially Court TV, helped to transform courtrooms, such as the one in which the state of California tried O. J. Simpson for murder, into television soundstages. Court TV featured more than 1,000 hours of live, in-court coverage of the fifteen-month Simpson criminal trial.

How well did the U.S. Supreme Court fit into this changing legal-cultural environment? Awkwardly or not at all might be a simple answer, subject to minor qualifications.

The high court, of course, remained situated within the larger cultural terrain. *Dickerson v. U.S.* (2001), for example, illustrated how pop-cultural imagery could travel through Sherwin's feedback loop into Supreme Court decisions. Responding to claims that the Miranda procedures were not constitutionally required, a majority of the justices upheld their validity. As one opinion insisted, the Miranda ritual, so familiar to anyone who watched American TV shows and movies, had "become embedded in routine police practice to the point where the warnings have become part of our national culture."

The Court's continuing ban on cameras suggested, though, that the justices remained more comfortable with print than with electronic media. Members of the Court continued to write books for the popular market, such as Chief Justice Rehnquist's histories, and memoirs as different as Justice William O. Douglas's politically pointed *Go East Young Man* and Justice Sandra Day O'Connor's nostalgic account of growing up on an Arizona ranch. Particularly contentious episodes, such as the nomination hearings for Robert Bork and Clarence Thomas and the furor surrounding the presidential election of 2000, sparked successful books about the Court. Yet few of these volumes attracted either the sales or the attention gained by works about other institutions or by other public figures. Ironically, no book by or about any justice did as well as *The Tempting of America* (1991), a bitter jeremiad by Bork, whose 1987 appointment to the Supreme Court had failed to clear the Senate.

The Court, in the eyes of popular chroniclers, seemed ill suited for the tell-all genre. Most authors respected the cultural cocoon that had been spun by those who worked at the Court and seemed content with telling all too little about the justices. Beginning around the turn of the twentieth century, there had been, according to the historian Michael Kammen, "a gradual increase in public interest, even curiosity," about Court members. "Serious" writers (academics or otherwise) of the post–World War II era, however, generally looked at the Court through an institutionally focused lens. They saw nine judges largely wedded to doctrinal debate. A work might vociferously criticize doctrinal niceties, but few saw the justices doing something other than pondering high constitutional theories and principles, such as engaging in old-fashioned vote trading, in political partisanship, or in personal feuding. Works that broke the mold, such as *Nine Men* (1955), by maverick Yale Law School professor Fred Rodell, risked being dismissed as trivia or something worse.

Gideon's Trumpet (1964), by Anthony Lewis, exemplified the prevailing fashion. It told of how an indigent Florida prisoner, Clarence Earl Gideon, set in motion an appeal that was argued all the way to the Supreme Court (Plate B.13). Perhaps taking his view of the law from popular legal dramas, such as *Perry Mason,* Gideon had wrongly claimed that the Constitution guaranteed him a lawyer, even though he himself lacked the money to hire one, a claim at odds with prevailing doctrine. The Warren Court's liberal majority had been seeking a case in which it could establish such a rule, and the Court did so, unanimously, when it decided *Gideon v. Wainwright* (1964). Every Court watcher had expected this result, but Lewis's account skillfully added dramatic tension by switching its focus from the obscure Gideon to the high-powered Washington lawyer (and future Supreme Court Justice) Abe Fortas, who argued the appeal before the high court. Casting the justices as members of a venerable institution that can create a more just society through the magic of constitutional doctrine, *Gideon's Trumpet* brought a celebratory and heroic image of the Supreme Court into the popular realm. Rivaling the fictive *To Kill a Mockingbird* (1962) for its ability to garner praise from both lay and professional critics, *Gideon's Trumpet* has migrated from being a best-selling popular account of the U.S. Supreme Court at work to becoming the best-known popular history of the Warren Court era.

Several more acerbic books did crack the popular market and even gained grudging recognition from segments of the legal-scholarly community. These included *The Brethren* (1979), probably the best-selling Supreme Court book of all time (released during the post-Watergate fascination with "insider histories" of recent events), and the much less successful *Closed Chambers* (1998). They also drew criticism for, avowedly, emphasizing the political and the personal over the doctrinal and for, implicitly, encouraging former clerks at the Court to betray the informal code of silence that surrounded internal relationships among the justices. *Wild Bill* (2003), perhaps the first judicial biography to qualify for the pathography genre, relentlessly catalogued the personal and sexual foibles of Justice William O. Douglas. Even though it intrigued the legal-constitutional cognoscenti, especially those with their own "Wild Bill" tales, the book generated much less popular attention than comparable volumes about governmental officials who had served somewhere other than the U.S. Supreme Court.

General-market books about the Court seemed to track popular views, at least as pollsters and political scientists could see them. On the one hand, polling data suggested that most people knew little about the Court or its members. The fight "to save the nine" during the 1930s, for example, apparently left little imprint on popular memory. Surveys indicated that few adults even knew how many justices sat on the Court. Survey respondents found it much easier to identify jurists, such as Joseph Wapner and "Judge Judy," who presided over popular TV tribunals, than the chief justice of the United States. On the other hand, most people still held the Court in much higher esteem than either Congress or the presidency. A celebratory popular account such as *Gideon's Trumpet*, in other words, was destined for a much longer shelf life than one such as *The Brethren*.

This dominant tendency — to celebrate an institution about which most people remained ignorant — existed within a popular milieu in which the Court had a relatively low profile, especially in the electronic media. A center of Washington culture at the turn of the nineteenth century, the Court failed to attract anything like the visibility that other legal institutions commanded in the early-twenty-first-century's visually dominated mediascape. Although the contentious nominations of Bork and Thomas generated extensive TV and radio coverage, these two media largely ignored subsequent, less controversial nominations to the high court during the 1990s.

Even the reality-programming trend that swept through popular culture at the end of the twentieth century bypassed the Supreme Court. Of course, its very mode of operation — no more than a single hour of public argument about any one case and secret deliberations behind the fabled red velvet curtain — hardly attracted TV's reality auteurs. Indeed, no other appellate-level court — state or federal — had satisfied the media's appetite for real-time programming. The absence of cameras inside the Marble Palace also made it virtually impossible to wrap even the most celebrated Supreme Court case within a viewer-friendly documentary-style package. As of 2003, even PBS's *American Experience* series, which routinely used moving and still pictures in documentaries on a wide range of historical topics, had never done a program that focused on the Supreme Court, a justice, or even a landmark case.

The niche network C-SPAN, which carried various documentary-style features on the Supreme Court, tried the hardest to show the justices at work. It supplemented audiotapes of oral arguments on those rare occasions when the Supreme Court permitted their same-day (but still delayed) release with artistic renderings of the *mise en scène* in the Court's chambers. The resulting media product hardly rivaled the dramatic immediacy of images from *inside* the Simpson and other notorious trials. At best, TV cameras could portray events *outside* the Court building. A familiar, mediated ritual quickly developed. Groups interested in particular cases marshaled their forces, deployed their best (or shrillest) advocate before the microphones, and, finally, offered their attorneys to the media after an oral argument had concluded or a decision had been announced. Except for the handful of cases, such as *Bush v. Gore* (2000), that attracted crews and commentators from other networks, the limited popular appeal of C-SPAN meant that Supreme Court programming qualified, on its best days, as jurisprudence for the hundred thousands rather than for the millions.

Those who developed fictive programming for movies and television also struggled to frame the Supreme Court as effectively — and as profitably — as they could other institutions of the federal government. Although blockbusters, such as *Thirteen Days* and *The West Wing*, have been set in the White House, commercial projects featuring the Supreme Court have always struggled to find a sizable popular audience. In the wake of the success of *The West Wing*, for example, two TV networks scheduled Supreme Court dramas for the 2002–2003 season. Both embraced the narrative frame that had structured earlier Court-centered novels, such as Allen Drury's *Decision* (1983). They followed a new justice who joins a fictive Court that vaguely resembles the contemporary one, providing the audience with a point of entry into an unfamiliar place where people speak in a strange legalistic way. As in Hollywood's musicals of the 1930s, the newcomer soon discovers what goes on backstage. CBS's *First Monday*, with an ensemble cast that included James Garner as the folksy chief justice, fully exploited its poetic license. The first episode, for instance, portrayed a trial-level litigant being allowed to sit alongside attorneys during the oral argument before the Supreme Court. Staggering through a season-long run, with a minimal TV audience, *First Monday* still did far better than ABC's *The Court*. Even after appointing Sally Field as its new chief justice and winning plaudits for its stab at realism, *The Court* remained in session for only three episodes.

These two examples seemingly confirmed the perils of creating a mass, popular production about the Supreme Court. At least since *Talk of the Town*, the Supreme Court has appeared best suited for a supporting rather than a starring role in visual productions aimed at a substantial audience. Writers have occasionally tapped the Court, for example, to appear as one locale in a broader story line. The murder of two fictional Supreme Court justices — one a liberal in the mode of William J. Brennan and the other a conservative vaguely resembling William Rehnquist — does kick off

The Pelican Brief (1992). Although obtaining new justices seems the ostensible goal of the dual murders, the opening operates more as an Alfred Hitchcock–style McGuffin, a largely arbitrary plot device to set a filmic story in motion, than as the narrative's focal point. Other movies that might have emphasized the role of the Supreme Court followed a similar course. *All the President's Men* (1976), which depicted the most minor of players in the Watergate drama, relegated the Supreme Court (and its opinion in *U.S. v. Nixon* [1973]) to a walk-on role. Newspaper headlines, at the end of the movie, provide the only images of how the Court intervened at a crucial moment in this seminal constitutional episode.

Decisions by the Supreme Court between 1954 and 1973, which produced considerable popular political controversy at the time, have inspired several made-for-TV movies, but these were aimed at rather specialized audiences. Thus, even such decisions as *Brown v. Board of Education* (1954), *Gideon v. Wainwright* (1964), and *Roe v. Wade* (1973) could not yield film features with the appeal of real-life "political" movies, such as *Mr. Smith Goes to Washington* (1939), *Thirteen Days* (2000), or even *Dave* (1993) and *Legally Blond 2* (2003).

These films, for instance, eschewed the megastar casting used in most political movies and in *Talk of the Town. Roe vs. Wade* (1989), which traced the legal strategy that preceded the 1973 abortion decision by the badly split Burger Court, employed a large ensemble cast. Films that looked back to the era of the Warren Court featured major, if but aged, stars. *Separate But Equal* (1991), which highlighted the litigation that produced the *Brown* decision, cast Sidney Poitier as Thurgood Marshall and Burt Lancaster (in one of his final film roles) as his prosegregationist opponent John W. Davis. Significantly, lesser-known character actors played members of the Warren Court. *Gideon's Trumpet* (1980), starring Henry Fonda and Jose Ferrer, represented a later version of the Warren Court in a similar manner.

Gideon's Trumpet, based on the Lewis book, remains the most celebrated of these limited-market movies. By giving the role of Gideon to Fonda, a major Hollywood star long identified, both on- and off-screen, with social-justice causes, the movie could associate years of filmic imagery and Hollywood lore with its images of the Warren Court at work. The casting of John Houseman as Chief Justice Warren and Jose Ferrer as Abe Fortas capitalized on their earlier legal roles in *The Paper Chase* (1973) and *The Caine Mutiny* (1954). *Gideon's Trumpet,* in this sense, dispensed a thick dose of popular nostalgia to bolster its relatively thin view of the Supreme Court. Indeed, subsequent advertisements for revivals of this movie have elevated the iconic pop-cultural image of Henry Fonda's Gideon over that of the Supreme Court itself.

Looking "Up There"

One of the most colorful, even entertaining, of recent justices, Antonin Scalia, once used an analogy from the world of prize fighting to characterize the relationship between the Court and popular culture. When thrust into the popular arena, he quipped, the Court adopts a constitutional version of Muhammad Ali's "rope-a-dope" strategy: The justices allow opponents to beat on them until they get weary, from exertion, and can no longer sustain the larger battle. More elegant explanations have generally used (explicitly or implicitly) some version of the German cultural theorist Walter Benjamin's view of the effect that the process of "mechanical reproduction" might have on a once unique cultural image. Any product or practice can lose its aura — those priceless meanings linked to a single place — as a consequence of being copied and reproduced all across the visual marketplace, Benjamin theorized. The sense of uniqueness and authority that once enveloped its iconic image can begin to evaporate.

From this perspective, the Supreme Court has never, even during its most trying times in the popular spotlight, entirely lost its aura. As it has receded to the background of the twenty-first century's vast mediascape, the Court has generally maintained a more favorable image than most other institutions. At the same time, the Court has remained visible enough in the popular cultural realm so as not to risk appearing — at least to most people — to be a secretive, cabalistic body. As a fictive anarchist (a.k.a. Cary Grant) once said of an equally imaginary justice (a.k.a. Ronald Colman), the Supreme Court has most always appeared to look "fine up there," thereby assuring most people that the "country's in good hands." Jurisprudence for the hundreds may, in this sense, rest on popular images consumed by the millions.

—NORMAN L. ROSENBERG

FOR FURTHER READING AND RESEARCH

Although Michael G. Kammen's *A Machine That Would Go of Itself: The Constitution in American Culture* (New York, 1986) offers a much broader focus than the Supreme Court, it remains the best place to begin locating the high court in popular culture. The Court's image during the era of the "Republic of Letters" is elegantly discussed in Robert Ferguson, *Law and Letters in American Culture* (Cambridge, Mass., 1984).

The cultural place of the early-nineteenth-century Supreme Court is expertly illuminated in G. Edward White, *The Marshall Court and Cultural Change, 1815–1835* (New York, 1988), volume 3–4 of the *History of the Supreme Court of the United States* (the Oliver Wendell Holmes Devise). White's analysis can be supplemented with the discussion in two volumes by R. Kent Newmyer: *John*

Marshall and the Heroic Age of the Supreme Court (Baton Rouge, La., 2001) and *Supreme Court Justice Joseph Story: Statesman of the Old Republic* (Chapel Hill, N.C., 1985). On developments during the later nineteenth century, see Don Edward Fehrenbacher, *The Dred Scott Case: Its Significance in American Law and Politics* (New York, 1978); and Owen M. Fiss, *Troubled Beginnings of the Modern State, 1888–1910* (New York, 1993), volume 8 of the *History of the Supreme Court of the United States* (the Oliver Wendell Holmes Devise).

Maxwell H. Bloomfield, *Peaceful Revolution: Constitutional Change and American Culture from Progressivism to the New Deal* (Cambridge, Mass., 2000), offers the only book-length study of the Court's place in popular culture from the late nineteenth to the midtwentieth century. Different views of how Hollywood represented the post–New Deal Court in *Talk of the Town* (1942) are offered in Robert C. Post, "On the Popular Image of the Lawyer: Reflections in a Dark Glass," *California Law Review* 75 (1987), 379; and Norman L. Rosenberg, "Professor Lightcap Goes to Washington: Rereading *Talk of the Town*," *University of San Francisco Law Review* 30 (1996), 1083. L. A. Scot Powe's wide-ranging *The Warren Court and American Politics* (Cambridge, Mass., 2000) often touches on the Court's image in popular culture.

Norman L. Rosenberg looks at popular representations of the Warren-era case of *Gideon v. Wainwright* (1963) and also sketches a broader theoretical approach to law and popular culture in "Constitutional History and the 'Cultural Turn': Cross-Examining the Legal-Reelist Narratives of Henry Fonda," in Sandra F. VanBurkleo et al., eds., *Constitutionalism and American Culture: Writing the New Constitutional History* (Lawrence, Kans., 2002). Other studies in this vein, which look at, and also beyond, the Supreme Court while surveying the domains of popular culture, include Richard L. Sherwin, *When Law Goes Pop: The Vanishing Line between Law and Popular Culture* (Chicago, 2000). See also the essays edited by Austin Sarat and Jonathan Simon, collected under the general title "Beyond Legal Realism?: Cultural Analysis, Cultural Studies, and the Situation of Legal Scholarship," in *Yale Journal of Law and the Humanities* 13 (2001).

18

The Supreme Court and Election Returns

AT THE TURN of the twentieth century, Finley Peter Dunne wrote a popular newspaper column featuring the satiric observations and analysis of a fictional Irish American saloonkeeper, Mr. Dooley. Mr. Dooley's best-known insight is that "th' supreme coort follows th' iliction returns." Over time, this pithy conclusion achieved iconic status as one of the fundamental truths about the Court. But lurking beneath the statement was a profound question: why?

Justices of the Supreme Court have life tenure and their salaries can't be cut. Justices can be removed only by conviction following impeachment, and that has never happened. So why would their decisions follow the election returns? One common answer is that parties that win elections get to appoint justices, and justices are likely to vote with the party that appointed them. Second, the same intellectual and social forces that influence the electorate also influence judges. Third, periodically, the party in power cares so much about a result that it threatens the independence of the judiciary. Each answer — appointments, society, and power — is certainly plausible.

The party that controls the presidency gets to control the appointments to the Supreme Court. Deaths and retirements are random but constant; if one party wins more elections than the other, it can expect to appoint a majority of the justices on the Court. On average, a vacancy occurs somewhat over every two years, so a president can expect two appointments per four-year term. If the same party wins three consecutive presidential elections, it can expect between five and six appointments and a majority of the Court. In fact, there is not a single time in American history when a party winning three consecutive presidential elections did not get at least five appointments to the Court.

Much as we may try to insulate the justices from everyday politics, we cannot insulate or isolate them from American society. They will see, hear, and read the things that other relatively affluent, well-educated East Coast–based Americans see, hear, and read. Thus, the same intellectual and social forces that move American thought generally, and elections periodically, will also impact on the judiciary and cause change there too. This reflects the natural evolution of legal doctrine over time. Society changes; so do judicial results.

Although impeachment has never occurred, threats to the Court itself have. Individual justices are independent, but the judiciary itself is not. The Constitution protects judges; it does not protect the judiciary. Jurisdiction of all federal courts, the Supreme Court included, may be enlarged or cut back (and the latter has happened). So, too, the size of the courts, even that of the Supreme Court, can be varied. Indeed it has, from a low of six to a high of ten justices. Justices would naturally prefer not to be sitting on a Court that the political branches are trifling with for partisan reasons.

Thus, Mr. Dooley's observation has several plausible explanations. A more modern view, which began to emerge during the Warren Court era, is that Mr. Dooley is now obsolete. This view holds that whatever the Court once did, the modern Court no longer follows the election returns. Instead, it protects minorities — those who cannot find protection via the ballot. Our objective here is to test how well these various views explain the Court's decisions over time.

First Impressions

Mr. Dooley offered his observation in 1901 after the Court's decisions in the *Insular Cases* (1901). He concluded that the Court had ratified the results of the 1900 election, in which William McKinley defeated William Jennings Bryan, because a major issue between the two candidates (and parties) had been whether the United States would (or could) become an imperial power. The voters said yes, returning substantial Republican majorities in both the House and the Senate in addition to reelecting McKinley. The Court said yes, too.

Imperialism had been in play throughout the 1890s, with an increasing number of Republicans believing that the United States should acquire overseas territories, whereas Democrats held to the continental republic. The outcome of 1898's "splendid little war" (the Spanish-American War) resulted in Spain's ceding its claims to the Philippines and Puerto Rico to the United States, even though acquisition of them had not been a primary prewar objective. Everyone agreed that those territories were not headed for statehood; given the racist assumptions of the era, successfully assimilating the dark-skinned inhabitants of these islands was deemed impossible.

Democrats claimed that holding colonies was corrupting and unconstitutional. The Revolutionary War had been fought to free Americans from overseas rule, and it was unthinkable that America should now attempt to become a colonial power. Because American institutions could not be transplanted to the Philippines, the islands could not become a state; therefore, their acquisition was unconstitutional. The entire argument was compressed into a single phrase in the Democrats' 1900 platform: "the Constitution follows the flag."

Republicans wanted none of the "lesser America" that the Democrats espoused. Republicans believed that a great country would, like England, France, and Germany, have a colonial empire. The Constitution, they claimed, offered no barriers to this, because the right to acquire territory is an inherent incident of sovereignty.

The parties' positions were reiterated in the 1900 election, and Bryan made anti-imperialism (along with his old standby of free silver and attacks on the soulless "trusts") a cornerstone of his campaign. "The imperialistic idea is directly antagonistic to the ideas and ideals which have been cherished by the American people since the signing of the Declaration of Independence. A nation can not endure half republic and half colony." McKinley and his running mate, war hero Theodore Roosevelt, beat Bryan by 137 electoral votes — a slightly greater margin than in the 1896 outcome.

The issue of the Constitution and the flag reached the Court in the *Insular Cases*, and based on precedent, the Democrats seemed to have the better of the argument. Just three years earlier, in *Thompson v. Utah*, Justice John Marshall Harlan had written for the Court that the Sixth Amendment right to a jury trial was fully applicable in a territory because the Constitution governed all actions by Congress. Perhaps even more relevant was Chief Justice Roger Taney's opinion in *Dred Scott v. Sandford* (1857), which held that there were no second-class (white) Americans. When citizens entered a territory, they took their constitutional rights with them because, obviously, Congress has no power to nullify the Constitution. Significantly, in a seldom-read part of his opinion, Taney found that the power to acquire territory was to be implied from the power to admit new states. Like the Democrats in the debates of the aftermath of the Spanish-American War, Taney believed that any acquired territory had to be moved toward statehood and equal participation in our national institutions. "No power is given to acquire a territory to be held and permanently governed in that character."

Taney's views garnered only four votes in the *Insular Cases*. For the majority, the choice of either granting the inhabitants of the islands full political rights in our society or else relinquishing control over the islands was untenable. Like the Republicans, the Court's majority believed that a great power needed an empire, and they invoked John Marshall's phrase "the American empire." Territorial acquisition was inherent in sovereignty (and not, as Taney held, limited by or implied from the power to admit new states); therefore, Congress could determine as it pleased the status of territories virtually unaffected by the Constitution. If Congress wished to pave the way for statehood, as it had with the nineteenth-century continental expansion, it could. If Congress wished to leave the territories as colonies, it could do that. Congress had chosen the latter, and that was its prerogative.

There is a lot more policy analysis than constitutional analysis in the *Insular Cases,* and no single opinion commanded five votes. *Dred Scott* was declared to be no problem, because the Civil War had "produced such changes in judicial, as well as public sentiment, as to seriously impair the authority of that case." Mr. Dooley interpreted that as a justice saying: "If I cudden't write a betther wan with blinderhers on, I'd leap off th' bench. This horrible fluke iv a decisions throws a gr-reat, an almost dazzlin' light on th' case. I will turn it off." Then he offered his most famous remark that "no matther whether th' constitution follows th' flag or not, th' supreme coort follows th' iliction returns."

Mr. Dooley did not say why, but the best explanation for the *Insular Cases* is a combination of the Court's being influenced by the same social and intellectual forces that led to McKinley's reelection and the enthusiasm for becoming a colonial power, as well as twenty-five years of appointments that had given the Republicans six of the nine seats on the Court. (The Republicans voted 4–2 for imperialism; the Democrats were 2–1 opposed.)

As the *Insular Cases* show, the various possible explanations for Mr. Dooley's observation can, and therefore should, be tested by examining other instances of Court behavior involving significant change. Opportunities abound: In the decade following Franklin Roosevelt's victory over Herbert Hoover, for example, the course of decisions offers interesting variations on Mr. Dooley. Furthermore, the Court's composition—absolutely unchanged through 1937 and then virtually remade by 1942—sheds important light on the explanations. Similarly, major cases in the constitutional canon—*Marbury v. Madison* (1803), *Dred Scott v. Sandford* (1857), *Brown v. Board of Education* (1954), *Roe v. Wade* (1973), and *Bush v. Gore* (2000)—all offer additional insight into the possibilities of Mr. Dooley. Finally, instances of strong doctrinal shift—domestic security 1954–1962 under Chief Justice Earl Warren; capital punishment 1967–1976 under both Warren and his successor, Warren Burger; and the New Federalism after 1994 under Chief Justice William Rehnquist—can be analyzed for the light they shed. What do these various situations reveal about the influence of "th' iliction returns"?

The New Deal Court

The Court that decided all New Deal cases through 1937 consisted of three voting blocs. Four justices were so totally opposed to initiatives designed to alleviate the effects of the Great Depression that they became known as the "Four Horsemen of Reaction." Three justices were liberals generally sympathetic to New Deal measures. In the middle were Chief Justice Charles Evans Hughes and Justice Owen Roberts, both Republican appointees of President Hoover. For the New Deal to prevail at the Court, both had to vote with the liberals; any time one joined the Four Horsemen, the New Deal lost.

Accommodating Experimentation: 1934

Initially, the liberals prevailed in major cases as both Hughes and Roberts joined them to give states extra latitude to deal with the Great Depression. These 1934 cases — *Nebbia v. New York* and *Home Building and Loan v. Blaisdell* — represented a sharp break with the past.

Nebbia is a classic in presenting the old order against the new. New York imposed price controls on milk. A half-century of precedent held that price controls were valid only when imposed on a "business affected with the public interest." Prior cases showed that very few businesses fell within that special category. In essence, price regulation was valid for monopolies and state-granted franchises, but that was it. Therefore, under existing doctrine, the New York law should have been unconstitutional. Roberts held instead that there was "no closed class or category of business affected with a public interest" and that all the phrase meant was that the legislature had to have an adequate reason for wishing to control prices. In so holding, Roberts was rejecting the rigid system of classification that had previously been developed and substituting instead the idea that the limits imposed by the due process clause were "only that the law shall not be unreasonable, arbitrary or capricious." Similar reasoning could easily support the constitutionality of a minimum wage and much more.

Blaisdell was a response to falling agricultural prices and deflation in the Midwest. The Great Depression left many farmers unable to meet their mortgage payments, and at several judicial sales, there were serious threats of violence to prevent anyone except the defaulting landowner from bidding on the property. To stem the lawlessness and to help the landowners who could not meet their obligations, Minnesota passed a Mortgage Moratorium Law. By any standard, the law impaired the obligation of contract (in violation of Article I, section 10) because the creditor was getting neither the monthly payments nor, in default, the property.

In a stunning opinion, Hughes upheld the law by emphasizing the social and economic changes that the United States had undergone in the 150 years since the Constitution was adopted. The Court stated bluntly that times had changed since the framing and so had constitutional meanings. It is difficult to find a more modernist statement of a living constitution. Applied consistently, such a worldview would have found all the various New Deal actions valid because they, too, were attempting to cope with unprecedented economic distress.

Checking the New Deal: 1935–1936

The 1934 elections constituted the rarest of off-year elections, one in which the president's party swept to an even larger share of power. Democrats added nine senators to give them a total of sixty-nine, the greatest margin in American history; Democrats gained only thirteen House seats because they already had overwhelming control. As in the Senate, they enjoyed more than 70 percent of the chamber's members after the election. Finally, at the state level, Republicans were reduced to seven governorships.

The 1934 results, coming on the heels of those two years earlier, should have sealed the victory of the progressive constitutional doctrine announced in *Nebbia* and *Blaisdell*. Instead, the Court — or, more accurately, Roberts (and, to a lesser extent, Hughes) — shifted ground and began to invalidate everything in sight, an unprecedented ten federal statutes, nine of which had passed in 1934 and 1935. The major 1935 decision invalidated the National Industrial Recovery Act, the cornerstone of the New Deal economic program and a statute that Roosevelt had labeled as one of the most important in the nation's history. In another 1935 case, Roberts's opinion invalidating the Railroad Retirement Act embraced all the intellectual assumptions that had been driving the Four Horsemen.

A year later, the Court, through Roberts, struck down major New Deal initiatives dealing with conditions in agriculture and energy production. The Agricultural Adjustment Act, with both taxing and spending provisions, attempted to stabilize farm prices by curtailing farm production. The Court found the AAA unconstitutional because Congress had invaded state authority over local issues. The fact that the same problems were everywhere and therefore affecting the nation's general welfare was deemed irrelevant, simply "a widespread similarity of local conditions."

Congressional efforts to stabilize the coal industry by preventing strikes met a similar fate. Provisions limiting hours and providing for a minimum wage were held to exceed the Constitution's commerce power. It did not matter whether strikes greatly affected the national economy. Because mining was a local activity, it was left to the states.

State statutes were no less immune from judicial scrutiny and, it turned out, no more able to control wages. Adhering to the holding of *Adkins v. Children's Hospital* (1923), *Morehead v. New York ex rel. Tipaldo* (1936) invalidated a New York statute setting a minimum wage for women and children. Minimum-wage laws, *Adkins* had explained, required an employer to subsidize the employees, and that forced extraction was a violation of due process of law.

The Court Switches: 1937

Everything changed again in 1937. *Morehead* was expressly overruled in *West Coast Hotel v. Parrish.* Now the Court saw failure to pay a minimum wage as a societal subsidy to the employer and therefore appropriate for legislative correction. Next, the National Labor Relations Act was sustained. It turned out that preventing strikes that affected the national economy could be reached via the commerce clause. Finally, the Court sustained both unemployment compensation and old-age benefits under the Social Security Act. Similar conditions throughout the nation made the problem fit for national action.

Liberalism Triumphant: 1942

The New Deal revolution was completed in 1942 with *Wickard v. Filburn,* which allowed Congress to regulate wheat to be used on the farm where it was grown. If one retreated to 1937 (much less 1935 and 1936), the idea that the commerce power could reach Farmer Filburn's wheat would have been unthinkable. In *Schechter Poultry* (1935), in which the NIRA was invalidated, regulations dealing with chickens that came from Pennsylvania, were purchased in Manhattan, and then slaughtered in Brooklyn were found beyond national power. A unanimous Court held that control of slaughtered chicken was local and therefore beyond the commerce clause. In *Wickard v. Filburn,* the wheat never entered interstate commerce; it went from one place on Filburn's farm to another place on his farm. The Court nevertheless unanimously ruled that this was covered by the commerce clause. The most fundamental constitutional question of the era went from 0–9 to 9–0 in no more than seven years.

Explanations

Nebbia and *Blaisdell* look like natural outgrowths of the 1932 election, in which the country turned to the Democrats in the search for solutions to the Great Depression. Just a few years earlier, both cases would have come out differently. Mr. Dooley could have concluded that the 1932 elections and the Great Depression influenced the Court.

What can explain the shift between 1934 and the next two years? One thing is absolutely certain: It can't be Mr. Dooley. There is no better example of the Court's going counter to the election returns. Maybe, just maybe, one can argue that the Great Depression created conditions for which experimentation was necessary, and thus *Blaisdell* and *Nebbia* authorized states, as little laboratories, to experiment. But the various New Deal measures threatened basic constitutional structures and limits. Extra power in state governments is one thing; extra power in the federal government is dangerous.

In June 1936, the Court had seemed poised to strike down by votes of 5–4 or 6–3 everything the New Deal passed; in June 1937, everything was constitutional by a 5–4 vote. What had happened was FDR's landslide re-election in November, carrying every state except Maine and Vermont, and his stunning proposal in February to add justices to the Supreme Court. If successful, Roosevelt would have immediately been able to add six yes justices to the existing nine, thereby guaranteeing that all New Deal legislation would be declared constitutional (Plate B.7). Success would also have guaranteed that the Supreme Court would be less worthy of respect. Within everyone's memory was the British Liberal government's threatened packing of the House of Lords to prevent it from blocking important legislation. The Lords had acquiesced but were neutered in the process. The Court-packing plan threatened a similar result: a permanently wounded Supreme Court.

Roberts got the message. In 1937, he abandoned voting with the Four Horsemen and instead voted to sustain government action designed to deal with the economy. With the changed results and the benefit of one of the Four Horsemen's retirement, the Court-packing plan died in the summer heat. And Roberts became forever known as the "switch in time that saved nine."

Under the circumstances, Roberts had two choices. He could yield and live to fight another day in a better political climate for the Court. Or he could fight, lose, and finish his career as a dissenter on the diminished Supreme Court. Although fighting the good fight is heroic, seeing an institution one reveres — and believes has accomplished much good — harmed is more than unattractive; it is tragic. Maybe it was possible to find a third option. Virtually any contested constitutional question has two sides with strong arguments supporting each. Maybe a switch is less a switch than an appreciation that the Constitution was not as clear as previously thought. Then the jurist and the institution can continue with their heads held high. Roberts, in fact, deeply disputed and resented the charge that he had switched, even though many scholars, including the author, believe it true.

Roberts claimed that he had believed that the minimum-wage laws were constitutional well before the Court so held in *West Coast Hotel* (1937). He stated that he would have voted to overrule *Adkins* in *Morehead* but that the dissenters offered instead weak distinctions and that he could not agree with them. Rejecting the influence of the Court-packing plan on his actions, he noted that the vote in *West Coast Hotel* occurred well before FDR unveiled the plan. Important scholars agree and have offered a lively defense of his actions, combining several elements. First, statutory drafts-manship as well as administration lawyering had been particularly bad in the cases in which Roberts voted against the New Deal. By 1937, standards in both areas had improved substantially. Second, the early-1900s legal and intellectual worldview that provided the constitutional background for the New Deal dealt with legal events as if they belonged in discrete categories. This essentialist view of law had been eroding, however, and the Great Depression accelerated the trend. Roberts was the youngest of the justices, one of the two still in his twenties when the century began, and was thus more likely to embrace a modernist position. Third, he had already accepted the necessary intellectual framework to support the New Deal by 1934 with his important opinion in *Nebbia*.

Nevertheless, the vote on *West Coast Hotel* was held after FDR's landslide, and the votes on the NLRA and the Social Security Act did come after the Court-packing plan was announced. If Roberts had always "been there," ready to embrace the new order, how could anyone explain his time-out during 1935 and 1936, when he always voted with the majority in striking down the New Deal statutes? Poor lawyering and bad statutory drafting seem quite stretched as explanations, considering that his 1935 and 1936 opinions involving the Railroad Retirement Act and the AAA fully embraced the intellectual assumptions of the old order. Roberts's only extrajudicial explanation for those votes talked of the Court, not himself. "Looking back, it is difficult to see how the Court could have resisted the popular urge for uniform standards throughout the country — for what in effect was a unified economy."

Roberts might not have been the key vote had the normal appointments cycle played out during Roosevelt's first term when he became the first president to serve a full term without getting a single appointment to the Court. The composition of the Court in 1936 was the same as Hoover had left it in

1932: five Republicans and four Democrats, based on four Republican presidencies and Wilson's two terms. Nevertheless, one of the Republicans, Harlan Fiske Stone, was a staunch liberal, whereas two of the Democrats — James McReynolds and Pierce Butler — comprised half of the reactionary Four Horsemen. Had FDR garnered a retirement from the then seventy-five-year-old Willis Van Devanter in 1934 and had the new justice voted with the New Deal, Roberts's vote would not have mattered, in most cases, and "1937" might have occurred earlier, once again proving Mr. Dooley right and saving Roberts from the epithet he hated.

The complete liberal lurch after 1942, whereby the Court simply abandoned restraints on economic legislation, is fully explained by the argument that the Court follows the election returns: By then, Roosevelt had appointed seven Democratic justices to the Court, and each of the Four Horsemen retired. These younger New Dealers were fully compatible with modern conditions and the need for government action to control the economy. Thus, in the long run, it seems, Mr. Dooley is surely right.

Depending on where one stops between 1933 and 1942, there is evidence for all three possibilities behind Mr. Dooley's observation, as well as one situation, 1935–1936, inconsistent with it. Furthermore, had we looked at other areas — notably, the Court's decision in *Carolene Products* (1938)— we could have seen an incipient beginning for the idea that the Court protects minorities. In other words, the New Deal offers something for everyone. So it is appropriate also to look before and after that turbulent decade to see how Mr. Dooley fares.

Marbury v. Madison (1803)

The political crisis that produced *Marbury* also produced the first example of the elected branches' flexing their muscles at the Court. Without the election of 1800, *Marbury* would never have happened. The revolutionaries who won independence from Britain and then created the Constitution split into two factions during the 1790s. One, the Federalists, led by George Washington and then John Adams, had controlled the government from its inception. The other, Republicans, triumphed in the 1800 elections under their leader, Thomas Jefferson. In what turned out to be a peaceful, although tense, transition of power, the Federalists yielded the presidency but also created numerous new judgeships and sought to embed themselves in the national judiciary until they could return to elective power. Chief Justice Oliver Ellsworth retired, and Secretary of State John Marshall was confirmed as his replacement. Sixteen new life-tenured circuit judges were created by the Judiciary Act of 1801 and were swiftly confirmed. A statute organizing the District of Columbia created forty-two justices of the peace whose nominations by the lame-duck Adams had been speedily confirmed by the Senate. Secretary of State John Marshall had affixed the seal to the commissions, but five were not delivered before Jefferson took over the presidency.

Jefferson ordered the commissions not to be delivered, and William Marbury (Plate A.5) brought his famous mandamus action in the original jurisdiction of the Supreme Court. In its December 1801 term, the Court issued a show-cause order to Jefferson's secretary of state, James Madison. Congress responded by abolishing the Court's June 1802 term so that *Marbury* could not be heard before February 1803.

Chief Justice Marshall's famous *Marbury* opinion found, first, that delivery of a signed and sealed commission was not necessary for the office to vest; hence, Madison's refusal to deliver the commission was illegal. The opinion was a pointed rebuke to Jefferson, finding that he behaved as if this were not a government of laws but instead one of men. Were it not for Marshall's next move, holding that the Court had no jurisdiction because section 13 of the Judiciary Act of 1789 was unconstitutional, the Court would have ordered Madison to deliver the commission. He would not have done so, and, in that standoff with the popular and powerful Republican president, the Court was bound to lose. Marshall's celebrated genius is that he found a way to assert judicial power while avoiding a direct confrontation.

When that confrontation could not be avoided, the Court yielded to Jefferson — and the results of the 1800 election — in the profoundly underappreciated *Stuart v. Laird.* Decided six days after *Marbury, Stuart* dealt with the other "midnight judges," the sixteen circuit judges created by the Judiciary Act of 1801. Jefferson made its repeal his first legislative priority. He privately wrote that "lopping off the parasitical plant engrafted at the last session on the judicial body" was necessary because "from that battery all the works of Republicanism are to be beaten down and erased."

In the congressional debates and in the partisan press, Federalists claimed that life tenure during good behavior made repeal of the Judiciary Act unconstitutional and that repeal was an attack on the independence of the judiciary. Republicans responded that, because the Constitution provides for salaries only "during their Continuance in Office," stripping them of the office would end the need for payment. When the Repeal Act of 1802 passed, the Republican *National Intelligencer* exalted: "Judges created for political purposes, and for the worst of purposes under a republican government, for the purpose of opposing the national will, from this day cease to exist."

Federalists believed that now, only the judiciary could save the country from the Republicans, and many were anxious for the constitutional fight to begin. Some Republicans, too, relished the prospect, hoping to engage the Federalists in a battle that the defeated and unpopular party could not hope to win. Federalists had frequently warned that the Supreme Court would declare the Repeal Act unconstitutional, but Marshall, trying to protect judicial independence with the resources at hand, fully understood that the Federalists could not prevail, even though he believed that the Repeal Act was unconstitutional. Thus, *Stuart* meekly upheld the repeal, its three brief paragraphs never mentioning the constitutional issue as perceived by the Federalists. Instead, the Court stated that "Congress have constitutional authority to establish such inferior tribunals as they think proper; and to transfer a cause from one such tribunal to another. In this last particular there are no words in the Constitution to prohibit or restrain the exercise of legislative power."

Scott v. Sandford (1857)

The *Dred Scott* case was decided by a Court loaded with Democratic appointees because Democrats had controlled the federal government for most of the previous three decades. It is hardly surprising, therefore, that the *Dred Scott* majority upheld the Democratic Party's position on slavery in the territories. Nevertheless, almost from the moment of the decision itself, people have heaped anathemas on one or both of *Dred Scott's* conclusions that descendants of Africans could never be citizens and that Congress lacked power over slavery in the territories. Given the proximity of the decision to the Civil War and the two constitutional amendments repudiating the case, it is hardly surprising that Charles Evans Hughes's conclusion that *Dred Scott* was a "self-inflicted wound" on the Court has stuck.

Slavery had been a national issue since the Missouri Compromise had banned it in territories to the north of Missouri. With the territorial acquisition resulting from the Mexican War (1846–1848), slavery became *the* decisive national issue. The United States had gained substantial territories that one day would be states. One way or another, the North-South balance in the Senate would be affected. The land made cotton slavery unlikely, but the land was also south of the Missouri Compromise and therefore could create potential slave states.

In the immediate aftermath of the Mexican War, the issue was finessed in the omnibus Compromise of 1850. But behind that compromise was the unmistakable fact that party lines had evaporated and that 80 percent of the members of Congress had cast their votes not as Democrats or Whigs but rather as Northerners or Southerners. Four years later, the Kansas-Nebraska Act repealed the Missouri Compromise. The 1854 act was intended by its sponsor, Senator Stephen Douglas of Illinois, as a way of bridging the sectional gap on slavery by shifting the decision of whether a territory would be slave or free from Congress to the territory's settlers. Congress also tried to take the issue out of politics by constitutionalizing it and requesting that the Supreme Court decide the question of congressional power. As the political parties had found themselves unable to deal with the issue, perhaps the Court could settle it, and then the parties could go back to the economic debates that they were used to and for which they had been created. It was too late for the Whigs; they had been weakened by the Compromise of 1850 and did not survive to fight in 1856. The election was contested between the national Democrats and the new, purely sectional, Republican Party, which stood for just one thing: banning slavery from the territories. Not surprisingly, the Democrats prevailed.

The Court that accepted the invitation to settle the controversy consisted of representative lawyer-politicians. Only Peter Daniel of Virginia (who refused to eat food produced in the North or set foot on Northern soil) was outside the mainstream. Six of the remaining eight were Democrats, four of them from the South. All six (plus Daniel) held the Missouri Compromise unconstitutional because Congress lacked power over slavery in the territories. That was the view of the newly elected Democratic president, James Buchanan of Pennsylvania, who privately urged his fellow Pennsylvanian, Justice Robert Grier, to vote with the Southerners to hold the Missouri Compromise unconstitutional. That was the view of Stephen A. Douglas, the likely Democratic candidate for president after a Buchanan administration. That was the view of the decided majority of the Democratic Party — the sole surviving national, that is, nonsectional, institution in the United States. Ruling the other way, with the sectionally based Republicans, would have been unthinkable, not to mention irresponsible, as the South would have seceded, and Buchanan believed that the Constitution precluded stopping them.

With hindsight, virtually everyone, like Hughes, has decided that the Court should have ducked. But with slavery in the territories driving the country apart and shattering all the national institutions, would it have been responsible for the Court to sit this one out? Might not the failure to even try at the time of the country's greatest need also be seen as a "self-inflicted wound"? The case for ducking is either the historically fallacious assumption that *Dred Scott* caused the Civil War or the belief that the Civil War was inevitable so the Court should preserve its place and reputation for its aftermath. Neither seems particularly apt.

Dred Scott was more than following the 1856 election returns, although Buchanan had influenced both and was enthusiastic about the results of both. It was the outgrowth of Democrat victories in most of the elections from Andrew Jackson onward, from which the party had gained a large majority on the Court. *Dred Scott* may have been wrong, but Democrats both North and South supported it (Plate A.8).

Dred Scott neither caused nor hastened the Civil War. It was a product of its times; slavery in the territories was destroying the country, and only one result could offer any hope. The Court gave that one result, but events — especially Buchanan's wholly irresponsible decision late that year to support statehood for Kansas under the Lecompton fraud that denied the residents of Kansas a vote on the proslavery constitution (and against the will of the overwhelming majority of residents) — were beyond the Court's control. Lecompton fueled the Republican belief that *Dred Scott* was part of a Southern conspiracy to make slavery a national institution.

Brown v. Board of Education (1954)

If *Dred Scott* is the most universally condemned case, *Brown* is the most universally praised. *Brown* is an example of intellectual and social forces pointing the Court in a single direction, although the Court needed an assist to achieve unanimity.

Without Dwight Eisenhower's victory in the 1952 elections, Earl Warren would not have been chief justice, and *Brown* might not have been the same. Yet civil rights was an issue both parties had ignored in 1952.

The legal challenge to segregation had been coming at least since World War II. American soldiers, especially African American soldiers, could not be expected to fight Nazi racism in Europe and then ignore Southern racism in America. Virtually everyone could see the parallels; it was simply a question of when something would be done.

Major-league baseball, the national pastime and a white preserve, was desegregated in 1947. Jackie Robinson was first to cross that color line, but the Brooklyn Dodgers did not stop with one African American and thereafter became the National League's dominant team. A major cultural institution could be desegregated successfully.

In 1948, Minneapolis Mayor Hubert Humphrey gave a rousing speech to the Democratic National Convention, demanding that the party make a strong commitment to civil rights. When the convention agreed, the Deep South, led by South Carolina Governor Strom Thurmond, bolted the party. But Harry Truman won without the Dixiecrats, and he then ordered the armed forces desegregated. A major party could overcome its past and the military could change.

As the cold war heightened, segregation became America's Achilles' heel, and in *Brown*, the United States filed a brief that urged the Court to see segregation in the context of the cold war. "The United States is trying to prove to the people of the world, of every nationality, race and color, that a free democracy is the most civilized and most secure form of government yet devised by man." The Soviet Union, in its arguments to Third World countries, consistently emphasized racial discrimination in the United States, and other countries "cannot understand how such a practice can exist in a country which professes to be a staunch supporter of freedom, justice, and democracy." Segregation was a "constant embarrassment" that "jeopardizes the effective maintenance of our moral leadership of the free and democratic nations of the world." That brief was filed by the Truman Department of Justice; a new brief, filed by Eisenhower's, did not backtrack.

Thurgood Marshall, head of the NAACP Legal Defense Fund, had determined that the time was right to overrule *Plessy v. Ferguson.* Yet when *Brown* was first argued, he was proved wrong. The justices were hopelessly split on an issue when they desired (and perhaps needed) unanimity. Four justices believed that segregation was per se unconstitutional. Three— Kentuckians Chief Justice Fred Vinson and Stanley Reed and Texan Tom Clark—believed *stare decisis* (and therefore separate but equal) should prevail. The positions of the other two, Felix Frankfurter and Robert Jackson, are difficult to determine, but a 6–3 decision on such a momentous issue would be risky.

In order to buy more time, Frankfurter suggested new briefing and reargument devoted to ascertaining the circumstances surrounding adoption of the Fourteenth Amendment and the relationship between legislative and judicial power under the amendment, as counsel for Virginia had denied that even Congress could touch state segregation. During the summer recess, Vinson died of a heart attack. Frankfurter commented privately to his law clerks that it was "the first indication that I have ever had that there is a God." Thus, the popular California governor, Earl Warren, whom Eisenhower had previously promised the first seat to open on the Court, replaced Vinson. He changed the dynamics of the decision.

Warren requested that no vote be taken and hardened positions avoided. Instead, *Brown* would be discussed weekly at conference and individually among the justices. But when he offered his views, the other justices knew that *Plessy* was doomed, for Warren made it clear that he believed segregation could be sustained only on the fallacious theory of Negro inferiority. "We must act, but we should do it in a tolerant way." There were five votes, and Frankfurter happily made a sixth; Clark, always liking to vote with his chief, added a seventh. Jackson was willing to go along, although he might have written separately but for a heart attack that hospitalized him for six weeks. Reed was the lone holdout. Eventually, as the months passed, Warren met with Reed and went for the clinching argument: "Stan, you're all by yourself in this now. You've got to decide whether it's really the best thing for the country." Reed switched, and *Brown* was unanimous.

Brown is often portrayed as the Court protecting a minority, but that ignores the fact that only the white South objected. *Brown* is best explained as a response to a changed social and intellectual climate — the fight against Nazism, the propaganda needs of the cold war, African American migration to the North, changes in the Democratic Party, the desegregation of national institutions. In mid-twentieth-century America, *Plessy* could not be reaffirmed, no matter what Vinson, Reed, and Clark initially thought. Replacing Vinson with Warren validated Thurgood Marshall's conclusion that the time was right for ending *Plessy*'s regime (Plate B.11).

Roe v. Wade (1973)

Like *Brown*, *Roe* was a result whose time seemed right. But unlike *Brown*, in which the decision was not unexpected, *Roe* came out of the blue.

Roe nationalized and constitutionalized the debate on abortion. That debate was less than a decade old and previously had been carried on separately in various state legislatures considering whether to modify or eliminate the existing legal bans on abortion. Initially, doctors were the primary figures in the debate. Then, in the late 1960s, they were supplanted by the growing women's movement.

The newly formed National Organization for Women (NOW) offered a women's bill of rights in which abortion was a fundamental right and should be available on demand. By the time *Roe* was decided, more than a quarter of the states had liberalized their laws, and four, including New York, had gone all the way to the NOW position. Under California's liberalized law, signed by Governor Ronald Reagan, the number of legal abortions increased 2,000 percent, from 5,018 to 116,749, in four years.

The takeover of the abortion debate was only one feature of a movement for equality whose time was truly right. In 1970, Congress considered the Equal Rights Amendment (ERA). It was favored by President Richard Nixon and former President Lyndon Johnson and sailed through the House by a 350–15 vote. But the amendment bogged down in a Senate committee, largely over the issue of whether the military draft would have to include women. In the next Congress, the amendment easily won March 1972 passage. That day, Hawaii ratified; a day later, four states ratified; two more followed suit the next day. By the beginning of 1973, thirty of the necessary thirty-eight states were aboard. At least six (and perhaps all) of the justices were sure that the ERA would be swiftly ratified. The four Democratic holdovers from the Warren Court were so impatient that they tried to render it irrelevant by holding that the Fourteenth Amendment already gave women equal rights with men.

Women had successfully and much more quickly built an equal rights movement to parallel the civil rights movement for African Americans, and it was in this climate that the Court decided *Roe*. Not only were the justices swept along with the rest of the country, but also the issue of women's rights was one on which they could be successfully lobbied: by their wives and daughters. It was almost as unthinkable to vote against equal rights as it would have been twenty years earlier to vote for separate but equal. Essentially, with elites in both political parties favoring equal rights and abortion rights, the justices had little trouble going along and no incentive not to.

Bush v. Gore (2000)

Of all the cases we have considered here, *Bush v. Gore* is the easiest to explain, although at one level, it is a decisive slap at Mr. Dooley, for it obviously didn't follow the election returns. Depending on one's viewpoint, *Bush v. Gore* either validated the 2000 election returns or created them. The *Brown* and *Roe* explanation fails because no social or intellectual climate influenced the Court and country to intervene in a state election recount. But the third alternative — appointments over time — has remarkable explanatory power. Twenty-seven years had elapsed between LBJ's nomination of Thurgood Marshall and Bill Clinton's of Ruth Bader Ginsburg. In between came four Nixon appointments, one by Gerald Ford, three by Ronald Reagan, and two by the elder Bush. The Court that decided *Bush v. Gore* was nominally 7–2 Republican. But far more important, of those seven, five were conservative Republicans. Those five first stayed the Florida recount and then provided the votes to end the recount, electing the younger Bush president.

Additional Changes in Court Behavior

All these major cases point to the conclusion that Mr. Dooley was wrong if he was asserting that a single intervening election could change the Court, but at least the latter two seem at odds with a Court protecting those who cannot prevail in elections. Three additional switches in Court behavior merit consideration in determining the best explanation: the anti-Communist domestic-security cases between 1954 and 1962, capital punishment from 1967 to 1976, and the New Federalism dating from 1995.

Domestic Security

The Court's domestic-security decisions from 1954 through 1957 reflect an initial overreading of the message the Senate was deemed to have sent when it condemned Joseph McCarthy. After Congress made it clear that the Court had overstepped its boundaries, the Court retreated, just as it had in 1937.

The Court had sustained all the important aspects of the domestic-security program as quickly as it got cases. In 1954, the Court even upheld a suspension of a medical license for reasons that had nothing to do with the ability to practice medicine but instead were undergirded by the doctor's support for the loyalists in the Spanish Civil War. Then in December 1954, the Senate condemned McCarthy for his many excesses in the name of fighting and (unsuccessfully) finding domestic Communists. Thereafter, the Court started to dismantle the domestic-security program.

In 1956, the Court issued two major decisions. In *Slochower v. Board of Higher Education*, it held that a tenured employee could not be dismissed simply for taking the Fifth Amendment when asked about prior Communist activities. In *Pennsylvania v. Nelson*, the Court reversed the conviction for sedition of the head of the Communist Party in western Pennsylvania and essentially held that state sedition laws, existing in forty-two states, were all preempted by the federal Smith Act. Both of these decisions were sharply criticized by the organized bar and, more important, in Congress.

During the Court's next term, twelve cases were decided that involved Communists, and the Communists prevailed in every one. The Court outraged the organized bar by holding that state bar associations could not refuse admission solely on the ground of past membership in the Communist Party. The Court construed the advocacy provisions of the Smith Act in such a way as to make future prosecutions impossible. In *Jencks v. United States*, it ordered that raw FBI files be made available to defense counsel in perjury cases. In *Watkins v. United States*, it verbally slapped the House Un-American Activities Committee (HUAC) around, suggesting the unconstitutional vagueness of "Un-American" and stating that there was no valid power to expose individuals as current or former Communists merely to "expose for exposure's sake." Because that was all HUAC did, *Watkins* threatened the very existence of HUAC.

Congress was busy dealing with the first civil rights act to pass in seventy-five years and could not focus legislatively on all that the Court had done except to quickly pass a single statute — the Jencks Act — that clarified the duties to pass FBI files to defense counsel. J. Edgar Hoover had demanded the clarification, and given his power and reputation, he got it quickly.

A year later, the Court was far more circumspect and indeed gutted *Slochower* by allowing an employee who took the Fifth to be fired for insubordination (instead of simply for taking the Fifth). That was insufficient to appease a very angry congressional coalition of Southerners, on the one hand, and national security conservatives, on the other, who were furious about what the Court had done. They came within a hair of stripping the Court of jurisdiction in cases dealing with communism. Chief Justice Warren observed that the "legislation, evoking as it did the atmosphere of the Cold War hysteria, came dangerously close to passing."

The Court reversed course immediately. In 1959, it undid *Watkins* and ruled that HUAC's governing resolution was not too vague and that no court could determine whether HUAC was exposing individuals for exposure's sake. In 1961, the Court revisited the bar cases and found that an applicant must answer questions about past communism so that the bar could determine fitness to practice. The Court also sustained over a First Amendment challenge the Subversive Activities Control Board's order to the Communist Party to register. Finally, a year later, the Court initially voted to allow Florida to use Communist-hunting tactics on the NAACP. Then Justice Charles Whittaker followed his doctor's orders and retired. The NAACP case was put over to the following term and, with Frankfurter also retired, the Court changed the outcome and over the next four years invalidated the domestic-security program virtually in its entirety.

Looking back, one can see that the Court may have taken a false signal from the Senate's condemnation of McCarthy and concluded that McCarthyism was also condemned. When, in 1958, the Court had the domestic-security program in shambles, Congress reacted by giving the Court a near-death experience. The Court retreated until well into President John Kennedy's term. Interestingly, in the 1958 elections, seven Republican senators who had voted against the Court were defeated by liberal Democrats. And, of course, liberal Democrats prevailed in the 1960 elections. But the Court itself did not respond to these new circumstances until Kennedy made his second nomination (Arthur Goldberg) to the Court.

Capital Punishment

The Court believed that Americans wished an end to capital punishment and declared its practice unconstitutional. When it was clear that the Court had misread the country, the Court switched to again uphold the constitutionality of capital punishment.

Stripping out the double negatives, both the Fifth and Fourteenth Amendments textually authorize the taking of life so long as due process is accorded the defendant. Thus, as late as 1965, the official position of the American Civil Liberties Union (ACLU) was that capital punishment did not present a civil liberties issue. Nor had the Court spoken a word on the issue — possibly because the Constitution did so explicitly. Nevertheless, the number of executions in the United States had been declining steadily. In the 1940s, the nation averaged 128 executions per year; in the 1950s, the average was 72; from 1960 to 1962, it was 48, and that dropped to 21 in 1963. The drop in executions was matched in the polls by an increasing belief that capital punishment ought to be abolished. In 1967, the year that the Court started deciding capital cases, two men were executed. There were no further executions for a decade.

The Court commenced its capital punishment jurisprudence with a blockbuster by holding unconstitutional the jury-selection procedures that most states used in capital cases. To that point, "death-qualified" juries had been created by striking for cause any potential jurors who were opposed to capital punishment. The decision dealt such a blow to the existing regime that many experts thought that no jury would ever give the death penalty, but the Court was not through. It was poised to make yet another radical change in the system by holding that states must give jurors standards by which to choose which defendants deserved death and which did not. The justices believed that that task was impossible and therefore by requiring it, they would end capital punishment. But Justice Abe Fortas's resignation and Warren's retirement intervened, and in *McGautha v. California* (1971), a 6–3 Court upheld standardless sentencing.

Seemingly stunned by what they had done — six hundred death-row inmates now faced execution — the justices voted to consider whether capital punishment as practiced was cruel and unusual punishment. In *Furman v. Georgia* (1972), a 5–4 Court held that it was. The majority consisted of the five Warren Court holdovers; the dissenters were the four appointees of President Nixon.

Although each of the five in the majority wrote separately and offered five different reasons why capital punishment as practiced violated the Constitution, the outcome of *Furman* was a revisiting of *McGautha*, which required the states to provide standards for jurors in the exercise of their ultimate discretion. Justice Thurgood Marshall would have gone further and held that capital punishment under any circumstances violated the Constitution because the death penalty "shocks the conscience and sense of justice of the people" and "is morally unacceptable to the people of the United States at this time in their history." Justices William O. Douglas, Potter Stewart, and Byron White did not go so far but did not believe they had to. Stewart felt that the moral authority of the Court's pronouncement would end the issue. States would not revisit capital punishment, and the Court would never again have to face the issue. Even the dissenting Chief Justice Warren Burger agreed; privately, he predicted that there would never be another execution in the country.

How wrong they were. Over the next four years, thirty-five states and the federal government enacted new death-penalty laws. And the Court bowed to that legislative judgment, with only the two remaining members of the liberal wing of the Warren Court dissenting. *Gregg v. Georgia* (1976) explained that the claim in *Furman* was predicated primarily on the proposition that "standards of decency had evolved to the point where capital punishment could no longer be tolerated." That had proved incorrect. "The most marked indication of society's endorsement of the death penalty for murder is the legislative response to *Furman*." The Court's makeup was basically the same, but the justices' understanding of their countrymen had been proved wrong. The justices started by following the polls; they ended by following the election results.

The New Federalism

Federalism — the very existence of states as a limit on federal power — ceased to be a constitutional factor after 1937. Then, after the Republicans took control of Congress in the 1994 elections, a majority of the Court found federalism a viable limit on national power.

Fedcralism was a casualty of both the new order after 1937 and segregation. States were something the South had. Between 1937 and 1995, only two federal statutes were found beyond congressional power in relation to the states. One case so holding was overruled; the other wasn't that important. But in 1995, the Court reinitiated limits on federal power vis-à-vis the states and did so in striking down a recent, politically popular statute, the Gun Free School Zones Act. Subsequent cases knocked out the Religious Freedom Restoration Act, the Brady Bill (on background checks for gun purchasers), the Violence Against Women Act, and damage remedies against state governments under both the Age Discrimination Act and the Americans with Disabilities Act.

The rationales offered by the Court varied. In the cases striking the Gun Free School Zones and Violence Against Women Acts, there was neither commerce nor the crossing of a state line; the Brady Bill commandeered local officials to do the federal work; the Religious Freedom Restoration Act invaded the Court's role as final expositor of the Constitution; the damage remedies went against the right of states to claim sovereign immunity in any court.

If the rationales varied, the statutes did not. All were the type of statutes that Democrats adore — rights creating (except for the Brady Bill, which was almost as good because it stripped rights from a group Democrats loathe) — and the type that Republicans cannot oppose without causing themselves political difficulty. Furthermore, all were passed by Congresses with Democratic majorities in both houses. Finally, all were struck down after the Republicans took control of the House of Representatives following the 1994 elections. Those elections may not have been the signal to strike down these statutes, but the results guaranteed that the Court would suffer no consequences from doing so.

Conclusions

Mr. Dooley was on the money in saying that the Court follows the election returns, but no single explanation encompasses why that is so. The dominant reason is that election victors get to appoint and confirm judges. When a party wins enough elections, it controls the judiciary. Additionally, the same factors that influence politicians and elections influence judges as well. They are independent but not cocooned off from American society. Finally, but only on rare occasions, election victors overtly flex their muscles at the Court such that the justices must take notice. Thus, although elections surely matter in predicting Court developments, they matter in different ways.

Of the cases examined here, three — *Marbury, Stuart v. Laird*, and *Bush v. Gore* — were direct results of presidential elections and would not have existed without the elections. On two additional occasions — the Court-packing crisis in 1937 and the domestic-security cases after 1958 — when the Court abruptly changed directions, outcomes were the direct result of the winners' in the previous election threatening judicial independence. *Stuart v. Laird* is also a case in which judicial independence was at issue. A number of cases seem to directly follow the election returns: *Dred Scott*, the *Insular Cases*, the reinstatement of capital punishment, and the New Federalism. Finally, several cases — *Brown, Roe*, and *Furman* (albeit briefly) — are examples of an idea whose time apparently had come.

What does this analysis demonstrate? Far from the feel-good civics lecture that the Court is busy protecting those who cannot protect themselves, the Court is revealed as a majoritarian institution. It is moved by the same social, intellectual, and political factors that move voters. Because of the regularity of retirements and appointments, the personnel of the Court maintain a reasonably accurate reflection of the state of American politics.

To return one last time to Mr. Dooley: The *Insular Cases* were no fluke; Mr. Dooley and his candidate lost on the issue of imperialism, fair and square. Perhaps Mr. Dooley shouldn't have taken his defeat so hard. But perhaps he couldn't resist. Finley Peter Dunne had risen to national prominence for his lampooning of the imperialists during the Spanish-American War. Thus, he once wondered whether the Philippines were islands or canned goods and opined that Roosevelt's account, *The Rough Riders,* should have been titled instead *Alone in Cubia.* Without Dunne's disappointment, Mr. Dooley might never have had the opportunity to be a lasting American sage.

—LUCAS A. (SCOT) POWE, JR.

FOR FURTHER READING AND RESEARCH

In his seminal article, "Decision-Making in a Democracy: The Supreme Court as a National Policy-Maker, *Journal of Public Law* 6 (1957), 279, Robert Dahl offered a terse reason why Mr. Dooley was correct: "It would appear . . . somewhat unrealistic to suppose that a Court whose members are recruited in the fashion of Supreme Court Justices would long hold to norms of Right or Justice substantially at odds with the rest of the political elite." John Hart Ely's *Democracy and Distrust* (Cambridge, Mass., 1980) offers an elegant view of the Court as protecting minorities who cannot protect themselves in the political process. Ely's operative assumption was that he was describing the Warren Court. The most complete study of the era — Lucas A. Powe, Jr., *The Warren Court and American Politics* (Cambridge, Mass., 2000) — shows that to be unfounded; the Warren Court was a functioning part of Kennedy-Johnson liberalism of the mid- and late 1960s. Mark A. Graber demonstrates that the Court tends to declare laws unconstitutional only after receiving fairly explicit invitations to do so by members of the dominant national coalition: "The Nonmajoritarian Difficulty: Legislative Deference to the Judiciary, *Studies in American Political Development* 7 (1993), 35. For discussions of the politics surrounding the case studies offered in the text, see William E. Leuchtenburg, *The Supreme Court Reborn* (New York, 1995); Barry Cushman, *Rethinking the New Deal Court* (New York, 1998); James F. Simon, *What Kind of Nation* (New York, 2002); Kenneth Stampp, *America in 1857* (New York, 1990); Powe, *The Warren Court and American Politics;* and Mark A. Graber, *Rethinking Abortion* (Princeton, N.J., 1996).

Appendix A

Supreme Court Personnel: 1789 to the Present

The Jay, Rutledge, and Ellsworth Courts

NAME	SWORN IN	LEFT COURT
Jay, John	**October 1789**	**Resigned June 1795**
Rutledge, John	February 1790	Resigned March 1791
Cushing, William	February 1790	Died September 1810
Wilson, James	October 1789	Died August 1798
Blair, John	February 1790	Resigned October 1795
Iredell, James	May 1790	Died October 1799
Johnson, Thomas	August 1792	Resigned January 1793
Paterson, William	March 1793	Died September 1806
Rutledge, John	**August 1795**	**Rejected December 1795**
Cushing, William	February 1790	Died September 1810
Wilson, James	October 1789	Died August 1798
Blair, John	February 1790	Resigned October 1795
Iredell, James	May 1790	Died October 1799
Paterson, William	March 1793	Died September 1806
Chase, Samuel	February 1796	Died June 1811
Ellsworth, Oliver	**March 1796**	**Resigned October, 1800**
Cushing, William	February 1790	Died September 1810
Wilson, James	October 1789	Died August 1798
Iredell, James	May 1790	Died October 1799
Paterson, William	March 1793	Died September 1806
Chase, Samuel	February 1796	Died June 1811
Washington, Bushrod	February 1799	Died November 1829
Moore, Alfred	April 1800	Resigned January 1804

The Marshall Court

NAME	SWORN IN	LEFT COURT
Marshall, John	**February 1801**	**Died July 1835**
Cushing, William	February 1790	Died September 1810
Paterson, William	March 1793	Died September 1806
Chase, Samuel	February 1796	Died June 1811
Washington, Bushrod	February 1799	Died November 1829
Moore, Alfred	April 1800	Resigned January 1804
Johnson, William	May 1804	Died August 1834
Livingston, Brockholst	January 1807	Died March 1823
Todd, Thomas	May 1807	Died February 1826
Duvall, Gabriel	November 1811	Resigned January 1835
Story, Joseph	February 1812	Died September 1845
Thompson, Smith	September 1823	Died December 1843
Trimble, Robert	June 1826	Died August 1828
McLean, John	January 1830	Died April 1861
Baldwin, Henry	January 1830	Died April 1844
Wayne, James M.	January 1835	Died July 1867

The Taney Court

NAME	SWORN IN	LEFT COURT
Taney, Roger B.	**March 1836**	**Died October 1864**
Story, Joseph	February 1812	Died September 1845
Thompson, Smith	February 1823	Died December 1843
McLean, John	January 1830	Died April 1861
Baldwin, Henry	January 1830	Died April 1844
Wayne, James M.	January 1835	Died July 1867
Barbour, Philip P.	May 1836	Died February 1841
Catron, John	May 1837	Died May 1865
McKinley, John	January 1838	Died July 1852
Daniel, Peter V.	January 1842	Died May 1860
Nelson, Samuel	February 1845	Retired November 1872
Woodbury, Levi	September 1845	Died September 1851
Grier, Robert C.	August 1846	Retired January 1870
Curtis, Benjamin R.	October 1851	Resigned September 1857
Campbell, John A.	April 1853	Resigned April 1861
Clifford, Nathan	January 1858	Died July 1881
Swayne, Noah	January 1862	Retired January 1881
Miller, Samuel F.	July 1862	Died October 1890
Davis, David	December 1862	Resigned March 1877
Field, Stephen J.	May 1863	Retired December 1897

The Chase Court

NAME	SWORN IN	LEFT COURT
Chase, Salmon P.	**December 1864**	**Died May 1873**
Wayne, James M.	January 1835	Died July 1867
Catron, John	May 1837	Died May 1865
Nelson, Samuel	February 1845	Retired November 1872
Grier, Robert C.	August 1846	Retired January 1870
Clifford, Nathan	January 1858	Died July 1881
Swayne, Noah	January 1862	Retired January 1881
Miller, Samuel F.	July 1862	Died October 1890
Davis, David	December 1862	Resigned March 1877
Field, Stephen J.	May 1863	Retired December 1897
Strong, William	March 1870	Retired December 1880
Bradley, Joseph P.	March 1870	Died January 1892
Hunt, Ward	January 1873	Retired December 1880

The Waite Court

NAME	SWORN IN	LEFT COURT
Waite, Morrison R.	**March 1874**	**Died March 1888**
Clifford, Nathan	January 1858	Died July 1881
Swayne, Noah	January 1862	Retired January 1881
Miller, Samuel F.	July 1862	Died October 1890
Davis, David	December 1862	Resigned March 1877
Field, Stephen J.	May 1863	Retired December 1897
Strong, William	March 1870	Retired December 1880
Bradley, Joseph P.	March 1870	Died January 1892
Hunt, Ward	January 1873	Retired December 1880
Harlan, John Marshall	December 1877	Died October 1911
Woods, William B.	January 1881	Died May 1887
Matthews, Stanley	May 1881	Died March 1889
Gray, Horace	January 1882	Died September 1902
Blatchford, Samuel	April 1882	Died July 1893
Lamar, Lucius Q. C.	January 1888	Died January 1893

The Fuller Court

NAME	SWORN IN	LEFT COURT
Fuller, Melville W.	**October 1888**	**Died July 1910**
Miller, Samuel F.	July 1862	Died October 1890
Field, Stephen J.	May 1863	Retired December 1897

Bradley, Joseph P.	March 1870	Died January 1892
Harlan, John Marshall	December 1877	Died October 1911
Matthews, Stanley	May 1881	Died March 1889
Gray, Horace	January 1882	Died September 1902
Blatchford, Samuel	April 1882	Died July 1893
Lamar, Lucius Q. C.	January 1888	Died January 1893
Brewer, David J.	January 1890	Died March 1910
Brown, Henry B.	January 1891	Retired May 1906
Shiras, George, Jr.	October 1892	Retired February 1903
Jackson, Howell E.	March 1893	Died August 1895
White, Edward D.	March 1894	Promoted February 1910
Peckham, Rufus W.	January 1896	Died October 1909
McKenna, Joseph	January 1898	Retired January 1925
Holmes, Oliver Wendell	December 1902	Retired January 1932
Day, William R.	March 1903	Retired November 1922
Moody, William H.	December 1906	Resigned November 1910
Lurton, Horace H.	January 1910	Died July 1914
Hughes, Charles E.	October 1910	Resigned June 1916

The White Court

NAME	SWORN IN	LEFT COURT
White, Edward D.	**December 1910**	**Died May 1921**
Harlan, John Marshall	December 1877	Died October 1911
McKenna, Joseph	January 1898	Retired January 1925
Holmes, Oliver Wendell	December 1902	Retired January 1932
Day, William R.	March 1903	Retired November 1922
Lurton, Horace H.	January 1910	Died July 1914
Hughes, Charles E.	October 1910	Resigned June 1916
Van Devanter, Willis	January 1911	Retired June 1937
Lamar, Joseph R.	January 1911	Died January 1916
Pitney, Mahlon	March 1912	Resigned December 1922
McReynolds, James C.	October 1914	Retired January 1941
Brandeis, Louis D.	June 1916	Retired February 1939
Clarke, John H.	October 1916	Resigned September 1922

The Taft Court

NAME	SWORN IN	LEFT COURT
Taft, William H.	**July 1921**	**Retired February 1930**
McKenna, Joseph	January 1898	Retired January 1925
Holmes, Oliver Wendell	December 1902	Retired January 1932

Day, William R.	March 1903	Retired November 1922
Van Devanter, Willis	January 1911	Retired June 1937
Pitney, Mahlon	March 1912	Resigned December 1922
McReynolds, James C.	October 1914	Retired January 1941
Brandeis, Louis D.	June 1916	Retired February 1939
Clarke, John H.	October 1916	Resigned September 1922
Sutherland, George	October 1922	Retired January 1938
Butler, Pierce	January 1923	Died November 1939
Sanford, Edward T.	February 1923	Died March 1930
Stone, Harlan F.	March 1925	Promoted July 1941

The Hughes Court

NAME	SWORN IN	LEFT COURT
Hughes, Charles E.	**February 1930**	**Retired July 1941**
Holmes, Oliver Wendell	December 1902	Retired January 1932
Van Devanter, Willis	January 1911	Retired June 1937
McReynolds, James C.	October 1914	Retired January 1941
Brandeis, Louis D.	June 1916	Retired February 1939
Sutherland, George	October 1922	Retired January 1938
Butler, Pierce	January 1923	Died November 1939
Sanford, Edward T.	February 1923	Died March 1930
Stone, Harlan F.	March 1925	Promoted July 1941
Roberts, Owen J.	June 1930	Resigned July 1945
Cardozo, Benjamin N.	March 1932	Died July 1938
Black, Hugo L.	August 1937	Retired September 1971
Reed, Stanley F.	January 1938	Retired February 1957
Frankfurter, Felix	January 1939	Retired August 1962
Douglas, William O.	April 1939	Retired November 1975
Murphy, Frank	February 1940	Died July 1949

The Stone and Vinson Courts

NAME	SWORN IN	LEFT COURT
Stone, Harlan F.	**July 1941**	**Died April 1946**
Roberts, Owen J.	June 1930	Resigned July 1945
Black, Hugo L.	August 1937	Retired September 1971
Reed, Stanley F.	January 1938	Retired February 1957
Frankfurter, Felix	January 1939	Retired August 1962
Douglas, William O.	April 1939	Retired November 1975
Murphy, Frank	February 1940	Died July 1949
Byrnes, James F.	July 1941	Resigned October 1942

Jackson, Robert H.	July 1941	Died October 1954
Rutledge, Wiley B.	February 1943	Died September 1949
Burton, Harold H.	October 1945	Retired October 1958
Vinson, Frederick M.	**June 1946**	**Died September 1953**
Black, Hugo L.	August 1937	Retired September 1971
Reed, Stanley F.	January 1938	Retired February 1957
Frankfurter, Felix	January 1939	Retired August 1962
Douglas, William O.	April 1939	Retired November 1975
Murphy, Frank	February 1940	Died July 1949
Jackson, Robert H.	July 1941	Died October 1954
Rutledge, Wiley B.	February 1943	Died September 1949
Burton, Harold H.	October 1945	Retired October 1958
Clark, Tom C.	August 1949	Retired June 1967
Minton, Sherman	October 1949	Retired October 1956

The Warren Court

NAME	SWORN IN	LEFT COURT
Warren, Earl	**October 1953**	**Retired June 1969**
Black, Hugo L.	August 1937	Retired September 1971
Reed, Stanley F.	January 1938	Retired February 1957
Frankfurter, Felix	January 1939	Retired August 1962
Douglas, William O.	April 1939	Retired November 1975
Jackson, Robert H.	July 1941	Died October 1954
Burton, Harold H.	October 1945	Retired October 1958
Clark, Tom C.	August 1949	Retired June 1967
Minton, Sherman	October 1949	Retired October 1956
Harlan (II), John Marshall	March 1955	Retired September 1971
Brennan, William J., Jr.	October 1956	Retired July 1990
Whittaker, Charles E.	March 1957	Retired March 1962
Stewart, Potter	October 1958	Retired July 1981
White, Byron R.	April 1962	Retired June 1993
Goldberg, Arthur J.	October 1962	Resigned July 1965
Fortas, Abe	October 1965	Resigned May 1969
Marshall, Thurgood	October 1967	Retired June 1991

The Burger Court

NAME	SWORN IN	LEFT COURT
Burger, Warren E.	**June 1969**	**Retired September 1986**
Black, Hugo L.	August 1937	Retired September 1971
Douglas, William O.	April 1939	Retired November 1975

Harlan (II), John Marshall	March 1955	Retired September 1971
Brennan, William J., Jr.	October 1956	Retired July 1990
Stewart, Potter	October 1958	Retired July 1981
White, Byron R.	April 1962	Retired June 1993
Marshall, Thurgood	October 1967	Retired June 1991
Blackmun, Harry A.	June 1970	Retired August 1994
Powell, Lewis F., Jr.	January 1972	Retired June 1987
Rehnquist, William H.	January 1972	Promoted September 1986
Stevens, John Paul	December 1975	
O'Connor, Sandra Day	September 1981	

The Rehnquist Court

NAME	SWORN IN	LEFT COURT
Rehnquist, William H.	**September 1986**	
Brennan, William J., Jr.	October 1956	Retired July 1990
White, Byron R.	April 1962	Retired June 1993
Marshall, Thurgood	October 1967	Retired June 1991
Blackmun, Harry A.	June 1970	Retired August 1994
Powell, Lewis F., Jr.	January 1972	Retired June 1987
Stevens, John Paul	December 1975	
O'Connor, Sandra Day	September 1981	
Scalia, Antonin E.	September 1986	
Kennedy, Anthony M.	February 1988	
Souter, David H.	October 1990	
Thomas, Clarence	October 1991	
Ginsburg, Ruth Bader	August 1993	
Breyer, Stephen	August 1994	

Appendix B

Supreme Court Justices, 1789–2004: Biographical Information

Abbreviations Used in "Noteworthy Opinions" Sections

m (**majority opinion**) An opinion written by one judge and joined by a majority of the judges on the Court

d (**dissenting opinion**) An opinion written by a judge who disagrees with the result in a case

c (**concurring opinion**) An opinion by a judge who agrees with the result in a case but not necessarily with the reasoning used to reach it

c/d (**concurring in part/dissenting in part**) An opinion in which the authoring justice concurs with a portion of the prevailing opinion and dissents from another portion

s (**seriatim opinion**) Each justice's opinion as delivered seriatim, or individually; used primarily in the earliest years of the Court

pl (**plurality opinion**) If no opinion in a case can muster the support of a majority of the justices, the opinion prevails that is supported by the largest number of justices.

pc (**per curiam decision**) An opinion issued in the name of the Court rather than specific justices; generally short but not necessarily unanimous and may be accompanied by dissenting opinions

---

HENRY BALDWIN
BORN: January 14, 1780, New Haven, Connecticut
TENURE ON COURT: January 1830–April 1844
DIED: April 21, 1844, Philadelphia, Pennsylvania
NOTEWORTHY OPINIONS: *Ex parte Crane* (1831-d), *United States v. Arredondo* (1831-m), *Holmes v. Jennison* (1840-c)

FROM A POLITICALLY PROMINENT New England family, Henry Baldwin graduated from Yale in 1797. He studied law and settled in Pittsburgh, where he developed a prestigious practice and gained a reputation for thorough preparation and restraint in his briefs. Baldwin served on the local Public Safety Council during the War of 1812 and was elected to Congress in 1816. In Congress, he was a strong defender of Andrew Jackson's Seminole War activities. Twice reelected, Baldwin resigned his seat in 1822 because of poor health and for the next several years campaigned heavily for Jackson's presidency. With Jackson's success in 1828, Baldwin expected a federal position. He was nominated to the Supreme Court one year later. After one term and seven dissents, Baldwin expressed a desire to resign, but Jackson urged him to remain. Soon thereafter, Baldwin disappointed Jackson by supporting the constitutionality of the Bank of the United States. Baldwin's relations with his colleagues were often strained, and he suffered from bouts of mental illness, once causing him to miss an entire term. Although he attempted to carve out a constitutional vision that would mediate between a states' rights doctrine and federalism, Baldwin's jurisprudence had little impact on constitutional law. His final years on the Court were marked by illness and financial trouble.

★ ★ ★

PHILIP P. BARBOUR
BORN: May 25, 1783, Orange County, Virginia
TENURE ON COURT: March 1836–February 1841
DIED: February 25, 1841, Washington, D.C.
NOTEWORTHY OPINIONS: *New York v. Miln* (1837-m), *Kendall v. United States* (1838-d), *Holmes v. Jennison* (1840-d)

BORN INTO A once wealthy Virginia plantation family, Philip Barbour taught himself law. He passed the bar and developed a successful practice in Kentucky. In 1812, Barbour was elected to the House of Delegates of Orange County, Virginia. Two years later, he won a seat in Congress. In Washington, Barbour was a chief supporter of Jackson's actions in the Florida war against the Seminoles and a strong opponent of the Bank of the United States and restraints on the expansion of slavery. He served as speaker (1821–1823) during one of his five terms. In 1824, Barbour accepted a seat on the Eastern District Court of Virginia but returned to the House in 1827 at the urging of his constituents. With Jackson's victory in 1828, Barbour was appointed federal judge for the district of eastern Virginia. In 1832, he was nominated by Southern delegates for the vice presidency but withdrew his name in favor of Jackson's own choice, Martin Van Buren. In 1835, Jackson nominated Barbour, along with Roger Taney as chief justice, to the Supreme Court. In his five years on the Court, Barbour supported Taney's modifications of the Marshall Court's nationalism but did not have a chance to develop a strong independent judicial record of his own. Barbour's tenure was cut short by his untimely death in 1841.

★ ★ ★

HUGO L. BLACK

BORN: February 27, 1886, Harlan, Alabama
TENURE ON COURT: August 1937–September 1971
DIED: September 25, 1971, Bethesda, Maryland
NOTEWORTHY OPINIONS: *Korematsu v. United States*
(1944-m), *Adamson v. California* (1947-d), *Everson v.
School Board* (1947-m), *Youngstown Sheet & Tube Co. v.
Sawyer* (1952-m), *Barenblatt v. United States* (1959-d),
Engel v. Vitale (1962-m), *Gideon v. Wainwright* (1963-m),
Griffin v. County School Board (1964-m), *Griswold v.
Connecticut* (1965-d)

HUGO L. BLACK entered medical school in 1903 but soon transferred to the University of Alabama Law School, where he received his law degree in 1906. After passing the bar, he established a practice in Ashland, Alabama. In 1907, a fire destroyed Black's office, and he opened a new firm in Birmingham, where he remained for the next twenty years, excepting his service as a captain in World War I (1917–1919). In 1927, he was elected to the U.S. Senate and was reelected six years later. Black lobbied for New Deal legislation and supported President Roosevelt's Court-packing plan. His work caught Roosevelt's attention, and Black was nominated to the Supreme Court in 1937. After his confirmation but before he took his seat, Black admitted that he had been a member of the Ku Klux Klan.

Black's judicial philosophy involved strict adherence to what he considered to be the plain meaning of constitutional text. His philosophy led him to positions that are difficult to fit within the liberal/conservative framework. Black believed that the Constitution absolutely protected free speech but not "expressive conduct," and he demanded a strict separation between church and state. He supported total incorporation of the Bill of Rights, one of the many issues on which Black and Justice Felix Frankfurter sharply disagreed. Black consistently opposed substantive due process, segregation legislation, and a constitutionally protected right to privacy. Although few other justices held such absolute views, Black's opinions were influential. He resigned from the Court in 1971, following a stroke, and died eight days later.

★ ★ ★

HARRY A. BLACKMUN

BORN: November 12, 1908, Nashville, Illinois
TENURE ON COURT: June 1970–August 1994
DIED: March 4, 1999, Arlington, Virginia
NOTEWORTHY OPINIONS: *Roe v. Wade* (1973-m),
*Virginia Pharmacy Board v. Virginia Citizens
Consumer Council, Inc.* (1976-m), *Garcia v. San Antonio
MTA* (1985-m), *Bowers v. Hardwick* (1986-d), *Ward's
Cove Packing v. Atonio* (1989-d), *Webster v. Reproductive
Health Services* (1989-c/d), *Sale v. Haitian Centers
Council* (1993-d)

RAISED IN MINNESOTA, where he attended grade school with his future colleague Warren Burger, Harry A. Blackmun was awarded a scholarship to Harvard from the Harvard Club of Minnesota. He graduated with a degree in mathematics in 1929 and received his law degree from Harvard in 1932. After a yearlong clerkship with the Eighth Circuit Court of Appeals, Blackmun joined a Minneapolis firm, where he remained until 1950. During that time, he also taught courses at the University of Minnesota Law School and the St. Paul College of Law. In 1950, Blackmun became in-house counsel to the Mayo Clinic in Rochester, Minnesota.

President Eisenhower appointed Blackmun to the Eighth Circuit in 1959. In 1970, President Nixon nominated Blackmun to the Supreme Court in his third attempt to fill Abe Fortas's seat. Although Blackmun's circuit record and initial opinions on the Court suggested conservatism, he soon emerged as a liberal voice. Despite the apparent shift in ideas, Blackmun claimed that it was the Court that had shifted, not him.

Blackmun's most famous opinion, *Roe v. Wade,* spoke for the Court in establishing the right to abortion. He consistently upheld this right, often in dissent, as the Court worked in later decisions to reduce *Roe's* impact. He also contributed to the Court's constitutional protection of commercial speech, although he subjected First Amendment claims to a balancing test. In 1994, Blackmun declared that he could no longer defend the constitutionality of the death penalty. He retired the same year and died five years later at the age of ninety.

★ ★ ★

JOHN BLAIR
BORN: 1732, probably in Williamsburg, Virginia
TENURE ON COURT: February 1790–October 1795
DIED: August 31, 1800, in Williamsburg, Virginia
NOTEWORTHY OPINIONS: *Chisholm v. Georgia* (1793-cs),
Penhallow v. Doane's Administration (1795-s)

ONE OF AMERICA'S lesser-known Founding Fathers, John Blair studied law at the Middle Temple in the mid-1750s. He practiced law and was a legislator in the colony of Virginia, then became active in the Revolutionary movement. Blair was a central figure in Virginia's constitutional framing in 1776. He sat on the bench of several state courts between 1777 and 1789, including the supreme court of appeals. Blair represented Virginia at the federal Constitutional Convention of 1787. Washington chose his nominees to the fledgling Court as representative of geographical regions, a practice that many later presidents have followed. Blair's solid reputation in Virginia politics made him a logical choice.

Blair participated in the Court's first important decision, *Chisholm v. Georgia,* which controversially limited state sovereignty. He also took a strong position in the circuit hearing of *Hayburn's Case,* which, when affirmed by his brethren, established a precedent that helped to ensure that Court decisions would not be subject to executive or legislative review. Blair's support of the efforts of this early Court to secure its independence and the right of judicial review are considered his only noteworthy contributions.

★ ★ ★

SAMUEL BLATCHFORD
BORN: March 9, 1820, New York City
TENURE ON COURT: April 1882–July 1893
DIED: July 7, 1893, Newport, Rhode Island
NOTEWORTHY OPINIONS: *Chicago, Milwaukee &
St. Paul Railway v. Minnesota* (1890-m), *Counselman v.
Hitchcock* (1892-m), *O'Neil v. Vermont* (1892-m)

SAMUEL BLATCHFORD GAINED acceptance at Columbia College at the age of thirteen and passed the bar in 1842. The young lawyer entered public life by serving the Union as a loyal Republican during the Civil War, and he earned his first federal bench appointment soon after the war's end. After ten years on the Southern District Court of New York (1867–1878) and five years on the Court of Appeals for the Second Circuit (1878–1882), he was an uncontroversial choice for nomination to the Supreme Court by President Arthur. As in his federal circuit days, Blatchford was better known for his tireless work habits than for the brilliance of his opinions. Indeed, on issues of civil rights and economic liberties, he was rather obviously inconsistent.

Blatchford's greatest contributions to the Court may have been his intense productivity and coalition-building skills. He authored more than four hundred majority opinions during his eleven-year tenure. He also championed the practice, later termed "substantive due process," of using the due process clause of the Fourteenth Amendment to invalidate state regulation of the marketplace. Although history does not remember him as a remarkable jurist, Blatchford was, Chief Justice Waite commented, a "good worker."

★ ★ ★

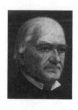

JOSEPH P. BRADLEY
BORN: March 14, 1813, Berne, New York
TENURE ON COURT: March 1870–January 1892
DIED: January 22, 1892, Washington, D.C.
NOTEWORTHY OPINIONS: *Bradwell v. Illinois* (1872-c),
Slaughterhouse Cases (1873-d), *Civil Rights Cases*
(1883-m)

UNLIKE MOST OTHER JUSTICES, Joseph Bradley had not held any public office prior to his Court appointment. He studied law with a local firm after graduating from Rutgers College in 1836 and spent the next thirty years among the elite of Newark as a railroad attorney. Bradley was nominated to the Court as a result of an 1869 statute that allowed the president to appoint new justices as soon as a sitting judge retired or died rather than waiting until there were only seven on the bench.

Critics have charged that Grant used this statute to pack the Court with Republicans who might support the constitutionality of his favored Legal Tender Acts.

Regardless of Grant's reasons for nominating him, Bradley made significant contributions to constitutional law, especially in his selective interpretation of the Fourteenth Amendment and the Civil Rights Act of 1875. He argued that white male workers had protection under the due process clause but that women did not and that blacks were constitutionally protected from state, but not social, discrimination. However, Bradley won praise for refusing to use the Fourteenth Amendment to protect private corporations from state regulation, notwithstanding his corporate past. Despite his acceptance of stereotypes popular in his day, Bradley was renowned for his broad intellect and range of interest. In 1877, he sat on the commission to resolve the controversy surrounding the Hayes-Tilden presidential election. Bradley's twenty-two-year tenure will be remembered for its contribution to the development of the field of commercial law.

★ ★ ★

LOUIS D. BRANDEIS

BORN: November 13, 1856, Louisville, Kentucky
TENURE ON COURT: June 1916–February 1939
DIED: October 5, 1941, Washington, D.C.
NOTEWORTHY OPINIONS: *International News Service v. Associated Press* (1918-d), *American Column and Lumber Co. v. United States* (1921-d), *Truax v. Corrigan* (1921-d), *Whitney v. California* (1927-c), *O'Gorman and Young v. Hartford Fire Insurance Co.* (1931-m), *Erie Railroad Co. v. Tompkins* (1938-m)

LOUIS D. BRANDEIS graduated from Harvard Law School at the age of twenty and opened a Cambridge law office with a Harvard classmate. He remained active in Harvard affairs throughout his life and was one of the founders of the *Harvard Law Review*. Brandeis was part of the generation that pioneered in changing the role of lawyer from simple advocate to that of counselor, a person whom the client would consult ahead of taking action. In his practice, Brandeis believed firmly in knowing, as he put it, "all the facts that surround." Courts had to decide cases not only on formalistic legal rules but also in light of the social and economic conditions surrounding the case.

Throughout his career, Brandeis tried to get legislatures and courts to understand those conditions. In his famous brief in *Muller v. Oregon* (1908), he devoted a scant two pages to legal precedent and more than one hundred pages to explaining why the Oregon legislature believed that a law regulating the working hours of women was necessary. Called the "People's Attorney," Brandeis worked without fee for social-justice causes, such as lower insurance costs and better industrial conditions, and was a generous philanthropist.

Brandeis was also attracted to the Zionist movement not because he, as a Jew, wanted to leave the United States but for what he saw as early Zionism's Jeffersonian idealism. In 1914, he accepted the chairmanship of the U.S. Zionist movement. Brandeis had campaigned for Woodrow Wilson in 1912, and in 1916, despite the potential for controversy over Brandeis's Jewish heritage and reputation as a radical reformer, Wilson nominated him to the Supreme Court. After five months of committee hearings, Brandeis's appointment was confirmed.

On the Court, Brandeis the successful advocate and teacher refused to disappear behind Brandeis the justice. Just as he had attempted to instruct courts on the legitimacy of reform legislation during the Progressive era, he used his Supreme Court opinions to educate not only his brethren but also the legal academy and profession. Brandeis was critical of the popular view that law was grounded in conceptual absolutes, and he opposed privileging the right of contract over the remedying of social ills. He was also a strong supporter of the priority of civil rights, such as privacy and speech. His willingness to consider legal experimentation, however, was tempered by a constrained sense of the scope of judicial review, and he argued for the courts in economic matters to defer to the judgment of the political branches in determining policy. His opinions also emphasized the primacy of the legislature in determining policy. Brandeis is often remembered for his dissents, many of which presaged later developments in constitutional law. However, Brandeis spoke for the Court in 454 of his 528 opinions.

★ ★ ★

WILLIAM J. BRENNAN, JR.

BORN: April 25, 1906, Newark, New Jersey
TENURE ON COURT: October 1956–July 1990
DIED: July 24, 1997, Arlington, Virginia
NOTEWORTHY OPINIONS: *Jencks v. United States* (1957-m), *Cooper v. Aaron* (1958-m), *Baker v. Carr* (1962-m), *Sherbert v. Verner* (1963-m), *New York Times v. Sullivan* (1964-m), *Shapiro v. Thompson* (1969-m), *Paris Adult Theatre v. Slaton* (1973-d), *Craig v. Boren* (1976-m), *Rutan v. Republican Party of Illinois* (1990-m)

SON OF A NEW JERSEY LABOR LEADER, William J. Brennan, Jr., graduated from the University of Pennsylvania in 1928 and received his law degree from Harvard in 1931. After passing the bar in 1932, Brennan joined a Newark law firm and specialized in representing management in labor disputes. He served in the Army during World War II and was a member of the staff of the Under Secretary of War. In 1949, Brennan was appointed to the newly created New Jersey Superior Court. Over the next three years, he was elevated to the Appellate Division of the Superior Court, then to the State Supreme Court.

Brennan was one of the few public figures to speak out against Senator McCarthy's hunt for Communists. In 1956, President Eisenhower gave Brennan a recess appointment to the Supreme Court. Three months later, Brennan was nominated formally. McCarthy cast the only vote against confirmation.

Eisenhower would later express regret at the appointment. Brennan was a staunch opponent of "original intent" in constitutional interpretation and advocated an adaptable approach geared toward protecting the dignity of individuals. Known for his conciliatory style, he worked hard to gain majority support for his views on issues of gender discrimination, affirmative action, freedom of expression and religion, criminals' rights, legislative reapportionment, welfare, the death penalty, and the separation of church and state. Throughout, he was guided by concern for fair procedure, understood expansively, supplemented by what he called the "Rule of Five"—that it takes five votes to get the Court to do anything. Brennan's efforts were largely successful during the Warren Court, but during the Burger and Rehnquist Courts, his positions encountered mounting conservative opposition. Nevertheless, Brennan was so central to the work of the Supreme Court throughout his tenure that some scholars think that the entire period of the Warren and Burger Courts should in fact be called the Brennan Court. After thirty-three years of service on the Court, Brennan retired in 1990. He died seven years later, at the age of ninety-one.

★ ★ ★

DAVID J. BREWER
BORN: June 20, 1837, Smyrna, Asia Minor (modern Turkey)
TENURE ON COURT: December 1889–March 1910
DIED: March 28, 1910, Washington, D.C.
NOTEWORTHY OPINIONS: *Budd v. New York* (1892-d), *Reagan v. Farmer's Loan and Trust Co.* (1894-m), *In re Debs* (1895-m), *Muller v. Oregon* (1908-m), *Berea College v. Kentucky* (1908-m)

AFTER GRADUATING FROM Yale (1856) and the Albany Law School (1858), David J. Brewer followed the example of his uncle, Justice Stephen Field, and headed west to the new territories. Brewer established a law practice in Kansas, representing railroad and business interests. He served in several state political and legal offices before he won a seat on Kansas's First Judicial District in 1865. Brewer was elected to the Kansas Supreme Court in 1870 and served for fourteen years. In 1884, President Arthur appointed him to the Eighth Circuit Court. Five years later, President Harrison nominated Brewer to the Supreme Court.

Although his judicial record had been relatively liberal in his earlier years on the Kansas bench, Brewer's circuit court opinions displayed a growing conservatism that solidified in his years on the Supreme Court. An advocate of substantive due process in the economic sphere, Brewer opposed many of the labor and social movements of his day. Although he was occasionally flexible on immigration and women's labor issues, as in his acclaimed opinion in *Muller v. Oregon,* his reasoning is today considered paternalistic. He spoke for the majority in upholding charges against labor activist Eugene Debs during a period in which his conservative views, usually to the right of both the public and many of his colleagues, expressed the nation's fears of class protest. Brewer died suddenly at the age of seventy-three.

★ ★ ★

STEPHEN G. BREYER

BORN: August 15, 1938, San Francisco, California
TENURE ON COURT: August 1994–present
NOTEWORTHY OPINIONS: *United States v. Lopez*
(1995-m), *Richardson v. McKnight* (1997-m), *United
States v. Balsys* (1998-d), *Stenberg v. Carhart* (2000-m)

RAISED IN SAN FRANCISCO, Stephen G. Breyer chose to attend Stanford University to remain close to his family. He graduated in 1959 and won a Marshall Scholarship, which allowed him to travel to Oxford, where he attended Magdalen College and received a B.A. in 1961. Breyer took his law degree in 1964 from Harvard Law School, where he also edited the *Law Review*. Justice Arthur J. Goldberg selected Breyer as his law clerk during the 1964 term, and Breyer had the opportunity to assist in drafting Goldberg's opinion in *Griswold v. Connecticut*. He spent the next three years working as an aide on antitrust cases for the Department of Justice. In 1967, Breyer joined the faculty at Harvard Law School, where he taught until 1994. During the Watergate investigation, Breyer served as an assistant to prosecutor Archibald Cox. He remained in Washington at Senator Ted Kennedy's request to provide legal counsel to the Senate Judiciary Committee, and in 1979 was elevated to chief counsel. Breyer worked hard to end government airline regulation while serving as the Judiciary Committee's counselor and gained Republican friends in the Senate. President Carter appointed Breyer to the U.S. Court of Appeals for the First Circuit in 1980. A decade later, he was named its chief judge. From 1985–1989, Breyer was a powerful member of the U.S. Sentencing Commission, which drafted federal sentencing guidelines. In 1990, Breyer became a member of the Judicial Conference. President Clinton nominated Breyer to the Supreme Court in 1994. Breyer is considered pragmatic and moderate in his views. On the conservative Court, he has emerged as one of the more liberal members.

★ ★ ★

HENRY B. BROWN

BORN: March 2, 1836, South Lee, Massachusetts
TENURE ON COURT: January 1891–May 1906
DIED: September 4, 1913, New York City
NOTEWORTHY OPINIONS: *The Oregon* (1895-m), *Pollock
v. Farmers' Loan & Trust Co.* (1895-d), *Plessy v. Ferguson*
(1896-m), *Holden v. Hardy* (1898-m), *Insular Cases*
(1902-m)

HENRY B. BROWN graduated from Yale in 1856 and then traveled in Europe before returning to study law at Yale and Harvard. Like many other New Englanders, Brown migrated west, settling in Detroit, Michigan, where he was admitted to the bar. In 1861, he became a U.S. marshal and gained experience in maritime and admiralty issues through his exposure to the Detroit federal court district. Brown avoided service in the Civil War by hiring a substitute, a common practice that did not prevent President Lincoln from appointing him as an assistant U.S. attorney in 1863. In 1875, President Grant appointed Brown to the federal district court of Michigan. In 1890, President Harrison nominated him to the Supreme Court. Brown specialized in admiralty and patent law. His record on substantive due process and issues of taxation and commerce during the period shows a moderate stance. His judicial approach emphasized factual analysis over precedent or principle, and he avoided extremes.

Brown is most famous for his heavily criticized majority opinion in *Plessy v. Ferguson*, which upheld the Jim Crow statutes. At the time, however, the case drew little public attention, and Brown's opinion was considered moderate. Brown authored more than 450 opinions during his tenure on the Court. He retired in 1906 because of eye trouble but remained active, lecturing and writing on legal issues until his death in 1913.

★ ★ ★

WARREN E. BURGER
BORN: September 17, 1907, St. Paul, Minnesota
TENURE ON COURT: June 1969–September 1986
(Chief Justice)
DIED: June 25, 1995, Alexandria, Virginia
NOTEWORTHY OPINIONS: *Harris v. New York* (1971-m),
Lemon v. Kurtzman (1971-m), *Reed v. Reed* (1971-m),
Swann v. Charlotte-Mecklenburg Board of Ed. (1971-m),
Wisconsin v. Yoder (1972-m), *Miller v. California*
(1973-m), *United States v. Nixon* (1974-m), *South
Dakota v. Opperman* (1976-m), *Richmond
Newspapers v. Virginia* (1980-pl), *Immigration and
Naturalization Services v. Chadha* (1983-m), *Nix v.
Williams* (1984-m)

BY 1931, AFTER six years of night classes, Warren Earl Burger, who came from a modest background, had managed to graduate from the University of Minnesota and to earn a law degree from the St. Paul College of Law. Burger went on to practice with a St. Paul law firm for the next twenty years and was active in local and national Republican politics. In 1953, President Eisenhower appointed Burger assistant attorney general in charge of the Civil Division of the Department of Justice. Three years later, Eisenhower named him to the U.S. Court of Appeals for the District of Columbia Circuit, where he served fourteen years. Seeking a "law and order" judge to replace Earl Warren as chief justice, President Nixon approved of Burger's outspoken criticism of *Miranda* and other Warren Court criminal rights expansions and nominated Burger to the Supreme Court's highest seat in 1969. Ironically, five years later, Burger would speak for the Court in its unanimous decision to uphold a subpoena for the Watergate papers, leading to Nixon's resignation.

Burger was an advocate for "strict construction" in constitutional interpretation. His votes helped to reduce, but not overturn, Warren-era limitations on police and prosecutorial actions. Burger also worked to limit access to the federal courts for litigants seeking to institute social change and to reduce the inefficiencies that bogged down the federal judiciary. However, this conservative chief justice who called for judicial restraint presided over a Court remembered for its extension of rights to women, the disabled, and other disadvantaged groups, as well as its activism on social issues, such as abortion and the separation of church and state. In 1985, President Reagan appointed Burger to head the Commission on the Bicentennial of the U.S. Constitution. Burger retired from the Court the following year and continued to direct the commission until 1992.

★ ★ ★

HAROLD H. BURTON
BORN: June 22, 1888, Jamaica Plain, Massachusetts
TENURE ON COURT: October 1945–October 1958
DIED: October 28, 1964, Washington, D.C.
NOTEWORTHY OPINIONS: *Morgan v. Virginia* (1946-d), *Henderson v. United States* (1950-m), *Beilan v. Board of Education* (1958-m)

HAROLD H. BURTON graduated from Bowdoin College in 1909 and Harvard Law School in 1912 and then moved to Ohio to practice law. Over the next seventeen years, he practiced in Cleveland, Utah, Idaho, and then Cleveland again. Burton interrupted his private practice to serve as an Army lieutenant during World War I. He was elected to the Ohio state legislature in 1929. Beginning in 1935, he served three consecutive terms as mayor of Cleveland. In 1941, Burton was elected to the Senate and four years later was tapped by President Truman for the Supreme Court.

The Court was deeply divided at the time, particularly over the merits of judicial restraint or judicial activism. Burton was the only Republican appointed to the Supreme Court from 1933 to 1953, a period of Democratic control of the presidency and the Senate. He tended toward judicial restraint, and when Fred Vinson replaced Harlan Stone as chief justice, this view gained influence. Burton was a moderate conservative, more liberal than Truman's other appointees, with a tendency to uphold government authority against expanding civil liberties jurisprudence and increases in labor movement power. By the early 1950s, Burton joined the Court's increasingly united front on striking down discriminatory practices in schools and voting booths. With the liberal direction of the Court under Chief Justice Earl Warren solidifying in the mid-1950s, however, Burton's more conservative views left him somewhat marginalized. Suffering from Parkinson's disease, he retired at age seventy.

★ ★ ★

PIERCE BUTLER
BORN: March 17, 1866, Dakota County, Minnesota
TENURE ON COURT: January 1923–November 1939
DIED: November 16, 1939, Washington, D.C.
NOTEWORTHY OPINIONS: *Olmstead v. United States* (1928-d), *United States v. Schwimmer* (1929-m), *Morehead v. New York ex rel. Tipaldo* (1936-m), *Railroad Commission v. Pacific Gas & Electric Co.* (1938-d)

PIERCE BUTLER, an Irish Catholic born on St. Patrick's Day, attended Carleton College and graduated in 1887. He was admitted to the bar one year later, after studying law at a St. Paul firm. In 1891, Butler was made assistant county attorney; two years later, he was elected county attorney and served until 1897. During this time, Butler joined a law partnership, which became successful representing railroad companies. He was elected president of the Minnesota State Bar Association in 1908. In 1910, Butler was appointed to represent the government in a number of antitrust cases. He also served as a regent of the University of Minnesota from 1907 to 1924, where he advocated the dismissal of "unpatriotic" professors during World War I. In 1922, on Chief Justice Taft's recommendation, President Harding nominated Butler to the Supreme Court. Although Senate progressives opposed Butler's conservative economic views, his appointment was confirmed.

Butler's judicial philosophy centered on laissez-faire economics, patriotic civic duty, and morality. He was also a strong supporter of criminal due process. Butler consistently opposed government attempts to regulate workers' hours or wages, and in the 1930s, he and three other justices (Van Devanter, Sutherland, and McReynolds) formed a conservative bloc that opposed every piece of New Deal legislation that came before them. Butler died at the age of seventy-three, while still serving on the Court.

★ ★ ★

JAMES F. BYRNES
BORN: May 2, 1879, Charleston, South Carolina
TENURE ON COURT: July 1941–October 1942
DIED: April 9, 1972, Columbia, South Carolina
NOTEWORTHY OPINIONS: *Edwards v. California* (1941-m), *Taylor v. Georgia* (1942-m)

JAMES F. BYRNES left school at the age of fourteen to work as a law clerk in a Charleston law firm. He became a court reporter in 1900. Byrnes followed the nineteenth-century path to the bar by reading law with a local judge rather than attending law school. He was admitted to the bar in 1903 and established a practice in Aiken, South Carolina. Byrnes was elected solicitor for his judicial circuit in 1908 and won a congressional seat two years later. He lost a Senate bid in 1924 but successfully ran again in 1930. Byrnes worked closely with Roosevelt during his presidential campaign of 1932 and continued to advise him in office. He was re-elected to the Senate in 1936. In 1941, Roosevelt nominated Byrnes to the Supreme Court.

Byrnes served on the Court for only one term. He spoke for the majority in sixteen cases but did not write a single concurring or dissenting opinion. With the onset of World War II, Roosevelt tapped Byrnes to assist him in preparing emergency legislation; in October 1942, Byrnes resigned from the Court to accept a series of wartime appointments. Roosevelt referred to Byrnes as his "assistant president." In 1945, President Truman appointed him secretary of state, although he resigned in 1947. In 1950, Byrnes ran successfully for governor of South Carolina on a moderate prosegregation platform. He died in 1972, at the age of ninety-two.

★ ★ ★

JOHN A. CAMPBELL
BORN: June 24, 1811, Washington, Georgia
TENURE ON COURT: April 1853–April 1861
DIED: March 12, 1889, Baltimore, Maryland
NOTEWORTHY OPINIONS: *Marshall v. Baltimore and Ohio Railroad* (1854-d), *Dodge v. Woolsey* (1856-d), *Dred Scott v. Sandford* (1857-c)

BY THE AGE of eighteen, John Campbell had graduated from Georgia's Franklin College, attended three years at West Point, and passed the bar. He moved to Alabama to open his practice and established a reputation as the state's leading attorney. He was twice offered, though he declined, a seat on the state supreme court. Campbell served two terms, 1837 and 1843, in the Alabama legislature. After the death of Supreme Court Justice McKinley in 1853, President Fillmore failed in three attempts to fill the post. The empty seat was passed to President Pierce, who nominated Campbell on the recommendation of the eight incumbent justices.

Although he lacked judicial experience, Campbell's extensive legal scholarship and talent were remarkable. His dissents on issues of corporate citizenship rights and interpretation of the contract clause were especially noteworthy. A Southerner and strict constructionist, Campbell often joined with Justices Daniel and Catron to form a states' right bloc. As sectional tensions increased, Campbell initially worked to prevent war. When hostilities broke out, however, he resigned and returned to Alabama, where he joined the Confederate government as assistant secretary of war. Briefly jailed after the war, Campbell was pardoned by President Johnson and moved to New Orleans to resume law practice. He became an active member of the Supreme Court bar, arguing more than forty cases, including the famous *Slaughterhouse Cases* (1873).

★ ★ ★

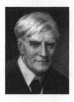

BENJAMIN N. CARDOZO

BORN: May 24, 1870, New York City
TENURE ON COURT: March 1932–July 1938
DIED: July 9, 1938, Port Chester, New York
NOTEWORTHY OPINIONS: *Snyder v. Massachusetts*
(1934-m), *Baldwin v. Seelig* (1935-m), *Carter v. Carter*
Coal Co. (1936-c/d), *Palko v. Connecticut* (1937-m)

HOMESCHOOLED by tutors, notably Horatio Alger, Benjamin N. Cardozo was admitted to Columbia University at the age of fifteen. He graduated in 1889 and studied law at Columbia. Cardozo passed the bar in 1891 before obtaining a law degree and practiced appellate law with his older brother. He remained in private practice in New York for twenty-three years. In 1914, Cardozo was elected to the New York trial court. Later that year, the governor of New York appointed him to fill a replacement position on the state's highest court. Three years later, Cardozo was elected to an associate seat on that bench and in 1926 became chief judge. New York's highest court afforded Cardozo rich opportunity to use his talents: Rapid industrial and commercial change required the judges of the nation's most populous and economically significant state to reexamine many old common-law doctrines. In a series of landmark decisions, such as *MacPherson v. Buick Motor Co.* (1916), Cardozo and his exceptionally able brethren transformed much of the common law to respond to modern social and economic conditions. Cardozo also established himself as a significant legal thinker in four books: *The Nature of the Judicial Process* (1921), *The Growth of the Law* (1924), *The Paradoxes of Legal Science* (1928), and *Law and Literature* (1931), all of which remain standard works. In 1932, following an unprecedented bipartisan showing of support from political, intellectual, and media leaders for his appointment, President Hoover nominated Cardozo to the Supreme Court.

Elected soon after Cardozo's appointment, President Roosevelt's New Deal policies solidified the liberal and conservative blocs on the Court. Although Cardozo, along with Justices Brandeis and Stone, sympathized with Roosevelt's economic regulation, his liberal record was inspired by a theory of judicial restraint rather than social experimentation. Cardozo's decisions are considered particularly significant in the realms of civil liberties and commerce clause interpretation. Nevertheless, his contributions to the law before he ascended the nation's highest bench were more significant than his work on the Court itself. Cardozo's innovative decisions as a judge of the New York Court of Appeals and his brilliant writings as a legal philosopher are probably his most enduring legacies. His six-year Supreme Court tenure (1932–1938), cut short by poor health culminating in a major stroke in January 1938, was too brief to enable him to make a major mark on an institution in which greatness unfolds slowly over the course of service typically measured in decades. Cardozo was unable to return to the bench after suffering his stroke and died several months later at the age of sixty-eight.

★ ★ ★

JOHN CATRON

BORN: 1786, probably Pennsylvania
TENURE ON COURT: May 1837–May 1865
DIED: May 30, 1865, Nashville, Tennessee
NOTEWORTHY OPINIONS: *License Cases* (1847-d), *Piqua Branch of the State Bank of Ohio v. Knoop* (1854-d), *Dred Scott v. Sandford* (1857-c)

LITTLE IS KNOWN of John Catron's early years. His family may have moved from Pennsylvania to Virginia, where Catron is known to have spent his childhood, and then to Kentucky. Catron served under General Jackson in the War of 1812; in 1818, three years after passing the bar, he moved to Nashville to practice law. In 1824, Catron was offered a seat on Tennessee's Court of Errors and Appeals, the state's highest court. Seven years later, he was appointed its chief justice. When the state's courts were reorganized in 1834, the Court of Errors and Appeals was abolished, and Catron briefly returned to private practice. A strong Jackson supporter, he managed the 1836 Tennessee campaign for Jackson's designated successor, Martin Van Buren. On his last day in office, President Jackson nominated Catron to one of the two new seats on the Supreme Court.

Although most agree that Catron was an influential figure in nineteenth-century jurisprudence, there is some doubt about his precise position in the political spectrum of the Taney Court. Some argue that he was an extremist in favor of slavery and states' rights; others, that he developed a moderate jurisprudence. What is not disputed is Catron's support of both old Southern and Western expansionist interests. With the onset of the Civil War, Catron put the Union and his Western interests ahead of the protection of slavery. He did not support secession and continued to ride the circuits until Confederate vigilantes confiscated his property and ran him out of Tennessee. Catron died just after the fall of the Confederate Army.

★　★　★

SALMON P. CHASE

BORN: January 13, 1808, Cornish, New Hampshire
TENURE ON COURT: December 1864–May 1873 (Chief Justice)
DIED: May 7, 1873, New York City
NOTEWORTHY OPINIONS: *Ex parte Milligan* (1866*), *Test Oath Cases* (1867-d), *Ex parte McCardle* (1869-m), *Hepburn v. Griswold* (1870-m), *United States v. Klein* (1872-m)

---

* Chase wrote a separate opinion, with which three other justices concurred, in *Ex parte Milligan*. He agreed with the order of the Court, written by Justice Davis, but dissented from Davis's reasoning.

SALMON P. CHASE was raised in Ohio but returned to New Hampshire to attend Dartmouth College. He graduated in 1826 and moved to Washington, D.C., to read law. Chase was admitted to the bar in 1829 and established his practice in Ohio. He was active in the antislavery movement and the Free-Soil Party and gained a reputation for defending runaway slaves. In 1848, the Ohio legislature elected Chase to the U.S. Senate, where he helped to form the Republican Party. In 1855, he was elected governor of Ohio and served two terms. Chase made an unsuccessful bid for the presidency in 1860 and was instead reelected to the Senate. He resigned after two days when he was named President Lincoln's secretary of the Treasury. Chase proposed the national bank system but clashed with Lincoln and resigned in June 1864. Six months later, President Lincoln fulfilled his promises to Radical Republicans by nominating Chase to succeed Roger Taney as chief justice.

Chase assumed leadership of the Supreme Court at a time when it was demoralized by the *Dred Scott* decision (1857) and the nation was coping with the Civil War. Chase, who did not approve of military rule over the South, took a moderate stand on most Reconstruction cases. He saw Reconstruction as primarily a political rather than a judicial issue and worked to avoid a direct clash with Congress. Chase presided over the 1868 impeachment proceedings of President Johnson, angering many of his old radical friends in the process and spurring Chase's rejection of the Republican Party. He never stopped seeking the presidency and unsuccessfully sought the Democratic nomination in 1868. Chase suffered a series of strokes in 1870, and although his health improved during his final terms, he died in 1873 at the age of sixty-five.

★ ★ ★

SAMUEL CHASE
BORN: April 17, 1741, Somerset County, Maryland
TENURE ON COURT: February 1796–June 1811
DIED: June 19, 1811, Baltimore, Maryland
NOTEWORTHY OPINIONS: *Ware v. Hylton* (1796-m), *Calder v. Bull* (1798-m)

AT AGE TWENTY-TWO, Samuel Chase had already established a flourishing law practice in Maryland. As political opposition to British imperial policy in North America intensified, he became a prominent anti-British agitator and was a signer of the Declaration of Independence. Chase was a committed delegate to the Continental Congress during the Revolutionary War, although he gained notoriety from a botched financial scheme, and the state legislature refused to reappoint him. He soon returned to public life and eventual appointments to several Maryland bench positions. Chase was initially an outspoken opponent of the federal Constitution, fearing that the new system would favor wealthy merchants, but later changed his views and became a supporter of the Federalist Party. Despite his turbulent reputation, Washington named Chase to the Supreme Court in 1796.

Although Chase's opinion in *Calder v. Bull* established the dominant interpretation of the ex post facto clause, history remembers him best as the first and only sitting justice to face impeachment. The 1804 impeachment proceedings responded to his enforcement of the Alien and Sedition Acts, as well as to his virulent attack on Congress the previous year, for its repeal of the 1801 Judiciary Act. Despite President Jefferson's behind-the-scenes efforts against him, the Senate did not convict. Chase's near brush with impeachment had, at the least, the effect of revealing the depth of Jefferson's antipathy toward the Marshall Court. Chase remained on the Court for seven years after his trial but maintained a lower profile.

★ ★ ★

TOM C. CLARK
BORN: September 3, 1899, Dallas, Texas
TENURE ON COURT: August 1949–June 1967
DIED: June 13, 1977, New York City
NOTEWORTHY OPINIONS: *Garner v. Board of Public Works* (1951-m), *Watkins v. United States* (1957-d), *Jencks v. United States* (1957-d), *Mapp v. Ohio* (1961-m), *Heart of Atlanta Hotel, Inc. v. United States* (1964-m)

FOLLOWING SERVICE in World War I, Tom C. Clark attended the University of Texas and received his law degree in 1922. For the next fifteen years, he practiced law in Dallas, serving as Civil District Attorney of Dallas from 1927 to 1932. In 1937, he joined the Justice Department as special assistant to the U.S. attorney general for war risk litigation and, later, antitrust issues. Clark was promoted to assistant attorney general in 1943 and worked closely with Senator Harry Truman. As president, Truman appointed Clark attorney general in 1945, a post Clark used to propose vigorous antitrust policies and oppose communism and strong labor unions. Truman then nominated him to the Supreme Court in 1949 to replace libertarian Justice Frank Murphy. Clark's appointment was controversial, as some liberals accused him of lacking concern for civil liberties.

On the bench, the central issues for Clark were national security and antisubversion. He fought consistently, with varying degrees of success, for broad national authority to combat communism. Clark was more sympathetic to civil liberties in other areas. He spoke for the Court in *Mapp v. Ohio*, which extended Fourth Amendment protections to the states, and he joined Chief Justice Warren in making desegregation a Court priority. When his son, Ramsey, was appointed U.S. attorney general in 1967, Clark retired to avoid the appearance of a conflict of interest. He remained active in the federal judiciary, serving as chairman of the Federal Judicial Center and occasionally accepting invitations to sit as a replacement judge on various circuit courts of appeals, until his death in 1977.

★ ★ ★

JOHN H. CLARKE

BORN: September 8, 1857, New Lisbon, Ohio
TENURE ON COURT: October 1916–September 1922
DIED: March 22, 1945, San Diego, California
NOTEWORTHY OPINIONS: *Abrams v. United States*
(1919-m), *United States v. Reading Railroad* (1920-m),
American Column and Lumber Co. v. United States
(1921-m), *United Zinc Co. v. Britt* (1922-d)

FOLLOWING GRADUATION FROM Western Reserve College in 1877, John H. Clarke studied law with his father. He was admitted to the bar in 1878 and joined his father's firm. Two years later, Clarke moved to Youngstown, Ohio, to establish his own practice, specializing in corporate law. He also bought a local newspaper, the *Vindicator,* which became a successful Progressive paper. As a member of a local literary society, Clarke gained statewide recognition for his lectures on Lowell and Shakespeare. In 1897, Clarke moved to a Cleveland law firm. He lost a bid for the U.S. Senate in 1903 and another in 1914. After thirty-five years of practicing law, he was appointed by President Wilson to the U.S. District Court for northern Ohio in 1914. Two years later, Wilson appointed Clarke to the Supreme Court.

Clarke's judicial philosophy opposed big business and trusts and was supportive of labor and the poor. Although his trust-busting stance was consistent, Clarke's record on civil liberties was mixed. He supported the protection of due process rights for immigrants and a broad interpretation of Fourth and Fifth Amendment privacy rights. On First Amendment issues, such as antigovernment speech, Clarke upheld federal prosecutions. Surprising all and disappointing liberals, Clarke resigned from the Supreme Court in 1922, claiming that he found work on the bench unsatisfying. He lived to the age of eighty-seven and spent many of his remaining years campaigning for American participation in the League of Nations.

★ ★ ★

NATHAN CLIFFORD

BORN: August 8, 1803, Rumney, New Hampshire
TENURE ON COURT: January 1858–July 1881
DIED: July 25, 1881, Cornish, Maine
NOTEWORTHY OPINIONS: *Knox v. Lee* (1871-d), *Loan
Association v. Topeka* (1875-d), *Hall v. DeCuir* (1878-c)

LARGELY SELF-EDUCATED, Nathan Clifford passed the bar in 1827 and moved to Maine to establish his practice. He became active in state politics, representing rural Democrats, and was elected to four terms in the state legislature (1830–1834). Clifford was appointed state attorney general in 1834, then won a seat in the U.S. House in 1838. He served two terms but lost his reelection bid in 1843. President Polk appointed Clifford U.S. attorney general in 1846 and U.S. minister to Mexico in 1848. He returned to his Maine practice the following year. In 1857, President Buchanan nominated Clifford to the Supreme Court. Clifford's relative inexperience and Southern sympathies made him a controversial choice, and he was confirmed by only a slim margin in 1858.

During his tenure, Clifford authored nearly four hundred opinions, most on cases concerned with maritime and commercial law. Despite his strong states' rights beliefs, Clifford was not a secessionist; he remained loyal to the Union throughout the Civil War years. Clifford coined the phrase "equality is not identity," which would influence the "separate but equal" logic of *Plessy v. Ferguson* (1896). In 1876, Clifford served on the commission to decide the contested presidential election between Hayes and Tilden. Although Hayes won, Clifford thought the election illegitimate. His health and sanity worsening, Clifford refused to resign until a Democrat was president. His death in 1881 denied him his wish.

★ ★ ★

BENJAMIN R. CURTIS
BORN: November 4, 1809, Watertown, Massachusetts
TENURE ON COURT: December 1851–September 1857
DIED: September 15, 1874, Newport, Rhode Island
NOTEWORTHY OPINIONS: *Cooley v. Board of Wardens of the Port of Philadelphia* (1852-m), *Lafayette Insurance v. French* (1855-m), *Den ex Dem. Murray v. Hoboken Land & Improvement Co.* (1856-m), *Dred Scott v. Sandford* (1857-d)

BENJAMIN CURTIS GRADUATED from Harvard in 1829 and went on to Harvard Law School, where he was a student of Justice Joseph Story. He graduated in 1832 and passed the bar a few months later. Curtis began his career in Northfield, Massachusetts, then returned to Boston in 1834 to join his cousin in practice. In 1845, he was appointed to replace Story as a Harvard Corporation fellow. Four years later, Curtis won a seat in the Massachusetts House, where he stood behind then Senator Daniel Webster's conservative policy of accommodating sectionalism. When a Supreme Court seat opened in 1851, Webster, now President Fillmore's secretary of state, suggested Curtis.

Curtis served only six years, but his jurisprudential contributions were significant. In his first term, Curtis authored the Court's opinion in *Cooley v. Board of Wardens* (1852), which forged a consensus around a flexible interpretation of the commerce clause. Curtis also wrote on issues of due process jurisprudence, the "citizen" status of corporations, and the scope of federal powers in admiralty cases. On the New England circuit, he consistently enforced the unpopular Fugitive Slave Act. However, Curtis may be best known for his strong dissent in *Dred Scott v. Sandford* (1857). He resigned from the Court soon after, claiming that the salary was inadequate and the circuit duties difficult, and returned to private practice. He had many opportunities to argue before the Court and, memorably, before the Senate during President Andrew Johnson's impeachment trial.

★ ★ ★

WILLIAM CUSHING

BORN: March 1, 1732, Scituate, Massachusetts
TENURE ON COURT: February 1790–September 1810
DIED: September 13, 1810, Scituate, Massachusetts
NOTEWORTHY OPINIONS: *Chisholm v. Georgia* (1793-cs),
Ware v. Hylton (1796-c), *McIlvaine v. Coxe's Lesse*
(1808-m)

BORN INTO A politically and socially prominent family, Cushing graduated from Harvard College in 1751 and was admitted to practice in 1755. His first bench appointment, as a Massachusetts probate judge and justice of the peace, was secured through his father's influence, as was a later appointment (replacing his father) to the Massachusetts Superior Court. A supporter of the Crown, Cushing was not eager for revolution, but he switched allegiances as the conflict became imminent. He retained his superior court post but under a new title. From 1777 to 1789, he served as chief justice of the highest state court in Massachusetts. Perhaps motivated by the disorder of Shays's Rebellion, which he had witnessed in western Massachusetts, Cushing was a devoted supporter of constitutional ratification. Washington saw Cushing, with his extensive judicial experience, as an obvious choice to represent Massachusetts on the new Supreme Court. Despite his impressive credentials, however, Cushing displayed little ambition on the Court and wrote only nineteen opinions. Following Chief Justice John Jay's resignation and the Senate's rejection of John Rutledge, Cushing was confirmed as Jay's replacement but declined to take the position. His twenty-year tenure was the longest of any of Washington's appointees, but his impact on the Court was minimal and in later years was further reduced by the effects of age.

★ ★ ★

PETER V. DANIEL

BORN: April 24, 1784, Stafford County, Virginia
TENURE ON COURT: January 1842–May 1860
DIED: May 31, 1860, Richmond, Virginia
NOTEWORTHY OPINIONS: *Prigg v. Pennsylvania*
(1842-c/d), *Searight v. Stokes* (1845-d), *West River Bridge
Co. v. Dix,* (1848-m), *Propeller Genesee Chief v. Fitzhugh*
(1852-d), *Dred Scott v. Sandford* (1857-c)

PETER V. DANIEL received his primary education from private tutors on his family's Virginia plantation. In 1805, after a year at the College of New Jersey (now Princeton University), Daniel moved to Richmond to study law with the prominent legal and political figure Edmund Randolph. Daniel passed the bar in 1808 and was elected to the state legislature the same year. Occupying a series of posts in state politics, Daniel established himself as a leader in Virginia politics. A close friend and political ally of Martin Van Buren, Daniel was influential in his state's decision to support Van Buren's nomination for the vice presidency in 1832. In 1936, as a reward for his loyalty, President Jackson appointed Daniel to a bench post on the

U.S. district court of eastern Virginia. Five years later, President Van Buren, with only a few days left in office, nominated Daniel to the Supreme Court, and he was sworn in in January 1842.

Daniel's agrarian and antifederal views were more extreme than those of any of his colleagues. In admiralty and federal commerce cases, in which he argued against extending federal power, he was often a lone dissenter. Daniel's concurring opinion in *Dred Scott v. Sandford* is representative of his narrow constructivism, although also of his thorough preparation and legal knowledge. Although his views had been mainstream in earlier years and still had many adherents in the South, his resistance to any form of nationalization placed him in opposition to the main trends of mid-nineteenth-century America. Daniel died in 1860, days after Virginians voted to secede.

★ ★ ★

DAVID DAVIS
BORN: March 9, 1815, Cecil County, Maryland
TENURE ON COURT: December 1862–March 1877
DIED: June 26, 1886, Bloomington, Illinois
NOTEWORTHY OPINIONS: *Ex parte Milligan* (1866-m),
Burke v. Miltenberger (1874-m)

RAISED IN MARYLAND, David Davis studied at Kenyon College in Ohio, read law in Massachusetts, studied a year at Yale's law school, and then moved back west to Illinois to establish a practice. In 1835, Davis met state representative Abraham Lincoln, and the two became close friends. Davis won a seat in the state legislature in 1844. At the 1847 Illinois constitutional convention, Davis successfully pushed for the popular election of judges. The following year, he was himself elected to a bench post under the new system and served fourteen years. In 1856, like many other former Whigs, Davis joined the Republican Party. He campaigned for Lincoln's failed Senate bid and was a central figure in his 1860 presidential bid. The 1862 reconfiguration of judicial districts allowed Lincoln to nominate an Illinois justice to the Supreme Court, and Davis was appointed.

Although Davis's vote was crucial to many Civil War–related cases, he authored only one historic decision, *Ex parte Milligan*, in which he argued that the wartime military tribunals were unconstitutional. Davis was an opponent of Democratic efforts to resist Reconstruction, as well as Radical Republican attempts to enforce it. Dissatisfied with the Court, he coveted the presidency and was nominated by the Labor Reform Party in 1872. Davis resigned in 1877 to accept a U.S. Senate seat. His move to the Senate was controversial, as it took him out of the running for the fifteenth (and tie-breaking) place on a commission charged with resolving the 1876 presidential election dispute. Davis served one term in the Senate before retiring to Bloomington, where he died three years later.

★ ★ ★

WILLIAM R. DAY

BORN: April 17, 1849, Ravenna, Ohio
TENURE ON COURT: March 1903–November 1922
DIED: July 9, 1923, Mackinac Island, Michigan
NOTEWORTHY OPINIONS: *Dorr v. United States*
(1904-m), *McLean v. Arkansas* (1909-m), *United States v.
Union Pacific Railway Co.* (1912-m), *Hammer v.
Dagenhart* (1918-m), *Minnesota ex rel. Whipple v.
Martinson* (1921-m)

WITH THREE GENERATIONS before him serving on state supreme courts, William R. Day's decision to practice law was no surprise. Day studied law at the University of Michigan and passed the bar in 1872. While practicing in Canton, Ohio, for twenty-five years, he befriended a fellow attorney, William McKinley. In 1886, Day was elected to Canton's Court of Common Pleas by both Democrats and Republicans, but he resigned owing to the low pay. Soon after winning the presidency in 1896, McKinley appointed Day assistant secretary of state and two years later, secretary of state. Day left McKinley's cabinet to serve as a delegate to the Paris Peace Conference, which ended the Spanish-American War. In 1899, McKinley appointed Day to the Sixth Circuit's court of appeals, where he shared the bench with future Justices William Taft and Horace Lurton. Four years later, President Roosevelt nominated Day to the Supreme Court.

Day's constitutional philosophy emphasized a federalism with distinct and separate functions for state and national governmental powers. He followed Chief Justice Fuller's 1895 interpretation of the commerce clause, distinguishing manufacturing from commerce, with only the latter subject to federal regulation. Day's approach positioned him between the Progressives, who sought federally protected labor reform, and those who defined commerce strictly in terms of transportation. At the age of seventy-three, Day resigned. He briefly served on a commission to adjudicate World War I claims, then left public life shortly before he died in 1923.

★ ★ ★

WILLIAM O. DOUGLAS

BORN: October 16, 1898, Maine, Minnesota
TENURE ON COURT: April 1939–November 1975
DIED: January 19, 1980, Bethesda, Maryland
NOTEWORTHY OPINIONS: *Federal Power Comm. v. Hope
Natural Gas Co.* (1944-m), *Dennis v. United States*
(1951-d), *Zorach v. Clauson* (1952-m), *Griswold v.
Connecticut* (1965-m), *Adderley v. Florida* (1966-d),
Sierra Club v. Morton (1972-d)

WILLIAM O. DOUGLAS was raised in Yakima, Washington. He entered Whitman College in 1916, but military service in World War I interrupted his studies. Douglas graduated in 1920 and taught for two years before studying law at Columbia University. On graduation in 1925, he practiced law, first in New York, then in Yakima. Douglas returned to New York in 1928 to teach law at Columbia, then went to Yale University in 1929 to teach. In 1936, President Roosevelt appointed him to the Securities and Exchange Commission, and he was named chairman the following year. Roosevelt nominated Douglas to the Supreme Court in 1939.

The hostile relationship between Justice Felix Frankfurter, who championed judicial restraint and a nonpolitical role for the Court, and Douglas reportedly poisoned the atmosphere on the Court. Douglas, who avoided doctrinal labels, did not rank consistency and *stare decisis* highly among his legal principles and sought instead to decide each case in relation to its social, political, and economic context. He was an ardent advocate of free speech and a strong opponent of racial discrimination. In his most famous opinion, *Griswold v. Connecticut*, Douglas established a penumbral right of privacy protected by the Constitution. Representative Gerald Ford unsuccessfully attempted to have him impeached in 1970, in part because Douglas had financial associations with the Parvin Foundation, an organization connected to gambling interests. However, the attempt focused on Douglas's unorthodox lifestyle, including his four marriages, vocal environmental and antiwar beliefs, and comments on U.S. foreign policy during travel abroad. Ironically, Douglas submitted his resignation to President Ford five years later, after a severe stroke. In his record-breaking thirty-six years on the Court, Douglas served under five chief justices and wrote more than 1,200 opinions. In addition, he published thirty-one books, including a two-volume autobiography, and numerous articles.

★ ★ ★

GABRIEL DUVALL
BORN: December 6, 1752, Prince George's County, Maryland
TENURE ON COURT: November 1811–January 1835
DIED: March 6, 1844, Prince George's County, Maryland
NOTEWORTHY OPINIONS: *Queen v. Hepburn* (1813-d),
Prince v. Bartlett (1814-m), *Boyd's Lessee v. Graves*
(1819-m), *Walton v. United States* (1824-m), *Le Grand v. Darnall* (1829-m)

GABRIEL DUVALL ENTERED public life and completed his studies during the Revolutionary War. He was appointed clerk of the Maryland Convention in 1775 and remained clerk to the Maryland House after the state government was created in 1777. He was admitted to the bar in 1778. During the Revolutionary War, Duvall served as an administrator, and later a private, in the Maryland militia. He was elected to the Maryland State Council in 1782 and to the Maryland House of Delegates in 1787. Although selected as a delegate to the Constitutional Convention, he and the other Maryland delegates chose not to attend. In 1794, he was elected to the U.S. House of Representatives. Duvall resigned two years later to accept the position of chief justice of Maryland's General Court. In 1802, President Jefferson appointed Duvall the first comptroller of the Treasury. Nine years later, with two open seats on the Court, Madison nominated Joseph Story and Duvall, two justices with remarkably different legacies.

Duvall was the more experienced judge, but Story made by far the more substantial contribution to the direction of constitutional law under the Marshall Court. Duvall, in comparison, wrote only seventeen opinions in twenty-three years on the bench. The majority of his writings dealt with issues of public accounts. Duvall lost his hearing in his last decade on the bench but refused to resign. Only when assured that Roger Taney, also from Maryland, would be nominated in his place would Duvall depart, at the age of eighty-two.

★ ★ ★

OLIVER ELLSWORTH

BORN: April 29, 1745, Windsor, Connecticut
TENURE ON COURT: March 1796–October 1800 (Chief Justice)
DIED: November 26, 1807, Windsor, Connecticut
NOTEWORTHY OPINIONS: *United States v. La Vengeance* (1796-pc), *Wiscart v. Dauchy* (1796-m)

A CALVINIST EDUCATED for the ministry, Oliver Ellsworth was drawn instead to law and politics. After graduating from the College of New Jersey (now Princeton University), he established a successful practice. Ellsworth entered politics in 1773 as a Connecticut state legislator. A delegate to the first Continental Congress, Ellsworth also served as a delegate to the Constitutional Convention. His proposal for a bicameral legislature, with one house chosen on the basis of population and the other with equal representation by state, led to the Great Compromise of July 16, 1787, and allowed the Convention to complete its work. Ellsworth was chosen as one of Connecticut's first senators by the state legislature. His greatest accomplishment in the Senate was his authorship, along with future Justice William Paterson, of the Judiciary Act of 1789, which established the federal court system. When John Jay resigned as chief justice in 1795 and the Senate rejected the nomination of John Rutledge, Washington next turned to Cushing, who declined the post after the Senate confirmed him. After Cushing turned down the position, Washington named Ellsworth.

During his short tenure as chief justice, Ellsworth began the practice of issuing single opinions of the Court rather than providing individual seriatim decisions, a practice Marshall would embrace. In 1799, President Adams asked Ellsworth, although still on the bench, to travel to France to accompany two other envoys in order to negotiate a treaty. The trip was difficult, and Ellsworth's health suffered immensely. He sent his resignation from France, aware that he would be unable to resume his duties on his return.

★ ★ ★

STEPHEN J. FIELD
BORN: November 4, 1816, Haddam, Connecticut
TENURE ON COURT: May 1863–December 1897
DIED: April 9, 1899, Washington, D.C.
NOTEWORTHY OPINIONS: *Cummings v. Missouri*
(1867-m), *Slaughterhouse Cases* (1873-d), *Munn v. Illinois*
(1877-d), *Pennoyer v. Neff* (1878-m), *Sinking Fund Cases*
(1879-d)

AFTER GRADUATING FROM Williams College in 1837, Stephen Field studied law under his brother. He followed the gold rush to California and became a frontier lawyer and politician. In 1850, Field won a seat in the new California state legislature, where he helped to draft the state's criminal and civil codes. After a failed 1851 state senate bid, Field returned to private practice. In 1857, he was elected to the state supreme court; two years later, he was promoted to chief justice. Federal redistricting in 1863 produced a tenth judicial district, accompanied by a new seat on the Supreme Court. A pro-Union Democrat, Field was a politically astute choice for Abraham Lincoln.

Field's early attachment to the "free labor" tradition of Jacksonian Democracy, combined with his experiences in California, helped forge his distinctive jurisprudence. Fundamental attachment to an ethic of individual initiative bred a dogmatic jurisprudence preoccupied with the protection of property and entrepreneurial liberty. On the Supreme Court, Field was the driving force behind what later became known as laissez-faire constitutionalism — limited government with respect to matters involving economic freedom and the rights of property. In this vein, Field's most influential contribution to constitutional law was his broad interpretation of the Civil War amendments to apply to property interests. Field's dissents developed into a theory of substantive due process that was incorporated into law by the end of the nineteenth century. However, he resisted efforts to interpret the equal protection clause in a way that would give special attention to the plight of racial discrimination. In 1866, during Reconstruction, Congress restructured the circuit system and designated what had been the Tenth Circuit as the Ninth Circuit. Field was assigned to this newly structured Ninth Circuit. A decade later, he sat on the commission charged with resolving the 1876 presidential election dispute. Field himself entertained presidential ambitions several times but was never a serious contender. Although in poor health and mentally frail in his final years on the bench, Field was determined to surpass John Marshall's tenure record. He succeeded, breaking Marshall's record by one month before retiring in 1897. In all, Field wrote 620 opinions for the Supreme Court, 57 for the federal circuit court, and 365 for the state supreme court. He died in April 1899, two years after he retired from the Court.

★ ★ ★

ABE FORTAS
BORN: June 19, 1910, Memphis, Tennessee
TENURE ON COURT: October 1965–May 1969
DIED: April 5, 1982, Washington, D.C.
NOTEWORTHY OPINIONS: *Brown v. Louisiana* (1966-m),
Fortson v. Morris (1966-d), *In re Gault* (1967-m), *Time Inc.
v. Hill* (1967-d), *Tinker v. Des Moines Independent Com-
munity School District* (1969-m)

THE SON OF a cabinetmaker, Abe Fortas received full scholarships to both Southwestern College, in Memphis, and Yale Law School. After graduating from Yale in
1933, Fortas joined the faculty and served as an assistant professor of law until
1939. From the mid-1930s to the mid-1940s, he held a series of positions in the New
Deal administration. In 1946, Fortas and two associates established a law partnership in Washington, D.C., specializing in corporate law. One of his clients was Congressman Lyndon Johnson, to whom Fortas became a close advisor. In 1963, Fortas
argued the right to court-appointed counsel before the Supreme Court in *Gideon v.
Wainwright*. Two years later, Johnson, now president, appointed Fortas to the
Supreme Court.

He established himself as an influential justice, adding the fifth vote to Chief
Justice Warren's liberal bloc in anti–loyalty oath cases and *Miranda*. Fortas specialized in juvenile court law and worked to extend Bill of Rights protections to the
states. A defender of First Amendment speech in most arenas, Fortas drew the line
at flag burning and media invasion of personal privacy. Fortas remained a close advisor to Johnson while on the Court. In 1968, Johnson nominated Fortas to the chief
justiceship but withdrew the nomination in the face of a Senate filibuster. In 1969,
Life magazine revealed that Fortas had accepted and then returned a large fee from
an indicted stock manipulator. Although Fortas denied any wrongdoing, he resigned from the Court to avoid a likely impeachment effort. He continued to practice law until his death in 1982.

★ ★ ★

FELIX FRANKFURTER
BORN: November 15, 1882, Vienna, Austria
TENURE ON COURT: January 1939–August 1962
DIED: February 22, 1965, Washington, D.C.
NOTEWORTHY OPINIONS: *Minersville School District v.
Gobitis* (1940-m), *West Virginia Board of Education v.
Barnette* (1943-d), *Adamson v. California* (1947-c), *Dennis
v. United States* (1951-c), *Rochin v. California* (1952-m),
Sweezy v. New Hampshire (1957-c), *Baker v. Carr* (1962-d)

FELIX FRANKFURTER'S FAMILY emigrated to New York in 1894, when he was
twelve years old. Frankfurter graduated from the College of the City of New York in
1902 and received his law degree from Harvard in 1906. After a year in private
practice, Frankfurter was appointed assistant U.S. attorney for the Southern

District of New York. He served four years (1910–1914) as a legal officer in the War Department, then accepted a faculty position at Harvard Law School. Frankfurter resigned in 1917 to serve in a variety of federal posts during World War I. He returned to Harvard at the war's end and became famous as a prominent public intellectual on legal matters. He was an advisor and friend to President Roosevelt on New Deal policy issues. Roosevelt nominated him to the Supreme Court in 1939.

Although conservatives were upset at the appointment of a justice with a strong liberal background, liberals were displeased when it became clear that Frankfurter could not be counted on to seek liberal outcomes. A New Deal progressive, Frankfurter was a strong believer in judicial restraint and the popular will as expressed through the legislature. He was hesitant to rule against state law and saw the Court as a nonpolitical institution. After twenty-three years on the Court, Frankfurter resigned in 1962, citing ill health, and died three years later. Many of Frankfurter's important rulings were overturned during the 1960s and 1970s.

★ ★ ★

MELVILLE W. FULLER
BORN: February 11, 1833, Augusta, Maine
TENURE ON COURT: October 1888–July 1910 (Chief Justice)
DIED: July 4, 1910, Sorrento, Maine
NOTEWORTHY OPINIONS: *Pollock v. Farmers' Loan & Trust Co.* (1895-m), *United States v. E. C. Knight Co.* (1895-m), *Lottery Case* (1903-d), *Loewe v. Lawlor* (1908-m)

AFTER A CHILDHOOD in Augusta, Melville W. Fuller graduated from Bowdoin College in 1853. He read law with a local attorney and attended lectures at Harvard Law School for six months before passing the bar. In 1856, following a year of practice in Augusta, Fuller moved west to Chicago, where he established a firm and became involved in Democratic politics. Opposed to the secession of the Confederate states, as well as to abolition, Fuller managed Stephen Douglas's presidential campaign against Lincoln in 1860. Fuller was elected to one term on the Illinois state legislature in 1863. Fuller's legal practice became very successful in the postwar years, and he was elected president of the Illinois State Bar Association in 1886. President Cleveland nominated Fuller chief justice in 1888. Although the confirmation hearings were contentious, with some Republicans viewing his loyalty to the Union as suspect, Fuller's appointment was confirmed a few months later.

Known for his genial manner and humorous temperament, Fuller was a skillful Court manager. He lobbied for legislation that established the circuit court of appeals system to lighten the Court's overloaded docket and became the first chief justice to seek federal judiciary reform through legislation. A Jacksonian Democrat, Fuller advocated state autonomy, property rights, and free trade. Although he interpreted the Fourteenth Amendment's due process clause broadly with respect to economic rights, Fuller saw race relations as within the purview of state, rather than federal, regulation. In his final years on the bench, Fuller developed a strong friendship with Justice Oliver W. Holmes. Fuller died of a heart attack in his home in 1910.

★ ★ ★

RUTH BADER GINSBURG
BORN: March 15, 1933, Brooklyn, New York
TENURE ON COURT: August 1993–present
NOTEWORTHY OPINIONS: *United States v. Virginia* (1996-m), *Baker v. General Motors Corp.* (1998-m), *Buckley v. American Constitutional Law Foundation* (1999-m), *Bush v. Gore* (2000-d), *Stenberg v. Carhart* (2000-c)

RUTH BADER GINSBURG excelled in school and received scholarship aid to Cornell University. She graduated first in her class and attended Harvard Law School, later transferring to Columbia Law School, where she earned her LL.B. in 1959. Ginsburg was the first woman to sit on the law review of both of her graduate institutions. From 1959 to 1961, she served as a law clerk to a New York federal judge. Following a two-year project with Columbia on Swedish law, Ginsburg joined the faculty of Rutgers Law School. In 1972, she was hired by Columbia Law School, where she became its first female tenured law professor, and taught until 1980.

Ginsburg was active in feminist political and legal causes. She served as general counsel of the ACLU from 1973 to 1980 and was responsible for establishing its Women's Rights Project. In the 1970s, Ginsburg, with the ACLU, argued seven sex discrimination cases before the Supreme Court and won six. President Carter appointed Ginsburg to the U.S. Court of Appeals for the D.C. Circuit in 1980. Two years later, Antonin Scalia joined this bench, and the two future justices established a close friendship, if not a shared judicial vision. In 1993, President Clinton nominated Ginsburg to the Supreme Court.

Ginsburg continues to take strong positions on sex discrimination cases, although in most other areas of jurisprudence, her record has been moderate. Ginsburg's opinions are noted for their eloquence and accessibility, as well as for their marks of judicial restraint.

★ ★ ★

ARTHUR J. GOLDBERG
BORN: August 8, 1908, Chicago, Illinois
TENURE ON COURT: October 1962–July 1965
DIED: January 19, 1990, Washington, D.C.
NOTEWORTHY OPINIONS: *Aguilar v. Texas* (1964-m), *Escobedo v. Illinois* (1964-m), *New York Times Co. v. Sullivan* (1964-c), *Griswold v. Connecticut* (1965-c)

ARTHUR J. GOLDBERG graduated from Northwestern University in 1928, received his law degree from Northwestern in 1929, and began to practice labor law with a local firm. Goldberg first gained national recognition representing the

Chicago Newspaper Guild in a 1938 strike. He left his practice to serve in the Office of Strategic Services during World War II. After the war, Goldberg returned to his practice and in 1948 became counsel to the United Steelworkers of America. He was chief architect of the 1955 merger of the American Federation of Labor and the Congress of Industrial Organizations. Goldberg advised John F. Kennedy during his 1960 presidential campaign and was named secretary of labor in 1961. The following year, Kennedy appointed him to the Supreme Court.

Like Chief Justice Warren, Goldberg strongly supported equal rights for minorities, the rights of the accused, and freedom of expression. Goldberg's 1971 book, *Equal Justice*, detailed his commitment to the principle of equality. His judicial work demonstrated his conviction that the courts had the responsibility of protecting minorities unsupported by legislatures, a view that his colleagues who supported judicial restraint vigorously opposed. Goldberg also specialized in labor and antitrust law and advocated an expanded role of the federal government in these areas. In 1965, Goldberg left the Court to accept the U.S. ambassadorship to the United Nations. He retired from this post in 1968 and, after a failed campaign for New York governor, returned to Washington. Goldberg spent his last twenty years writing, teaching, and practicing law.

★ ★ ★

HORACE GRAY

BORN: March 24, 1828, Boston, Massachusetts
TENURE ON COURT: January 1882–September 1902
DIED: September 15, 1902, Nahant, Massachusetts
NOTEWORTHY OPINIONS: *United States v. Lee* (1882-d), *Elk v. Wilkins* (1884-m), *Juilliard v. Greenman* (1884-m), *United States v. Wong Kim Ark* (1898-m)

HORACE GRAY, born to an esteemed but no longer wealthy Boston family, studied at Harvard Law School and graduated in 1849. In 1851, he established a successful law practice. Gray was also the court reporter for Massachusetts Supreme Judicial Court before becoming, at age thirty-six, the youngest appointee in its history. He was promoted to chief justice in 1873. During his seventeen years on the state court, Gray wrote more than 1,300 opinions. President Garfield considered Gray for the Supreme Court in 1881 but died before filling the seat. As soon as he took office, President Arthur appointed Gray.

The Court that Gray joined was moving from Reconstruction to a new set of issues: industry, immigration, and post-Reconstruction negotiation of state/federal relations. Although known for his scholarship and knowledge of precedent, Gray wrote few innovative opinions. He rarely dissented alone, believing that dissents reflected poorly on the Court. Although Gray's support of greenbacks in *Juilliard v. Greenman* settled the question of the congressional issue of paper money during peacetime, his support for federal power was inconsistent, as was his concern for civil rights. Gray is most noted for his role in *Pollock v. Farmers' Loan & Trust Co.*, which ruled against the constitutionality of a 2 percent income tax. During the first hearing, there was a stalemate (with one justice ill), but in the final verdict, one justice switched decisions. Although Justice Shiras was suspected at the time, many scholars now point to Gray. Gray resigned in July 1902 because of ill health and died two months later.

★ ★ ★

ROBERT C. GRIER
BORN: March 5, 1794, Cumberland County, Pennsylvania
TENURE ON COURT: August 1846–January 1870
DIED: September 25, 1870, Philadelphia, Pennsylvania
NOTEWORTHY OPINIONS: *License Cases* (1847-d), *Passenger Cases* (1849-c), *Woodruff v. Trapnall* (1850-d), *Marshall v. Baltimore and Ohio Railroad Co.* (1854-m), *Prize Cases* (1863-m)

ROBERT C. GRIER was educated by his father, the supervisor of a Pennsylvania academy, and continued his studies at Dickinson College. On his father's death in 1815, Grier took over the academy, studying law in his spare time. He passed the bar in 1817 and was then able to support his widowed mother and ten younger siblings on his legal fees. Grier established a reputation as a loyal Jacksonian Democrat and received a state court judgeship in 1833, a position he held for thirteen years. Grier was nominated by President Polk to the Supreme Court seat opened up by Justice Baldwin's death two years earlier, a seat President Tyler had been unable to fill because of Senate rejections of his nominees.

Grier was a staunch defender of state autonomy in most instances, including slavery cases, but his nuanced view of federal commerce issues distinguished him from more extreme states' rights justices. He was well respected by Chief Justice Taney and wrote a fair number of influential opinions. Prodded by President Buchanan, Grier supported Taney's opinion in *Dred Scott,* although he professed a more moderate view himself. Despite his states' rights principles, Grier was not sympathetic to the secessionists and argued in favor of Lincoln's wartime policies in the *Prize Cases.* Failing health prevented Grier from riding his circuit after 1862. Facing criticisms of his competence, Grier took the advice of his colleagues and resigned in 1870. He died within the year.

★ ★ ★

JOHN MARSHALL HARLAN
BORN: June 1, 1833, Boyle County, Kentucky
TENURE ON COURT: December 1877–October 1911
DIED: October 11, 1911, Washington, D.C.
NOTEWORTHY OPINIONS: *Civil Rights Cases* (1883-d), *Hurtado v. California* (1884-d), *United States v. Texas* (1892-m), *Pollock v. Farmers' Loan & Trust Co.* (1895-d), *Plessy v. Ferguson* (1896-d), *Insular Cases* (1901-d), *Adair v. United States* (1908-m)

NAMED FOR THE famous chief justice, John Marshall Harlan studied law at Transylvania University and apprenticed under his father. He passed the bar in 1853 and established himself as a prominent Kentucky attorney. He served a one-year term, in 1858, as a county judge but lost his campaign for a U.S. House seat the following year. Although raised in a slave-owning family, Harlan supported the Union cause. He formed a volunteer brigade and served with distinction during the Civil War. Harlan won the state attorney general seat in 1863. Formerly a Whig, a Know-Nothing, and a Constitutional Unionist, Harlan embraced emancipation and the Republican Party in the late 1860s. President Hayes appointed him to the commission to resolve the Louisiana state election disputes that arose following the contested presidential election of 1876. The following year, Hayes nominated Harlan to the Supreme Court.

A reliable defender of property rights, Harlan's views were consistent with those of national conservatives on most matters of constitutional law. His strong views on commercial nationalism, however, put him at odds with those on the Court interested in imposing limits on national power and led to numerous dissents. Dissent also characterized Harlan's position in civil rights cases, later seen as prophetic. The pattern began in the *Civil Rights Cases* (1883), in which Harlan complained that his colleagues had gone out of their way to find technical reasons why Congress had no power to pass the Civil Rights Act of 1875. Some of Harlan's most memorable language can be found in his dissent in *Plessy v. Ferguson* (1896). The rest of the Court was happy to hide behind the legal fiction that racial segregation was a relatively benign regulation — impacting blacks and whites equally — but Harlan insisted that the statute in question subordinated blacks, in violation of the constitutional principle that "in the eye of the law, there is in this country no superior, dominant, ruling class of citizens." On most matters in which he voiced a dissenting opinion — the constitutionality of segregation, Congress's authority to pass civil rights legislation, the national government's power to regulate manufacturing, and the application of the Bill of Rights to the states — Harlan's opinions would be adopted by his successors. His reading of the Fourteenth Amendment promoted nationalization of the Bill of Rights, a significant contribution to civil rights and citizenship law. Harlan's death in 1911 marked the end of a thirty-four-year tenure.

★ ★ ★

JOHN MARSHALL HARLAN (II)
BORN: May 20, 1899, Chicago, Illinois
TENURE ON COURT: March 1955–September 1971
DIED: December 29, 1971, Washington, D.C.
NOTEWORTHY OPINIONS: *NAACP v. Alabama ex rel. Patterson* (1958-m), *Barenblatt v. United States* (1959-m), *Reynolds v. Sims* (1964-d), *Miranda v. Arizona* (1966-d), *Boddie v. Connecticut* (1971-m), *Cohen v. California* (1971-m)

NAMED AFTER HIS grandfather, also a Supreme Court justice (1877–1911), John Marshall Harlan graduated from Princeton in 1920. He was a Rhodes Scholar for three years at Balliol College, Oxford, before earning a law degree from New York Law School in 1924. Harlan joined a successful New York law office and remained with the firm for twenty-five years, although he left briefly to serve in the Air Force during World War II. From 1951 to 1953, Harlan was chief counsel to the New York State Crime Commission. In 1954, President Eisenhower appointed him to the Second Circuit Court of Appeals. Harlan served only ten months before Eisenhower nominated him to the Supreme Court.

Harlan's opinions have been noted by both supporters and detractors for their thorough and intellectually engaged analysis. Sometimes called a "lawyer's judge," he took care to elaborate on the implications of his opinions for practicing attorneys. Although a conservative committed to judicial restraint and suspicious of centralized government, Harlan's peers did not consider him dogmatic. He carefully examined the particulars of each case and was willing to acknowledge error in his own past judgments. Harlan's views, especially his unwillingness to interpret the Fourteenth Amendment as incorporating the Bill of Rights, often placed him on the minority side of the civil liberties decisions issued from the Warren Court. Harlan retired in poor health in 1971 and died soon after.

★ ★ ★

OLIVER WENDELL HOLMES, JR.
BORN: March 8, 1841, Boston, Massachusetts
TENURE ON COURT: December 1902–January 1932
DIED: March 6, 1935, Washington, D.C.
NOTEWORTHY OPINIONS: *Lochner v. New York* (1905-d), *Abrams v. United States* (1919-d), *Schenck v. United States* (1919-m), *Truax v. Corrigan* (1921-d), *Buck v. Bell* (1927-m), *Tyson & Brother v. Banton* (1927-d)

JUSTICE OLIVER WENDELL HOLMES is regarded almost universally as the greatest judge and the greatest legal thinker in American history. The only justice of the Supreme Court to have been the subject of a best-selling historical novel, a hit Broadway play, and a Hollywood movie, Holmes continues to be held up by senators during confirmation proceedings as the very model of what a Supreme Court justice should aspire to be. Holmes graduated from Harvard College in 1861 and immediately joined the Union Army. He served three years during the Civil War, was wounded three times, and always considered his years in the military formative. After the war, Holmes returned to Harvard and earned a law degree. He was admitted to the bar in 1867, joined a Boston law firm, and remained in practice for the next fifteen years. In addition, Holmes briefly taught law at Harvard, edited the *American Law Review,* and lectured at the Lowell Institute. In 1881, Holmes published a series of his Lowell lectures as a book, *The Common*

Law, that gained him international recognition. Holmes's thesis was that the life of the law is experience rather than logic. The following year, Holmes was appointed to the U.S. Supreme Judicial Court of Massachusetts, where he served for twenty years, the last three as chief justice. President Roosevelt nominated Holmes to the Supreme Court in 1902. Holmes served twenty-nine years and retired at the age of ninety, making him the oldest justice to date to have served on the Court.

Holmes's writings had brilliantly demonstrated that judging inescapably entailed policymaking. Holmes the judge followed through the implications of this insight. If judging was an exercise in policy choices, there was much to be said for judges' avoiding those choices in favor of more representative institutions. This was a major bulwark of Holmes's powerful defense of judicial restraint. Yet Holmes was neither much of a liberal nor a democrat. Instead, he was a moral nihilist, a firm believer in "might makes right," who suggested for his own epitaph, "Here lies the supple tool of power." Celebrated by generations of reformers, Holmes himself was not a social reformer but a Social Darwinist. It was respect for brute power, as much as insight into the policymaking nature of adjudication, that led Holmes to give state legislatures and Congress vast discretion to legislate in behalf of their visions of the general welfare.

Because he dissented so forcefully when the Court voted to strike down progressive social reforms under the banner of "liberty of contract," Holmes was idolized by progressive reformers. But for every Holmes decision taking a "liberal" position in respect of the interests of poor and working-class Americans, there exists another upholding the suppression of civil liberties or blithely injuring racial minorities' pursuit of equal justice. Holmes's initial postwar opinions for the Court concerning the suppression of antiwar speech, for example, read the First Amendment narrowly and upheld the government's power to punish and imprison dissidents in those cases. It was the influence of Brandeis and the urgings of liberal admirers that seemed to prompt Holmes, in dissent, to transform his own earlier precedents into a First Amendment test providing substantial protection for dissident speech. In race cases, there was no such transformation. The lesson of "experience" seemed to be that if the white South, as the "dominant forces of the community," wanted to subordinate black citizens under the thinnest cover of formal-legal equal treatment, the federal courts could or should do nothing about it. Nor did Holmes have any constitutional scruples about upholding a statute that, in Holmes's description, authorized the superintendent of a mental institution to sterilize "any patient afflicted with hereditary forms of insanity [or] imbecility." Here, Holmes was not simply deferring to legislative judgments better informed than he about local needs, practices, and exigencies but advancing eugenics, the only vein of progressive-era reform in which Holmes truly believed.

★   ★   ★

CHARLES EVANS HUGHES
BORN: April 11, 1862, Glens Falls, New York
TENURE ON COURT: October 1910–June 1916; February 1930–July 1941 (Chief Justice)
DIED: August 27, 1948, Cape Cod, Massachusetts
NOTEWORTHY OPINIONS: *Bailey v. Alabama* (1911-m), *Houston, East & West Texas Railway Co. v. United States* (1914-m), *Stromberg v. California* (1931-m), *Schechter Poultry Corp. v. United States* (1935-m), *DeJonge v. Oregon* (1937-m), *NLRB v. Jones & Laughlin Steel Corp.* (1937-m), *West Coast Hotel v. Parrish* (1937-m)

CHARLES EVANS HUGHES graduated from Brown and earned a law degree from Columbia in 1884. He practiced in New York City for twenty years and briefly taught law at Cornell (1891–1893). In 1905, Hughes was appointed counsel to a state utility investigation and gained national attention by exposing corporate corruption. He was elected governor of New York the following year and effectively promoted Progressive causes during his two terms. President Taft nominated Hughes to the Supreme Court in 1910. He served six years but resigned in 1916 to run for president. Hughes narrowly lost the election to Woodrow Wilson and returned to his law practice. He was President Harding's secretary of state from 1921 to 1925 and served as a U.S. delegate to the Permanent Court of Arbitration from 1926 to 1930. In 1930, President Herbert Hoover nominated Hughes chief justice of the United States.

Hughes supported the protection of free speech, labor organization, and equal rights for blacks, setting many civil liberties precedents, but he was more conservative on economic issues. In the midst of the Great Depression, the Hughes Court struck down several key pieces of New Deal legislation. In return, Roosevelt threatened to enlarge the Court. Soon after, Hughes led the Court in producing decisions that supported Roosevelt's Social Security Act and the Wagner (National Labor Relations) Act, and the Court-packing plan was defeated. As his successor, Harlan Fiske Stone, wrote of Hughes's tenure: "One may search in vain for a period in the history of the Supreme Court in which the burden resting on the Chief Justice has been so heavy or when his task has been more beset with difficulties." Hughes retired in 1941, citing age and ill health. He would live on to the age of eighty-six, dying in 1948.

★ ★ ★

WARD HUNT
BORN: June 14, 1810, Utica, New York
TENURE ON COURT: January 1873–January 1882
DIED: March 24, 1886, Washington, D.C.
NOTEWORTHY OPINIONS: *United States v. Reese* (1876-d), *Pennoyer v. Neff* (1877-d)

AFTER GRADUATING FROM Union College in 1828, Ward Hunt studied law and worked as a clerk in the office of a Utica judge. Hunt passed the bar in 1831 and opened his own Utica practice. In 1838, Hunt served one term in the state legislature as a Jacksonian Democrat. Five years later, he was elected mayor of Utica. Hunt was one of the founders of the New York Republican Party (1855–1856) and was elected to the New York Court of Appeals in 1865. In 1869, the New York court system was reorganized. Hunt became a commissioner of appeals, a position he held until President Grant nominated him to the Supreme Court three years later.

Hunt wrote few major opinions in his six years of active service. His most noteworthy contribution was a dissent in *United States v. Reese.* The majority opinion invalidated the 1870 Enforcement Act's intended federal protection of Fifteenth Amendment voting rights for blacks. Hunt's dissent revisited the Radical Republican reasoning behind the act — a rare reminder of the themes of racial equality that had reigned only a decade earlier. Despite this brave dissent, he voted with the majority in several other cases that crippled black civil rights. Hunt is often known by law students for his dissent in *Pennoyer v. Neff,* famous for its persuasiveness and citation of precedent. A paralyzing stroke in 1879 left Hunt unable to perform his duties. However, he would not resign until Congress passed a bill granting him an early pension. Hunt resigned the day the bill became law.

★ ★ ★

JAMES IREDELL
BORN: October 5, 1751, Lewes, England
TENURE ON COURT: May 1790–October 1799
DIED: October 20, 1799, Edenton, North Carolina
NOTEWORTHY OPINIONS: *Chisholm v. Georgia* (1793-d),
Calder v. Bull (1798-c)

BORN AND EDUCATED in England, James Iredell emigrated to America in 1768. While working as a comptroller in a North Carolina customs house, Iredell studied law, opening a private practice in 1770. Sympathetic to the colonists' complaints, he left his post in 1776 to join the independence movement. He was appointed to the newly created North Carolina Superior Court in 1777 and later served as the state's attorney general. As a delegate to North Carolina's ratification convention, he gained the attention of prominent Federalists, including George Washington. Iredell was not Washington's first choice for the new Supreme Court but was selected only after another nominee, Robert Harrison, declined. However, Iredell's judicial experience and Federalist leadership credentials were recognized as strong recommendations for one of the South's seats.

Despite the limited number of cases presented in the early years, several of Iredell's opinions were noteworthy. The best known may be his dissenting opinion in *Chisholm v. Georgia,* in which the Court found that state conduct fell within federal jurisdiction. The uproar caused by the case led the states to ratify the Eleventh Amendment. Scholarly opinion varies on the implications of this dissent. Some commentators claim that his positions were the germ of what would become known as the doctrine of states' rights. Others, citing Iredell's strong Federalist views, argue that Iredell dissented on pragmatic and political grounds, recognizing the dangers to the Union that lay in threats to the independence of the states during such turbulent times.

★ ★ ★

HOWELL E. JACKSON
BORN: April 8, 1832, Paris, Tennessee
TENURE ON COURT: March 1893–August 1895
DIED: August 8, 1895, West Meade, Tennessee
NOTEWORTHY OPINIONS: *Mobile and Ohio R.R. v. Tennessee* (1894-m), *Pollock v. Farmers' Loan & Trust Co.* (1895-d)

HOWELL E. JACKSON graduated from West Tennessee College in 1849 and studied law at the University of Virginia and Cumberland University. He was admitted to the bar and established a law practice in Memphis in 1859. Although he was not a secessionist, Jackson served the Confederacy during the Civil War. In 1875, he was appointed to a provisional supreme court, the Court of Arbitration for West Tennessee, established to resolve the many cases created by the war. In 1880, Jackson was elected to the Tennessee state legislature and in 1881 to the U.S. Senate, where he became close with President Grover Cleveland and future President Benjamin Harrison. He resigned his Senate seat to accept a Sixth Circuit bench post in 1886. In 1891, he became a judge of the circuit's newly established Court of Appeals. Recommended to President Harrison by his friend Justice Henry Brown, Jackson was nominated to the Supreme Court in 1893.

An expert in patent law, Jackson was busy in his first term but authored few constitutionally important opinions. In 1894, Jackson contracted tuberculosis. Still ill in May 1895, he missed the hearings in *Pollock v. Farmers' Loan & Trust Co.*, a case involving the legality of the federal income tax. As the other eight justices were deadlocked, Jackson returned to Washington to listen to the rehearing and cast the deciding vote. Jackson's protax opinion was in the minority, however, as the final vote was 5–4 to overturn the tax. He never recovered from his illness and died a few months later.

★ ★ ★

ROBERT H. JACKSON
BORN: February 13, 1892, Spring Creek, Pennsylvania
TENURE ON COURT: July 1941–October 1954
DIED: October 9, 1954, Washington, D.C.
NOTEWORTHY OPINIONS: *Wickard v. Filburn* (1942-m), *West Virginia State Board of Education v. Barnette* (1943-m), *H.P. Hood Sons, Inc. v. Du Mond* (1949-m), *Youngstown Sheet & Tube Co. v. Sawyer* (1952-c)

ROBERT H. JACKSON completed his two-year course of study at Albany Law School in one year, graduating in 1912. However, Jackson's apprenticeship with a local law firm provided him with his legal training. He established a practice in Jamestown, New York. Although he was active in local politics, Jackson quickly realized that he preferred law to elected office. In 1934, following Franklin Roosevelt's election as president, Jackson moved to Washington, D.C., to become general counsel to the Bureau of Internal Revenue. From 1935 to 1941, Jackson served successively as assistant to the attorney general, solicitor general, and U.S. attorney general. In 1941, Roosevelt nominated Jackson to the Supreme Court. Jackson would have been nominated earlier had Roosevelt not found him more valuable in his cabinet.

Jackson's opinions are often quoted, for he was an accomplished literary craftsman. His judicial philosophy is not easily categorized, although he valued federalism and feared a turn toward unitary government. Jackson made a significant contribution to First Amendment jurisprudence with his opinion in *West Virginia State Board of Education v. Barnette*. While on the Court, he served as Chief U.S. Prosecutor at the International War Crimes Tribunal in Nuremberg, Germany, from 1945 to 1946. Jackson served on the Court until he died in 1954 at age sixty-two.

★ ★ ★

JOHN JAY
BORN: December 12, 1745, New York City
TENURE ON COURT: October 1789–June 1795
DIED: May 17, 1829, Bedford, New York
NOTEWORTHY OPINIONS: *Chisholm v. Georgia* (1793-s),
Georgia v. Brailsford (1794-m), *Glass v. The Sloop Betsey*
(1794-m)

BORN TO A prominent New York mercantile family, John Jay graduated from King's College (now Columbia University) at age eighteen and passed the bar four years later. Growing tension with the British drew Jay's attention from his successful New York law practice, and he committed himself to political service. In addition to numerous other public roles, Jay was a New York delegate to the First and Second Continental Congresses, chief justice of New York's superior court from 1777 to 1778, and president of the Continental Congress from 1778 to 1779. From 1782 to 1783, he helped negotiate the Treaty of Paris, which ended the war with Great Britain. A strong nationalist, Jay wrote five of the *Federalist Papers*. George Washington, his close friend and political ally, was delighted when Jay accepted the position of first chief justice.

Jay hoped to use the new Court as a tool for enhancing the legitimacy of the United States in the eyes of the international community but found to his disappointment that the fledgling Court was ineffectual. Still, the Jay Court confronted the first constitutional challenge (*Chisholm v. Georgia*) and used it to support national sovereignty over state objections.

While in Britain negotiating the unpopular economic compromise that came to be known as the Jay Treaty, Jay was nominated governor of New York by local Federalists. He won the election and resigned from the Supreme Court in 1795. In 1800, President John Adams once more nominated Jay to the Court, and the

Senate confirmed him. But he declined the commission, citing his own ill health and the weakness of the Court.

★ ★ ★

THOMAS JOHNSON

BORN: November 4, 1732, Calvert County, Maryland
TENURE ON COURT: September 1791–January 1793
DIED: October 26, 1819, Frederick, Maryland
NOTEWORTHY OPINIONS: *Georgia v. Brailsford* (1792-d)

A SUCCESSFUL BUSINESSMAN and lawyer prior to the Revolutionary War, Thomas Johnson was also a prominent, though largely overlooked, figure in revolutionary politics. He served as a delegate to the First and Second Continental Congresses, nominated Washington to the commander-in-chief post, and organized supplies and men for the war. When Maryland held its first free elections in 1777, Johnson was elected governor, a position he held for three terms. During the postwar 1780s, Johnson worked for ratification of the Constitution and for Washington's presidential candidacy but longed to return to his family and business interests. He accepted the position of chief judge of Maryland's General Court in 1790. On Justice Rutledge's resignation several months later, Washington nominated Johnson to the Court. Johnson accepted the post reluctantly, concerned that circuit riding would affect his health and disrupt his business. He would serve the shortest term of any justice: less than eighteen months.

Johnson will be remembered as an early dissenter on the Supreme Court, as he voted (along with Justice Cushing) to deny Georgia's request for an injunction in *Georgia v. Brailsford*. This would be the only known opinion Johnson issued of the cases that were before the Court that term. He resigned in 1793, citing as the primary cause the difficulties of circuit riding. Although he remained active in business, Johnson declined Washington's offer of secretary of state. In his later years, Johnson befriended Roger B. Taney, the future chief justice, who was then a young lawyer and witnessed his will.

★ ★ ★

WILLIAM JOHNSON

BORN: December 27, 1771, near Charleston, South Carolina
TENURE ON COURT: May 1804–August 1834
DIED: August 4, 1834, Brooklyn, New York
NOTEWORTHY OPINIONS: *United States v. Hudson and Goodwin* (1812-m), *Anderson v. Dunn* (1821-m), *Green v. Biddle* (1823-d), *Gibbons v. Ogden* (1824-c), *Ogden v. Saunders* (1827-d), *Craig v. Missouri* (1830-d)

SON OF A Revolutionary War veteran and state legislator, William Johnson was raised during wartime. These civic lessons remained with Johnson, who returned to South Carolina after graduating first in his class at the College of New Jersey (now Princeton University). Admitted to the bar in 1793, he was elected to the state legislature as a Democratic-Republican one year later. After three consecutive terms in office, Johnson was elected judge to the state's highest court. As Thomas Jefferson's first appointment to the Supreme Court, in 1804, he would face a Court dominated by Federalist Chief Justice Marshall.

Johnson's entire thirty-year tenure was spent on the Marshall Court. Johnson issued more dissents than any other justice under Marshall and more opinions than any but Justice Story and Marshall himself. Johnson's occasional nationalism infuriated Jeffersonians, whereas his deference toward elected state and federal legislatures angered the Federalists. The imagination and originality of many of his opinions, and the legal discussions in his correspondence with Jefferson, offer a rich legacy for historians of constitutional law. Johnson established dissent as a legitimate form of constitutional opinion and formulated a rights-oriented conception of the federal court system. Although he stood with Marshall in advancing national powers that he deemed necessary for the Union's survival, Johnson increasingly advocated state autonomy in his (mainly dissenting) opinions.

★ ★ ★

ANTHONY M. KENNEDY
BORN: July 23, 1936, Sacramento, California
TENURE ON COURT: February 1988–present
NOTEWORTHY OPINIONS: *Skinner v. Railway Labor Executives Assoc.* (1989-m), *Illinois v. Perkins* (1990-m), *Planned Parenthood v. Casey* (1992-pl/pc), *Ramdass v. Angelone* (2000-pl)

AS THE SON of a prominent Sacramento lawyer, young Anthony M. Kennedy grew up around such figures as future Chief Justice Earl Warren. He was a pageboy for the state senate in junior high and assisted in his father's law office during high school. After spending his final year studying at the London School of Economics, Kennedy graduated from Stanford University in 1958 and received his law degree from Harvard Law School in 1961. Kennedy was admitted to the California bar in 1962 and began to practice with a San Francisco office. On his father's death in 1963, Kennedy returned to Sacramento to take over his firm. He also taught law at the McGeorge School of Law, University of the Pacific, from 1965 to 1988. Kennedy assisted then Governor Ronald Reagan in drafting a state tax proposal in 1966. In 1975, on Reagan's recommendation, President Ford appointed Kennedy to the Ninth Circuit Court of Appeals, where he served for twelve years. He also served on the board of directors of the Federal Judicial Center during this time. President Reagan nominated Kennedy to the Supreme Court in November 1987, following the Senate defeat of his first nomination, Robert Bork, and the withdrawal of his second choice, Douglas Ginsburg. Although generally known as a conservative, Kennedy's case-by-case approach and coalition-building skills have made him in recent years a pivotal figure on the Rehnquist Court, voting often with centrist Justices O'Connor and Souter.

★ ★ ★

JOSEPH R. LAMAR

BORN: October 14, 1857, Cedar Grove, Georgia
TENURE ON COURT: January 1911–January 1916
DIED: January 2, 1916, Washington, D.C.
NOTEWORTHY OPINIONS: *Gompers v. Bucks Stove and Range Co.* (1911-m), *Diaz v. United States* (1912-d), *United States v. Midwest Oil* (1915-m)

JOSEPH R. LAMAR studied law at Washington and Lee University in Virginia, then clerked for a Georgia attorney. He was admitted to the Georgia bar in 1878. From 1880 to 1910, Lamar alternated between practicing law in Georgia and serving in public positions. During this period, he also wrote scholarly essays on legal history. In 1886, Lamar was elected to the state legislature, where he served two terms. In 1893, the governor appointed him commissioner to codify Georgia laws. Lamar was elected to the Georgia Supreme Court in 1903 but resigned two years later to return to his practice. In 1910, after meeting him briefly on a vacation to Georgia and hearing of his glowing state reputation, President Taft nominated Lamar to the Supreme Court.

Few divisive constitutional issues faced the Court during the five years that Lamar served. His judicial philosophy favored laissez-faire economics and administrative authority, especially executive power. He wrote few dissents and generally supported the moderate majority that Taft placed on the bench. Although Lamar is not remembered by many legal scholars and historians, his contemporaries considered him one of the strongest members of the Court during his brief tenure. Lamar died of heart failure in 1916.

★ ★ ★

LUCIUS Q. C. LAMAR

BORN: September 17, 1825, Eatonton, Georgia
TENURE ON COURT: January 1888–January 1893
DIED: January 23, 1893, Macon, Georgia
NOTEWORTHY OPINIONS: *In re Neagle* (1890-d), *McCall v. California* (1890-m), *Marshall Field & Co. v. Clark* (1892-c)

BORN TO A FAMILY of landed aristocrats, Lucius Quintus Cincinnatus Lamar graduated from Emory College in 1845. After passing the bar in 1847, he practiced law in Georgia and Mississippi and became involved in sectional politics. Lamar was elected to a Mississippi seat in the U.S. House in 1857 as a states' rights Democrat. He resigned from Congress on the eve of the Civil War and served two years in the Confederate Army. When the war was over, Lamar returned to his practice in Mississippi. He became a leading spokesman of reconciliation and received a pardon for his Confederate activities. In 1872, Lamar was reelected to the U.S. House and five years later won a seat in the Senate. During his second term, Lamar resigned from the Senate to accept President Cleveland's offer of appointment as secretary of the Interior. Then, in 1887, Cleveland nominated Lamar to the

Supreme Court. Lamar was confirmed by a close vote in 1888 over the objections of Senate Republicans, but the bitterness of his confirmation process revealed the depth of residual sectionalism during the postwar era.

Lamar's judicial philosophy reflected a belief in rigorous separation of powers, strong interstate commerce, and suspicion of executive power. Although he had only four active years on the bench before he died, Lamar's presence on the bench as the Court's first Confederate is noteworthy.

★ ★ ★

HENRY BROCKHOLST LIVINGSTON
BORN: November 25, 1757, New York
TENURE ON COURT: January 1807–March 1823
DIED: March 18, 1823, Washington, D.C.
NOTEWORTHY OPINIONS: *Dugan v. United States* (1818-m), *United States v. Smith* (1820-d)

HENRY BROCKHOLST LIVINGSTON was among three Supreme Court justices to come from one of New York's most influential families. John Jay, the first chief justice, was his brother-in-law; Smith Thompson, his immediate successor, married into the family. After graduating from the College of New Jersey (now Princeton University) in 1774, Livingston joined the Continental army and fought in the Revolution. He passed the bar in 1783 and was elected to the New York Assembly three years later. Although Livingston had supported ratification, he aligned himself with Jefferson's antifederalism movement in the 1790s. In 1802, he was appointed to the New York Supreme Court, where he was considered an able and outspoken judge. When Supreme Court Justice Paterson of New Jersey died four years later, Livingston's political views and state affiliations recommended him to Thomas Jefferson as a replacement.

But Jefferson's attempts to contain the Federalist tendencies of the Marshall Court were little helped by Livingston's appointment. Among such powerful figures as Marshall and Story, Livingston's voice was rarely heard. The weakening of Livingston's Jeffersonian views is often attributed to the strength of Marshall's persuasive skills, although some scholars speculate that the antifederalism espoused in his middle years was opportunistic. In sixteen years on the Court, he produced fewer than fifty opinions, mainly on commercial issues or in the field of prize law, of which only eight were dissents.

★ ★ ★

HORACE H. LURTON
BORN: February 26, 1844, Newport, Kentucky
TENURE ON COURT: January 1910–July 1914
DIED: July 12, 1914, Atlantic City, New Jersey
NOTEWORTHY OPINIONS: *Coyle v. Smith* (1911-m), *Henry v. A.B. Dick Co.* (1912-m), *United States v. Terminal R.R. Association* (1912-m)

HORACE H. LURTON'S family moved from Kentucky to Tennessee when he was a child. In 1859, he traveled to Douglas University (now defunct) in Chicago but left his studies when the Civil War broke out. Lurton joined the Confederate Army and was captured by Union soldiers in 1862. He escaped but was recaptured the following year. When Lurton fell ill in prison, his mother successfully petitioned President Lincoln for a pardon. Although he always identified himself as a Democrat, the war was Lurton's last involvement with partisan politics. He graduated from Cumberland Law School in 1867 and established a practice. In 1875, Lurton was appointed to the Sixth Chancery Division of Tennessee but resigned after three years for financial reasons. Lurton was elected to his state's supreme court in 1886 and became its chief judge in 1893. Later that year, President Grover Cleveland appointed Lurton to the Sixth Circuit's Court of Appeals, where he served for sixteen years alongside William Howard Taft and future Justice William Day. His nomination in 1909 was the first of President Taft's five appointments to the Supreme Court.

Lurton became known for his courtesy, moderation, and respect for precedent. He consistently voted to uphold the Sherman Act, although he also supported jurisprudence that excepted "reasonable" trusts. Lurton's traditionalism and short tenure prevented him from making any major contributions to constitutional law. He died of a heart attack after four years on the bench.

★ ★ ★

JOSEPH McKENNA

BORN: August 10, 1843, Philadelphia, Pennsylvania
TENURE ON COURT: January 1898–January 1925
DIED: November 21, 1926, Washington, D.C.
NOTEWORTHY OPINIONS: *Magoun v. Illinois Trust and Savings Bank* (1898-m), *Adair v. United States* (1908-d), *Hipolite Egg Co. v. United States* (1911-m), *German Alliance Insurance Company v. Lewis* (1914-m), *Bunting v. Oregon* (1917-m), *United States v. United States Steel Corporation* (1920-m)

JOSEPH McKENNA'S IRISH immigrant family left Philadelphia when he was a child to settle in California. Made head of the household at age fifteen by his father's death, McKenna worked odd jobs, studied law, and passed the bar in 1865. McKenna aligned himself with the Republican Party and was elected county district attorney in the same year. In 1875, he served one term in the state legislature. Following two failed bids, McKenna won a congressional seat in 1885 and served four terms. He allied himself with powerful Republicans Leland Stanford and William McKinley and was appointed to the Ninth Circuit Court of Appeals in 1892. When McKinley won the presidency in 1896, he made McKenna his attorney general. One year later, McKinley nominated him to the Supreme Court.

McKenna's relative inexperience and strong party ties made the appointment controversial. Although he would spend twenty-seven years on the Court, McKenna did not develop a particularly consistent judicial philosophy. His interpretation of the Fourteenth Amendment's due process clause, a significant area of constitutional law during his tenure, varied from case to case. However, McKenna's advocacy of broad federal police powers under the commerce clause, another constitutional issue disputed by his Court, did not waver. In his final years on the bench, McKenna's mental capacities diminished to the point that he was asked several times to rewrite his opinions. He resigned in 1925 and died the following year.

★ ★ ★

JOHN McKINLEY

BORN: May 1, 1780, Culpeper County, Virginia
TENURE ON COURT: January 1838–July 1852
DIED: July 19, 1852, Louisville, Kentucky
NOTEWORTHY OPINIONS: *Lane v. Vick* (1845-d),
Pollard's Lessee v. Hagan (1845-m)

SOON AFTER JOHN McKINLEY's birth, his family joined the many Virginians heading west to sparsely populated Kentucky. McKinley taught himself law and passed the bar in 1800. In 1818, McKinley moved his practice to Huntsville, Alabama. When Alabama became a state the following year, McKinley ran for a circuit judge post but lost. In 1820, however, McKinley was elected to the state legislature and two years later was in the running for a Senate seat but once more lost. Initially a supporter of Henry Clay, Jackson's growing popularity attracted McKinley's attention. His support of Jackson finally brought him a U.S. Senate seat in 1826, but he lost his reelection bid and in 1831 returned to the state House. McKinley fought against the Bank of the United States and generally supported Jacksonian policy, popular positions that earned him a congressional seat in 1832. He did not run for reelection, opting to return to the state legislature once more in 1836. McKinley was again elected to the Senate in 1837 but did not have a chance to serve, the newly elected President Van Buren offering him one of two new seats on the Supreme Court.

Once on the Court, McKinley adhered to his states' rights doctrine, dissenting in those cases in which a corporation was granted citizen status or the federal government attempted to make claims in the territories. He wrote few opinions, and none concerned major issues of constitutional law. In 1845, McKinley's health deteriorated. His final years on the bench were spent in relative obscurity.

★ ★ ★

JOHN McLEAN

BORN: March 11, 1785, Morris County, New Jersey
TENURE ON COURT: January 1830–April 1861
DIED: April 4, 1861, Cincinnati, Ohio
NOTEWORTHY OPINIONS: *Wheaton v. Peters* (1834-m),
Briscoe v. Bank of Kentucky (1837-m), *Cooley v. Board of
Wardens* (1852-d), *Pennsylvania v. Wheeling Bridge Co.*
(1852-m), *Dred Scott v. Sandford* (1857-d)

JOHN MCLEAN WAS born in New Jersey but during his childhood moved with his family to Virginia, then Kentucky, and finally to the Ohio frontier. Despite having little formal education, McLean studied law and began to practice in 1807. He also printed a weekly newspaper, the Lebanon *Western Star*, for several years, which led him into Ohio politics. McLean was elected to Congress in 1812 and strongly supported President Madison's war measures. Although he was reelected, McLean resigned from the House in 1816 to take a seat on the Ohio Supreme Court. In 1822, President Monroe appointed him commissioner of the General Land Office and the following year, postmaster general. McLean was President Jackson's first Supreme Court nominee, confirmed in March 1829 but not sworn in until January 1830.

McLean did not fully associate himself with Jackson's policies. Distancing himself from Jacksonian Chief Justice Taney, McLean opposed slavery, tended to defer to federal sovereignty, and supported congressional regulation of commerce. His dissent in *Dred Scott v. Sandford* led some Northerners to suggest him as a presidential candidate. Associated with many different parties in his thirty-one-year tenure, McLean did not view partisan politics as inappropriate to the bench; he was discussed as presidential candidate numerous times. Although he wrote many majority opinions (247 in all), few of them addressed constitutional issues. McLean died of pneumonia one month after Lincoln's inauguration.

★ ★ ★

JAMES C. MCREYNOLDS
BORN: February 3, 1862, Elkton, Kentucky
TENURE ON COURT: October 1914–January 1941
DIED: August 24, 1946, Washington, D.C.
NOTEWORTHY OPINIONS: *Berger v. United States* (1921-d), *Meyer v. Nebraska* (1923-m), *Pierce v. Society of Sisters* (1925-m), *Nebbia v. New York* (1934-d), *Gold Clause Cases* (1935-d), *Ashwander v. Tennessee Valley Authority* (1936-d)

JAMES C. MCREYNOLDS graduated from Vanderbilt University in 1882 and received his law degree from the University of Virginia in 1884. After a brief stint as a secretary to a U.S. senator, McReynolds settled in Tennessee and established a law practice. He lost a bid for Congress in 1896 and returned to private practice and teaching law. In 1903, President Roosevelt appointed McReynolds assistant attorney general. He served four years and earned a reputation as a "trustbuster." In 1913, President Wilson appointed him U.S. attorney general. When McReynolds's well-known temper brought controversy to the cabinet, Wilson sought a way to remove him and in 1914 nominated McReynolds to the Supreme Court.

McReynolds combined conservatism with strong libertarianism, opposing monopolies as well as the growth of federal government. He wrote seminal civil liberties opinions for the Court, striking down nativistic state laws that interfered with the teaching of foreign languages and parochial education. McReynolds was one of the four conservative members of the Court, dubbed the Four Horsemen, who consistently opposed Roosevelt's New Deal programs. A vocal anti-Semite, his racist and sexist views are equally well documented. On his death in 1946, McReynolds, a bachelor, willed his significant wealth to various charities.

★ ★ ★

JOHN MARSHALL

BORN: September 24, 1755, Prince William County, Virginia
TENURE ON COURT: February 1801–July 1835 (Chief Justice)
DIED: July 6, 1835, Philadelphia, Pennsylvania
NOTEWORTHY OPINIONS: *Marbury v. Madison* (1803-m), *Dartmouth College v. Woodward* (1819-m), *McCulloch v. Maryland* (1819-m), *Gibbons v. Ogden* (1824-m), *Cherokee Nation v. Georgia* (1831-m), *Barron v. Baltimore* (1833-m)

JOHN MARSHALL WAS the first of fifteen children born to a leading Virginia frontier family. In 1780, following five years of service in the Revolutionary War, Marshall studied law with George Wythe at the College of William and Mary. Marshall moved his law practice to Richmond and was elected to the state legislature eight times between 1782 and 1797. At the Virginia ratification convention of 1788, Marshall supported the Constitution. After turning down several positions in the new government, he traveled to France as one of the envoys sent on the 1797 diplomatic mission that brought on the "XYZ" affair. Marshall was elected to the U.S. House in 1799 and in 1800 was appointed secretary of state by President John Adams. Immediately following Jefferson's victory in the 1800 presidential election, Adams named Marshall chief justice of the United States. Marshall continued to serve as secretary of state for the remainder of Adams's term and did not give up his cabinet position until after Jefferson's inauguration.

Marshall is considered by many to have exerted the greatest influence on the Court of any chief or associate justice. His desire to strengthen the Court's power by presenting a united front rather than seriatim opinions, as well as his logical style of opinion writing, defined the Court's image during its crucial early years. Besides his leadership, Marshall's greatest contribution may have been the firm establishment of judicial review of state and federal law. His broad interpretation of the interstate commerce clause, which significantly expanded the scope of federal power over the states, was characteristic of Marshall's Federalist views. His constitutional vision dominated the Court for thirty-four years, to the dismay of states' rights advocates, such as Thomas Jefferson. Although Marshall experienced health problems in his final years, he was reluctant to leave the Court for fear that President Jackson's replacement would undermine his work. Marshall died at the age of seventy-nine while still serving on the Court.

★ ★ ★

THURGOOD MARSHALL

BORN: July 2, 1908, Baltimore, Maryland

TENURE ON COURT: October 1967–June 1991

DIED: January 24, 1993, Washington, D.C.

NOTEWORTHY OPINIONS: *United States v. Wilson* (1975-m) *Regents of the University of California v. Bakke* (1978-c/d), *Harris v. McRae* (1980-d), *Donovan v. Dewey* (1981-m), *Oliver v. United States* (1984-d), *Skinner v. Railway Labor Executives' Association* (1989-d), *Florida v. Bostick* (1991-d)

THURGOOD MARSHALL GREW UP experiencing Southern segregation. After graduating from Lincoln University in Pennsylvania, he was barred by race from attending Maryland's state law school and so commuted to Howard University Law School in Washington, D.C., where he came under the influence of the demanding academic dean Charles Hamilton Houston. Marshall struggled to sustain a private law practice in Baltimore during the Depression. In 1936, Houston recruited him to the NAACP's legal staff. In 1939, Marshall succeeded his mentor as the NAACP's chief lawyer and for more than twenty years spearheaded the NAACP's efforts to end racial segregation, arguing more than thirty cases before the Supreme Court, including *Brown v. Board of Education* (1954). Referring to the litigation campaign that culminated in *Brown*, Chief Justice Rehnquist would observe on Marshall's death that he was perhaps the only Supreme Court justice of the late twentieth century who would have had a large place in the history books even if he had never sat on the Supreme Court.

Marshall's path to the Court began in 1961, when, over the objections of southern Democrats in the Senate, President Kennedy nominated him to the Second Circuit Court of Appeals. In 1965, President Johnson named him U.S. solicitor general; two years later, Thurgood Marshall became the first African American Supreme Court justice. Marshall joined the Court at the height of the Warren Court's liberal activism, but within a few years, Marshall's liberal views would more often appear as dissents, as appointees of Presidents Nixon and Reagan gained power in the 1970s and 1980s. Marshall viewed law with an eye to the impact of decisions in daily practice, especially for socially disadvantaged groups. He strongly opposed the death penalty and supported affirmative action and other measures that aimed to erode discrimination and its effects. The only justice with significant experience in criminal defense, Marshall also worked hard to broaden the rights of criminal defendants.

Marshall wrote some important First Amendment opinions, but his major doctrinal contribution came in his articulation of the so-called sliding-scale approach to equal protection law. Prevailing doctrine divided classifications into the rigid categories of suspect and nonsuspect and interests into the equally rigid division of fundamental and ordinary. Marshall argued that equal protection analysis should instead carefully balance the nature of the classification, the kind of interest affected, and the reasons the government had for its actions. Within the Court, colleagues found Marshall engaging and — particularly on issues of race and criminal justice — a person whose views carried great moral authority. But the job as justice never quite suited him. An outgoing man who felt isolated from social contacts on the Court, Marshall never devoted a great deal of attention to the Court's work. When his friend William Brennan retired in 1990, Marshall lost the one person on the Court who kept his spirits up. A large man with large appetites, it became more difficult for him to carry his weight easily as he aged. He retired in poor health in 1991 and was an outspoken critic of the Rehnquist Court in his remaining years. Marshall died of heart failure in 1993.

★ ★ ★

STANLEY MATTHEWS
BORN: July 21, 1824, Lexington, Kentucky
TENURE ON COURT: May 1881–March 1889
DIED: March 22, 1889, Washington, D.C.
NOTEWORTHY OPINIONS: *Hurtado v. California* (1884-m), *Poindexter v. Greenhow* (1885-m), *Yick Wo v. Hopkins* (1886-m)

STANLEY MATTHEWS GRADUATED from Kenyon College, Ohio, at the age of sixteen. He moved to Tennessee and passed the bar in 1842. From 1851 to 1853, he served as a county judge. Matthews was elected to the Ohio Senate in 1855 and became a federal attorney in 1858. He served in the Union army during the Civil War but resigned in 1863 to take a seat on the Superior Court of Cincinnati. Two years later, Matthews returned to private practice, including service as midwestern chief counsel to financier Jay Gould. In 1876, he served as counsel to the Hayes-Tilden Electoral Commission and acted as Hayes's representative in negotiating the Compromise of 1877. Later that year, he was appointed to fill a vacancy in the U.S. Senate. Matthews's Supreme Court nomination, announced in the last days of Hayes's presidency, was extremely controversial. Republicans disapproved of Matthews's prewar willingness to prosecute abolitionists, whereas Democrats were angered at his support of Hayes. The Senate refused to act on the nomination until President Garfield renominated Matthews in May.

Besides his controversial nomination, Matthews is remembered for his interpretation of the Eleventh Amendment. He argued that, although states could not be sued under the Constitution, agents of the state could be. Although he followed the majority in denying federal protection to black civil rights, Matthews's opinion for the Court in *Yick Wo v. Hopkins* overturned a San Francisco city ordinance on the ground that, despite its neutral appearance, its intention and application were racially biased against Chinese immigrants. Illness forced Matthews to miss much of the 1888 term, and he died the following year.

★ ★ ★

SAMUEL F. MILLER

BORN: April 5, 1816, Richmond, Kentucky
TENURE ON COURT: July 1862–October 1890
DIED: October 13, 1890, Washington, D.C.
NOTEWORTHY OPINIONS: *Hepburn v. Griswold* (1870-d),
Slaughterhouse Cases (1873-m), *Davidson v. New Orleans*
(1877-m), *United States v. Lee* (1882-m), *Ex parte
Yarbrough* (1884-m), *Wabash v. Illinois* (1886-m)

SAMUEL MILLER EARNED a medical degree in 1838 and became a practicing
Knox County, Kentucky, physician. He grew interested in law and passed the bar in
1847. An advocate of gradual manumission for slaves, Miller left Kentucky in 1850,
when it became clear that Kentucky was deepening its commitment to slavery. He
settled in Iowa, where he soon joined the ranks of the state's leading attorneys.
Miller left the Whigs to join the Republican Party in its early years. He lost his bid
for the state senate in 1856 but by 1860 was considered the leading Republican
figure in Iowa. His friends in Congress successfully lobbied President Lincoln on
Miller's behalf when a new Court seat was created for the western circuit in 1862.

Miller was an influential justice during the turbulent Civil War and postwar period, writing more than six hundred opinions, nearly one hundred on constitutional
issues. Although he was a civil rights proponent and nationalist, Miller's constitutional theory made regulation of commerce a higher priority than expansion of black
civil rights. He developed constitutional law to support state regulatory powers, as
in his narrow interpretation of the Fourteenth Amendment's due process clause in
the *Slaughterhouse Cases*. This position strictly limited the meaning of national citizenship, a significant disappointment for freedmen. Overall, Miller's judicial philosophy was marked by an attempt to balance a defense of the rights of the individual with protection of the public good. Miller's reading of the Fifteenth Amendment
was largely responsible for the extension of federal protection to black voting rights.
Although he was considered for the chief justiceship and the presidency at various
times, Miller died in 1890 while still serving as an associate on the Court.

★ ★ ★

SHERMAN MINTON

BORN: October 20, 1890, Georgetown, Indiana
TENURE ON COURT: October 1949–October 1956
DIED: April 9, 1965, New Albany, Indiana
NOTEWORTHY OPINIONS: *United States ex rel. Knauff
v. Shaughnessy* (1950-m), *United States v. Rabinowitz*
(1950-m), *Adler v. Board of Education of the City of New
York* (1952-m), *Terry v. Adams* (1953-d)

SHERMAN MINTON RECEIVED a law degree from Indiana University in 1915 and
an additional degree from Yale University Law School in 1917. He established a law
firm in New Albany, Indiana, and spent the next fifteen years in private practice. In
1933, Minton was appointed counselor to Indiana's Public Service Commission.

A year later, he ran successfully for the U.S. Senate as a New Dealer. He actively supported President Roosevelt's Court-packing plan. Minton lost his reelection bid, but Roosevelt appointed him to the White House staff as an administrative assistant in charge of coordinating military agencies. Later that year, Minton was appointed to the U.S. Court of Appeals for the Seventh Circuit, where he served eight years. President Truman, a close friend of Minton's from his Senate years, nominated him to the Supreme Court in 1949.

At the time, many believed that he would join Justice Hugo Black in the liberal bloc. However, the New Deal era had given Minton a narrow vision of the role of the Court, and during his tenure, he came to be regarded as one of the most conservative members of the Court. Minton tended to give a large leeway to Congress in most matters, especially in civil liberties claims. The decisive factors, according to his judicial philosophy, were legislative power and judicial restraint. In the area of religious and racial discrimination, major issues that came before him on the Court, Minton believed that states did not have the power to discriminate, whereas private citizens did. Minton retired in 1956, owing to ill health.

★　★　★

WILLIAM H. MOODY

BORN: December 23, 1853, Newbury, Massachusetts
TENURE ON COURT: December 1906–November 1910
DIED: July 2, 1917, Haverhill, Massachusetts
NOTEWORTHY OPINIONS: *Employers' Liability Cases*
(1908-d), *St. Louis, Iron Mountain, and Southern Railway
v. Taylor* (1908-m), *Twining v. New Jersey* (1908-m)

WILLIAM H. MOODY graduated from Harvard in 1876 and briefly attended Harvard Law School. He completed his legal studies with a Boston law firm and was admitted to the bar in 1878. Moody established a successful practice in Haverhill, Massachusetts, specializing in corporate law. He served as a city solicitor from 1888 to 1890, then was elected district attorney for the Eastern District of Massachusetts. Moody prosecuted Lizzie Borden's murder trial in 1892; Borden was acquitted, but the notorious trial won Moody national recognition. In 1895, he won a special election to Congress and was reelected for three consecutive terms. Moody left Congress in 1902 to accept an appointment as secretary of the Navy under President Roosevelt, with whom Moody had become close. From 1904 to 1906, he served as U.S. attorney general. Roosevelt nominated Moody to the Supreme Court in 1906, in hope that his appointment would tip the conservative Court's balance in favor of liberal nationalism.

Moody's judicial philosophy, as seen in his brief tenure, was that of a Roosevelt progressive. He favored broad interpretations of the commerce clause and hoped to see constitutional law modernized to meet the needs of an industrialized nation. However, Moody was stricken with rheumatism in 1908 and could not attend the 1909 term. He resigned the following year, after Congress passed a statute granting him retirement benefits, and lived for seven more years as an invalid.

★　★　★

ALFRED MOORE

BORN: May 21, 1755, Brunswick County, North Carolina
TENURE ON COURT: April 1800–January 1804
DIED: October 15, 1810, Bladen County, North Carolina
NOTEWORTHY OPINIONS: *Bas v. Tingy* (1800-s)

AFTER COMPLETING A Boston education, Alfred Moore returned to North Carolina to study law under his father, a prominent state judge. He served as a captain during the War for Independence, and in 1782, his wartime efforts won him a seat in the state senate, which elected him attorney general of the state that same year. Moore's Federalist views were not popular in North Carolina during the 1780s, and he lost his bid to become a delegate to the state's first ratification convention but served on the second convention. An attempt to win a Senate seat in 1795 also failed, although by only one vote. In 1798, the North Carolina General Assembly elected Moore a Superior Court judge. When Justice Iredell died in 1799, President Adams nominated Moore to the Supreme Court as a replacement from Iredell's home state. During his four-year tenure, he wrote only one opinion. Moore resigned in 1804, citing the difficulties of circuit riding, and spent his final years helping to establish the University of North Carolina.

★ ★ ★

FRANK MURPHY

BORN: April 13, 1890, Harbor Beach, Michigan
TENURE ON COURT: February 1940–July 1949
DIED: July 19, 1949, Detroit, Michigan
NOTEWORTHY OPINIONS: *Thornhill v. Alabama* (1940-m), *Hirabayashi v. United States* (1943-c), *Korematsu v. United States* (1944-d), *Wolf v. Colorado* (1949-m)

FRANK MURPHY WAS raised Irish Catholic in a small Protestant town north of Detroit. He graduated from the University of Michigan in 1912 and took a law degree in 1914. After passing the bar, Murphy clerked with a Detroit law firm for three years. In World War I, he served briefly with the American forces in Europe. On his return in 1919, Murphy became assistant district attorney for Detroit, then served on the Recorder's Court of Detroit from 1923 to 1930. Murphy was elected mayor of Detroit in 1930. He strongly supported Roosevelt's 1932 presidential campaign. Soon after Roosevelt's inauguration, in 1933, Murphy was appointed governor general of the Philippines. After his return in 1936, he was elected governor of Michigan and served two years during a period of intense labor struggle. Murphy lost his reelection bid in 1938, and Roosevelt appointed him U.S. attorney general. In 1940, he was named to the Supreme Court of the United States.

Murphy remained a staunch liberal on the bench. He advocated a "preferred position" for the First Amendment and opposed religious bigotry and racism wherever he perceived it. During World War II, he was the only justice to report for duty, serving as an infantry officer at Fort Benning, Georgia, when the Court broke for recesses. Although Murphy briefly supported Japanese internment, he later was a strong dissenter on the issue. Murphy died in 1949, having significantly expanded civil liberties jurisprudence.

★ ★ ★

SAMUEL NELSON

BORN: November 10, 1792, Hebron, New York
TENURE ON COURT: February 1845–November 1872
DIED: December 13, 1873, Cooperstown, New York
NOTEWORTHY OPINIONS: *Dred Scott v. Sandford*
(1857-c), *New York ex rel. Bank of Commerce v. Commis-*
sioners of Taxes (1863-m), *Prize Cases* (1863-d)

SAMUEL NELSON WAS intended for the ministry, but after his 1813 graduation from Middlebury College, Vermont, he decided to pursue law. He clerked in Salem, New York, and passed the bar in 1817. Nelson established a successful practice in Cortland, New York, and became active in politics. In 1821, he was a county delegate at the state's constitutional convention. He was appointed judge of New York's Sixth Circuit Court two years later. In 1831, Nelson was advanced to the state's supreme court and eventually became its chief justice. After Supreme Court Justice Smith Thompson's death in 1843, President Tyler considered numerous candidates for the vacant seat. Two were rejected by the Senate before Tyler proposed Nelson.

Nelson's was a moderate Democratic voice as tensions between North and South grew. His opinion in *Dred Scott* was initially supposed to speak for the majority. Nelson had decided the case without raising the citizen status of free blacks or the constitutionality of congressional authority to outlaw slavery in the new territories. Chief Justice Taney's broader opinion, which took up these controversial points, became the final majority view; Nelson filed his opinion as a separate concurrence. During the Civil War, Nelson remained in Washington and for a brief period worked as a negotiator between the two sides. Although Nelson wrote 347 opinions in his twenty-seven years on the Court, his jurisprudence was marked by restraint and precision rather than landmark decisions. He resigned owing to ill health in 1872 and died one year later.

★ ★ ★

SANDRA DAY O'CONNOR

BORN: March 26, 1930, El Paso, Texas
TENURE ON COURT: September 1981–present
NOTEWORTHY OPINIONS: *Strickland v. Washington*
(1984-m), *Oregon v. Elstad* (1985-m), *Florida v. Bostick*
(1991-m), *New York v. United States* (1992-m), *Planned*
Parenthood v. Casey (1992-pl/pc), *Tuan Anh Nguyen v. INS*
(2001-d)

RAISED ON AN Arizona ranch, Sandra Day O'Connor graduated from high school at sixteen. After receiving a B.A. from Stanford University in 1950, she completed the university's law program in two years. Failing to find private-sector work after graduation, except for a secretarial offer, O'Connor turned to public service and became a county attorney for San Mateo, California. From 1954 to 1957, she worked as a civilian attorney for the U.S. Army in Germany. When she returned to the United States, she established her own private practice in Phoenix, Arizona. After her second child was born, O'Connor spent five years as a full-time mother, charitable volunteer, and Republican Party worker. She returned to law as an assistant state attorney general in 1965. Four years later, O'Connor was named to fill a vacancy in the state senate; she held the seat in the next two elections. O'Connor was elected to a county bench position in 1975 and appointed to the Arizona Court of Appeals in 1979. Expectations that a woman would be nominated to the Supreme Court had grown throughout the 1970s, and in the final weeks of his 1980 presidential campaign, Ronald Reagan promised to name a woman to "one of the first Supreme Court vacancies in my administration." When Justice Potter Stewart informed the administration in 1981 that he planned to retire, Reagan reminded his aides of his campaign pledge. Chief Justice Warren Burger had recently met O'Connor at a judicial conference abroad, and he called her to the attention of the administration. As a judge and a legislator, O'Connor had built a tough-on-crime record that appealed to the White House, but her legislative record on abortion was ambiguous, giving some conservatives pause. Liberals, meanwhile, contested her lack of support for feminist issues. Nonetheless, O'Connor was confirmed by the Senate in a 99–0 vote, making her the first female associate justice in the history of the Court.

Initially, many assumed that she would follow Rehnquist, with whom she had attended law school. But although O'Connor often joined the conservative bloc, she frequently tempered her support with a narrower concurring opinion. Except in cases of sexual discrimination, O'Connor has tended to resist judicial activism, emerging in the 1990s as a centrist and a coalition builder.

★ ★ ★

WILLIAM PATERSON
BORN: December 24, 1745, County Antrim, Ireland
TENURE ON COURT: March 1793–September 1806
DIED: September 9, 1806, Albany, New York
NOTEWORTHY OPINIONS: *Penhallow v. Doane's Administrators* (1795-s), *Hylton v. Ware* (1796-c), *Calder v. Bull* (1798-c), *Stuart v. Laird* (1803-m), *Simms v. Slacum* (1805-d)

WILLIAM PATERSON EMIGRATED with his family to New Jersey while still a child. He graduated from the College of New Jersey (now Princeton University) in 1763, studied law, and was admitted to the bar in 1769. Paterson became active in state politics with the onset of the Revolutionary War. Although his judicial career was not negligible, Paterson's primary influence on the American court system stems largely from accomplishments during his political career. At the Philadelphia Convention of 1787, Paterson proposed the New Jersey Plan of Union, a section of which added a federal judiciary and stated that the acts and treaties established under the new Constitution would be considered the "supreme law" of the states. Two years later, while serving in the Senate, Paterson coauthored the Judiciary Act of 1789. Washington's nomination of Paterson to the Supreme Court rewarded him for these contributions.

Paterson and the other strong Federalists on the bench eventually came under public attack for their vigorous interpretation of the Sedition Act. While on circuit, Paterson informed the jury in *U.S. v. Lyon* (1799) that judges, not juries, determine the constitutionality of the Sedition Act. Paterson's zeal cost him any chance to be chief justice, President Adams instead nominating his secretary of state, John Marshall. Paterson handled the situation gracefully and became a friend and ally of the powerful Chief Justice Marshall. The zealous federalism of his earlier years on the bench gave way to a reputation for nonpartisan equity. Paterson's health never recovered from a carriage accident in 1805, and he was largely absent from the Court during his final years.

★　★　★

RUFUS W. PECKHAM
BORN: November 8, 1838, Albany, New York
TENURE ON COURT: January 1896–October 1909
DIED: October 24, 1909, Altamont, New York
NOTEWORTHY OPINIONS: *White v. United States* (1896-m), *Allgeyer v. Louisiana* (1897-m), *Maxwell v. Dow* (1900-m), *Lochner v. New York* (1905-m)

RUFUS W. PECKHAM STUDIED law with his father, a prominent New York attorney, judge, and Democratic politician. He passed the bar in 1859 and joined his father's firm. In 1869, Peckham was elected to the post of Albany County District Attorney. He joined the upstate Democratic faction in opposition to the Tammany Hall Democrats of New York City and in 1881 led the movement to prevent the Tammany delegation from sitting at the Democratic state convention. The same year, he was named Albany's corporation counsel. Peckham was appointed to the New York Supreme Court in 1883 and elected to the court of appeals three years later. In 1895, President Cleveland nominated him to the Supreme Court.

Peckham's tendency toward judicial activism and outspoken advocacy of a laissez-faire capitalist conception of liberty of contract were components of the judicial conservatism emerging from the sitting Court. Peckham helped to shift these views into the majority. In his opinion for the majority in *Lochner v. New York,* which elicited a famous dissent from Justice Holmes, Peckham argued against state workplace regulation, on the basis of his interpretation of substantive due process. Although Peckham invoked the Fourteenth Amendment to protect economic rights, he shared the majority's conservative view that the civil rights of blacks, of criminals in state courts, and of laborers were not similarly protected. Later Courts would reject much of Peckham's jurisprudence. He died at the age of seventy while still serving on the bench.

★　★　★

MAHLON PITNEY

BORN: February 5, 1858, Morristown, New Jersey
TENURE ON COURT: March 1912–December 1922
DIED: December 9, 1924, Washington, D.C.
NOTEWORTHY OPINIONS: *Coppage v. Kansas* (1915-m),
Frank v. Mangum (1915-m), *Hitchman Coal and Coke Co.
v. Mitchell* (1917-m), *Mountain Timber Co. v. Washington*
(1917-m), *Pierce v. United States* (1920-m)

MAHLON PITNEY GRADUATED from Princeton University, where he was classmates with Woodrow Wilson, in 1879. Pitney then studied law with his father and practiced in Dover, New Jersey, before returning to Morristown to run his father's firm. Success in private practice led to a congressional seat in 1894 and reelection two years later. Pitney resigned to accept a New Jersey Senate seat, serving as president in 1900. The following year, Pitney was appointed to the New Jersey Supreme Court, sacrificing a promising gubernatorial bid to accept the position. In 1912, Pitney became the last of President Taft's five appointees to the Supreme Court. Pitney's antilabor record at the state level made his nomination unpopular among progressive Republicans in the Senate.

Pitney is remembered primarily for his opinions in several high-profile labor cases, although he also specialized in tax issues. His antiunion stance was somewhat tempered by his willingness to grant state police powers in cases involving workmen's compensation or maximum-hours laws. On questions of civil liberties, Pitney's judicial philosophy was similarly complex. Although, for example, he upheld the constitutionality of convictions under the Espionage Act, he voted against mandatory segregation and discriminatory voting statutes. In 1922, Pitney suffered from a stroke that left him unable to perform his duties. He retired and died two years later.

★ ★ ★

LEWIS F. POWELL, JR.

BORN: September 19, 1907, Suffolk, Virginia
TENURE ON COURT: January 1972–June 1987
DIED: August 25, 1998, Richmond, Virginia
NOTEWORTHY OPINIONS: *Kastigar v. United States*
(1972-m), *San Antonio Independent School District v.
Rodriguez* (1973-m), *Stone v. Powell* (1976-m), *Regents of
the University of California v. Bakke* (1978-pl), *Solem v.
Helm* (1983-m), *Batson v. Kentucky* (1986-m), *Bowers v.
Hardwick* (1986-c)

IT IS NO surprise that Lewis F. Powell, Jr., would often counsel his law students to return home after graduation and play a role in community affairs. After Powell had received his B.A. and law degree from Washington and Lee University in 1931 and a master's degree from Harvard Law School in 1932, he had done just that himself. Powell joined a Richmond law firm and remained until 1971, eventually becoming a senior partner. After serving in World War II, Powell resumed his law practice and was active in Richmond local government, chairing the Richmond School Board through the 1950s desegregation crisis. President of the American Bar Association from 1964 to 1965, he also served on several presidential commissions on crime and defense in the late 1960s. In 1969, President Nixon tapped Powell for the Supreme Court, but he declined. Two years later, Nixon offered again, and he accepted.

Powell took pride in keeping an open mind about cases and maintaining a moderate position amid the ideological battles taking place in the 1970s and 1980s. Joining an ideologically divided Court, Powell's vote was decisive in the Court's first confrontation with abortion, affirmative action, and gay rights. In many 5–4 decisions regarding the separation of church and state, Powell also found himself carving out a compromise with his swing vote. After his retirement in 1987, he turned to teaching and occasionally sat in for federal judges. Powell died of pneumonia in 1998, at the age of ninety.

★ ★ ★

STANLEY F. REED
BORN: December 31, 1884, Minerva, Kentucky
TENURE ON COURT: January 1938–February 1957
DIED: April 2, 1980, Huntington, New York
NOTEWORTHY OPINIONS: *United States v. Rock Royal Cooperative* (1939-m), *Smith v. Allwright* (1944-m), *Adamson v. California* (1947-m), *Beauharnais v. Illinois* (1952-d)

AFTER EARNING TWO bachelor's degrees, Stanley F. Reed studied law at the University of Virginia and Columbia University, traveled to the Sorbonne in 1909 for additional courses, and then returned to Maysville, Kentucky, and established a law practice. From 1912 to 1916, he also served in the state legislature. Reed was an Army lieutenant during World War I, after which he returned to private practice. In 1929, President Hoover appointed him counsel to the Federal Farm Board. Three years later, President Franklin Roosevelt elevated Reed to counsel for the Reconstruction Finance Corporation. In 1935, after a short stint assisting the attorney general, he was named solicitor general. Reed argued the constitutionality of New Deal policies to a resistant Supreme Court. In 1938, President Roosevelt nominated Reed to a Court that had abandoned its opposition to state and federal regulatory authority.

As an economic progressive, Reed generally supported labor rights and New Deal programs. On other issues, such as antisubversion legislation, Reed was considered a conservative. He did not see many limits to congressional or presidential power when there were national security concerns. However, Reed's deference to governmental judgment tended to remain at the federal level; he was less likely to support state and local regulations over constitutional objections. Reed retired from the Court at the age of seventy-two. He served briefly as President Eisenhower's chairman of the Civil Rights Commission. Reed lived to the age of ninety-five, making him the longest-lived justice to date.

★ ★ ★

WILLIAM H. REHNQUIST

BORN: October 1, 1924, Milwaukee, Wisconsin
TENURE ON COURT: January 1972–September 1986;
September 1986-present (Chief Justice)
NOTEWORTHY OPINIONS: *Hustler Magazine v. Falwell*
(1988-m), *Planned Parenthood v. Casey* (1992-c/d),
United States v. Ramirez (1998-pc), *Dickerson v. United
States* (2000-m), *Boy Scouts of America v. Dale* (2000-m),
Bush v. Gore (2000-c)

AFTER SERVING IN World War II with the Army Air Corps, William H. Rehnquist entered Stanford University on the G.I. Bill. He graduated in 1948 with a B.A. and an M.A. in political science and went on to earn a second master's degree from Harvard University. Rehnquist then attended Stanford's Law School and graduated first in a class that included his future colleague Sandra Day O'Connor. He served as a law clerk to Justice Robert Jackson for the 1952–1953 term. Rehnquist settled in Phoenix, Arizona, to practice law and became involved in Republican politics. In 1969, President Nixon appointed him to an assistant attorney general position in the Department of Justice. Two years later, Nixon nominated Rehnquist to the Supreme Court of the United States. In 1986, after Rehnquist had served fifteen years as an associate justice, President Reagan elevated him to chief justice.

In his early years on the Court, Rehnquist's opinions were to the right of most of his colleagues, including other Republican appointees, and he was often a lone dissenter. By the time he was nominated chief justice, however, many of Rehnquist's earlier dissents reflected views that had gained majority support. As a result, he held significant power on the Court. Despite liberal opposition to the nomination, Rehnquist's appointment was supported by a solid majority of the Senate. As chief justice, Rehnquist worked to overturn much of the Warren Court's legacy, particularly in the area of criminals' rights. His views began to show some moderation, however, after the emergence of a centrist bloc made up of Justices O'Connor, Souter, and Ginsburg qualified the court's capacity to assemble conservative majorities consistently. Late in 2004, deteriorating health forced Rehnquist to abstain for several months from active participation in the Court's routines. Although he returned to hear oral arguments in March 2005, the chief justice's early retirement is thought inevitable.

★ ★ ★

OWEN J. ROBERTS

BORN: May 2, 1875, Philadelphia, Pennsylvania
TENURE ON COURT: June 1930–July 1945
DIED: May 17, 1955, Chester Springs, Pennsylvania
NOTEWORTHY OPINIONS: *Grovey v. Townsend* (1935-m)
United States v. Butler (1936-m), *Herndon v. Lowry*
(1937-m), *Korematsu v. United States* (1944-d)

OWEN J. ROBERTS GRADUATED from the University of Pennsylvania in 1895 and received his law degree three years later. He established a successful law practice in Philadelphia, specializing in railroad and banking law. Until 1919, Roberts also taught law part-time at his alma mater. From 1924 to 1930, Roberts served as a special U.S. attorney investigating the Teapot Dome scandal and gained national attention from his successful prosecution of Albert Fall, President Harding's secretary of the Interior. Although Roberts had no judicial experience, President Hoover nominated him to the Supreme Court in 1930 after the Senate rejected John J. Parker, Hoover's first nominee.

Roberts held a key swing vote in many cases involving New Deal legislation. He voted with his conservative colleagues to overturn a number of New Deal policies, including a state minimum-wage law in *Morehead v. Tipaldo* (1936), although his reasoning was generally centrist. Many scholars do not see a clear theoretical foundation for his positions, and his opinion of Roosevelt's economic legislation softened over time. Roberts famously changed his position on the minimum wage one year later, after President Roosevelt was reelected in a landslide. It is also difficult to find a consistent judicial philosophy in Roberts's record on civil rights and civil liberties. One innovation he authored was the distinction between the "clear and present danger" and the "bad tendency" tests of the limits of freedom of speech. Roberts dissented fifty-three times in his final year on the Court, citing frustration with the liberal justices appointed by Roosevelt. He retired and served as dean of the University of Pennsylvania Law School from 1945 to 1951. He died four years later, at the age of eighty.

★ ★ ★

JOHN RUTLEDGE
BORN: September, 1739, Charleston, South Carolina
TENURE ON COURT: February 1790–March 1791;
August 1795–December 1795 (Chief Justice, recess appointment)
DIED: July 18, 1800, Charleston, South Carolina
NOTEWORTHY OPINIONS: *Talbot v. Janson* (1795-s),
United States v. Peters (1795-m)

JOHN RUTLEDGE STUDIED law with a prominent South Carolina attorney, then traveled to London to study at the Inns of Court. He was admitted to the English bar in 1760 and returned to South Carolina the same year. A state delegate to all the crucial colonial congresses, Rutledge represented South Carolina planters and their economic interests. His moderate views on separation from Great Britain led him to clash, before and during the war, with more radical advocates of independence. Rutledge was a strong wartime commander of South Carolina and played a large part in returning the state to postwar order. As delegate to the Philadelphia Convention of 1787, Rutledge was a key contributor to the construction of the Constitution. Most notably, the supremacy clause of Article VI was added on his motion. Rutledge resigned from his post as chief justice of South Carolina's Chancery

Court to accept Washington's nomination to the first bench of the Supreme Court. He resigned from the Supreme Court after serving only one year, but four years later, after Chief Justice Jay's resignation, Rutledge successfully petitioned Washington for the chief justice nomination.

Scandal over his scathing public critique of the Jay Treaty marred his reputation, however, and a Federalist backlash brought rejection in the Senate after Rutledge had completed four months on the bench under a recess appointment. He had heard only two cases at the Supreme Court. His resignation from the first Court and the rejection of his second nomination, combined with the dearth of cases during his brief tenure, do not allow for a generous reading of Rutledge's contribution to the Supreme Court.

★ ★ ★

WILEY B. RUTLEDGE
BORN: July 20, 1894, Cloverport, Kentucky
TENURE ON COURT: February 1943–September 1949
DIED: September 10, 1949, York, Maine
NOTEWORTHY OPINIONS: *Schneiderman v. United States* (1943-c), *Thomas v. Collins* (1944-m), *In re Yamashita* (1946-d), *United States v. United Mine Workers* (1947-d)

DURING HIS EARLY YEARS, Wiley B. Rutledge's family moved successively to Texas, Louisiana, and then North Carolina in search of a climate that might remedy his mother's tuberculosis. When she died in 1903, the family settled in Tennessee. Rutledge attended Maryville College in Tennessee for three years and then transferred to the University of Wisconsin, graduating in 1914. Rutledge taught high school and took law courses but contracted tuberculosis himself. Recovering, he received his law degree from the University of Colorado in 1922. Rutledge practiced law for two years with a firm in Boulder, Colorado, before returning to academics. For the next fifteen years, he was a professor of law and dean at a succession of law schools. In the mid-1930s, Rutledge publicly supported President Roosevelt's New Deal policies, including his Court-packing plan, and critiqued the Supreme Court for resisting social welfare programs. In 1939, Roosevelt appointed Rutledge to the U.S. Court of Appeals for the District of Columbia Circuit. Four years later, Roosevelt nominated him to the Supreme Court.

Rutledge was a strong liberal voice on the bench, with a deep belief in protecting civil liberties. He was especially concerned with the right of the accused under the Bill of Rights. Rutledge wrote more than 170 opinions during his six years on the Court. His tenure was cut short by a cerebral hemorrhage at the age of fifty-five.

★ ★ ★

EDWARD T. SANFORD

BORN: July 23, 1865, Knoxville, Tennessee
TENURE ON COURT: February 1923–March 1930
DIED: March 8, 1930, Washington, D.C.
NOTEWORTHY OPINIONS: *Gitlow v. New York* (1925-m),
Corrigan v. Buckley (1926-m), *Whitney v. California*
(1927-m)

EDWARD T. SANFORD GRADUATED from the University of Tennessee in 1883 and went on to earn three degrees from Harvard University and a Ph.D. from Tennessee. After passing the bar in 1888, Sanford studied in France and Germany for one year before returning to Knoxville, where he established a law practice. He was active in public charities and many educational organizations and also taught law at the University of Tennessee from 1898 to 1907. In 1905, Sanford became special assistant to the attorney general to prosecute trust violations. Two years later, he was appointed an assistant attorney general. In 1908, Sanford was selected for the District Court bench for the Middle and Eastern Districts of Tennessee, where he served for fifteen years. In 1923, Sanford became President Harding's fourth Supreme Court nominee in two years.

Sanford's judicial views were generally moderate. Like his close friend Chief Justice Taft, with whom he voted consistently, he held precedent in high regard. Sanford made an important contribution to civil liberties jurisprudence in his freedom-of-speech opinions, implying that the Fourteenth Amendment applied First Amendment protections against the states as well as the federal government. He also worked toward strengthening antitrust law and could usually be found siding with the public interest in antitrust cases. Sanford died suddenly in 1930, at the age of sixty-four, just hours after the death of Taft.

★ ★ ★

ANTONIN E. SCALIA

BORN: March 11, 1936, Trenton, New Jersey
TENURE ON COURT: September 1986–present
NOTEWORTHY OPINIONS: *Illinois v. Rodriquez* (1990-m),
California v. Hodari (1991-m), *United States v. Williams*
(1992-m), *United States v. Virginia* (1996-d), *Stenberg v.
Carhart* (2000-d), *Alexander v. Sandoval* (2001-m)

RAISED IN QUEENS, Long Island, by first-generation Italian parents, Antonin E. Scalia graduated from Georgetown University in 1957 and from Harvard Law School in 1960. After a year abroad, Scalia moved to Cleveland, Ohio, and practiced there until 1967, when he joined the faculty of the University of Virginia Law School. In 1971, Scalia took a leave from his teaching post to work in Washington. Over the next five years, he served as counsel on a number of governmental committees and as an assistant legal advisor to the executive. When President Carter came to the White House in 1976, Scalia left government service. After a short stint at a conservative think tank, Scalia returned to teaching in 1977 at the University of

Chicago Law School. In 1982, President Reagan appointed Scalia to the U.S. Court of Appeals for the D.C. Circuit. Four years later, Reagan nominated him to the Supreme Court of the United States.

Combative and gregarious, Scalia has earned a reputation for being the Court's most dynamic personality. Scalia's philosophy centers on judicial restraint, bright-line legal distinctions, and strict interpretation of the Constitution. Although generally one of the most conservative sitting justices, Scalia has surprised many with his positions in some free-speech cases, most surprisingly his swing vote on a Texas flag-burning case that earned him the ire of many conservative supporters.

★   ★   ★

GEORGE SHIRAS, JR.
BORN: January 26, 1832, Pittsburgh, Pennsylvania
TENURE ON COURT: October 1892–February 1903
DIED: August 2, 1924, Pittsburgh, Pennsylvania
NOTEWORTHY OPINIONS: *Brass v. North Dakota* (1894-m), *Swearingen v. United States* (1896-m), *Wong Wing v. United States* (1896-m), *I.C.C. v. Alabama Midland Rail Co.* (1897-m), *Knoxville Iron Co. v. Harbison* (1901-m)

GEORGE SHIRAS, JR., STUDIED at Ohio University and Yale, graduating from the latter in 1853. Shiras returned to Yale's Law School but quit to study law in the office of a local judge. After three years of private practice in Iowa, he opened his own law office in Pittsburgh. Shiras's legal reputation grew along with the iron and steel industry. Although his major clients were industrial corporations and railroad companies, Shiras remained independent of political or economic influence, often acting against large corporations as well as for them and never holding public office or bench seat during his thirty-seven years of private practice. In 1892, Shiras's political neutrality won him nomination to the Supreme Court from President Harrison, who was at the time embroiled in Republican factional disputes.

On the bench, Shiras clung to the center. He tended toward liberal views on civil rights issues, supporting due process for Chinese immigrants and upholding the First Amendment, but voted with the majority in *Plessy v. Ferguson* and other Jim Crow cases. Shiras was also more restrained than some of his colleagues in overturning state statutes regulating commerce. Shiras is remembered for his role in the *Pollock v. Farmers' Loan & Trust Co.* (1895) controversy, regarding the constitutionality of a 2 percent income tax. During the first hearing, there was a stalemate (with one member ill), but after a rehearing before the full Court, one justice had switched decisions. Shiras was suspected at the time, with much press, but many scholars now point to Justice Gray. When he took his seat on the bench, Shiras had vowed to step down at age seventy. He kept his word.

★   ★   ★

DAVID H. SOUTER

BORN: September 17, 1939, Melrose, Massachusetts
TENURE ON COURT: October 1990–present
NOTEWORTHY OPINIONS: *Planned Parenthood v. Casey*
(1992-pl/pc), *National Endowment for the Arts v. Finley*
(1998-d), *United States v. Morrison* (2000-d), *Bush v. Gore*
(2000-d)

WHEN HE WAS eleven years old, David H. Souter's family moved from Massachusetts to the farmhouse in New Hampshire that remained his primary residence until his appointment to the Supreme Court. Souter graduated from Harvard University in 1961 with a degree in philosophy. He spent the following year as a Rhodes scholar at Magdalen College, Oxford. Souter received his law degree from Harvard Law School in 1966. He was admitted to the bar and joined a law firm in Concord, New Hampshire. In 1968, Souter became an assistant attorney general of New Hampshire and in 1971, deputy attorney general under Warren Rudman. In 1976, Souter took Rudman's place as New Hampshire's attorney general. During these years, Souter also served on numerous public policy and crime commissions and was active in New Hampshire historical societies. Souter was appointed to New Hampshire's Superior Court in 1978. He served as an associate justice of the state's Supreme Court from 1983 to 1990, when President Bush appointed him to the First Circuit Court of Appeals. Just three months later, on now Senator Rudman's recommendation, Bush nominated Souter to the Supreme Court. Souter, with his devotion to rural New England, love of rare books, and fastidious manners, is often characterized as a nineteenth-century personality. Although conservatives hoped that he would join Chief Justice Rehnquist and Justices Thomas and Scalia in trying to overturn the legacy of the liberal precedents of the 1960s and 1970s, Souter has tended toward a centrist position.

★ ★ ★

JOHN PAUL STEVENS

BORN: April 20, 1920, Chicago, Illinois
TENURE ON COURT: November 1975–present
NOTEWORTHY OPINIONS: *Payton v. New York* (1980-m),
Maryland v. Garrison (1987-m), *Webster v. Reproductive
Health Services* (1989-c/d), *Reno v. ACLU* (1997-m), *Clinton
v. City of New York* (1998-m), *City of Chicago v. Morales*
(1999-m), *Santa Fe Independent School District v. Doe*
(2000-m)

JOHN PAUL STEVENS earned his B.A. from the University of Chicago in 1941. After service in World War II with a Navy code-breaking team, he graduated from Northwestern University School of Law in 1947, with the highest grades in the school's history. Stevens was recommended as a law clerk to Justice Rutledge for the 1947–1948 term. In 1949, he returned to Chicago to practice law and remained for more than twenty years. An antitrust specialist, Stevens left briefly to serve as counsel in 1951 to a congressional subcommittee studying monopoly power and from

1953 to 1955 to another studying antitrust law. He also taught law at both of his alma maters. In 1969, his reputation for integrity won him the position of general counsel to a special commission appointed by the Illinois Supreme Court to investigate the conduct of its judges. The following year, President Nixon appointed Stevens to the Seventh Circuit Court of Appeals. In 1975, President Ford nominated Stevens to the Supreme Court. With the Watergate scandals a recent memory, Ford hoped that a moderate nominee with a spotless reputation would restore confidence in Washington. The Senate confirmed the appointment unanimously. Although moderate and independent in his voting patterns, the Court's conservative shift during his tenure has made Stevens appear ever more liberal.

★ ★ ★

POTTER STEWART

BORN: January 23, 1915, Jackson, Michigan
TENURE ON COURT: October 1958–July 1981
DIED: December 7, 1985, Hanover, New Hampshire
NOTEWORTHY OPINIONS: *Elkins v. United States* (1960-m), *Abington School District v. Schempp* (1962-d), *Jacobellis v. Ohio* (1964-c), *Jones v. Mayer Co.* (1968-m), *Coolidge v. New Hampshire* (1971-m), *Gregg v. Georgia* (1976-m)

POTTER STEWART WAS born into an affluent Cincinnati family. Although his family was affected by the Depression, Stewart was able to graduate from Yale College in 1937. After a year of study abroad, he enrolled in Yale Law School and graduated in 1941. Stewart briefly joined a New York law firm but was called to duty in the Navy several months later. In 1945, he returned to New York and then to Cincinnati to practice law. He was twice elected to city council and then returned to private practice. President Eisenhower appointed Stewart to the Sixth Circuit Court of Appeals in 1954, where he served for four years. In 1958, Eisenhower awarded Stewart a recess appointment to the Supreme Court, and he was formally nominated early in 1959.

Stewart's was the swing vote on an equally divided Warren Court for the first few years of his tenure. Although his vote lost some significance when the activist bloc gained a solid majority, Stewart continued to vote independently. He consistently supported First Amendment claims but was also a strong believer in dual federalism and states' rights. He will be remembered for defining pornography with the now famous line from his opinion in *Jacobellis v. Ohio:* "I know it when I see it." Narrow decision making was characteristic of his opinions; he was as concerned to show what was not being decided as what was. Stewart retired at the relatively youthful age of sixty-six to spend time with his family. He spent his final years recording legal texts for the blind and working occasionally as a judge in the courts of appeals.

★ ★ ★

HARLAN FISKE STONE

BORN: October 11, 1872, Chesterfield, New Hampshire
TENURE ON COURT: March 1925–July 1941; July
1941–April 1946 (Chief Justice)
DIED: April 22, 1946, Washington, D.C.
NOTEWORTHY OPINIONS: *United States v. Butler* (1936-
d), *United States v. Carolene Products Co.* (1938-m), *Min-
ersville School District v. Gobitis* (1940-d), *United States v.
Darby* (1941-m)

HARLAN F. STONE GRADUATED from Amherst College in 1894. After teaching high school science for one year, he studied law at Columbia University. In 1899, Stone was admitted to the bar and joined a New York law firm. For the next twenty-five years, he divided his time between his successful practice and a professorship at Columbia Law School, where he was also dean for thirteen years (1910–1923). In 1924, President Coolidge appointed Stone U.S. attorney general. The following year, Coolidge nominated him to the Supreme Court. Stone spent sixteen years as an associate justice and was then nominated chief justice by President Roosevelt in 1941.

Stone's legal philosophy centered on judicial restraint, seen as a distinction between what the Court finds unconstitutional and what it finds merely undesirable. He often found himself opposing the conservative "Four Horsemen" in a liberal bloc with Justices Holmes and Brandeis. In the famous fourth footnote to his opinion in *Carolene Products* (1938), Stone flagged a new direction for the Court after its confrontation with the New Deal, introducing the "preferred position doctrine," the notion of a higher standard of judicial review in matters of civil rights and civil liberties than in cases involving economic regulation. As chief justice, Stone struggled to lead a Court with the highest rates of dissent in American history. Consistently, he sought to prevent the Court from acting as a legislative body. In all, Stone served twenty years on the Court. He died in 1946, at the age of seventy-three.

★ ★ ★

JOSEPH STORY

BORN: September 18, 1779, Marblehead, Massachusetts
TENURE ON COURT: February 1812–September 1845
DIED: September 10, 1845, Cambridge, Massachusetts
NOTEWORTHY OPINIONS: *Martin v. Hunter's Lessee*
(1816-m), *Van Ness v. Pacard* (1829-m), *Charles River
Bridge v. Warren Bridge* (1837-d), *Prigg v. Pennsylvania*
(1842-m), *Swift v. Tyson* (1842-m), *United States v. The
Amistad* (1841-m)

OFTEN CONSIDERED THE "most learned scholar" ever to sit on the Court, Joseph Story graduated from Harvard College in 1798. The youngest justice to be appointed to the Court, Story had already served as a U.S. congressman and speaker of the Massachusetts House, successfully argued a case before the Supreme Court, and even published a book of poetry before his nomination. To replace William Cushing,

President Madison was seeking a justice from Massachusetts, preferably one who would help shift the Court away from its Federalist orientation. Story, a rising Essex County Democratic-Republican with a brilliant legal mind, was Madison's fourth choice.

Once on the bench and exposed to the influence of Chief Justice Marshall, who quickly became his closest friend and ally, Story turned into an avid nationalist. In partnership with the chief justice, Story became the key contributor to the Marshall Court's consensus-oriented, nationalistic development of constitutional law. Story's contribution to both the Marshall and Taney Courts left an indelible mark on legal history. Still, throughout, he retained a distinctive voice through his expertise on issues of commerce and property; his New England circuit decisions, notably in maritime law; his extrajuridical writings and professorship at Harvard; and his behind-the-scenes political activity. Story's work on the Court was of a piece with his broader mission to make law and legal science the directing force of republican government in the new nation. He pursued this goal to such good effect that he has been called "the most commanding legal figure of his age." In particular, as Dane Professor of Law at Harvard, he trained the young minds who became the next generation's lawyers and judges. He published his lectures in a massive outpouring of treatises and commentaries that went through numerous editions and translations.

None of his writings was more important than his three-volume *Commentaries on the Constitution* (1833), dedicated to Chief Justice Marshall. Published at the height of the nullification crisis, the *Commentaries* (quoting copiously from the chief justice's opinions) sought to vindicate the nationalist interpretation of the Constitution set forth during the Marshall Court's golden age and to defend the Supreme Court's role as the final arbiter of conflicts between federal and state jurisdictions. More than any other work, it is responsible for Marshall's enduring reputation as "the great chief justice."

After Roger Taney succeeded Marshall as chief justice, Story's position on the Court changed to one more of isolation and opposition. He found himself passionately dissenting in important cases arising from the contract and commerce clauses. Although he remained an influential voice on the Taney Court, Story eventually determined to resign his judicial appointment and devote himself fully to teaching and scholarship. Death in 1845, only months before his announced retirement, prevented him from acting on his intention.

★ ★ ★

WILLIAM STRONG

BORN: May 6, 1808, Somers, Connecticut
TENURE ON COURT: March 1870–December 1880
DIED: August 19, 1895, Lake Minnewaska, New York
NOTEWORTHY OPINIONS: *Bigelow v. Forrest* (1870-m),
Knox v. Lee (1871-m), *Blyew v. United States* (1872-m),
Strauder v. West Virginia (1880-m)

SON OF A Presbyterian minister, William Strong graduated from Yale in 1828 and moved to New Jersey to teach. He read law with a local attorney while continuing his legal studies at Yale. Strong passed the bar in 1832 and opened a law office in Pennsylvania. He established himself as a railroad counsel and served two congressional terms (1847–1851) as an antislavery Democrat, later joining the Republican Party. In 1857, he was elected to the state supreme court. After more than a decade on the bench, Strong returned to private practice for financial reasons. Strong was one of President Grant's controversial Supreme Court appointees of 1870. Grant's Legal Tender Act had been ruled unconstitutional by a seven-member Court. When Grant awarded the empty seats to Strong and Joseph Bradley, both supporters of his legal-tender policy, he was accused of Court packing. The Court's earlier decision was reversed in *Knox*, with Strong writing the majority opinion. Generally, however, Strong sided with the conservative wing of the Court against government intervention in the economy. Although blacks won few legal victories after the war, Strong spoke for the majority in two cases in which federal protection, albeit limited, against racial discrimination was upheld. He sat on the commission charged with resolving the 1876 presidential election dispute. Strong resigned in 1880 while still of sound mind and body, presumably to set an example for colleagues who were less able. His final years were spent teaching law at Columbian University (now George Washington University) and in active involvement with Presbyterian Church affairs.

★ ★ ★

GEORGE SUTHERLAND
BORN: March 25, 1862, Buckinghamshire, England
TENURE ON COURT: October 1922–January 1938
DIED: July 18, 1942, Stockbridge, Massachusetts
NOTEWORTHY OPINIONS: *Adkins v. Children's Hospital* (1923-m), *Powell v. Alabama* (1932-m), *Carter v. Carter Coal* (1936-m), *Jones v. Securities and Exchange Commission* (1936-m)

IN 1864, WHILE George Sutherland was an infant, his family migrated from England to Utah. In 1878, after earning his own tuition money, Sutherland entered Brigham Young University but left school in 1881. He then studied law for one year at the University of Michigan before returning to Utah, where he established a law practice in Provo and, ten years later, in Salt Lake City. When Utah was admitted to the Union in 1896, Sutherland was elected to the new state legislature. In 1900, he was elected to the U.S. Congress, served one term, and then campaigned for a U.S. Senate seat, which he won in 1904. Sutherland served two terms but lost his bid for a third after passage of the Seventeenth Amendment determined that Senate elections be decided by popular vote. Sutherland campaigned for Harding in 1920, and President Harding rewarded him with a Supreme Court nomination two years later.

"Freedom of contract" was formative in Sutherland's judicial philosophy. During his first term, in *Adkins v. Children's Hospital*, he reinvoked the substantive due process views of the *Lochner* Court to overturn a D.C. minimum-wage law for women and children. Sutherland is best known as the intellectual leader of the Four Horsemen, the four-justice bloc that opposed the social experimentation of FDR's New Deal programs. He also left his mark on constitutional law through decisions on defendants' rights to counsel and foreign relations, among other important issues. Sutherland retired soon after the Court, threatened by FDR's Court-packing plans, overturned *Adkins* in *West Coast Hotel v. Parrish* (1937). He died four years later, at the age of eighty.

★ ★ ★

NOAH H. SWAYNE

BORN: December 7, 1804, Frederick County, Virginia
TENURE ON COURT: January 1862–January 1881
DIED: June 8, 1884, New York City
NOTEWORTHY OPINIONS: *Osborn v. Nicholson* (1872-m), *Slaughterhouse Cases* (1873-d), *Springer v. United States* (1881-m)

AFTER PASSING THE bar in 1823, Noah Swayne's antislavery views led him to move to Ohio, a free state, where he was appointed county prosecuting attorney. He served two terms in the state legislature (1829, 1836) and was appointed to a federal attorney post by President Jackson in 1830. Swayne returned to private practice in 1839 and served as counsel in several fugitive slave cases. As the dispute over slavery in the territories worsened, Swayne split from the Democrats and became one of the first converts to the new Republican Party. During the Civil War, he was active in state mobilization and was a strong Unionist. With the death of Justice McLean of Ohio in 1861, Swayne mustered enough political backing to win a Supreme Court nomination from President Lincoln.

Although Swayne authored few historical opinions, his vote was crucial in many cases involving the Lincoln administration's wartime policies and the expansion of federal powers. Swayne was a consistent champion of African American civil rights, campaigning from the bench for passage of the Fifteenth Amendment. His most noteworthy opinion, in *Springer v. United States*, upheld the constitutionality of the Civil War income tax. Swayne lobbied unsuccessfully for the chief justice post twice during his tenure — after the deaths of Roger Taney and Salmon Chase. His health and mental faculties began to deteriorate in 1870s, but he refused to resign until President Hayes pressured him in 1881. Swayne died three years later.

★ ★ ★

WILLIAM HOWARD TAFT

BORN: September 15, 1857, Cincinnati, Ohio
TENURE ON COURT: July 1921–February 1930 (Chief Justice)
DIED: March 8, 1930, Washington, D.C.
NOTEWORTHY OPINIONS: *Truax v. Corrigan* (1921-m), *Bailey v. Drexel Furniture Co.* (1922-m), *Adkins v. Children's Hospital* (1923-d), *Carroll v. United States* (1925-m), *Myers v. United States* (1926-m)

WILLIAM HOWARD TAFT is the only person in American history ever to have occupied the offices of both president and chief justice. After graduating from Yale College in 1878, Taft went on to Cincinnati Law School and passed the bar in 1880. In 1887, he was appointed a judge of the Ohio Superior Court and, two years later, as U.S. solicitor general. From 1892 to 1900, Taft served on the Sixth Circuit. He was named civilian governor of the Philippines in 1901 and secretary of war in 1904. Taft preferred the bench to politics but was nevertheless elected president of the United States in 1908. Including Chief Justice Edward White, Taft appointed six justices to the Supreme Court during his single term. After his reelection defeat in 1912, Taft lectured and taught at Yale. On White's death in 1921, President Harding nominated Taft chief justice.

Taft was a judicial reformer whose chief contribution to the Supreme Court was his concern for administrative efficiency. He was successful in advocating legislation to give the Court greater control of its docket, centralize federal judicial communications, and enhance the powers of the chief justice. He also campaigned successfully for a new Supreme Court building. Taft's view of judicial power was expansive; on social and economic issues, however, Taft was more conservative. He embraced Social Darwinism and fought to protect private property from government encroachments. Initially successful in achieving near unanimity on the bench, Taft's ideological differences with such progressives as Brandeis and Holmes became more pronounced during his tenure. Taft retired from the Court in 1930 and died soon after.

★ ★ ★

ROGER BROOKE TANEY

BORN: March 17, 1777, Calvert County, Maryland
TENURE ON COURT: March 1836–October 1864 (Chief Justice)
DIED: October 12, 1864, Washington, D.C.
NOTEWORTHY OPINIONS: *Charles River Bridge v. Warren Bridge* (1837-m), *Bank of Augusta v. Earle* (1839-m), *License Cases* (1847-m), *Luther v. Borden* (1849-m), *Dred Scott v. Sandford* (1857-m)

ROGER BROOKE TANEY was born into a wealthy, slave-owning Maryland family whose fortune came from tobacco. He graduated from Dickinson College, Pennsylvania, in 1795 and then studied law with an Annapolis judge. He was admitted to the bar in 1799. In the same year, he was elected to the Maryland state legislature as a Federalist; in 1816, he was elected to the state senate. In 1823, Taney moved to Baltimore, where he continued to practice law. In 1824, he broke with the Federalists to support Andrew Jackson, who appointed Taney U.S. attorney general in 1831. Taney received a recess appointment as secretary of the Treasury in 1833, but the Senate failed to confirm the appointment. Early in 1835, Jackson nominated Taney to the Supreme Court, but the Senate refused to consider the matter. Following Marshall's death in July 1835, however, Jackson nominated Taney again, this time to be chief justice. Changed in composition by the November 1834 elections, the Senate confirmed Taney in March 1836.

Taney held to a mixed philosophy of the proper relation of state and federal power. Although he strongly supported President Jackson against state nullification threats, Taney tended to defer to the states on questions of slavery. Despite his contributions to other areas of jurisprudence, such as corporate and commercial law, Taney's primary legacy is his infamous opinion in *Dred Scott*. In an intentionally wide-reaching opinion, Taney held that neither slaves nor free blacks could be citizens and, additionally, that Congress had no authority to prevent slavery from entering the territories. By overturning the 1820 Missouri Compromise, Taney hoped to end the controversy over slavery. But the decision failed miserably and, according to many historians, helped precipitate the Civil War. In his final years on the Court, Taney did all that he could to thwart President Lincoln. He died in the minority on the Court, ignored by Lincoln and held in contempt by many citizens.

★ ★ ★

CLARENCE THOMAS
BORN: June 23, 1948, Pinpoint, Georgia
TENURE ON COURT: October 1991–present
NOTEWORTHY OPINIONS: *Kansas v. Hendricks*
(1997-m), *Jones v. United States* (1999-m), *Mitchell v. Helms* (2000-m), *Stenberg v. Carhart* (2000-d)

RAISED IN A poor Georgia community, Clarence Thomas excelled in school and entered a Missouri seminary in 1967 to prepare for the priesthood. Disappointed with the racial prejudice he experienced there, Thomas attended the College of the Holy Cross and graduated in 1971. Thomas received a law degree from Yale Law School in 1974 and was admitted to the Missouri bar the same year. He joined the staff of state Attorney General John Danforth, working on tax law. When Danforth was elected to the Senate, Thomas shifted to the private sector. From 1979 to 1981, Thomas served as a legislative assistant to Senator Danforth. Although lacking background in civil rights jurisprudence, Thomas was appointed assistant secretary for civil rights in the Department of Education in 1981. In 1982, Thomas was named chairman of the Equal Employment Opportunity Commission, where he supported President Reagan's opposition to affirmative action remedies. President George H. W. Bush appointed Thomas to the U.S. Court of Appeals for the D.C. Circuit in 1990. The following year, Bush nominated Thomas to the Supreme Court to replace Thurgood Marshall, the first African American Supreme Court justice. Thomas's opposition to affirmative action and to a civil rights agenda divided the black community. Controversy increased when a former employee, Anita Hill, testified to the Senate that Thomas had sexually harassed her. The Senate nevertheless confirmed his nomination 52–48. The youngest member of the Court, Thomas has aligned himself with Justice Scalia, who is considered the Court's most conservative member.

★ ★ ★

SMITH THOMPSON

BORN: January 17, 1768, Dutchess County, New York
TENURE ON COURT: February 1824–December 1843
DIED: December 18, 1843, New York City
NOTEWORTHY OPINIONS: *Ogden v. Saunders* (1827-d), *Cherokee Nation v. Georgia* (1831-d), *Kendall v. United States* (1838-m), *Prigg v. Pennsylvania* (1842-c/d)

SON OF A prominent Anti-Federalist, Smith Thompson graduated from the College of New Jersey (now Princeton University) in 1788, then studied law under the famous jurist James Kent. After entering practice in 1792, Thompson married into a powerful New York political family, the Livingstons. He won a seat in the New York legislature in 1800 and was one of the delegates appointed to the state constitutional convention the next year. Although Thompson served briefly as a district attorney, he was promoted to the bench of the state supreme court so quickly that he did not prosecute a case. He shared the bench with future Supreme Court Justice Henry Brockholst Livingston, who was also his cousin by marriage; another Livingston in-law; and his former mentor, Kent. In 1818, Thompson was appointed secretary of the Navy by President Monroe, possibly owing to his friendship with rising politician Martin Van Buren. Five years later, following the death of Brockholst Livingston, Monroe offered Thompson the vacant Supreme Court seat. Thompson, however, was aiming for the presidency and delayed his response for months, enduring public criticism. Thompson accepted the offer only after his presidential candidacy failed. Thompson's political ambitions were the subject of criticism again in 1828, when he ran for governor of New York without leaving the Court. An advocate of states' rights, Thompson was a frequent opponent of the Marshall Court's federalizing tendencies. In his later years on the bench, under Chief Justice Taney, Thompson developed his position through a theory of concurrent powers.

★ ★ ★

THOMAS TODD

BORN: January 23, 1765, King and Queen County, Virginia
TENURE ON COURT: May 1807–February 1826
DIED: February 7, 1826, Frankfort, Kentucky
NOTEWORTHY OPINIONS: *Preston v. Browder* (1816-m), *Watts v. Lindsey's Heirs* (1822-m), *Riggs v. Tayloe* (1824-m)

ORPHANED AT A young age, Thomas Todd was raised by a bankrupt guardian. After a short stint in the American Army at age sixteen, Todd finished his schooling in 1783 at Virginia's Liberty Hall Academy (now Washington and Lee University). Todd studied law with a distinguished Virginia statesman, Harry Innes, in exchange for tutoring Innes's daughter, and later accompanied the Innes family to Kentucky, where he played a major role in the campaign for statehood. After passing the bar in 1786, Todd became known for his skill in land and title litigation. When Kentucky became a state in 1792, Todd held a variety of state positions — secretary to the new legislature, then clerk to the state supreme court. In 1801, Todd was elevated to the bench of the court and in 1806 became its chief justice. In 1807, an amendment to the Judiciary Act of 1789 created a new federal Western Circuit, together with a corresponding new seat on the Supreme Court. President Jefferson sought recommendations from the Tennessee, Kentucky, and Ohio congressional delegations, and Todd's name appeared on every list. But Todd disappointed Jefferson's hopes that he would quell Marshall's federalism. Instead, his knowledge of common law and experience in resolving complex contract conflicts were put in the service of the Marshall Court's efforts to strengthen federal power. Frequently ill, Todd missed five full terms of the Court and issued few opinions of his own, with only one dissent in nineteen years on the bench.

★ ★ ★

ROBERT TRIMBLE

BORN: November 17, 1776, Berkeley County, Virginia (now West Virginia)

TENURE ON COURT: June 1826–August 1828

DIED: August 25, 1828, Paris, Kentucky

NOTEWORTHY OPINIONS: *The Antelope* (1827-m), *Ogden v. Saunders* (1827-d)

RAISED ON THE Kentucky frontier, Robert Trimble studied at Bourbon Academy and the Kentucky Academy. He read law and entered private practice in 1800. Having quickly established a solid reputation for logical and fair, if not brilliant, argumentation, Trimble was elected to the Kentucky House in 1802. Owing to the poor pay or perhaps dislike for politics, he did not run again and returned to private practice to support his wife and ten children. He briefly sat on the Kentucky Court of Appeals (1807–1808) but again resigned for financial reasons. In 1817, however, Trimble accepted President Madison's nomination to be federal district judge for Kentucky. Trimble's nomination to the Supreme Court in 1826 provoked some opposition, as he was a strong believer in federal powers, and five senators voted against him. He was John Quincy Adams's only bench appointment.

It is widely held by legal scholars that Trimble could have made important contributions to constitutional law if he had sat longer on the Court. He wrote 16 of the 103 opinions issued during his tenure and concurred with Chief Justice Marshall in nearly all of the others. Trimble's most important opinion was delivered in *Ogden v. Saunders,* in which he deviated from his Federalist stance to uphold the constitutionality of a New York bankruptcy law. Trimble's promising career on the Court was cut short by illness, and he died shortly after completing his second term.

★ ★ ★

WILLIS VAN DEVANTER

BORN: April 17, 1859, Marion, Indiana
TENURE ON COURT: January 1911–June 1937
DIED: February 8, 1941, Washington, D.C.
NOTEWORTHY OPINIONS: *Second Employers' Liability Cases* (1912-m), *United States v. Sandoval* (1913-m), *New York Central v. Winfield* (1917-m), *McGrain v. Daugherty* (1927-m)

SHORTLY AFTER TAKING a law degree from the University of Cincinnati in 1881, Willis Van Devanter moved to the Wyoming Territory, where he represented railroads and developed expertise in public land law, water rights, and Indian claims. An active Republican, he served in several territorial and local judicial and political posts. In 1890, President Harrison appointed Van Devanter chief justice of the territory's supreme court, although he resigned the following year to return to his more lucrative private practice. In 1897, President McKinley appointed him assistant attorney general. Seven years later, President Roosevelt selected him for an Eighth Circuit judgeship, and in 1910, despite the opposition of Progressives angered by his tight railroad connections, President Taft nominated Van Devanter to the Supreme Court.

Although his colleagues regarded Van Devanter as an important contributor to deliberations, he wrote comparatively few opinions. In a rare deviation from his usual conservative stance, Van Devanter spoke for the Court in holding railroad companies liable for employee injuries. But his conservative leanings grew over the course of his tenure; by the 1930s, Van Devanter's judicial philosophy was considered reactionary by some. Indeed, Van Devanter is best known as one of the "Four Horsemen," the four Court members who consistently opposed President Roosevelt's economic programs. He retired in 1937 and sat on the U.S. District Court in New York until his death four years later.

★ ★ ★

FREDERICK M. VINSON

BORN: January 22, 1890, Louisa, Kentucky
TENURE ON COURT: June 1946–September 1953 (Chief Justice)
DIED: September 8, 1953, Washington, D.C.
NOTEWORTHY OPINIONS: *Shelley v. Kraemer* (1948-m), *Sweatt v. Painter* (1950-m), *Dennis v. United States* (1951-m), *Youngstown Sheet & Tube Co. v. Sawyer* (1952-d)

FREDERICK M. VINSON graduated from Centre College, Kentucky, with a B.A. in 1909 and earned his law degree two years later. In 1911, Vinson was admitted to the Kentucky bar and began to practice, first in Louisa and then in Ashland. He served as a city attorney and a commonwealth attorney before winning a U.S. House seat in 1924. Vinson was elected to six terms in Congress and was a key figure on the Ways and Means Committee, where he was an active supporter of New Deal legislation. President Roosevelt appointed him to the District of Columbia Court of Appeals in 1937. During World War II, Vinson was appointed to a succession of important administrative and advisory positions. Soon after the war's end, President Truman appointed him secretary of the Treasury and in 1946 nominated him to be chief justice of the United States.

Truman hoped that Vinson's personality would help to unite a fractious Court. He was widely regarded as affable, patient, respectful of the views of others, and skilled at forging compromises. However, the divisions on the Court were largely ideological, and Vinson's best efforts did not significantly alter the situation. Judicially, Vinson supported expansion of the commerce clause and the strengthening of government powers. His interpretation of the "clear and present danger" standard for applying the First Amendment rejected the "preferred freedoms" doctrine of his civil libertarian colleagues and significantly limited the range of protected speech. Although Vinson worked to undermine racial discrimination, he resisted overturning "separate but equal" entirely, a move his successor would make in *Brown*. Vinson died of a heart attack at the age of sixty-three.

★ ★ ★

MORRISON R. WAITE
BORN: November 29, 1816, Lyme, Connecticut
TENURE ON COURT: March 1874–March 1888 (Chief Justice)
DIED: March 23, 1888, Washington, D.C.
NOTEWORTHY OPINIONS: *United States v. Cruikshank* (1876-m), *United States v. Reese* (1876-m), *Munn v. Illinois* (1877-m), *Stone v. Farmers' Loan & Trust Co.* (1886-m)

SON OF A state supreme court chief justice, Morrison R. Waite graduated from Yale College in 1837. He moved to Ohio the following year to read law with a local attorney and was admitted to the bar in 1839. Waite practiced in Maumee City until 1850, then moved to Toledo, where he practiced until 1874. Waite ran for Congress unsuccessfully in 1846 and 1862 but won a seat on the Ohio General Assembly in 1849. In 1871, President Grant appointed Waite as one of three U.S. representatives to negotiations in Geneva with Great Britain regarding British assistance to the Confederacy during the Civil War. Waite gained national recognition by helping the United States to win $15.5 million in compensation. When he returned from Europe, Waite won a seat at the Ohio Constitutional Convention of 1873 and was selected to serve as its president. During the convention, to Waite's surprise, President Grant nominated him to be chief justice of the United States. Waite was Grant's sixth choice, the others all dismissed as cronies.

Waite's patience, geniality, and managerial skills helped mold a remarkably united Court. The opinions of his Court were the first sustained interpretations of the Civil War amendments. Waite tended to defer to state power in civil rights cases, leaving Southern blacks with little federal protection. In the area of the new industrial economy, Waite's test of "public interest" for state regulation of property guided the Court's review of state business regulation for decades. Although Waite suffered a breakdown in 1885, he continued to work, drafting opinions until his death of pneumonia in 1888.

★ ★ ★

EARL WARREN
BORN: March 19, 1891, Los Angeles, California
TENURE ON COURT: October 1953–June 1969 (Chief Justice)
DIED: July 9, 1974, Washington, D.C.
NOTEWORTHY OPINIONS: *Brown v. Board of Education* (1954-m), *Reynolds v. Sims* (1964-m), *Miranda v. Arizona* (1966-m), *Loving v. Virginia* (1967-m), *Walker v. Birmingham* (1967-d)

RAISED IN BAKERSFIELD, Earl Warren graduated from the University of California, Berkeley, in 1912 and received a law degree in 1914. He practiced in law offices around the San Francisco Bay area before serving as an Army lieutenant in World War I. In 1919, Warren became deputy city attorney of Oakland; the following year, deputy district attorney of Alameda County. In 1925, he was appointed to an interim seat as district attorney of Alameda County, a post he kept until 1938. In 1938, he was elected attorney general of California and was responsible for initiating Japanese internment during World War II, a decision he would later regret. In 1942, he was elected governor of California. Warren was a popular governor, the first California governor twice reelected. Warren received the Republican nomination for the vice presidency in 1948. He sought the presidential nomination in 1952 but did not win it. In September 1953, President Eisenhower nominated Warren chief justice of the United States in a recess appointment, and he was confirmed the following year.

Warren joined a fractious Court that had recently begun hearing cases on segregated public facilities. He used his strong leadership skills to bring together his colleagues in a unanimous decision to strike down segregation. His admirers remember the Warren Court as a revolutionary period in which the Court established itself as the guardian of democratic values and procedures. Warren's critics, on the other hand, saw the least democratic branch of government usurping power from the democratically elected branches. All agree that Warren was a strong judicial leader who transformed the Court and constitutional jurisprudence during his fifteen-year tenure. Warren retired in 1969 and died five years later.

★ ★ ★

BUSHROD WASHINGTON

BORN: June 5, 1762, Westmoreland County, Virginia
TENURE ON COURT: February 1799–November 1829
DIED: November 26, 1829, Philadelphia, Pennsylvania
NOTEWORTHY OPINIONS: *Dartmouth College v. Woodward* (1819-c), *Green v. Biddle* (1823-c), *Mason v. Haile* (1827-d), *Ogden v. Saunders* (1827-m)

FAVORED NEPHEW OF the childless George Washington, Bushrod Washington was also close with another towering figure of American history, John Marshall, whom he met while studying at the College of William and Mary. Marshall left in 1780 to practice law; Washington fought in the Virginia campaign and then studied law under the future Justice James Wilson. Years later, when Washington moved his practice to Richmond, he and Marshall were often opposing counsel before the Virginia court of appeals. When Justice Wilson died, President Adams first offered the appointment to Marshall, who declined but accepted Adams's nomination as chief justice two years later. Washington was then offered the post.

His legacy on the Court is aptly summarized in Justice William Johnson's famous observation that Marshall and Washington "are commonly estimated as one judge." Washington rarely issued dissents, as he shared Marshall's concern to protect property rights and limit state sovereignty. Still, he occasionally offered a more moderate or politically sensitive view, and his individual contribution was not entirely negligible. Washington's consistent citation of precedent enhanced the legitimacy of *stare decisis*. His opinion in the circuit case of *Corfield v. Coryell* (1823) was the first to interpret the privileges and immunities clause. After thirty-one years of diligent service to the Court, Washington died in Philadelphia, where he was performing his circuit duties.

★ ★ ★

JAMES M. WAYNE

BORN: January 1, 1790, Savannah, Georgia
TENURE ON COURT: January 1835–July 1867
DIED: July 5, 1867, Washington, D.C.
NOTEWORTHY OPINIONS: *Louisville Railroad Co. v. Letson* (1844-m), *Waring v. Clarke* (1847-m), *Passenger Cases* (1849-c), *Dodge v. Woolsey* (1856-m), *Dred Scott v. Sanford* (1857-c)

THE TWELFTH OF thirteen children, James M. Wayne entered the College of New Jersey (now Princeton University) at the age of fourteen and graduated in 1808. By 1811, Wayne had finished his law studies and entered practice. He served as captain of a volunteer militia in the War of 1812, was elected to the state legislature in 1815, and became mayor of Savannah in 1817. In 1819, Wayne was appointed to the Savannah Court of Common Pleas and then to the local superior court. Wayne left the bench in 1828 to run for Congress and served three terms as a Jacksonian

Democrat. When Justice William Johnson, another Southerner, died in 1834, Wayne received the nomination from President Jackson.

Wayne established a judicial record in commercial and admiralty cases that demonstrated his firm belief that the Constitution granted Congress the power to regulate commerce. He also helped to develop jurisprudence supporting corporations as legal entities. Wayne's record on slavery was more ambiguous. Although a Unionist, Wayne was also a Southerner and a slave owner. Despite his general support of slavery as an institution and his agreement with Chief Justice Taney's opinion in *Dred Scott*, Wayne refused to join the Confederacy or to abandon the Court during the Civil War. He was labeled a traitor in Georgia, and the Confederate Army seized his property. Although he considered the war a rebellion, Wayne did not support the punitive measures of Reconstruction. He died before many of these measures were enacted and was buried in Savannah.

★ ★ ★

BYRON R. WHITE
BORN: June 8, 1917, Fort Collins, Colorado
TENURE ON COURT: April 1962–June 1993
DIED: April 15, 2002, Denver, Colorado
NOTEWORTHY OPINIONS: *Miranda v. Arizona* (1966-d),
*Camara v. Municipal Court of the City and County
of San Francisco* (1967-m), *Reitman v. Mulkey* (1967-m),
Roe v. Wade (1973-d), *Regents of the University of
California v. Bakke* (1978-c/d), *Bowers v. Hardwick*
(1986-m), *California v. Greenwood* (1988-m)

IN 1938, BYRON "Whizzer" White graduated from the University of Colorado as valedictorian and star football player. He accepted a Rhodes scholarship to study at Oxford University but deferred to play a season of professional football. White attended Oxford for one year and then enrolled at Yale Law School. After Pearl Harbor, he left Yale to serve in the South Pacific as a naval intelligence lieutenant. White completed his legal studies after the war; on graduation in 1946, he was selected for a coveted law clerkship under Chief Justice Vinson. He returned to Colorado in 1947 and spent the next fourteen years in private practice. White was active in his friend John F. Kennedy's 1960 presidential campaign; in 1961, Kennedy appointed him deputy attorney general. The following year, Kennedy nominated White to the Supreme Court. White disappointed many Kennedy supporters with his centrism during the height of Warren Court liberalism. His dissents in *Miranda v. Arizona* and *Roe v. Wade* and his majority opinion in *Bowers v. Hardwick* are just a few examples of opinions that angered liberals. White supported integration and black voting rights but would not grant individual rights claims in most cases. Scholars have found it difficult to categorize White within the conventional conservative/liberal framework. Trained in legal realism, White was less concerned with writing theoretically justified opinions than with the practical functioning of law. He retired in good health after thirty-one years on the Court and occasionally served as an appeals judge in his final years.

★ ★ ★

EDWARD D. WHITE

BORN: November 3, 1845, Lafourche Parish, Louisiana
TENURE ON COURT: March 1894–December 1910;
December 1910–May 1921 (Chief Justice)
DIED: May 19, 1921, Washington, D.C.
NOTEWORTHY OPINIONS: *McCray v. United States*
(1904-m), *Employers' Liability Cases* (1908-m), *Standard Oil Co. v. United States* (1911-m), *Guinn v. United States* (1916-m)

BORN AND RAISED on a Louisiana plantation, Edward D. White traveled north to Georgetown College in Washington, D.C., for his education. White's studies were interrupted by the start of the Civil War, and he returned home at age sixteen to join the Confederate Army. In 1863, White was captured by Union troops. Although he was released later in the year, he remained in Louisiana. At the end of the war, White read law and attended the University of Louisiana. He was admitted to the bar in 1868 and established a law practice in New Orleans. White became active in Louisiana politics and was elected to the state senate in 1874. He served on the Louisiana Supreme Court for one year (1879–1880) but had to step down when a rival instituted an age requirement of thirty-five for the position. White returned to his practice until 1891, when the state legislature approved his nomination to fill a vacancy in the U.S. Senate. Three years later, President Cleveland nominated White to the Supreme Court.

White had served for sixteen years on the Court when, in 1910, President Taft nominated him chief justice of the United States. He was the first associate justice to be directly elevated to chief justice. Known as an amiable and generous colleague, White fostered a cooperative spirit on the Court. On commerce and trade, White generally opposed the intrusion of the federal government into state regulatory activities. White's most lasting contribution to constitutional jurisprudence is often considered to be the "rule of reason" he adopted to distinguish between legal and illegal monopolies in antitrust cases. This standard was used throughout most of the twentieth century. Although suffering from cataracts, White would not give in to Republican pressure to retire. He died at the age of seventy-six while still serving on the Court.

★ ★ ★

CHARLES E. WHITTAKER

BORN: February 22, 1901, Troy, Kansas
TENURE ON COURT: March 1957–March 1962
DIED: November 26, 1973, Kansas City, Missouri
NOTEWORTHY OPINIONS: *Lehmann v. Carson* (1957-m),
Staub v. City of Baxley (1958-m), *Kinsella v. Singleton*
(1960-c/d), *Chapman v. United States* (1961-m)

AFTER HIS MOTHER DIED, sixteen-year-old Charles E. Whittaker left high school to work on the family farm. A few years later, with tutoring and a part-time job in a local firm, he was able to qualify and pay for studies at the University of Kansas City Law School. Whittaker passed the bar in 1923 and earned his law degree the following year. Whittaker joined the Kansas City law firm where he had worked as an office boy and in 1932 became a partner. He remained in private practice for the next thirty years and served one term as president of the Missouri Bar Association. His peers recommended him to President Eisenhower, who appointed him to a Missouri district court in 1954. Two years later, Eisenhower elevated him to the Eighth Circuit Court of Appeals. After only eight months in that post, he was nominated by Eisenhower to the Supreme Court.

Unfortunately, Whittaker did not possess the intellectual or technical skills needed for the position. His conservative views were rarely explained, and he occasionally produced contradictory decisions. Although he worked hard, Whittaker's vision of the issues at stake in particular cases was often narrow. He resigned after collapsing from exhaustion in 1962. In 1965, Whittaker was hired as counsel to the General Motors Corporation. He also served as special counsel to the Senate Committee on Standards and Conduct in 1966. Whittaker eventually returned to private practice in Kansas City, where he died in 1973.

★ ★ ★

JAMES WILSON

BORN: September 14, 1742, Carskerdo, Fifeshire, Scotland
TENURE ON COURT: October 1789–August 1798
DIED: August 21, 1798, Edenton, North Carolina
NOTEWORTHY OPINIONS: *Chisholm v. Georgia* (1793-s),
Ware v. Hylton (1796-c)

BORN IN SCOTLAND and educated at St. Andrews, James Wilson arrived in America in 1765. He began his legal studies and patriotic activities soon after, moving about Pennsylvania to expand his clientele as well as the readership of his radical pamphlets. Although he was not an early supporter of independence, Wilson signed his name to the Declaration of Independence. Later, as a delegate to the 1787 Convention, Wilson advocated a range of issues, such as abolition of property qualifications for voting, the supremacy of national government, popular election of the legislative branches and the executive, and the creation of a supreme court endowed with powers of judicial review. In Pennsylvania, Wilson worked tirelessly for ratification of the federal constitution, although most of his measures had not been included. Washington rewarded him with a nomination to the first Supreme Court in 1789.

Wilson was a strong supporter of judicial review and tended to uphold the power of the national government, although he wrote few opinions. Wilson also accepted a professorship in law at the College of Pennsylvania in the fall of 1790 and gave lectures on American law while remaining on the bench. Although he envisioned a larger scholarly project, Wilson's lectures lasted only a year. Despite the promise of his early career, Wilson's personal ambition and related financial crises sullied his reputation. Passed over twice for the position of chief justice, Wilson's mishandled investments brought massive debt, and his final years were spent fleeing jail and creditors.

★ ★ ★

LEVI WOODBURY

BORN: December 22, 1789, Francestown, New Hampshire
TENURE ON COURT: September 1845–September 1851
DIED: September 4, 1851, Portsmouth, New Hampshire
NOTEWORTHY OPINIONS: *Jones v. Van Zandt* (1847-m), *Planters' Bank v. Sharp* (1848-m), *Luther v. Borden* (1849-d), *Passenger Cases* (1849-d)

LEVI WOODBURY GRADUATED from Dartmouth College in 1809, then studied at Litchfield Law School for one year, making him the first Supreme Court justice to have attended law school. In 1812, Woodbury passed the bar and began to make a name for himself in New Hampshire legal and political circles. At the age of twenty-seven, he was appointed to a state supreme court seat, where he served for five years. A strong supporter of states' rights, Woodbury aligned himself with Jacksonian Democrats. Over the next three decades, he served as governor of New Hampshire (1823–1824), state legislator (1925), U.S. senator (1825–1831; 1841–1845), secretary of the navy (1831–1834), and secretary of the Treasury (1834–1841). With the death of Justice Story in 1845, President Polk made Woodbury a recess appointee to the Supreme Court, an appointment confirmed by the Senate in January 1846.

Woodbury continued to embrace states' rights on the bench, although he occasionally broke from this view. Like many Jacksonian Democrats, Woodbury combined his resistance to the expansion of federal powers with support for federal protection for the rights of slaveholders and Southern interests. This position was popular among conservative Northerners and many Southerners, and Woodbury nearly won his party's presidential nomination in 1848 with this platform. Although he failed, he remained politically ambitious, and it is likely that he would have won and accepted the 1852 nomination. But Woodbury died in 1851, having served only six terms on the Court.

★ ★ ★

WILLIAM B. WOODS

BORN: August 3, 1824, Newark, Ohio
TENURE ON COURT: January 1881–May 1887
DIED: May 14, 1887, Washington, D.C.
NOTEWORTHY OPINIONS: *United States v. Harris*
(1883-m), *Presser v. Illinois* (1886-m)

WILLIAM WOODS GRADUATED from Yale in 1845 and returned to Ohio to study law, passing the bar in 1847. Woods established a practice and was elected mayor of Newark, Ohio, in 1856. The following year, he won a seat as a Democrat in the state legislature. Although he denounced Republican policies as the Civil War approached, Woods was pivotal to Ohio's defense of the Union when the war arrived. After advancing to the rank of major general in the war, Woods resettled in Alabama and became a leading Republican. In 1868, he was elected to the bench of Alabama's Southern Chancery Court. The following year, President Grant appointed Woods to the Fifth Circuit Court of Appeals. In 1880, President Hayes nominated him to the Supreme Court.

Woods's judicial experience made his nomination uncontroversial. As a circuit judge, Woods had developed a broad application of the Fourteenth Amendment, but when he reached the Supreme Court, he reversed his earlier view, most notably in his majority opinion in *United States v. Harris* overturning the Civil Rights Enforcement (Anti-Klan) Act of 1871. This reversal has contributed to the historical view of Woods as inconsistent in judicial philosophy. Woods usually sided quietly with the majority and issued only eight dissents. He wrote more than two hundred opinions in his brief tenure, related mostly to equity issues. His activity on the Court was cut short by sudden illness in 1886. Woods died the following year.

NOTE ON SOURCES

Printed: Bernard Schwartz, *A History of the Supreme Court* (New York, 1993); Melvin I. Urofsky, ed., *The Supreme Court Justices: A Biographical Dictionary* (New York and London, 1994); Leon Friedman and Fred Israel, eds., *The Justices of the Supreme Court, 1789–1978: Their Lives and Major Opinions*, 5 volumes (New York and London, 1980); Clare Cushman, ed., *The Supreme Court Justices: Illustrated Biographies, 1789–1993* (Washington, D.C., 1993); Maeva Marcus, ed., *The Documentary History of the Supreme Court of the United States 1789–1800* (New York, 1985–).

Online: Columbia Encyclopedia at www.bartleby.com; The Federal Judges Biographical Database from the Federal Judicial Center at http://air.fjc.gov/history/judges_frm.html; Oyez: U.S. Supreme Court MultiMedia at www.oyez.org; Supreme Court Historical Society at www.supremecourthistory.org; and (for current justices in particular) www.washingtonpost.com/wp-srv/nation/sidebars/supremecourt/justicebios.htm, and articles cited therein. See also, generally, www.findlaw.com and www.law.cornell.edu/lexicon.

Appendix C

The Supreme Court's Budget: 1790 to the Present

NOTE ON SOURCES

For the period 1789 to 1929, budget figures were compiled from a year-by-year examination of all appropriations bills passed by Congress, as recorded in the U.S. *Statutes at Large*. Only appropriations specifically intended for Supreme Court personnel, materials, or property were included. For example, appropriations to purchase law books for the justices were included, but appropriations to purchase copies of the *Supreme Court Reports* for the Justice Department's use were not included.

For the period 1930 to 2003, figures were taken from the Office of Management and Budget, *Budget of the United States Government* (1932–1962), and *Appendix to the Budget* (1963–2001), as reproduced, with annotation, in Lee Epstein et al., *The Supreme Court Compendium: Data, Decisions and Developments* (Washington, D.C., 2003), Table 1–9, where readers will also find estimates for 2002–2003.

YEAR	SALARY AND EXPENSES	BUILDING AND OTHER	TOTAL
1789	—	—	—
1790	$21,500	—	$21,500
1791	$21,500	—	$21,500
1792	$21,500	—	$21,500
1793	$21,500	—	$21,500
1794	$21,500	—	$21,500
1795	$21,500	—	$21,500
1796	$21,500	—	$21,500
1797	$21,500	—	$21,500
1798	$21,500	—	$21,500
1799	$21,500	—	$21,500
1800	$21,500	—	$21,500
1801	$21,500	—	$21,500
1802	$21,500	—	$21,500
1803	$21,500	—	$21,500
1804	$21,500	—	$21,500
1805	$21,500	—	$21,500

(*continued*)

YEAR	SALARY AND EXPENSES	BUILDING AND OTHER	TOTAL
1806	$21,500	—	$21,500
1807[a]	$25,000	—	$25,000
1808	$25,000	—	$25,000
1809	$25,000	—	$25,000
1810	$25,000	$20,000	$45,000
1811	$25,000	—	$25,000
1812[b]	$25,556	—	$25,556
1813	$25,000	—	$25,000
1814	$25,000	—	$25,000
1815	$25,000	—	$25,000
1816[c]	$25,000	—	$25,000
1817	$25,000	—	$25,000
1818	$27,000	—	$27,000
1819[d]	$33,000	—	$33,000
1820	$33,000	—	$33,000
1821	$33,000	—	$33,000
1822	$33,000	—	$33,000
1823	$33,000	—	$33,000
1824	$33,000	$640	$33,640
1825	$33,000	—	$33,000
1826	$32,000	—	$32,000
1827	$34,000	$450	$34,450
1828	$33,000	—	$33,000
1829	$33,000	—	$33,000
1830	$33,000	—	$33,000
1831	$33,000	$400	$33,400
1832	$33,000	—	$33,000
1833	$39,000	—	$39,000
1834	$36,000	$800	$36,800
1835	$36,250	—	$36,250
1836	$36,000	$500	$36,500
1837[e]	$36,000	$400	$36,400
1838	$45,000	—	$45,000

a. A new federal circuit is created, comprising Tennessee, Kentucky, and Ohio, and a seventh justice is added to the Court.

b. Congress grants the justices use of the Library of Congress for research purposes.

c. Congress authorizes government publication and distribution of Supreme Court Reports. The Court appoints its first official Reporter.

d. Congress raises the justices' salaries from $4,000 (chief) and $3,500 (associate) to $5,000 (chief) and $4,500 (associate).

e. Congress adds two more federal circuits and raises the number of Supreme Court justices to nine

YEAR	SALARY AND EXPENSES	BUILDING AND OTHER	TOTAL
1839	$42,000	—	$42,000
1840	$42,000	—	$42,000
1841	$42,000	—	$42,000
1842	$42,000	—	$42,000
1843 [f]	$20,500	$650	$21,150
1844	$42,350	—	$42,350
1845	$42,300	$1,750	$44,050
1846	$42,300	—	$42,300
1847	$42,300	$867	$43,167
1848	$42,300	—	$42,300
1849	$42,300	—	$42,300
1850	$42,300	—	$42,300
1851	$42,300	—	$42,300
1852	$42,300	—	$42,300
1853	$42,300	—	$42,300
1854	$42,300	—	$42,300
1855	$42,300	$5,000	$47,300
1856 [g]	$57,245	—	$57,245
1857	$55,800	$800	$56,600
1858	$55,800	$500	$56,300
1859	$55,800	$1,000	$56,800
1860	$55,800	—	$55,800
1861	$55,800	$25,000	$80,800
1862	$55,800	$500	$56,300
1863 [h]	$55,800	—	$55,800
1864	$40,300	$1,833	$42,133
1865	$62,800	$1,214	$64,014
1866	$68,800	$8,000	$76,800
1867 [i]	$68,500	—	$68,500
1868	$62,356	$15,000	$77,356
1869 [j]	$52,000	$1,400	$53,400
1870	$55,000	—	$55,000

(continued)

f. The Supreme Court switches to the July 1–June 30 fiscal year.

g. Congress raises the justices' salaries from $5,000 (chief) and $4,500 (associate) to $6,500 (chief) and $6,000 (associate).

h. The Judiciary Act of 1863 establishes the Tenth Circuit in California/Oregon and adds a tenth justice.

i. Office of the Marshal of the Supreme Court is created at an annual salary of $3,500.

j. The Judiciary Act of 1869 establishes the size of the Court at nine members and provides first pension guidelines for judges. Circuit-riding responsibilities of justices are reduced. (With the establishment of the circuit courts of appeals in 1891, the justices' circuit-riding responsibilities became entirely optional.)

YEAR	SALARY AND EXPENSES	BUILDING AND OTHER	TOTAL
1871[k]	$67,500	$2,000	$69,500
1872	$78,500	—	$78,500
1873[l]	$82,500	—	$82,500
1874	$113,500	$2,500	$116,000
1875	$121,500	—	$121,500
1876	$121,500	—	$121,500
1877	$124,500	—	$124,500
1878	$133,000	—	$133,000
1879	$140,364	—	$140,364
1880	$150,364	—	$150,364
1881	$133,364	—	$134,364
1882	$130,864	—	$130,864
1883	$149,000	—	$149,000
1884	$126,000	—	$126,000
1885	$119,000	—	$119,000
1886	$108,313	—	$108,313
1887	$120,400	—	$120,400
1888[m]	$112,900	—	$112,900
1889	$123,400	$2,000	$125,400
1890	$121,786	$2,500	$124,286
1891	$126,812	$1,000	$127,812
1892	$124,356	—	$124,356
1893	$125,268	—	$125,268
1894	$126,668	—	$126,668
1895	$124,660	$2,300	$126,960
1896	$124,508	—	$124,508
1897	$124,356	$4,600	$128,956
1898	$126,204	$3,165	$129,369
1899	$134,324	$13,033	$147,357
1900	$129,008	$4,751	$133,759
1901	$128,520	$3,285	$131,805
1902	$128,524	$155,650	$284,174
1903[n]	$136,997	—	$136,997
1904	$153,036	—	$153,036

k. Congress raises the justices' salaries from $6,500 (chief) and $6,000 (associate) to $8,500 (chief) and $8,500 (associate).

l. Congress raises the justices' salaries from $8,500 (chief) and $8,000 (associate) to $10,500 (chief) and $10,000 (associate).

m. Stenographic clerks are added to the Court, one for each justice, at an annual salary of $1,600 each.

n. Congress raises the justices' salaries from $10,500 (chief) and $10,000 (associate) to $13,000 (chief) and $12,500 (associate).

YEAR	SALARY AND EXPENSES	BUILDING AND OTHER	TOTAL
1905	$150,764	—	$150,764
1906	$152,909	—	$152,909
1907	$156,264	—	$156,264
1908	$153,429	$7,500	$160,929
1909	$159,675	$120	$159,795
1910	$168,760	$6,500	$175,260
1911[o]	$155,335	—	$155,335
1912	$185,395	$3,000	$188,395
1913	$189,263	—	$189,263
1914	$182,840	—	$182,840
1915	$181,640	—	$181,640
1916	$214,713	—	$214,713
1917	$185,420	—	$185,420
1918	$200,220	—	$200,220
1919	$185,243	—	$185,243
1920	$217,846	—	$217,846
1921	$238,243	—	$238,243
1922[p]	$223,244	—	$223,244
1923	$257,148	$5,000	$262,148
1924	$253,520	—	$253,520
1925	$254,220	—	$254,220
1926[q]	$252,060	—	$252,060
1927	$319,920	$1,500,000	$1,819,920
1928	$361,873	$10,000	$371,873
1929	$345,920	$293,741	$639,661
1930	$343,420	—	$343,420
1931[r]	$343,420	$1,050,000	$1,393,420
1932	$343,420	$3,750,000	$4,093,420
1933	$324,500	$1,000,000	$1,324,500
1934	$315,173	$3,490,000	$3,805,173

(continued)

o. The Judiciary Act of 1911 abolishes U.S. circuit courts and transfers their jurisdiction to district courts; codifies salaries of the Court reporter and marshal and outlines their expenses; establishes the Supreme Court budget separately from the rest of the federal budget; and grants the justices a $2,000 pay raise, from $13,000 (chief) and $12,500 (associate) to $15,000 (chief) and $14,500 (associate).

p. Chief Justice Taft founds the Judicial Conference—a group consisting of the Supreme Court justices and all the district court judges—to meet biannually to discuss the problems of the judiciary.

q. Congress authorizes the secretary of the Treasury to find a site for the construction of the new Supreme Court building in Washington, D.C., and raises the justices' salaries from $15,000 (chief) and $14,500 (associate) to $20,500 (chief) and $20,000 (associate).

r. Construction of the new building begins on Capitol Hill, continuing through 1934. Congress also appropriates $50,000 to purchase printing plates for volumes 1–265 of the *Supreme Court Reports*.

YEAR	SALARY AND EXPENSES	BUILDING AND OTHER	TOTAL
1935	$358,830	$30,348	$389,178
1936	$486,000	$49,080	$535,080
1937	$508,500	$55,000	$563,500
1938	$470,900	$60,000	$530,900
1939	$479,160	$61,500	$540,660
1940	$504,000	$62,500	$566,500
1941	$500,000	$65,000	$565,000
1942	$601,460	$70,017	$671,477
1943	$569,161	$70,566	$639,727
1944	$642,214	$76,600	$718,814
1945	$652,959	$80,000	$732,959
1946	$668,500	$104,100	$772,600
1947	$801,906	$121,231	$923,137
1948	$852,920	$122,800	$975,720
1949	$990,400	$190,700	$1,181,100
1950	$944,100	$152,000	$1,096,100
1951	$1,080,800	$159,200	$1,240,000
1952	$1,152,050	$172,500	$1,324,550
1953	$1,189,550	$174,100	$1,363,650
1954	$1,193,236	$174,100	$1,367,336
1955	$1,194,985	$350,800	$1,545,785
1956	$1,294,285	$367,400	$1,661,685
1957	$1,361,285	$201,500	$1,562,785
1958	$1,423,835	$218,200	$1,642,035
1959	$1,519,800	$219,200	$1,739,000
1960	$1,536,000	$347,000	$1,883,000
1961	$1,642,000	$287,000	$1,929,000
1962	$1,712,000	$284,000	$1,996,000
1963	$1,752,000	$323,000	$2,075,000
1964	$1,853,000	$355,000	$2,208,000
1965	$2,195,000	$305,000	$2,500,000
1966	$2,270,000	$319,000	$2,589,000
1967	$2,305,000	$324,000	$2,629,000
1968	$2,356,000	$334,000	$2,690,000
1969	$2,602,000	$361,000	$2,963,000
1970	$3,138,000	$410,000	$3,548,000
1971	$3,746,000	$502,000	$4,248,000
1972	$4,180,000	$561,000	$4,741,000
1973 [s]	$4,719,000	$1,109,000	$5,828,000

s. The 1973–1975 figures include supplementary appropriations for buildings and grounds of $95,000, $75,000, and $372,000, respectively.

YEAR	SALARY AND EXPENSES	BUILDING AND OTHER	TOTAL
1974	$5,353,000	$1,568,000	$6,921,000
1975	$5,892,000	$1,376,000	$7,268,000
1976	$6,582,000	$1,454,000	$8,036,000
1976[t]	$1,576,000	$196,000	$1,772,000
1977	$7,732,000	$831,000	$8,563,000
1978	$8,691,000	$1,588,000	$10,279,000
1979	$9,690,000	$1,475,000	$11,165,000
1980	$10,363,000	$2,182,000	$12,545,000
1981[u]	$11,840,000	$2,213,000	$14,053,000
1982	$11,635,000	$1,654,000	$13,289,000
1983	$12,675,000	$2,000,000	$14,675,000
1984	$13,635,000	$2,571,000	$16,206,000
1985	$14,143,000	$2,242,000	$16,385,000
1986	$14,399,000	$2,223,000	$16,622,000
1987	$15,513,000	$2,336,000	$17,849,000
1988	$15,247,000	$2,110,000	$17,357,000
1989	$15,901,000	$2,131,000	$18,032,000
1990	$17,497,000	$4,369,000	$21,866,000
1991	$19,083,000	$3,453,000	$22,536,000
1992	$20,787,000	$3,801,000	$24,588,000
1993	$22,286,000	$3,320,000	$25,606,000
1994	$23,000,000	$2,850,000	$25,850,000
1995	$24,000,000	$3,000,000	$27,000,000
1996	$26,000,000	$3,000,000	$29,000,000
1997	$27,000,000	$3,000,000	$30,000,000
1998	$29,000,000	$3,000,000	$32,000,000
1999	$31,000,000	$4,000,000	$35,000,000
2000	$36,000,000	$6,000,000	$42,000,000
2001	$39,000,000	$9,000,000	$48,000,000
2002[v]	$42,000,000	$68,000,000	$110,000,000 (est)
2003	$48,000,000	$54,000,000	$102,000,000 (est)

t. The federal government moves the end of the fiscal year from June 30 to September 30, necessitating the one-time addition of a transitional fiscal quarter.

u. Figures include a one-time appropriation of $645,000 for acquisition of property to add to the Supreme Court's grounds.

v. The 2002–2003 estimates reflect substantial increases in funding for buildings and grounds, attributable to major renovation work on the Supreme Court building and increased security provisions following the terrorist attacks of 2001.

Index

Illustration Credits

All illustrations used in Appendix B are from the Collection of the Supreme Court of the United States (courtesy Jerry Goldman www.oyez.org). They include the work of the following artists: Eben F. Comins (Benjamin N. Cardozo); Earle Clarke Daniel (Peter V. Daniel); Ashur B. Durand (Smith Thompson); C.J. Fox (Harlan F. Stone); George P.A. Healy (Philip Barbour, Joseph Story, Roger Brooke Taney); John Hesselius (Thomas Johnson); Robert Hinckley (John Rutledge); Lewis Thomas Ives (Henry B. Brown); Matthew Harris Jouett (John McKinley, Thomas Todd); Ruth Koppang (John Blair); Adrian Lamb (Samuel Blatchford, Bushrod Washington); Edmund C. Messer (Joseph P. Bradley); Rembrandt Peale (John Marshall); C. Gregory Stapko (William Cushing, Henry Brockholst Livingston, Alfred Moore, William Paterson, Robert Trimble); Thomas Sully (Henry Baldwin); Robert S. Susan (James Wilson); Larry Dodd Wheeler (Gabriel Duvall); William Wheeler (Oliver Ellsworth).

INSERT ILLUSTRATIONS

Plate A-1: After portrait by Gilbert Stuart. Collection of the Supreme Court of the United States. *Plate A-2:* Collection of the Supreme Court of the United States. *Plate A-3:* Published in the *Philadelphia Monthly Magazine,* 1798. The Library Company of Philadelphia. *Plate A-4:* Photograph by Robin Miller, 2003. Independence National Historical Park. *Plate A-5:* Photograph by Vic Boswell from original portrait. Collection of the Supreme Court of the United States. *Plate A-6:* Architect of the Capitol. *Plate A-7:* Photographer Unknown. Collection of the Supreme Court of the United States. *Plate A-8:* *Harper's Weekly,* v. 3, 23 July 1859, p. 479. Library of Congress, Prints and Photographs Division LC-USZ62-132561. *Plate A-9:* "Arraigned at Indianapolis for Treason." Photograph by Indiana Historical Society, C5136. *Plate A-10:* Library of Congress, Prints and Photographs Division LC-USZ62-21202. *Plate A-11:* Library of Congress, Prints and Photographs Division LC-USZ62-95372. *Plate A-12:* "Our Overworked Supreme Court," by J. Keppler, *Puck,* 9 December 1885, pp. 232–33. Library of Congress, Prints and Photographs Division LC-USZC4-436. *Plate A-13:* "Wampole's Preparation of Cod Liver Extract." Reproduced courtesy of Timothy G. Crowley, Esq. *Plate A-14:* Drawn by Carl J. Becker. *Harper's Weekly,* v. 32, 28 June 1888, p. 61. Library of Congress, Prints and Photographs Division LCUSZ62-1249.1.14. *Plate A-15:* "On a Populistic Basis. A Forecast of a Popocratic Victory to the Supreme Court of the United States," by William Allen Rogers. *Harper's Weekly,* 12 September 1896, p. 889. Library of Congress, Prints and Photographs Division LC-USZ62-116355. *Plate B-1:* *The Evening Star,* 11 October 1907. Library of Congress, Prints and Photographs Division LC-USZ62-10544. *Plate B-2:* Arthur Estabrook Papers. M. E. Grenander Department of Special Collections and Archives, University at Albany, SUNY. *Plate B-3:* © Underwood & Underwood/CORBIS. *Plate B-4:* *Architecture* 1936. *Plate B-5:* Collection of the Supreme Court of the United States. *Plate

B-6: Museum of the City of New York. *Plate B-7:* "New Deal Plan for Enlarged Supreme Court," by Clifford Berryman for the *Washington Evening Star,* 10 February 1937. © 1937, *The Washington Post.* Reprinted with permission. Photograph from Library of Congress, Prints and Photographs Division LC-USZ62-10831. *Plate B-8:* Columbia/The Kobal Collection. *Plate B-9:* Library of Congress, Prints and Photographs Division LC-USE623-D-OA-000145. *Plate B-10:* "Inherent Powers," editorial cartoon by Art Bimrose, *The Oregonian,* Wednesday, 4 June 1952. *The Oregonian* © 1952, Oregonian Publishing Co. All rights reserved. Reprinted with permission. Photograph from Library of Congress, Prints and Photographs Division LC-USZ62-98627. *Plate B-11:* © Bettmann/CORBIS. *Plate B-12:* Photograph by Harris & Ewing. Collection of the Supreme Court of the United States. *Plate B-13:* National Archives Building, Washington, D.C. *Plate B-14:* Photograph by Harris & Ewing. Collection of the Supreme Court of the United States. *Plate B-15:* Photograph by Bob Pileggi. Reproduced courtesy of Lambda Legal Defense.